The Stalingrad Cauldron

The Stalingrad Cauldron

Inside the Encirclement and Destruction of the 6th Army

Frank Ellis

University Press of Kansas

Published by the University Press of Kansas (Lawrence, Kansas 66045), which was organized by the Kansas Board of Regents and is operated and funded by Emporia State University, Fort Hays State University, Kansas State University, Pittsburg State University, the University of Kansas, and Wichita State University

Library of Congress Cataloging-in-Publication Data

Ellis, Frank, 1953–
The Stalingrad cauldron : inside the encirclement and destruction of the 6th Army / Frank Ellis.
pages cm. — (Modern war studies)
Includes bibliographical references and index.
ISBN 978-0-7006-1901-6 (cloth : alk. paper)
1. Stalingrad, Battle of, Volgograd, Russia, 1942–1943. 2. Germany. Heer. Armee, 6—History. 3. Germany. Heer. Panzer-Division, 16—History. 4. Germany. Heer. Infanterie-Division, 76—History. 5. Germany. Heer. Infanterie-Division, 94—History. 6. World War, 1939–1945—Regimental histories—Germany. 7. World War, 1939–1945—Prisoners and prisons, Soviet. 8. Prisoners of war—Soviet Union. 9. Prisoners of war—Germany—History—20th century. 10. Stalingrad, Battle of, Volgograd, Russia, 1942–1943—History—Sources. I. Title.
D764.3.S7E55 2013
940.54'21747—dc23
2013002055

British Library Cataloguing-in-Publication Data is available.

Printed in the United States of America

10 9 8 7 6 5 4 3 2 1

The paper used in this publication is recycled and contains 30 percent postconsumer waste. It is acid free and meets the minimum requirements of the American National Standard for Permanence of Paper for Printed Library Materials Z39.48-1992.

Then it was 2 February 1943, the fall of Stalingrad. I came home from school, and my little sister was playing very quietly in the children's room. The door to the living room was ajar, and I saw our mother sitting bent over in front of the small radio. Tears were running down her cheeks. I knew at once what had happened. I opened the door and ran up to her. Without a word she stroked my hair. I shall never forget my mother's pain.

—*Annemarie Müller-Andreesen*

CONTENTS

PREFACE

From the moment I started to take an interest in World War II and the war on the Eastern front I was mesmerized by the struggle of German 6th Army to seize the city and the sacrificial efforts of the Red Army to thwart German ambitions on the Volga. I determined that at some stage I would make my own contribution to the body of literature on the subject, following in the footsteps of some very well-known and expert historians, such as John Erickson, Earl Ziemke, Joachim Hoffman, Antony Beevor, Manfred Kehrig, and David Glantz. Due credit must also be paid to the Russian scholars and archivists, among them M. M. Zagorul'ko and Major General V. A. Zolotarev and especially those in the Russian Security Service, the Federal'naia sluzhba bezopasnosti (FSB), who have devoted themselves to the enormous task of sifting and processing hitherto-classified Soviet material and placing it in the public domain, a process that started in 1991 and that still has a long way to go. I owe a huge debt to the many Russian scholars and archivists who have labored long and hard in this area. Without the vast flood of new material, there would have been no point in writing this book.

It is not just new material entering the public domain from former Soviet archives that justifies another book on Stalingrad. There is also still a great deal of material in German archives that can yield insights. For example, the German military archives in Freiburg-im-Breisgau have recently acquired six volumes of reports, diaries, and *Erlebnisberichte* put together by former members of 76th Infantry Division. This material was originally submitted to Jochen Löser when he undertook to write *Bittere Pflicht*, the divisional history. These supplementary volumes proved to be a valuable source for some of the themes examined in this book. Published German divisional histories are also an exceptionally valuable source, and none of the main ones has been translated into English. Even where they are referred to in English-language works, the references are perfunctory, suggesting only a superficial familiarity with, or interest in, the German text. Another surprise from the past that has only recently come to light is the film diary *Mit der Kamera nach Stalingrad: Filmtagebücher deutschen Soldaten 1941/42* (*With the Camera to Stalingrad: Film Diaries of German Soldiers 1941–42*, 2009). The diaries were edited by Michael Kuball and the film taken by Wilhelm Bleitner and Götz Hirt-Reger. The diaries show the journey taken by 29th Infantry Division (mot.) as the division fights its way across Russia through the first winter, eventually ending up in Stalingrad. It contains remarkable footage and is accompanied by commentary from former members of the division. The whole diary can be viewed on the Internet and is available on DVD.

This study is not a detailed operational account of the battle, such as that found in the work of Manfred Kehrig, John Erickson, and, more recently, David Glantz. My study is more tactical and personal, more concerned with some of the lesser-known detail than with the bigger operational picture. In chapter 1 I have put together an overview of the battle dealing with some of the main themes: recent publications on Stalingrad; some recent films and documentaries on the battle; the nature of the terrain and weather; the impact of cold; fighting in the urban and steppe environment; the impact of Stalin's Order № 227 (and related orders); the role of 10th Rifle Division Narodnyi Komissariat Vnutrennikh Del (NKVD) in the defense of the city; the question of German war crimes with reference to Dulag-205; and capture and captivity.

Chapters 2, 3, and 4 are my translations of documents: the remnants of German divisional war diaries and recollections of survivors dealing with the participation of 16th Panzer Division, 94th Infantry Division, and 76th Infantry Division. Where necessary I have added notes to highlight certain points. As far as I am aware, this is the first time these documents have been translated from German into English. It may also be the first time they have been cited in any study of the battle. I have found no references to these diaries in any major or recent scholarly works. Nor do the names of Major Grohe, Hauptmann Krell, Major von Alvensleben, and Lt. Dr. Elsner von Gronow—the officers responsible for compiling these documents—appear in any of the major works on Stalingrad. The lack of any reference to these diaries is a surprising omission. All three are substantial, and all of them yield insights on the nature of the battle after the encirclement: on weather, tactics, weapons, internal disputes, the effects of cold and reduced rations, the high quality of German junior leaders, and an astonishing sense of duty. All these aspects amply justify the inclusion of full translations of these diaries. They make compelling reading.

This book is a study of a number of themes that, though not specific to Stalingrad, have their own Stalingrad footprint. Sniping was a specialized form of infantry warfare that was practiced by both sides on the Eastern front. To begin with, training, initiative, and the brutal lessons inflicted by the Finns

Central to the urban battle is the need to recognize the moment when the transition from local successes to a systematic advance can begin and deeper penetration can be achieved. In fact, the ability to recognize this moment of opportunity is regarded as a key element in offensive leadership. Critical is the personal presence and example of leaders at all levels: "All leaders are to keep as close as possible to their men as their command tasks permit."[61] The authors recognize that urban warfare disrupts the normal organizational structures and establish a clear operational principle: "Combat in a conventionally and organizationally structured regime is the exception: the formation of combat groups comprising all arms is the rule."[62] The next-most-important element is to achieve the most effective combination of all arms, the most effective ratio of infantry to combat engineers, and where necessary the deployment of heavy infantry weapons and assault guns.

A striking feature of German infantry doctrine was the emphasis on the initiative of junior leaders. In the urban environment it is critical for local and wider success. "Merkblatt für den Ortskampf" (General guidelines for the urban battle) provides a detailed summary of this junior leader doctrine, in some ways a succinct summary of the doctrine of *Auftragstaktik*: "Success depends most of all on the independent conduct of junior leaders. It is important to keep them thoroughly briefed about what is happening beyond their own immediate mission, beyond the connections of the planned operation. This is not only the precondition for independent operational conduct but is also the most expedient in the sense of the entire operation."[63]

The basic operational principle identified is that the heavy weapons, typically assault guns, are deployed so as to make it possible for the assault troops to reach and neutralize the objective, whereupon the conditions are met for a further advance under cover of heavy weapons fire. The urban setting means that the precise location of enemy positions will not always be known. In such circumstances firing on likely enemy positions (*auf Verdacht*) will be very frequent. Red Army ambushes from the rear and flanks had taught the Germans the need to have troops in reserve, following behind the main advance, whose primary task was the elimination of enemy stay-behind parties. The language in "Merkblatt für den Ortskampf" suggests that the Germans regarded these sorts of delayed ambushes as unacceptable, somehow dishonorable. The task of the cleanup groups (*Säuberungstrupps*) "is to destroy overlooked nests of resistance and immediately to crush any renewed resistance behind the front line. Exceptional severity is required."[64] Once an objective has been taken, a thorough check of the area is to be carried out with the aim of eliminating any concealed enemy. “Merkblatt für den Ortskampf” reveals a complete awareness of the special problems associated with urban warfare and confirms the importance attached by the Wehrmacht to the role of highly trained and qualified junior leaders in all phases of war. As the conduct of the urban battle in Iraq (2003–2011) attests, German lessons and insights are by no means dated. The U.S. Marine Corps, for example, lays exceptional stress on flat command structures and high-quality junior leadership in the urban battle.

Inside the city, as German infantry losses mounted, the role of the Luftwaffe became ever more important in helping to maintain the offensive power of the German infantry. Lieutenant General Vasilii Chuikov attempted to counter the contribution of the Luftwaffe to the German offensive by moving his men as close as possible to the German line. He reasoned that German pilots would be reluctant to attack Red Army positions if there was a good chance that their bombs would hit German soldiers. Moving closer to the German lines would also have the same effect on German artillery observers, who would have to take the possibility into account that their shells might hit German troops. As David Glantz has argued,[65] the approach adopted by Chuikov suggests a cool, analytical appraisal of the battlefield, yet his adoption of these methods was not risk-free. First, if German artillery observers were going to have to think very carefully about the risks of laying down fire so close to their own lines, the same problem arose for Soviet fire controllers—or possibly not, given the Soviet approach to losses. Second, the reduced distance between the lines made things easier for would-be Soviet deserters. One possible advantage of reducing the impact of the Luftwaffe and the German artillery would be an enhanced role for German infantry support weapons, whose crews were vulnerable to snipers. What emerges from a study of the Soviet and German conduct of the urban battle is that both sides were being forced to adapt and change. With their highly trained junior leaders and their doctrinal emphasis on initiative, the Germans were well placed to implement the necessary changes. For the Red Army, these changes were more challenging because they weakened not only the power of the commissars and other political appointees but also of senior and midlevel army commanders. Urban warfare cannot be micromanaged. Chuikov recognized that the battle would be won or lost by his junior leaders and that they had to be trusted. Their time had come.

In his study of the methods adopted by the Red Army inside Stalingrad to counter the Wehrmacht, David Stone argues that the manner and the effectiveness of these measures provide clear evidence that the view of the Red

Army as being unimaginative and lacking initiative is outdated and wrong. This false view is, he says, primarily inspired by German sources, not Soviet. It is also interesting to note that British propagandists perpetuated the view, going back to World War I, that the German military machine was made up of mindless, goose-stepping zombies who just obeyed orders. An army so constituted would not have overwhelmed the British and French in six weeks in the summer of 1940 nor reached the steppes of Central Asia. Much the same kind of thinking colored British assessments of the Imperial Japanese Army and led directly to the fall of Singapore. Underlying these clearly false assumptions about German and Japanese soldiers was an idea, widespread even now, that initiative and flexibility are exclusively products of a liberal-democratic society.

Much of the blame for the view that the Red Army was full of "stolid and faceless Russian soldiers"[66] lies with Soviet military propagandists who created and disseminated a picture of a mass modern army that would easily deal with any invader in very short order. The purges, the execution of able Red Army commanders, and the institution of commissars also support the view that initiative was regarded with suspicion by the party and that the Red Army could not be trusted. The consequences of dual command are well established; it stifled initiative, wasted time, led to tactical opportunities not being grasped, and undermined the confidence of the rank and file in its officers. In short, it was a disastrous impediment when fighting an enemy of the quality of the Wehrmacht. Perhaps these brutal realities, which had been evident since the start of the war, finally persuaded the party that the institution of commissars had to go. The abolition order was issued at the height of the battle (9 October 1942).[67]

It is undoubtedly flattering for Wehrmacht veterans to believe that they were defeated by sheer weight of numbers and not necessarily by the skill of their opponents, but this does not mean that the German assessment of the Red Army was wrong or hopelessly biased. For example, in a secret intelligence summary (29 August 1942) concerning enemy intentions for the autumn and winter of 1942, and certainly not intended to provide an unduly glowing appraisal of the German Army at the expense of its opponent, Reinhard Gehlen, the head of Fremde Heere Ost, acknowledges that the Soviet high command was learning tried and tested lessons from the Germans in the conduct of operations: the formation of tank corps, concentrated use of airpower, the formation of operational assault groups, and the deployment of tanks so as to exploit gains in the assault. However, his view of intermediate and junior commanders was bleak—these lower command strata had continued to deteriorate—and this had an impact on the Soviet conduct of operations.[68] German generals interviewed after the war and writing memoirs naturally had an interest in playing up the numerical and matériel advantages of the Red Army. However, German staff officers preparing daily reports of Red Army attacks on their positions had to submit reports based on the facts, not on wishful thinking. These reports acknowledge clearly and openly the severity of the fighting and the tenacity and skill of their opponents. Yet they also recognize that Soviet initiative and tactical considerations were all too often sacrificed in favor of mass infantry attacks, which were easily broken up, with very heavy losses inflicted by the Germans. In fact, this feature of Soviet infantry tactics—mass attacks pressed home regardless of losses—consistently and regularly appears in German memoirs and novels, often well after the war. In my opinion, these accounts cannot simply be dismissed as the bias of German veterans. The provisions of Order № 227 also confronted Soviet commanders at all levels: Did they press home an attack and take huge losses, or did they withdraw and incur accusations of cowardice?

Stone notes a number of examples of Soviet cities being defended in their surrounding fortifications—Odessa, Sevastopol, Tula, and Leningrad—and makes the point that before Stalingrad there were no cases for the Red Army "to grasp the nature of extended urban warfare or explore the inherent defensive potential of cities."[69] Soviet intervention in the Spanish Civil War suggests that there were lessons to be learned not just about the importance of tactical airpower and its role in cities but also about the nature of urban warfare. General Alexander Rodimtsev, the commander of 13th Guards Rifle Division at Stalingrad, had served in Spain as a military adviser, winning the award Hero of the Soviet Union. He had every opportunity to make out some of the contours of future urban warfare and how such a battle might be conducted.

Iurii Rybalkin's study *Operatsiia «X» Sovetskaia voennaia pomoshch' respublikanskoi Ispanii, 1936–1939* (Operation "X": Soviet military assistance to republican Spain, 1936–1939, 2000) leaves no doubt that the Red Army did have the chance to assess the nature of urban warfare in advance of the German invasion. Rybalkin shows that the lessons and experiences of Soviet intervention were intensively studied by the Soviet general staff. The study was not confined to Soviet sources; they paid attention to all articles published in the foreign press, which were translated. Novels by Western authors based on personal experiences were also translated. I take it for granted that George Orwell's *Homage to Catalonia* (1938) would have been studied very carefully.

Good practice was disseminated as widely as possible throughout the Red Army. Among some of the detailed studies of the war planned by the military-history section of the Soviet general staff were *Oborona Madrida* (The defense of Madrid) and *Nekotorye vyvody iz opyta voiny* (Some conclusions from the experience of the war).[70] Before he was arrested and executed, Marshal Mikhail Tukhachevskii had analyzed the effectiveness of Soviet equipment supplied and set out his conclusions in a briefing document, *Takticheskie zadaniia po provedeniiu opytov v «X»* (Tactical tasks in the implementation of lessons in "X").[71] The fact that an "enemy of the people" had written the document would have inhibited its lessons being disseminated.

Urban warfare was one of the distinguishing features of the Spanish Civil War, and the siege of Madrid provided the future adversaries in the Great Fatherland War with some idea of what they could expect. For example, Rybalkin notes that the defense of Madrid was accorded the highest priority in terms of the provision of men and equipment and that Soviet advisers played a major role in the measures taken to defend Madrid. Among the defensive measures was the construction of three reinforced lines. The first was to be about 20–35 kilometers (12–22 miles) from the city center, a second at a distance of 12–14 kilometers (7–9 miles), and a third at a distance of 6–8 kilometers (4–5 miles). The result of these and other defensive measures was, in Rybalkin's words, that "soon Madrid was in actual fact converted into a distinctive reinforced region. Engineer obstacles were erected not only on the approaches to the city but also in the streets of the city itself."[72]

In the Great Fatherland War, the end phase of the battle for Rostov-on-Don, which involved street fighting in fortified zones, adumbrates the sort of conflict awaiting German 6th Army and Chuikov's men in Stalingrad and what might have befallen the Germans had they been forced to fight for the streets and buildings of Leningrad and Moscow. The task of clearing out the Soviet resistance in Rostov was given to the German 125th Infantry Division. The approach adopted by Oberst Alfred Reinhardt, the commander of 421st Regiment, one of the units tasked with clearing out the Soviet resistance, was to clear the buildings systematically and in coordinated fashion, with a second wave of troops cleaning out any Soviet ambush parties that might attack the lead German troops from the rear. So bitter was the nature of the fighting that German wounded had to be protected or they would be killed by Soviet troops. The enemy in this final phase was units of the NKVD. Paul Carell, drawing on the report of the street fighting written by Reinhardt, assesses the measures adopted by the NKVD units as follows:

> What these specialists in street fighting had made of Rostov was unimaginable. The streets have been torn up and the paving has been piled up to make barricades a meter thick. The side streets are blocked by deep brick bunkers. Rolls of barbed wire and mines make any stealthy approach completely impossible. House doors are bricked up and the windows filled up with sandbags and turned into fire positions, and the balconies are used as machine-gun nests. Snipers occupy well-camouflaged positions on the rooftops. And in the cellars there are tens of thousands of Molotov cocktails.[73]

Stone also challenges the standard view that tanks would be of little use in urban warfare. Large-scale deployment of tanks in fast-moving columns supported by mechanized infantry can be used in the early stages of an attack on a city if the defenders can be taken by surprise so that they have no time to organize effective defenses. Cities and large built-up areas organized in advance for antitank defense are another matter. Once roads are blocked by rubble and obstacles, mined, and covered by effective antitank fire, the advantages of armor are severely negated: movement is canalized; junctions, interdicted by preregistered artillery fire and antitank weapons, become ambush sites; and bridges can be blown after armored vehicles have crossed, thus trapping tanks where they can be destroyed piecemeal by tank-killing squads. That Chuikov's use of tanks in the city identifies a niche use—the Germans eventually did the same—and demonstrates perspicacity and improvisation is clear enough, but it is not conventional tank warfare. The deployment of low numbers of tanks, either dug in as strong points or used to cover short distances in support of infantry, is an example of guerrilla warfare waged with tanks.

The nature of the fighting outside the city, the quality of German leadership, the exhausting battles, and the general evolution of the campaign can be derived from two German reports that deal with small-unit actions. The first is the battle for height 61.6; the second deals with the defensive battles of 3rd Battalion Grenadier Regiment 203 under the exemplary leadership of Hauptmann Gerstenberg. The defensive battles over which Gerstenberg presided cover the period from 15 October to 26 November 1942; that is about a month before and a week after the Soviet counteroffensive. The two actions were not unique; many such actions were being fought, some won and some lost, throughout the entire Kessel, but they typify the attritional nature of the battle and, despite all the often brilliant improvisational measures adopted by the Germans, how they were slowly losing and succumbing.

The battle for height 61.6 deals with a planned deployment carried out by 3rd Battalion of Grenadier Regiment 203, 76th Infantry Division, during the night of 26 November 1942. Late in the afternoon the battalion is ordered to break contact with the enemy as soon as it is dark. "Battalion" is something of a misnomer because the unit's total strength is only about 160 men. In other words, this is a severely depleted battalion. Weapons and ammunition do not seem to be a problem (there are a total of three frontline reserves of ammunition). Tinned rations have been stockpiled, and the battalion has amassed a huge array of digging equipment: 200 hundred long spades, 400 short spades, 200 pickaxes, 25 crosscut saws, 150 shovels, and 10 wood hammers. In addition, winter clothing has been issued so that each man, in addition to his normal-issue leather boots, also has his felt boots. The main problem is lack of vehicles and pack animals to move all the necessary equipment. The move, determined by the consequences of the Soviet counteroffensive, is something of a cruel blow because a great deal of effort went into preparing winter accommodations, in direct contact with the enemy, which now have to be abandoned.

Red Army pressure on the battalion's position has steadily increased since 20 November 1942. The report cites the exemplary leadership of the company commanders, Leutnant Hannig, Leutnant Kressin, and Oberleutnant Bente, whose companies inflicted heavy losses on the Red Army. By 26 November 1942 there are some 550–600 Red Army dead to the front of Oberleutnant Bente's company's sector. With its left boundary position against the Don River, the battalion is now coming under fire from the other bank. Luckily, since it was not yet properly frozen, the Don still constitutes a major obstacle to Red Army movement.

Such is the friction in war that the move to height 61.6 is delayed, the final move out starting at 2100 hours. However, the bulk of the battalion is not able to move out until 2400 hours. The rearguard is ordered to fire off ammunition that cannot be carried, and this may well assist the battalion in breaking contact. Nevertheless, the night march is an ordeal for heavily laden and exhausted troops, as the report notes:

> Only by the harshest discipline and a relentless treatment toward every soldier, particularly toward the weaker ones, was it possible to ensure that the battalion moved out at 0100 hours and to hope that it could break contact and reach the new forward edge of the battle line before it became light. The battalion marched in the following order: 9th Company, 12th

> Company (remnants), headquarters, 10th Company, and 11th Company. During the day of 26 November 1942 it had thawed. Toward evening it became cold, accompanied by a storm and rain. The tracks immediately froze. The fine rain made the roads smooth with ice and very difficult to use. The temperamental and well-fed Romanian cavalry horses became even more edgy. Weak from exhaustion, the soldiers with their heavy packs, additional equipment, ammunition, sleeping blankets, and winter clothing could hardly stay on their feet because of the sheet ice. They fell, and they did not get up again. Their comrades, following behind, staggered helplessly over them as they headed along without bothering about them. At the end of the marching column, apart from the appointed liaison Feldwebel between the companies, there was an officer (Leutnant Fröhlich) with two very energetic Feldwebel attached, who relentlessly collected up soldiers lying on the ground.[74]

In spite of the setbacks the battalion reaches its destination, the village of Kisslov, before first light. Meanwhile, the Russians are making ready to attack. Oberleutnant Bente leads the remnants of the battalion onto height 61.6, planning to hold it. The Germans move the four remaining light howitzers onto the rear slope (with a total of only twenty shells). Eight machine-gun groups are deployed. The crews are under orders to withdraw only on the authority of the combat group commander. The first Soviet attack at 0800 hours on 27 November 1942 is broken up, but there are signs that German morale is cracking. Soldiers from 384th Division, out of ammunition, try to abandon the position.

Toward 1000 hours height 61.6 is subjected to a Soviet bombardment that lasts for about one and a half hours. The main Soviet assault follows, with tanks and about 1,000 men. The attack is broken up. The Russians then attack the height from all sides, probing for any weak links. As if the Soviet assault were not enough, the weather changes dramatically. To cite the report:

> Toward 1430 hours a snowstorm, unprecedented so far this year, set in, darkening the whole horizon. Morale-wise, the men of the combat group were weakened further. The snowstorm was icy cold and caused the first cases of frostbite. For the most part, nobody had gloves or any head protection. Brought on by this sudden winter storm, the breech mechanisms of the machine guns froze solid, as did the rifle chambers. To make matters worse, the Russians chose this moment for their attack in

> regimental strength, with tanks in support. The men occupying height 61.6 were physically and morale-wise finally no longer able to cope with the situation. Some surrendered. The majority, having abandoned their weapons, ran toward the main position. Even force of arms could achieve nothing more.[75]

German wounded now start to increase. In the report due tribute is paid to the efforts of a German doctor to save lives: "This young doctor, as far as his age was concerned, he may have been about 28 years old, achieved something extraordinary on 27 November 1942. With shirts and underclothing from our own dead or from Russians, he dressed his wounded and severely wounded comrades."[76] Eventually three Soviet T-34 tanks and accompanying infantry reach the top of height 61.6. In the words of the report, "An unearthly picture: broad daylight, yet blacked out by the snowstorm and then these dark, primordial monsters."[77] In the ensuing defensive battle, which lasts about twenty minutes, some 800–1,000 Soviet soldiers are killed. The defensive battle has been won. The problem now facing the German defenders is that there is no food, and ammunition is almost exhausted as well. Renewed Soviet attacks can also be expected. At one stage the sole effective small arms are pistols. Since by 0100 hours on 28 November 1942 neither orders nor any resupply of ammunition and food have arrived, the order is given to break out to the south.

The report freely acknowledges that many soldiers have reached the physical and psychological breaking point; that hunger and cold have rendered them more or less indifferent to discipline. In fact, there are hints that one of the German officers, Leutnant Mikulasch, has fallen short of what his superiors are entitled to expect. The report notes that "the entire sector was scoured and Leutnant Mikulasch was discovered alone in the area and did not know where his combat group had got to."[78]

Earlier in the report it was noted that vehicles that had barely covered 2 kilometers (1.2 miles) and that were laden with equipment and heavy mortars have "for unexplained reasons" been abandoned by Leutnant Mikulasch. Again, after contact is made with a combat group under command of an officer from 384th Infantry Division, Oberleutnant Sygar, there is still no news of Mikulasch's combat group. What clearly emerges from this account of the battle for height 61.6, one of any number of such battles being played out, is that the example and role of junior leaders, noncommissioned officers (NCOs), and officers are critical. Even in extremis these continue to remain among 6th Army's core strengths.

The defensive battles conducted by 3rd Battalion, Grenadier Regiment 203 under command of Hauptmann Gerstenberg underline the role of effective leadership in the unfavorable conditions now facing the Germans. The battalion, consisting of about 200 men, is responsible for a sector with a linear frontage of about 3.5 kilometers (2 miles). Its left wing was the river Don. The position the battalion now occupies provides inadequate accommodations and, crucially, lacks defense in depth. Worse still, as the report notes, "no built-in positions for machine guns or other weapon positions or accommodations were in evidence at all. Movement to and between the individual positions was only possible in darkness, since the entire battalion sector could be seen by the Russians, who at the nearest points were only about 150 meters away."[79]

On assuming command of the battalion, Hauptmann Gerstenberg took a number of measures to raise the battalion's combat effectiveness: digging equipment and building material were made available; support troops from the pay staff and supply personnel were deployed to raise manpower as well as *Hiwis*; the battalion was tactically reorganized to take into account the terrain and enemy; and the battalion's firepower was increased by the deployment of all available weapons, including captured ones. Finally, Hauptmann Gerstenberg sought to harden the defensive will and the morale of each soldier. He initiated a training regimen to raise the standard of replacement troops, continually monitored the battalion's progress, and ensured that accommodations and the provision of rations were up to standard. Evidence for the effectiveness of these measures is the fact that enemy fighting and reconnaissance patrols have been successfully repelled in the battalion's sector, and right up to the moment when the position is evacuated on 26 November 1942 the enemy has failed to achieve any breakthrough. Most enemy casualties have been incurred—500–600 on the Don sector—in frontal attacks on the battalion's forward lines.

Threatened by the enemy from the west bank of the Don, the battalion defensive line has to be reorganized. In the words of the report, which bears witness to the tactical impact of the asymmetry of Russian riverbanks, "In order to counter the threat from the west bank of the Don, the battalion's main forward battle line had to be extended by 2 kilometers [1 mile] at 90 degrees to the left rear. This extended line was also held without breaking. In view of the weak forces and the unfavorable terrain conditions (the enemy's side of the Don was much higher and as a result dominated the whole time), this was a notable feat."[80]

The consequences of Gerstenberg's leadership and drive were far-reaching. The battalion's position was the cornerstone of the German defense between the Don and the Volga and had to be held. That the position was held made it possible for the last remaining German troops to be pulled back from the west bank of the Don. Furthermore, confident that Gerstenberg's sector was secure, the regiment was able to deploy its available reserves to contain an enemy break to the right. That 6th Army did not collapse into chaos and that German order and discipline more or less held for as long as they did inside the Kessel is largely due to the many outstanding officers of the caliber of Hauptmann Gerstenberg, Oberleutnants Bente and Sygar, and Leutnants Hannig and Kressin.

German success in these steppe defensive battles was enormously assisted by unimaginative Soviet methods of attack, as can be seen in the account of Albrecht Appelt, a Stalingrad veteran and survivor:

> One day, the enemy facing us climbed out of his trenches and attacked us at a range of 300 meters. It looked like a black-dotted island in the middle of the snow-covered steppe that was moving toward us. Their leader, on horseback, rode, for us most unusually, not at the front but behind the attackers. For us the distance was still too great, but not for the artillery. The very first ranging shell tore a large, round hole among the ranks of the attackers. Now the horseman, like a sheepdog, raced up and down from left to right behind his company and once again from right to left. The next shell tore a further hole, and wilder still, with raised pistol, the slave driver herded these poor wretches forward. When our whole battery fired, only a few remained; nevertheless, they were driven to a pointless death. With the last salvo the rider came off his horse. Nothing moved anymore; nobody stood up. About 100 to about 150 sons, fathers, and husbands, dead or badly wounded, lay on the battlefield: the madness of war![81]

The lack of imagination in the prosecution of Soviet infantry attacks as a factor contributing to German defensive successes has been astutely analyzed by Jochen Löser: "We were fortunate insofar as the Russians invariably attacked on the same position, according to the same scheme and mostly at the same time."[82] Two consequences of this mechanistic approach adopted by the Red Army were that first, the bravery of its soldiers was squandered; and second, losses were much higher than they needed to be.[83] A particularly telling criticism by Löser is that the Red Army seldom exploited any local successes. He concludes, therefore: "Had they pressed more energetically against the

German divisions withdrawing back toward Stalingrad when forming the Kessel, then they would have been able to finish the battles at that time."[84] This assessment is entirely consistent with a lack of initiative on the part of Soviet commanders: they did what they were ordered to do and no more. At the tactical level this was and remained a crucial distinction between Soviet and German junior leaders and one that would often determine the outcome of local engagements.

Horst Zank, a battalion commander in 673rd Grenadier Regiment of 376th Infantry Division whose battalion faced many such Soviet attacks, was also highly critical of Soviet assault tactics.[85] Typically the Soviet infantry would approach the German positions seated on T-34 tanks so as to avoid being exhausted by a march through deep snow. With no protection, the Soviet infantry would then be shot off the tanks by the concentrated fire of machine guns and small arms. In response to the heavy losses, the Soviet infantry changed strategies so that they advanced behind the tanks as they approached the German positions. Once the Soviet tanks were knocked out or immobilized, the Soviet infantry had to stay behind them or continue the assault across open ground, slowed down and exhausted by deep snow and once again vulnerable to the withering fire of well-sited German machine guns. In these Soviet-style mass attacks, launched with scant regard for loss of life, the Germans had all the advantages. They could observe the attacks being formed up and were able to identify the main lines of advance well before the Soviet infantry got anywhere near their positions. The obvious solution would have been to launch attacks in which the Soviet infantry advanced to contact under cover of darkness, thus denying the Germans the advantages of daylight. The silent approach to contact, with artillery and tank support available after contact had been made and the firefight had started, would have emulated the classic methods pioneered by Hermann Geyer and used by the German Army in the Ludendorff offensives of March–July 1918 in World War I. With no shortage of manpower, artillery, and tanks, there was a very good chance that these infiltration methods would have worked had they been applied. However, fortunately for the Germans, these sorts of silent advances to contact at night required very high standards of junior leadership, which were lacking in the Red Army. So, with some exceptions, the mass daylight attack regardless of losses remained the preferred option for Red Army commanders.

There is some evidence that Soviet assault methods were being modified in order to penetrate German defenses. A memorandum drawn up by Grenadier Regiment 178 notes that Soviet units are putting together assault units numbering about thirty men each and made up of the best and most combat-experienced soldiers. These small groups are led by especially bold commissars and officers and equipped with numerous weapons suited for close-quarters fighting. Such a Soviet assault group approaches the German position under cover of darkness. Concentrated mortar fire is laid on the German positions, and the positions are assaulted as soon as the weight of fire is transferred to a neighboring position. The report's author specifies the following countermeasures to deal with these night attacks: (1) complete and continual observation of the forward terrain; (2)listening posts in front of the forward line; (3) increased readiness of all positions, quick-reaction units, and reserves; (4) reinforcement and checking of the wire obstacles in front of the positions; (5) laying artillery fire and the fire of heavy-infantry weapons on the likely enemy start lines about 200 meters in front of the German position under fire once heavy preparatory fire has been identified; (6) automatic counterattack.[86] As sound as these countermeasures were, they could not be sustained in undermanned and exhausted units. Nor did dwindling reserves of artillery and mortar ammunition permit such an expenditure of fire.

Night fighting also had its distinct features and varied according to whether it took place on the steppe, in the open, or in the very close confines and rubble of the city. Cloud-free night skies made binoculars highly effective at night, especially with snow on the ground, so reconnaissance patrols could observe the terrain in front of them before making their tactical movements. Moonlight in such conditions meant that any kind of movement had to be made with extreme caution using any available cover, such as folds in the ground and gullies, as would be the case in daylight. Thick fog on the steppe made the use of compasses by day and night essential, and frequent listening stops were required. In such conditions any encounters with the enemy were sudden, brutal, and short. The victors were those who were aggressive and seized the initiative. The same applied in the city, but night encounters there were made worse by the disorienting effect of buildings and rubble, the ease with which the soldier could be separated from his fellows, and his own sense that he was alone. His perception of his own vulnerability was heightened. Viktor Nekrasov, Stalingrad veteran and author of *V okopakh Stalingrada* (*In the Trenches of Stalingrad*, 1946), describes the psychological strain and peculiarities of the night battle: "A battle of individuals: in such circumstances the soldier is everything. His power is unlimited. Initiative, audacity, instinct, sixth sense, resourcefulness all decide the outcome. Here there is no mass, self-abandoning passion, as in a daytime attack. No feeling of comradeship. No comforting 'hurrahs' that shut off the fear and inspire. . . . No horizon. And no way back. You don't know what's in front, what's behind your back."[87]

German War Crimes: The Case of Dulag-205

For all its horrors and bloodletting, Stalingrad is not generally associated with German war crimes on the Eastern front. However, the Soviet view, which remains unchanged in the Russian Federation, was that the Germans did commit war crimes at Stalingrad. The most serious case of war crimes committed by 6th Army at Stalingrad of which I am aware concerns the death of well over 3,000 Red Army soldiers in Dulag-205 between October 1942 and January 1943. The first reference to this camp in the secondary literature is made in *Stalingradskaia epopeia*.[88] Dulag-205 was a transit camp (*Durchgangslager* in German) located close to the village of Alekseevka and about 5 kilometers (3 miles) from Gumrak, one of the main airfields in 6th Army's rear area. Today Gumrak is Volgograd's main airport, about 24 kilometers (15 miles) west of the city.

On 31 January 1943 Dulag-205 was overrun by the Red Army, and the German officers responsible for the camp's administration were captured: the camp commandant, Oberst Rudolf Körpert (1886–1944); the deputy camp commandant, Hauptmann Carl Frister (1896–1944); the officer responsible for work details, Hauptmann Kurt Wohlfahrt (1893–1944); the officer in charge of the camp's construction group, Hauptmann Richard Seidlitz (1887–1944); the head of camp security, Rotmeister Fritz Müsenthin (1889–1944); and adjutant to the commandant Oberleutnant Otto Mäder (1895–1944). All were interrogated by SMERSH officials, and an initial investigation, which included witness testimony from prisoners, concluded that the German camp staff had presided over the deliberate mass killing of Soviet prisoners of war. Prisoners lived in filthy conditions without proper sanitation, without access to water, and with thoroughly inadequate food. They were subjected to arbitrary beatings and shootings. So bad was the provision of food that starvation ensued and cannibalism became a major problem, especially as the weather turned colder.

On 18 September 1944 Körpert and his staff were formally arrested, and on 23 September 1944 General Lieutenant Mikhail Belkin, the head of SMERSH on the 3rd Baltic front, upheld the charges of "mass extermination of Soviet citizens."[89] The hearing opened on 9 October 1944. The tribunal's findings concerning Körpert's running of Dulag-205, are reproduced here in full for the first time:

1. That the prisoner-of-war camp that existed from the beginning of September 1942 within the area under control of the German 6th Army in the region of Stalingrad, the so-called Dulag-205, was laid out in an open field. On the territory of the camp several bunkers were constructed in which it was not possible to accommodate more than 500 prisoners. Moreover, the number of prisoners and civilians who were placed in the camp reached 4,000 and beyond. A consequence of such unbelievable overcrowding was that people could not sleep lying down. There were no bunks of any kind in the shelters. Several armfuls of rotten grass were thrown in the shelters to be used as bedding. In the cold months of November–December 1942 and January 1943 the bunkers were not heated. Those people who could not be accommodated in the bunkers had to remain in the open field without any fuel for lighting fires. In these conditions wounded prisoners were kept, as well as those who were suffering from respiratory diseases, malnutrition, exhaustion from physical work, and beatings.

   Those directly guilty for the creation of these inhuman conditions of accommodating prisoners of war are the accused: the camp commandant Körpert, the deputy commandant Frister, the commandant's assistant Müzenthin, the adjutant Mäder, and the head of the construction group Seidlitz.
2. That the food for the prisoners was the scraps from the kitchens of German soldiers and sometimes the corpses of dead horses, which were thrown into the camp. Water was not delivered to the camp, and the prisoners were forced to use dirty snow collected inside the camp. Additionally, no fuel was brought to the camp, which forced the prisoners to use fuel from the clothes of the dead in order to make fires for preparing the "food" comprising leftovers and dead horses. And when there was insufficient clothing to be taken from the dead they used their own uniforms. However, even this "food" made up of scraps and horses was of a miserable quantity. As a consequence of the starvation in the camp, prisoners were reduced to cannibalism. Despite this, rations were not given to the prisoners.

   Those directly guilty for creating these inhuman conditions for the prisoners are the camp commandant Körpert and the adjutant Mäder, under whose control came the camp transport, which should have been used to secure the delivery of fuel and water to the camp.
3. That German soldiers of the camp's headquarters company tormented the

prisoners on a daily basis, beat them, and removed their warm clothing, keeping it for themselves.

On the instructions of the accused Frister and Müsenthin, with the consent of Körpert, the prisoners were terrorized by dogs, allegedly for the purposes of maintaining order in the camp.

Apart from the persons named, the accused Mäder, who as the commander of the headquarters company permitted the beating of prisoners by soldiers under his command, is also guilty of tormenting prisoners and beating them.

4. That exhausted, starving, and ill prisoners were dispatched to do heavy, exhausting work on the construction of defenses and on building roads. When these exhausted and ill prisoners, weakened from work, sat down to rest or collapsed, they were beaten by the guards and frequently shot dead on the spot. And when this happened none of the soldiers guilty of murder were ever subjected to any kind of punishment.

   The camp commandant Körpert and Wohlfahrt, the head of the camp's work allocation detail, bear responsibility for this inhuman and criminal treatment of the prisoners.

5. That on the direct orders of the camp commandant, the accused Körpert, two prisoners were executed who had committed no crime at all in the camp and were killed merely because in a conversation they expressed indignation between themselves about the evil acts that were carried out by the camp administration. The criminal deeds of all the accused in their sum total created in the camp those inhuman conditions as a consequence of which more than 3,000 Soviet prisoners of war died from starvation, beatings, and executions.

By the evil deeds described the accused have committed a crime provided for by Article 1 of the Decree of the Presidium of the Supreme Soviet of the USSR of 19 April 1943.

Being guided by Articles 319 and 320 of the Criminal Procedural Code and the Decree of the Presidium of the Supreme Soviet of the USSR of 24 May 1944, the Military Tribunal—

HAS SENTENCED:

KÖRPERT Rudolf, FRISTER Carl, MÜZENTHIN Fritz, MÄDER Otto, SEIDLITZ Richard, and WOHLFAHRT Kurt, on the basis of the Decree of the Presidium of the Supreme Soviet of the USSR of Article 1 of 19 April

> 1943, to the highest measure of criminal punishment—TO BE SHOT. The sentence is final and shall not be subject to appeal.[90]

Körpert, Frister, Müzenthin, Mäder, Seidlitz, and Wohlfahrt were all executed on 13 October 1944. They had earlier been permitted to submit written notes requesting clemency.

The decree of the Presidium of the Supreme Soviet of the USSR referred to in the sentence was one of the primary Soviet documents setting out the need for tracking down war criminals among German and Axis formations (Italian, Romanian, Hungarian, Finnish) and inflicting retribution, as can be seen from its full title: "Concerning the Punitive Measures to Be Applied to the German-Fascist Criminals Guilty of the Murders and Tortures of the Soviet Civilian Population and Red Army Prisoners of War and to Spies, Traitors of the Motherland from among Soviet Citizens, and Their Accomplices."[91] The decree provided for sentences of between fifteen and twenty years of forced labor for those found guilty of aiding and abetting the German occupation forces and their allies. Sentences of the military courts attached to divisions were to be carried out immediately. Paragraph 5 of the decree provided for the public hanging of those sentenced to death. The provisions of the 1926 Rossiiskaia Sovetskaia Federativnaia Sotsialisticheskaia Respublika (Russian Soviet Federated Socialist Republic [RSFSR]) Criminal Code also applied. The number of Soviet citizens convicted for these crimes was greater than the number of those from enemy occupation forces. For example, of the total of 81,780 persons who were charged with war crimes between 1943 and 1952, the number from enemy forces was 25,209.[92]

Capture and Captivity

The march into captivity, or marches undertaken in captivity, is one of the defining experiences of prisoners of war of all belligerents in World War II. For example, British memoir literature based on experiences in Japanese captivity contains many detailed accounts of the miseries endured on long marches and even short marches by poorly fed soldiers in tropical heat and humidity. For Americans, the defining experience in the Far East was the Bataan death march. The march into captivity is also a propaganda opportunity for the captors. In *The Railway Man* (1995) Eric Lomax, who was captured after the fall of Singapore, recalls that the prisoners were subjected to a carefully orchestrated march for Japanese camera crews: "Every able-bodied prisoner had to line a route which included all the main roads in the Changi area, 50,000 of us standing two deep, strung out for miles around the camp. A cortège of open cars drove past, preceded by a camera crew in the back of an open lorry. They were making their propaganda film for home consumption, and we were the extras."[93] Experiences of Allied prisoners captured by the Germans were not as bad, but bad enough. In his unpublished memoir, *A Bandsman and Barbed Wire: Experiences and Recollections, May 1941–May 1945*, Kenneth R. Macdonald, who survived the sinking of HMS *Gloucester* during the battle of Crete in 1941, recollects the long, exhausting marches that his fellow prisoners and he endured under a hot Greek sun.[94] Moreover, in 1945, as the Third Reich was collapsing, parts of Central and Eastern Europe became a seething mass of people on the move. Millions of civilians, slave laborers, Allied prisoners of war heading west, displaced persons, and refugees were fleeing in search of hope and salvation.

This march into captivity and subsequent death is also an unforgettable part of the Soviet war experience, especially in 1941 and 1942. Millions of Soviet prisoners captured in huge encirclement operations were marched into large camps that were little more than hastily improvised barbed-wire pens exposed to the weather, where they died of starvation, cold, and disease. And as the Red Army retreated, civilians fled too. On the Briansk front in September 1941, Grossman witnessed the flight of civilians and soldiers, and it made a profound impression on him:

> I thought that I had seen a retreat, but I had seen nothing like this; I could not even have imagined it. It was exodus, something out of the Bible! The vehicles are moving in rows of eight; there is the hysterical whining noise of dozens of lorries all trying at the same time to pull themselves out of the mud. Huge herds of sheep and cows are being driven across the fields. Further on you can hear the scraping of horse-drawn carts, thousands of trailers covered in colored cloth, wood, and tin plate in which were refugees from Ukraine. Still further there are huge masses of people on foot carrying sacks, bundles, and suitcases. This is no flood; this is no river: this is the slow movement of an ocean, and the width of this movement was hundreds of meters to the right and left. From underneath the canopies on the carts peer the white and black heads of children, the biblical beards of Jewish elders, the scarves of peasant women, the hats of Ukrainian uncles, black-haired girls and women. And what calm there is in their eyes, what wise grief, what a feeling of fate, of a universal

> catastrophe! In the evening the sun appears from behind the many-layered blue, black, and gray clouds. Its rays are wide and huge. They stretch from the heavens to the ground, just like in those paintings by Doré depicting the terrible biblical scenes of those harsh divine forces descending to earth. In these wide yellow rays the movement of these old men, women carrying little children, the herds of sheep, and soldiers is something that seems so majestic and tragic that for some brief minutes I have the very real sense of our having been taken back to the times of biblical catastrophes.[95]

Having endured two and a half months of fighting on ever-dwindling rations after the encirclement, psychologically worn down and with physical reserves exhausted, Axis soldiers were about to confront another ordeal—a series of ordeals, in fact—for which a large part of them were ill prepared and from which they would perish. The German collapse at Stalingrad is powerfully recorded in Soviet newsreel footage showing long lines of starving and freezing German and Romanian soldiers, often clad in improvised footwear and bizarre combinations of military and civilian clothing—anything to beat the cold—marching into captivity. That this footage was primarily intended for propagandistic purposes takes nothing away from its profoundly moving scenes of human degradation and the catastrophe that had finally overwhelmed the German 6th Army and its allies. The propaganda humiliation inflicted on the British by the Japanese after the fall of Singapore seems mild by comparison.

All the German memoirs written by survivors record the horrors of the march from Stalingrad to various assembly points and railway lines for onward transport to camps. Typically these marches to the nearest railway line were in the range of 150 to 200 kilometers (93 to 124 miles), a grim ordeal for malnourished and exhausted soldiers under winter conditions. One of the best accounts of these ordeals is provided by Dr. Hubert Haidinger. Immediately after the surrender Haidinger reports that prisoners in his contingent were kept standing all night in the Tsaritsa gully. The dreaded march started at first light: "No food, nothing to drink. Dirty snow and urine-yellow ice were all there was to quench the unbearable thirst."[96] Cold, exhaustion, and lack of food—and all too often no food or water—were not the only trials to which the soldiers were subjected. On the way to the various assembly points and railheads there were stops. During these pauses the German prisoners could expect to be robbed by guards and civilians of boots, clothing, watches—anything of value, and in the material poverty of the Soviet Union, just about anything they had was valuable. In these harsh weather conditions, loss of clothing was tantamount to a death sentence.

Along with frostbite injuries, Haidinger reports that the main medical problems were typhus, lung infections, and intestinal disorders. Once in a camp, postmortems were ordered to ascertain the causes of the many deaths. The results were obvious:

> The first cut alone in the cheek provided an unequivocal diagnosis: death from starvation. The fat body of the cheek (*corpus adiposum buccae*), the human body's very last reserve of fat, was absorbed and disappeared. Body weight was well under 40 kilos [88 pounds]. When opening the abdominal captivity, one was confronted with a picture of contents like pure, transparent glass. It was forbidden to write starvation as the diagnosis of death, and in its place one wrote dystrophy, what means much the same as malnutrition.[97]

Confirmation of Haidinger's point that any mention of starvation was forbidden by the Soviet camp administrators can be found in a Russian source. Khristoforov notes that a study commissioned by the NKVD and other Soviet agencies concluded that dystrophy, as noted by Haidinger, was the main cause of death in captivity. He writes: "The mortality of prisoners due to alimentary dystrophy (the complete exhaustion of an irreversible nature of the internal organs because of degeneration), wounds, and frostbite amounted to 80.5 percent of the general total of mortality cases."[98]

Horst Zank, having been captured in a failed escape attempt, was taken to Dubovka on the Volga, about 50 kilometers (31 miles) north of Stalingrad. He refers to Dubovka as "the death chamber" and notes that it was not uncommon for a man to wake up and find that the soldier next to him had died in the night. Common to most of the German memoirs is the observation, also noted by Allied prisoners of the Germans and Japanese, that soldiers lost the will to live and died: "It is something indescribable and deeply shocking to have to follow the decreasing will to live and weakening of strength that is linked to it."[99] If they survived the great waves of death that struck down so many in the first six months after capture, prisoners, especially the NCOs and other ranks, were liable for heavy work details. Stone breaking and forestry were standard. Prisoners of all ranks, especially senior officers, were subjected to intense pressure—food was a very powerful incentive—to join Soviet front organizations such as the Bund Deutscher Offiziere (BDO, Alliance of German officers) and Nationalkomitee Freies Deutschland (NFD, National committee of free Germany). I shall return to this problem when dealing with the specific case of Oberst Arthur Boje, but perhaps the most perplexing aspect of this Soviet pressure to secure the collaboration of German officers is why decorated and brave soldiers would agree to work for Soviet propaganda aims. Zank, in common with Boje, tends to see this as a question of character, or lack thereof.

Zank also explains collaboration on the part of German officers as a mixture of naked opportunism and status-seeking, what one might call the will to power. He argues that the need to be admired (*Geltungsbedürfnis*) and personal ambitions were decisive factors. He draws an interesting parallel between the Soviet Union and Nazi Germany: "It is therefore no matter of chance that more than a few of those who in the Third Reich or in the party or in one of its organizations occupied leading positions at different levels also here belong to the ranks of functionaries in the anti-Fascist movement."[100] Such is the extent to which some members of the BDO have internalized the aims and ambitions of their Soviet captors that they started to refer to Red Army successes as "ours."[101] Especially painful for Zank and his fellows who did not collaborate with the Soviet authorities must have been the fact that many of the generals in the BDO had been captured at Stalingrad and lent their names to undermining the German war effort. With one or two exceptions, Zank is highly critical of German doctors in Soviet captivity. As a group they seem to have succumbed to the demands made on them by the Soviet authorities and did not aggressively intercede for the well-being of German prisoners. By contrast, Zank writes very favorably of Russian doctors and their efforts to ameliorate the lot of German prisoners.

Perhaps with memories of what had befallen the millions of Red Army prisoners in the winter of 1941–1942, German soldiers, despite Soviet promises of good treatment if they surrendered, feared the prospect of captivity. Escape was an option, and some of the memoirs provide details of serious preparations and actual attempts. Horst Zank made two attempts. Ration bombs (*Verpflegungsbomben*), which were being dropped by the Luftwaffe right up to the end, made it possible to create a reserve of tinned food and bread.[102] Paulus's chief of staff, Generalleutnant Schmidt, even informed Zank that plans were afoot to set up ration depots near Kalach and that orders had been given to rescue any escapees by plane. Zank and his fellow escapees manage to acquire skis and snowshoes, but their first attempt is aborted after they set off a mine. For the second attempt Zank and his three companions, Oberleutnant Gerhard Kaiser and Oberfeldwebels Drieschner and Kurek, make for the Volga and then move north along the frozen river. At the end of their first night they sit out the day in an abandoned bunker, though they are lucky not to be discovered by two Russians. By first light at the end of the second night they are still moving about and are seen and eventually captured. They have got as far as the village of Vinnovka, which is about 15 kilometers (9 miles) north of Stalingrad on the high ground overlooking the river.

Gerhard Dieckhoff records that three officers equipped with skis and winter clothing, Oberleutnants Knabe, Mickein, and von Heynitz, made an escape attempt. Like the Zank group, they had to abandon their first attempt. A second attempt was made, but Dieckhoff notes that "nothing more was heard of them."[103] In 100th Jäger Division, Oberst Franz Neibecker, the commander of Infantry Regiment 227, gave the order that those who wanted to make a breakout attempt to reach the west were free to do so. Neidhardt notes that very few made the attempt, and the reasons were clear enough: "Quite apart from the lethargy, it was above all a question of their poor physical condition that deterred the men from this hazardous undertaking. Moreover, hardly any of them were aware that the German lines—not, as was widely believed at the time, immediately on the other side of the Don—at this time had already been pulled back about 200 kilometers [124 miles] farther west."[104]

According to Carell, many small groups of German soldiers tried to break out of the Kessel and get back to German lines. He says that lone groups were still being spotted by air crews in mid-February. Thereafter the sightings ceased. Carell reports that one German soldier, Unteroffizier Nieweg, did succeed in getting back to German lines but was killed within twenty-four hours of returning.[105] There is reliable evidence that at least one German soldier, Feldwebel Michael Horvath, who served in the military police unit of 100th Jäger Division, did escape, though after he had been captured, from Stalingrad. Captured on 31 January 1943, Horvath, a Russian speaker, was used by the Red Army as an interpreter. He remained with the Soviet Infantry Regiment 207, part of 51st Guards Division, when it was transferred to the region of Orel. It was from there that he escaped on 10 March 1943 and reached the German lines.

In keeping with standard German practice, Horvath was required to provide statements about what had happened and what he had seen. He confirms the harrowing treatment of German prisoners after the surrender:

> The behavior of Russian soldiers toward our wounded German soldiers was despicable. Immediately after they were captured they fell upon our

> people, officers as well, like hyenas and robbed them. They especially wanted money, watches, and jewelry. Those who refused or hesitated were badly treated and forced to hand over what they had. Fur hats, gloves, felt boots, and overcoats were especially sought after and were taken from the prisoners without any consideration of the prevailing cold weather. I myself saw a prisoner standing barefoot in the snow, another without anything on his head, and an officer moving about in just the regulation shirt without an overcoat. After they were captured our prisoners were given bread, which was immediately torn away from them by Russian soldiers after it had been distributed.[106]

Horvath claims that badly wounded German soldiers were shot by the Russians. He reports that later, when he was being held as a prisoner at the headquarters of a Soviet regiment, a Russian woman with anti-Bolshevik sentiments told him that she had seen German wounded stripped of their clothing and then shot. In his two statements, which he made on returning to German lines, Horvath reported that Soviet commissars and officers made it clear that German medical personnel were needed primarily to care for Red Army sick and wounded. A feature of the divide-and-rule policies that the Soviet authorities would adopt in their formation of the BDO and anti-Fascist propaganda is also reported by Horvath. Soldiers from his division were separated according to whether they were *Ostmärker* (soldiers from the eastern border regions of Germany) or *Altreichsdeutsche* (soldiers from Austria and the Sudetenland): the *Ostmärker* were being used as cleanup squads in Stalingrad, which was regarded as preferential treatment, whereas the rest were to be sent to Siberia.

One aspect of the aftermath of 6th Army's destruction on the Volga concerns the fact that the National Socialist (NS) regime dealt with the need to maintain morale on the home front by keeping news of German prisoners to an absolute minimum. This strategy necessarily placed thousands of wives, mothers, sons, and daughters, for whom the loss of fathers and sons and the uncertainty were individual catastrophes, at odds with the regime. That large numbers of 6th Army were now in Soviet captivity inspired the hope, however desperate, that perhaps a loved one had not been killed or succumbed to cold but was alive and that maybe he would one day return home. These relatives desperately wanted news.

An especially valuable account of how OKH and other institutions reacted behind the scenes to the defeat and the insatiable desire for news on the part of next of kin is provided by Mady von Schilling. From February 1940 to the end of February 1943 she was a secretary attached to Replacement Battalion 178 in Potsdam and thus had very close links with 178th Infantry Regiment and 76th Infantry Division. After the loss of 6th Army, OKH established an Arbeitsstab Stalingrad, commanded by Count Alfred Waldersee, which dealt with a range of administrative tasks arising from the defeat, one of which was to try to ascertain who had been killed in the last days inside the Kessel and who might have survived. Von Schilling was appointed Waldersee's secretary. Her account of her work reveals that the NS regime was more concerned with the propaganda aftermath of the defeat than with the welfare of German prisoners in Soviet captivity.

Von Schilling reports that shortly before Whitsun (Pentecost) 1943 she was visited by General Friedrich von Rabenau, a friend of General Walter Heitz and his wife. Heitz, the commander of VIII Army Corps, had been captured at Stalingrad. According to Rabenau, Frau Heitz had received a very long letter purporting to be from her husband. From the letter's contents there are no doubts that her husband was the author. In the letter Heitz informs his wife that German prisoners are now permitted to receive mail and packages and that their relatives should be writing. According to von Schilling, it is official policy to make people believe that the Russians do not take prisoners at all. This policy is intended to ensure that German soldiers will fight stubbornly and to deter mass desertion. Consequently, the contents of the Heitz letter, she warns Rabenau; are subversive and dangerous because, if the contents are true, the letter exposes official policy as false.

Just how a letter from a captured German general managed to reach his wife from a camp inside the Soviet Union is not made clear. One explanation is that Heitz wrote the letter at the behest of the NKVD and that it was smuggled into Germany via neutral diplomatic channels. If that is so, it suggests that Heitz may well have joined the BDO. This possibility would seem to be completely ruled out, however, by Oberst Arthur Boje's glowing and admiring assessment of Heitz's behavior as a prisoner—Heitz died in captivity in 1944—characterizing him as the most steadfast of all the Stalingrad generals.[107] So the letter may have been a forgery, but it was based on intimate knowledge of the Heitz household. Whatever the origins of the letter, the urging of large numbers of Germans to write letters is clearly intended to embarrass the German government and has all the hallmarks of a well-organized NKVD propaganda operation. Moreover, given Heitz's hostility to von Seydlitz–Kurzbach for collaborating with the NKVD-sponsored BDO and his own rejection of the BDO, a forged letter reaching Germany would imply, as perhaps it was intended to do, that Heitz was working for the NKVD and thus to besmirch his reputation for upright behavior in captivity.

The contents of this explosive letter were, however, soon making the rounds because von Schilling's superior, oblivious to the caution of his secretary, had written to Baroness Beaulieu, the wife of a regimental commander in 29th Infantry Division (mot.), informing her of what he knew. The baroness passed on the news in a letter to a friend. This letter was then duplicated so that relatives became aware that letters could be sent to German prisoners. According to von Schilling, other letters, somehow smuggled across the lines, reached Germany and were destroyed. However, before the letters were destroyed a list was compiled noting the name of each sender and the date of dispatch. Undeterred by official policy, von Schilling, noting that various Germans of all ranks are making radio addresses over Soviet radio, made the dangerous proposal to her superior that they maintain a file of the speakers' names and the dates of such broadcasts. This was extremely risky not only because it involved listening to enemy radio broadcasts, which was forbidden in wartime Germany, but also because the list—written evidence—confirmed the proscribed act.

Inevitably it came to the attention of the German authorities and Goebbels that prisoners' letters from the Soviet Union had reached Germany. In a series of announcements placed in the press—*Völkischer Beobachter* and *Angriff*—relatives were encouraged to send letters intended for German prisoners of war to a special post-office box, from which letters would be collected and handed over to the International Red Cross and the Turkish Red Crescent. According to von Schilling, however, all the letters so received were destroyed. The regime's ploy was not risk-free because if the offer of passing on letters had come to the attention of the International Red Cross, that organization would have been in a position to expose the fact that, despite its willingness to assist, no letters had been received from the German authorities. Von Schilling writes that the whole idea "was simply a means or attempt to calm the public."[108] It is perhaps a measure of von Schilling's isolation from the regime's atrocities (or a refusal to face up to them) that she can regard the destruction of these letters as one of National Socialism's great abuses.[109] Deceiving the relatives and families of soldiers in this way and then destroying the letters—the fact that they were burned in an oven possesses a gruesome significance in the light of Nazi war crimes—was undoubtedly a despicable act (despicable regimes commit despicable acts), but it is an absolute nonevent when compared to the misery, suffering, and evil that had been inflicted on millions of people all over the Eastern front and which 6th Army prisoners were experiencing as they stumbled and marched into Soviet captivity.

One aspect of these letters and the broadcasts made by German officers and others who joined the BDO is how their relatives were treated in Germany. For example, Boje records that Oberst von Beaulieu, the commander of the artillery regiment in 29th Infantry Division (mot.), was suborned by the NKVD and joined the BDO.[110] Given the NKVD intention to use these defections for propaganda purposes, von Beaulieu's role in the BDO would have come to the attention of the German authorities, and one assumes that his wife would have been made aware of her husband's collaboration with the enemy. NS Germany had no equivalent of Stalin's vindictive Order № 270, but toward the end of the war, especially after the attempt on Hitler's life on 20 July 1944, Himmler was eager to apply the policy of *Sippenhaft*, which determined that families were liable for acts committed by close relatives.

Those who survived Soviet captivity, in some cases for as long as thirteen years, returned to a divided Germany, each part on a different side in the Cold War. Some, as in the case of Friedrich Dettmer, returned to East Germany, which was then in the Soviet occupation zone. We can take it for granted that those who returned home faced enormous difficulties as they tried to adapt to a Germany that had changed in all kinds of ways. The sorts of support mechanisms, not perfect by any means, that today's soldiers take for granted did not exist. Soldiers were alone with their thoughts and memories. In fact, they were something of an embarrassment in a society, in the case of West Germany, that just did not want to be reminded of the Nazi past and was more concerned, not surprisingly, with rebuilding a shattered economy. One particular problem is highlighted by Horst Zank. Having withstood an attempt to incriminate him as a war criminal and finally returned home in December 1949, Zank is assailed by thoughts on how and why he survived—even whether he deserved to survive. This sense of survivor guilt is a major theme in much of the camp literature based on experiences in Nazi camps, for example, in the work of Primo Levi and Viktor Frankl.

Conclusion

Whereas the Soviet Union after 1945 celebrated the victories and soldierly qualities of the Red Army in the Great Fatherland War, a tradition taken over by the Russian Federation, Germans, for understandable reasons, have been reluctant to acknowledge the military prowess of the Wehrmacht or the combat units of the Waffen SS lest it be interpreted as a manifestation of neo-militarism or lack of repentance for National Socialist crimes. Politically this reluctance may have helped Germany's post-1945 rehabilitation, but it has led to the ignoring and evasion of some fundamental historical and military truths.

As David Glantz makes very clear in the first volume of his Stalingrad trilogy, the German army did not simply turn up at Stalingrad in August 1942: it had to fight its way there against determined opposition. If, as some Wehrmacht survivors believe, the Red Army's retreat to the Volga was a planned withdrawal implemented to lure German 6th Army into a trap, then it was a costly military maneuver for the Red Army. Yet the battles to secure and to clear the Great Don Bend exacted a severe toll on 6th Army and undoubtedly exacerbated its supply and manpower problems in the city. That 6th Army reached Stalingrad on the Volga, the start of Central Asia, was itself an outstanding military achievement, a brilliant demonstration of high-speed warfare, toughness, planning, and, to use the German word, *Daraufgängertum* (offensive, aggressive spirit). Encircled and in crisis, it adapted; its remarkable junior leadership achieved wonders of command and improvisation in appalling conditions that undoubtedly made it possible for 6th Army to hold out as long as it did. After 6th Army's collapse the Nazi propaganda machine made much of the fact that the British had more or less surrendered without a fight at Singapore, consigning a vast fortress to Germany's ally, whereas 6th Army had held fast in Fortress Stalingrad until the end. The Nazi propaganda may be shrill, but its point that Lieutenant General Arthur Percival had failed to do his duty is uncomfortably close to the truth.

The next three chapters, translations of German war diaries, presented here in English for the first time, reveal in forensic detail how three of 6th Army's divisions, 16th Panzer Division, 94th Infantry Division, and 76th Infantry Division, responded to the challenges of exhausting victory and looming defeat.

2 16th Panzer Division inside Fortress Stalingrad, 19 November 1942–2 February 1943

This account of 16th Panzer Division's operational history at Stalingrad, "16th Panzer Division's Battle inside Fortress Stalingrad over the Period from 19 November 1942 to 2 February 1943," was compiled by Leutnant Dr. Elsner von Gronow and is based on the various reports (*Erlebnisberichte*) prepared by those who served inside the Kessel. In his *Geschichte der 16. Panzer-Division*, Wolfgang Werthen notes that a provisional history of 16th Panzer Division was put together in Italy (1943) by Major von Alvensleben and Lt. Dr. Elsner von Gronow, but Major von Alvensleben's name does not appear on the German original of this document. This account forms part of the archive holdings of the Bundesarchiv-Militärarchiv in Freiburg-im-Breisgau. Its BA-MA archival reference is RH 27-16/52 (Der Kampf der 16. Panzer-Division in der Festung Stalingrad in der Zeit vom 19. November 1942 bis 2. Februar 1943).

Preface: Russia, January 1944

A layer of snow has once again enveloped Russia's wide plains and marshy woods. In the ranks of 16th Panzer Division, comrades fight who were with us in Stalingrad. After the summer and autumn battles in Italy, we are once again in Russia.[1]

For the friends of those who remained in the Stalingrad Kessel, the following pages should evoke memories of the time of a heroic battle of our old, proud 16th Panzer Division. In 1940 we were in France, and in 1941 and 1942 we fought in south Russia! In the huge encirclement battles of Kiev and Kharkov, 16th Panzer Division led by General Hube made its reputation.

The Wehrmacht report dated 31 January 1943 referred to the proud feats of arms of 16th Panzer Division, now one of the divisions in the army, led by General of Panzer Troops Hube, that defeated the Russians at Pogrebishche.

And now, how to revive the memory of the dreadful weeks at Stalingrad of a year ago? In these critical months the caring thoughts of those at home accompanied their loved ones every hour of the day. Where in the homeland worry threatened to crush someone or other, 3,000 kilometers (1,864 miles) to the east in the snow and ice a new hero arose. The weak will have their spirits revived for all time by the cast of mind that this battle to the very end has nurtured among the very best, and which emerges from their letters.

Roll of Honor

Holders of the Knight's Cross in 16th Panzer Division who fell and remained at Stalingrad:

1. Generalmajor Angern, divisional commander since October 1942 and during the battles in Stalingrad
2. Major Dormann, commander of the Motorcyclist Unit K16
3. Hauptmann Mues, commander of Armored Reconnaissance Battalion, Regiment 64, killed in an attack on Rynok on 17 November 1942
4. Oberleutnant Berger, 10th Company, Antiaircraft, Panzer-Grenadier Regiment 79. Oberleutnant Berger died of the severe wound he received on 24 November 1942. On 27 November 1942 he was buried in the Cemetery of Heroes at Stalingrad.

The Road Taken and the Battles Fought by 16th Panzer Division from 22 August to 19 November 1942

The huge encirclement battle at Kalach ended in victory on 17 August 1942. The Great Don Bend is essentially free of enemy. In the battles of July and August 1942, 16th Panzer Division won new fame. On 8 August 1942 our division destroyed its one thousandth Russian tank.

In the night of 22–23 August 1942, 16th Panzer Division assembles on the west bank of the Don on the main Don highway in order to cross the 140-meter-long army bridge 40 kilometers (25 miles) northeast of Kalach, sometime toward 0340 hrs. On the west bank of the Don, next to this bridge, lies the village of Lutchenskii. On the east bank the route leads to Peskovatka. On the evening of 22 August 1942 a fast-moving combat group has already crossed the Don and formed a bridgehead.

On 23 August 1942 the march of the combat group proceeds on the eastern side of the Don with a thrust to the north for three hours and then farther to the east; then a turn is made to old boundaries: the Tartar burial mounds, the Stalingrad–Moscow railway line, and farther in the direction of the northern part of Stalingrad. In the evening the Volga is visible. The division takes up an all-around defensive position on a narrow piece of ground 5 kilometers (3.1 miles) west of Latashanka and Rynok. At 1000 hours on 24 August 1942

Latashanka is under our control. A platoon of engineers[2] takes out some 8.5-cm antiaircraft guns dug in on the flanking high ground southwest of Latashanka, as a consequence of which a thrust into the Latashanka area and down to the Volga is made possible. Combat Group Strehlke has been given the task of reaching the Volga bank and then occupying it to a width of 8 kilometers (5 miles). Other parts of the division are to head toward the village of Rynok, the southern edge of which is overlooked and dominated by Spartakovka. The commander of this south front is the commander of Panzer Grenadier Regiment 64. From a lack of fuel, the attempt to occupy the village of Rynok, practically free of any enemy, is abandoned. It is stormed by motorcyclists and engineers on 27 August but has to be given up again on 29 August.

Members of 9th Company, 2nd Panzer Regiment, and of Panzer Engineer Battalion 16 are the first Germans in this war to reach the Volga!

As so often before, 16th Panzer Division is on this occasion cut off from any communication from the outside world for several days. On orders from the Führer, we hold the positions that were reached on 23 and 24 August in the north of Stalingrad. German formations following on are to clear the region between the Don and the Volga.

In the following months, in the same sector, 16th Panzer Division holds the so-called North Switch Position and the Volga bank at Vinnovka, fighting against Russian attacks and landing attempts. On 16 September 1942 Generalmajor Hube hands over command of the division to Oberst von Ahrenstorff (commander of Panzer Grenadier Regiment 79). Two weeks later he is followed by Generalmajor Angern, who then leads the division for the next four months. Generalmajor Hube receives command of XIV Panzer Corps.

Days of quiet are interrupted by days of fighting. The German Wehrmacht report of 31 October 1942 singles out the especially great achievements of our division and reports the sinking of 14 combat and freight vessels on the Volga by our 16th Panzer Division!

Some bridgehead positions in the north of Stalingrad are still in Russian hands. The village of Rynok is one such bulwark. The Führer orders that these bridgeheads be attacked. On 15 November 1942 in the North Switch Position we are relieved by 94th Infantry Division and afterward change position to the region of Rynok. A great many have already taken part in the attack on Rynok on 15 October. Will the attack in the murderous battle for Stalingrad lead on this occasion to a victorious outcome?

In dense fog, at first light on 17 November 1942, the division's attack on

Rynok gets under way. Advancing from the north, assault engineers roll up the line of Russian bunkers leading up to the Volga. The bunkers are systematically destroyed without any significant losses. To the right of them, grenadiers with attached engineers and armored cars launch their assault on the village. Some platoons penetrate on the western edge of Rynok and surprise the Russians. The men of the 64th Regiment also manage to penetrate the southern part of the village. In dense fog, Russians heading back to Rynok come across 6th Company, Panzer Grenadier Regiment 64, so that nobody now knows what is happening. A part of 6th Company breaks its way east through to the Volga, then advances to the north and there establishes contact with the attacking combat group. Hauptmann Mues, the commander of our Armored Reconnaissance Battalion, known to us all from countless battles as one of the bravest, meets a hero's end on this day from a severe wound.

As a result of the strong Russian defense the attack comes to a standstill. The assault troops await the support of our armored regiment, which has been held up by a minefield. This supporting attack is also unable to get the operation going again. Toward midday the assault troops, covered by tanks, withdraw. Another attack is due to be launched with the onset of darkness. The various groups of units of our division that penetrated the village are brought back or are destroyed in street battles. On 19 November 1942 the forward position on the west edge of Rynok that was won in this battle is once again evacuated.

The ground has already frozen rock hard so that digging in is made very difficult. Each one of us longs for a return to the well-built bunkers in the North Switch Position that was constructed in the past few months and into which 94th Infantry Division moved when we were relieved.

No further attacks on Rynok take place because the military situation in the rear of the German Stalingrad front has meanwhile changed. Since the beginning of November it has been known to the German leadership that 4th Russian Reserve Army has the task of encircling the German troops in Stalingrad and on the Kalmyk steppe by means of an attack along the line of the Don to the south (see the intelligence section report, 16th Panzer Division, dated 5 November 1942. Statement of a Ukrainian first lieutenant, commander of 1st Battalion, Rifle Regiment 1049, Vasil' Belda, who together with his headquarters was captured by our armored engineers during a landing of Russian forces in Latashanka on 1 November 1942).[3] In order to avert, and to deal with, the danger, all available forces have to be withdrawn from the north front and from the Rynok operation. On 19 November 1942, gunboats on the Volga are still being bombarded by us. On 20 November 1942 all ammunition that cannot be removed to the west as part of the ordered operation is fired off against similar targets.

Before the beginning of this November operation on the Don, the German forces on the Stalingrad North Switch Position were deployed in the following manner: the biggest part of the east front along the river itself and in Stalingrad is occupied by XI Corps. Our 16th Panzer Division forms the northeast corner of the German defensive system (XIV Corps) Farther to the west they join up with 3rd and 60th Motorized Infantry Divisions. In the period from the middle of August to the end of November, superb positions have also been constructed on the sectors of these formations.

In the east the autumn of 1942 was unusually mild. Up to the beginning of November no snow fell.[4] Nor did it freeze.

The Counterblow to the West at the End of November 1942 (20–26 November 1942)

At the beginning of November the standing Russian forces in the Beketovka bridgehead (south of Stalingrad) were constantly being reinforced. These Russian forces went over to the attack and achieved the breakthrough. The Russians also managed to achieve a breakthrough between Katschalinskaia and Kletskaia (northeast corner of the Great Don Bend). As a consequence of this, the German forces bordering to the east and the Italian 8th Army linking up in the west were both adversely affected. A crisis occurred on the defensive front at Stalingrad. When the Russian forces heading from the southeast and from the north joined up on about 21 November 1942 at Kalach, they launched a tank thrust with about 120 tanks into the rear of the German forces at Stalingrad. This undoubtedly dangerous crisis in the days around 25 November 1942 was remedied with little concern. When on 20 November 1942 crucial forces had to be withdrawn from the north front and from the defensive front being held by LI Army Corps on the Volga—and with them the main part of 16th Panzer Division, in order to deploy against the Russian forces that had broken through—the Führer transferred command of the eastward defensive front to Generalleutnant von Seydlitz, the general commanding LI Corps. As a result, XI Corps (Generalleutnant Strecker) was subordinated to him [von Seidlitz].

Early on 20 November 1942 the alarm is raised. All troops assemble at Orlovka. In the large ravine west of Rynok the supply lines assemble and are to follow on later. Decimated companies are replenished by disbanding other units. A combat group that has been formed from the division marches out by 0500 hours in the direction of the Don bridge at Pestkovatka, north of Kalach. On 21 November 1942 the march to the new area of operations is continued. Advance parties are sent out ahead toward Ssuchanov. The Lisha sector is then scheduled to be reached and held so that a link can be later established with the German forces standing farther to the west. Ssuchanov is known to everyone in the division. On 23 July 1942 Combat Group Lattmann, when heading into the Great Don Bend, reached Ssuchanov, approaching from western Businovka, and on 28 July 1942 Combat Group Reinisch arrived there via Manoilin–Jerik. Ssuchanov lies 40 kilometers (25 miles) west of the Don bridge at Golubinka, which is important for the German resupply. The bridge is crossed in the evening of 21 November 1942. The march continues on the Don Heights highway. The Heights highway is covered with sheet ice. The tanks have no antiskid chains fitted to their tracks. In the night, our tank drivers perform wonders. "We make a sled journey with our tanks the like of which we have never experienced before." Again and again the armored cars keep skidding right across the road into the ditches. Sometimes we can manage only a few meters up a slope. With the slightest movement of the steering mechanism, the tank slides straight back down the hill again. From ahead the news reaches us that the Russians have already arrived in Ssuchanov. Our drive forward still manages to reach the village. The march destination is, however, finally changed. By turning to the southwest the Russians are encountered in several forward thrusts. The Russians move forward and, by turning to the east, want to take the German counterattack in the flank. Masses of Romanians and individual German units and supply trains flood toward us. Russian tank forces have already penetrated to the Don Heights highway. Southwest of Golubinka, in an area of streams, a prepared position is supposed to have been occupied. On the march there the point of the division suddenly turns back. The commander of the forward battalion has received an order via radio with the instruction, once again, to turn immediately in an easterly direction to cross the Don at Golubinka. Some hours later, after the return march, this order is, as a result of a check at corps headquarters, explained as a misunderstanding. Once again a turn is made. A high position west of Golubinka is occupied.

Meanwhile, the Don Heights highway has been further blocked by the moving columns of our tank division, elements of 24th Panzer Division, and supply columns. (Fourteenth Panzer Division, which took part in the advance of XIV Panzer Corps, is deployed farther to the north on height 222.) The enemy, who has quickly moved forward, lays down a barrage of artillery and mortar fire on the Heights highway.

During the night of 22–23 November 1942 there is a move to the east with the aim of gaining a cohesive front as a bridgehead position with the center in Bolschanabatovskii. Fire from one of the artillery sections of our artillery regiments virtually destroys a strong Russian cavalry formation north of Golubinka. This formation pushes forward from the direction of height 222 to the south right up to the Don in the night of 22–23 November. When our divisional commander, General Angern, from his command post in the morning sun, catches sight of the masses of cavalry once again wheeling from the Don to the north, he personally rushes off in great haste across the field to 2nd Company, Panzer Artillery Regiment 16, which is close by in its position. Fire orders are given. A few minutes later everything is in total rout, and a mass of human and horse bodies are smashed. Fourth Battery (heavy flak artillery) helps to clear the road ahead of enemy.

During these days the overwhelmingly strong enemy, pushing from the west, is time and time again brought to battle, held, and weakened by Combat Group Dormann. The Führer acknowledges the achievements in these battles with the award of the Knight's Cross to Major Dormann. In a counterattack launched across an area of streams, several of our tanks are set alight by antitank fire when crossing the high ground. Another start line in readiness for a new tank attack is set up in a flat hollow in front of the area of streams. In dead ground the final preparations are made for the attack. Another 5 tanks are lost in the attack. These are irreplaceable losses in matériel for an encircled army, and irreplaceable losses in men. Oberleutnant Bartscherer, who with his 9th Company, Panzer Regiment 2, was one of the first to reach the Volga on 23–24 August 1942, is killed. That was three months ago today. . . . A further attack launched by us against the stream area at last light is repulsed. The tank regiment, with an armored car company and a battery of self-propelled guns, organizes itself for defense on the secured heights. On 25 November 1942, in the region of the Don Heights highway, Panzer Grenadier Regiments 64 and 79, the reconnaissance section, and the motorcyclists are involved in heavy fighting.

Under the cover of local attacks we withdraw to the bridgehead position, which on 25–26 November 1942 is occupied as follows (from left to right): 16th, 24th, and 14th Panzer Divisions to the west and XI Corps to the north. In the night of 24–25 November 1942 the ground freezes rock hard. On 25 November 1942 enemy mortar fire, especially among Panzer Grenadier Regiment 64, causes heavy casualties. Toward evening much weaker Russian infantry and tank forces probe forward. All 7 attacking tanks are knocked out. Two-cm antiaircraft guns, antitank guns, and infantry guns destroy the attacking infantry. Meanwhile, strong Russian formations seize part of the Heights highway farther to the south. For elements of the 16th Panzer Division, the return journey to the Don bridge is postponed. Out of the chaos of the fleeing allies, individual vehicles attempt to escape to the east over the frozen Don and in the attempt sink in. About 700 German vehicles are unable to get out, fall into Russian hands, and are destroyed. A section of our Panzer artillery regiment is finally able to extricate itself from the cauldron (southeast of Malitsch). A lack of fuel means that in all the sections and battalions, vehicles have to be destroyed. Indeed, for the time being, we are planning on a breakthrough and continued marching to the west. So even before the decision to withdraw back to Fortress Stalingrad was made, all vehicles on 23–24 November 1942 that would be unable to make the estimated 170 kilometers (106 miles) to the west, from a lack of fuel or for other reasons, are blown up or burned. This means that a wide range of equipment that over the next two months could have been of great assistance is destroyed. What a marvelous stroke of luck that our Panzer regiment on 22–23 November 1942 was able to refuel on a field airstrip at Golubinka. As a result, it is no longer necessary to destroy the division's most important heavy weapons. The counterorder, "Return east to Fortress Stalingrad," which is issued by the army's supreme leadership, signifies the temporary abandonment of any attempt to break the ring surrounding 6th Army from the inside. To the west of the encircled front there are insufficient German forces ready for a counterattack.

Other formations must also fight their way back to the bridge. In complete darkness the strong Russian forces are penetrated. In the early-morning hours of 25 November 1942 and in the following days, the bridge is crossed once again in an eastward direction. The last units cross the Don on 27 November 1942 at Lutschenskii in the direction of Stalingrad. On 25 November 1942 a Russian operation supported by armor, which tried to advance on the bridge after crossing the iced-up Don from the southwest, was repulsed. This thrust posed a great danger because the retreat of XI Corps to Stalingrad that meanwhile had been ordered could have been jeopardized by it. The Russian battalion was repulsed with heavy losses. Over 300 Russian dead were counted. Company Mutius, with elements of other companies under command, has the task of protecting the bridge so as to guarantee the passage of 16th Panzer Division and the whole of XI Corps. At 0330 hours on 27–28 (?) November 1942 the combat bridge that was built by German engineers is due to be blown. Toward 0310 hours the bridgehead is pulled back. As final protection, a platoon remains on the right bank of the Don. After the destruction of all military installations at the same place, it is reported to Hauptmann Strack that all German soldiers have left the west bank of the Don. So the bridgehead that was held for three days with a very heavy consumption of ammunition is given up after completion of the mission. The removal of 3rd Section, Artillery Regiment 16, to the east bank of the Don had already occurred in the night of 24–25 November 1942. On the morning of 26 November 1942 1st and 3rd Sections also move back to the east, probably without 5th Battery, which on this day remains in position 3 kilometers (1.9 miles) west of the Don. The remaining elements close up on the Tartar burial mounds.

After the evacuation of the bridgehead at Lutschenskii, our division heads once again in column to the east and on 27 November 1942 occupies the former positions of 3rd Infantry Division (mot.) on the rail embankment west of Stalingrad. At this time rumor has it that the enemy has taken Kalach and has reached the eastern bank of the river across the undamaged bridge. The troops are still not aware that the enemy has joined up with the Russian lead columns, which, approaching from the southeast, have penetrated the switch position at Beketovka.

The original aim of the operation west of the Don cannot be attained. The ring around Stalingrad is closed. This fact alarms no one because it is part of the normal circumstances in modern mobile warfare.[5]

On 24–25 November 1942, 2nd Panzer Regiment, which with divisional headquarters and the division's combat group has pushed ahead farthest to the west, moves once again onto the east bank of the Don with other elements of the division; to the south, in fact. A reception area aimed at the Russians who are now attacking there is to be occupied with elements of 3rd Infantry Division (mot.). A construction battalion that had been involved in heavy fighting for a built-up area is relieved. On 25 November 1942 the Russians transfer the concentration of their attacks to the region of Dimitrievka in order to split the German forces standing between the Don and the Volga into two Kessels. These attacks are repulsed.

On 26 November 1942 3rd Section, Panzer Regiment 2, is placed under the command of XIV Panzer Corps (General Hube). The rest of the regiment is once again deployed in the old North Switch Position within the framework of 16th Panzer Division, to where our division has moved in a column from the Don to the Volga. The town of Kalach, which lies to the south of the operational area of 16th Panzer Division and in which our Workshop Company 3 is situated, has already been lost on 21 November 1942. A group of Russian tanks, coming from Chir, broke through onto the Don Heights highway. They also seized the important Don bridge at Kalach. All the vehicles in Workshop Company 3 were lost (300 vehicles were being repaired there). The loss of the Kalach bridge was made possible by a misunderstanding. In the area west of Kalach there were still hundreds of Russian tanks, mainly T-34s remaining from the battles that had occurred from the end of July to the beginning of August 1942. At that time our Panzer division had captured countless T-34s. These tanks were only partly burned out. Many had been rendered immobile by hits from antitank guns or from other minor damage and had been abandoned by their crews. The destruction of the bridge had not been carried out because we were hourly expecting the return of an existing German section of about 20 captured T-34s. It was realized too late that the tanks that came rolling over the bridge did not belong to the section of captured tanks but were in fact the point of the Russian tank column.

The Don has frozen. The Russians are pressing hard with all forces across the river. In the varied and unequal battles there is a constant falling back toward Stalingrad. Our division—now without Combat Group Strack and 3rd Battalion, 2nd Panzer Regiment but with 24th Panzer Division and 60th Infantry Division (mot.)—belongs to XI Corps. Twenty-fourth Panzer Division is situated in the North Switch Position on the Volga, joining up to the west with 16th Panzer Division. Sixtieth Infantry Division (mot.) lies farther to the west in the old positions that it earlier held. Unfortunately, there are many more Russians in the well-built bunkers that we put up for the winter. Sometime toward the end of November divisional headquarters moves to the Grismaia gully. The positions in the North Switch Position are generally not as favorable as they were two weeks before. During the relief operation the positions were squeezed back, especially the northeast corner at Vinnovka.

The west front of the fortress is defended by XIV Panzer Corps. General Hube commands it right up to the moment of his departure on 18 January 1943. From the middle of January the old headquarters staff officer of 16th Panzer Division, our Oberstleutnant Müller, has been in the Kessel as the headquarters staff officer of XIV Panzer Corps.

VIII Corps defends the northeast corner of the fortress between XIV Panzer Corps and our XI Corps.

In the move back to the old positions at the end of November, we are without the combat group led by Hauptmann Strack, which was retained by General Hube in order to reinforce XIV Corps. The combat group is formed from elements of 16th Panzer Division that, as a consequence of losing their heavy equipment, have already been deployed as infantry. In addition to these two companies, an armored car reconnaissance company, put together from two companies of Hauptmann Mues's battalion and a platoon of engineers of Panzer Engineer Battalion 16, are also under the command of Hauptmann Strack. Since 1 December 1942 Combat Group Strack has been held as a counterattack reserve not far from the Pitomnik airfield in a gully at Dubiniki. As of 1 December 1942, XIV Corps holds the line roughly from Marinovka in the south via Karpovka, Dimitrievka, and Baburkin in the north. Elements of 24th Panzer Division are also there. Farther to the south are divisions of XIV Panzer Corps: 14th Panzer Division, 3rd Infantry Division (mot.), and 44th Infantry Division.

The division's advance party, which set off on 20 November toward the southeast to the planned winter quarters on the Don, reaches the area south of Kalach before the arrival of the Russians (at Poistenspinskii and Podemkinskaia). Major von Burgsdorff, the commander of Panzer Grenadier Regiment 64, assumes command. On arrival in the area of the winter accommodations, the situation regarding the enemy, which has suddenly changed, means that some quick decisions must be made. All heavy weapons are deployed with the main part of the division. A defense of the winter quarters by the weak advance party offers little chance of success. A retreat toward Morosovskaia over the blocked bridge position at Demkin is no longer an option. On 23 November 1942 these remnants of the division move via Zymlianskaia to the west. At the eleventh hour the deployment by this formation of 16th Panzer Division rescues a part of the division. These divisional remnants are now located in the sector of IV Panzer Army. Strength is about 2,200 men, including 400 Russian auxiliaries (*Hilfswillige*). Combat Group Burgsdorff, which since 22 December 1942 has been deployed at Morosovskaia, consists of about 300 men at this time. Four weeks earlier (27 November 1942) a combat group under the command of Oberleutnant Sedlmayer had already been deployed toward Plesnovskii to secure the Don (5:30:144),[6] to which on 3 December 1942 an additional 16 soldiers returning from leave have been allocated. Additional combat groups operating as infantry have also been detailed, such as one under the command of Hauptmann Rabe (2:16) to 6th Army headquarters.

In the winter of 1942–1943 Combat Group von Burgsdorff, considerably reinforced by old soldiers from 16th Panzer Division who were once again returning to Russia, has continually helped to hold up the red flood in countless battles and won everlasting glory.

On 23 November 1942, in Losnoi, Oberst Krumpen (commander of Panzer Grenadier Regiment 64) assumes command of the division's remnants.

The rest of the division, which has played no part in the counterattack on Lisha and has remained at Rynok, moves out three days later as an advance party to the winter quarters to the rear on the Don. It encounters the encirclement front that has meanwhile been set up by the Russians and so returns hard to the north of Orlovka into the ravine terrain and assembles there.

In the newly formed North Switch Position of Stalingrad the positions of 16th Panzer Division as of 29 November 1942 can be cited as follows: the division's right wing north of Gorodische on the railway line that leads into Spartakovka is formed by Panzer Grenadier Regiment 79. Panzer Grenadier Regiment 64 links up with Panzer Grenadier Regiment 79. Motorcyclist Unit K16 links up to the left of Panzer Grenadier Regiment 64, with its left wing about 6 kilometers (3.7 miles) west of the old divisional cemetery (northwest from the old divisional command post). The artillery is situated in the area of Orlovka. The Panzer engineer battalion is located in the gullies to the north of Orlovka. It is involved in laying mines and strengthening the fire positions. It suffered especially heavy losses in the battles for Rynok.

That the northeast wing of the fortress, held by 16th Panzer Division until the middle of November, was withdrawn in this one week of the Don operation is especially unfavorable. All the bunkers and the transit position built between September and October are left to the Russians, who now occupy good accommodations. At the end of November, the grenadiers have no chance of digging out the hard-frozen ground and building any bunkers. So we lie without cover in the open terrain. Ninety-fourth Infantry Division, which in this decisive week was deployed in the North Switch Position, is relieved and deployed to plug the gaps in the sectors of 16th and 24th Panzer Divisions.

16th Panzer Division's Battles from 1 December to Christmas 1942

In the course of the battle in the period from the beginning of December to Christmas 1942, defensive battle successes against countless Russian attacks directed against the front line held by 16th Panzer Division could be reported. In our sector of the front our own large-scale attacks ceased. In the context of the whole situation, they were not required. The forward edge of the battle area was for the time being occupied and free of any gaps. Only later, when the shortage of forces became ever more perceptible, and for this reason all the fronts also had to be concentrically withdrawn, were the bulk of the hedgehog defensive positions formed. Attacks were repelled by us between 4 and 6 December. From 6 to 8 December 1942, the Russians tried to wear down our defensive front by means of nonstop attacks. On 8 December, toward 0800 hours, under heavy fire, a tank attack with mounted infantry was launched. Fifth Motorcyclist Company bore the brunt of this attack. Our own artillery and rocket launchers could do nothing from lack of ammunition. Fire trench after fire trench was rolled up. Finally this attack spread out onto the sector of Panzer Grenadier Regiment 64. Initially there was a retreat. The enemy was then ejected in a counterattack. We destroyed 6 enemy tanks. The old forward edge of the battle line was once again in our possession.

On 10 December the Russians paid dearly with losses of tanks for a similar attack in the sector of Panzer Grenadier Regiment 79. A Russian attack on 11 December resulted in minimal loss of terrain. A great deal of activity on the part of enemy fighting patrols over these weeks meant that the German grenadiers did not get much rest. As preparation for his local attacks, the enemy used primarily mortars and heavy guns. In these attacks, Russian tanks were always being destroyed, and penetrations in our line were always being cleaned out. Fire from heavy enemy artillery did not lead to severe casualties, whereas our machine guns reaped a rich harvest from the attacking Russians. One of the counterattacks, which was completely successful, took place on 20 December under the command of Oberleutnant Knörzer. This quick-reaction group was made up of engineers and men from 1st Company, Panzer Grenadier Regiment 64. Leutnant Strunk, the commander of the armored platoon of 3rd Company, Panzer Engineer Battalion 16, who received special recognition in the divisional order, was killed in this operation.

Combat Group Strack, 1 December 1942–1 January 1943

We want to take a brief look back at the fate of Combat Group Strack, which came from 16th Panzer Division and helped to defend the fortress's west front against the Russian onslaught.

In the night of 3–4 December 1942 an enemy penetration occurred at Baburkin and to its north at a depth of about 6 kilometers (3.7 miles) and a width of about 8 kilometers (5 miles). On 5 December the whole of Combat Group Strack was deployed with the task of cleaning out this break-in (on board armored reconnaissance cars). The combat group managed to clean the break-in with just a small enemy wedge in Baburkin and to get the riflemen—part of 24th Panzer Division—back into their positions once again. On

6 December, Combat Group Strack made a renewed attempt to clear the approximately 2-kilometer-deep (1.2-mile-deep) enemy penetration at Baburkin that still remained. Because of a lack of fuel, the armored reconnaissance car squadron had to be deployed in an infantry role. The target of the attack was a height north of Baburkin, which was stormed and captured in a few minutes. As a consequence of an enemy counterattack that occurred with infantry and the heaviest tanks from the north and was launched at our flank while our attack was under way, our attack was defeated. There were heavy losses among our ranks. After our left flank had already been turned, Hauptmann Strack gave the order to withdraw. This intention was noted by the Russians. Together with some of the troops that had broken through, they swung around with the aim of encircling our troops. No systematic withdrawal was now possible. Every man ran for his life. In order to avoid even greater losses, Oberleutnant von Mutius, while falling back, tried to get the formation back. He kept shouting, "Break contact!" Severely wounded, he departed his comrades as a hero. On 27 November 1942 he was the last German officer to cross the bridge over the Don at Lutchenskii toward the east and into the fortress. Heavy weapons and ammunition were in short supply. Those parts of Combat Group Strack that had escaped the encirclement moved for the time being to a reception area, finally handing this over to 24th Panzer Division, and once again assembled in the Dubininki ravine, where they remained until 1 January 1943. On that day Combat Group Strack was disbanded. The grenadiers were allocated to Combat Group Dormann and 24th Panzer Division. The whole of the armored reconnaissance car company was placed under the command of 24th Panzer Division and, owing to a lack of fuel, was deployed as infantry to the west of Karpovka linking up on the right with parts of 24th Panzer Division and on the left with a Cossack platoon and some ground personnel. Toward 2200 hours on 10 January 1943 Karpovka was evacuated. Our exhausted grenadiers had to abandon the biggest part of the vehicles to the enemy, who, toward 2100 hours, attacked from the north. Ten armored reconnaissance cars were lost. On 14 January 1943 the position that had been taken up at Karpovskaia station also had to be given up after we had suffered heavy losses. Details concerning the future fate of the old soldiers of 16th Panzer Division who were fighting there have not come to light.

Meanwhile, on all fronts of the fortress, the situation had become much worse. Everywhere in the middle of January there were shortages of ammunition and rations. Care for the wounded and sick was also becoming much more difficult. A member of Combat Group Strack writes:

On 14th January the Russians launched a major attack. We had occupied a former Russian position. Here the enemy charged us in vain. Because of a lack of ammunition we opened fire only at very close range. In one of these attacks I received a stomach wound at 1300 hours from a round fired by a Russian rifleman. Obergefreiter K. and Gefreiter R. at great risk to their lives took me 2 kilometers [1.2 miles] to the rear on a ground sheet. Along with several other wounded I was loaded onto a truck and taken in the direction of the airfield. Three kilometers [1.9 miles] before our journey's end the fuel ran out, and on orders the vehicle had to be destroyed. The wounded were left to their fate. Crawling, I made my way to the airfield. It was now night. I received my first medical help in a large tent. Several tents were hit by showers of bombs from Russian planes and blown away. On this day the enemy was only about 12 kilometers (7.5 miles) away from our last airfield.

Christmas in Stalingrad!

The day the post came was always the main holiday for German soldiers. Even in normal times the mood was always lifted by any letter from home, and how much more our encircled comrades needed mail over the Christmas period of 1942 in the ice and snow. And in Stalingrad as well, every soldier wanted to send a letter to his family at home, which was due to make its way out of the Kessel by plane for Christmas. What joy broke out when on 4 December every soldier was allowed to send a Christmas letter! The transport situation did not permit a large-scale exchange of letters. In the bunkers and in the trenches the mail, which could not be flown out, piled up. Many an exhausted soldier waited for mail from home and wrote and wrote with numb fingers when fighter planes, snipers, and Stalin organs left any quiet moments.

In IAsinovtaia, the large loading station north of Stalino, the post meant for 16th Panzer Division had been piling up since the middle of November. From 12 January 1943 the remaining troops of 16th Panzer Division, at that moment not encircled in the fortress, were deployed to sort the post so that it could be flown into the Kessel.

Christmas 1942!

For some days a thin layer of snow had covered the bodies of our fallen comrades, who lay around in large numbers to the front and in between the positions. The wish of all the soldiers, who are spending Christmas Eve in

Russia for the second time, is to be able to eat one's fill again. In the evening the divisional commander turned up on the position, said a few encouraging words to each soldier, and handed out cigarettes. The Christmas surprise came later. Each soldier received a whole loaf, cigarettes, cigars, chocolate, and supplementary tinned rations. The joy was great, and in places a Christmas carol could be heard coming from the bunkers. "*No Christmas tree decorates our bunker, and our candles were the tracers that soared into the sky.*" And no matter, every unit tried its best to impose some mark of Christmas on these days. The most wonderful present of all was the extra bread. . . .

Celebrations also took place in the field hospitals in the Kessel:

> I will never forget the visit of Hauptfeldwebel W. and Oberfeldwebel K. on Christmas Eve in the field hospital. They brought me some cigarettes and a slab of chocolate. I could have howled for joy. For the most part I owed it to these good items that I became able to be moved in the next few days. There was practically nothing to eat in the field hospital, and there was nothing at all for any special diets.

Not all the units enjoyed peace in the position on 24 December. The holiday also brought massive Russian attacks.

The second day of the holiday, in particular, was due to be honored by some fresh coffee beans, writes one storeman: "However while the coffee was being prepared an enemy fighter put a bullet through the pot so that the priceless liquid was lost."

From the other side one could hear the screeching of a Russian loudspeaker, which by means of the usual waffle and promises was supposed to break the defensive morale of the German soldier. On 25 December a ferocious snowstorm set in. It was barely possible to leave the bunker. One could hardly see ten paces. Into this appalling weather enemy artillery shells continued to drone, along with the booming of mortars and the thundering of the Stalin organs, which penetrated to the marrow of one's bones. Blow after blow caused the deeply frozen ground to shudder. We were wide awake, and we knew that on that day the long-prepared-for attack would come. Out of the gray-white floating mass of snow, tank after tank, with trucks in between packed full of infantry, pressed forward against our positions. We fired while the ammunition lasted. Nevertheless, the enemy onslaught could not be stopped. The men in the bunkers defended themselves in a mood of despair. In the end, any survivors tried to reach the infantry gun position situated to our rear. In the sector of Panzer Grenadier Regiment 64, an 88-mm antiaircraft gun was sited well forward. Although the riflemen detailed to provide close protection were either dead or wounded, the gun crew managed to hold out and in a very short space of time succeeded in taking out 13 enemy tanks. The gun was destroyed with the last hand grenade, and the crew withdrew to the assembly area.

"I could not get the rest of my Christmas rations out of the snow hole."

The Battles in Fortress Stalingrad, 25 December 1942–20 January 1943

In a huge snowstorm, 25 December sees the long-prepared-for major Russian attack, which costs us heavy losses in men, matériel, and terrain. The few armored vehicles that are still available are at this time held in reserve for counterattacks. In dense, driving snow wave after wave of enemy rolls against the thinly occupied lines of the men of 16th Panzer Division. In the end our ranks are thinned out. Everyone is so exhausted from hunger that a withdrawal to the reception area has to be started. The withdrawal of the men from Panzer Grenadier Regiment 64 is covered by 2-cm-caliber guns of 10th Company (antiaircraft), 64. Time and time again the enemy is forced into temporary cover. One gun after another then falls silent from a lack of ammunition. The gun crews fight man to man with the Russian infantry. There are heaps of enemy dead in front of the guns, but the sheer weight of enemy tells in the end. The last men of the antiaircraft platoon are killed in close-quarters battle. The time gained by the fire of the antiaircraft cannons is enough for us to re-form our units in the reception area. The renewed enemy attack encounters firm resistance and remains pinned down on the high ground of our infantry gun position. In the evening our armored reconnaissance car squadron and some tanks of 14th Panzer Division support a counterattack that secures the infantry gun position. The number of Russian dead is huge, but our own losses are shockingly high as well. In spite of some gain in terrain the enemy does not manage to achieve his hoped-for penetration of our defensive system.

In the last week of December the enemy brings his attacks to a halt. The enemy does, however, maintain heavy artillery fire, and the number of enemy air attacks increases.

The soldiers who are on their way to the Christmas field service at the division's command post north of Gorodische have to be stood to. They are immediately deployed to destroy the enemy groups that have broken through and to defend the regimental command post of Panzer Grenadier Regiment 64.

In the last days of the year, our own counterattacks, above all on the left wing of the division on the lines of K-16 (Motorcyclist Battalion 16), do not achieve the desired success. Every loss of a bunker position has the severest consequences since there is an absence of cover in the terrain. The exhausted soldiers have no chance of building new, warm bunkers in the hard, frozen ground.

About New Year numerous units are put together and replenished by other units, also from neighboring divisions (for example, 60th Infantry Division's [mot.] construction battalion). One can put the number of soldiers from supply services, resupply units, artillery units, antiaircraft units (without guns and ammunition), and so on who are gradually being deployed as infantry in Fortress Stalingrad at about 70,000 to 80,000. About the end of December and the beginning of January, training courses take place in many units. The most important subjects are use of terrain, dealing with tanks, and use of the machine gun.

Already in the first days of the New Year there are strong enemy attacks supported by tanks. Our own counterattacks can no longer drive the Russians out of the positions into which they have broken through. The losses of Panzer Grenadier Regiments 64 and 79 in these severe battles are made good by members of the supply services and artillery, and so on.

On 4 January 1943 a field church service is held.

On 4 and 5 January our counterattacks fail to achieve any decisive result.

Not only on our division but also on other locations along the front, Russian attacks occur over the period from 8 to 10 January that are quite clearly intended to bring about the collapse of the German defense in the shortest possible time. From the west the thrust is aimed in the direction of Karpovka via Marinovka. In our divisional sector, on 10 January, about 4 regiments attack, parts of the Russian 99th, 116th, 299th, and 343rd Rifle Divisions. We count about 800–900 Russian dead, take 16 prisoners, and capture 4 tanks. At various times the enemy launches about 20 attacks, of which there are 6 alone in the sector of Combat Group Dormann and 10 in the sector of Combat Group Dörnemann. The Russians are again thrown out of all 10 break-in positions. Our losses amount to about 90 men, of whom 22 are killed. In the corps order of the day of XI Army Corps, dated 12 January 1943, General of Infantry Strecker acknowledges the achievement:

> Supported by elements of 24th Panzer Division and 60th Infantry Division (mot.), 16th Panzer Division, in three days of severe fighting, repelled all

> attacks of the enemy in an operation of the highest military professionalism and with it achieved a major defensive success for the entire defense of this decisive position. I express my gratitude and my acknowledgment to both the leadership and the troops. If we continue to maintain our courage, the final victory will be ours.

After the daily situation report for 13 January—on this day there is anything from −15 to −25 degrees (5° to −13°F) of frost—the division on this day is not compelled to give up ground on any position. The division's front line runs in large platoons, as on the evening of the first day of the battle. With the existing weak forces, any gaps that arise in the line are isolated by the rapid deployment of tanks and armored reconnaissance cars in mobile defense.

Generalleutnant von Seydlitz (LI Corps, to which XI Corps was subordinated), the commander of the defensive front on the Volga, also especially praises the performance of our Panzer division in his order of the day dated 13 January 1943:

> Yesterday 16th Panzer Division, in a bitter contest, repulsed the most severe and repeated attacks of an enemy numerically many times superior, thus holding on to all its positions. The success is to be evaluated all the more highly when in the division's front numerous soldiers were deployed who, only a few days ago, were drawn from the artillery, signal companies, and supply units. The division's victorious defensive battle—in particular, however, the heroic stance of these troops drawn from the noninfantry units, who could not be given a thorough training for the battle or could not be thoroughly imbued with the infantry spirit—proves what men are able to do whose heart is in the right place and who are led by brave officers, who themselves stick it out to the utmost in a spirit of fearless dedication.

In the days leading up to 20 January there is severe fighting for the strongpoints 16–19 in the left sector of 16th Panzer Division. In the right sector there is a degree of calm. Enemy preparatory positions can be identified along the entire front line.

At this time 60th Infantry Division (mot.), which is fighting parallel with our Panzer division, systematically disengages from the enemy. Owing to a lack of fuel, the heavy vehicles have to be left behind. On 20 January the left wing of 60th Infantry Division (mot.) is located 2 kilometers (1.2 miles) southeast of Borotkin.

On 20 January our Panzer division's situation as regards tanks is as follows:

1 Panzer Battalion, 3 Panzer Regiment (long),[7] is operational. Detached to 24th Panzer Division.

3 light field howitzers are deployed as antitank guns. The following are also still operational:

1 antitank (7.62 cm)
2 antitank, 88 mm
6 medium antitank guns
1 heavy antitank gun
1 platoon (27 men) from 3rd Battalion, Regiment 544, at division as a reserve

From 16 to 20 January only 66 shells for the light field howitzers come into the fortress: several thousand have already been used! On 17 January in the Rossoshka valley another 4 of our tanks have to be destroyed because of a lack of fuel. On 18 January a total of only two Heinkels land (Gumrak), both without fuel.

The vulnerability of tanks and motorized divisions to the inadequate provision of fuel is obvious. This circumstance leaves a permanent stamp on the many battles of modern war. In actual fact we never had large amounts of fuel in Russia. But these few examples show what difficulties the ever more exhausted troops have to overcome because of the shortage of fuel, which is so absolutely necessary for their vehicles.

Complete reports concerning the losses in these battles around the middle of January are unavailable. On 20 January, for example, 16th Panzer Division reports a loss of 4 officers and 72 men (of which 3 officers and 49 men are wounded). For the period from 17 to 20 January 1943 the following losses are noted in a follow-up report:

2 officers killed; 13 NCOs and soldiers killed
3 officers wounded; 31 NCOs and soldiers wounded
The high number of 63 men missing

At this time our Panzer division, already severely weakened, loses on average about 100 men per day. Some of those reported as missing have almost certainly fallen into Russian hands. Those with light wounds receive treatment in their units.

How is the morale among the troops at this moment? What thoughts motivate the braver ones? Does everything seem to them to be a pointless sacrifice, or does the soul create new strength where the halfhearted see only empty wells? On 14 January a *Hauptmann* whose deployment in our division has frequently led to particular success wrote the following:

> I have a few moments of peace for myself. I want to use the time in order to express my thanks for the greetings delivered by Leutnant Braun (K/16) who has safely flown in. Four very hard days are behind us. Since 8 January the Russians have been hurling themselves against our sector with 5 divisions and have left—thank God!—neighboring units on the left and right completely alone. Penetrations and counterattacks follow on, one after another. On the sixth day of the attacks—several attacks a day from regimental down to company strength—the division is able to record a proud defensive success. For the most part, the line has been held. At the moment I write these lines, a report has just arrived of another strong attack. Dörnemann and Dormann are in fine fettle. They are both outstanding combat group commanders. The contributions of all the men are indescribable. I would not like to enumerate all the factors that make combat here so hard. There are a lot of them, physical and psychological. That virtually all our soldiers have so far overcome them is an inestimable achievement. Some future tribute to the unique "Elite of the Army Kessel" in the history of the German Army cannot stress this enough. Only he who himself has withstood the strain of the Kessel will be able completely and totally to honor them. The strain is a constant factor but one that changes like atmospheric pressure. One's physical constitution (rations, the degree of cold, whether one is wounded, and much more) and the not inconsiderable attrition of forces on the edge of the Kessel cause the pointer to climb up the scale. But such strain also has something positive, especially if it can be evaluated later and also then used in one's own work. The essence of being reveals itself more clearly than hitherto. Many indistinct ideas become concrete and can be expressed objectively, orally or even in writing. The pale colors of one's memory become fresh and alive once again, and with it powerful. The whole richness of one's past

life, with all its joy and beauty, with the fullness of good fortune, reveals itself and forces out the inner wealth and the tangible value of thankfulness so as to meet fate.

The hunger for beauty makes the sun shine all the brighter. The light itself bathes the endless white expanses with golden brilliance and conjures up a peaceful, cozy corner out of a plain and simple earth bunker. And if the present should let us down, then thousands of memories step into its place, enticing us into a realm of beauty.

A handful of weak men break under the strain (for example, the best people with a hitherto faultless leadership steal like magpies or shirk and so on). The stronger ones are drawn taut like a bow, in order, after it has been drawn, to surge even higher and to live with ever more strength for something greater, more worthwhile.

Here the individual, as if in a final rehearsal, is able to test himself to find out whether he possesses that inner composure that makes him the master of every situation. He is able to identify whether he can distinguish all unimportant things from what matters, whether from that pedestal of firm self-confidence he can view everything from above, the inaccessible height of which causes the depressions of little and ordinary men to be lost in the depth of the eye.

This time makes one more experienced, more generous but at the same time much more severe toward everything that sins against the cause. And the time makes one harder because, once again, it forcibly underlines the fact that there are certain times when only naked and brutal violence can help—even in the service of the ideal.[8]

Russian Propaganda and the Morale of Our Troops

Russian propaganda had no success among the soldiers at Stalingrad. It was an experience of this war that enemy propaganda had an impact only on those people who did not have to bear the greatest burdens in this war. If the Russians could not achieve their goals by force, they dropped leaflets on which the situation inside the Kessel was depicted in order to break the inner composure and the morale of the German soldier. No inquiries were required in order to ascertain the use to which these leaflets were put. . . .

The names of prisoners were broadcast over loudspeakers if comrades had been overpowered by the enemy. The rest were called upon by the loudspeaker to surrender. However, the effect of Russian propaganda broadcasts was mainly favorable. The *Landser* could once again have a good laugh.

The letters in December bore, overwhelmingly, a mood of confidence. Unconditional trust in the Führer and the help that was expected from him was expressed in these letters. In fact, there was a very widespread belief in the Kessel that the Führer had been there himself. On 25 December 1942 a comrade wrote: "But despite everything we will hold out and on top of that show our teeth to the enemy until the victory is finally ours."

When the stand-to sounded to the south, it was believed that Manstein's army and Hoth were on their way and that the encirclement was at an end. In January the psychological state caused by a lack of mail from home, the awareness of one's own powerlessness, insufficient rations, and the cold became many times worse. Intestinal illness, jaundice, and cases of fainting increased. The performance of the doctors was frequently praised.

Many dead and fallen comrades lay about, but there was no strength to dig a grave for one's dearest comrade. So many of the letters dealt finally with thoughts of parting. Many of these letters were written to the accompaniment of tears. On 7 January 1943 it was written in a letter: "With this cold our relief troops cannot advance, and apart from that, the ring round the Kessel is already too wide and too strong. Our losses are great. Many have already died of exhaustion."

On 14 December 1942 the order was read out according to which Manstein's army had mounted a relief operation. Everything was looking good! We would soon be in winter quarters and off on leave. Many had had no leave since autumn 1940, for more than two years.

The formations (6th and 22nd Panzer Divisions, and finally 306th Infantry Division and 11th Panzer Division) under the command of Generaloberst Hoth, which had started to press forward west of Aksay in the direction of the Stalingrad Kessel, made only very slow progress against the exceptionally strong enemy defense. On 18 December 1942 they reached the Myshkovo sector, about 40 kilometers (25 miles) from the encircled front.

After the failure of this advance, the fate of the encircled army in Stalingrad was sealed.

When the soldiers of our Panzer-Grenadier Regiment 64 listened to the noise of severe fighting coming from the south of the Kessel on 29 and 30 December 1942, the word went around that 6th Panzer Division was supposed to be trying to break the ring at that point. New hopes, new disappointments. . . .

"One may well have worries, but one must not become soft." So the letters of comrades who remained in Stalingrad also provided a heroic portrait of the morale of our glorious division.

The Enemy's Situation

During the entire Stalingrad battles the enemy's situation was enormously more favorable than ours. The withdrawal of the Russians in the region of the Great Don Bend in July 1942 created behind the German lines a vast open area with the sparsest communications in Europe. In September 1942—far too late indeed—the German construction industry was given the task of delivering and releasing large amounts of material for road construction. This material was due to be used for improving the delivery of supplies in the area of the Great Don Bend.

Every downpour of rain, every thaw, rendered the roads in that area likely to collapse due to the fact that there were no roads at all that were built on foundations of gravel, let alone any based on asphalt or concrete. There was a total absence of gravel and hard rock. In such circumstances, the railway system provided better services.

On the Volga from Baku via the Caspian Sea and Astrakhan, the Russians were able to deliver any amount of desired fuel in the battle region with a minimum of effort—fuel that reached us only after 2,000 kilometers (1,242 miles) by rail and then a further 1,000 kilometers (621 miles) in vehicles. River traffic on the Volga was at times accurately bombarded by our tanks and the guns of Artillery Regiment 16 in the North Switch Position at Vinnovka. The amount of supplies allocated to the German formations in Stalingrad and directly delivered by rail via Tsurovikino was never very substantial and covered only the very short period from the end of September to the encirclement in the middle of November.

If the Russians had withdrawn to Stalingrad and the Caucasus with the intention of seeking a decisive battle in areas that, from the point of view of communications infrastructure, were favorable for them yet unfavorable for the attacker, then they had calculated correctly. It was much easier for Russia to tolerate the loss of the culturally and agriculturally neglected provinces in the Great Don Bend, which did not have good soil everywhere, than to do without Ukraine or the expanses of land that had been lost in 1942 after the battle of Kharkov.

On 10 January the Volga had finally frozen up. The ice-free Volga had made it possible to bring in large transport ships up- and downstream, but an uninterrupted stream of new matériel and fresh troops now came rolling across the ice. The final blow on the encircled Stalingrad army could be prepared.

With their advance through the Great Don Bend in the middle of November 1942, the supply of Russian troops was improved by the capture of German ration dumps and supply lines. This could have been of decisive significance because at this time, indeed on the Russian side as well, long and endangered supply routes had to be surmounted. When on 22 November 1942 the Russian cavalry attack on the Don Heights road came under the fire of our artillery, tanks, and the sustained machine gun of Panzer Grenadier Regiment 64, large amounts of German cigarettes, German chocolate, and items of German clothing were found on Russian prisoners when they were searched. "In the last few days," a *Gefreiter* wrote home regarding this, "the Russians must have made fantastic progress."

General value judgments concerning the Russians' combat capabilities can hardly be made. At any rate it can be pointed out that even at a time when the situation of the encircled German army was hardly favorable, Russian deserters still came. Thus, even on 8 January 1943 Grenadier Regiment 79 was able to report taking deserters as prisoners.

The number of Russian *Hilfswillige* employed in 16th Panzer Division, who in many a critical situation took up arms against the Bolsheviks, was considerable. Later, outside of Russia, they also proved themselves.

Supplies

From the middle of November the encircled army had to rely on aircraft for resupply. A minimum of 500 metric tons (551 tons) of ammunition, fuel, and rations per day were required in the fortress. This resulted in transport requirements that the German air force was unable to meet. Five hundred transport aircraft as a daily average could be deployed from a long distance. The effective level of the aircraft was impaired by the fact that they had to carry all the necessary fuel with them to the fortress for the return journey. One hour's flying time meant that a transport aircraft must have engine performance of 2,000 horsepower and 500 kilograms (1,102 pounds) of fuel. Even today the resupply of large encircled formations over a long period remains a difficult problem to solve.

At the end of November in the region between the Volga and the Don there were about 10 operationally effective airfields. Countless wounded had taken off from the airfield at Pitomnik on their way home. However, as early as 28 December 1942 this airfield was the scene of infantry battles and could be held only until the beginning of January. Likewise, the airfields at Orlovka in the north and at Gumrak and Alekseevka in the south were of great importance. The aircraft regularly took wounded and mail to Germany after their supplies had been unloaded. A wounded soldier wrote:

> On 11 December [1942] the weather was clear, and there was an opportunity to take off. At the crack of dawn the JU-52s and the Heinkel 111s were already landing. They brought out the wounded and dropped off ammunition and rations. Although the airfield was constantly being bombed and strafed by Russian fighters, our pilots took off. In the afternoon I had the opportunity to take off in a Heinkel 111. After we had been flying for about 10 minutes we were attacked by Russian fighters. When we flew over the Russian positions we took some weak antiaircraft fire. A plane in our formation was brought down. Toward 2200 hours we landed at an airfield in Morosovskaia. More wounded arrived after a few days who had been able to get through after their plane had been shot up and forced to make an emergency landing.

About 13 wounded can usually be transported in a JU-52; in a Heinkel 111 up to about 9 wounded.

In the middle of January nearly all airfields were within range of Russian batteries. The landing strip on the improvised airfield at Stalingradskii was constantly being torn up by some of the heaviest bombs. On 17 January, despite good opportunities for landing, only 15 Heinkel 111s landed by day. No resupply plane landed on 18 January, although all ground installations were clear; the pilots had reported the contrary to the earlier pilots on the Pitomnik airfield, which had meanwhile been given up. So this was not true. It bears witness to their lack of operational readiness.

Twenty-eight resupply aircraft had landed on 20–21 January. Up to 1700 hours on 21 January 41 metric tons (45 tons) of supplies had arrived: the equivalent of 3 goods wagons for a fighting army. Night landings were still secure on the Gumrak airfield. Hour after hour and day after day the airfields were under fire from masses of bombs and machine-gun fire from Russian planes against which nothing could be done. Already for some months it had been forbidden to fire at attacking Russian planes so as to conserve ammunition. *Everything* had to be deployed in the land battle. On 18 January 1943 only two Heinkels landed. On 19 January only 6 Heinkels and 1 Condor landed. A few aircraft dropped ration containers, which were not easily found in the snowdrifts. In many cases the exhausted German soldiers were repeatedly unable to dig them out and could no longer bring the desperately needed rations to their positions.

Many aircraft that had broken up on landing lay on the airfield. Even in December Russian planes in their day attacks were being shot down by the handful of German fighters. Because of the constant Russian air attacks, resupply goods were immediately taken away from the airfield. Since the planes when they left would be full of wounded, a great many empty ration containers were assembled on the airfield.

On 1 February 1943 an improvised landing site for a Stork in the north of the Kessel was still usable. It was, however, no longer in use.

It was not possible to bring in sufficient bread by air. Already on 29 November 1942, in one unit, one loaf was being issued for 10 men a day. Other units were still able to fall back on hidden rations in January. At the beginning of December the consumption of horseflesh was permitted. He who wanted to get moving and had no fuel exchanged a little horseflesh with hungry drivers for a few liters of fuel. "Our horse has already been slaughtered, as there was no feed left and it was too weak to drag along the sled with rations."

The rations situation for the troops who were in Fortress Stalingrad and, in particular among 16th Panzer Division, had over the period from the middle of November 1942 to the middle of January 1943 developed as follows. Since the beginning of September 1942 our divisional ration branch had been situated in Marinovka. It received the rations from 6th Army's rations depot at Chir, which was situated on the railway line west of the Don not far from the bridge. From there, finally, 15 trucks, each one loaded with about 2.5 metric tons (2.8 tons) of rations, arrived on 21 November in Marinovka. At this time the Russian advance was already about 20 kilometers (12.4 miles) south of Marinovka at Businovka. The divisional supply headquarters of 24th Panzer Division, which had been in Businovka, pulled back to Marinovka. However, already on 22 November 1942, toward 1030 hours, a Russian tank column approached from the southwest, probably from Kalach. There were 30 tanks with mounted infantry. Quite by chance a column of German rocket launchers that was passing through the area laid down fire on the Russian tanks, whereupon the tanks turned farther to the west. The division's rations were rescued! At midday the transport of all material to Pestovatka was started (the total length of the journey was 32 kilometers [20 miles]). The material was now to be the supply foundation of 16th Panzer Division, which was pushing to the west over the Don. Six trucks loaded with bread from the bakery company, which arrived shortly before the encirclement, traveled with this column. By afternoon the column was back from Pestovatka and could be reloaded. The Karpovka stream, on the north bank of which Marinovka is situated, had become the forward edge of the battle line. Eventually, however, it was still possible to remove all rations from the old distribution point, which was situated in the territory to the south of Karpovka. On 24 November 1942 the Russians were already in Illarinovskii, 10 kilometers (6.2 miles) northwest of Marinovka. On 26 November 1942, therefore, the last supplies in the camp had to be brought all the way back to the east in the area of the Stuka airfield near the Voroshilovo camp to Peskovatka.

From 26 November 1942 the army ordered that rations were to be halved and that the bread ration per man was 200 grams (7 ounces) per day. Sixteenth Panzer Division had sufficient rations up to about 20 December 1942, for about another four weeks. The provision of bread and meat caused concern, to be sure, since our bakery and butchers were outside the Kessel, along with the reserves of livestock and flour. These units were situated on the Don south of Kalach in the area of the region designated as winter quarters. For example, 305th Infantry Division had rescued huge reserves of livestock, somewhere in the region of 800–900 animals, by getting them across the Don toward Stalingrad. On 28 November 1942 16th Panzer Division received 25 animals. Likewise, the units of the division that had once again been deployed in the North Switch Position repeatedly received slaughtered animals from the butcher company of 305th Infantry Division.

Over the period from 22 to 29 November 1942 the divisional ration branch was able to keep about 165 metric tons (182 tons) (about 20 kilos [44 pounds] per man) out of the hands of the fast-moving Russian advance. Whereas 16th Panzer Division in terms of rations for the immediate future was in a favorable situation, other units, for example, 376th Infantry Division, had arrived in the fortress without any significant holdings of rations. Thus, on 29 November 1942, 70,000 ration portions were given to 376th Infantry Division. During this time the scattered remnants of other divisions were fed from our rations reserves. About 1 December 1942 coffee and tea could still be freely issued. A constant stream of lightly wounded arrive at the divisional ration center for the Pitomnik airfield and were fed. About 2,000 men waited to be taken away, and they received only sparse rations. Seventy-sixth Infantry Division could for the time being help out with flour, and the bread for our division was baked by the bakery company of 305th Infantry Division.[9] Thus, the divisions were able to assist one another. Some were well provisioned for the winter.

The individual soldiers baked bread partly in their mess tins with the addition of lemonade powder, which was part of the special issue for tank crews. The wheat was ground in mortars, as we had often seen being done among the primitive Russian peasants. With these reduced allowances the division was still able to feed itself up to about 8 January 1943. Thereafter rations were substantially reduced week after week.

Since the beginning of December most of the soldiers in our division had either felt or straw footwear; all members of combat groups did. Also, all available winter clothing had been issued in good time. The men in the trenches, crews in combat vehicles, and wounded—in all a total of about 1,600 men—each received a whole loaf, 3 cigars, and 10 cigarettes (from army stores) at Christmas. To the combat groups, whose strength at this time amounted to about 1,000 men, 200 liters (53 gallons) of red wine could also be issued. In ascertaining the number of men in the trenches, who after Christmas received 300 grams (10.5 ounces) of bread per day, a strict standard had to be adhered to. The number of men in the trenches receiving bread amounted to about 1,000; the entire rations strength of our division at Christmas amounted to about 7,000–8,000 men. In several units of the division the standard allocations from the divisional rations branch were supplemented by an issue of rations that had been saved earlier. On 18 and 20 January 1943 members of the division who had been flown out of the Kessel reported that these additional rations were still available among elements of the division on 18 January.

On 9 January 1943 our supply regiment was disbanded. Somewhere about 20 January rations were issued direct from divisional headquarters to the units. Since 12 January the division's rations branch had been located in a gully on the south edge of Stalingrad; the headquarters of 6th Army (Generaloberst Paulus) was not far away from there. At army headquarters, which had assembled for a withdrawal and which shortly before Christmas stood some 40 kilometers (25 miles) southwest of the encirclement ring, were countless vehicles loaded with rations and army stores that were due to be immediately allocated to 16th Panzer Division by Hauptmann Mulder. However, none of this made it into the fortress. If only there had not been the severe frost along with the hunger! All too often the food arrived in the position frozen, especially the coffee. The *Feldwebel*, the last wounded soldier of Hauptmann Mues's battalion to be flown out of the fortress on 15 January, received a bullet wound in the stomach on 14 January. He had been fighting for the previous 6 days completely without food. So he survived the otherwise fatal wound!

From a field that lay behind the position and whose ears of corn protruded from the snow, soldiers collected additional rations. Wheat and millet ears were threshed, and in the dugouts the corn was cooked with water. He who was lucky found a dead horse and cut off a large piece for his meal. Over and over again one heard the complaint: if only there was a bowl of watery soup and 2 pieces of crispbread a day!

After these sacrifices the bravest of the brave entered into the final battle.

The Final Resistance! 20 January–3 February 1943

On the north front, in front of 16th Panzer Division's positions, the enemy is getting stronger. Above all there is fighting for the strongpoints on the left wing. On 20 January 1943 enemy attacks on the east front against the left wing of 16th Panzer Division are still in progress. At the same time the Kessel is becoming narrower from drawing back under the strong enemy pressure. As a direct result of the losses that cannot be made good, the lines are becoming weaker and weaker, and so everything must be drawn back. The Russians push eastward from Bol'shaia Rossoshka to just before Nadezhda (see map). Once again, as a consequence of the lack of fuel, men and equipment remain behind. In such a way, the very raw material of battle is constantly being reduced. On 22 January 1943 the west front between point 453 and both sides of Voroponovo is ripped open. The Russians advance 15 kilometers (9.3 miles) deep and stand 3 kilometers (1.9 miles) west of Gumrak. The west front is occupied only by a series of strongpoints.

On 23 January 1943 fighting is already under way for the Gumrak airfield. In addition, the airstrip at Stalingradskii is no longer usable. The remnants of IV Army Corps and the remnants of XIV Panzer Corps take up all-around defense in the southern part of Stalingrad, where on 25 January they begin to offer their final resistance. VIII Army Corps and XI Army Corps, 16th Panzer Division, and 5 other divisions pull back their forward lines. The gaps between these groups and the hedgehog[10] in the southern part of Stalingrad can no longer be closed.

On 24 January 1943 those fighting on the north front of the fortress go back to the east via Gorodishche in order to form a hedgehog in the Red October Tractor Works. There the remnants of 1st Romanian Cavalry Division and 20th Romanian Infantry Division are also holding out shoulder to shoulder with their German comrades. Since December 1942 some attached Romanians have also been fighting with 16th Panzer Division, or they have been deployed on construction work because they no longer possess any weapons.

On 25 January 1943 strong enemy attacks that are carried out with unimaginable artillery and tank superiority squeeze the north Kessel, in which our 16th Panzer Division stands, still further. The southern half of the west edge can only be held in the line 7 kilometers (4.3 miles) south of Gorodishche to 3 kilometers (1.9 miles) east of Sadovaia. The remnants of 371st Infantry Division are still fighting on the railway line between Pevorino and Red October and seal the front to the south. The Volga front remains unchanged (LI Corps). According to its report XI Army Corps is conducting the battle with only a handful of heavy weapons, with little ammunition, and without rations along the line Spartakovka to the north of Orlovka and up to the area of Gorodishche. The north Kessel still has an average diameter from 8 to 10 kilometers (5 to 6.2 miles) in both directions. The entire city area is being incessantly ripped up by the heaviest enemy air attacks. The Russian pilots are often able to take off daily from the airfields on the east bank of the Volga and to attack any target without encountering resistance. The number of unattended wounded, starving, and scattered soldiers increases by the hour.

On 26 January 1943 XI Corps is thrown back to the south on the territory close to the west of Red October.

The pulling back of 100th Jäger Division brings about the collapse of the south front. The remnants of IV Army Corps are destroyed. The exhausted soldiers have to leave the larger part of their machine-gun ammunition behind. As a consequence, the catastrophic lack of ammunition becomes even worse (100th Jäger Division belongs to LI Corps. Since December this corps has been holding the east front. The divisions of LI Corps stand in the following sequence from north to south: 389th Infantry Division, 305th Infantry Division, 79th Infantry Division, 100th Jäger Division, and 71st Infantry Division). The formations of the former west front are no longer combat-effective.

On 27 January 1943, 3 enemy tanks are destroyed; the same on 30 January. In the following night the north front, on which the remnants of our proud 16th Panzer Division are performing further heroic resistance, has to be taken back to the line from the southern part of Spartakovka—the north edge of Stalingrad—west edge of Barrikady. At this time 6th Army has no further communication with XI Army Corps.

The defense of the city area is being made exceptionally difficult by the presence of 40,000 wounded and displaced soldiers. The few physically able leaders make every effort to form units from the scattered remnants with which they still offer resistance, they themselves fighting in the front line. The following extracts of radio messages from 6th Army headquarters to OKH, dated 26 January 1943, confirm how senior officers offered an example to their men to the very end.

0820 hours: The front of IV Army Corps south of Tsaritsa is breaking up from superior enemy attacks. The last report from there at 0700 hours that on Point 467 Generals Pfeffer, von Hartmann, Stempel, and Oberst i.G. Grome, with a handful of men, standing upright on the railway embankment and shooting at the mass of Russians surging forward from the west.

0940 hours: At 0800 hours General von Hartmann, the commander of 71st Infantry Division, was killed in close-quarters battle by a bullet in the head.

1205 hours: Generalmajor Stempel, commander of 371st Infantry Division, and Oberstleutnant Andrack, the adjutant of IV Army Corps, killed.

General von Drebber, the commander of 297th Infantry Division, overrun at his command post by Russians.

Since 28 January 1943 no food at all can be given to the sick and wounded so that those fighting can be fed with the minuscule remaining rations. Somewhat improved rations on 29 January 1943 as a consequence of the air and land defensive successes once again raise the morale of 16th Panzer Division.

The command of XIV Panzer Corps (south Kessel) is taken in the farthest forward line and smashed. One reckons with the possibility that XI Corps can hold out for a few more days in the tractor works. Army headquarters and the remnants of Grenadier Regiment 194 are able to offer final resistance in the multistory building. On 30 January 1943 6th Army headquarters forms a hedgehog position in an area of 300 meters around the Red Square.

The last remnants recognize that there is no chance of any relief. Eight to 10 of our groups, among them probably some determined men of 16th Panzer Division, break out of the north Kessel in a southwest direction in order, via Nizhne–Chirskaia, to reach some of the German formations still committed to a relief.

On 31 January 1943 the supreme commander of the glorious 6th Army is promoted to field marshal.

On 31 January 1943 a counterattack with the aim of removing enemy penetrations is only partly successful. There are heavy losses from enemy bombardment. The ammunition of heavy weapons is consumed. After the report at 0800 hours on 1 February 1943, heavy enemy artillery begins preparation on the south and southwest fronts of the north Kessel. A major attack is expected.

On 2 February 1943 XI Army Corps fights the unequal battle to the end. Afer 0920 hours there are no further radio messages.

After superhuman sacrifices the remnants of the southern group are destroyed on the anniversary of the national socialist revolution.

Over and over again the fresh Bolshevik masses rush forward over the bodies of the fallen, until on 3 February 1943 the last soldier in the group of General of Infantry Strecker is overwhelmed.

True to his intention, the commander of 16th Panzer Division does not fall into Russian hands. Meanwhile, Oberst Krumpen, at the headquarters of the remnants of 16th Panzer Division in Konstantinovka, on 27 January 1943 announces the following: "General Hube is pushing ahead with the creation of a new 16th Panzer Division with the remnants of the glorious old 16th Panzer Division."

In April and May 1943 the new 16th Panzer Division is re-formed in France. There are new feats of arms in Italy. Only rarely is anything said about the old comrades who remained in Stalingrad. That's the way soldiers do things. The present demands everything from us. For the "young ones," we wish that they had known the old Stalingrad comrades of the first 18 months of the Russian war.

Rainy autumn of the Italian uplands.
Wrapped in his sleeping blanket, the old soldier of the 16th,
As before in the great ravine in front of Rynok,
Lies pressed to the ground in its plowed furrow.
Pause in the battle.
Night and stars invite contemplation.
And so from time to time one communes
With those who remain in Stalingrad.
In the battle to the very end
Your example stands
Complete and bright in the memory
And above our future.
So you have become more to us
Than the good comrade of earlier campaigns:
A genuine glory,
Which quietly and with the time
Lies around you like a coat of honor.

3 "And There Are No Pages That Tell of These Heroic Deeds": 94th Infantry Division

This account was written by Hauptmann Rudolf Krell (1911–1970), who served with the 94th Infantry Division (commanded by Generalleutnant Pfeiffer). Krell joined the division when it was first formed in 1939. From June 1942 until the middle of November 1942 he was the aide-de-camp at the divisional headquarters. Thereafter he was the regimental adjutant of Grenadier Regiment 267, which was part of Kampfgruppe Müller. Krell was captured on 2 February 1943 in Dubovka and was convicted by the North Caucasus Military Tribunal in Stalingrad (November 1949). No details of the specific charges or any evidence are available. He spent thirteen years in Soviet captivity and finally returned home on 16 January 1956 as one of the nonamnestied prisoners. Having written his first draft, Krell sent copies to former members of 94th Division for comments. The full title of this draft was *Geschichte der 94 Infanterie Division: Kampf um Stalingrad 21.11.1942–2.2.1943*. Attached to the document are comments from former officers. Krell's document is referred to as "chapter 5," which suggests that it was intended to be a chapter in a monograph dedicated to Stalingrad. The diary forms part of the archive holdings of the Bundesarchiv-Militärarchiv in Freiburg-im-Breisgau. Its BA-MA archival reference is RH 26-94/113 (Beiträge zur Geschichte der 94. Inf. Div. bei den Kämpfen um Stalingrad 1942–43).

I. Preface

History should not burden memory but facilitate understanding
—Gotthold Lessing

No official document can make known for posterity the brave struggle of German soldiers inside the Stalingrad Kessel during the last weeks and days. In accordance with the situation, the war diaries with their appendixes had to be destroyed in order to deny the enemy any information. Subsequent Soviet captivity made it impossible to preserve any material of documentary value for the future. Only the verbatim radio messages of 6th Army and the corps that were received by Supreme Headquarters of the Armed Forces remain. Even today the drama and tragedy of 6th Army's and XI Army Corps's desperate battle speak to us from the records. But caution is always advisable before using these radio messages as authentic proof. It is precisely here that politically motivated literature seeks to find support through additions, omissions, and changes in the text. Almost without exception the entire postwar literature that has so far been published concerning the struggle of 6th Army is subject to many errors and lack of information, as a consequence of which false conclusions are drawn. Uncertainty, falsehood, and defamation distort the historical factual basis, even more so in that many a writer, without embarking upon any consideration of evidence, bases himself on the sources of predecessors that are already imbued with errors.

Out of all this, for purposes of objective reporting, are only the living eyewitnesses, of whom there are less and less and who are competent for the task. Further preconditions would be a good memory, an insight into the command structure, and a concern for the highest possible level of objectivity and factual grounding in the depiction and evaluation of the circumstances.

The chronicler, Rudolf Krell (born 1911), was a member of 94th Infantry Division from the moment it was established in 1939. He served on the Siegfried Line, then took part in the French and Russian campaigns. He emerged from Infantry Regiment 276 as a company commander in 1st Battalion and then 2nd Battalion, Infantry Regiment 276 (winter position 1941–1942). With the start of the offensive against Stalingrad from June to the middle of November 1942, he served as orderly officer in the command section of 94th Infantry Division and during the Kessel phase served as regimental adjutant of Grenadier Regiment 267 (Combat Group Müller). On 2 February 1943, with the combat troops in the north Kessel of XI Army Corps, he entered Soviet captivity. His last rank was Hauptmann (captain) on the reserve. He returned home on 16 January 1956 after 13 years in captivity.

Since the author of this chapter belonged to Combat Group Müller during the period being reported, he is especially familiar with the events in this regiment's sector. Therefore, he requests understanding for the fact that he is unable to depict the same level of detail in the course of events among other units of 94th Infantry Division

The author died suddenly of a heart attack while on a convalescent trip to the south Tyrol on 9 January 1970.[1]

II. North Switch Position I

Defense and defensive actions over the period 21 November 1942–24 January 1943. Consideration of the situation map "Stalingrad and Surrounding Area" (see attachment[2]) makes it clear that the retention of the North Switch Position before Stalingrad was "especially important" for the defense of 6th Army inside the Kessel. At this point the important and essential lines of communications with the central Russian landmass are severed (the railway line Kotluban–Pensa–Moscow, respectively, Kazan, the lower Volga region, the main road link Ersovka–Stalingrad, and on to the north). Also situated here are spot heights 93.2, 135.4, 144.20, 147.6, and 145.1 ,possession of which must make it easier for the attacker to capture Stalingrad north (the tractor works). The North Switch Position was intended to secure these heights. An enemy breakthrough of this line would mean the loss of Stalingrad within the shortest possible time. This situation is given precedence in order to underline, with all possible force, the significance of 94th Infantry Division's combat mission at this critical juncture in the defense.

On 23 November 1942 94th Infantry Division was deployed for the defense (in the north of the pocket). Deployment of the division's units was as follows:

Grenadier Regiment 274 (on the boundary with 389th Infantry Division), Orlovka gully north of the tractor works—western edge of Spartakovka—closing up toward the north with Engineer Battalion 194, Bicycle Troop 194, and the rest of 3rd Battalion, Regiment 276 (west edge of Rynok)

Grenadier Regiment 267 (after the relief of 16th Panzer Division) on the right wing of North Switch Position I (to a distance of about 4 kilometers [2.5 miles] in the direction of the Volga)

Divisional Command Post, height 135.5 "Fuchsbau" (Fox earth)

Artillery Regiment 194 and Antitank Section 194, attached to the regiments

Engineer Workshops 194, Stalingrad South

Divisional rations camp and Supply Battalion 194, Marinovka

Field Replacement Battalion 194, Marinovka (Hauptmann Zeugner)

At this time the 94th Infantry Division was under the command of LI Army Corps (General von Seydlitz-Kurzbach, chief of staff Oberst i.G. Clausius).

1. Description of North Switch Position I

The general course runs with the right wing from the Volga (reference point 717 north of Akatovka) and farther in a westerly direction via reference points 416–424 over the high ground 129.6–112.2–111.1, then farther to the west via the stopping point 564 km (a way marker on the railway line Gumrak–Kotluban).

This position was built up as early as August 1942 with the front to the north by units of XIV Panzer Corps. The construction of reinforced positions and the incorporation of obstacles to strengthen the defense created outstanding combat conditions for the defender. Barbed-wire obstacles running nearly the entire length, mining of the ground to the front, the inclusion of listening and forward posts, strengthened fighting positions linked by crawl trenches, construction in depth of the main battlefield, secure winter dugouts, well-constructed observation posts on their own high points, reinforced fire positions for the heavy weapons, and the construction of secure winter tank garages out of which the combat vehicles were also able to function as artillery offered, by way of comparison, a model position that could not have been better demonstrated on an exercise area. The natural terrain was skilfully exploited—the dominant heights were in our possession, whereas the attacker was compelled to move on the flat steppe with gently rising ground without being able to find any cover. Excellent use was made of the available forward slopes. Even at middle or long ranges every enemy attack, often in the forming-up areas of more distant gullies, could be smashed.

2. Deployment of Grenadier Regiment 267 in North Switch Position I

While 16th Panzer Division was being relieved in the middle of November 1942, Grenadier Regiment 267 was deployed in this section of the front with a width of about 6 kilometers (see map diagram).

On the right: elements of 16th Panzer Division with Engineer Battalion in Volga position north from reference point 717, then turning farther into North Switch Position I to the west for about 4 kilometers (2.5 miles).

On the left: a special-purpose Luftwaffe battalion (Hauptmann Matho). (Note: This special-purpose Luftwaffe battalion consisted of three companies of air-landing troops and one company of paratroopers. It was the remnants of a battalion of Luftwaffe Regiment "Stahel." As a consequence of the incorporation of the disbanded 2nd and 3rd Battalions, Matho [1st Battalion] was almost completely up to strength in manpower. The battalion had exceptional firepower at its disposal [among other things 5-cm and 7.5-cm antitank guns]; it also had snipers, and every trooper was armed with either an assault rifle[3] or a machine pistol. In the infantry role the firepower was remarkable, especially in close-quarters battle and counterattacks. Morale was very high. The troops consisted of volunteers only. In the rear the battalion had a full complement of the most up-to-date combat vehicles. The setup regarding command was absurd. After 16th Panzer Division had been relieved, the battalion remained in the North Switch Position. Its existence was unknown to the army and corps leadership, and it was "forgotten." Concerning "leadership," it came under immediate command of VIII Air Corps [General Fiebig].

On the basis of the very good relations of 267's regiment command with Hauptmann Matho, who in respect of leadership was in something of a state of limbo, the regimental command later managed with the assistance of XI Army Corps to get this outstanding battalion incorporated into Grenadier Regiment 267 as a third battalion in the middle of December 1942. By this means the battalion became part of the army and was withdrawn from VIII Air Corps.)

Grenadier Regiment 267, actual formation from the middle of December 1942.

1st Battalion, commander Oberleutnant Krüger (adjutant Oberleutnant Bernhard)
2nd Battalion, commander Oberleutnant Braun (adjutant Leutnant Siegert)
3rd Battalion, commander Hauptmann Matho (special-purpose Luftwaffe, 1st Battalion)

The relations with Hauptmann Matho remained very good right up to the end of the fighting on 2 February 1943.

With the addition of reserves from Field Replacement 194th Battalion, it was possible to raise the frontline strength of 1st and 2nd Battalions/267 to about 650 men, to which could then be added the full complement of the Luftwaffe battalion (temporarily under command).

Allocation of heavy weapons during the deployment in North Switch Position I.
Grenadier Regiment 267 possessed the following:

1 battery of heavy field howitzers, Artillery Regiment 194
1 section of light field howitzers, Artillery Regiment 194

1 battery of heavy antiaircraft guns, 9th Antiaircraft Division (in a ground role[4])
1 battery of light mortars, Mortar Regiment 51 (Oberstleutnant Westerburg)
1 battery of heavy mortars, Mortar Regiment 51 (Oberstleutnant Westerburg)
3 repaired tanks of 16th Panzer Division dug in for use as artillery
2 platoons of light close-support infantry guns
1 platoon of heavy close-support infantry guns, 13th Company/267
14th Company/267 equipped with 5-cm antitank guns (German) and 7.5-cm antitank guns (French)

Ammunition state. Artillery ammunition: running short; mortar ammunition: plentiful; small-arms ammunition: freely available.

In this outstanding position Grenadier Regiment 267 (reinforced) felt itself well able to deal with every enemy attack.

Grenadier Regiment 276 merely consisted of the remnants that had been put together in 3rd Battalion/276. Before that this brave Silesian regiment had had to help out other divisions in crisis moments in the battles in the city area on the orders of LI Army Corps. In the course of these special operations in the street fighting and ruins north of the Tsaritsyn ravine and later in the capture of the smashed industrial area, the Red Barricades, the tried-and-tested assault companies of this regiment under the command of other divisions, had successfully rolled up and broken through the enemy's trench system. Its commander, Major Rittner, was decorated for particular bravery with the Knight's Cross!

Third Battalion/276 (the rest of the regiment) was situated, with a construction battalion under command and Bicycle Troop 194, in a defensive position west of Rynok in a relatively quiet location. Major Rittner was on Knight's Cross leave, and at this time the battalion was led by Oberleutnant Krause.

Engineer Battalion 194 (Commander Major Gerisch) was situated to the south of this position, linking up in front of the west edge of Spartakovka, likewise in a much quieter section.

Grenadier Regiment 274 was located north of the tractor works linking up with 389th Infantry Division in front of the Orlovka ravine, wheeling toward spot height 93.2 (Pilz/Mushroom) in an exposed position. Its mission was to secure the northern boundary of the tractor works, to defend the unfavorable terrain north of the Orlovka ravine, and to counter the enemy's frequent fighting-patrol attacks (often in regimental strength) that came from the Soviet Spartakovka bridgehead. As a consequence of the nature of the terrain, the regiment's heavy weapons only had a limited effect, so the regiment had constantly to parry enemy attacks or breakthroughs. This situation demanded not only the men's courage and nerve but also many bloody sacrifices that individually were not high but constant. The skilled leadership of the regimental commander, Oberst Brendel, always knew how to hold this sector despite the numerical superiority of the enemy. The regiment remained in this position right up to 24 January 1943, after which, as part of the late sealing of the northern pocket, the left wing was turned in.

It is necessary to depict the deployment and formation of 94th Infantry Division in such detail from about 23 November 1942 since only then can everything that follows be better understood.

3. Overview

From everything it emerges that in the later course of the battle and events Grenadier Regiment 267 became part of the battle's center of gravity as well as in the actual battle and, as a consequence, of the later, unjustified measures taken by LI Army Corps.

In the defense of the Stalingrad Kessel the regiment was at times assigned a key position.

At this juncture the combat strength of 94th Infantry Division can be assessed, numerically, at about 35 percent, whereas the firepower of the troops in attack and defense can be rated as very high. The regiments and the sections had an exceptional hard core of junior leaders and officers who had much combat experience from the division's long eastern campaign. A large number of the junior leaders came from our own troops. Before being deployed at the front, the reserve from the battalions under preparation, insofar as the current situation permitted, was in 194th Field Training Battalion, commanded by Hauptmann Zeugner (Marinovka) and Oberfeldwebel Gustav Strauß, one of our most experienced specialists in the area of street and house fighting (on 30 October 1942, after a successful breakthrough to the Volga in the southern part of the city, he was decorated with the Knight's Cross) and trained in the specific demands of infantry combat (close-quarters battle, sentry duty, immediate and set-piece counterattacks, and individual combat). With the return of the convalescents, who, in any case, were part of the division's hard core, the combat strength was further enhanced. Members of the rear services had, as early as the winter battles of 1941–1942, demonstrated that they were capable of being used in operations on the front line. The regiments' and sections' command elements were very well adapted to the changing combat conditions to which the long experience at the front also contributed. The cooperation of the command elements meant that the heavy (attached) assault guns, army-level artillery, battery guns, mortar units, antiaircraft guns in a ground role, assault pioneers, and armor-piercing weapons were all in high readiness.

Ninety-fourth Infantry Division would have rightly been able to characterize itself as an elite division of 6th Army. It was full of élan and courage in the attack and steadfast in defense.

III. The Unauthorized Order of LI Army Corps (General von Seydlitz) to Abandon North Switch Position I and the Consequences of Same (the So-Called Seydlitz Order)

Grenadier Regiment 267 is situated in the above-named forward edge of the battlefield in defense. Apart from some enemy fighting patrols, which are repulsed well before our own line, the enemy initiates no large-scale attacks in this sector. The regiment uses the time to increase its combat effectiveness through creating greater defense in depth in the rifle companies, training the reserves in the ways of the front, and replenishing weapons and ammunition or getting hold of the ammunition left behind by the relieved 16th Panzer Division. Heavy weapons are registered on the assigned areas (artillery targets). The entire firepower of the heavy artillery (army and antiaircraft) is placed together under the control of Oberstleutnant Borsdorf (commander, Heavy Section 194). The rifle companies are familiarized with their own mine obstacles in front of the forward edge of the battlefield (paths through the minefields). Positions close to neighboring units are strengthened.

The mood of the troops is confident.

Early on the morning of 23 November 1942 the regimental adjutant of 267 is summoned by the operations officer of 94th Infantry Division to divisional headquarters (spot height 135.5, "Fuchsbau"). Orally, the order is given that North Switch Position I is, on the order of LI Army Corps (General von Seydlitz), to be evacuated in the night of 23–24 November 1942! The reinforced [Panzer] Grenadier Regiment 26 is to take up a defensive position during the night on the Orlovka position along the railway line Spartovka–Kotluban and, in fact, in front of spot heights 135.4 and 144.2. (reference point 722, about the center of the regiment). This rallying point is to be maintained for 24 hours. Beginning on the northeast front in a southwesterly direction, 6th

Army intends to break out. Scouts are to be dispatched ahead immediately in order to ascertain further rallying positions along the stretch of railway Gumrak–Kotluban with the front to the west.

After the regimental adjutant had returned to regimental headquarters, battalion commanders and unit leaders of the subordinated, allocated, and attached troop elements were summoned so that they could be notified verbally to receive orders that were being prepared. The regimental order was set down in writing and issued toward 1500 hours. The preparations that affected the rear services were initiated. The regimental leadership repeatedly tried in vain to make contact with the unit on the right concerning the withdrawal. This was bound to come to nothing because the relevant headquarters staff could no longer be found! The regimental adjutant of 267 personally searched for the commander of the unit on the left, Hauptmann Matho of the Luftwaffe special-purpose battalion, in his headquarters. Up to then Matho had not received this withdrawal order from any superior commander, which indeed was hardly surprising, since his battalion from a command point of view existed in a state of limbo and all fundamental questions over the disposal of the battalion were still under consideration by VIII Air Corps. (This dual command was grotesque but nevertheless existed.) Hauptmann Matho did not mince his words: he called the order "madness" and expressed himself in words that would be inappropriate to reproduce. His outrage stemmed from his sense of Prussian background and was thoroughly justified. ("The forgotten battalion"!) Matho was then advised immediately to inquire of VIII Air Corps using his long-range radio equipment!

1. The Uncovering of the Unauthorized Withdrawal Order of LI Army Corps

As a result of the inquiry it turned out that VIII Air Corps (General Fiebig) had no knowledge of any imminent breakout attempt! We shall try and get some information and get back to you! [Emphasis in original.]

An answer never followed.

As was demonstrated by later military-historical research, VIII Air Corps immediately passed Matho's inquiry on to the supreme command so that OKH/OKW [Oberkommando der Wehrmacht, German supreme high command] learned of the withdrawal order before the headquarters of 6th Army learned of it. General Paulus first heard of anything when, as a consequence of General von Seydlitz's unauthorized acts, he was notified just before the fait accompli of a withdrawal from North Switch Position I.

Hauptmann Matho was one of those rare men who could make the correct decisions with lightning speed. He immediately placed his battalion under the command of the regimental leadership of Grenadier Regiment 267, and a firm, soldierly comradeship—come what may—was sealed with the regimental adjutant. The adjutant had also passed every test in exemplary fashion right up to his capture on 2 February 1943. This represented a great strengthening of the regiment's combat capability, which was urgently required. Matho immediately ordered his motorized transport, which was set up in his rear echelon, to get ready to move (and also his motorized radio transport, the half-tracked prime movers for the antitank guns, MTW [personnel transport vehicles], and half-tracked motorbikes). This motorized transport made it possible, together with the other combat vehicles of Regiment 267, for nearly all the regiment's guns to get mounted up in order, when drawing back, to be a fast reserve in contact with the additional heavy weapons (motorized) in mobile deployment or to be able to operate independently, should the situation arise, as a reinforced grenadier regiment. The subordinated, allocated, and attached heavy weapons (mortars, antiaircraft guns, the remaining assault guns, the three overhauled panzers that used to belong to 16th Panzer Division) had likewise inadvertently been left out by the issuing of the order of LI Army Corps. For a brief spell these assets were subordinated to the regiment, and the unit leaders were especially pleased to have this support. The firepower of this strengthened regiment (motorized), the striking power of the tested battalions, and the high mobility gave all hope for something like a planned breakout (if such had to be)

2. Change of Position to the Rear

After the onset of darkness on 23 November 1942 the rifle companies, unnoticed by the enemy, broke contact. The removal of the heavy weapons from their fire positions then ensued in relay. The route to the rear was the main road Ersovka–Orlovka. A light frost and minor snow cover were minor impediments. The change of position to the rear was carried out according to plan in a few hours. Those tasked with reconnoitering the designated holding position for "Tempo 2" had already been dispatched in the afternoon. The Orlovka position was occupied according to plan. The heavy weapons took up fire positions behind the battery positions, spot heights 135.4 and 144.2, in order to maintain a view over the area to the front. Before the onset of first light the rearguards broke contact *unobserved by the enemy* [emphasis in the original].

The regiment dug in at the new position.

With the onset of darkness on 23 November, among the western neighboring units, as a consequence of the withdrawal order, the destruction of war material started inducing panic. In a real-life auto-da-fé ammunition was blown up and war matériel was burned and destroyed during the night. Throughout the night the whole line of the front on North Switch Position was characterized by the explosions of ammunition dumps and the flames of destruction.

The destruction of this matériel was paid for later. [Emphasis in original.]

It shall be emphatically stated here that Grenadier Regiment 267 and indeed the other formations of 94th Infantry Division took no part in this destruction. Every piece of equipment, all weapons, and ammunition vehicles were taken back in exemplary fashion to the Orlovka position.

In the period of first light of 24 November the taking up of further positions in the direction of the right and left units was still running its course in order to make contact. This was in vain. From the unit on the left none of our troops could be found for several kilometers. As it later turned out, this division had moved considerably farther than 94th Infantry Division, as a consequence of which contact had been lost. The left-hand battalion (Matho) lengthened its line as far as possible and assumed protection for the flanks. Likewise, none of our own troops could be seen. An engineer battalion that hitherto had occupied a position on the north Volga front had clearly withdrawn beyond the ordered boundary line. After this the flank on the right was likewise exposed.

Divisional command had Engineer Battalion 194, 3rd Battalion/276, Bicycle Troop 194, and the construction battalion swing out with the right wing to the west so that in the course of the afternoon (24 November) contact was established. Only as late as midday, did the enemy attempt a hesitant reconnaissance in force that was immediately repulsed by heavy weapons. At the same time further preparations for the next redeployment phase were taken, which, according to orders, ought to have started with the onset of darkness (Tempo 2).

3. "Stop the Whole Thing!"

During the late morning of 24 November 1942 the regimental command received an order from divisional headquarters of 94th Infantry Division: *The troops are to assume the defense where they now stand!*

For the men, above all, the meaning of this was quite clear: the Kessel was not going to be given up. Everyone breathed a sigh of relief, for everyone was certain that a withdrawal in such a rush would have meant disaster for all concerned.

The high command was already well aware of these events as a result of Matho's radio signal. There, presumably no one appreciated the background to the events. Because of their misjudgment, General von Seydlitz received an order in the evening of 24 November 1942 from the supreme command that he was now responsible for the entire leadership of the Volga front and the North Switch Position. So he was now required once again to bring together all the troop fragments, which on the basis of his movement order were still heading toward the southwest, and deploy them on the front. For 94th Infantry Division nothing was required since this division had carried out the given order and was in contact with the enemy.

Military discipline and order remained intact in this noble division, and the unconditional trust of the soldiers in the divisional leadership was—as always—also here affirmed.

4. Description of the Orlovka Position (North Switch Position II)

The position ran across the slopes of the north-facing heights 135.4–144.2–147.6 (to reference point 722). Third Battalion of Regiment 267 was deployed on the right, 2nd battalion in the middle, both slightly separated by the main road Ersovka–Orlovka and 1st Battalion (Matho) on the left. The single-line railway Tractor Works–Spartovka–Kotluban ran in front of the named high feature (not indicated on the 1:100,000 map). The future forward edge of the battlefield ran along this flat permanent railway line in a hollowed-out depression from about a half to 1 kilometer (.3 to .6 mile) behind the railway feature. It formed a marked forward-slope position, which, as far as defense is concerned, is often problematic. Advantages and disadvantages more or less cancel one another out. The terrain to the front was lightly sloping steppe, which for a great distance could be seen from every part of the position. The sole start lines available for an attacker were located in distant gullies, which could be taken out by our own heavy weapons. There were old Soviet field positions on the gently declining forward slope with the front toward the enemy that were pitiful. That in the position available material from the railway (sleepers, track, and sand) was suited to the construction of one's own position needs to be grasped. The observation posts for the heavy weapons as well as the listening and ranging units were set up on the heights. The artillery could operate favorably from hidden fire positions. To the rear was the strongpoint of the nearby township Orlovka and nearby, and running parallel to the front, the Orlovka gully, which made it possible to bring up reserves unobserved. A part of the supply services was located here.

Regimental headquarters of Grenadier Regiment 267 (with the regimental bicycle platoon, engineer platoon, supply platoon, and medical platoon) was located in a side ravine running north-south immediately south of the village of Orlovka. Administrative facilities such as laundry, delousing, baths, and kitchens were in Orlovka under the control of Hauptfeldwebel Herzog. The forward signal communications center "Urban"[5] was located at regimental headquarters (to "Urban" one went north of Gumrak). Rations and supply loading were north of Gumrak, and the main supply strongpoint was at Marinovka.

Already with the move into North Switch Position II, construction work was under way, even if with fairly modest infantry means. The commander of Engineer Battalion 194 formed a construction detail out of a Ukrainian construction battalion, Organisation Todt,[6] and so on, which brought in engineer stores from the engineer park 194 (among other things heavy material for support and cover) and dug in reasonably well. Measures were taken to secure fireplaces and wood. Experiences from the winter of 1941–1942 were evaluated. After the battle-positions accommodations had been built, they were provided with shallow communications trenches and later with deep communications trenches. The old Russian positions in front of the forward edge of the battlefield were leveled in the night, and as far as it was possible they were filled in and mined. In the course of several weeks the entire sector was protected with wire and mined so that from the middle of December the regiment possessed a superb defensive position.

The description has been so detailed since this regiment was able to hold the position for over two months in spite of all major attacks.

Grenadier Regiment 274 was not included in the rearward move. Only measures of a precautionary nature had been carried out. The regiment holding the old position remained, furthermore, in a relatively quiet sector. Here one did not have to reckon with major attacks. Nevertheless, the danger always existed that the enemy could exploit surprise successes in order to expand the same with a view to a breakthrough toward Stalingrad north. The same also applied for 3rd Battalion/276 and the deployed elements of the division to the north of it.

5. The Consequences of the Seydlitz Order for the Enemy

The redeployment of Regiment 267 during the night of 23–24 November was completed unobserved by the enemy. It was only in the afternoon (24 November) that the enemy initiated a cautious reconnaissance. This resulted in heavy losses for the enemy in the area to the front of our positions, and he was repulsed without any losses for us. A counterattack secured a number of prisoners. Their statements revealed the surprise of the local Russian command as well as their opinion that no grounds existed for the German troops to evacuate such good positions. Also, they found the previous night's "fireworks" inconceivable. Fortunately, the Russian leadership had not recognized this weak phase and had, therefore, not exploited it.

In the postwar literature that has concerned itself with the battle for Stalingrad, the thoroughly superficial and, in part, malicious assertion is made that the "withdrawal from the North Switch Position led to total destruction and, from that, to the partial disintegration of 94th Infantry Division." This depiction is pure fiction and has its origins in the imaginations of people who took no part. It can only be characterized as a perversion of the true facts! The true reasons that led to the "disintegration" of 94th Infantry Division are elsewhere. These will be dealt with below. The fact of the matter is that not a single loss on our side was incurred as a result of the rearward move to North Switch Position II. No soldiers were wounded or killed in action. No history of the war can be dealt with using this line of polemics.

Of interest is the statement of a senior Soviet officer made during captivity in the Oranki camp (Gorkii) in the summer of 1943. During the battles for Stalingrad this officer had had some insight into the leadership of the Don front (Rokossovskii). In conversation with Oberstleutnant Westerburg (commander of mortar regiment), he explained "that the biggest mistake of the German leadership was committed as a consequence of the voluntary relinquishment of the North Switch Position, which in the end, according to Russian opinion, contributed perfectly to the complete liquidation of the Kessel." This judgment from the enemy may be seen as a flashback to the unauthorized withdrawal order of General von Seydlitz.

IV. Group Pfeiffer and Group von Lenski

1.

In the course of organizational regroupings Group Pfeiffer was created by a corps order of LI Army Corps at 2000 hours on 21 November 1942 (in this report we shall be referring back to this date). The newly formed group under the command of 94th Infantry Division commander General Pfeiffer had now to exercise responsibility for the Volga front north (from the tractor works) and the North Switch Position up to the railway line south of Kotluban with 94th Infantry Division, 3rd Infantry Division (mot.), and 60th Infantry Division (mot.) under command. Total length of the front was about 35 kilometers (22 miles).

Countering the major attack against North Switch Position II. Early on 25 November 1942 the enemy initiated a large-scale attack against the weakest position, Road Construction Battalion 501 to the right of Grenadier Regiment 267. The location of the breakthrough was on the so-called strip of woods about 3 kilometers (1.9 miles) east of Orlovka between height 135.4 and 101.3 at a depth of over 3 kilometers. The line of advance was aimed at the tractor works.

As early as 25 November 1942 the enemy had been fortunate in identifying the current weakness of the north front of "Fortress Stalingrad," and 94th Infantry Division spread out over a wide front and attacked it with superior forces. The breakthrough occurred at the division's weakest point, which had been identified by the enemy. This was the sparsely occupied sector of Road Construction Battalion 501; the low combat effectiveness of this exposed wing of the division was only too well known.

This battalion had to be drawn in to the newly occupied Orlovka position after "Tempo 1" since Grenadier Regiment 267 had an open flank on the right and this, as a result of its own overstretched location, could not be covered.

According to the Seydlitz Order provision had been made for the fact that the sector to the right of Grenadier Regiment 267 up to Spartakovka should assume command of those elements of 16th Panzer Division that had remained in the Volga north position. These units exploited the apparently obvious trend to withdrawal but withdrew much farther than parts of 94th Infantry Division!

Consequently the command of 94th Infantry Division was forced to cover this sector by Road Construction Battalion 501 in order, at the very least, to get it secured by men in uniform and armed with Dutch rifles. This measure would have been sufficient for the course of one night, had Tempo II been started. As a result of the army's total-halt order, that is, from OKW, the command of 94th Infantry Division was now confronted with the fact of having to set up immediately, without sufficient men and equipment, a "permanent front" at a length of over 12 kilometers (7.5 miles) out of a holding position that had been planned for only 24 hours.

This was asking far too much of the division's leadership and troops! *That Seydlitz Order of 23 November 1942 gave the enemy the opportunity to attempt a breakthrough here that was also exploited.* [Emphasis in original.]

Containment, counterattack, and regaining the position. Third Battalion/276, Engineer Battalion 194, and Motorcycle Squadron 194 managed to contain the break-in. The combined fire of artillery and mortars was able for the time being to support the containment. The construction battalion had minor combat value and was completely destroyed. Assault parties of Grenadier Regiment 274 with other parts of the division just about managed to hold.

At 1030 hours 24th Panzer Division is issued an order from 6th Army to move immediately from the Don Bend and head in the direction of Orlovka. Toward evening elements of 24th Panzer Division reach Rossoshka, where they take up their Panzer section from the Pestovatka area (the bulk of the division). Already in the night of 25–26 November Group von Scheele (Panzer Grenadier Regiment 26 and Cavalry 4 of 24th Panzer Division) has made contact with Group Pfeiffer, and on the morning of 26 November a counterattack with these strong forces of 24th Panzer Division is initiated. At 1200 hours the enemy is ejected from the break-in area and the old position is regained. Oberst von Scheele is severely wounded in this attack.

2.

The right wing of North Switch Position II was taken over by the new formation Group von Lenskii (24th Panzer Division) to create a uniform defense of this cornerstone of the Volga and north front on 27 November 1942.

As a result, the subordination to Group Pfeiffer no longer applied. Of its own troops only Grenadier Regiment 267 remained to the command of 94th Infantry Division. On the basis of the 6th Army order, Regiments 274 and 276 along with the earmarked sections were removed from the authority of 94th Infantry Division!

Operational formation of Group von Lenski from 27 November 1942 (Generalmajor von Lenski, commander 24th Panzer Division):

24th Panzer Division (new formation in battle groups with the incorporation of elements from 94th Infantry Division)

Combat Group Brendel (commander Oberst Brendel), Grenadier Regiment 274, reinforced, the rest of Grenadier Regiment 276, Engineer Battalion 194, and Bicycle Troop 194

Combat Group von Below (commander Oberst von Below, adjutant Oberleutnant von Burkersroda), with reinforced Panzer Grenadier Section (Rittmeister von Gotz, Cavalry 4) and formed from the rest of Panzer Grenadier Regiment 21 and Motorcycle Rifle Section 4, 2nd Battalion, Panzer Grenadier Regiment 26, quick-reaction unit made up from Panzer Artillery Regiment 89, Panzer Section (commanded by Rittmeister Thiel), and equipped with 8 Panzers Mk. IV (long-barrel)

389th Infantry Division (Generalmajor Magnus)

27 November 1942. Early on 27 November Combat Group von Below (supported by Panzer Section Thiel) mounted an attack toward the north, cleared the rest of the break-in, and laid a new forward edge of the battle area about 2 kilometers (1.2 miles) to the north in a more favorable position. At 0830 hours the aim of the attack was achieved. The local break-in of the enemy in the afternoon [day before] was contained.

28 November 1942. The enemy occupying a break-in position was thrown back in a counterattack. The enemy left behind 30 dead and 80 prisoners. Three enemy tanks were destroyed.

In the area of Group Pfeiffer the enemy attacks, as on the previous day, Grenadier Regiment 267 on the right wing in order to secure height 135.4. With the support of Tank Destroyer Section 40 (24th Panzer Division) and the good use of heavy antitank weapons (self-propelled) and the light 51-mm mortars of the 3rd Battalion, these dangerous attacks could be repulsed by the regiment.

29 November 1942. The newly formed Combat Group Müller moved to the defensive sector of 24th Panzer Division connecting to the west.

Combat Group Müller (Oberstleutnant Julius Müller [commander Grenadier Regiment 267, 94th Infantry Division], adjutant Oberleutnant Krell [final rank Hauptmann])

Formation: Grenadier Regiment 267 with Luftwaffe Battalion Matho, elements of Artillery Regiment 194, 3rd light mortar Battalion 51, 1 battery of heavy 51-mm mortars, assault company Kellerman

Thus from 29 November 1942 Group von Lenski is divided into three combat groups:

Combat Group Brendel (Grenadier Regiment 274, the rest of 276, et al.)
Combat Group von Below (consisting of elements of 24th Panzer Division)
Combat Group Müller (Grenadier Regiment 267 reinforced et al.)

The group's artillery counterdefensive fire is being newly regulated by bringing the reinforced Artillery Regiment, 389th Infantry Division into play.

The artillery commander of Group von Lenski will be the commander of Artillery Regiment 194, Oberstleutnant Borsdorf (Artillery Regiment 389, Infantry Division, with elements of Panzer Artillery Regiment 89, Artillery Regiment 194, and heavy and light cannon).

Group von Lenski's entire antitank defense is also being newly formed; additional antitank weapons from neighboring divisions are being attached, and with that hitherto questionable gaps in the terrain most suited to tanks are being closed.

30 November 1942. Reconnaissance probes are repulsed along the entire north front. Toward 1100 hours the enemy attacks 1st Battalion, Grenadier Regiment 267, with the strongest possible forces in the direction of height 135.4 and tears a gap between Combat Group Müller and Combat Group von Below. At 1400 hours, by means of an immediate counterstroke of Panzer Section Thiel, K4, and 2nd Company, Panzer Grenadier Regiment 26, the line is restored and improved. The enemy fully recognizes the importance of height 135.4. Afterward he makes endless attempts with the exploitation of favorable terrain to seize the decisive height from the northeast and east. Simultaneously, enemy advances follow against the "white house" west of Rynok (Engineer Battalion 194, 3rd Battalion/276) and against the left wing of Combat Group Müller (Matho's battalion), which are pushed back.

1 December 1942. At daybreak there are heavy attacks from enemy artillery with salvoes from Stalin organs on the entire forward edge of the battle area. Then there are enemy advances that everywhere collapse in the fire of heavy weapons. There is a local attack on Matho's battalion (Grenadier Regiment 267) against the left wing of Combat Group Müller. The break-in can be cleared by a counterattack.

Large-scale enemy movements on the northern horizon of the steppe (south of Ersovka) with the enemy in excess of divisional strength in an east-west direction, as well as heavy convoy traffic, are observed. Even with its greater range the heavy gun battery cannot reach the enemy.

Fire from enemy artillery and guns is very heavy. There are losses on the forward edge of the battlefield. About 60 Romanians are attached to Combat Group Müller for deployment as infantry; they are allocated to the rifle companies. As a result of their unwillingness to fight, the results are bad, they are only a burden for the troops. Onset of heavy snowfall and severe frost.

2 December 1942. At 0800 hours independent command of Group von Lenski is dissolved.

The newly arrived general commanding XI Army Corps takes over the north front (Commander General Strecker, chief of staff Oberst i.G. Groß-curth) with the following: 24th Panzer Division, 16th Panzer Division, and 60th Infantry Division (mot.).

3.

Simultaneously Group Pfeiffer was disbanded. By bringing in the constant stream of reinforcements, the units of 94th Infantry Division were separated from one another, as a consequence of which the necessity arose *tactically to split up* 94th Infantry Division so that at the defensive flashpoints the defense could be conducted in a uniform manner.

In accordance with the supply regime the units of 94th Infantry Division continued to be looked after by the Quartermaster Section of 94th Infantry Division. Hauptmann Toepke, the quartermaster (Ib), was subordinated to the quartermaster of XI Army Corps for that purpose.

2 December 1942. At 0800 hours Group Pfeiffer passed on the order concerning all the units still under command to XI Army Corps. From 0800 hours on 2 December 1942 the command section of 94th Infantry Division (with Signals Section 194 minus the deployed elements and headquarters of Panzer Destroyer Section 194) was at the disposal of 6th Army for special purposes.

11 December 1942. Whole elements of 94th Infantry Division deployed in the sector of 24th Panzer Division were also subordinated to 24th Panzer Division.

30 December 1942. Sixth Army ordered that, tactically and as regarded resupply, 94th Infantry Division was to be incorporated into 16th and 24th Panzer Divisions.

Therefore, Grenadier Regiment 274 and Grenadier Regiment 276 should be allocated to 24th Panzer Division in accordance with its combat formation, and Grenadier Regiment 267 joined 16th Panzer Division on the same basis. Twenty-fourth Panzer Division would gladly have had the latter regiment as part of its formation as well.

Grenadier Regiment 267 remained tactically, and in accordance with ration demands, subordinated to 24th Panzer Division. So as not to jeopardize the painstakingly constructed defensive plan, the combat reorganizational measures for the regrouping that were ordered by 6th Army are not implemented.

The regiments and sections of 94th Infantry Division that were deployed in the defense plan of 24th Panzer Division remained with 24th Panzer Division, which was welcomed by all men of 94th.

In the situation report of 24th Panzer Division, the chief of staff, Oberstleutnant i.G. von Menges, regarding this noted: "This dissolution order was a very sore point for 94th Infantry Division after it had fought so bravely and after it had discharged its duty in such a magnificent fashion."

By means of this dividing up, as well as in 24th Panzer Division, headquarters and units were all mixed together. The combat strength could be raised by about 1,231 men. Of this body of men about 600 were allocated to Grenadier Regiment 267 such that the frontline strength of the strengthened regiment at the beginning of January 1943 amounted to about 1,200 men (Combat Group Müller).

A Correction

All the interpretations of the postwar period that were peddled about the battle for Stalingrad, that 94th Infantry Division had been destroyed by the withdrawal from North Switch Position I, are false and even slanderous. These sorts of mistaken judgments simply pay no regard to the facts and at the same time, by doing this, tendentious objectives are clearly being pursued. The mere use of the expression "dissolution" is misleading. The infantry regiments and sections remained extant; the Quartermaster Section of the 94th, moreover, supplied their units and beyond that, additionally and from their own means, 24th Panzer Division, among others, also by an issue of meat from their own horse reserves. The entire supply network of Supply Battalion 194 not only supplied, furthermore, the units of 94th Infantry Division but also the attached heavy weapons units. The combat vehicles still retained the Sword of Saxony as the tactical divisional emblem of 94th Infantry Division, and right up to the very end, on 2 February 1943, the members of the division were always referred to as the men of the 94th. In actual fact Grenadier Regiments 267 and 274 experienced a relative increase in combat strength that reached the levels at the start of the offensive in July 1942 (above all, this is the case regarding Combat Group Müller as the main regimental force).

De jure the 94th Infantry Division no longer existed under this designation. De facto, however, its now divided units, which in the sector of 24th Panzer Division (XI Army Corps) were self-contained under their own tactical emblems of the crossed swords, remained deployed to the very end.

4. Continuation from Paragraph 2

3 December 1942. Exploiting the early-morning fog, the enemy achieves a major break-in on the left wing of Combat Group von Below (boundary line with Combat Group Müller). After a heavy artillery bombardment the enemy attacks the all-important spot height 135.4 with a force of about 200 men—behind which there is a blocking company—and occupies it. Right up to the artillery position in Orlovka base no German soldier stands anymore. Leutnant Köhler 6/26 (24th Panzer Division) with a handful of assembled soldiers attacks the enemy in close-quarters battle, breaking in from the flank, destroys about 100 Soviets, and pushes with his small group into the blocking company, which after losses of about 20 men is thrown back. After a subsequent cleanup operation with additional forces, height 135.4 is once again in our possession. Leutnant Köhler is decorated with the Knight's Cross.

Height 135.4 is constructed as a switch line (strongpoint) and occupied with our own strong forces.

Two strong enemy advances from Spartovka against I/274 of Combat Group Brendel are repulsed with heavy losses for the enemy.

As a precautionary measure the construction of two rear positions, the Orlovka switch and the Gorodische position, which, should the need arise, could be taken up by Combat Groups Müller and von Below, begins under the control of Major Gerisch (Engineer Battalion 194).

4 December 1942. A Russian attack against Grenadier Regiment 267 (Combat Group Müller) is broken up by our defensive fire just before midday.

5 December 1942. An enemy reconnaissance probe is repulsed by Luftwaffe Battalion Matho (Combat Group Müller).

6 December 1942. Quiet.

7 December 1942. In the night the enemy brings up reinforcements (motorized) against North Switch Position. Renewed attack against Grenadier Regiment 274 (Combat Group Brendel), which breaks down.

8 December 1942. An enemy forming-up point in the northern part of Spartakovka is broken up by artillery fire.

During the day frequent attacks in front of Grenadier Regiment 267 (Combat Group Müller), particularly against the left wing of Matho's battalion and height 135.4 (boundary position with Combat Group von Below), are repulsed. On the boundary position, after heavy preparatory fire, the enemy succeeds in penetrating to a depth of 100 meters. In a counterattack the enemy is thrown back by tanks (Tank Section Thiel); despite strong counteraction the enemy remains in the front of the forward edge of the battle area on the ground.

9 December 1942. Repeated enemy attacks, above all against the 3 battalion sectors of Grenadier Regiment 267, are repulsed. The fighting on the east wing of Combat Group Müller is especially severe. The enemy is repulsed in furious close-quarters battles. In order to reinforce these permanent pressure points with greater forces, stronger positions in the boundaries between Combat Groups Müller and von Below are ordered. Combat Group Below is better situated as regards forces and takes over a short section of this sector from 3rd Battalion/267, which is overstretched. Romanian soldiers are constantly being brought in and are deployed as construction units in the building of the position in the combat groups and in Engineer Company 40.

10 December 1942. Every last man is brought in order so as to strengthen the positions at night and create better accommodations in the severe cold (field bunkers). The heights that run close behind the front are further reinforced as strongpoints. The Orlovka switch and the Gorodische position are being urgently extended.

In front of Grenadier Regiment 267's sector, enemy reconnaissance probes are being repulsed. Heavy attacks on the left neighbor (16th Panzer) are repulsed with the support of Panzer Section Thiel.

11 December 1942. After the lack of enemy success in the last few days there are no serious attacks.

In this day's Wehrmacht report the defensive successes on this front are given due acknowledgment.

The troop-support services of numerous deployed elements of 94th Infantry Division are under the command of 24th Panzer Division (see more above).

Losses since deployment on this part of the front north Stalingrad amount to the following:

Among elements of 24th Panzer Division:
13.8 percent of the frontline strength in officers
20.4 percent in NCOs and men
Among elements of 94th Infantry Division under command:
10.2 percent of the frontline strength in officers
23.6 percent in NCOs and men

In the course of 15 days this means that an average of one-fifth of the frontline strength has been lost that cannot be replaced. Also, the shortage of ammunition, minimal rations, and the unfavorable weather conditions are an especially severe test for the small infantry forces that are being reduced on a daily basis.

It is a trial that is being surmounted by all in a clear understanding of the situation.

12 *December* 1942. Enemy forming-up positions in front of Combat Group Brendel (Grenadier Regiment 274) are smashed, and a strong fighting patrol is repulsed. Harassing fire across the entire northern sector.

13 *December* 1942. In front of the position enemy reconnaissance patrols are repulsed at night. There is harassing fire.

14 *December* 1942. In the early-morning hours and in the afternoon enemy fighting patrols, above all near Combat Group Müller, are again repulsed: isolated enemy tank advances that do not reach the forward edge of the battlefield. Very bad weather, fog, fine rain, warm.

15 *December* 1942. Enemy reconnaissance patrols are repulsed. Enemy air activity is increasing and dominates the air space. Ground fog.

16 *December* 1942. Russian reconnaissance patrols are repulsed in the night, at times destroyed. Enemy forming-up point in front of Combat Group Brendel is broken up by fire.

17 December 1942. Heavy enemy fire, above all on the all-important height 93.2 (Pilz), which is occupied by Battalion Kannengießer (Grenadier Regiment 274). Behind the forward edge of the battlefield further strongpoints are being built. Captured weapons and ammunition are being secured in order to make good gaps and save our own ammunition.

Combing the communications and the rear services in order to make up the frontline strength. Sudden severe frost.

18 December 1942. Quiet.

19 December 1942. Enemy reconnaissance patrols are repulsed in front of Combat Group Brendel. Using loudspeakers and leaflet propaganda, the enemy makes a vain attempt to undermine our combat morale. These sorts of attempts achieve nothing. The German soldier knows what is ordered regarding this bait, and in any case he knows what his duty is.

20 December 1942. Harassing fire increases on Combat Group Brendel.

21 December 1942. Concentrated harassing fire on the strongpoints of Combat Group Brendel. The Gorodische position, which has been highlighted as a possible defensive position, is further examined and work on strengthening it is started. It is uncertain whether and when the position will be occupied. It is better to hold the current well-constructed position than to withdraw to the reduced and still not fully completed position, regardless of the morale of the troops.

The infantry is still only about 20 percent mobile. The horse-drawn artillery of 94th Infantry Division is completely immobile. Huge numbers of horses perish from a lack of fodder on a daily basis. They are slaughtered before they die and for the last month they have been the division's sole source of meat.

In the event of having to clear the position at short notice one will have to reckon with a heavy loss of equipment.

22 December 1942. Harassing fire above all on the sector of Combat Group Brendel. For the eventuality of a withdrawal of the division, measures are under way for taking Combat Group Brendel and the remaining vehicles of 94th Infantry Division and of 24th Panzer Division. In this eventuality it would be possible with all assistance to take away all the artillery of Artillery Regiment 194. As a result, all the horse contingent, motorized vehicles of Luftwaffe Battalion Matho, the mortar batteries, and any surviving trucks (German and captured) would be assigned to Combat Group Müller.

23 December 1942. Quiet.

24 December 1942. Heavier fire on Combat Group Brendel.

Through skilled management of resources on the part of the division's quartermasters and the comradely assistance of 94th Infantry Division, which still retains some army goods inside the "Fortress," the division manages to get every man small rations of bread, chocolate, and cigarettes. The quartermaster of 94th Infantry Division manages, through rationing (silo wheat), to give every man a loaf of army bread for Christmas. Christmas day will be spent in the trenches and the bunker accommodations. The bulk of the soldiers have received no mail from home since the middle of November.

The trust of the soldiers in the leadership and in an imminent relief remains unchanged. Even here, in a constructed defensive position, the German soldier considers himself to be superior to the enemy.

25 December 1942. Heavy bombardment on Combat Group Brendel. Concentrated break-in on the left unit of 16th Panzer Division that is mainly concentrated against heights 147.6 and 145.1. Fifteen tanks of Panzer Section Thiel (24th Panzer Division) are able to clear the break-in.

26 December 1942. After heavy preparatory fire the Russians attack Combat Group Brendel at 0400 hours. The heavy attack is repulsed in close-quarters battle and counterattacks. Further enemy preparations are destroyed by fire. The local break-in can be cleared before the onset of nightfall. On this day the losses in Combat Group Brendel amount to 45 killed and wounded, which means about one-third of the battalion's combat strength. The combat group's last reserves have to be deployed in order to cover the losses. Indications of further attacks are evident. Group Thiel (Armored 2nd Company, Cavalry 4) has once again to clear a break-in on its left neighbor (16th Panzer Division). Because of enemy superiority, this is not completely successful.

In order to raise the combat strength two artillery sections of Artillery Regiment 194 are merged into one section. Those remaining are attached to the combat groups as infantry (Quick-Reaction Company Kellermann in Grenadier Regiment 267, the rest to Grenadier Regiment 274).

27 December 1942. In the night enemy probes are repulsed. Heavy fire, during the day up to 400 shells on 2 to 3 of the most important strongpoints of Combat Group Brendel, above all on Pilz (height 93.2). With an attack at 0600 hours the enemy achieves a minor local break-in, which is immediately cordoned off.

28 December 1942. Toward 0400 hours, after heavy preparatory artillery fire, the Russians once again, with 4–5 companies, attack the decisive strongpoints of Combat Group Brendel. The attack is repulsed everywhere. In the afternoon the minor local break-in position of the day before, after thorough preparation, is again cleared. During the process 52 enemy dead are counted. A Russian counterattack that is immediately initiated is repulsed.

29 December 1942. Enemy fighting patrols repulsed in front of Combat Group Brendel. Later, heavy artillery fire on this sector.

30 December 1942. Three fighting patrols are repulsed in front of Combat Group Brendel. In accordance with an incoming 6th Army order, the parts of 94th Infantry Division are to be incorporated in 24th and 16th Panzer Divisions with immediate effect. In this severe defensive battle the 6th Army order is only of theoretical significance. A tactical realization in the formation of the defense plan is not possible because of the pressure of the situation (see further above).

As a result of men being made available from the dissolution and merging of rear units and divisional headquarters staff, Combat Groups Müller and Brendel have their combat strength raised by an additional 1,231 soldiers.

31 December 1942. After dark in the evening of 30 December 1942 the Russians attack the decisive strongpoints, above all Pilz (height 93.2) in the middle of Combat Group Brendel (Grenadier Regiment 274), three times. Defense through close-quarters battle. Divisional reserve, 3/Armored Engineer Battalion 40 is deployed in platoon strength and removes the enemy on Pilz so that it is once again in our hands. At 0530 hours the forward edge of the battlefield with heavy own losses is once again in our possession. Combat Group Brendel can look back with special pride on its defensive successes.

Effective 30 December 1942, as a result of a new combat organization, the units of 94th Infantry Division receive an increase in manpower that raises their frontline strength to 1,231. These numbers are not included in Table 3.1.

As of 1 January 1943 the total combat strength is 3,386.

Table 3.1 *Frontline Strength, 31 December 1942*

Unit and Attachments	Total
Combat Group von Below, 24th Pz. Div, 2/21, 2/26, K4	659
Combat Group Brendel (Grenadier Regt. 274), 94 ID.	604
Combat Groups Müller (Grenadier Regt. 267) and Matho, 94 ID	654
Tank Destroyer Section 40 (24th Pz. Div)	238
Total strength	2,155

A comparison of the strength ratio (frontline strength) between 94th Infantry Division and 24th Panzer Division clearly reveals that:

94th Infantry Division = two-thirds of the frontline strength
24th Panzer Division = one-third of the frontline strength

The units of 94th Infantry Division amount to about two-thirds of the frontline strength of 24th Panzer Division and form the flank regiments of 24th Panzer Regiment. On these points the enemy conducts the full weight of his constant attacks, in order, on these positions, to tear up the front and to seize the city of Stalingrad in one move. Not for nothing are the regiments of 94th Infantry Division deployed on the exposed flank positions. The leadership of both 24th Panzer Division and XI Army Corps knows that such front positions can be held only by tried-and-tested infantrymen with their existing "professional qualification." The deployed, mainly active, and willingly serving soldiers of the Panzer division belong to a highly regarded troop formation but one that is designed to show its full potential primarily in mobile warfare. It proves, therefore, that this was taken into account by the leadership: the integration of both divisions followed by the replenishment of the infantry regiments, which has subsequently proven to be correct, since in these regiments particularly the experience and the know-how in defensive battles is to be found in deployment on the immediate front.

5. Experiences and Lessons

Once again it was shown that in defense, closely controlled infantry could repel every enemy attack, often where the enemy had a tenfold numerical advantage, when it staunchly carried out its battle task and did not allow itself to be influenced by the enemy's temporary penetration successes. To be sure, defense forces must immediately be deployed in a counterattack. A flanking containment from the defense's own position often achieved faster success than a frontal counterattack, which as a rule resulted in greater casualties. The latter method demands too much in terms of time and expenditure of effort, such that the enemy is able to secure a foothold using heavy infantry weapons—which are invariably brought along by gun crews in order to provide all-around defense—and with these same heavy weapons is then able to push on with his attack.These weapons should be taken out when the enemy advances!

Infiltrated reconnaissance patrols and trained fighting patrols that took the enemy by surprise (particularly at night or during fog) confused the enemy by short bursts of fire from their assault weapons. Fighting patrols in the enemy's known preparation areas (at night) induced panic and result in minor or no losses for our side. In the forward edge of the battle area dug-in sniper positions with alternate positions (6 rifles fitted with telescopic sights per rifle company) kept the enemy and his forward lines at a distance. When he attacked, the enemy's officers and junior leaders, when identified, could be eliminated.

Bring armor-piercing weapons *to* the forward edge of the battle area (forward line). These weapons must have an impact *before* an enemy tank has broken through.

The use of explosive grenades fired from antitank guns destroyed massed attacks well before the forward edge of the battlefield (the infantry's artillery). Widespread use of captured weapons (the Soviet "*Ratschbumm*"), for which the ammunition was everywhere, strengthened the defensive power of the forward line. Virtually every infantryman had trained himself in the use of this weapon.

The Use of Small Arms

Soviet machine pistol (very reliable) used as a backup weapon.

Soviet assault rifle (10 rounds) with the appropriate ammunition (phosphorus, explosive and tracer). These were in great numbers there; they just had to picked up.

Soviet 12-cm mortar (superheavy). This was used in the forward edge of the battlefield. Soviet T-34s were dug in behind the line; with their moving turrets, they could be used as artillery.

Siting of Soviet bar mines in front of the forward line.

Here the sort of improvised means with which the infantry's fighting power was strengthened in order to make good the gradually diminishing supplies (replenishment) of our infantry weapons and ammunition should be flagged. None of this was envisaged in the *Army Manual of Regulations*.

The strengthened construction of strongpoints in a system of secured battle positions with the siting of heavy weapons on high ground to the rear proved itself to be successful (securing the depth of the main battlefield in accordance with the *Army Manual of Regulations*).

In the last 6 weeks the cooperation of the heavy weapons (artillery, mortars, heavy antiaircraft guns deployed in the ground role) with infantry had worked out superbly. Above all, the mortars of the 11/Mortar 53 unit and the batteries of heavy mortars broke the momentum of enemy attacks or smashed the enemy's forming-up zones. These magnificent weapons had a plentiful supply of ammunition so that they were always on call. This weapon played a substantial role in the success of the defense.

In the all-arms cooperation of experienced frontline arms of service, such high performances were attained, which would scarcely have been reached in peacetime, and demonstrated by elite units on the training ground!

The communications network in the permanent front North Switch Position II. A preliminary point: the communications network in the defensive plan did not correspond with the conventional rules of the communications service. Special conditions, however, require special measures when the task demands it and when the resulting success provides belated justification.

The old main signal routing between regimental headquarters, Infantry Regiment 267 (in front of the forward divisional headquarters of 94th Infantry Division), and the still existing Signal Control Urban (Leutnant Urban, Signals Battalion 194) north of Gumrak station with all its long-distance communications (among others to Grenadier Regiment 274, right flank) still came under Signal Control Urban's control This signal routing was transmitted to the other units of 24th Panzer Division (heavy weapons sections) and on to the units on the right and left through a distribution network. An integrated communications system was created within these signal routes so that radio conferences arising from tactical requirements (heavy weapons, deployment of reserves, situation briefings) could be conducted. In addition, Signal Control Urban had a direct line to headquarters, XI Army Corps, that could be connected in case of an emergency. It could also be connected to the neighboring division on the left, Hauptmann Holl/Infantry Regiment 276 (16th Panzer Division). In exceptional circumstances the communication links of 24th Panzer Division (Headquarters Section) could be used to contact regimental headquarters in the event that the communication had any immediate bearing on the enemy situation (permitted by 6th Army's signal order). The rifle companies maintained a direct link by line across the forward edge of the battlefield that was on switched on during an enemy attack. By this means the regimental command had a direct link to the forward edge of the battlefield so that the necessary measures for supporting the front could be initiated. In addition, the Command Section, 24th Panzer Division, had its own voice net linking up with the regiments and LI Army Corps. Signals Battalion 194 installed a forward signal communication link (Leutnant Urban) with two exchanges at the regimental headquarters of 267. Radio communications existed as follows: 24th Panzer Division to the regiments, signal reporting head (Leutnant Urban) to Grenadier Regiment 267, Grenadier Regiment 267 to Grenadier Regiment 274, Combat Group von Below, and those sections that were equipped with radio: mortar, artillery, Tank Section Thiel, and Tank Destroyer Section (mot.) 40 with frequency changes. The voice net between regimental headquarters 267 and the battalions, the battalions and the rifle companies was activated only when under direct enemy attack.

A list of code names was used with frequent changes. Radio traffic was kept to a minimum as the enemy listened in to the net.

All these measures made a contribution to a flexibly conducted defense!

V. Further Defensive Actions (January–February 1943)

In the New Year there was minimal enemy activity. Heavier harassing fire from Russian artillery on our own artillery positions. Further building work undertaken above all in the Orlovka ring, which cordons off, for a distance of about 3 kilometers (1.9 miles), the broken gully terrain of the upper Orlovka from height 144.2 toward reference point 431 (Wegespinne) in order to stop a likely enemy break-in on the left-hand unit (16th Panzer Division). Work on strengthening the positions—using engineering equipment—of fire positions, living accommodations, and communications trenches was carried out.

During the first weeks of January the enemy shifted the thrust of his heavier attacks against 16th Panzer Division, since he assumed that he would encounter a less rigorously conducted defense. Focus of the attacks was against the right wing, height 147.6. These attacks also fell on the left flank of Matho's battalion (boundary) and were immediately repulsed in vigorous counterattacks.

In order to secure the left flank of 24th Panzer Division, which as a consequence was always threatened, the remainder of Grenadier Regiment 276 (3rd

Battalion) and I/Panzer Grenadier Regiment 79 with combat group leaders Hauptmann Krause and company commander Hauptmann Holl were now detached from 16th Panzer Division to defend height 147.6. With this, combat troops of 94th Infantry Division who were expected to hold out took over this sector of 16th Panzer Division. Troop support services were subordinated to 16th Panzer Division and allocated to tactical cooperation with Grenadier Regiment 267 in order to be able to conduct the defense at this new focal point in a uniform manner.

During the night and at first light, and on his own initiative, Hauptmann Matho undertook strong fighting patrols with a company of paratroopers way in front of the forward edge of the battlefield in enemy positions in order to clean out the forward area. This caused panic and confusion among the enemy. Apart from lightly wounded we suffered no losses. The attacks against his sector weakened moreover so that Hauptmann Matho was able to remove one company out of the forward line as a reserve and boundary security.

General of Infantry Strecker (commander of XI Army Corps) concerned himself personally with the well-being of Grenadier Regiment 267 (Combat Group Müller). The commander Oberstleutnant Müller and General Strecker have been friends since peacetime (1936), when Strecker was Müller's regimental commander. Every few days he would call in to see his "Julius" at regimental headquarters 267 in order to find out for himself how the troops were doing. As a result, much in the way of reinforcements came the regiment's way. The well-being of the men of 94th Infantry Division was close to the commanding general's heart.

General Strecker ordered that the administrative headquarters of XI Army Corps be disbanded; the corps signal section be reduced; and the army units subordinated to them, insofar as these were without equipment, be allocated to Grenadier Regiment 267 as an infantry reserve as part of the front reorganization. By means of this the combat strength of the regiment could be replenished and assault companies under the leadership of infantry officers could be newly trained. The regiment received additional assault rifles and machine guns (MG-42s). For a long time Oberstleutnant Müller had been suffering from a severe stomach complaint that had recently deteriorated such that he could take only small amounts of food. The divisional doctor ordered that he be flown out of the pocket immediately. At the same time he suffered an increasingly severe weight loss, and for days on end he was confined to lying down. Oberstleutnant Müller rejected the idea of being flown out of the pocket since he wanted to remain with the men of his regiment in order to share their fate. As a result the main burden of regimental command fell to the regimental adjutant, for whom the commander acted in essence merely as an adviser. Three attempts (announced) to get Oberstleutnant Müller awarded the Knight's Cross failed since petty reservations of the personnel section at Supreme Army Headquarters concerning the justifications always found some formal shortcoming. The deserved promotion to full colonel was submitted but failed to reach him. On 3 May 1943 Oberstleutnant Müller died in Soviet captivity in the Oranki prison camp. May this serve as an obituary for one of the best regimental commanders of 94th Infantry Division!

The first week in January. Once again the heavier attacks preceded by heavy fire are made against Battalion Kannengießer on "Pilz" (height 93.2). The enemy seeks complete control of this dominating height in order to attain possession of the northern part of Stalingrad by a breakthrough on the Combat Group Brendel sector. Artillery Group Borsdorf lays concentrated fire on the enemy's familiar forming-up positions on the west edge of Spartakovka and destroys the massed attacks. Immediate counterattacks can prevent break-ins. Renewed strengthening work of strongpoints, above all with regard to cover from artillery, is carried out in Combat Group Brendel. Combat von Below's sector is quieter.

The second week in January. With forces that are becoming ever stronger the enemy attempts to seize height 147.6 (left unit). As experienced infantry officers, the strongpoint commanders Hauptmann Krause and Hauptmann Holl (3rd Battalion/276) succeed in holding this height by the use of all their forces. These attacks are repeated on a daily basis, increasing in strength. The enemy manages to gain temporary possession of this height. Tank Section Thiel (with 6 remaining Mark IV lg.); the assault company of 24th Panzer Division; and the reserve company of Matho's battalion, which is thrown in, are able to recapture the height.

It is clear to all concerned that an enemy breakthrough on heights 93.2, 135.4, 144.2, and 247.6 [*sic*] means the loss of Stalingrad!

Under command of Rittmeister von Dreßler, 24th Panzer Division forms a strong combat group out of the artillery sections, the remains of Panzer Engineer Battalion 40, freed-up elements of the Panzer Supply Section 8, and Tank Destroyer Section 40 in order to retain the Orlovka Switch position. Combat Group von Dreßler moves to the Orlovka Switch to take up permanent defense of the left wing on the defensive front of 24th Panzer Division. At the same time the question arises as to how much longer the defense on the left unit (16th Panzer Division) can hold. The reserve assault companies of 24th Panzer Division are being transferred as assault groups behind the ring in the west Orlovka gully.

Yet again there are reconnaissance patrols against the boundary of Combat Group Müller/Combat Group von Below, which are repulsed in front of the main battle line.

10 *January 1943: Large-scale assault on Combat Group Müller.* As early as the previous evening and during the night there were clear signs of the enemy's major preparations. A lot of noise from tanks and the many lights from trucks all pointed to this. Prisoners who had been taken in the night (who were permitted to run back) stated that new troop formations with many tanks had arrived. Supported by measures taken by the command of 24th Panzer Division, the combat group got ready for a major defensive battle. Quite obviously the enemy wanted to initiate a major breakthrough into the Kessel.

On the morning of 10 January 1943 the Russians attacked the main front line of Combat Group Müller with a large formation in a southerly direction from the area of Ersovka. Approximately 80 heavy tanks with infantry on board formed up out of shooting range for a frontal attack. They were accompanied by infantry moving between the tanks in at least regimental strength. Behind them were heavily laden infantry in large groups on numerous trucks. On the snow-covered steppe the attack was pushed forward hesitantly, supported by salvoes from Stalin organs. The weather was cold in the clear light. At a suitable range our own heavy mortar batteries, the light mortars, and heavy and light gun batteries opened fire on the attacking enemy. In such a way the accompanying regiments (mot.) that were coming up behind were forced together and destroyed. The tank-mounted infantry got into position, mainly in the snow holes and were forced to ground by the fire of heavy infantry weapons and the bombardment of light mortars and comprehensively taken out. The remnants of the tank formation (not in any depth) were hit by the fire of antitank weapons and heavy antiaircraft guns at intermediate range, with the mass destroyed. The rest fled.

Statements from prisoners confirmed that this large formation was a Soviet tank corps that had just arrived at the Stalingrad front. The tanks, supplied on the basis of the Lend-Lease Pact, had just been handed over by the Soviets' American allies and were straight out of the factory. The Soviet tank crews were not familiar with the Sherman and operated this Allied equipment very badly. The numerous trucks, GM Studebakers, were also American. Likewise as a consequence of Lend-Lease, the Red Army soldiers were physically in a much better condition.

Toward the afternoon the enemy once again put everything together and put his attack plan into effect. This attack was also destroyed in front of the main positions.

During the evening a large Soviet fighting patrol managed to penetrate the lines of the right company of Combat Group Müller. The enemy was repulsed in close-quarters battle with heavy losses on our side. In defending the position both the company and platoon commanders were killed as well as a large number of the section commanders. The company armorer (a determined Obergefreiter) organized the remnants of the company and placed them under his command. With the survivors he succeeded in recapturing the position in bitter close-quarters fighting. Assault Company Kellermann reinforced the situation with a counterattack, mopping up the area in front of the forward position. The enemy left his dead, about battalion strength, behind. This brave and hitherto unprepossessing Obergefreiter had more than discharged his duty. The regiment put him in charge of the company, and he was promoted to sergeant. Nor did he let anyone down afterward. A recommendation for the Knight's Cross was not processed by 6th Army headquarters. For this performance he was only awarded the Iron Cross First Class by Regiment 267.

Comment: This comprehensive depiction should make clear that these men with their high morale—at this time three weeks before the end—managed to repulse an overwhelmingly powerful enemy and to destroy him. And there are no pages that tell of these heroic deeds.

11 January 1943. With the last tanks of his unit (about 20) and supporting infantry the enemy attempts again to punch through the forward edge of the battlefield on the boundary between 1st and 2nd Battalions/267. This attack follows the same pigheaded set of "rules" as the day before. Once again the enemy attack is smashed with heavy losses for the enemy. Only a handful of tanks manages to withdraw. Our own losses are minimal.[7]

Quiet in Combat Groups von Below and Brendel.

12 January 1943. The enemy transfers the weight of his attacks in North Switch Position II farther to the west onto the sectors of 16th Panzer Division and 60th Infantry Division (mot.). In possession of height 145.1, the enemy clearly now wants to take height 147.6, which is being defended by 3rd Battalion/

Grenadier Regiment 276, by reinforced attacks. This is also critical for Combat Group Müller, since this battalion abuts the left wing of 24th Panzer Division. Holl's battalion always manages to throw the enemy back. Wotha's battalion (16th Panzer Division) successfully supports the defense to the left of Holl's battalion.

On this day, on his own request, Rittmeister von Dreßler (24th Panzer Division) is flown into the Kessel and assumes responsibility for the entire defense of the transferred elements of the Orlovka ring, which is now in a state of combat readiness (Combat Group Dreßler has a combat strength of about 600). Heavy artillery weapons are regrouped so these weapons can be used in any enemy breakthrough in front of the Orlovka ring and in the nearby gullies. Attacks are expected from there.

13–20 January 1943: A synopsis. With strong forces the enemy attempts to punch a hole through the left wing of North Switch Position II in order to take the northern part of the city in one move. Here the attacks supported by numerous tanks especially hit the right wing of 16th Panzer Division (neighbor of Matho's battalion). Over and over again, the already assembled assault companies (squadrons) of 24th Panzer Division have to throw back in counterprobe or -attack the infiltrated enemy in front of 16th Panzer Division (as temporary help). To this end Motorcycle Rifle Section 4 (Rittmeister von Götz) from the sector of Combat Group von Below is also removed in order to eject the enemy from the area immediately to the front of the Orlovka position. The enemy has already, in part, gone firm in the upper part of Orlovka in the gully system that runs to the north. The position can only be, once again, cleared in bitter close-quarters battle. The enemy attacks reach their peak on 18 and 19 January. The Orlovka position and also 3rd Battalion/276 and height 147.6 have been able to hold their own.

Our artillery has expended all its ammunition. The freed-up crews fill up the gaps that arise in the assault companies. Light and heavy mortars can continue to be used with good effect since there is available ammunition.

Three of our tanks (Tank Section Thiel) and some self-propelled antitank guns have been restored to good condition and play an essential part in the successful defense.

In the combat groups of 24th Panzer Division there are heavy enemy reconnaissance probes on the entire sector, which are repulsed in front of our lines.

Sixth Army has ordered that a preparatory line making use of earlier enemy positions along the length of the Gorodishche gully be quickly built and reinforced on the northern edge of Stalingrad with the front to the west. The defense installations are to be prepared under command of Major Kempter (389th Infantry Division) with the use of local resources.

On 17 January the great Stalingrad pocket has already been squeezed in from the west by about half from numerically superior numbers of Russian assault troops. Now the North Switch Position is held only in its reduced west flank by 113th Infantry Division.

21–24 January 1943. Enemy pressure on the North Switch Position eased up. Isolated enemy groups in the gullies in front of the Orlovka position were crushed. Sixteenth Panzer Division was able to make a dent between heights 145.1 and 147.6 and regain the old forward edge of the battlefield. Third Battalion, Grenadier Regiment 276, (Hauptmann Holl) over this period proved itself in the defense of height 147.6. The enemy failed to capture this decisive height. Wounded could no longer be moved back as there was no longer any means of transport. The combat vehicles were filled with the last reserves of fuel. After these practically uninterrupted defensive battles, 16th Panzer Division was hardly in a situation to hold the North Switch Position any longer. The combat groups of 24th Panzer Division were moreover in a strained situation. However, they were still able to carry out their defensive task for the time being.

Assessment of the Period 1–24 January 1943. In spite of frequent attacks on the sector of 24th Panzer Division the enemy failed to achieve a breakthrough. The following decisions were vindicated:

1. The deployment of the tried-and-tested infantry regiments of 94th Infantry Division with their experience in the forward line in order to defend the forward edge of the battlefield. Their tenacity in holding the position and their calmness confirmed the quality of these troops for the higher command.
2. The integration of units of an infantry division into a tank division to leave the defensive line to the infantry units, whereby these units with the allocated reserves were equipped to a considerable level of combat strength.
3. The dissolution in good time of elements of 24th Panzer Division (apart from panzer grenadiers), insofar as these elements were relieved of the tasks of mobile warfare by the needs of a permanent front.

The dissolution of the respective units followed in relay after the period of their usefulness had expired. Smaller formations of assault groups (squadrons, sections) that bore the names of their current commanders were formed therefrom. This task suited these groups, which were now used as infantry very well indeed, especially in the counterattack. The reason was that 24th Panzer Division came from the former (East Prussian) 1st Cavalry Brigade, which in the winter of 1941–1942 was reequipped as a type-1942 tank division. In cavalry battles deployment on foot and fighting as infantry were applied whereby the roles of attack and defense were carried out. Its strength lay in aggressively led attack or in counterattack that suited the cavalry ethos: "No hesitation; ride on ahead! So they rode, fought, and died, every man a hero!" The individual soldier, including those in rear-line units, had a solid training in infantry weapons. The overwhelming part of the soldiers, NCOs, and officers were volunteers.

Chief of staff Oberstleutnant von Menges, who served in the headquarters staff of 24th Panzer Division, himself came from a cavalry regiment and knew what could be entrusted to his tank comrades and what sort of tasks were suitable for the infantry. The cooperation of regimental headquarters of 94th Infantry Division with that of 24th Panzer Division was good throughout, and the significance of the attached infantry was always taken into account.

The execution of the defense at the center point in North Switch Position II, with its huge strains when compared with the average performance of men, fell on the best parts of the combat troops, above all the officers. The consequence was a repeated and shockingly high rate of loss of the most outstanding front soldiers who had passed through peacetime training and whose replacement was impossible.

The initiative, the willingness to make decisions, and the skill and boldness of the junior leaders alongside the quality, endurance, and bravery of the troops were now more than ever decisive for the deployment of the forces and for the outcome of the fierce battles.

The senior leadership had consciously to impose upon itself a severe restriction in its influence on battle actions, above all in defense. As a rule, it had to satisfy itself with the task of ensuring that sufficient artillery support for the defensive battles was available, to prepare the construction of rear positions, and above all to get the necessary combat forces and equipment to the regimental commanders (combat groups) in good time that the heavily engaged troops required for holding the defense, and in extremis for counterattacks.[8]

VI. North Kessel XI Army Corps (General Strecker)

Defense of the North Kessel from 25th January 1943 to 2nd February 1943

On 24 January 1943 the Russians advanced with strong tank and infantry forces from northwesterly and westerly directions to the area north of Gorodische.

Sixth Army Headquarters ordered that in the night of 24–25th January our own forces were to be removed from North Switch Position II in order, with the onset of first light on 25 January, to defend Stalingrad north on the Gorodische gully with the front to the west. Equipment that could not be moved as well as any classified material was to be destroyed.

The Extraction from North Switch Position II in the Night of 24–25 January 1943

The enemy's breakthrough with strong formations to the west through the rear defensive system running along North Switch Position II, the breakthroughs in the positions of 113th Infantry Division and 60th Infantry Division (mot.) into their rear areas, and further strong penetrations of the front on 16th Panzer Division's lines threatened to turn the flank of the right wing of North Switch Position II from the rear. For the time being the Orlovka switch position (Rittmeister Dreßler) is able to tie up the enemy, who had broken through in front of the sector. In the last few days, with the assistance of Combat Group Wotha (16th Panzer Division), any enemy that brakes through is repeatedly ejected from the ravines of the Orlovka Gully in attritional close-quarters battles. The line of the main Russian blow now headed in front of the Orlovka position, reaching out toward the south in the direction of Gorodische. As a consequence of this, on 24 January 1943, the threat arose that the intact right flank of north switch position II, close to the lost hinterland, now hung in the ballance, and with the lost hinterland hung in the balance and with it the north part of Stalingrad and the possibility that the entire city area could fall into the enemy's hands without a fight.

The Divisional Order of Ia 24th Panzer Division Headquarters (Summary)

In order to mount a new defense along the Gorodische ravine (the western edge of Stalingrad north) the division, with all elements, is to move to this prepared position with the front toward the west in the night of 24–25 January 1943. The move out of North Switch Position II shall begin in the evening with the left wing of the division. To this end, 3rd Battalion/276 is placed under the command of 24th Panzer Division. Joining up with one another, Combat Groups Müller and von Below and the left wing of Combat Group Brendel are to drop off to the south until they reach the Orlovka stream. The movements of the combat groups are to be harmonized in such a way that elements of Combat Group Brendel, following Combat Groups von Below and Müller, moving in the direction of the Orlovka stream, are to reach the north part of the Gorodische ravine in order to infiltrate themselves there into the new position. Guides from 389th Division will be waiting. The remaining parts of the assault groups (quick-reaction units) are, with immediate effect, to come under the command of Combat Group Müller as well as 3rd Battalion/276. Officers and men of the artillery units (with elements under command) are, effective immediately, to come under the command of Combat Group von Below. Weak rearguards are to remain in North Switch Position II and to follow before first light. The Orlovka ring is to be defended by Combat Group Dreßler until such time as the move of the combat groups through the Orlovka ravine is complete. To that end, Combat Group Dreßler is to be under the command of Combat Group Müller.

The regimental command of Combat Group Müller shall remain in the regimental battlefield headquarters south of the village of Orlovka in order to oversee the move out of the west divisional elements until such time as the withdrawal of 3rd Battalion/276 and its own combat group has taken place. The regimental command (with headquarters protection) together with Combat Group von Dreßler shall move out last. Execution of this order is to be reported to division at the appropriate time.

All wounded are to be taken via the main casualty clearing station of 24th Panzer Division to the rear of the new position. All war matériel that cannot be moved is to be destroyed.

In order to strengthen future firepower the troops are to equip themselves with extra close-quarters battle weapons (captured enemy machine pistols, light mortars, and hand grenades) and are to take the greatest possible quantity of small-arms ammunition with them, loaded on each soldier.

With immediate effect and without delay, supply units in the Orlovka ravine are to be dissolved (apart from medical services) and to be allocated to Combat Group Brendel through their leaders as infantry forces.

Until the end of the night divisional headquarters shall remain north of Gorodische and from there shall deploy north to tractor works early on 25 January.

The Move Out

The move out of the positions of North Switch Position II was put into effect with the onset of darkness, in echelon order, to the Orlovka ravine, which was situated to the rear. The move started on the right wing with the incoming units of Combat Group Brendel. Combat Group von Dreßler was able to break contact with the enemy only with difficulty since the strong enemy immediately attempted to rush into the Orlovka ravine in an easterly direction.

Rearguards (von Dreßler), which included reinforced Cycle Platoon 267 and reinforced Engineer Platoon 267, defended the strongpoint around regimental headquarters 267 (the area to the south of Orlovka village with its gully complex) as long as 3rd Battalion/276 (Hauptmann Holl) and the headquarters of Grenadier Regiment 267 (headquarters of Combat Group Müller) were able to function as battle headquarters, in order to break contact as the last unit in the night. Regimental Headquarters 267 loaded up engineer and signals equipment, additional close-quarters weapons, and ammunition on several half-tracked vehicles of the light mortar section. Likewise several sacks of wheat grain (taken from the silo) were loaded up as the last rations reserve for the regiment.

The combat groups were able to break contact together with the rearguards from North Switch Position II in such a way that the move remained for the time being undetected by the enemy. Only von Dreßler's rearguards had to pull back, fighting a delaying action. The combat groups were able to take up the new Gorodische position along this ravine while there was still some darkness.

Combat Group von Below succeeded through tactically forceful measures in bringing the last two VI (1) tanks in the night, unnoticed by the enemy, out of North Switch Position II. These last tanks of the German Wehrmacht in the battle for Stalingrad were deployed in the north of the Kessel in the sector of Combat Group von Below, operating in hidden fire positions. Leutnant Sylla (1st Squadron, Panzer Regiment 24) defended this sector with these heavy armored weapons right up to the end of military operations.

The execution of the withdrawal was implemented in exemplary order, during which the troops maintained complete discipline. This outstanding performance was achieved by the command and troops after two months of the most severe defense in the Kessel. It indicates the high quality of the entire personnel comprising 24th Panzer Division and not least 94th Infantry Division.

Extent and Situation of the New Position

Orlovka gully north of a settlement—bend in Orlovka ravine—ravine in the main Gorodische ravine (with the front to the north)—along the east edge of the Gorodische ravine for about 3 kilometers (1.9 miles) to the west—then (with the front to the west, opposite Three Corner Wood) veering away to the Volga in front of the Barricades settlement.

Along the length of the Gorodishche ravine were well-built battle positions with covered bunkers, in part linked by communications trenches. The defense installations were rim positions situated on the ravine to a depth of 30 meters. The depth of the ravine faced the enemy so that any advancing enemy climbing the counterslope and at the foot of the ravine could be effectively dealt with from fire and grenade-throwing positions that were situated above. The defender possessed all the advantages. These defensive positions were organized in rows close together above the ravine. The Gorodische ravine had a width of about 50 to 100 meters. The walls of the ravine were very steep (caused by erosion). Any enemy who attacked from a westerly direction, even before he could reach the ravine, had to descend a long forward slope (Three Corner Wood with sparse undergrowth) in order merely to reach the natural obstacle of the ravine (in our own attacks aimed at capturing the tractor works in the autumn of 1942 this current position, then defended by the Russians, had been called "the Acropolis"). No matter; these defensive installations, particularly on the right wing of the Gorodishche, were well laid out and well built. Beyond the first wing the number of constructed positions dropped sharply so that there the defense was conducted in part from snow bunkers.

Organization of the Defense

(Link up with 389th Infantry Division) Combat Group Brendel—Combat Group von Below—Combat Group Müller with Luftwaffe Battalion Matho on the left wing. Motorcycle Section 4 (Rittmeister von Götz), small contingent of 16th Panzer Division—the rest of 305th Infantry Division (?).

Strength of 24th Panzer Division = Frontline strength (25 January 1943), approximate:

Combat Group Brendel (with units under command, including the remainder of 3rd Battalion/276 = c. 450

Combat Group von Below (with units under command) = c. 400

Combat Group Müller (with units under command, including Motorcycle Section 4) = c. 800

No reserves; all units are deployed in the forward lines. Total = c. 1,650 men.

Provision of Weapons

After the construction of the position, 389th Infantry Division had deposited infantry weapons and any extant ammunition, partly in the battle positions, from its surplus equipment. This equipment was supplemented by the transferred weapons and various calibers of ammunition of the combat groups, by means of which a stockpiling in and on behalf of the forward lines was accomplished. Infantry guns (*Ratschbumms*) situated in concealed positions were used, for which there was a copious supply of ammunition. These weapons were able to make an impact on the immediate area to the front (Three Corner Wood). Extant and dug-in T-34s and superheavy Soviet 12-cm mortars were likewise directed at the enemy. Combat Group von Below dug in the last two tanks (Mark IV) in order to defend their sector of the forward edge of the battlefield. These tanks successfully repelled all attacks right up to the general end of the battle and were destroyed by Leutnant Sylla himself in the enemy's last attack.

Combat Headquarters (up to 2 February 1943)

Twenty-fourth Panzer Division, tractor factory north, concrete cellar under the sheet-metal workshop, close to the headquarters of XI Army Corps and 389th Infantry Division (Generalmajor Lattmann)

Combat Group Brendel, ruins of the high-rise building near Dzerzhinskii Place, tractor works main gate

Combat Group von Below, in the tractor works settlement

Combat Group Müller, initially in the west part of the settlement, later with Grenadier Regiment 544, 389th Infantry Division, about 2 kilometers (1.2 miles) south of Dzerzhinskii Place

General Situation with the Closing of the North Kessel, XI Army Corps (Strecker)

In the last days, the enemy, with strong formations, has succeeded in turning the left flank of North Switch Position II with a thrust to the east, as a consequence of which the biggest part of our troops defending that location have been annihilated. The rest of 16th Panzer Division and all the combat groups of 24th Panzer Division (with units under command) has managed to occupy a new defensive front in a firm position on the western edge of Stalingrad north. This new defensive front has stopped the offensive thrust of the enemy, who is now forced to regroup for further attacks on Stalingrad north.

In the north Kessel, XI Army Corps the following are deployed. On the Volga front: 389th Infantry Division (approximately from the brickworks running along the Volga to the east to the entry of the Orlovka ravine, then veering to the west on the southern edge of the Orlovka to the high-rise buildings); 24th Panzer Division with Combat Group Brendel to the entry of the Gorodishche ravine, farther into this ravine for about 1 kilometer (.6 mile), then joining up with about a 2-kilometer (1.2-mile) stretch of Combat Group von Below's sector (with the front to the northwest), then linking up along the southeastern edge of this ravine (Gorodishche ravine) with a front length of about 4 kilometers (2.5 miles), then Combat Group Müller to the "Pig Ravine," on the left wing of which are situated Motorcycle Rifle Section 4 (Rittmeister von Götz) and what remains of a 16th Panzer Division combat group.

The attempt to close the Kessel defense veering off south to the Volga has been unsuccessful because 305th Infantry Division is no longer able to take over this sector. Apparently this division no longer retains a coordinated command structure. No enemy attacks have taken place on this "open" front position.

On 26 January 1943, beginning with reconnaissance probes and in the afternoon with heavier attacks, the enemy attempts to achieve a breakthrough on the combat groups' positions. All attacks are broken up with bloody losses for the enemy. The Volga front of 389th Infantry Division is quiet. Via the field kitchens of 389th Infantry Division, which since late autumn have been located in the Volga position, some hot food is brought up to the front. XI Army Corps arranges a drop position for ration canisters in Dzerzhinskii Place, which is to be marked by searchlights for the night drop.

On 27 January 1943 the enemy moves against the Gorodische ravine (Three Corner Wood) with massive artillery and moves on the forward slope into the position with, among other things, heavy-caliber weapons. This is effectively dealt with by our artillery (using Soviet *Ratschbumms* and dug-in T-34s). Forming-up positions of strong infantry units in regimental to divisional strength are observed. Throughout the day there are massed bombing attacks carried out by the Russian air force, which, with heavy American bombers (Lend-Lease

Flying Fortresses), attempt without respite to smash the Kessel. Outposts, primarily in the interior of the Kessel and at the edges of positions of our own infantry, are not hit. In the afternoon there are renewed heavy attacks in tractor works north and on Combat Group Müller (Gorodishche ravine), which are repelled with many enemy losses. Toward evening it proves possible to supply the combat troops with some hot and dry rations (from ration canisters).

Battlefield headquarters of Combat Group Müller (Grenadier Regiment 267) located in the tractor works settlement, receives a direct hit from a heavy aircraft bomb, which smashes through the still existing first floor and cellar. Practically all the men in the cellar are killed by this direct hit (signals platoon and the rest of the engineer platoon and cycle platoon as well as assault reserve and the rest of the headquarters personnel). Only 6 survivors who were in a corner of the cellar are able to get out of the rubble. These are: regimental commander, regimental adjutant, regimental medical officer Dr. Hauser, engineer Oberfeldwebel Peters, regimental runner Obergefreiter Freyer, and 1 man from the supply platoon. About 40 fallen comrades meet their end here.

The headquarters is transferred to Grenadier Regiment 544 (389th Infantry Division), where in the spirit of comradeship regimental commander Major Maltzan provides accommodations for the bombed-out regimental headquarters of 267 in the cellar ruins of his regimental headquarters. Major Maltzan makes men and equipment available by means of which the regimental headquarters is once again operational. Grenadier Regiment 544 still has some rations reserves (mainly coming from the ration canisters that were dropped on the Volga ice), and it is possible to get some hot and dry rations delivered to Combat Group Müller by rations carriers. Many soldiers of 389th Infantry Division who volunteer to deliver the rations to 24th Panzer Division in this comradely manner are wounded or killed in the process. Major Maltzan (regimental adjutant Oberleutnant Schlüter) hands over new radio equipment to the regimental command of 267, newer models (improved portable radios), of which 12 sets are installed in Combat Group Müller in the Gorodishche position in the battle positions of the sector commanders. As a result, the regimental command now has firm radio contact with the forward line. Major Maltzan is a peacetime comrade of Oberstleutnant Müller, and his comprehensive comradely help can be explained by this connection.

On 28 January 1943 there is further, exceptionally heavy artillery bombardment from heavy and some of the heaviest-caliber guns in the region of the north Kessel. During the day there is uninterrupted aerial bombing from aircraft flying in and out without pause. In the Kessel it is almost impossible to move outside cover. On the Volga front weak attacks across the ice are repulsed. In the sector of 24th Panzer Division there are heavy and repeated Soviet infantry attacks, aimed above all against Combat Group Müller, which are repelled with heavy losses for the enemy. The mass of the attackers is destroyed by hand grenades from the throwing positions above the ravine (rim position) as soon as they reach the bottom of the ravine. Here the bodies of the Red Army soldiers pile up, but even more attacks are launched over their bodies. On the left wing of Combat Group Müller, Motorcycle Section 4 (Rittmeister von Götz) clears the Pig ravine of an enemy breakthrough and improves the flank protection. Above all the paratroopers of Matho's battalion fight superbly. In counterattacks they bravely throw the enemy back, thereby relieving the pressure on the left wing. To the south the front cannot be closed with our resources. Attempts to make contact with 305th Infantry Division to find out what is happening come to nothing. Nothing can be ascertained about this division. Fortunately no enemy attacks are taking place on this sector.

Since 24 January 1943, 24th Panzer Division has issued no further orders to the combat groups! In the evening the regimental adjutant of 267 searches for divisional headquarters in the tractor works. The officer in charge of the headquarters section, Oberstleutnant i.G. von Menges, is dying. An artillery splinter has penetrated his lungs through the back. One has to say the final good-bye to the tried-and-tested headquarters officer of 24th Panzer Division, who also had the interests of the regiments of 94th Infantry Division close to his heart and whose leadership qualities always gave the troops new strength. The successor and former divisional quartermaster, Hauptmann Wünsche-Steude, had more than enough experience for the task, while his divisional commander, Generalmajor von Lenski, showed no more thirst for action. While the dedicated troops fought so bravely, in order, if necessary, to shed the last drop of blood, here one had to acknowledge a complete failure of duty.

The War Pursued a Course of Its Own

A "dissolution" in the ranks of the troops (*combat* troops), that is, from the bottom upward, which partly took place in November 1918, is completely out of the question in this corps. True to their oath, the troops fight to the last breath, as the law orders!

On 29 January 1943 the enemy once again brings his massed artillery to the forward slope of the Three Corner Wood in a fire position. The numerous batteries lay their barrels on open sights on the battle positions to bombard them directly, in order to shoot out the crews. Our losses are heavy. Enemy infantry attacks against the Gorodische position are repelled with hand grenades, with heavy enemy losses. There are once again unsuccessful attacks against Motorcycle Section 4 and Matho's battalion. On 389th Infantry Division's sector it is relatively quiet. The main thrust of the enemy attacks ensues from the westerly direction of Three Corner Wood. There are heavy bomber attacks on the center of the Kessel.

On 30 January 1942 there are constant heavy enemy attacks on the defense line of 24th Panzer Division, above all on the corner position of Combat Group Brendel. All attacks are repulsed, with heavy losses for the enemy. Heavy artillery fire on the entire Kessel and heavy air raids. As on every evening, our own air force drops rations (in boxes and sacks from the hatch), which are not always accurate. At this time the enemy has set up decoy drop zones. Only a small part of these rations reaches the soldiers in the forward line (see above). There are isolated instances when rations dropped in the wrong place can be collected by our men on nighttime patrols. In the evenings brave ration runners of 389th Infantry Division bring warm rations to the comrades in the forward trenches of 24th Panzer Division. The ration runners are volunteers. There are heavy losses.

Among Combat Group Müller there are already heavy losses by aimed fire of Soviet batteries on the battle positions, the locations of which are in Three Corner Wood. Infantry ammunition is brought up from the reserves of 389th Infantry Division.

The enemy conducts a propaganda march at the very least in full divisional strength through the Three Corner Wood in a south-north direction. In spite of the relatively short distance the enemy cannot be brought under fire with our own weapons, which lack the range. Every Red Army soldier marches past with a red banner attached to a fixed bayonet. The formation marches in orderly fashion in battalion-strength columns.

On 31 January 1943, as on the day before, there are enemy attacks and artillery bombardment. Losses in the battle positions as a result of directly laid artillery fire are already very heavy. These losses cannot be replaced. As a consequence, our own defense on the Gorodische position is becoming weaker in places. However, 389th Infantry Division remains in its relatively quiet sector. The Russians only dare to undertake small-scale harassing attacks across the Volga ice, which are easily repelled. The weight of the attacks comes out of the northwest!

On 1 February 1943 enemy activity is the same as the day before. Toward midday there is drum fire from all the enemy's artillery pieces and nonstop carpet bombing. Infantry ammunition is starting to run low. Moreover, the battle positions are being continually shot to pieces, by means of which much bigger gaps are being torn open. For the past few days the wounded in the forward line have been without medical care, since there is no possibility of getting them to the rear.

Field dressings among the combat troops have run out. In places the troops have used up all their ammunition. They help one another. The positions can no longer be supplied with ammunition.

On the positions of Combat Groups Brendel and von Below enemy penetrations are repulsed in close-quarters battle, in part with cold steel. The front is bleeding to death, and it is now only a matter of a few hours until the overwhelming enemy flood rolls over everything.

However, the combat troops, the biggest part of which have already sacrificed their lives for the homeland, discharge their duty, loyal to their oath!

On the evening of 1 February 1943, in the aftermath of the enemy's destructive fire, the combat group commanders understand that their soldiers can hold out only for a few more hours. In all probability tomorrow will bring the death blow. Already, in the early evening, a delegation of officers under command of Rittmeister von Götz turns up at the headquarters of their divisional commander, Generalmajor von Lenskii, whose headquarters is located in the tractor works. The divisional commander offers this delegation of officers nothing more than his dejected opinions—the expected outcome; the receipt in the next few hours of instructions concerning the further conduct of the troops had failed to appear—but as regards orders for the hours ahead concerning the further conduct of the troops, there is nothing.

The commander of Grenadier Regiment 267, Oberstleutnant Müller, rightly demands at this hour a clear decision of his superiors concerning the further conduct of the troops entrusted to his care for the hours ahead. As a consequence of his illness, Oberstleutnant Müller is so gravely weakened that he is physically prevented from reaching the tractor works under the enemy's heavy and effective fire. To this end he delegates his regimental adjutant, provided with full powers to seek out General Strecker, with whom he has been friends for many years. General Strecker's final orders concerning the conduct of the troops should be demanded. Divisional commanders could, should the situation require it, and according to ancient custom, simply be informed concerning this intention.

On the evening before the end, the regimental adjutant with his escorts, the engineer Oberfeldwebel Peters, and the tried-and-tested regimental runner Obergefreiter Freyer reach the divisional headquarters of 24th Panzer Division through the ruins of the tractor works and under heavy bombardment toward 2100 hours. The divisional commander, Generalmajor von Lenskii, is briefly informed that the troops themselves will make immediate contact with XI Army Corps. The general considers it advisable to get in touch and to take the commander of 389th Infantry Division, Generalmajor Lattmann, along. The latter is indignant at this disturbance because he has already retired to his bed. He nevertheless brings himself around to the idea of coming along to the corps commander (in a nearby concrete cellar of the sheet-metal workshop).

VII. The Battle Expires

In the headquarters of the XI Army Corps commander (overall commander for the north Stalingrad Kessel), the following attended the discussion:

Commander of XI Army Corps, General Strecker
Chief of staff, Oberst i.G. Großcurth
Assistant adjutant, Leutnant von Arnim
Commander of 24th Panzer Division, Generalmajor von Lenskii
Commander of 389th Infantry Division, Generalmajor Lattmann[9]
Regimental adjutant of Grenadier Regiment 267, Hauptmann Krell

General Strecker relieved the regimental adjutant of Grenadier Regiment 267 of the normal military formalities and afforded complete freedom to speak in order to learn of the justifiable concerns of his friend Julius (Oberstleutnant Müller) in this difficult hour.

The point was made that the fate of the encircled troops in the morning hours of the next day could already be decided in the event that measures to further strengthen the front were not immediately taken by the commander. During the previous weeks the combat troops had been worn down by the constant heavy enemy attacks on the front, as a consequence of which the defense capacity had been weakened by the high losses. Holding out further against these attacks could be a matter of only a few hours or days at the most. With his huge superiority the enemy had already, by means of the direct and indirect action of the heaviest weapons and the almost unremitting attacks, above all on Combat Group Müller, inflicted such heavy losses that the outcome hung by a few threads. Moreover, apart from a large number of wounded who were not receiving medical attention, the combat group also had exhausted soldiers who were simply not in the situation to aim their weapons at the enemy. In spite of all this, the combat morale on the front line remained unbroken.

Because of his hurling massed forces, it was pointed out that here in the Kessel the enemy was also hemorrhaging lives, and his losses in relation to our own amounted to twenty times greater. A higher rate of attrition could, likewise, be attributed to the enemy himself.

Without a doubt the OKW placed a justified hope on the possibility of holding the Kessel longer. At this time XI Army Corps was under the command of OKH and in direct contact with the same by means of a radio transmitter link. It was precisely for this reason that the combat morale of the frontline troops, even the few left, remained intact, for nothing, even at this hour, could shake their trust in the supreme command. Among the troops there was a saying: "As long as the organ is playing, the church is not finished!"

At this juncture in the discussion the commander was informed by a speaker from the troops that the defenders were well aware of the task, the shared responsibility for reestablishing the southern sector (Army Group A and the Chir front) through their own operations, and rejected a voluntary abandoning of the battle.

In the middle of this discussion a radio message from the supreme command was received with a clear order: "Capitulation is out of the question; the battle is to be fought to the last round."

After this both divisional commanders engaged in a discussion with the chief of staff about "whether this last round was de jure or whether it had already been shot off de facto," whereupon Generalmajor Lattmann urged immediate capitulation.

General Strecker considered himself to be bound by his orders and pointed out to his divisional commanders that capitulation was out of the question! [Emphasis in original.]

To this end the chief of staff fell silent.

Generalmajor Lattmann stated briefly that this was "futile."

Defense against the enemy in the north Kessel with all its bloody sacrifices did not appear "futile" to those fighting on the front, as it did to Generalmajor Lattmann, especially since there was a clear mission of tying down several Soviet armies in order to facilitate the construction of a defensive line on the entire endangered southern front. Moreover, the enemy's offensive power was to be weakened and to be consumed by the constant heavy losses sustained in hurling himself against our defense. Additionally, the commander well understood that by the possession of Stalingrad the rail link from the Persian Gulf to central Russia (the so-called A-A line), which was so important to the enemy, was at that point cut and with that the enemy was denied the opportunity of using the vast amount of war matériel sent as part of Lend-Lease.

Finally, the German soldier has been taught throughout the centuries to stand fast where it is "hopeless." In the thousand-year history of all peoples, this attitude has always been demanded of soldiers as a self-explanatory duty and celebrated as such. The "futile" concept stems in any case from the terminology of the enemy's conduct of psychological warfare, and it was stunning to hear Generalmajor Lattmann in this place and at this time, among others, keep availing himself of this word "futile."

After all this another two hours was spent among the higher commanders solely concerned with how the frontline troops should be discharged without capitulating so as to carry out the last order.

VIII. The Last Order

To this end, on 1 February 1943 toward 2300 hours, the senior general and commander of the Kessel arrived at the following decision:

On 2 February 1943 from 0300 hours, flags bearing the red cross are to be flown in all combat positions and dugouts in which there are wounded. [Emphasis in original.]

This order was directly handed to the regimental adjutant of Regiment 267 for immediate transmission to the troops. The regimental leadership gave this, the final, corps order over the radio (only partly operational), and it was attempted, using runners, to inform the deployed combat groups of 24th Panzer Division. This order was only deliverable insofar as the short time frame and enemy activity permitted.

On 2 February 1943 in the morning a major enemy attack was launched against the positions of 24th Panzer Division on the entire sector. Initially, in order to probe for the weakest points, the attack was conducted very hesitantly. Bitter defense conducted by the last positions, in part counterattacks carried out by the remains of the squadron, Combat Group von Below in the housing quarter, Motorcycle Section 4, and Luftwaffe Battalion Matho, as well as from nests of resistance in Combat Group Müller. At the end of the battle, the battalion, which two months before had been full strength, consisted of 1 officer (Hauptmann Matho) and 8 men! In the course of the early morning the Red Army soldiers gradually managed to achieve such strong penetrations that these, as a result of the knocked-out defenses, were being exploited to achieve breakthroughs. The northwest front of the Kessel on the Gorodische ravine was being, always hesitantly, penetrated and took the enemy into the rear of 389th Infantry Division.

The last shots of the "Great Battle of Stalingrad" were exchanged. On both sides the weapons fell silent.

It is a falsification of historical truth to claim that the Stalingrad Kessel capitulated. Not even the former enemy asserts this. In the *Large Soviet Encyclopedia*, vol. 1 (Moscow, Gosizdat, 1952 edition), on page 750, it is stated objectively and historically accurately: "On 2 February 1943 the German Army group at Stalingrad ceased to exist."

Out of responsibility to their starved, ammunition-depleted, and in part wounded subordinates, isolated sector and unit leaders sought in the last hours of the final battle to avoid further unnecessary loss of life.

But it is guaranteed that:

a. Neither in the south Kessel on 31 January 1943 were capitulation negotiations conducted or signed by Generalfeldmarschall Paulus or any representative authorized by him, nor
b. Did any such negotiation or any signing by General Strecker or any representative on behalf of the north Kessel occur!

The defenders of the north pocket bore the burden of the battle to the last on themselves alone. From their conception of their duty alone did they derive the courage and strength to repel and to bleed white the hundred-times-stronger enemy.

May history just once tell us of their feat of arms!

4 Eternal Glory: The End of 76th Berlin-Brandenburg Infantry Division

Covering the period from 1 October 1942 to 23 January 1943, this detailed war diary was compiled by Major Grohe with the assistance of other 76th Infantry Division officers who, like Grohe, were flown out of the Kessel before the final German collapse. The other three officers were Hauptmann Löser (flown out 20 January 1943), Major von Rochow (flown out 21 January 1943); and Major Boening (flown out 14 November 1942). As Grohe notes in his introduction, the war diary (*Kriegstagebuch*) of the 76th Infantry Division up to the end of September 1942 survived, but from 1 October on, large parts are missing. Grohe acknowledges that his personal recollections of the Kessel end on 29 November 1942, the day he was flown out. What follows after this date is therefore a reconstruction with all the potential biases that come with such a project. The document was put together between July 1943 and January 1944 under the auspices of the German Army's Military-Historical Section. The diary forms part of the archive holdings of the Bundesarchiv-Militärarchiv in Freiburg-im-Breisgau. Its BA-MA archival reference is RH 26-76/40 (Kriegstagebuch der 76 I.D. vom 01.10.42–23.01.43).

War Diary of 76th Infantry Division: Introduction

The war diary of the 76th Infantry Division is complete for the period up to 30 September 1942. After 1 October 1942 specific official archives are missing. The suggestion is that they were lost as a consequence of the conditions that obtained at the time in the Stalingrad Kessel. The 76th Infantry Division belonged to 6th Army and up to 2 September 1942 was under the command of LI Army Corps, then VIII Army Corps.

In the following the attempt will be made to reestablish the war diary of the 76th Infantry Division from 1 October 1942. The following material is available:

1. Records from 6th Army up to 19 November 1942
2. Records of the Quartermaster's Section VIII Army Corps up to December 1942

3. Records of Grenadier Regiment 178 and Infantry Regiment 230 (infantry regiments of 76th Infantry Division), which only, however, cover the period from October to November and the beginning of December 1942.

Furthermore, I (Major Grohe) must confine myself to what I experienced up to 29 November 1942 (when I was flown out of the Kessel) and to the experiences of officers who were flown out of the Kessel after this time. Valuable cooperation was rendered by the following:

1. Hauptmann Löser (flown out 20 January 1943)
2. Major von Rochow (flown out 21 January 1943)
3. Major Boening (transferred to the Führer's reserve at Army Headquarters, 14 November 1942).

On 21 August 1942 (formation of the bridgehead at Vertiachii) 76th Infantry Division was under the command of LI Army Corps within the framework of 6th Army and deployed in the direction of Stalingrad. Up to 28 August 1942 the division fought in the general direction of the southeast to the Rossoshka Valley, was then deployed toward the north, and was now deployed in the North Switch Position (right flank on the boundary with XIV Panzer Corps, at that time located at Kotluban). The ensuing defensive battles were the most severe that the division had yet had to withstand in the course of the war with Russia (deployment on 22 June 1941 in Moldavia) and the entire campaign. In these battles the division covered its banners with immortal glory: 13 Russian rifle divisions and 7 Russian panzer brigades failed to achieve any successful breakthrough on the reinforced positions of 76th Infantry Division. The following official figures [shown in Tables 4.1 and 4.2[1]] impart some idea of the scale of the exceptionally severe fighting:

Table 4.1 *German 6th Army Ammunition Expenditure, September 1942*

Type of Ammunition Expended	Amount Expended
Rounds of infantry ammunition	20,035,863
Armor-piercing shells	575,828
Infantry support weapon shells	116,932
Shells of all types	752,747
Mines laid	14,932
Hand grenades thrown	178,066

Table 4.2 *German 6th Army Combat Losses on the North Don–Volga Front (Switch Position Stalingrad), 13 September–14 November 1942*

Rank	Killed in Action	Wounded	Missing	Total
Officers	56	172	2	230
NCOs & other ranks	2,481	8,988	340	11,809
Total	2,537	9,160	342	12,039

Since crossing the Don (21 August 1942) and up to 16 October 1942, 6th Army in both offensive and defensive operations has inflicted the following losses on the enemy [Table 4.3].

Our own air force has shot down 1,705 enemy aircraft. Antiaircraft and army formations have shot down 269 enemy aircraft. [Table 4.4 shows 6th Army losses during this period.]

On 5 October 1942 headquarters of VIII Army Corps reported the following losses for the period from 23 August 1942–30 September 1942 for the divisions subordinated to it (76th Infantry Division first came under the command of VIII Army Corps on 3 September 1942, so its considerable losses in the period 21 August–2 September 1942—at that time under the command of LI Army Corps—are not included in the numbers of men and horses[2] lost [cited in Tables 4.5 and 4.6].

1 October–31 October 1942

1 October 1942. Divisional headquarters located at Bolshii Nabatov. Weather: by day sunny and warm, by night cool, down to 0°C (32°F). Beginning 30 September 1942 and ending 1 October 1942 the division was relieved by 113th Infantry Division in its previous position (North Switch Position, Stalingrad,

Table 4.3 *Losses Inflicted on the Enemy by German 6th Army While Crossing the Don, 21 August 1942–16 October 1942*

Category of Enemy Loss	Number
Prisoners of war	57,800
Tanks destroyed	1,950
Destroyed/captured enemy guns	805
Armed motorboats	10
Other vessels	14

Table 4.4 *6th Army Losses, 21 August–16 October 1942*

Rank	Killed in Action	Wounded	Missing	Total
Officers	239	821	8	1,068
NCOs and other ranks	7,456	30,360	1,127	38,943
Total	7,695	31,181	1,135	40,011

Don-Volga, both sides of Kotluban) in order to be replenished and reorganized. Expected length of this relief period is some 8–10 days.

The bulk of the division will be accommodated in the Golubaia Valley, some elements will remain in and around Vertiachii, and others will head to Barburkin in the Rossoshka Valley. The accommodations of the regiments and divisional sections are approximately as follows:

Grenadier Regiment 203 in Golubinskaia
Grenadier Regiment 178 in Baburkin
Fusilier Regiment 230 in Malo-Mabotovskii and Kartlui
Artillery Regiment 176 with its sections with the respective infantry regiments
Reconnaissance section in Illarionovskii
Signals section in Tsokarevka
Tank destroyer section in Tsokarevka
Engineer battalion in the Don Forest, about 2 kilometers (1.2 miles) downstream from Vertiachii on the left bank of the Don (see attachment 1)[3]
Light Engineer column and motorized supply of the battalion on the western exit of the Antonova and Vertiashchevskaia gully
Divisional supply officer in Vertiachii

Table 4.5 *VIII Army Corps Men, Killed, Wounded, and Missing, 23 August–30 September 1942*

Division	Killed	Wounded	Missing	Total Losses
76th Inf. Div.	402 (17)	2,373 (74)	44	2,819
305th Inf. Div.	179	540	29	748
384th Inf. Div.	171	698	11	880
389th Inf. Div.	69	284	25	378
Total	821	3,896	109	4,825

Table 4.6 *VIII Army Corps Horses, Killed, Missing, and Captured, 23 August–30 September 1942*

Division	Killed	Missing	Captured	Total Losses
76th Inf. Div.	1,083	39	132	1,254
305th Inf. Div.	595	11	550	1,156
384th Inf. Div.	268	7	61	336
389th Inf. Div.	390	16	161	567
Total	2,336	73	904	3,313

Divisional quartermaster, all supply troops (trucks and motorized columns, ammunition and ration distribution centers, medical companies, and so on) remain in their earlier accommodations areas, that is, in and around Vertiachii

Grenadier Regiment 178, the third battalion of which, with elements of 14th Company under its command, had already been relieved in the night of 30 September 1942 by a battalion of Infantry Regiment 261 of 113th Infantry Division, is to be relieved in the night of 1 October 1942 by further battalions of Infantry Regiment 261 and to march into the area of Barbukin. Arrival is scheduled in the period before midday. Outlook for accommodations is very bad, since the area is already overcrowded with elements of 389th, 113th, and 100th Infantry Divisions.[4]

Fusilier Regiment 230 had already been relieved in the night of 30 September 1942 and is bivouacked in the western part of the Vertiachevskaia gully. On 1 October 1942 before midday the marching elements are to be loaded on trucks of the divisional supply officer and deployed in the area of Malo-Mabotovski-Kartuli. Opportunities for accommodations are likewise limited. Supply units are bivouacked in the Don Forest.

Hauptmann Löser (adjutant of Fusilier Regiment 230, later commander of 3rd Battalion Fusilier Regiment) reports:

Sometime during the night when Fusilier Regiment 230 was being relieved, very strong enemy attacks had to be repulsed in the line, along with an enemy break-in on the regiment's right flank, which on the afternoon of 30 September 1942 followed on with tanks and was cleaned up with assault guns and elements of the regiment's assault reserves. The

> battle for Stalingrad's North Switch Position, in the course of which, as a consequence of the violence of the fighting, the entire Grenadier Regiment 203 and the bulk of Grenadier Regiment 178, along with a motorized section, an engineer battalion, and a reconnaissance section under its command, were placed under the command of the regiment, came to an end. The division should be regarded as having been bled white. The battalion's strength (effective combat strength) is about 50 men; 9th Company of Fusilier Regiment 230 consists of 1 officer, 1 NCO, and 4 soldiers (the effective combat strength at the start of the battle for the Stalingrad North Switch Position was 60 soldiers). Having been relieved, the leaders and men of the division are exceptionally exhausted, both physically and psychologically.[5]

2 October 1942. Weather as yesterday. Grenadier Regiment 203 is to be transferred to Golubinskaia. Infantry are to be transported by truck. Supply units are to march over the Akimovskii bridge, Don main road, Bolshii Nabatov. The march is about 45 kilometers (28 miles). Accommodations are partly in houses and gardens and partly in small wooded areas.

The regiments have left rearguards, who must guard the assembled reserves of wood and straw, in the former accommodations of the supply parties.

3 October 1942. Weather as yesterday. At 0900 hours all commanders and leaders of the supply units are summoned to divisional headquarters in Bolshii Nabatov. The divisional commander, Generalmajor Rodenburg, announces that, in accordance with the Führer's order, all supply and ration units as well as the regiments' supply parties and sections are to hand over a minimum of 50 percent of their strength of NCOs and soldiers to the infantry regiments. Captured Russians (*Hilfswillige*) are to be used as replacements. The order is to be carried out by 10 October 1942.

4 October 1942. Weather as yesterday. Commander's conference at division in Bolshii Nabatov in the presence of General of Artillery Heitz. The infantry regiments are to be brought up to the strength of two battalions. As a consequence, the infantry regiments are now to be organized as follows:

Grenadier Regiment 178, 1st and 2nd Battalion, 3rd Battalion to be disbanded

Grenadier Regiment 203, 1st and 3rd Battalion, 2nd Battalion to be disbanded
Fusilier Regiment 230, 1st and 3rd Battalion, 2nd Battalion to be disbanded

Hauptmann Löser reports:

After presenting those members of Fusilier Regiment 230 who had earned it with the Iron Cross (First Class), the divisional commander takes a meal prepared by the field kitchen with a group of officers from the regiment (about 20). He thanks the regiment for its operations and stresses that the regiment had been the heart of the defense in the North Switch Position Stalingrad, and without the outstanding drive of its commanders the defensive successes of the division would have counted for nothing. Company commanders are to be provided for the regiment from the army reserve.

Major Schön is to become commander of 2nd Battalion, Grenadier Regiment 178. Hauptmann Gerstenberg is to be transferred to Fusilier Regiment 230.

5 October 1942. Weather as yesterday. The divisional commander drives to Grenadier Regiment 203 in Golubinskaia. A meeting with the officers of Grenadier Regiment 203, 2nd Battalion, Artillery Regiment 176. There he shares stew with men in a meadow on the bank of the Don.

6 October 1942. Weather as yesterday. Divisional order to the regiments and sections to the effect that in the period from 8 to 11 October 1942, 76th Infantry Division is to relieve 305th Infantry Division.

Grenadier Regiment 178 is to take over the section between the Kotluban gully (exclusively) and the line P.90.3—Panshchinov Station and with it the right flank of the division. Grenadier Regiment 203 is to take over the division's left flank and to extend its left flank to the east bank of the Don east of Akatov.[6] Fusilier Regiment 230 has the middle sector of the division.

The divisional order, which to be sure is consistent with its original only in its sense, runs more or less as follows (reconstructed by Hauptmann Löser).

Divisional Order for the Relief of 305th Infantry Division in Period from 8 to 11 October 1942 in the Sector to the East of the Don

1. The enemy in field positions shows no intentions of attacking at the present time. However, at all times one must reckon with strong attacks. At the present time there are no signs of preparation for any attack.
2. To be deployed are: on the right Grenadier Regiment 178, center Fusilier Regiment 230, and on the left the reinforced Grenadier Regiment 203 (cycle section under its command).

   (Possible) sector boundaries: right toward 113th Infantry Division—west edge of Kotluban ravine, between Grenadier Regiment 178 and Fusilier Regiment 230. Point 80.7 south of the Vertiachii-Kotluban road, point 86.2, 5 kilometers (3 miles) southeast of Panshchino, between Fusilier Regiment 230 and Grenadier Regiment 203, point 61.6, 1 kilometer (.6 miles) southeast of Zolotoi Rog, point 56.8, 2.5 kilometers (1.6 miles) southeast of Verkhnei Gniloi, southeast corner of Panshchino. Left toward 384th Infantry Division, eastward edge of Akatov, east bank of Don. For forward edge of battle area, see map sketch, attachment 2.
3. Artillery Regiment 176 is instructed to cooperate with the infantry regiments as follows: Section 1 with Grenadier Regiment 178, Section 2 with Grenadier Regiment 203, Section 3 with Fusilier Regiment 230.

   The batteries of Artillery Regiment 53 (army heavy guns) are told off for cooperation with Artillery Regiment 176. Captured British guns are to be allocated to Artillery Regiment 176.

   The following tasks are to be dealt with: combating enemy batteries in the area of Panshchino and to the southeast the destruction of enemy attacks.

   Areas designated for harassing and direct fire (one battery allocated for each task) are to be agreed with the infantry regiments, and the fire plan is to be delivered to divisional headquarters as soon as possible. The aim is to achieve the maximum concentration of fire.
4. Antitank defense: parts of tank destroyer Section 176 are to be allocated to one company of the infantry regiments. Antitank concentration areas are point 13.2 and point 56.8.
5. Construction and strengthening: Engineer Battalion 176 is to detail one company for cooperation with the infantry regiments. The extant building materials of 305th Infantry Division are to be used for this

purpose. Continuous wire obstacles (concertina barbed wire) are to be established as soon as possible. Mines are especially required on the regimental boundaries. Squads are to be detached to the infantry units in order to instruct them in the construction of dugouts. Every effort must be made to complete a continuous communications trench running throughout the entire divisional sector as soon as possible. Battalions and regiments are responsible for the junctions to the right. Wood for bunkers is to come from the divisional quartermaster.

6. Tactical command: the defense of the division's sector is set in a position linked by trenches to strongpoints. Position and strongpoint commanders as well as their second-in-commands are to be identified by name. In spite of the lack of reserves it must be ensured that assault reserves—up to section strength—from the company command posts are available. At regimental command posts assault reserves are to be formed from the cavalry platoon, engineer platoon, and heavy machine-gun and mortar platoons of the disbanded battalions. (These are to be trained close to the regimental command posts, and the commanders are to be allocated to all company sectors. The order concerning the winter mobility of this company is to follow.) Every penetration of the main battle line must be countered with an immediate counterattack from the position and the reserves in depth.

   All observation positions for heavy weapons and all battalions are to maintain observation logs, which are to be checked on a daily basis by the commanders. In such a way complete observation of enemy ground must be achieved.

7. Communications: Signals Section 176 is to provide secure wire and radio communications to the infantry regiments, Artillery Regiment 176, and Engineer Battalion 176. Then radio silence.

8. Divisional command post: northeast part of Vertiachii.

   Major Gehrke, commander of 3rd Battalion Fusilier Regiment 230, is to be transferred to the Führer's reserve at Army Headquarters. Hauptmann Gerstenberg, formerly commander of 2nd Battalion Grenadier Regiment 178, is to be transferred to Grenadier Regiment 203.

   After having been inspected and welcomed by General Rodenburg to the division, the battalion in waiting (76/9) is to be allocated primarily to the infantry regiments. It arrived in Lobinskii on 5 October 1942. The convalescent section of the battalion in waiting had already been transported to the division on 25 September 1942 by truck, since it had suffered heavy losses in the Switch Position south of Kotluban.

The units can send small groups on leave, who should be able to reach Iasinovotaia station in 27 hours from Tschir station. Trains for those on leave depart from there.

7 October 1942. Weather: windy and cold. Sandstorms in the evening, rain during the night. Notification from 6th Army via the Army High Command has been received that we should not count on receiving any significant replacements of troops before the New Year and that we shall have to adjust to this state of affairs and do everything in spite of this to raise and to maintain combat strength.[7]

With this in mind the following measures are to be implemented as quickly as possible:

1. The complete disbanding of individual units and formations and the disbanding and reduction of supply trains.
2. Replacement of German soldiers by Russian auxiliaries (prisoners of war) in positions that do not require to be occupied by combat troops.[8] In many units this process is well advanced. Further measures are nevertheless required.
3. Incorporation of all German soldiers freed as a consequence into the infantry and the formation of special frontline units. See attachment 4.

Hauptmann Löser reports:

About 90 prisoners are allocated to the infantry regiments from the division's prisoner assembly point. Among the supply trains these replace German soldiers with auxiliaries and form, in accordance with the order, labor squads in the engineer platoons (about 30 men to each). The latter take the prisoners into account and receive their rations on the returns. The auxiliaries receive the same rations as German soldiers though without the special supplements.

The division orders that a training squad be put together in Maloabatovski under the command of Oberleutnant von Manthey (divisional assistant adjutant). With this in mind the battalions are to provide weapons and trainers from the disbanded battalions. The squad has the task to instruct junior leaders and to retrain selected junior leaders from the signals and artillery as infantry soldiers.

8 October 1942. Weather: sunny, cold at night, frost down to –2°C (36°F. The relief of elements of 305th Infantry Division (artillery) requires the deployment of elements of artillery from 76th Infantry Division as early as in the night of 7–8 October 1942. The advance parties of the regiments and sections move into position. Preparation of the regiments and sections for departure on 9 October 1942.

The commanders as well as those in charge of the heavy weapons set off to the new sectors in order to be briefed by 305th Infantry Division. Since a total of only 7 battalions (including the bike section) are at the division's disposal for the relief of 9 battalions, every battalion has to assume responsibility for an additional company sector during the relief.

9 October 1942. Weather as yesterday. Midday Grenadier Regiment 178 moves out of its former accommodations to the rest and preparation area in the Antonova ravine. From 1700 hours the regimental command post is at the command post of Infantry Regiment 578 in the Gerassimova ravine 1.2 kilometers (.75 mile) northwest of Gnilovka. In the evening units of the regiment set off to relieve units at the forward edge of the battle area.

Supply trains of Grenadier Regiment 203 and Fusilier Regiment 230 reach their new accommodations areas in the course of 10 October 1942 via the Don Heights highway and bridges at Akimovskii and Lutshchinskii.

Regimental order of Grenadier Regiment 178 from 8 October 1942 for the relief. See attachment 5.

Via telephone the division informs regiments and sections that the position that they are taking up is to be the winter position.

10 October 1942. Weather: changeable, cloudy and windy. By 0145 hours the relief of Infantry Regiment 578 by Grenadier Regiment 178 is complete. The companies of Grenadier Regiment 203 and Fusilier Regiment 230 are taken on trucks, respectively, to the area around Vertiachii and the Antonova ravine. The relief follows on the evening of 10 October and the night of 11 October 1942.

From 1830 hours the divisional command post is in the northeast part of Vertiachii; 76th Infantry Division assumes command at 1800 hours.

Allocation of Grenadier Regiment 178 is as follows: 1st Battalion on the right, 2nd Battalion on the left. For the operational allocation of 2nd Battalion Grenadier Regiment 178, see attachment 6.

For position sketches of 2nd Battalion Grenadier Regiment 178, see attachments 7 and 8.

Engineer Battalion 176:

1st Company to Grenadier Regiment 203
2nd Company to Grenadier Regiment 178
3rd Company to Fusilier Regiment 230

For battalion command post and company command posts, see sketches, attachment 9.

The engineer battalion has assumed responsibility for the mine obstacles in front of 305th Infantry Division. The 4th Squadron of Road-Construction Battalion 540 has been attached to 76th Infantry Division. This Road-Construction Battalion 540 was under the command of VIII Army Corps. The 4th Company of the battalion was accommodated on the western edge of Vertiachii. In cooperation with Engineer Battalion 176 its tasks were primarily:

1. Construction of concertina barbed wire obstacles and the like
2. Construction of deep dugouts
3. Felling and preparation of wood
4. Road maintenance

For additional information, see attachment 12.

For a list of officers' appointments in the Signals Section 176, see attachment 13.

11 October 1942. Divisional command post is at Vertiachii. Weather as the day before. The relief of 305th Infantry Division by 76th Infantry Division is complete. For operational formation of the division, see attachments 2 and 10.

The commander in chief of 6th Army turns up with the general commanding VIII Army Corps at the command post of 76th Infantry Division. The commander of 76th Infantry Division, Generalmajor Rodenburg, receives the Knight's Cross of the Iron Cross from the hand of the supreme commander. In conferring this distinction the commander in chief mentions the division's part in the battle at Kalach, the securing of the bridgeheads for the attack on

Stalingrad, and the division's heroic defensive battles south of Kotluban. The divisional commander makes a brief speech.

The regiments start work on the further construction on the forward edge of the battle area with great enthusiasm. The main emphasis of the construction work is placed first of all on improving the positions and the communications trenches. At the same time measures are also taken to secure wood for building (Don Forest) and boards (Stalingrad). Securing this wood is made difficult as a result of a lack of fuel and the poor state of the horses.

The deployment of the engineer battalion: the focus of its work was setting out obstacles in front of the forward line of the battle area (antitank and antipersonnel mines and wire). Some elements were detached to the regiments to provide guidance in the construction of dugouts. With the assistance of *Hilfswillige*, work on the construction of the forward trenches was undertaken. The aim was to set up obstacles in the depth of the forward line of the battle area, for example, an antitank ditch (not carried out; see attachment 11).

The front is relatively quiet. As a consequence of enemy fire Grenadier Regiment 178 sustains losses (2 men killed, 3 wounded).

12 October 1942. Weather: generally clear and dry. Work on the forward edge of the battle line. During the night Grenadier Regiment 178 picks up 6 deserters. The division's state is reported to 6th Army Headquarters via VIII Army Corps as follows:

6 infantry battalions: 1 medium strength, 5 average, 100 percent mobile
Artillery: 9 light batteries, 2 heavy batteries, 100 percent mobile
Engineer battalion: average, 70 percent mobile

The division is fully suited for defense.
For operational formation of the regiments, see attachment 10.

13 October 1942. Weather: overcast, rain in the afternoon but becoming brighter. Enemy digging activity in front of the sectors, weak artillery fire and harassing fire from mortars. A mobile delousing center is set up at 1st Medical Company 176 at the main casualty clearing station on the Vertiachii southeast exit. In small groups, the units of the division are withdrawn and deloused. After the German soldiers have been deloused, the Russian auxiliaries are also deloused. The construction of the position and the dugouts is carried out with the greatest enthusiasm. The same goes for the construction of dugouts for the baggage parties and accommodations for the horses. In addition, poor-quality fields of grain and grass, which still remained in the surrounding area the still remaining, were combed in order to secure a supply of feed for the horses.

Concerning the dropping of Russian paratroops in the Kalach area, see attachment 14.

14 October 1942. Weather: generally clear and cool. In front of the division's sector enemy digging activity, above all in the depth of his main battle area. Otherwise nothing to report.

Towards 0200 hours a man of 3rd Company, Grenadier Regiment 178, according to the statement of an accompanying auxiliary, was captured by the Russians while bringing up rations. He lost his way with the *panje* wagon.

15 October 1942. Weather: clear before midday; afternoon increasing clouds, dry. No noteworthy battle activity to report.

Hauptmann Löser reports:

> We receive the divisional order to make the regiments' assault reserves mobile for winter conditions. Formation of 2 infantry platoons per reserve with 1 heavy-platoon man-portable radio. Provision of skis, large transport sleds, and small sledges is to follow. It is also planned to issue Finnish tents. Later on it is also planned to withdraw the cycle section and to deploy it as a divisional reserve and an additional winter-mobile formation.

Sixth Army Headquarters distributes the order dated 11 October 1942 and the information sheet for guidance concerning behavior toward Cossacks (see attachment 15).[9]

16 October 1942. Weather: variable, cloudy, cool. During the night an enemy reconnaissance patrol of about 8 men was repulsed in front of Fusilier Regiment 230's positions. Otherwise the night passed quietly in the divisional sector. Enemy busy digging in trenches.

Losses: 1 soldier killed, 7 NCOs and soldiers wounded, 4 soldiers in field hospital, 1 soldier missing.

Army order concerning Führer Order Number 1 on account of raising combat strength:

1. The order issued by 6th Army Headquarters on 6 October 1942 regarding the raising of combat strength is still completely valid.
2. The actual strength of the high commands, divisional headquarters, are to be reduced by 10 percent and, additionally, the command appointments at these headquarters are to be canceled.
3. There is to be a comprehensive replacement of German soldiers by Russian auxiliaries; see attachment 16.

Hauptmann Gerstenberg is to become commander of 3rd Battalion Grenadier Regiment 203

Oberleutnant Busse is to become adjutant of Grenadier Regiment 203

Hauptmann Isberner is to become commander of 1st Battalion Grenadier Regiment 203.

Regarding the battalion and detachment commanders' course in Antwerp from 26 October 1942 to 21 November 1942, notification is given that the following officer will attend: Hauptmann D. R. Geissler, 4th Battery, Artillery Regiment 176. Rank and seniority, 1 May 1942–1943 Jr.

17 October 1942. Weather: variable, cloudy, clear, dry, road conditions good. Enemy mortar fire. The night passed without incident. During the day weak artillery and mortar fire, harassing fire that grew in intensity on the right flank of Grenadier Regiment 203 in the afternoon. Minimal air activity on both sides of the front.

Losses: 1 soldier killed, 7 soldiers wounded.

18 October 1942. Weather: overcast, low-lying clouds, persistent, at times heavy rain. The night completely quiet along the entire divisional sector. The enemy continues work on the construction of his positions.

Two rafts, each with a 1-ton load, being towed away by the enemy downstream on the Don in the region of Nizhnii Akatov, are detonated by tracer rounds.

In the course of the day weak enemy artillery and mortar harassing fire.

Losses: 3 soldiers killed, 7 soldiers wounded.

19 October 1942. Weather, persistent rain, heavy snow showers, roads passable only with convoy truck. An enemy reconnaissance patrol of about 12 men which was probing the area around point 46.8 was repulsed with losses. Otherwise, apart from minimal harassing fire, the night passed quietly. Throughout the day both sides applied harassing fire. No major incidents.

Losses: 1 soldier killed.

One deserter picked up on position of 2nd Battalion, Grenadier Regiment 178, states that he belongs to Rifle Regiment 8/92 of 298th Rifle Division.

The average combat strength of the rifle companies amounts to about 45 men all ranks.

In accordance with the report to 6th Army Headquarters dated 19 October 1942, the state of the division is:

6 infantry battalions: 1 medium strength, 5 average, 100 percent mobile
Artillery: 9 light batteries, 2 heavy batteries, 100 percent mobile
Engineer battalion: average, 70 percent mobile

The division is fully suited for defense.

20 October 1942. Weather: cloudy, clear in parts, windy, routes clear of dry snow. Weak enemy artillery and mortar harassing fire. Minimal air activity on both sides of the front.

Losses: 3 NCOs and soldiers killed, 3 NCOs and soldiers wounded, 10 NCOs and soldiers in field hospital.

Supply journeys to Stalingrad in trucks cannot be resumed again because the roads are still impassable from mud.

Intensified combing of the supply units and supply trains.

Quick-reaction companies are set up.[10]

21 October 1942. Weather: dull, windy, hollows and depressions still under mud; otherwise routes for unloaded vehicles generally passable. Night passed without incident. Minimal enemy artillery harassing fire throughout the day. Afternoon: a great deal of enemy activity in front of the division's sector. Intense activity in enemy trenches. Minimal air activity on both sides of the front.

Losses: 1 soldier killed, 1 soldier wounded.

One deserter picked up by 1st Battalion, Grenadier Regiment 178. He says he belongs to 298th Rifle Division; see attachment 17.

Fusilier Regiment 230 reports that a continuous obstacle of concertina barbed wire has been laid in front of 1st Battalion with a breadth of 1,200 meters.

22 October 1942. Weather: variable cloudy, rain in the morning, brightening up in the afternoon, windy. Routes passable for loaded vehicles.

The divisional commander goes to 2nd Battalion, Grenadier Regiment 178. Day and night pass without incident.

A Russian floating mine detonates against one of the supports of the former bridge at Akatov.

Losses: 1 soldier wounded, 2 soldiers ill.

Great loss of life among the horses, since there is little fodder available and poor provision of shelter.

23 October 1942. Weather: morning clear, afternoon cloudy, cool, dry. Unsupported routes continue to dry out, and in certain hollows there are places suitable for all vehicles. The night passed without any special incidents. Air attacks and bombs dropped in the Vertiachii area. Before midday isolated and weak harassing artillery fire. Heavier mortar and antitank fire in the sector of Grenadier Regiment 203. Enemy digging in along the entire divisional front.

Losses: 1 soldier killed, 6 soldiers wounded.

Order of 6th Army Headquarters dated 22 October 1942 passed on from VIII Army Corps to the division concerning the need to render our own weapons unusable when there is any danger of these weapons falling into the hands of the enemy and the need to hold on to gun positions and places where stores are held; see attachment 18.[11]

As a result of a huge shortage of officers to fill positions, the division puts no names forward for the company commander's course at Döberitz (3–30 November 1942). Ill, the regimental commander of Grenadier Regiment 178 Oberst von Bissing is admitted to the field hospital. Formerly the commander of 2nd Battalion Grenadier Regiment 178, Major Schön assumes command of the regiment.

24 October 1942. Weather: bright, mainly cloudless, dry. Limited enemy harassing fire during the night. A lot of enemy air activity over the division sector. Bomb attacks on Vertiachii. A lot of enemy vehicle traffic in front of the center of the division.

Losses: 1 soldier killed, 5 soldiers wounded, 3 soldiers admitted to field hospital.

One deserter on position of 7th Battalion, Grenadier Regiment 178.

The division reports ration and combat strength (minus troops from general reserve). As of 18 October 1942 the status is as follows: ration strength (including 2,776 Russians): 12,125;[12] attached units: 5,706 [Table 4.7].

Table 4.7 *76th Infantry Division Combat Strength, 18 October 1942*

Arm of Service	Number
Infantry	2,702
Artillery	1,263
Engineer battalion	233
Tank destroyer section	230
Cycle section	104
Signals section	277
Total	4,809

For an assessment of the division's ration situation, see the division's report to VIII Army Corps, Quartermaster's Section, dated 24 October 1942 (attachment 19).

Hauptmann von Stocki, formerly of Fusilier Regiment 230, assumes command of 2nd Battalion, Grenadier Regiment 178.

25 October 1942. Weather: bright and clear. Yesterday, at last light and in the night, there was a great deal of enemy air activity and bombing; otherwise the night passed without incident. Enemy artillery and mortar harassing fire throughout the day in the middle of the sector and on the left flank, increasing to bombardment strength.

In terms of infantry activity the enemy is quiet. Vigorous enemy construction work along the entire divisional front.

Losses: 1 soldier killed, 4 soldiers wounded.

6th Army commander in chief turns up toward 1200 hours at the divisional command post in Vertiachii. From here, accompanied by an assistant adjutant, he goes to height 302 south of the position of Fusilier Regiment 230 and then to the regimental command post of Grenadier Regiment 178. The commander in chief ascertains that the regiment has dug itself in well throughout and takes note of the fact that there is a shortage of digging tools, especially of long-handled pickaxes and shovels. On the way back, toward 1415 hours, the commander in chief makes a brief stop at the divisional command post.

The company and platoon commanders of the quick-reaction companies are allocated to the positions of the infantry regiments.

Second Battalion, Grenadier Regiment 178, reports the status of the construction work on the positions; see attachment 20.

26 October 1942. Weather: sunny and clear, cold at night. Reconnaissance patrol from 5th Battalion, Grenadier Regiment 178, establishes that there are Russians digging some 500–600 meters in front of the forward edge of the battle area. The enemy is laying mines in front of his own positions.

Apart from weak harassing fire and lively air activity the enemy in the division's sector is quiet.

Losses: 1 soldier killed, 1 soldier wounded, 5 soldiers admitted to field hospital.

The state of the division as of 26 October 1942 is reported as follows:

6 infantry battalions: 1 medium strength, 5 average, 100 percent mobile
Artillery: 9 light batteries, 2 heavy batteries, of which 4 batteries are 100 percent mobile, 7 are immobile
Engineer battalion: average, 60 percent mobile

The division is fully suited for defense.

General army order concerning the opportunities for placing vehicles under cover: cover must be produced quickly and in the simplest form. From considerations of camouflage and concealment and in order to save wood for building, the sites are to be dug into the ground and to be provided with well-camouflaged exit ramps (corduroy tracks)[13] and to be usable in any weather. Additionally, they must, as far as is possible, be sited so as to be protected from the wind. This order has only just been issued to the division because the position of VIII Army Corps and with it that of 76th Infantry Division has only very recently been designated as a winter position.

Grenadier Regiment 178 reports an increase in the number of dysentery cases. First Battalion Grenadier Regiment reports 1 deserter.

Order received from 6th Army Headquarters dated 26 October 1942: remaining squads in the region from the field administration headquarters troops Donez are to be checked and, as far as possible, to be disbanded based on an absolute scale of necessity. Weapons that are absolutely necessary may not exceed the scale of three men. Officers, NCOs, and soldiers made available are to be incorporated into the divisions with the greatest speed.

Seventy-sixth Infantry Division has left a resupply backup headquarters group of 15 men in Artemovsk.

27 October 1942. Weather: clear and dry. Plenty of enemy harassing artillery fire in the sector of Grenadier Regiment 203 and Fusilier Regiment 230. Harassing fire continues throughout the day and evening, primarily in the division's left sector. Plenty of Russian air activity.

Losses: 4 soldiers wounded.

Army order concerning the reduction in the number of signals troops:

1. Signals sections are to be maintained up to 90 percent of their equipment. It shall be left up to the divisions within the framework of this reduction whether to disband whole units or to apply this reduction evenly to the whole unit. Equipment that is freed up is to be dispatched to the army signals park.
2. Voice traffic is to be reduced by about 50 percent. As many field radios as possible are to be requisitioned and the equipment sent to division. Traffic between divisions is to be substantially reduced. Divisions must make do with 1920s units (20 valves).
3. From 1 November 1942 the divisions' signal and radio traffic are to be regulated by senior officers.
4. From 1 November 1942 teleprinter controls are to be set up by divisional signals officers. All unnecessary telex traffic is to be cut back.
5. Measures are to be taken to reduce the amount of signal traffic. Unnecessary radio traffic jeopardizes our security. There is evidence to suggest that the Russians carry out planned surveillance of our radio traffic.[14]

28 October 1942. Weather: sunny and dry. Since daybreak steady artillery fire. Toward 0200 hours an enemy reconnaissance patrol managed to break into a machine-gun nest of 3rd Platoon, 3rd Company, Grenadier Regiment 178. One soldier was wounded, 1 soldier was captured by the Russians, and the machine gun was taken away at the same time. During the course of an immediate counterattack the enemy suffered losses. Prisoners could not be taken. A counterattack up to our own minefields established that the terrain was free of enemy.

Throughout the entire night plenty of enemy activity with bombs dropped and attacks from on-board weapons.

Losses: 6 soldiers wounded, 4 soldiers ill.

In the course of the day minimal harassing fire from enemy artillery and mortars on division's sector. Enemy movement and identified batteries to the front of the division's lines are engaged with infantry weapons and antiaircraft guns.

In order to provide an overview of the relation between rations and combat strength and to check the status of the manner in which the order for raising the combat strength is being implemented, reports are to be submitted to 6th Army Headquarters signed by the divisional commanders by 10 November 1942 concerning the following:

1. Ration strength of the division (without Russians and attached units, which are to be provided separately)
2. Entire combat strength of the division broken down according to the combat strength of the infantry, artillery, engineer, cycle, tank destroyer, and signals sections, showing the number of each at the time
3. Breakdown of all soldiers on the ration strength other than those on the combat strength, with a statement of their tasks and formation. The entire sum of 2 and 3 must tally with the ration strength

The division has established a quick-reaction unit from supply troops. Total strength of 129 men and 9 light machine guns. The formation consists of a company headquarters platoon and three platoons.

In order to increase the combat strength the following must be implemented by 5 November 1942:

1. The return of all officers, NCOs, and soldiers to their units who had been seconded to divisional headquarters
2. A reduction of the actual strength of the remaining divisional strength by 10 percent
3. The replacement of further soldiers by Russian auxiliaries;
4. A reduction in the number of those soldiers and units in the division not immediately deployed in the fighting (a reduction of battalion and regimental headquarters by about 10 percent), reduction of the batteries to 3 guns (the fourth battery can be set aside as a general repair and material reserve), the disbanding of individual batteries, the formation of batteries of six guns. Reduction of the engineer battalions by discontinuing the posts that are not absolutely necessary: truck drivers, runners, clerks, and drivers; reduction of the signals section by about 10 percent. Reduction of the supply troops by merging vehicle and truck units so as to create bigger vehicle and truck supply units (saving leadership and supply train personnel) as well as setting aside individual transport units that are not required during the winter war.

Reduction of the support lines of all weapons by disbanding or setting to one side those that are not essential during the winter.

It is further ordered:

1. The replacement of all German soldiers by Russian auxiliaries in all units up to and including companies and batteries as drivers; codrivers; farriers; builders; technical and work personnel in construction and supply units; and, additionally, in machine-gun companies, raiding companies, and tank destroyer companies as ammunition carriers, in battalion and regimental headquarters as line layers in signal units, in engineer units as replacements for engineers not directly involved in the battle, in signals sections, and in all kinds of supply units. As a consequence, supervisory personnel and urgently required specialists will be freed up.

   The use of soldiers made available by means of the above mentioned measures:

   a. The immediate deployment of all infantry-capable soldiers with a sufficient level of training in infantry rifle companies
   b. The deployment of infantry-capable soldiers with insufficient infantry training, after a short period of training carried out by the division, in infantry rifle companies
   c. The gathering of infantry-capable soldiers as well as the last sons from the division's units into a divisional reserve battalion

Hauptmann Löser, the adjutant of Fusilier Regiment 230, assumes leadership of 3rd Battalion, Fusilier Regiment 230. Hauptmann von Stocki, hitherto commander of 2nd Battalion, Fusilier Regiment 230, assumes command of 2nd Battalion, Grenadier Regiment 178; and Oberleutnant Deschma, hitherto commander of 12th Company, is appointed adjutant of Fusilier Regiment 230.

Commanders' conference at division:

1. Order for the conduct of the battle in the winter of 1942–1943 (instructions concerning winter tasks; deployment of formations; leadership of the battle in winter positions; measures for maintaining fighting strength regarding men, horses, and equipment; and further guidelines for additional training during the winter)
2. The extent of the winter position

3. Setting up winter-mobile raiding parties and assault groups

See 6th Army Headquarters orders:

1. 29 October 1942 concerning combat in winter 1942–1943, attachment 21[15]
2. 30 October 1942 concerning direction of the battle in winter in connection with the Führer's orders, attachment 23[16]

In Golubinskii at 6th Army Headquarters on 28 October 1942 discussions concerning the supply situation took place at which the general quartermaster and army supply took part. Officers and NCOs from the front troops were also ordered to report. Oberleutnant Warstaedt, supply officer of Artillery Regiment 176, took part, among others from 76th Infantry Division, and gave a detailed report concerning the receipt of supplies from August to October 1942; see attachment 22.

29 October 1942. Weather: dry, light clouds. Night passed quietly, with minimal enemy artillery and mortar harassing fire. Plenty of enemy air activity with numerous bombing runs.

Losses: 1 soldier missing, 4 soldiers wounded.

Minimal enemy artillery harassing fire throughout the day. Plenty of enemy artillery harassing fire in the area of the Perepolnyi bridge. From 1830 hours Vertiachii is attacked by waves of enemy bombers. Divisional order: at night all troops are to sleep in cellars or bunkers. Sleeping in houses is forbidden.

30th October 1942. Weather: before midday overcast, afternoon light rainfall, routes are starting to get soft and wet. Enemy artillery fire on sector of Fusilier Regiment 230; otherwise minimal harassing fire.

Plenty of enemy air activity with numerous bomb attacks in the region of the Don bridges at Vertiachii and Akimovskii.

Losses: 4 soldiers killed, 1 officer wounded, 6 NCOs wounded, 2 soldiers ill.

Strong enemy movement throughout the day in front of the division's lines and minimal enemy artillery and mortar harassing fire.

Deserters say that bigger enemy attacks are planned for 6 and 7 November.

By 10 November 1942 the existing bandsmen who originally were combat troops but are no longer deployed in this capacity are to report to corps headquarters.

The band of Fusilier Regiment 230 has been closed down in the middle of October. Bandsmen and their instruments have been sent on leave.

Construction of a cinema in the northern part of Vertiachii (almost completely built into the ground). The engineer battalion is in charge of construction. Work has been carried out by prisoners of war and civilians.

31 October 1942. Weather: overcast and dry, routes passable. During the night enemy harassing fire and individual air attacks with bombs and machine guns on the forward edge of the battle area and the Vertiachii region and Don bridges.

Minimal enemy harassing fire in the divisional sector in the course of the day. No air activity.

Fifty-four men with Oberleutnant Kühler join Grenadier Regiment 178 as replacements from Germany.

About 30 convalescent men from Germany under the command of Leutnant Kandt join Fusilier Regiment 230. Leutnant Kandt is to take command of 10th Company as a replacement for Oberleutnant von Mühlen, who is ill.

Concerning the deployment of 76th Infantry Division, including all reinforcements and resupply units, see detailed overview attachment 24.

1 November–30 November 1942

1 November 1942. Weather: clear, dry, state of roads good. The time is once again set at Central European Time. It begins to get dark at 1530 hours.

In the night an enemy reconnaissance patrol is repulsed in front of Grenadier Regiment 203.

Losses: 1 soldier killed, 5 NCOs and soldiers wounded.

Enemy harassing fire throughout the day that is especially strong in the sector of Fusilier Regiment 230. Little air activity by either side.

Grenadier Regiment 178 reports 2 deserters.

For November Engineer Battalion 176 reports the following:

The work tempo is being accelerated. Existing mine obstacles are to be strengthened; all machine-gun positions are to be secured by tripwires and concealed charges. Various reconnaissance operations in strength are to be carried out in cooperation with the infantry. Concerning the provision of close-quarters antitank units with antitank mines (T-mines), see attachment 25.

Plans are being drawn up for a scaled relief of the companies (by groups) in order to carry out some intensive weapon training.

Orders for strongpoint defense from the main edge of the battle area into the depth of the battlefield (single machine guns, antitank weapons, gun positions, and so on).

2 November 1942. Weather: clear and dry, frost at night. In the sector of 1st Battalion, Grenadier Regiment 203, an enemy fighting patrol of about 15 men, which had succeeded in getting through a mine passage in front of our own position, was pushed back. The enemy managed to abduct a wounded German soldier.

In the remaining divisional sectors occasional enemy harassing fire. The rest of the night passed quietly.

Losses: 1 soldier killed, 8 NCOs and soldiers wounded.

Reduced enemy air activity.

On the order of the division, all sentry posts and machine-gun positions are to be protected by wire and to be fitted with booby traps.

Report concerning the status of the division as of 2 November 1942:

6 grenadier battalions: 6 average, 60 percent mobile
Artillery: 9 light batteries, 2 heavy batteries, of which 4 batteries are 100 percent mobile, 7 lack mobility
Engineer battalion: average, 60 percent mobile;
4 medium-caliber and 19 heavy antitank guns

The division is fully suited to defense.

3 November 1942. Weather: clear, no frost. An enemy reconnaissance patrol in the sector of 3rd Battalion, Fusilier Regiment 230, is repulsed. The enemy continues construction work and digging in on point 73.2. Otherwise the night passed without incident.

Losses: 3 men killed, 4 men hospitalized.

Weak enemy artillery and mortar harassing fire throughout the day in the divisional sector; little air activity by either side.

Regimental order of Grenadier Regiment 178 for the start of work for the period from 4 to 25 November 1942 dealing with construction work; see attachment 26.

4 November 1942. Weather: clear and frost-free, state of roads good. In the evening hours of the previous day, three enemy reconnaissance patrols repulsed. In places during the night there was plenty of artillery and mortar harassing fire. Plenty of enemy air activity during the night.

Losses: 6 men wounded.

A fighting patrol of 2nd Battalion, Grenadier Regiment 203, raided an enemy bunker at 1900 hours the previous day and brought in 6 prisoners.

Throughout the day lively enemy harassing fire on the division's left sector, though minimal. Little enemy reconnaissance activity on the high ground.

Second Battalion, Grenadier Regiment 178, reports: the construction of accommodations, to be sure without any internal fittings, more or less complete. The construction work leaves a great to be desired. As a result of the good weather the health of the troops has improved.

Regimental order of Grenadier Regiment 178 of 4 November 1942 concerning the linking up of boundary security; see attachment 27.

5 November 1942. Weather: clear and frost-free, state of roads good. At 0115 hours an enemy reconnaissance patrol of about 10 men was repulsed. Plenty of enemy air activity with some 80 bombs dropped in the divisional sector

Losses: 2 NCOs and soldiers killed, 6 NCOs and soldiers wounded, 3 NCOs and soldiers hospitalized.

Apart from artillery and mortar harassing fire throughout the day, nothing to report.

Deserters state that the Russians either on 6 or 7 November will attack on several positions. Division orders that all defensive measures are to be checked and that reserves are to be kept ready in the event of enemy penetration on threatened points on the front.

Elements of Tank Destroyer Section 670 that are to be deployed as a counterattack reserve are to be assigned.

VIII Army Corps orders that reports concerning the following topics are to be compiled:[17]

1. Combat on the steppe
2. Installations, construction, fighting in the current winter positions

   The experiences are to be complied from the following perspectives:

   a. leadership
   b. tactical combat
   c. weapon-technical
   d. miscellaneous

Regimental order of Grenadier Regiment 178 of 5 November 1942 regarding the heightening of defense and operational readiness on 6 and 7 November 1942; see attachment 28.

6 November 1942. Weather: overcast, midday light rain, turning heavy later. In the night an enemy fighting patrol of about 30 men was repulsed in front of Fusilier Regiment 230's lines. Plenty of enemy air activity with bombs dropped; our own reconnaissance patrols very active.

Regimental order of Grenadier Regiment 178 for 6 November 1942 concerning observation of the enemy, reporting, and evaluation of the identified enemy movements from the construction sites; see attachment 29.

Losses: 2 soldiers wounded.

Some enemy harassing fire throughout the day; otherwise no significant events to report.

One of our reconnaissance planes and a fighter were shot down by enemy antiaircraft fire in the divisional sector.

Regimental order of Grenadier Regiment 178 for 6 November 1942 regarding new Russian combat methods employed by fighting patrols; see attachment 30.

Hauptmann Löser reports:

> At the beginning of November enemy fighting patrols, particularly on the right and left flanks of Fusilier Regiment 230 as well as on the right flank and in the center of reinforced Grenadier Regiment 203, increase. From the many movements on the front and from the increase in deserters, a strengthening of the enemy can be identified. An increase in the number of enemy artillery batteries can be identified from the increase in artillery fire, particularly on the left sector of the division. Reconnaissance aircraft report accumulations of several hundred vehicles and tanks to the north of Kachalinskaia.[18]

As the divisional sector is only thinly occupied, VIII Army Corps refrains from pulling out further forces, which it had originally intended to do. The division has only 1½ to 2 companies of mobile reserves at its disposal.

Sometime in the near future 6th Army is to have a battalion of Turkic troops attached to each division. The setting up and initial training is being carried out by 162nd Infantry Division in the army's rear area. For the experiences of this division and suggestions for deployment as well as the formation, equipment, and state of the Turkic battalions, see attachment 31.[19] The Turkic battalion that has been designated for 76th Infantry Division is already under way. Arrival in Chir is expected sometime between 10 and 18 November 1942.

According to the weather reports, a rapid deterioration in the weather situation with heavy rain is to be expected. We are instructed by Corps that great emphasis is to be given to resupply, especially of ammunition.

7 November 1942. Weather: biting wind since midnight, onset of frost, –10°C (14°F). An enemy reconnaissance patrol of unknown strength was repulsed after a short firefight in front of Fusilier Regiment 230's position. One of our reconnaissance patrols from Grenadier Regiment 203 brought in 2 prisoners. 2nd Battalion, Grenadier Regiment 203, reports that the Russians were singing and flying red flags.

Losses: 4 soldiers wounded, 2 soldiers missing.

The day passed quietly in the division's sector. Minimal air activity.

Divisional order of 7 November 1942 in reference to antitank defense; see attachment 32.

Führer Order № 2, dated 6 November 1942, regarding possible Russian attacks on the occasion of the anniversary of the revolution is issued by 6th Army Headquarters; see attachment 33.[20]

8 November 1942. Weather: clear, frost down to –13°C (9°F). Apart from weak harassing fire and isolated reconnaissance patrol activity by both sides in the division's sector, the night passed quietly.

Losses: 1 soldier killed, 9 NCOs and soldiers wounded.

Again, apart from weak enemy artillery harassing fire, nothing significant to report. Minimal air activity.

Order from quartermaster, VIII Army Corps, dated 8 November 1942, in reference to reduction in consumption of fuel; see attachment 34.

9 November 1942. Weather as yesterday. In the night plenty of reconnaissance patrol activity by both sides. Four enemy prisoners brought in by Fusilier Regiment 230. Heavy enemy mortar fire on the sector of Fusilier Regiment 230 and a lot of enemy air activity. Bombs dropped in the region east and northeast of Vertiachii. On the position of 2nd Battalion, Grenadier Regiment 178, one of our own reconnaissance patrols set off a booby trap. Three men are lightly wounded.

Losses: 1 officer and 3 NCOs and soldiers wounded.

Throughout the day no significant activity.

As of 9 November 1942 the state of the division is as follows:

6 grenadier battalions: 2 middle strength, 4 average, 50 percent immediately mobile, up to 70 percent after bringing in horses from the recovery areas

Artillery: 9 light batteries, 3 heavy batteries, of which 3 light and 1 heavy are 100 percent mobile, 6 light and 2 heavy are not mobile

Engineer battalion: average, 60 percent mobile

4 medium-caliber and 21 heavy-caliber antitank guns

The division's reserve battalion has not been incorporated (130 men from the supply troops and so on told off for training, making soldiers available for battle)

The division is fully suited for defense.

Regimental Order of Grenadier Regiment 178, dated 9 November 1942, in reference to the appointment of quick-reaction unit commanders; see attachment 35.

10 November 1942. Weather: clear, light frost, good visibility. In ground in front of the divisional sector an enemy reconnaissance patrol was repulsed. Plenty of enemy air activity with bombs dropped; otherwise the night was quiet.

Losses: 2 soldiers killed, 2 soldiers wounded.

Weak enemy harassing fire throughout the day. In the division's sector plenty of digging and isolated enemy activity. Our artillery fires on enemy groups and enemy engaged in construction work.

At 1020 hours an enemy plane was shot down by a German fighter. A member of the crew was taken prisoner.

At 1930 hours fire from heavy infantry guns and the artillery of 1st Battery, Artillery Regiment 176, is put down on singing Russians in front of 2nd Battalion, Grenadier Regiment 178.

Officer appointments for 1st Battalion, Grenadier Regiment 178 as of 10 November 1942:

Commander, Major Gebauer; adjutant, Leutnant Bülow; battalion doctor, Dr. Kaller (until 20 November 1942 detached from headquarters at Dinafü[21]).

1st Company commander Oberleutnant von Clausing
2nd Company commander Leutnant Müller
3rd Company commander Leutnant Müller
4th Company commander Leutnant Welken

6th Army Headquarters orders that after 15 November 1942 the divisions are to hold themselves ready to collect the incoming reserve units and convalescent companies in Chir with motorized convoys.

VIII Army Corps announces that the 6th Army commander requests that the divisional commanders use every available opportunity to instruct their subordinate commanders that all arms are permanently obliged to assist the infantry and that all officers, NCOs, and men who have been attached or transferred to the infantry must be especially proud of the fact that they have been allocated to this arm of the service.

Report from 2nd Battalion, Grenadier Regiment 203, that the wire obstacle in front of the company sector is now fully restored.

11 November 1942. Weather: bright, light frost, visibility good. Apart from weak enemy harassing fire, the night passed without incident.

Losses: 1 soldier killed, 1 soldier wounded.

Weak enemy harassing fire throughout the day. Plenty of enemy movement in front of the divisional sector, apparently units being relieved. Minimal air activity.

The current rate of horse mortality in the army's zone, in particular east of the Don, will reduce the mobility of army formations to a minimum within the shortest possible time. In the army's zone in October, 6,400 horses perished, compared to 3,000 in the previous month.

In the night the company and platoon commanders of the division's quick-reaction companies called on the position of Grenadier Regiment 178. Grenadier Regiment 178 reports a deserter.

Divisional order, dated 11 November 1942, in reference to command arrangements № 3; see attachment 36.

12 November 1942. Weather: overcast, light frost. The night passed quietly with some weak enemy harassing fire.

Losses: 4 soldiers killed, 3 men wounded.

Heavier enemy harassing fire throughout the day. Enemy movement in front of the division somewhat weaker than the previous day. No enemy air activity.

A deserter from 49th Rifle Division on the position of Grenadier Regiment 178 says that the enemy has plans for an attack.

Leutnant Fröhlich assumes command of 2nd Battalion, Grenadier Regiment 203. Leutnant Hannig, hitherto commander of 2nd Company, will in effect become assistant adjutant at regiment headquarters of Grenadier Regiment 203 beginning 13 November 1942.

VIII Army Corps Quartermaster's Section presents its overview of the supply situation on 12 November 1942; see attachment 37.

13 November 1942. Weather: sunny, clear, temperatures below 0°C (32°F). Roads good. Minimal enemy harassing fire; otherwise the night passed without incident

Losses: 1 soldier wounded.

With the concentrated fire of three artillery sections, the division bombards attack-start positions being used by the enemy. According to statements from deserters, the attack is scheduled for first light, 13 November 1942 (south and southwest of Paniashchino). On Culture Station antiaircraft guns fired on accumulations of enemy troops of about 200 men. Additionally, our artillery successfully bombarded two enemy batteries immediately south of Paniashchino. Further, substantial movement in the enemy's main battle area across the division's entire front.

Minimal enemy harassing fire on the area of the Perepolnyi bridge. The enemy digging in front of the right flank and center of division.

Thirteen deserters.

The relationship between rations and combat strength shows a considerable shift to the benefit of the combat strength [see Tables 4.8–4.11] when

Table 4.8 *Combat Strength of 76th Infantry Division, 13 November 1942*

Arm of Service	Number
Infantry	2,697
Artillery	1,132
Engineer battalion	244
Tank destroyer section	224
Cycle section	201
Signals section	242
Total strength	4,740

Table 4.9 Seventy-sixth Infantry Division Troops Not Counted as Combat Strength, 13 November 1942

Function	Number
Divisional headquarters	136
Supply troops	1,413 (18%)
Attached combat units	1,734 (22%)
Total	3,283

Note: The numbers cited in Tables 4.8 and 4.9 total 8,023, which is the combined total of the division's combat strength (4,740) and troops not reckoned to be combat troops (3,283). As the manpower situation deteriorated, this distinction broke down.

compared to the last report, dated 24 October 1942, which can be attributed to the measures taken in the interim period to restore combat strength. Seventy-sixth Infantry Division reports a total ration strength of 8,023 and auxiliaries (4,988) and attached (3,045).

In the period from 3 October to 31 October 1942 losses amount to 226 officers, NCOs, and soldiers. These losses are not included in the total shortfall.

Leutnant Lenz, hitherto adjutant at Grenadier Regiment 203, assumes command of 12th Company, Grenadier Regiment 203.

VIII Army Corps orders that 76th Infantry Division have 100 men to release as a reserve fully equipped as riflemen for the setting up of an instruction unit for the company commander's course. This must include 1 officer, 2 platoon commanders, and 10 junior leaders selected as section commanders.

Table 4.10 *Breakdown of Those Attached to Combat Units of 76th Infantry Division, 13 November 1942*

Personnel Function	Number
Clerical	219
Vehicle and farrier	542
Weapons	103
Equipment	183
Technical	265
Supplies and Rations	345
Signals	31
Medical	46
Total	1,734

Table 4.11 *Shortages of Personnel Reported by 76th Infantry Division, 1 November 1942*

Rank	Number
Officers	157
Officials	24
NCOs	993
Others	5,591
Total	6,765

14 *November* 1942. Weather: bright, lighter frost, visibility good. Minimal harassing fire in the night. In the divisional sector enemy digging activity in the region of Culture Station was disrupted by the concentrated fire of heavy infantry weapons. At the same time an identified enemy command post in front of Fusilier Regiment 230 and an accumulation of 16 trucks near point 75.8 were successfully dealt with by guns and artillery.

Losses: 4 NCOs and soldiers killed, 1 soldier wounded.

Northeast of Verkhnii much stronger occupation of enemy positions identified.

At 1215 hours a formation of 12 bombers and 6 fighters attacked the area of Vertiachii with bombs and machine guns.

Major Boening leaves Engineer Battalion 176 and is transferred to the Führer's reserve at Army Headquarters Berlin.

During the night enemy relief operations were once again detected by Grenadier Regiment 178. Toward evening an order arrived from division that in the days ahead in the early-morning hours from 0300 to 0500 hours the highest state of emergency-readiness is to be maintained, since at this time, according to statements from deserters, enemy attacks are to be expected.

15 *November* 1942. Weather: cloudy, temperatures below 0°C (32°F), state of roads good. Isolated bombing raids in the night and weak enemy harassing fire in the division's sector. Two enemy reconnaissance patrols with a strength of 5–10 men were repulsed in front of the right flank of Grenadier Regiment 203. Otherwise a quiet night.

Losses: 1 soldier wounded.

Throughout the entire morning, movement, digging, and vehicle traffic in front of the division's sector. In the late afternoon on the right flank of Fusilier Regiment 230 an enemy fighting patrol of 20 men was repulsed. According to statements from deserters after a company command post had been taken out, an attack of other forces would follow. Our artillery bombarded possible forming-up points on both sides of Culture Station with concentrated fire, with the aim of destroying any attack.

Second battalion, Artillery Regiment 53, minus one battery, is to be placed under the command of 76th Infantry Division. Third and 4th Batteries of Antiaircraft Battalion 241 are, on the order of 6th Army Headquarters, to be withdrawn from the corps sector.

Cycle Section reports the completion of the bunkers and the communications trench for all deployed elements.

16 November 1942. Weather: bright, light frost, visibility good, state of roads good. In the night 2 enemy fighting patrols were repulsed in front of the right flank of Grenadier Regiment 203. In order to destroy likely enemy forming-up points based on information from deserters, our own artillery completed a fire mission on both sides of the Culture Station area. Apart from that the night passed quietly.

Losses: 1 soldier killed, 2 soldiers wounded.

In the divisional sector our reconnaissance patrols are successful. Sparse enemy movement. At 1700 hours an enemy reconnaissance patrol repulsed in front of 1st Battalion, Grenadier Regiment 178.

Isolated flights by enemy aircraft.

Regimental order of Grenadier Regiment 178, dated 16 November 1942, concerning further construction of strongpoints; see attachment 38.

On 16 November 1942 VIII Army Corps Quartermaster's Section issues instructions for supply on the basis of the order for the assignment and securing of the rear combat area; see attachment 39.

State of the division as of 16 November 1942:

6 grenadier battalions: 2 middle strength, 4 average, 50 percent (70 percent) mobile
Artillery: 9 light and 2 heavy batteries, of which 3 light and 1 heavy are 100 percent mobile 6 light and 1 heavy are immobile
Engineer battalion: middle strength, 45 percent (60 percent) mobile
4 medium and 20 heavy antitank guns (figures in brackets are valid after bringing of horses from recovery areas)

The following are unallocated: field reserve battalion with 900 men, divisional reserve company with 130 men. The division is fully suited to defense.

17 November 1942. Weather: overcast, rain, poor visibility at times, marked freezing up. During the night minimal activity by own and enemy reconnaissance patrols. In the sectors of Grenadier Regiment 203 and Fusilier Regiment 230 minimal machine-gun and mortar fire.

Losses: 3 NCOs and soldiers killed, 2 soldiers wounded, 2 men ill.

At 1400 hours enemy movement about 1.5 km to the left and forward of 2nd Battalion, Grenadier Regiment 178. Enemy dealt with successfully by our artillery.

Isolated enemy harassing fire throughout the day; otherwise the day passed quietly.

At 1630 hours a reconnaissance patrol of Grenadier Regiment 203 managed to get into an enemy trench.

18 November 1942. Weather: cloudy, temperatures above freezing, thin, slippery layer of ice formed on the frozen subsoil. Weak enemy artillery and mortar harassing fire. Enemy reconnaissance patrol repulsed; otherwise the night passed without incident.

Losses: 1 soldier killed, 1 soldier wounded.

Throughout the day heavy enemy harassing fire in the divisional sector.

Our artillery bombards enemy groups of about 100 men digging in at a distance of 1 kilometer (0.6 mile) northeast of Culture Station and to the west of point 67.6.

Enemy movement in the region of Culture Station, in the area of point 67.6 and point 56.8, and in the gully terrain northeast of point 67.6 observed. Partly dealt with by our artillery.

In the afternoon plenty of enemy artillery fire on the sectors of Grenadier Regiment 203 and Fusilier Regiment 230.

19 November 1942. Weather as the day before. In the evening of the day before toward 1830 hours an enemy fighting patrol of about 30 men was repulsed with heavy losses in the right sector of Fusilier Regiment 230.

Apart from some minor harassing fire the night passed quietly.

Losses: 2 soldiers killed, 2 soldiers wounded, 2 men missing.

Throughout the day enemy movements in the main battle zone were less than the day before. Normal level of harassing fire. No air activity.

It is known that on the left wing of the army's boundary heavy Russian attacks are being carried out on Romanian positions. In places these attacks have led to some deep penetrations.

Hauptmann Löser reports:

> Oberst Abraham, the commander of Fusilier Regiment 230, receives the Knight's Cross of the Iron Cross from the divisional commander. As a consequence of the state of his health, he is transferred to the Führer's reserve of 6th Army in order to assume command of the company commanders' school and the training units in the Kalach region. Oberstleutnant Hering replaces him and is appointed regimental commander. Colonel Abraham's departure is scheduled in the New Year. Oberstleutnant Hering is ill with jaundice. Major Lindow takes over command of the regiment until the middle of December (also, dates whether the change of command took place on 19, 20, or 21 November; not known).

20 *November* 1942. Weather: mild, light snowfall with slight warming. All leave for 6th Army blocked because the enemy, with heavy forces, has broken into the Don salient and into the area to the west.

On the order of the division the main area of Vertiachii for the rear elements of the division (divisional command posts, administrative centers for the regiments, the bulk of the supply trains, ammunition and rations-issuing centers, and so on) is laid out for all-around defense. A defensive plan has been organized that includes the four sectors, which are coordinated to cover the four points of the compass. The intended forward defensive positions are situated about 100 meters in front of the town perimeter and are well suited to the terrain. The positions are constructed for defense, and troops for the defense are recruited from the supply and rear-echelon units in and around Vertiachii. The positions are to be occupied only when the alarm has been given. A detailed emergency order has been drafted.

Commander of the defense sectors is Major Alpes; second-in-command is Hauptmann Grohe. The alarm will be given by division.

The Engineer Battalion reports the following: 1 platoon of 1st Company of the Engineer Battalion has been deployed to Grenadier Regiment 203 on the left-sector boundary of the division (Don) in order to secure the riverbank. The other platoon has had to provide infantry cover in the cycle squadron formation.

21 *November* 1942. Weather: overcast with ground fog and light frost. Before midday heavy enemy air activity, mainly fighter and reconnaissance flights. Enemy mortar and artillery fire becomes more and more intense.

Order from VIII Army Corps that a battalion must be kept ready for deployment to the defensive front that has been formed in the south of the Kessel.

Division issues warning order that 2nd Battalion of Grenadier Regiment 178 should prepare for withdrawal from the divisional front. The battalion is to be relieved by 2nd Company, Engineer Battalion 176; assault reserves of Regiments 178 and 230; and the headquarters of Engineer Battalion 176. (This undertaking was not carried out, as the pressure on the divisional sector intensified.)

The Russians have broken through with tanks from the north (from the region west of Kletskaia) into the Kalach area. On 22 November 1942 a counterattack by German tank formations is to be launched with the aim of encircling the enemy forces that have broken in. (This counterattack did not have the anticipated success because the Russians were markedly superior and the forces at our own disposal were very weak. As a result of the extremely small combat forces, only very limited troop contingents could be made available from the deployed divisions in the old front sectors. The state of the roads for bringing up the troops was exceptionally bad. There was insufficient fuel.)

22 November 1942. Weather, hoarfrost, light fog, –5°C (23°F). At 0530 hours our artillery carried out a fire mission with cooperation of 2–3 sections on areas deemed to be enemy forming-up positions in the low-lying terrain in front of the main forward line of the sectors of Grenadier Regiment 203 and Fusilier Regiment 230.

From 0600 to 0700 hours a concentrated rolling barrage of enemy artillery on the entire divisional sector, with the exception of Grenadier Regiment 178. At 0700 hours attack by enemy infantry from out of a smokescreen in the above sectors. In places the enemy manages to penetrate our forward line.

At 0900 hours, 2nd Company, Engineer Battalion 176, which is attached to Grenadier Regiment 176, is taken to Grenadier Regiment 203 in trucks.

At 1030 hours, as a consequence of a divisional order, the regimental assault reserve Grenadier Regiment 178 (engineer and mounted platoon) moved to 2nd Battalion, Grenadier Regiment 178, in order to be able to assist the right battalion of Fusilier Regiment 230.

At 1300 hours, as a consequence of a divisional order, this regiment's assault reserve is moved to Grenadier Regiment 230, since, after an artillery bombardment, another enemy attack on the break-in positions has occurred there.

At 1700 hours, as a result of successful counterattacks, the situation is restored up to a break-in position at the cycle section (a piece of trench line about 200 meters wide) and a smaller break-in position on the left battalion of Fusilier Regiment 230 (a strongpoint on the boundary of the right-hand 3rd Battalion).

Heavily replenished Russian penal companies have attacked in front of Fusilier Regiment 230.

Division informs the regimental command posts that 6th Army is encircled, as the enemy has also penetrated from the southeast through the Kalmuck steppe to the Kalach region. Along the length of the railway line to Stalingrad a south front is formed from Kalach to the east against enemy forces attacking from the region south of Stalingrad and the Kalmuck steppe.

As a consequence of the Russian break-in from the southeast, rear units of the division are affected. These are primarily the two workshop platoons of Workshop Company 176 in Liabitshchev; the 4th, 5th, and 6th Mobile Columns; and Veterinary Company 176. The workshop platoons remain outside the Kessel; nevertheless, the valuable installations, machine tools, and the like must be considered as lost. The 4th Mobile Column (accommodations in Sovetskii) lost nearly all its vehicles and horses and a great part of its men, killed and wounded. The 5th Mobile Column (accommodations in Marinovka) and the 6th Mobile Column (accommodations in Illarionovskii) were able to break through to the north of the Vertiachii area without significant losses of men, horses, and vehicles.

On 22 November 1942 VIII Army Corps Quartermaster's Section issues an order for the supply of the newly formed south front and general orders for supply; see attachments 40 and 41.

Toward evening a lot of noise from vehicles in front of the divisional sector, moving from east to west. Small forces (on average about 30 per group) from the supply parties are attached to the infantry regiments as reserves and deployed as security for the regimental command posts.

From a reconnaissance patrol of 6th Company, Grenadier Regiment 178, it is established that tracked vehicles coming from the west, north of point 80.7, turn toward the north and head away. Presumably it is a question of vehicles that have earlier driven from east to west, so they are likely to be supply vehicles and not tanks.

According to statements from prisoners, which were passed on to the regimental command posts from division, the Russians have suffered very heavy losses in today's attacks, and tomorrow's attacks, if at all, will be markedly weaker since reserves are allegedly unavailable. According to the same statements, the enemy artillery has used a great deal of ammunition, and only a few tanks are in Panshchino.

In the late evening salvoes of enemy artillery fire along the entire line of the division's sector.

Before midday the stand to signal for the defense of Vertiachii is given.

Effective 22 November 1942, the daily bread ration is reduced to 400 grams (14 ounces).

23 November 1942. Weather: temperature around freezing, visibility somewhat better than the day before. At first light enemy tank attacks against Grenadier Regiment 203 and Fusilier Regiment 230 on the exact positions against which attacks were launched on 22 November 1942. Line penetrated by some 16–20 tanks in the direction of Vertiachii.

By midday 12 enemy tanks knocked out with the help of assault-gun batteries. Two tanks manage to break through to Vertiachii. Their mounted infantry were shot off the tanks by the local defense. After shooting up the location, especially the northwest edge of the village, the tanks turn northeastward, returning to the front. The local defense was unable to destroy them because it had no armor-piercing weapons, nor were any T-mines or limpet mines available.

On this day, 4th and 6th Batteries of Artillery Regiment 176 knocked out 1 tank with each 5.5-cm gun battery.

The battalion command post of 1st Battalion, Fusilier Regiment 230—a number of trenches with accommodations organized in all-around defense and situated in completely flat steppe—is surrounded by 6 tanks with some infantry. Two to 3 tanks were destroyed, 2 in close-quarters battle by the battalion adjutant and a lieutenant from the battalion.

First Battalion has suffered heavy losses. In the counterattacks to regain possession of captured strongpoints Oberfeldwebel Pieper of Mounted Platoon, Fusilier Regiment 230, especially stood out. For this action he has been nominated for the Knight's Cross.

Soldiers separated from their units are gathered up and are allocated to the regiments and battalions as reinforcements. The allocation is made according to losses. Third Battalion, Fusilier Regiment 230, receives about 30 soldiers.

The separated remnants of soldiers are mainly from the infantry units of 384th Infantry Division.[22]

Toward 1500 hours in the sector of 2nd Battalion, Grenadier Regiment 178, an enemy tank approaches from the rear through our front. It takes direct hits from 3.7-centimeter (cm) antitank shells, which just bounce off.

The divisional front has held despite attacks yesterday. The enemy infantry were unable to follow the tank attacks with any significant forces.

The position of the local penetration on the cycle section (under the command of Grenadier Regiment 203) has expanded to about 300 meters. The cycle section becomes the assault reserve (cycle and engineer platoon) of Grenadier Regiment 178 and is then attached to 1st and 2nd Companies of Engineer Battalion 176. Additionally, 3rd Battalion, Grenadier Regiment 536, is attached to 384th Infantry Division. It is a question of a largely shattered battalion without any supply services and without adequate equipment, which has been transferred from the west Don bank to the east.

The local defense is standing to at the highest state of readiness. The designated positions have been occupied.

In the evening the divisional commander orders that all classified material is to be destroyed.

In front of the division's lines a total of 23 enemy tanks were knocked out. There were 12 Russian deserters.

24 November 1942. Weather, temperatures around 0°C (32°F), sunny, then overcast. With the onset of daybreak further enemy tank attacks in the same front sectors as on previous days. Penetration by a number of tanks in the direction of Vertiachii and the Don bridge at Perepolnyi. In the course of the day all are again pushed back, and the front with minor penetrations is again reestablished.

A total of 11 enemy tanks are knocked out in the division's sector. The enemy has notably reinforced his position in front of height 56.8.

On the previous evening a Russian tank is seen in the sector of 2nd Battalion, Grenadier Regiment 178, on the barbed-wire obstacle. In the morning, at a distance of about 700 meters in front of the main battle line, it is seen to be burned out. It has probably driven on one of its own mines.

During the night in the sector of 1st Battalion of Grenadier Regiment 178, deployed on the division's right flank, the enemy has removed some of our mines and cut the wire.

In the evening the remnants of the cycle squadron are withdrawn and a reserve platoon is formed from them. The squadron's position is taken over by 2nd Battalion, Grenadier Regiment 536 (384th Infantry Division), which is reinforced by 2nd Company, Engineer Battalion 176.

Scattered remnants of the 384th, 44th, and 376th Infantry Divisions as well as many Romanians deployed west of the Don come over the bridges at Perepolnyi and Akimovski to the eastern side of the Don.

Enemy artillery bombards Vertiachii.

On the order of VIII Army Corps, 76th Infantry Division collects ammunition for its light field howitzers 16 with its own vehicles from 384th Infantry Division (west of the Don).[23]

The division's requirement for mortar ammunition cannot be met at VIII Army Corps.

Reduction of rations effective 24 November 1942 to 300 grams (10.6 ounces) of bread.

The division's main casualty clearing station (1st Medical Company) at Vertiachii is overwhelmed with wounded. No more can be accepted.

25 November 1942. Weather: overcast, light frost. In the morning heavy enemy artillery fire and fire from enemy tanks on the break-in positions. Enemy tank attacks and the penetration of a single tank in the direction of Vertiachii are without success.

Nine enemy tanks are knocked out in the course of the day. Cycle Section 176 is reinforced with the addition of 33 soldiers from 376th Infantry Division.

Hauptmann Löser reports:

> The strongpoints on the forward edge of the battle area, which, as a result of the reduced strength, are often separated from one another by 150 to 200 meters and repeatedly encircled by the enemy, must simultaneously secure themselves some space in counterattacks. There are any number of acts of courage. In 3rd Battalion, Fusilier Regiment 230, an NCO (Unteroffizier Demke, 10th Company) with 1 soldier takes back a strongpoint that had been lost and occupied by 17 Russians. In the evening the positions of the weakened and heroically fighting Fusilier Regiment 230 (Battalion Gröning), situated on the left flank about 600 meters up the steep edge north of the Kotluban–Zolotoi Rog highway, are taken back.

On the west side of the Don the enemy has gained ground. The left flank of 3rd Battalion, Grenadier Regiment 203, must be withdrawn about 2 kilometers (1.2 miles) to the south.

In the late evening the division informs the regiments that 6th Army shall withdraw to the area around Stalingrad, since the divisions of XI Army Corps are practically without weapons and the Don Heights highway can no longer be held. The army of Generalfeldmarschall von Manstein and panzer corps of General Heim are under way as relief for 6th Army but are still some, respectively, 300 kilometers (186 miles) and 150 kilometers (93 miles) away. The supply lines of the regiments and sections are, effective immediately, to be transferred to the Rossoshka Valley. The withdrawal of the forward edge of the battle area should take place in about three days. Great difficulties are expected as a result of the reduced numbers of horses, the poor state of the existing ones, and the low reserves of fuel.

Quartermaster of 76th Infantry Division requests fuel from the Quartermaster's Section, VIII Army Corps, for the evacuation of Vertiachii; see attachment 42.

A 20-ton highway convoy and a 35-ton convoy from the corps supply commander 408 from VIII Army Corps are placed at the disposal of 76th Infantry Division for the evacuation of Vertiachii. JU-52 transport aircraft bring fuel and ammunition for armor-piercing weapons and take away 100 wounded from the Peskovatka field hospital and the main casualty clearing station at Vertiachii. About 1,200 wounded and ill still remain in Peskovatka and Vertiachii.

On 26 November 1942, 16 heavy trucks from VIII Army Corps are to be placed at the disposal of 76th Infantry Division as prime movers for moving the captured English and French guns in the division's sector.

The local defense of Vertiachii is continually deployed. The enemy artillery bombardment of Vertiachii ceases. The further influx of troop formations (overwhelmingly supply services), already in a partially disorderly state, from the divisions deployed west of the Don and from the Romanians on the east bank of the Don has come to a halt.

The defensive front in the west runs more or less on the Don Heights highway.

Second Medical Company, 176th Battalion, as well as pieces of divisional equipment left in Bolshii Nabatov can still be moved to the east bank of the Don.

On 20 November 1942 the Bakery Company of 176th Battalion, accommodated in Kaliakin on the west bank of the Don, evacuated its local accommodations and located a temporary bakery in the former pioneer camp on the east bank of the Don, about 1 kilometer (.6 mile) south of Vertiachii. In so doing, it managed to take with it not only all the equipment and vehicles but also a reserve of 200 tons of bread flour, about half. A further vehicle convoy across the ice of the partially frozen river was made ready and would have been possible if the flour stores had not been prematurely set alight by foreign security troops.[24]

On 22 November 1942, when the evacuation of Vertiachii and the left Don bank was ordered, the company set up the bakery in a small ravine 4 kilometers (2.5 miles) south of Bol'shaia Rossoshka and 5 kilometers (3.1 miles) northwest of the Pitomnik airfield. This position was maintained until 13 January 1943.

In the cemetery close to the forward edge of the battle area, mass graves have to be provided. With the high number of dead, the time for individual graves has passed.

26 November 1942. Weather as yesterday, with increasing frost and light snowfall. In the morning enemy tank attacks once again start primarily in the front of Grenadier Regiment 203 and Fusilier Regiment 230. Enemy tanks that penetrate the line are knocked out. The positions are held. The Russians suffer heavy and bloody losses. At midday there is a conference at division with the regimental adjutants who receive the divisional order for the withdrawal that is to take place in the night of 27 November 1942:

1. Third Battalion, Grenadier Regiment 203, is to be under the command of Battalion Gröning (1st Battalion, Grenadier Regiment 203), which has the task of securing the division's left flank and is to withdraw to the northern heights of Vertiachii with the front toward the north-west
2. 1st Battalion, Grenadier Regiment 203, and the regimental command post are to be transferred to the command post of Grenadier Regiment 178
3. Fusilier Regiment 230 is to go back with the left flank to height 61.6
4. Grenadier Regiment 178 is to remain in its old position

The disengagement of 3rd Battalion, Grenadier Regiment 203, was particularly difficult, as it was located the farthest to the northwest. Its combat strength now came to only about 160 soldiers. Despite all difficulties, it reached height 61.6 and fitted in with the existing defense setup (consisting overwhelmingly of units of 384th Infantry Division). The height was being held under the most difficult of conditions. In the course of the day it was soon totally surrounded by the Russians such that there was no link with division.[25]

In the course of the day a total of 12 enemy tanks were knocked out in front of the divisions.

Concerning the defensive operations of 3rd Battalion, Grenadier Regiment 203, for the period 15 October–26 November 1942, see attachment 43.

On 26 November 1942 6th Army Headquarters issues an order for dealing with stragglers; see attachment 44.

Since early morning, stores, ammunition, rations, and equipment have been taken to the Rossoshka Valley, Blizhnii, close to the Malaia Rossoshka Valley, and Vlasovka, by the regiments' supply services. In spite of heavy enemy artillery fire, the division's considerable reserves of ammunition, rations, and forage are evacuated and taken to the Rossoshka Valley.

From the afternoon of 26 November 1942 the divisional command post is located in the Antonova gully.

Vertiachii is under harassing fire from enemy artillery.

In the morning 1st Medical Company moves to Pitomnik. Second Medical Company takes over the main casualty clearing station in Vertiachii. The wounded are taken on trucks and sleds to Pitomnik.

27 *November* 1942. Weather: clear and frosty, snow in the afternoon. The withdrawal ordered by the division on 26 November 1942 is carried out until daybreak.

The evacuation of Vertiachii is continuing at an accelerated tempo, since the withdrawal of the front of the center and right divisional sectors, which has still to take place in the night, must be taken into account.

The divisional command post is in Antonova gully. The ability of 1st Battalion, Fusilier Regiment 230 (Battalion Gröning), to fight is in doubt. The battalion's fighting strength has been reduced to about 60 men. The right flank has been withdrawn to the steep edge such that the left flank of Fusilier Regiment 230 must defend itself against heavy flank attacks.

On 27 November 1942, 3rd Combat Group of Grenadier Regiment 203 has held out in spite of heavy enemy attacks. Three of our reconnaissance patrols that were sent out to establish contact with division did not return. Since the combat group had nearly exhausted all its ammunition, the commander, Hauptmann Gerstenberg, at 0100 hours on 28 November 1942, decided, together with those elements of his combat group that still able to move, to break through the encirclement, even more so when on 28 November 1942 a major Russian attack had definitely to be reckoned with. The breakout succeeded; see attachments 45 and 46 concerning the battle for height 61.6.[26]

From 1530 hours onward the remnants of XI Army Corps are withdrawn from the Don Heights highway to the east bank.

Divisional supply headquarters, Supply Company 176, the remnants of workshop company, truck convoys, Fuel Resupply Convoys 5 and 6, and the remnants of 4th Convoy are transferred to the Rossoshka Valley close to Vlasovka. After a few days these logistics units are transferred to a ravine about 4 kilometers (2.5 miles) south of the township of Bol'shaia Rossoshka and northwest of the Pitomnik airfield.

The main casualty clearing station at Vertiachii is evacuated by 2nd Medical Company 176. It is coming under enemy artillery fire.

Heavy but unsuccessful enemy infantry and tank attacks in the left sector of the division. The right sector of the division (Grenadier Regiment 178) continues to remain quiet. There are no communications with 3rd Battalion, Grenadier Regiment 203. Early on 27 November 1942 the cycle section is transferred via Vertiachii to the Antonova ravine as a corps reserve and remains here until 28 November 1942.

28 November 1942. Weather, clear, some frost, snow flurries in the night. Divisional headquarters is in the ravine on the northern edge of Malaia Rossoshka. In the night of 28 November 1942 the division, protected by strong rearguards, breaks contact with the enemy and moves to new positions in the approximate line of point 102.3, the summer camp 1 kilometer south east of Gnilovka and the Vertiachii heights. See sketch, attachment 2.

At 2130 hours 11 Company Grenadier Regiment 178, departs with the second battalions and the bulk of the 1st Battalion at 2200 hours 27 November 1942. At 2230 hours the regimental command post of Grenadier Regiment 178 is moved to the region 2 kilometers south west of point 137.2.

Operational formation of the division is as follows: Fusilier Regiment 230 on the right, Grenadier Regiment 178 in the center, Grenadier Regiment 203 on the left. On the right the division joins up with the 113th Infantry Division, on the left with the 44th Infantry Division.

Since the start of the evacuation from Vertiachii and the surrounding area, and up to the 31st December 1942, the rations office and the butcher company were situated in a wide ravine about 800 metres south east of the township of Baburkin, linking up to the east with the convoys of 76th Infantry Division. The division's quartermaster's section is situated in a dugout half way between Baburkin and the Pitomnik airfield. A platoon of Workshop Company 176 and the ammunition issuing center of the division are also located here. Field hospital 176 was accommodated on the south eastern edge of Bol'shaia Rossoshka.

The main casualty clearing station of the division is situated in Malaia Rossoshka.

The cycle section is moved to the area near Malaia Rossoshka as corps reserve, with a new formation of the same. The mounted squadron with a combat strength of about 50 men is under the command of Oberwachtmeister Wonde. The remnants of cycle and heavy squadrons, with a combat strength of about 70 men, are under the command of Oberleutnant von Olshausen with 2 combat groups: commander Major von Rochow, adjutant Leutnant von Jena, and medical officer Dr. Mangliers.

In the night of 27 November 1942 Artillery Regiment 176 changed positions and on 28 November 1942 moved, with all elements, to a position northwest of Malaia Rossoshka.

Very early in the morning of 28 November 1942 Hauptmann von Tresskow, with 5 vehicles, is in Vertiachii in order to fetch the remnants of stores from the divisional rations dump and ammunition from the issuing point. Only in the morning does Father Kayser set out for Baburkin in a convoy. Up to then he had been attending to the last wounded at the main casualty clearing station in Vertiachii. No wounded remain there.

The bridges over the Don at Akimovskii and Perepolnyi are blown; see attachment 11.

The day passes quietly, especially on the right wing of the division in the new position. Weaker enemy attacks are repulsed on the left wing.

Hauptmann Löser reports:

> While strong convoys heading southwest can be observed on the west bank of the Don, the enemy in the division's own sector, as a direct consequence of his unprecedented losses, has become far more cautious. The bringing up of reserves is observed. The withdrawal from the forward edge of the battle area ensues without any pressure from the enemy, although audible. All dugouts and some ammunition that cannot be removed are blown. A very black night: toward the end heavy driving snow mixed with rain sets in. The withdrawal runs via the Gerasimovka ravine. Orientation is very difficult, particularly since, in spite of repeatedly collecting the battalions, they get split up; as many vehicles can only be

> got going with exceptional effort, many have to be unloaded. The last remnants of 384th Infantry Division—some 300 men—with field kitchens pulled by teams of men drag themselves along: a terrible sight. Within the entire division the withdrawal as well as the order of march proceeded superbly. Losses on the withdrawal march were exceptionally small. The discipline of the troops had withstood one of its hardest tests.

29 November 1942. Weather: heavy snowfall before midday, clearing up in the afternoon, temperature around 0°C (32°F). The regimental rearguards are withdrawn in the early hours of the morning. At about 0500 hours they have completely moved to the new forward edge of the battle area.

The day passed generally without incident.

Setting up the new forward edge of the battle area and construction of positions. Cover for tanks was laid out by a construction battalion and unit advance parties. Further construction is very difficult because there is a lack of digging tools and wood. The earth has already frozen very hard.

The division's artillery is dispersed over the entire division sector, generally in positions about 4 kilometers (2.5 miles) behind the forward edge of the battle area.

In reference to the construction of the forward edge of the battle area, see attachment 11.

Hauptmann Löser reports:

> In the new position only a thin line consisting of a few machine-gun positions and fire trenches, as well as about 3–4 dugouts per battalion (old artillery observation posts), erected in the previous nights by Romanian and German work squads, are available.
>
> In the sector of 3rd Battalion, Grenadier Regiment 230, about 300 meters behind the forward edge of the battle area is an old battery position with 8 dugouts that are on the boundary between Fusilier Regiment 230 and Grenadier Regiment 178 and are to be fitted out as a support for a strongpoint by the battalion headquarters.
>
> In the sector of Fusilier Regiment 230 only the 3rd Battalion is deployed, since the 1st Battalion has suffered very heavy losses and has been deprived of most of its command stratum. After Hauptmann Müller has taken over command of the battalion as replacement for the ill Hauptmann Gröning, the battalion will be placed in old dugouts behind the right flank of the regimental sector in makeshift accommodations.

> There, in the event of an emergency after the opening up of the boundary leading to 113th Infantry Division, it will have the task of intervening or protecting south of point 102.3 (accommodations also there), the right flank of the division to the north. Replenishment of the battalion shall occur on an ongoing basis by supply-service units and artillery soldiers. The two officers—Hauptmann Müller and Oberleutnant Matschke—are to be joined by three young officers from the army's command reserve.
>
> The strength of the companies deployed in the battalions on the front amounts to about 45 men each, including the command staff. Getting warmed up is especially difficult for the men since only about a third of the warming-up areas are available for each company sector. In the daytime the troops cannot be relieved because they can be observed by the enemy. Since in this deserted position all work including communications trenches is complete, the battalion is at a bit of a loss. The next task will be to set about building dugouts with maximum efforts.
>
> When using infantry heavy weapons, particular attention is placed on the possibility and preparation of concentrated fire on practically every point in front of the main edge of the battle area, since artillery ammunition is in short supply and permission to open fire must come from division.

All units of the division have set themselves up for the winter in hard and arduous work in all kinds of ways (trenches, wire obstacles, mines, and dugouts) by tireless effort in the old positions east of the Don. In Vertiachii the supply and support units have created dugouts for men, horses, and vehicles in available village accommodations, in ravines, and on slopes. Wood, boards, stones, and the like had to be brought from far afield (from the Don and Stalingrad). The troops saw the second Russian winter coming and knew from last year what a winter in the East meant.

When the order to abandon the positions and accommodations arrived, the troops had more or less completed construction work. Once again the men had to place themselves many kilometers to the east of the enemy in steppe terrain, where hardly a house and bush, scarcely any cover at all, existed. The men knew what it meant to have to start all over again in the new position and under extremely unfavorable conditions (already winter with snow and ice and without significant reserves of wood and the like). Here the troops would have put a loading team to shame; in this regard they were without parallel. The troops showed what they were made of!

30 November 1942. Weather: overcast, intermittent snowfall. Enemy probing with small forces against the new forward edge of the battle area. Light enemy mortar harassing fire.

Grenadier Regiment 203 reconnoiters a switch position in the Zapadnovka ravine that will be built by a bridge construction battalion.

Enemy air activity, stand to on the position of 44th Infantry Division.

The division requests ovens, construction and roofing materials, and firewood from VIII Army Corps.

Army order in accordance with which 76th Infantry Division must hand over 2,200 shells for the light field howitzer 16 and 80 tons of flour to 44th Infantry Division.

1 December–31 December 1942

1 December 1942. Weather: clearer, frost, –15°C (5°F). The enemy is reinforcing positions in the Gerassimova and Antonova ravines. During the night the enemy has moved in many places up to 50 meters in the direction of the forward edge of the battle area. Throughout the day the enemy's attempts to attack our lines are thwarted by artillery and machine-gun fire.

At 1730 hours a fighting patrol of 5th Company, Grenadier Regiment 178, raided a nest of enemy without any own losses. Five enemy dead left behind.

Further construction work on the positions. The existing tank dugouts are expanded so as to take small groups (up to about 6 men). Out of this, strongpoints capable of taking several groups are formed.

Mines in two rows are laid along the entire front line of the forward edge of the battle area.

Formation of Grenadier Regiment 203 as follows:

Third Battalion, 1st Battalion left. Third Battalion is formed as follows:

10th Company on the right
11th Company on the left
9th Company in the center facing to the rear as switch position
Each battalion has a platoon from 14th Company attached

Hauptmann Löser reports:

The enemy probes forward cautiously, yet some 2–3 kilometers (1.2–1.9 miles) in front of the forward edge of the battle area; he nevertheless behaves in a very free-and-easy fashion, apparently aware of our shortage of ammunition. By day convoys of traffic, headquarters, and the setting up of strongpoints can be clearly identified. Enemy artillery begins to register its guns. The regiment's assault reserves of Fusilier Regiment 230 under the command of Oberfeldwebel Pieper are attached to 3rd Battalion. The defense resembles a series of strongpoints and is laid out in a line. Distance between the strongpoints is about 100–200 meters. Whereas in the sector of Fusilier Regiment 230 the command posts of the 1st and 3rd Battalions—both 300 to 500 meters behind the forward edge of the battle area and both constructed as strongpoints—form the depth of the position, in Grenadier Regiment 178 deployment occurs in depth within the battalions (deployment of 2–3 companies behind one another).

2 December 1942. Weather: heavy snowfall with persistent frost.
Hauptmann Löser reports:

At last light the enemy conducts a reconnaissance probe against the right wing of Fusilier Regiment 230 in company strength. The probe is repulsed with heavy enemy losses. The enemy leaves behind about 20 dead on the forward edge of the battle area. Two heavy machine guns are captured.

The VIII Army Corps quartermaster announces that the allocation of fuel from 6th Army is very small. VIII Army Corps only receives 2–5 cbm [cubic meters] per day.

3 December 1942. Weather: easing of the frost, fog.
Hauptmann Löser reports:

The men have created improvised warming-up points in their trenches with boards that were swiped during the night from the old dugouts in front of the forward edge of the battle area in between the enemy positions and were partly brought in with horse-drawn vehicles. The digging for the first dugouts has started. Romanian work details, soldiers from the construction battalions, and the divisional engineers are in support, and are preparing the ground with explosives.

The first cases of exhaustion (frost and hunger) occur. They are indicated by fainting fits, apathy, delirium, low body temperature, and very weak pulse [emphasis added].

Reserves are attached to the units. They are badly clothed and fed and in their demeanor compare badly with earlier times! The bulk of the cases of theft from comrades (mainly rations) is carried out by this lot. Nearly every three days there is a case in the battalion. Severe measures taken by the men and increased attention to welfare by the company commanders sort this out. The company commanders themselves issue the rations and assume all the frontline functions of the senior NCOs. Their assistance is unprecedented. In this way the replacements fit in with the units.

Every day the battalion loses some 6–7 men who report sick to the main casualty clearing station.

In the night Engineer Battalion 176 lays mines in front of the regiments' positions (for example, about 338 mines were laid in front of the sector of Grenadier Regiment 178. In the early hours of the morning a strong enemy fighting patrol in front of 1st Battalion, Grenadier Regiment 178, was destroyed. The enemy left 37 dead and badly wounded prisoners. Apart from this the day passed quietly.

According to a message from VIII Army Corps, mail is to be picked up by JU-52s. The army field post office loading center is situated at Field Post Office 408 (VIII Army Corps). Every soldier can send a letter (not over 20 grams [.7 ounce]) to be delivered. Aircraft have already brought mail into the Kessel.

The regimental command post of Grenadier Regiment 203 is located in the Zapadnovka ravine. The following are also accommodated here:

Command post of 2nd Battalion, Artillery Regiment 176 (Hauptmann von Damm)
1st Bridge Construction Battalion, which is working on the construction of the forward edge of the battle area and on the switch position
1 assault gun battery
Headquarters companies and regimental supply services
Combat-supply services for the battalions and for 13th and 14th Companies

Ninth Convoy and regimental supply services were sent to the Rossoshka Valley. Up to 16 January 1943 they were accommodated in a ravine south of Bol'shaia Rossoshka.

4 December 1942. Weather: thaw, rain toward evening. Enemy artillery and harassing mortar fire throughout the day in the entire divisional sector.

At 1400 and 1500 hours an enemy fighting patrol was repulsed in front of each sector of 1st and 2nd Companies of Grenadier Regiment 178.

Throughout the day heavy enemy infantry and tank attacks on 44th Infantry Division, which led to penetrations of our own forward edge of the battle area on points 115.4 and 124.5. In these battles 10 enemy tanks were knocked out.

Stand to was ordered in Grenadier Regiment 203.

Changes in 3rd Battalion, Grenadier Regiment 203: Leutnant Hannig is appointed adjutant. The former adjutant (Leutnant Mörup) takes over command of 12th Company, Grenadier Regiment 203. Leutnant Mikulasch becomes company officer for Oberleutnant Bente (9th Company, Grenadier Regiment 203). Oberleutnant Hoppe becomes assistant adjutant of Grenadier Regiment 203.

5 *December* 1942. Weather: rain. At 0130 hours a penetration by the Russians on one of the positions of the light-supply services of 1st Battalion, Grenadier Regiment 203, and 13th Company, Grenadier Regiment 203, is cleaned out by NCOs and soldiers in a counterattack: 20 prisoners taken, 40 enemy dead.

Enemy mortar and artillery harassing fire.

The situation in the lines of the neighboring division is restored by the deployment of our tanks.

The cycle section is moved behind Grenadier Regiment 203 as a corps reserve.

Toward evening the news arrives that Generalfeldmarschall von Manstein sent the following message to 6th Army: "Acknowledge your defensive achievement. Our help to you is certain!"

At 0500 hours penetration by the Russians in battalion strength on the position of 2nd Battalion, Grenadier Regiment 203. The penetration was cleaned out by 9th Company, Grenadier Regiment 203, in a counterattack. At 1000 hours, the forward edge of the battle area is once again in our hands.

On 5 December 1942, 3rd Battalion, Grenadier Regiment 203, has about 60 dray horses and one horse for riding available. On 10 January 1943 only 6 dray horses were available.

6 *December* 1942. Weather: foggy, temperature around freezing. Toward evening an enemy fighting patrol of about 10 men was destroyed in front of the positions of 5th Company, Grenadier Regiment 178.

An enemy fighting reconnaissance probe consisting of about 50 men toward the left wing of Fusilier Regiment 230 was repulsed.

Within the corps area at the present moment there are about 1,750 ill and wounded. About 200 a day can be flown out in JU-52s.

7 December 1942. Weather: snowfall. Artillery and mortar harassing fire. We are informed by VIII Army Corps that from 8 December 1942 the daily bread ration will be 200 grams (7 ounces).

The Cycle Section is removed from its stand-to task behind Grenadier Regiment 203 and marches back to Malaia Rossoshka. The section will remain there as a corps reserve.

Hauptmann Löser reports:

> The enemy—as a result of observation from higher positions—has registered his mortars and artillery (*Ratschbumm*)[27] so well on the battalion's positions and on the battalion's command post as well that every movement by day is impossible. The slit trenches offer only minimal protection from mortar fire. In 3rd Battalion, Fusilier Regiment 230, there is an additional bread ration from divisional reserves such that the daily handover amounts to 300 and 450 grams (10.5 and 14 ounces) of bread. As a consequence of a lack of horse fodder and the need for rations, the rate at which horses are slaughtered gets going in a big way. Every day there is an issue of some 3–4 mess tins of watery horseflesh soup.

8 December 1942. Weather: bright, strong westerly wind, –10°C (14°F). Strong enemy attacks on the positions of 44th Infantry Division.

Toward 1500 hours an enemy fighting patrol, which was mounted on 2 armored wagons, was repulsed in front of the positions of 6th Company, Grenadier Regiment 178.

In the morning, Cycle Section 176, reinforced by Cycle Squadron 384 of 44th Infantry Division, is told off as corps reserve.

First Battalion, Fusilier Regiment 230, which consists of very few of the NCOs and soldiers from the old battalion, replenished with supply-line drivers and artillery soldiers and the like, is removed from the formation of 76th Infantry Division and transferred to Malaia Rossoshka as a corps reserve. See also 29 November 1942, 20 December 1942, and 29 December 1942. Corps order regarding the even distribution of ammunition:

Seventy-sixth and 113th Infantry Divisions are each to hand over 100 rounds of 8-cm mortar shells and light-infantry shells to 44th Infantry Division. The heavy-weapons 13th Platoon, Fusilier Regiment 230, still has some 45 heavy-infantry shells. In each sector of Fusilier Regiment 230 the following are deployed in each mutually supporting strong point: 1 light-infantry weapons platoon and 1 heavy-infantry weapons platoon. At the battalion strongpoint there are: 1 heavy-antitank platoon at the battalion command post, 1 light-antitank platoon on the forward edge of the battle area. Twelfth Company has 11 heavy mortars (5 of which are Russian) partly organized as a battery. Third Battalion also has 7 heavy machine guns.

LI Army Corps designates 305th and 389th Infantry Divisions as sponsoring divisions of 76th Infantry Division regarding the supply of digging tools. Since the first two named divisions have remained deployed on the Stalingrad front, they are still relatively well equipped with material.

9 December 1942. Weather: cloudy, temperature around freezing. With the exception of salvoes fired from Stalin organs on the sector of Grenadier Regiment 203, a quiet day.

As a result of the bad flying weather over the past few days, the supply situation of 6th Army has deteriorated. For about the past week the midday issue of rations has been reduced by about half; see attachment 47.

Third Battalion, Grenadier Regiment 203, reports the first cases of death from exhaustion.

The division requests writing paper from corps.

10 December 1942. Weather: cloudless sky, sunny, –15°C (5°F). Midday some 2 kilometers (1.2 miles) in front of the positions of 2nd Battalion, Grenadier Regiment 178, an enemy bomber crashes.

As a result of the lack of horse feed and the shortage of shelter for the horses, the state of the animals has become very bad. Because of complete exhaustion and debilitation, many of the horses have to be slaughtered. Grenadier Regiment 178 reports 24 horses slaughtered; Fusilier Regiment 230 reports 30.

There is an emergency landing of a JU-52 between the front lines in front of the sector of Fusilier Regiment 230. The aircraft is set ablaze.

Father Kayser (divisional Catholic priest) reports:

> Photographs are taken for the *Wochenschau* on Pitomnik airfield. A low-level Russian air attack is filmed in which 3 JU-52s were shot down.

Only very small quantities of fuel remain for the vehicles so that only very small amounts of wood from Stalingrad—a trip of about 40 kilometers (25 miles)—can be brought in.

11 December 1942. Weather as yesterday. Nothing significant to report. In accordance with a corps order, the division is to grind 12.5 tons of grain in a mobile flour mill and receives 100 liters (26.4 gallons) of fuel for that purpose.

There is continual reconnaissance patrol activity by our troops. The Russians are situated some 800 meters away in front of 3rd Battalion, Grenadier Regiment 203. For the time being it seems that the enemy has deployed only poor troops in front of our positions. Apparently he has thrown his best troops farther to the south and southwest of the encirclement ring.

Hauptmann Löser reports:

> In accordance with the order, Fusilier Regiment 230 also sends out reconnaissance patrols every night. Those who report are volunteers. The enemy positions are reconnoitered, and enemy mines are removed to meet our heating needs.[28] The soldiers in the reconnaissance patrols receive small ration supplements from the regiment's reserve. Because of the 15 cm (6 inches) of snow (frozen), the reconnaissance patrols find it tough going. In the night because of heavy drifting of snow the trenches are covered over, and it is possible to find one's way between the strongpoints only by following wire. The men's clothing is frozen stiff. As a result of the fact that the felt boots cannot for the most part be exchanged, numerous cases of frostbite occur. It is just not possible to send those suffering with grade 1 frostbite back to the rear.
>
> There are special problems with weapon maintenance since there is no oil available. The pilots of a detached formation of the fighter squadron Udet based at the Pitomnik airfield visit the battalion, bringing them bread, candles, and machine-gun oil. A wonderful sense of comradeship is evident (within 4 weeks 5 fighters have shot down over 400 enemy aircraft).

12 December 1942. Weather: cloudy –10°C (14°F). Minimal enemy harassing fire with antitank guns and mortars throughout the day. On the eastern exits of the Antonova ravine, the enemy is digging in 4 antitank guns.

In the evening the divisional commander visits the command post of 3rd Battalion, Fusilier Regiment 230.

Formation of 3rd Battalion, Fusilier Regiment 230, is:

Commander Hauptmann Löser
Adjutant Oberleutnant Nichtweiss
9th Company commander Oberleutnant Nowotne
10th Company commander Leutnant Kandt
11th Company commander Leutnant Löper
12th Company commander Leutnant Giesel
10th Platoon commander Leutnant Offer

Regimental Headquarters, Fusilier Regiment 230:

Commander Major Lindow
Adjutant Oberleutnant Tessmar
Signals officer Leutnant Holl
Assistant adjutant Leutnant Burkheiser
13th Company commander Leutnant Baier/Leutnant Elspass
14th Company commander Leutnant Wietusch/Feldwebel Prüfke (officer candidate)

In his diary, Father Kayser notes that JU-52s on the Pitomnik airfield that were full of wounded were shot up by Russian fighter bombers.

13 December 1942. Weather: clear, temperature –15°C (5°F). Enemy harassing artillery fire throughout the day. Toward 1600 hours the munitions dump of Grenadier Regiment 178 receives a direct hit. Thirty armor-piercing antitank 3.7-cm shells and 280 illuminating shells are destroyed.

In revenge the strong enemy fire is immediately answered with infantry heavy weapons.

Cycle Section 176 is returned from 44th Infantry Division to its own division and is then placed as corps reserve in Malaia Rossoshka.

At division headquarters there are discussions about a planned operation in the direction of the southwest. See also attachments of VIII Army Corps Quartermaster's Section concerning setting up of vehicle transport parks 48, 49, and 50.

On 12 December 1942, 76th Infantry Division reports the following vehicle transport parks: 76 vehicles, of which 67 are petrol and 9 are diesel. The payload is about 160 metric tons (176 tons). At the first fuel-dispensing point the required fuel amounts to: 3,200 liters (845 gallons) of petrol (Otto) and 450 liters (119 gallons) of diesel. Location of the vehicles is Malaia Rossoshka.

The headquarters vet, Dr. Herbert, reports that today Headquarters Company of Grenadier Regiment 203 is cooking horseflesh for the first time. Until then, as a result of the careful management of supplies, beef from livestock had still been available.

14 December 1942. Weather: as the day before. Nothing significant to report. In the evening General Rodenburg visits the command post of 3rd Battalion, Grenadier Regiment 203.

Officer status of Grenadier Regiment 203:

Regimental headquarters commander Major von Spangenberg
Adjutant Oberleutnant Busse
Assistant adjutant Oberleutnant Hoppe, Oberleutnant Poellnitz
Regimental medical officer Dr.Vigelius
Head of Headquarters Company Hauptmann Aurich

1st Battalion:

Commander Hauptmann Isberner, adjutant Leutnant Schwerin
1st Company [no name cited]
2nd Company [no name cited]
3rd Company Leutnant Textor
4th Company [no name cited]

3rd Battalion:

Commander Hauptmann Gerstenberg, adjutant Leutnant Hannig
9th Company commander Oberleutnant Bente
10th Company commander Leutnant Kressin
11th Company commander Leutnant Mikulasch
12th Company commander Leutnant Mörup

15 December 1942. Weather: cloudy skies, frost. Nothing significant to report. Generalmajor Rodenburg received accelerated promotion to Generalleutnant. On the occasion of his promotion he issues an order for the day to all ranks of reinforced 76th Infantry Division; see attachment 51.

16 December 1942. Weather: clear –15°C (5°F). Toward 0800 hours, the enemy, with about 200 soldiers from the Antonova ravine, probes the forward edge of Grenadier Regiment 178's battle area. The enemy approaches to within 200 meters, and there, protected by snow walls, digs in. The limited artillery fire from 1st Company, Artillery Regiment 176, is unable to drive him away. There is only a small amount of ammunition available.

Enemy artillery and mortar fire across practically the entire divisional front.

In the evening a deserter states that on 17 December the Russians will attack with tanks and infantry after a preparatory artillery bombardment.

17 December 1942. Weather: clear –20°C (–4°F).

From 0530 hours onward enemy artillery fire on the sector of 2nd Battalion, Grenadier Regiment 178.

At 0645 hours 2 heavy enemy tanks head out of the Antonova ravine in the direction of 2nd Battalion. Additional tanks follow at greater distances until 6 are formed up in front of the forward edge of the battalion's main line. Fourteenth Company, Grenadier Regiment 178, deals with 2 tanks (a T-34 and a KV-Mk-1) and renders another 3 immobile. Five new tanks appear for those that have been taken out and with direct hits knock out both 5-cm-caliber antitank guns and a captured 4.5-cm gun.

Further antitank defense was not available. Because of the proximity of our own forward edge of the battle area, our own artillery cannot open fire. The tanks remain about 100 meters in front of the forward edge of the battle area in a small depression untouched by armor-piercing weapons. The tanks open effective fire on the most forward of the strongpoints on the forward edge of the battle area. At 0730 hours the tanks return to the Antonova ravine and soon come back with infantry on board and others following behind. Despite effective artillery fire they manage, accompanied by infantry, to penetrate the positions and to capture the 5 most forward dugouts of 6th Company, Grenadier Regiment 178, deployed on the left, and 3 dugouts of 5th Company, deployed on the right. The enemy occupies the captured strongpoints and brings up new forces. Some of the tanks head back to the ravine and support their infantry's battle from cover. Four enemy tanks remain at the forward edge of the battle area and add further heavy losses to 5th and 6th Companies. At 0900 hours an assault battery with its own onboard reserve company of the division attached to the regiment made ready to launch a flank attack against the tanks in the event of any further penetration. Owing to the flat, coverless terrain, the counterattack with the assault guns of the mounted reserve company and the reserve company of 2nd Battalion, Grenadier Regiment 178, is planned for 1500 hours (after the onset of darkness). However, toward 1230 hours, as there are reports of further losses from the forward companies of 2nd Battalion, the divisional commander orders that the assault guns immediately go into action. Swinging round from the far left, the guns attack the enemy tanks and at a range of 1,200 meters shoot up 3 tanks, rendering them immobile. The remaining tanks head off in the direction of the enemy and disappear in the Antonova ravine. The assault guns now turn around, without having driven the enemy infantry out of the forward edge of the battle area, and return to their start positions as well. A further operation came to nothing for a lack of fuel.

At 1700 hours a counterattack, accompanied by 2 other assault guns that have been allocated by the division, is conducted by the company command post of 6th Company, Grenadier Regiment 178, against the ensconced enemy infantry. The attack is completely successful. All the strongpoints of 5th and 6th Companies are recaptured, and at 1900 hours the forward edge of the battle line is once again completely under the control of 2nd Battalion, Grenadier Regiment 178.

During the last operation there was a heavy enemy bombardment by artillery, antitank weapons, and infantry weapons throughout the entire sector of Grenadier Regiment 178.

In the night, divisional and regimental engineers as well as construction troops (in all a total of 300 men) are deployed in order to construct a second line some 400 meters behind the current forward edge of the battle area, which the forward companies of 2nd Battalion, Grenadier Regiment 178, are to occupy. At the same time the minefields in front of 2nd Battalion's sector are relaid; see attachment 11.

On the position of Fusilier Regiment's right neighbor (113th Infantry Division), the enemy penetrates the line in company strength. The enemy is ejected in a counterattack.

18 December 1942. Weather: clear, –15°C (5°F). In the night superior enemy forces captured the strongpoint at the junction on the main road (right flank of 6th Company, Grenadier Regiment 178) and so once again have penetrated our forward line. An immediate counterattack ensues; it results in heavy losses and is unsuccessful.

In the period before midday the enemy also moves up close to another position on our forward line and toward midday penetrates other strongpoints of 5th Company, Grenadier Regiment 178, from which he is immediately ejected in counterattacks.

In the sector of 1st Battalion, Grenadier Regiment 178, there is plenty of artillery, antitank, and mortar harassing fire throughout the day. Some 400 meters in front of our main line the enemy builds snow walls, behind which he digs in.

Toward 1600 hours a counterattack conducted by 2 assault guns on the lost strongpoint at the junction fails with heavy losses as a result of the heavy enemy defense. One assault gun is immobilized by an antitank shell, and the other gun's feed mechanism is hit by a shell splinter. Leutnant Merz (commander 6th Company, Grenadier Regiment 178) is killed in action.

Throughout the entire evening there is heavy small-arms fire in the sector of 2nd Battalion, Grenadier Regiment 178.

Engineer and construction troops continue work on the new forward line designated for 2nd Battalion, Grenadier Regiment 178.

Two 7.62-cm antitank guns are pulled out of Fusilier Regiment 230's sector in order to be deployed in the defensive depth of Grenadier Regiment 178.

19 *December* 1942. Weather: clear and frosty, –10°C (14°F). Heavy enemy attack on the neighboring left division (44th Infantry Division) and to the left.

In the division's sector, generally quiet.

In the sector of 2nd Battalion, Grenadier Regiment 178, the forward line of the battle area is pulled back by about 300 meters to the right and left of the junction and now forms an open bend facing the northwest (to the junction), which is held by 2 of the strongpoints of 6th Company farthest to the right. Seventh Company is also deployed in the forward line. The regiment's engineer platoon becomes the battalion's reserve. The regiment's cycle platoon had already been deployed the day before in the sector of 2nd Battalion.

Hauptmann Löser reports:

> Major Lindow, the regimental commander of Fusilier Regiment 230, informs me that Manstein's army is expected in the next few days and that sometime around Christmas 2 of its divisions are due to attack across our divisional sector in the direction of the Don, in cooperation with forces expected from the southwest from the other side of the Don (in the area of the Great Don Bend), in order to encircle the besieging Russian armies. Infantry reconnaissance of the starting positions has already been carried

> out. Artillery positions for support of the breakthrough are ready. The operation is being kept top secret. (According to later news the leading columns of Manstein's army were at this time about 30 kilometers [19 miles] to the south of the southern edge of Fortress Stalingrad. Shortly afterward Manstein's army was deployed elsewhere because of the failure of the Italians, and with that the fate of Stalingrad was decided.)

The VIII Army Corps quartermaster reports that the bread supply sufficient for a daily ration of 200 grams (7 ounces) up to 23 December 1942 is secure.

20 December 1942. Weather as yesterday. At 0200 hours Hauptmann Gröning assumes command of 2nd Battalion, Grenadier Regiment 178.

At 0300 hours the command post of Grenadier Regiment 178 receives a report that at around midnight the enemy captured the left dugout of the two on the right in the old forward line of the 2nd Battalion, which was still held. A counterattack against this dugout launched at 0713 hours with artillery and infantry weapons breaks down under enemy fixed-line and defensive fire, with heavy losses.

In the sector of Grenadier Regiment 178, following on from the operation launched before midday, there is heavy enemy harassing fire from artillery and small arms.

Quieter throughout the day. Toward evening heavier enemy small-arms fire.

The troops, so long as they remain in position, including the battalion command post, receive additional rations consisting of the following: 1 bar of chocolate and 1 tin of mixed conserves per man to last for 3 days. These supplements are issued until 6 January 1943. After this was discontinued, an extra ration of 100 grams (3.5 ounces) of bread was issued so that the daily bread ration then amounted to 300 grams (10.5 ounces).

First Battalion, Fusilier Regiment 230 (see 8 December 1942), takes up an assembly point as corps reserve on an estate near Dmitrievka (sector of 44th Infantry Division).

Hauptmann Löser reports:

> In addition, small additional ration supplements are issued to battalion commanders for junior leaders and particularly weak, nevertheless valuable men from Fusilier Regiment 230 in order to maintain the most

valuable equipment as long as possible. Glucose and vitamin tablets are issued to all ranks.

21 *December* 1942. Weather: foggy, −2°C (28°F), snow during the night. Nothing significant to report. Concerning the work of the bakery company, Leutnant May reports the following:

After the bakery company had been transferred to the steppe ravines south of Bol'shaia Rossoshka, work was immediately started on setting up a new bakery. Within two days this was ready to start. Afterward accommodations, vehicle cover, and so on were built by the off-duty men as well as by the 40-strong prisoner-of-war platoon. Wood to run the bakery and wood for construction of the accommodations was brought in from Stalingrad south. Initially this was done with the bakery's own trucks and later with convoy vehicles until the bakery was set up.

At the start of the encirclement the rations branch of the division had food for 3 weeks' full issue. This strong reserve had been ordered bearing in mind the transport difficulties of the autumn mud and the winter. As the bulk of the divisions assembled in the northwest of the Kessel had lost their rations supplies and dumps, they had to be fed from the reserves of our divisions. The bakery company worked at a reduced level for the time being until the middle of December, then with further interruptions up to 21 December or 22 December 1942. Then production ceased for good since the last reserves of flour had been consumed, and pre-prepared bread was brought in by air. The men were then occupied with looking after the aircraft and equipment, improving the accommodations, and guard duty. As a consequence of the difficulties arising from the food-supply situation, the prisoners of war were soon handed over, with the exception of a small remnant, which was required to prepare dough, since as a result of the lack of fuel there was insufficient electricity to power the bread machines.

22 *December* 1942. Weather: clear, light snowfall. Nothing significant to report.

Leutnant May reports:

Since the units are well supplied with Wehrmacht radio receivers, German news broadcasts can be regularly received. The storage batteries are charged up by means of a light truck engine driven by a wind motor.

23 *December* 1942. Weather: windy, –5°C (15°F), overcast, light snowfall. The units make preparations for Christmas. There are still a few army goods available (toothpaste, toothbrushes, skin cream) which are to be distributed. Cakes are to be baked from the last of the flour.

24 *December* 1942. Weather, snow, windy, –20°C (–4°F). Third Battalion, Grenadier Regiment 203, organizes small-scale Christmas celebrations in the battalion bunker in small groups. An assistant priest (name unknown) says a few words to the men. He also goes to the men deployed in the forward positions.

The cycle section, which has not been deployed as corps reserve, reports having a Christmas celebration in which the Catholic priest of the division, Father Kayser, holds a Christmas church service.

25 *December* 1942. Weather: overcast, heavy frost, –20°C (–4°F). Against expectations the Russians are very quiet.

Headquarters veterinarian Dr Herbert reports: Today a holiday roast, braised roast beef, at Headquarters Company, Grenadier Regiment 203.

26 *December* 1942. Weather: clearer, otherwise as yesterday. The enemy continues to remain quiet.

Headquarters veterinarian Dr. Herbert reports: beef goulash with macaroni at Headquarters Company, Grenadier Regiment 203. It goes to show that a company that thinks ahead, is frugal even in the worst of times, and takes care to secure supplies can, even here under the conditions obtaining in the Kessel, conjure up surprises.

27 *December* 1942. Weather as yesterday. Nothing significant to report. At the request of the divisions, officers from Army Group Don are flown into the Kessel from the Führer's reserve; see attachment 53.

28 *December* 1942. Weather: thawed snow, temperature around freezing.

Major von Rochow, the commander of Cycle Section 176, reports:

Seventy-sixth Infantry Division had to take over the right battalion sector of the neighboring left division (44th Infantry Division). The cycle section is to be attached to this sector. In the evening it goes into the position again. The combat strength of the section amounts to about 150 men. It is to be deployed to the right of the squadron of Olshausen (heavy squadron and cycle company) and to the left of the mounted squadron. The combat-group platoon went into a position behind the left wing. A mixed antitank platoon is also to be attached.

The position was extremely unsatisfactory as it ran across a wide-open plain without any cover and was completely observed by the enemy. There was one heated dugout per squadron, and the bulk of the men were located in holes in the ground covered with groundsheets. Throughout daylight no man can show himself, since enemy snipers are alert. There are continual losses. Individual posts that are lost can always be recaptured in counterattacks. The position remained firmly in our hands right up to 10 January 1943.

Work is undertaken with all available resources on the construction of additional dugouts. After a few days the section command post is transferred to a channel running out of a ravine behind the right wing of the sector in order to facilitate control of the battle. At the end of December some 40 men from the artillery supply services are attached to the section as reinforcements, who, however, must be trained behind the position. At the beginning of January 1943 Hauptmann Blume and Oberleutnant Helmuth (Tank Destroyer Section 176) are attached to the section.

In this sector Cycle Section 176 was under the command of Grenadier Regiment 203; see also attachment 11.

29 December 1942. Weather as the day before. The strength of the supply troops must be reported to VIII Army Corps. Seventy-sixth Infantry Division submits the following details [Table 4.12].

Weapons: 35 machine guns (1913), 4 Russian machine guns, 870 rifles, and 150 pistols.

Supply troops in various locations:

1. Two platoons of the workshop company in Liabishchev
2. Command appointments: Tussow and Field Telephone 3 to Squadron 78, in the region of Chernyshchov (registration of captured equipment)

3. Butchery company: *sovkhoz* at Krasnyi skotovod
4. Horse recovery areas: Kalivatal and Zymlianskaia

The following divisions are part of VIII Army Corps: 376th Infantry Division, 113th Infantry Division, 76th Infantry Division, and 44th Infantry Division. [Table 4.13 shows the allocation of bread in VIII Army Corps from September through December 1942.]

In order to deal with the precarious situation regarding wood supplies, the necessary measures are taken by the Quartermaster's Section of VIII Army Corps; see attachment 52.

Dr. Kaller (junior doctor) reports: 1st Battalion, Fusilier Regiment 230, is taken by truck from Dmitrievka to a penetration point on the position of 44th Infantry Division in the area of Kazachii Hill (north of Dmitrievka). Officer posts in the battalion are:

Commander Hauptmann Müller
Adjutant First Leutnant Schlegel
Battalion medical officer Dr. Kaller
1st Company commander [no name cited]
2nd Company commander Oberleutnant Bahrding
3rd Company commander Leutnant auf der Heide
4th Company commander Oberleutnant Matschke

Battalion strength amounts to about 250 men, mainly soldiers from supply columns, from artillery and the like. The battalion attacks Kazachii Hill four times without being able to capture the hill. The Russians have a massive su-

Table 4.12 *Supply Personnel, 76th Infantry Division, 29 December 1942*

Arm of Service	Officers	Officials	NCOs	Soldiers	Total
Divisional supply and convoys	23	2	97	306	428
Administrative	2	9	22	103	136
Medical	14	8	59	271	352
Veterinary	3	1	22	102	128
Workshop platoon	0	1	1	30	32
Field post office	0	14	0	0	14
Total	42	35	201	812	1,090

Table 4.13 *Allocation of Bread in VIII Army Corps, 3 September–29 December 1942*

Period	Allocation
3 Sept.–21 Sept.	750 grams (26 ounces)
22 Sept.–22 Oct.	600 grams (21 ounces)
23 Oct.–7 Dec.	300 grams (10.5 ounces)
8 Dec.–29 Dec.	200 grams (7 ounces)

periority in artillery and have occupied the hill with light and heavy mortars and Stalin organs (rocket launchers). There is a huge shortage of ammunition in 44th Infantry Division. Signals communications are extremely inadequate. The battalion remains about 300 meters (snow holes) in front of the Russians but manages to hold these positions until the day it is relieved (7 January 1943).

The battalion returned to 76th Infantry Division in Malaia Rossoshka. It was about 40 men strong with 2 officers (Hauptmann Müller and Oberleutnant Schlegel, plus the battalion medical officer). In addition to the combat losses, casualties had occurred from frostbite and illnesses (stomach complaints and fevers).

30 December 1942. Weather as the day before.

In the last days of the old year there were no significant events. There is a constant stream of losses arising from illness, frostbite, and wounds.

31 December 1942. Weather: cloudy, temperature below 0°C (32°F).

Heavy artillery fire from the Russians at 2200 hours. Our artillery replies. At 2400 hours there is quiet.

Further combing of the supply troops. Per company there remains: 1 *Hauptfeldwebel*, 1 clerk, 1 farrier, 1 chief accountant, 1 NCO responsible for weapons and equipment, 2 drivers, and, in addition, the Russian auxiliaries. All the NCOs and soldiers made available were handed over to the front line. Each company has some 12 to 15 Russian auxiliaries (*Hilfswillige*). Only a handful of them desert so as to mix in with the civilian population in the ruins of Stalingrad.

Hauptmann Löser reports:

> On the basis of an Army order the 3 regiments as well as the 3 artillery sections of each division are to be disbanded and to be used to replenish

the other units of the division. Moreover, supply services and artillery units are to be once again thoroughly combed. Deadline for completion of all these measures is 1 January 1943. The regimental headquarters and headquarter companies of Fusilier Regiment 230 are to be incorporated into 3rd Battalion, Fusilier Regiment 230, together with the supply services and troops of 13th and 14th Companies, Fusilier Regiment 230, as infantry reinforcements. Tactically, and regarding provision of technical support, 3rd Battalion, Grenadier Regiment 230, is to be subordinated to Grenadier Regiment 178 under the designation "3rd Fusilier Battalion 230." Formerly regimental signals officer, Oberleutnant Holl moves to Grenadier Regiment 178 as liaison officer and assistant adjutant. Combat platoons of 13th and 14th Companies are likewise to be subordinated to 13th and 14th Companies of Grenadier Regiment 178. Tactically, however, they remain in the same subordinate and operational relationship with 3rd Fusilier Battalion.

Formerly commander of Fusilier Regiment 230, Oberstleutnant Hering, with his regimental command staff, takes over "Group Hering," a formation created from the division's artillery and supply troops with a strength of about 300–400 men. After brief training this formation was subordinated to 44th Infantry Division (on 15 or 16 January 1943, as far as I recall, Oberstleutnant Hering was relieved of this duty and for a short period before he was wounded was entrusted with other command tasks by division. The regimental adjutant Oberleutnant Tessmar was with him). Cycle Section 176 was tactically subordinated to Grenadier Regiment 203.

In the last days of December the already noted infantry reinforcements are allocated to 3rd Fusilier Battalion 230. Insofar as they are not infantry trained, they are to be trained by a battalion training team in dugouts behind the right wing of the sector (earlier the area of 1st Battalion, Fusilier Regiment 230) and sent to the companies when ready. After replenishment the strength of the companies is more or less as follows:

9th Company: 60 men
10th Company: 50 men
11th Company: 45 men
12th Company: 55 men

Leutnant May reports:

On 31 December 1942 the order to disband the supply troops arrived. In each unit there remained only a small residual squad made up from ill or older men who tended and guarded the equipment. The rations administration was transferred from the region of Baburkin to the accommodations of the bakery company in order to get closer to the airfield at Pitomnik on which the supply transports arrived. Some of the vehicles of the bakery company along with their drivers were attached to the rations administration for transport tasks. Up to then the vehicle convoys had been deployed to fetch wood from Stalingrad for the combat troops. However, with their handful of weakened horses, they had been unable for some time to accomplish this task. Incidentally, the men cleared snow from the streets and other places.

On 1 January 1943 the supply troops, depending on level of training, were allocated to 3 training companies. Any men with infantry training were immediately sent to make up the numbers of the fighting troops. Two of these training companies were accommodated in the former accommodations of the rations administration, the butcher company, and two convoy companies east of Baburkin and exercised in this terrain. Leutnant Gold from divisional supply command was the company commander of one training company; the other was commanded by Oberleutnant Fitzner with Leutnant Schopf, both of whom were likewise from the divisional supply command. At the same location were also two retraining companies for artillery soldiers in whose training participated, among others, Oberleutnant von Manthey. I can no longer recall the other names. Control of the training was exercised by Oberstleutnant Heering [sic]. The third training company of supply troops found itself as the emergency company at Malaia Rossoshka. Company commander was Oberleutnant Hucke from the 2nd Combat Vehicle Platoon and myself as company officer. Some of these training units were already deployed on 5–7 January 1943 in order to replenish the front. I do not know what became of them.

1 January–23 January 1943

1 January 1943. Weather: overcast, mild, temperatures around freezing. Leutnant Hannig reports no significant events on the front.

Start of training of the soldiers from the supply services in the area of the battalion command post. The battalion has received 6 soldiers as replacements from the artillery supply service.

Leutnant Brieger, 9th Company, Artillery Regiment 176, reports that Artillery Regiment 176 is disbanded. There are 3 batteries from the 1st Section and the whole 3rd Section. The men of 3rd Battery and Headquarters Battery of the 3rd Section are deployed as infantry. The men of 7th, 8th, and 9th Batteries go to 1st Section. Artillery Regiment 176 is from now on formed as follows:

1st Section with 1st, 2nd, 7th, 8th, and 9th Batteries
2nd Section with 4th, 5th, and 6th Batteries
4th Section with 10th, 11th, and 12th Batteries

Hauptmann Löser reports that New Year's Eve was spent in the same old way.

The disbandment of Fusilier Regiment 230 is complete. Although nearly all the remnants of the regiment have been absorbed in 3rd Battalion under their earlier proud designation, this move is nevertheless very painful for all the old members of the regiment when they recall the proud past of the regiment since the start of the war.

2 January 1943. Weather: thawing, 2° to 3°C (36° to 37°F). In accordance with the special authorization of 6th Army Headquarters (Paulus promotions), the following are promoted:

To Generalleutnant: Generalmajor Rodenburg, commander of 76th Infantry Division, effective from 1 December 1942
To Oberstleutnant: Major von Spangenberg, commander of Grenadier Regiment 203, effective from 1 December 1942; Major Schön, commander of Grenadier Regiment 178, effective from 1 December 1942
To Hauptmann: Oberleutnant Busse, Headquarters, Grenadier Regiment 230, effective from 1 December 1942; Oberleutnant Bente, 9th Company, Grenadier Regiment 230, effective from 1 December 1942; Oberleutnant Kockzius, O2 Headquarters, 76th Infantry Division, effective from 1 December 1942; Oberleutnant Münchow, Grenadier Regiment 178, effective from 1 December 1942; Oberleutnant Schäfers, 13th Company, Grenadier Regiment 203, effective from 1 January 1943; Oberleutnant Loth, Grenadier Regiment 203, effective from 1 January

1943; Oberleutnant Langewiesche, Artillery Regiment 176, effective from 1 January 1943; Oberleutnant Nowotne, Fusilier Regiment 230, effective from 1 January 1943; Oberleutnant Müller, Signals 176, effective from 1 January 1943; Oberleutnant Krause, Signals 176, effective from 1 January 1943

To Oberleutnant: Leutnant Loeper, Fusilier Regiment 230, effective from 1 December 1943 [sic]; Leutnant Kandt, Fusilier Regiment 230, effective from 1 December 1943 [sic]; Leutnant Pommering, 1st Company, Engineer Battalion 176, effective from 1 December 1942; Leutnant Arnold, 2nd Company, Engineer Battalion 176, effective from 1 December 1942; Leutnant Wolff, 5th Company, Artillery Regiment 176, effective from 1 December 1942; Leutnant Textor, 3rd Company, Grenadier Regiment 203, effective from 1 December 1942; Leutnant Giesel, 12th Company, Fusilier Regiment 230, effective from 1 December 1942

To Leutnant: Feldwebel Grapert, Grenadier Regiment 178, effective from 1 January 1943

3 January 1943. Weather: frost, –10°C (14°F). Small-scale Russian penetration on the position of Grenadier Regiment 203 is removed by a counterattack at last light.

Three assault guns at the regimental command post of Grenadier Regiment 203 are still operational.

Light antiaircraft (2-cm) guns have been deployed on the height with the battalion command post of 3rd Battalion, Grenadier Regiment 203, for use against infantry targets.

Hauptmann Löser reports that there are no significant events. From 30 of the attached artillery soldiers of 3rd Section, Artillery Regiment 176, a training platoon is formed, led by experienced infantry junior leaders.

4 January 1943. Weather: sunny, cold, –8°C (18°F). No significant events. At the request of the division, officers from the Army Group Reserve are flown into the Kessel. Leutnant Reinbeck, coming from Rostov via Pitomnik on 28 December 1942, reports to divisional headquarters and takes over command of 1st Quick-Reaction Company, Grenadier Regiment 203, which is deployed on the left wing of the division on the boundary with 44th Infantry Division; see attachment 53. Leader of 2nd Quick-Reaction Company, Grenadier Regiment 203, is Leutnant Mansfeld; after his death, Leutnant Leuschner.

5 January 1943. Weather: very cold, storm-force east wind, –25°C (–13°F) Nothing significant to report. Concerning the setting up and training of further training, retraining, and quick-reaction companies, see 31 December 1942.

6 January 1943. Weather: overcast, north wind, –10°C (14°F).

Leutnant Hannig of 3rd Battalion, Grenadier Regiment 203, reports: rations getting worse; no more extra chocolate. At the regimental command post of Grenadier Regiment 203, 2 training platoons have been formed, 1 for each battalion. They are recruited from the NCOs and soldiers of the disbanded Signals Section 176, an observation section, convoys from the divisional supply command, and the remnants of the battalion in waiting 76/10.

These training platoons exist in addition to the training and retraining platoons formed by the division.

7 January 1943. Weather: snow, –5°C (23°F). Headquarters veterinarian Dr. Herbert (Grenadier Regiment 230) reports: "At 0500 hours there was an enemy penetration of 44th Infantry Division at a width of 1½ kilometers (.9 mile). In the period from 1400 to 1500 hours the enemy penetration was cleared with the help of assault guns and the reserves of 5th Company, Grenadier Regiment 203."

8 January 1943. Weather: heavy snowfall, –5°C (23°F). Nothing significant to report.

Hauptmann Löser reports:

> During this period, the precise date escapes me, the neighbouring sector of 1st Battalion, Grenadier Regiment 178, is taken over by Fusilier Battalion 230. Grenadier Regiment 178 is withdrawn and had to be placed at the disposal of 44th Infantry Division as a consequence of its severe battles. Since 11th Company of Fusilier Battalion 230 has to be allocated to the Cycle Section on the same day, the new sector that is to be taken over has to be handed over to a company (Company Koglin) that has been formed from the battalion's training platoon and 1 platoon from each of the battalion's remaining companies. Eleventh Company's sector will be jointly taken over by 9th and 10th Companies.

9 January 1943. Weather: cloudy, –5°C (23°F). Leutnant Hannig reports: "A resupply JU-52 crashes in the sector of 3rd Battalion, Grenadier Regiment 203. Three occupants are dead."

Otherwise nothing significant to report.

10 January 1943. Weather: cloudy, then clearing, –10°C (14°F). Major von Rochow, Cycle Section 176, reports:

> At first light most heavy Russian artillery and mortar fire, particularly on the left neighboring divisions (44th and 371st Infantry Divisions). The cycle section likewise comes under fire. The sector of the mounted squadron is totally shot to pieces, with heavy losses. Of this squadron only Oberwachtmeister Wonde with 6 men remained. The position was lost to the enemy, since there were also deep penetrations on the positions of the left neighbor. A counterattack with assault batteries and the regimental reserves of Grenadier Regiment 203 had some success. Nevertheless, the position could not be held because of the sheer weight of enemy. The combat group's platoon and the subordinated antitank platoon were totally shot up. All the officers right up to the commander and adjutant are killed. Divisional reserves arrive in order to close off the deep Russian penetration: the remnants of a construction section with about 120 men, about 80 men from the supply units, elements from the construction battalions, elements of an assault-gun battery, and the final remnants of a small combat group and engineer company. With these forces the ravine terrain on both sides of the section's command post is occupied. Further Russian attacks were foiled with these forces. The section has sustained heavy losses from the enemy artillery bombardment, from its own counterattack, and from frostbite, such that up to 15 January 1943 only a handful of men remained.

Leutnant Hannig, 3rd Battalion, Grenadier Regiment 203, reports:

> Deployment of the training platoons from the regimental command post and the remnants of the engineer and mounted platoons on the regiment's left flank (cycle section). None of these men is ever seen again in the regiment. In front of Grenadier Regiment 230 there is increased enemy activity. Some tanks are seen, but there is no attack. Enemy attempts to approach were broken up by our own artillery.

Hauptmann Löser reports:

Deployed in the threatened flank of Grenadier Regiment 203, 11th Company is heavily shot up. The commander, Leutnant Burkheiser, is severely wounded. The company is taken over by Oberfeldwebel Zickel.

Hauptmann von Damm reports:

The Russians put down 1 hour of rolling barrage in hitherto unprecedented volume on the left neighboring division (44th Infantry Division).

Obergefreiter Petznick, 5 Company, Artillery Regiment 176, reports:

On 10 January 1943 the Russians, in unheard-of numbers, accompanied by several hours of rolling fire from guns of all calibers, but mainly from heavy-battery guns, as well as the deployment of tanks, attacked west of the fire position of 44th Infantry Division and are said to have penetrated the line in several places. During this time there occurred in the battery position a regrettable incident. In a bunker next to the captured guns two boxes of charges ignited and the whole bunker crew burned to death. Those who perished were attached soldiers (among them Stabswachtmeister Römer) and Leuenberg, a member of the battery. At this time the unit's fire position consisted of 7 guns: 3 light field howitzers 18 and 2 French and 2 English captured guns. The position was constantly exposed to heavy bombardment.

By day and night the Russians are increasing their air activity (the so-called sewing machines). The enemy drops masses of leaflets that call upon the troops to desert and to surrender.[29]

For Leutnant Reinbeck's comments, see attachment 53.

11 January 1943. Weather: overcast, –5°C (23°F). Strong north wind in the evening. Leutnant Hannig, 3rd Battalion, Grenadier Regiment 203, reports: "Hauptmann Gerstenberg is ill and is flown out from Pitomnik on 12 January 1943. Hauptmann Bente assumes command of the battalion. Two Russian tanks are knocked on the position of the cycle section."

First Quick-Reaction Company, Grenadier Regiment 203, receives the order to close gaps in the regiment's left flank with 44th Infantry Division; see attachment 53.

12 *January 1943*. Weather: strong north wind, –15° to –20°C (5° to –4°F), drifting snow, clearing up at midday.

Leutnant Hannig reports: "9th Company, Grenadier Regiment 203, is moved to 1st Battalion since enemy attacks are expected here. Still quiet in 3rd Battalion, Grenadier Regiment 203. Enemy artillery and mortar fire."

Leutnant Mansfeld, commander of 2nd Quick-Reaction Company, Grenadier Regiment 203, was killed in the evening during an operation on the regiment's left flank. Stand to is ordered for the entire regimental sector of Grenadier Regiment 203.

An attack by 1st Quick-Reaction Company, Grenadier Regiment 203 (division's left wing), on spot height 117.5; see attachment 53.

13 *January 1943*. Weather as the day before.

Increasing enemy mortar bombardment in the sector of Grenadier Regiment 203.

Feldwebel Bohnen, 14th Company, Grenadier Regiment 203, reports: "All guns and vehicles—with the exception of 1 vehicle and gun—are lost. Company is deployed tactically as infantry."

Hauptmann Löser reports:

> In a commanders' conference at the command post of 2nd Battalion, Grenadier Regiment 178, the warning order for the withdrawal to the new forward edge of the battle area is issued. In the night of 14 January 1943 ammunition reserves, boards, digging tools, and trench stoves are already being taken to the battalion command post.

Leutnant May reports:

> At this moment in time—13 January 1943—the rearward movement of the west Kessel front only really got going. The work in the rear did not seem to be under any threat. Among my colleagues at this time one still counted on the likelihood of further resistance leading to some kind of relief operation that, it was hoped, would occur in March. In our circle, which, after all, had no overview of the true nature of the situation, this appraisal of the options available to the enemy stemmed from the fact that in the

area occupied by the Russians that could be observed by us no really dangerous operations had been undertaken, and that the front sectors, with the exception of insignificant penetrations, had remained stable since the moment of the encirclement. Also, until now, the Russian air force had had no real successes with which we were familiar, although the ravines, everywhere packed full of vehicles, offered superb targets.

14 *January* 1943. Weather: clear, –10°C (14°F). In the night of 13–14 January 1943, 6th and 7th Batteries, Artillery Regiment 176, under the command of Hauptmann von Damm, are withdrawn from the divisional sector and handed over to 44th Infantry Division. The batteries each have 3 guns. The change of positions takes place with antiaircraft prime mover vehicles.

Leutnant Hannig, 3rd Battalion, Grenadier Regiment 203, reports:

> In the evening there is an adjutants' conference at the regimental command post. The preliminary order for the move to the forward edge of the battle area is issued. The new line is to run more or less in the line from the south edge of the Kotluban gully—point 1.8, high line 100—to the west edge of Vlassovka. The regimental command post is due to move into the old divisional command post. All reserves of ammunition, trench stoves, digging tools, and boards, etc., are to be taken to the old regimental command post, from where they shall be transported further in vehicles. The regiment has 100 liters (26 gallons) of fuel at its disposal for the move. On the evening of 14 January 1943, 6th and 7th Batteries, Artillery Regiment 176, execute another change of position toward the west edge of Malaia Rossoshka.

15 *January* 1943. Weather: clear, –20°C (–4°F).

Hauptmann von Damm (commander of 2nd Battalion, Artillery Regiment 176) reports as follows: "Deep Russian penetration of 44th Infantry Division. Since its left flank is seriously threatened, 76th Infantry Division must now change its position."

Leutnant Hannig, 3rd Battalion, Grenadier Regiment 203, reports:

> The relief order has not arrived. New adjutants' discussion at regiment. The intended main defensive line cannot be occupied since the Russians in the southwest near the 44th Infantry Division and to the left have penetrated too deeply. New main defensive line approximately 1 kilometer

(.6 mile) eastward of Bol'shaia Rossoshchka. The division's right and left flanks are strongly exposed (see the diagram, attachment 3). In order to bring about a withdrawal, the original, main defensive line should be held as a switch line by rearguard troops with a completed relief within 24 hours.

Major von Rochow, commander of Cycle Section 176, reports:

Redeployment of the main defensive line during the night of 15–16 January 1943 a few kilometers southeast from Bol'shaia Rossoshka. Horses and fuel for towing vehicles no longer available so that all the supply vehicles, the guns, and certain heavy weapons must be destroyed.

Hauptmann Löser reports:

The planned main defensive line—some 3 kilometers (1.9 miles) to the east of the old one—is being determined on the ground between the battery commanders and the regimental adjutant of Grenadier Regiment 178 and Grenadier Regiment 203. In the afternoon the order arrives to leave the former main defensive line and to move to the new main defensive line east of Bol'shaia Rossoshchka (see map, attachment 3). In the planned temporary main defensive line the rearguard of each battalion, a company (Battalion 230 has designated 9th Company) is to remain during 16 January.

With the onset of darkness, ammunition and the battalion's heavy weapons are to be removed in two trucks. Light-infantry guns have to be towed by teams of men. The withdrawal of the bulk of Battalion 230 ensues at 2000 hours without any interference from the enemy. So begins an exceptionally demanding night march. As a consequence of the poor food, the men are utterly exhausted and have to drag nearly all the ammunition and weapons. Each company has two small sledges, which barely manage to move through the deep snow and in the end have to be unloaded. Officers, NCOs, and men drag each other along, most supporting one another, as they head on. Twenty men of the battalion alone collapse from exhaustion and either die immediately or after they have been pulled along for about a kilometer and then left. That more men did not have to be left is entirely due to the battalion's incredible comradeship. In the battalion's supply area there is a short pause. The battalion commander orders all available iron rations to be handed out to the men. For the last time the field kitchens prepare some hot food, and then the entire cooking equipment, for which there is no transport at all, is destroyed.

16 *January* 1943. Weather: clear, sunny, –30°C (–22°F).
Leutnant Brieger, Artillery Regiment 176, reports:

During the night of 15–16 January 1943 there is a change of position to the new forward edge of the battle area east of Bol'shaia Rossoshka. Sixth and 7th Batteries, with two guns apiece firing at point-blank range, run out of ammunition. The guns are destroyed. The Russians are about 600 meters in front.

Early on 16 January 1942 Hauptmann Löser's battalion (Fusilier Regiment 230) will be encircled in Bol'shaia Rossoshka. The battalion is to hold its position until the evening of 17 January 1943, when it is to break through under its own strength to the division.

See Hauptmann Löser's report from 16 and 17 January 1943.
Leutnant Hannig, 3rd Battalion, Grenadier Regiment 203, reports:

At 0100 hours the move out of the old forward edge of the battle area begins. There are great difficulties with the withdrawal as a result of the men's being exhausted. Only two small sledges per company are available. Only two light-infantry guns remain in the regiment. In the withdrawal to the new forward edge of the battle area, the cohesion of the companies and battalion is lost. The men reach Bol'shaia Rossoshka only in small groups. The switch position is not occupied. Getting on for 0600 hours, Feldwebel Böhm finds himself here alone. Toward 1400 hours the Russians in vehicles are already southwest of Bol'shaia Rossoshka. The withdrawal route has all the signs of a hasty retreat: assault guns, antitank guns of all calibers, 88-millimeter (mm) antiaircraft guns, field kitchens, and vehicles have to be left where they are destroyed, since there is no fuel left.

On 16 January 1943 the first, much bigger Russian attack operations against 76th Infantry Division start, after the earlier attacks against the neighboring 44th Infantry Division on the left had already begun.

The formation of the division in the new forward edge of the battle area is as follows:

Aligned right with 113th Infantry Division is Grenadier Regiment 178 with two battalions and later Hauptmann Löser's battalion (230); left Grenadier Regiment 203 with 1st and 3rd Battalions and the Cycle Section on the left wing as reserve and under the command of Grenadier Regiment 230.

Left neighboring division is 44th Infantry Division. The following are subordinated to it:

1. Hauptmann Müller's battalion (the remnants of the earlier 1st Battalion, 230; see 29 December 1942)
2. Oberleutnant von Blomberg's battalion (the remnants of the disbanded 3rd Battalion, Grenadier Regiment 178, former supply train drivers, artillery men, and the like)

According to statements from the cycle section, Müller's battalion has not found the boundary with the heavily dispersed 44th Infantry Division.

Battalion von Blomberg, which has the right boundary with Grenadier Regiment 203, reported that there no longer exists any contact with Battalion Müller. The division is supposed to have heard no more from this battalion.

From the division's left wing, heavy Russian movement in a southeasterly direction is observed.

The airfield at Pitomnik had to be abandoned.

There was no further opportunity of bringing back the bulk of the wounded from the division's main casualty clearing station in the night of 15–16 January. They had to be left behind. The Catholic priest, Father Kayser, volunteered to remain with them.[30] See attachment 53.

Feldwebel Bohnen, 14th Company, Grenadier Regiment 203, reports: "When withdrawing the last gun, it had to be totally destroyed as a result of a hit. The last vehicle with small-arms ammunition and hand grenades was taken to Bol'shaia Rossoshka."

Obergefreiter Petznick, 5th Company, Artillery Regiment 176, reports about the withdrawal to the new main forward edge of the battle line:

> Around the middle of January the Russian ground attacks were launched with such violence and also with huge air support and by day and night that the recapture of the positions on the western edge of the Kessel as a result of deep enemy penetrations became inevitable. In view of this, all

the battalion's guns had to be destroyed, on the one hand because the enemy pushed forward with surprising speed and force and on the other hand because there were no prime movers with fuel available—we had been without horses for a long time. At this time all soldiers in the battalion were in an infantry role. All the other regiment's units had to destroy their guns and were allocated to individual combat groups, which functioned either independently or were used to strengthen the weakest infantry formations. There was now about 3 or 4 guns available, which were brought up to support the combat groups. One of these combat groups was the combat group "Hauptmann Jüttner." The remnants of 5 batteries belong to it. Henceforth the combat group was deployed on the northwest edge of the much smaller Kessel east of Bol'shaia Rossoshka. However, this position was so unsuitable that it had to be abandoned the next day or the day after, and the guns deployed there had to be destroyed after exhausting all their ammunition. The combat group's wounded and ill were led to the casualty clearing station in the direction of Stalingrad. As a consequence of the deployment of assault guns, this change of position, in spite of deep enemy penetrations to the left of the combat group—southeast of Bol'shaia Rossoshka, by all accounts on the position of Infantry Regiment 203—was carried out in a fairly orderly manner.

Hauptmann von Damm reports:

Second Company, Artillery Regiment 176, is disbanded, having destroyed its guns. The remnants are deployed as infantry with Grenadier Regiment 203. The following officers are available: Hauptmann von Damm, Oberleutnant Griesbach, Leutnant Lutter, Stabszahlmeister Meyer, Oberstabsveterinär Zühlke, and Dr. Bergenthal.

The Kessel has contracted in size to an enormous degree. From this moment in time there are no hopes at all of any relief operation, since:

1. There are no horses available
2 There is a shortage of fuel
3. Considerable losses of weapons and equipment can be noted

From Artillery Regiment 176 the following are still operationally capable: Oberst Boeck, Hauptmann Becker, Hauptmann Jüttner, Oberleutnant Buschmann, Oberleutnant Guth, Oberleutnant Enzelmann,

Oberleutnant Kleissmann, Oberleutnant Dangelmeyer, Oberleutnant Hellmich, Leutnant John, Leutnant Körmann, and regimental adjutant Hauptmann Strobl.

On 16 January 1943 the combat strength of the battalions of Grenadier Regiment 203 is cited by Major von Rochow as being about 80–100 men each and about 80 men in the cycle section.

The heavy supply trains of Grenadier Regiment 203, which hitherto had been located in the ravines south of Bol'shaia Rossoshka with 9th Light Convoy 176 were withdrawn after the vehicles and second-line transports had been destroyed, since the enemy had achieved a surprise penetration from the southwest.

At midday on 16 January 1943 the regimental command post of Grenadier Regiment 203 was transferred to the Polevoistan *sovkhoz* about 7 kilometers (4.3 miles) southeast of Bol'shaia Rossoshka. With the four remaining horses, the field kitchen of the headquarters company can still be moved to the regimental command post.

Hauptmann Löser reports:

> In the bright light of a sunny day the marching column, moving on to Bol'shaia Rossoshka, passes countless trucks, guns, and convoy vehicles that have been left behind. On several occasions Russian fighter aircraft attack. At the western edge of Bol'shaia Rossoshka, the divisional commander orders the commander of Fusilier Battalion 230 to halt and to prepare the area for defense. Two casualty clearing stations (including Field Hospital 176) with over 200 wounded are located in the village and are due to be taken away in vehicles. While individual battalion commanders are still assembling their battalions and other units of the division, including the supply units of other divisions flowing through the village, the enemy appears on the high ground to the east of the village with about 2 regiments. Together with his own battalion and the reassembled remaining 12 soldiers of 11th Company with a few gathered-up elements of the units marching through the village, the battalion commander manages to hold out against the surprise enemy attack. The field hospital is temporarily lost and is recaptured in a counterattack by 10th Company.
>
> In the evening the battalion (without rearguard 9th company), altogether about 90 men strong with the main casualty clearing stations in

the village, is encircled by about 3 Soviet regiments. Shortly before, the assistant adjutant, Oberfeldwebel Pieper, had been dispatched to the main battle line with a report and to fetch new orders, vehicles for the wounded, and radio equipment so as to contact the regiment. The battalion commander reported back that a comprehensive defense of the village, given the Russian superiority, was pointless and that a move to the main battle line was recommended once the wounded had been removed.

Oberfeldwebel Pieper, who, with a radio, 3 vehicles, and the order to move out, tried to break through to the battalion, is pushed back by the Russian encirclement ring and is killed. For this he later receives the Knight's Cross. The battalion commander decides, in view of the helpless wounded and the order to defend the village, to remain there. During the night of 16 and 17 January the battalion creates some space for itself and fools the enemy over its strength. Prisoners are brought in. The battalion adjutant is severely wounded. Without knowing anything about the regiment's withdrawal order, a forward observer of the artillery manages to contact the battalion in the night by radio and reinforces the battalion commander's resolve to stick it out. In the morning of 17 January 1943, practically the entire village is in the battalion's hands.

17 January 1943. Weather: sunny, windy, very cold, down to –35°C (–31°F). Hauptmann Löser reports further:

Exceptionally severe close-quarters battles rage throughout the day. Enemy strength rises to about 3,000–4,000 men. Tenth Company is ejected from the field hospital. The company, following orders, withdraws to the battalion command post, which is likewise being ferociously contested. Its commander, Oberleutnant Kandt, as well as nearly all the junior leaders, is killed. Likewise the battalion's medical officer, Dr. Möhlmann, is killed.

The artillery observer establishes radio communication, and the battalion is to break through to the main forward line. The battalion commander reports the onset of darkness at 1530 hours as the time for the attempt. The evening breakthrough succeeds with only a handful of losses. Those wounded who can march are taken; the rest have to be left behind.

Toward 1630 hours the battalion commander reports the battalion's arrival with 80 men, weapons, and wounded at the forward edge of the battle area to the divisional commander by telephone. The divisional commander, who like everyone else had already written the battalion off, expresses his appreciation.[31]

As a consequence of the enemy's linking up in the township situated in front of the forward edge of the battle area, attacks on the same had stopped and with that the laying of guns in the exposed terrain had significantly eased.

The veterinary surgeon Dr. Herbert reports:

At 0500 hours a Russian attack without heavy weapons on the regimental command post of Grenadier Regiment 203 is repulsed in a counterattack. Toward 0800 hours a new Russian attack with tanks is successful.

The command post is withdrawn to a ravine 500 meters east of the *sovkhoz*. The tanks disappear again. Increasing enemy antitank and mortar fire, greater losses. To the right the regiment has lost contact with the battalions. The Russians enter the gap. To the left there is tenuous contact with 44th Infantry Division.

Hauptmann von Damm reports:

The headquarters section with the headquarters battery was placed under the command of Grenadier Regiment 203 (regimental headquarters). We moved to a *kolkhoz* southeast of Bol'shaia Rossoshka. The Russians attacked here on 17 January 1943. Initially it was possible to throw the enemy out until such time, as under attack from 7 tanks, we had to move back to the command post of the neighboring regiment in the neighboring division owing to a lack of antitank weapons.

Leutnant Hannig reports:

Scattered remnants of the division, along with troops from other divisions and general reserve troops that had returned in the direction of the Gumrak railway line, are stopped by the military police and directed to an assembly point (intersection of the railway about 5 kilometers [3.1 miles] north-northwest of Gumrak and the Rossoshka road heading east toward the railway line). Weapons and ammunition were issued. Soldiers were then deployed in platoons on the main forward edge of the battle line.

In Gumrak there is a main casualty clearing station that is overcrowded with about 5,000 ill and wounded. There are many cases of frostbite among the ill and wounded, who with the best will can receive no attention in the overcrowded bunkers. The airfield from where the wounded are flown out is very close to the casualty clearing station. Only those wounded who are able to make their own way to the airfield are flown out because no transport of any sort is available.

The airfield is already under enemy artillery bombardment. Only Heinkels III still fly in and out.

Leutnant Brieger reports:

From 17 to 19 January 1943 the artillery command post was situated about 2 kilometers (1.2 miles) northeast of the east edge of Bol'shaia Rossoshka in the ravine heading in the direction of Hilfswirtschaft.[32] At that moment there are supposed to be a total of 2 guns available. The NCOs and soldiers of 7th, 8th, and 9th Batteries are under the command of Oberleutnant Neumann and are deployed as infantry at the forward edge of the battle area on the right wing of Grenadier Regiment 178. Major von Rotsmann is in charge of the infantry deployment of Artillery Regiment 176.

Major von Rochow reports:

The Russians move through the gap between 76th and 44th Infantry Divisions with infantry, artillery, and tanks into the Kessel. Grenadier Regiment 203 (1st and 2nd Battalions) and Battalion Blomberg are placed under the command of the commander of the cycle section, since there is no contact with the command post of Grenadier Regiment 203. The formation (Grenadier Regiment 203, Battalion Blomberg, the cycle section, and the miscellaneous remnants of units) of Combat Group von Rochow numbers about 350 soldiers. There are no more heavy-infantry weapons and armor-piercing ammunition available. As a result of the ammunition shortage, only isolated shells can be fired from a single gun. Exceptionally heavy losses occur as a result of the heavy enemy bombardment, especially since there are no proper positions available (only snow holes). Removal of the wounded and the resupply of the troops could be maintained—completely insufficiently—only by sledges. On 17 and 18 January 1943 no rations at all could be issued.

Leutnant Brieger, Artillery Regiment 176 reports:

> On 17 January 1943 there was no movement at on all on the part of the supply link. Therefore, iron rations were issued from the kitchens to each man. Each receives 1½ loaves and two tins—1 kilo (2.2 lbs)—of meat or sausage. The issued rations must last for 8 days.

18 January 1943. Weather as the day before (sunny, windy, very cold, down to −35°C [−31°F]).

Headquarters veterinary surgeon Dr. Herbert reports: "Regimental Command Post of Grenadier Regiment 203 is holding on. From first light onward there is enemy antitank and mortar fire with increasing severity. Oberstleutnant von Spangenberg is lightly wounded."

Hauptmann Löser reports:

> The enemy attacks, especially the right divisional sector, in large assault groups and is everywhere fought back. Battalion 230 is resting as quick-reaction unit. Ninth Company, which, as a result of a massive enemy superiority, had to infiltrate and fight through in rearguard fashion, breaks through to the battalion (still 25 men strong).

Leutnant Brieger, Artillery Regiment 176, reports:

> In the morning, the NCOs and men of 4th Battery, Artillery Regiment 176, under the command of Hauptmann Jüttner and Leutnant Rusch, march on the Bol'shaia Rossoshka road in an easterly direction. The field kitchen is drawn by teams of men. The task is to secure the division's left flank, deployed as infantry some 4 kilometers (2.5 miles) west of the division's ration dump in the direction of Pitomnik. In the afternoon the attack of 2 Russian tanks, coming from Pitomnik and heading in the direction of the division's ration dump, was repelled by Oberst Boek, Hauptmann Jüttner, and his artillerymen.
>
> From 17 to 20 January 1943 the divisional command post was situated in a ravine 2 kilometers (1.2 miles) west-northwest from the signal box on the rail line from Gumrak to Kotluban, at the junction of the Bol'shaia Rossoshka road.
>
> The road from Bol'shaia Rossoshka to Gumrak is strewn with trucks, all kinds of other vehicles, field kitchens, weapons, and pieces of equipment.

Obergefreiter Petznick, 5th Battery, Artillery Regiment 176, reports:

> On 18 January 1943 the combat group took up new positions in open terrain in the area of Gumrak (southwest). Here too the Russians attacked with ever stronger forces. Every day losses were incurred from enemy snipers. The combat group was able to maintain its position more or less up to 20 January 1943 with difficulty, and only then with the addition of reinforcements made up of the remnants from various units (with also, among others, a Ukrainian construction company with Hauptwachtmeister Strzebnick, formerly of 5th Battery, Artillery Regiment 176).

Leutnant Reinbeck, Grenadier Regiment 203, reports:

> On 18 January 1943 groups made up of frontline soldiers who were part of some withdrawal came to Gumrak. The forward lines in the direction of Bol'shaia Rossoshka were overrun by the Russians. The men—still no wounded—were, some of them, completely exhausted. There were cases in which they collapsed, lay there, and froze to death; see attachment 53.

19 January 1943. Weather: overcast, cold, still only –10°C (14°F). Major von Rochow, Cycle Section 176, reports: "An attack of weaker Russian forces, which continued up to 1900 hours in the evening, was repulsed."

Hauptmann Löser (commander, 3rd Battalion, Grenadier Regiment 230) reports:

> In the night of 18–19 January 1943 the battalion carries out a strenuous night march to the forward edge of the battle area in order to relieve Hauptmann Bente's 3rd Battalion, Grenadier Regiment 203. This is carried out by first light, though not all elements of the battalion have arrived.
>
> The battalion has occupied the position with about 80 men when, toward 0900 hours, some 300–400 Russians can be seen coming from the direction of Bol'shaia Rossoshka. These troops attack the battalion in several waves after being reinforced to about 500 men and after having brought antitank guns and heavy mortars into position.
>
> A battalion forward strongpoint is lost. The forward edge of the battle area (snow holes in completely open terrain and one bunker in which the radio is set up) is, despite the heaviest enemy bombardment, held. The

battalion commander is severely wounded. In the evening hours the battalion dwindles to about 50 men. A section of artillery men under the command of Oberleutnant Neumann as one group consisting of 20 men from the old 13th Company, Fusilier Regiment 230, under the command of Leutnant Baier, is incorporated into the battalion as reinforcements. Hauptmann Nowotne assumes command.

In the evening the Russians resume their attacks in the manner of shock troops. These fighting reconnaissance probes repeatedly occur throughout the night.

Toward 0300 hours these probes become stronger. The forming-up positions of stronger forces can be identified. Toward 0600 hours there is a renewed attack of about 200 men against the forward edge of the battle area. In the distance closed-up columns in battalion strength are observed moving in the direction of our front.

20 January 1943. Weather: overcast, cold, still only –10°C (14°F). Hauptmann Löser of 3rd Battalion, Fusilier Regiment 230, reports:

Although the battalion is completely exhausted (it had to spend 1 day and 2 nights in open terrain without any rations), this attack was brought to a halt some 150 meters in front of the forward edge of the battle area. As a consequence there ensued, as on the previous day, a heavy bombardment from mortars and antitank guns. The battalion commander, Hauptmann Nowotne, in the area of the prominent radio bunker was lightly wounded next to Oberleutnant Giesel. After this heavy-weapons bombardment and despite counterattacks from Oberfeldwebel Grothe, the enemy worked his way forward into the forward edge of the battle area. Enemy tanks that had broken through appeared from the rear. As these started to have an effect, the enemy broke into the forward edge of the battle area and wiped out the remnants of the battalion. According to Oberfeldwebel Grothe's report, Hauptmann Nowotne was killed in the course of this action.

Only a handful of wounded remained left in the battalion and from Fusilier Regiment 230. Three of them were flown out of the Kessel.

Major von Rochow, commander of Cycle Section 176, reports:

Early on 20 January 1943 heavy Russian mortar and antitank fire fell on the right wing of Hauptmann Isberner's battalion sector (1st Battalion,

Grenadier Regiment 203). Then 2 Russian tanks rolled up the biggest part of the sector. The battalion was almost completely destroyed. The remnants of Combat Group von Rochow moved away to the left. The command post (von Rochow) was shot to pieces. There were exceptionally heavy losses. Major von Rochow was wounded.

The division was unable to provide any kind of support whatsoever. The last survivors of the combat group, still about 100 men, were taken back to the command post of Grenadier Regiment 178.

The enemy did not follow, as his infantry was poor and his tanks abandoned the attack. Of the cycle section on 20 January 1943 there remained Leutnant von Jena and 30 NCOs and soldiers.

On 20 January 1943 the following soldiers were decorated with the Knight's Cross of the Iron Cross:

Oberst Boeck (Artillery Regiment 176)
Oberstleutnant von Spangenberg (Grenadier Regiment 203)
Major von Rochow (Cycle Section 176)
Hauptmann Löser (Fusilier Regiment 230)
Oberfeldwebel Pieper (Fusilier Regiment 230)

The positions held by officers in the regiments and sections can be seen from attachments 54–59. Insofar as they have not been hitherto cited in the war diary, they are as follows:

Attachment 54: Officer appointments, medical formations, approximately the end of October 1942
Attachment 55: Officer appointments, Grenadier Regiment 203, about the middle of January 1943
Attachment 56: Officer appointments, Artillery Regiment 176, up to 15 January 1943
Attachment 57: Officer appointments, Grenadier Regiment 230, up to 1 January 1943
Attachment 58: Officer appointments, Tank Destroyer Section 176, up to 10 October 1942, to 1 January 1943, and to 10 January 1943
Attachment 59: Grenadier Regiment 178, up to 18 January 1943
Attachment 60: a list of officer appointments put together by the postings

headquarters of 6th Army's 76th Infantry Division of all regiments and sections up to the end of 23 January 1943

21 *January* 1943. Weather: overcast, cold, still only –10°C (14°F). Obergefreiter Petznick, 5th Battery, Artillery Regiment 176, reports:

In the night of 21 January 1943, toward 0300 hours, the combat group (artillery men under the command of Major von Rotsmann) with extra reinforcements from an engineer group from the division and an assault gun, attempted to remove some of the smaller enemy penetrations—in part these had worked to within only a few meters from our strongpoint. The combat groups succeeded, if only temporarily, in pushing the Russians back, but a break-in into his line of bunkers was not possible.

On the morning of 21 January the Russians then attacked the combat group with a much greater number of tanks, among which there were several heavy T-34s, with the additional assistance of heavy battery guns. In the course of the exceptionally fierce battles, and after he had already been repulsed several times in hand-to-hand fighting, the enemy succeeded in completely overrunning the position before midday, as there was a complete absence of any armor-piercing shells for the heavy weapons. At its disposal the combat group had merely a machine gun and an infantry gun (at the bunker of Oberleutnant Guth and Wachtmeister [assistant adjutant] Rohloff) with about 30–35 shells, such that even this sole German gun (where it came from is not known—light field howitzer 18) in the whole area soon fell silent. In the individual strongpoints of the forward edge of the battle area, some 100–150 meters apart from one another, which at any one time were occupied by 2 soldiers lying in an open piece of ground, were a mere rifle per each man with little small-arms ammunition, and in the best cases there were 1 or 2 hand grenades available. At some time in the evening before, individual groups had searched for infantry ammunition and the like on abandoned vehicles before taking up position. When the Russians broke into the combat group's positions, a number of Russian tanks were, among them 3 T-34s, partly and only with hand grenades either destroyed or rendered immobile. At this point I myself was wounded, and I managed to drag myself to the bunker position, which still functioned as a command post. There, on the orders of a *Wachmeister* (assistant adjutant) of 4th Battery, I was taken to the rear to my former battery chief, Oberleutnant Wolff. Some time later he arranged for me to be taken to the main casualty clearing station.

From what my former battery chief told me, on the evening of 21 January 1943, I had no doubts that the combat group's position had been rolled up during the day and that those parts of the combat group located there were destroyed. Only 2 officers (Oberleutnant Holters and Oberleutnant Guth) as well as a radio operator and I, wounded, returned.

In the late afternoon of 21 January 1943 the Russians with tanks broke into the rear positions, and Oberleutnant Wolff, with the remnants of the combat group, primarily soldiers from 5th Battery, Artillery Regiment 176, launched a counterattack, which, with heavier losses (among others Wachtmeister Pantel killed and Wachtmeister Gutzeit severely wounded), met some temporary success.

In the night of 21 January 1943 the battle headquarters of Grenadier Regiment 178 is withdrawn to the Gumrak railway line (about 2 kilometers [1.2 miles] northwest of Gumrak).

On 21 January 1943 the divisional command post is situated eastward of the railway line, about 1.5 kilometers (.9 mile) east of Gumrak.

The divisional rations dump, which until 18 January 1943 had been located on the Bol'shaia Rossoshka–Gumrak road about 2 kilometers (1.2 miles) south of Shchishchlianki, could be dispersed.

The new forward edge of the battle area should in general follow the Gumrak-Kotluban railway line.

Concerning the battle of the Engineer Battalion 176 groups, see attachment 11.

The airfield was now under enemy artillery fire. It had to be abandoned on 22 January 1943.

22 January 1943. Weather: overcast, cold, still only –10°C (14°F).
Obergefreiter Petznick reports:

On 22 January 1943 the remnants of the division assembled not far from Gumrak on the railway line to Stalingrad, and I was ordered by Oberleutnant Wolff to set off to the main casualty clearing station in Stalingrad. At this moment in time, that is, the previous evening, only about 20 of 5th Battery were still operationally effective. Among others, these were:

Hauptmann Blaffert
Oberleutnant Wolff
Stabsfeldwebel Pankrath
Unteroffizier Grebe
Obergefreiter Spengler
Obergefreiter Fischer
Obergefreiter Bannhagel
Gefreiter Pätzold
Gefreiter Woytalla
Gefreiter Schiemann
Gefreiter Paschen
Gefreiter Teichmann

In the last few days, while on the way to Stalingrad, I was flown out from the airfield at Stalingradskii. I have heard nothing more of my comrades and have also heard nothing from them. Along the way I bumped into Oberst Boek, who indicated the way. Even though I never saw my comrades again, I am nevertheless quite certain that they, in accordance with their oath, fought the enemy to the very last.

23 January 1943. Weather: overcast, cold, still only –10°C (14°F).

The airfield at Stalingradskii, about 2 kilometers (1.2 miles) east-northeast of Gumrak, was operational on the afternoon of 22 January 1943. Up to the end of 23 January 1943, wounded were flown out of it. Thereafter flights in and out were no longer possible.

According to statements made by Feldwebel Michael Horvath, Military Police Squad 100 of 100th Jäger Division, which had last fought farther to the east of the 76th Infantry Division at the boundary of the northern part of Stalingrad, Gumrak is said to be have been abandoned in the night of 24–25 January 1943. It can be assumed that the final remnants of the 76th Infantry Division will have defended Gumrak up to this date and that they were totally destroyed here, or indeed that they were absorbed into the still more combat-powerful groups of 100th Jäger Division; see attachment 61.

The 76th (Brandenburg) Infantry Division, fighting in a blaze of glory since August 1942 right up to the last days of January 1943 in the formation of the 6th Army, enters into the heroic history of the German people. The greatest that there has ever been in martial achievement and man's greatness, in war and in peace, will remain forever the heroic song of the soldiers of Stalingrad.

On 3 February 1943 the Supreme Command of the German Army makes the following announcement:

> The Battle for Stalingrad is at an end. Loyal to its oath to the very last breath, 6th Army under the exemplary leadership of Generalfeldmarschall Paulus has succumbed to the vast superiority of the enemy and the unfavorable conditions. Its fate is also shared by an Antiaircraft Division of the German Luftwaffe, two Romanian divisions, and a Croatian regiment, which in the spirit of true comradeship with their comrades of the German Army have discharged their duty to the utmost. At this time it is still not possible to depict the course of the operations that have led to this end. But one thing can today be said: the sacrifice of the army was not in vain. As the bulwark of the historical European mission, it shattered for many weeks on end the onslaught of six Soviet armies. Completely surrounded by the enemy, it held united, in the ensuing weeks of the most severe struggle and the hardest deprivations, against the strong enemy forces. In so doing it gave the German leadership the time and the opportunity to take the necessary countermeasures on the implementation of which the fate of the entire Eastern front depended. Entrusted with this task, 6th Army has also in the end held out, when with the duration of the encirclement and the continuation of the operations, the Luftwaffe in spite of the exceptional efforts and the severest losses was unable to guarantee a comprehensive resupply via the air, and the possibility of being relieved increasingly and finally disappeared for good. Surrender, twice demanded by the enemy, received a proud rejection. Beneath the banner of the swastika, which remained visible on the highest ruins of Stalingrad, the final battle came to an end. Generals, officers, NCOs, and men fought shoulder to shoulder to the last round. They perished so that Germany should live. Their example will exert a lasting influence, far into the future, in spite of all the false Bolshevik propaganda to the contrary. The divisions of 6th Army are already indeed in the process of being formed anew.

General der Panzertruppen, Friedrich Paulus (1890–1957), German 6th Army Commander, June 1942, promoted Generalfeldmarschall 31st January 1943. Bundesarchiv, Bild 183-B24575/Fotograf: Heinz Mittelstaedt

German soldier in a trench under rolling stock. Note the narrowness of the slit trench and the use of pieces of railway sleepers to provide extra and immediate cover when required. Overall this position offers good overhead protection but is likely to attract the attention of enemy snipers. Bundesarchiv, Bild 101I-218-0520-26/Fotograf: Klintzsch

German reconnaissance patrol in the suburbs of Stalingrad. Bundesarchiv, Bild 101I-218-0526-36/Fotograf: Seibold

German soldier, having checked the burning remnants of a T34, moves to avoid exploding ammunition. Bundesarchiv, Bild 101I-218-0527-12/Fotograf: Seibold

The soldier observing from this tank turret would have been a prime target for Soviet snipers. The building in the rear is most likely the Grain silo, the scene of bitter close-quarters battles.
Bundesarchiv, Bild 101I-218-0528-30/*Fotograf:* Propagandakompanien der Wehrmacht

A classic Stalingrad photo which conveys something of the professionalism of German 6th Army and the exceptionally high quality of its junior leaders.
Bundesarchiv, Bild 116-168-600/*Fotograf:* Kurt Heine

German machine-gun position set up on a captured Red Army position. The MG 34 and later versions gave enormous fire power and tactical flexibility to the German infantry. The role of the gun commander was critical. Bundesarchiv, Bild 183-B22163/Fotograf: Kurt Heine

Ration carriers bring food to the forward German positions. Soviet raiding parties would infiltrate under cover of darkness and attempt to snatch one of these soldiers. They were also routinely targeted by Soviet snipers. Bundesarchiv, Bild 146-2006-0106/Fotograf: Friedrich Germann

Trenches and dugouts among ruins which had to be systematically cleared of enemy at high cost to the Germans, October 1942. Bundesarchiv, Bild 183-B22436/Fotograf: Bauer-Altvater

This ruined house was referred to by the Germans as the "German castle in the Tsaritsyn valley". It was rumoured that the former owner was of German descent. On the side of the valley the house occupied a tactically important position, commanding a good field of view. Note the Volga in rear. Bundesarchiv, Bild 183-B22800/Fotograf: Kurt Heine

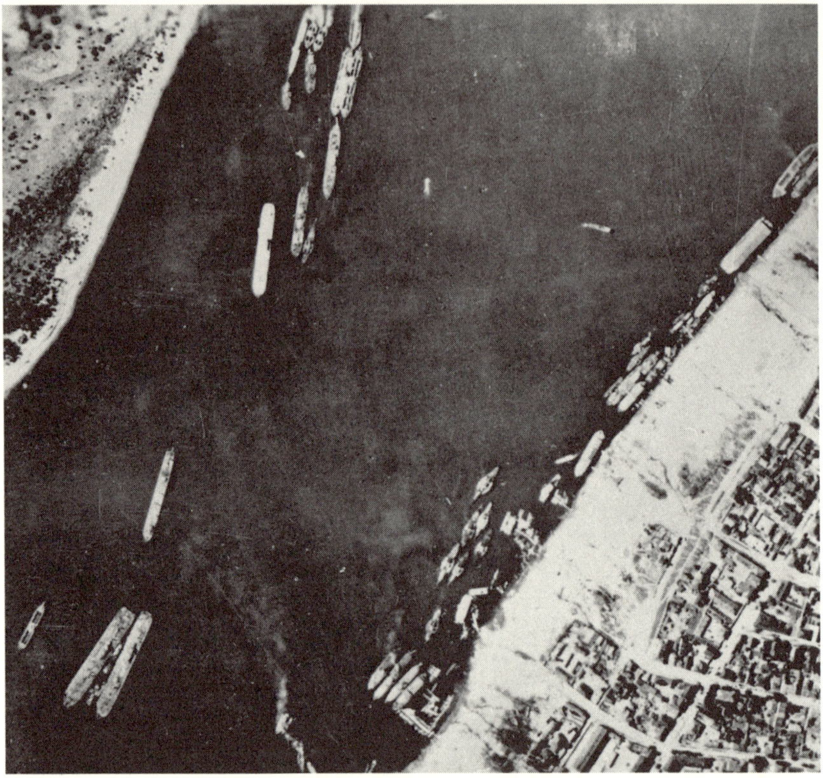

An excellent aerial view of the Volga, showing its width. The Volga was a major communications and supply route. Bundesarchiv, Bild 183-B22651/Fotograf: o.Ang

General Vasilii Chuikov (1900–1982), commander of 62nd Army in his command post, November 1942. RIAN-00051713, Photographer, Zelma

Soviet troops initiating an assault from a communications trench. Bundesarchiv, Bild 183-R76599/Fotograf: Allgemeiner Deutscher Nachrichtendienst

German infantry and an assault gun in a forming up position making ready for an assault on height 102. Note the steep-sided balkas which are a topographical feature of this part of Russia. Bundesarchiv, Bild 183-B26922/Fotograf: Herber

A German machine-gun position overlooking the Volga and a possible landing position for a Soviet assault. Imperial War Museum, HU005172

In quiet spells the Germans conducted sweeps of the giant factories, which were often full of imported German plant and machinery. This picture conveys some idea of the conditions in which the urban battle, the inner-factory battle, was waged. Bundesarchiv, Bild 183-B29903/Fotograf: Herber

A powerful image of a German grenadier, November 1942. The original caption stressed the determination of the German soldiers. Bundesarchiv, Bild 183-B29906/Fotograf: Herber

October 1942, Ju 87 Stuka over Stalingrad. The width of the Volga is apparent. As the German infantry lost men, the role of the Luftwaffe became crucial to maintaining German offensive power. Bundesarchiv, Bild 183-J20509/Fotograf: Opitz

---

→

A German signpost: "Transit for vehicles of all types forbidden. Road under enemy observation and fire." Imperial War Museum, HU005176

October 1942, Ju 87 Stuka over Stalingrad having just attacked its target. Bundesarchiv, Bild 183-J20511/Fotograf: Opitz

A remarkable photograph of Soviet troops under fire on the steppe, September 1942. The soldier in the foreground appears to be have been hit by flanking fire and the soldier on the hay, having identified the enemy, is returning fire. RIAN-00059099, Photographer: Alexander Kapustianskii

An excellent view of the terrain dropping away to the Volga from the top of height 102, Mamaev kurgan and thus the critical importance of this feature for both sides, 12th February 1943. RIAN-00169358, Photographer: Zelma

Members of Soviet ethnic minorities working for the German army. Inside the Kessel these troops played a major role in helping German 6th Army to prolong its resistance. Bundesarchiv, Bild 101I-218-0506-09A/Fotograf: o.Ang

German sniper, Stalingrad, September 1942. Bundesarchiv, Bild 101I-218-0517-24/Fotograf: Dieck

A Soviet volunteer working for the Germans. Note the improvised harness for carrying fuel and water containers. In the city these men, immediately identifiable as deserters, were prime targets for snipers. A grim fate awaited them after the German collapse. Bundesarchiv, Bild 101I-218-0518-32/Fotograf: o.Ang

A local Stalingrad woman preparing food in an improvised oven in a balka, *October 1942. If access to food was guaranteed, working for the Germans was an attractive option.* Bundesarchiv, Bild 169-0351/Fotograf: o.Ang

Refugees from Stalingrad camping in the open. Many of them had been forcibly evacuated from the city by both sides. Bundesarchiv, Bild 101I-617-2574-03/Fotograf: Propagandakompanien der Wehrmacht - Heer und Luftwaffe/Ollig

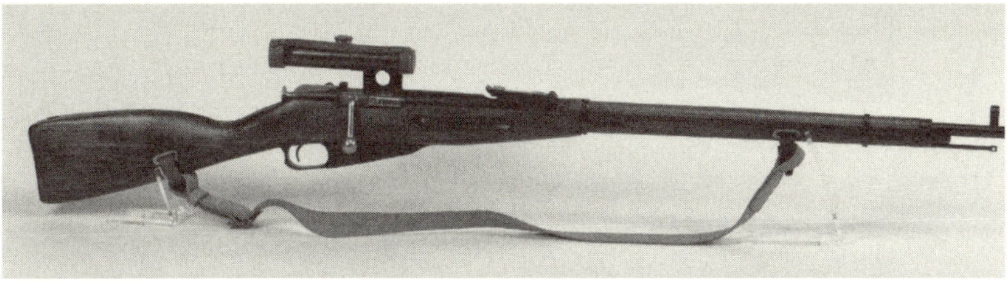

The Soviet, Mosin-Nagant rifle (1891/1930) with telescopic sight. Imperial War Museum, FIR008268

Improvised straw footwear worn by German soldiers that offered some protection from the cold. Imperial War Museum, UNI012917

Russian civilians fleeing the city with what they can carry or transport, September 1942. Bundesarchiv, Bild 183-B29111/Fotograf: Bauer-Altvater

German sniper, Stalingrad, September 1942. Bundesarchiv, Bild 169-0526/Fotograf: o.An

Vasilii Zaitsev (left) briefing two other snipers, December 1942. RIAN-00000456, Photographer, Zelma

General Chuikov, commander of 62nd Army holding Vasilii Zaitsev's rifle. K. Gurov, Army Council looks. Zaitsev stands on the far right. Unidentified officer in rear, December 1942. RIAN-00009681, Photographer, Zelma

Hero of the Soviet Union, sniper Nikolai Il'in, the most successful Stalingrad sniper, and M. Lama in the rear. Both men are armed with the semi-automatic Tokarev rifle. At short ranges in the urban environment the semi-automatic rifle was more than adequate for the Heckenschütze but sniping at longer ranges required a bolt rifle. RIAN-00665558, Photographer unknown

Indigenous women and children from the southern steppe zone, summer 1942. The bewildered faces of these children make a profound impression. Bundesarchiv, Bild 101I-218-0513-09A/Fotograf: Propagandakompanien der Wehrmacht - Heer und Luftwaffe

The pious invaders: a church service in the field, August 1942. Bundesarchiv, Bild 169-0950/Fotograf: o.Ang

A column of German prisoners on their way to prison camps. Large numbers died en route. Bundesarchiv, Bild 183-E0406-0022-010/Fotograf: o.Ang

A young, wounded and exhausted German prisoner of war under guard. The battle over, the ordeal of captivity was about to begin. Bundesarchiv, Bild 183-EO406-0022-011/Fotograf: ADN-Zentralbild/Archiv

A meeting of the NKVD-sponsored front organisation, the National Committee for a Free Germany. Sitting right is Erich Weinert (1890-1953), German Communist and the Committee President and to his left sitting, General Walther von Seydlitz-Kurzbach (1888-1976), the former commander of LI Corps, 6th Army. Bundesarchiv, Bild 183-PO926-309/Fotograf: Allgemeiner Deutscher Nachrichtendienst – Zentralbild

A German propaganda poster which was used in January 1943 as the end in Stalingrad approached. The poster shows the giant siege mortar, Thor. The caption reads: "The military genius of the Führer, the bravery of our soldiers and the superiority of such weapons shall decide this war!" Bundesarchiv, Plak 003-009-223/Fotograf: Erasmusdruck, Berlin; Franz Eher Nachf., München

Soviet tanks and infantry advancing over the snow. Imperial War Museum, RUS001656

Vasilii Grossman, 11th September 1951, just over a year before the full weight of the party apparatus would be directed at Grossman after the publication of his Stalingrad novel, For a Just Cause. RIAN-00005461, *Photographer:* Riumkin

Soviet war correspondents, June 1943, among them Vasilii Grossman, rear left. Grossman's Stalingrad articles made him a household name and out of his experiences at Stalingrad grew the great epic novel Life and Fate, *the tribute to* Mother Russia. RIAN-881051, *Photographer:* Minsker

Statue of the Mourning Mother, The State Historical Museum, Mamaev kurgan, Volgograd, 1964. The sculptor was Evgenii Vuchetich. RIAN-697773, Photographer, David Sholomovich

5 K-98 vs. Mosin M 1891/1930: German and Soviet Snipers at Stalingrad and on the Eastern Front

Here every man is happy just to get through the day in one piece. Again, today, another four of our men have been killed by head shots. There is something quite dreadful with these snipers. . . . Today our telephone link was not disrupted; by that I mean that it was not shot up, cut up, or otherwise made useless. This makes us happy since we have constantly to repair the line, and the Russians shoot at us all day with snipers and mortars

—Obergefreiter Wilhelm Gütinger, Stalingrad, 29 December 1942

The concentration of large numbers of German and Soviet troops in the urban areas of Stalingrad opened up huge opportunities for the deployment of snipers by both sides, yet the general perception of urban fighting in Stalingrad, relentlessly propagated by Soviet accounts and often amplified by Western historians, remains that Soviet snipers dominated the battlefield and that the Germans were completely outclassed by their enemy in this specialized form of infantry warfare. There are two reasons to doubt this view. First, it grossly underestimates the demonstrated flexibility and adaptability of German 6th Army (and indeed the Wehrmacht) in responding to unexpected threats on the Eastern front. Second, it ignores the possibility that Soviet claims for the number of kills achieved by their snipers at Stalingrad (and elsewhere on the Eastern front) could be fabricated (as were the number of German planes being shot down and tanks destroyed) for purposes of morale and wartime propaganda. For example, Soviet sources maintain that such was the success of Soviet snipers Anatolii Chekhov, Viktor Medvedev, and especially Vasilii Zaitsev, and the apparent inability of German 6th Army to cope with them, that German headquarters in Berlin was compelled to dispatch the sniper instructor Major Konings (Конингс/Konings in the Russian, not Кониг/Konig/König) in order to track down and kill Vasilii Zaitsev in the ruins of Stalingrad. The Soviet view was, and the Russian view still is, that Zaitsev was victorious in this duel. In this chapter, I consider the nature of sniping (often misunderstood by military historians); the general use of snipers by the Red Army on the Eastern front; the role they played in the propaganda war against the Germans; and, finally, based on published and archival sources, whether the duel between Zaitsev and Konings took place or whether the tale must be seen a masterpiece of wartime (and postwar) Soviet propaganda.

Introduction

The art of sniping provides an excellent example of how the lessons of war, which are learned at a cost in lives, can be forgotten when hostilities cease or are deemed to be redundant by one former belligerent, only to be eagerly adopted and modified by another. In World War I, after the German attempt to break through to Paris failed and the long period of trench warfare ensued, the German Army made excellent and deadly use of precision rifle fire against the Anglo-French armies. Well-equipped, imaginative in their use of ground, and tactically adept, German snipers dominated their opponents' sectors, ensuring that the death toll from a series of single rifle shots steadily rose. According to Major H. Hesketh-Prichard, who was largely responsible for dealing with the German sniper threat in 1914, the German Army was equipped with about 20,000 telescopic sights, with an allocation of 6 sights per company.[1] Regarding British losses, Hesketh-Prichard notes that "in early 1915 we lost eighteen men in a single battalion in a single day to enemy snipers."[2] Hesketh-Prichard's assessment convinced him that there were two pressing reasons for countersniping. First, there were considerations of simple arithmetic, the compound interest of prolonged, efficient execution: "Now if each battalion in the line killed by sniping a single German in the day, the numbers would mount up. . . . In a war of attrition the sniper on this count alone justifies his existence and wipes out large numbers of enemy."[3] Second, there was the question of morale, or, to use his spelling, "moral": "If your trench is dominated by enemy snipers, life in it is really a very hard thing, and moral must inevitably suffer."[4] Under the tutelage of Hesketh-Prichard and like-minded officers, sniping courses and schools were set up behind the lines, and eventually the threat from German snipers was reduced to an acceptable level.

It is perhaps understandable that the two main exponents of sniping in World War I—Britain and Germany—came to regard sniping as something that was unique to, and grew out of, the static conditions of 1914–1918 and thus as a military art whose requirements had been rendered redundant by the more mobile forms of warfare being intensely studied and pioneered in the 1920s. This was certainly not the case in the Soviet Union. The first Russian translation of Hesketh-Prichard's comprehensive sniper training manual appeared in 1924[5] and undoubtedly influenced future developments in the Soviet approach to sniping. Yet some credit must go to the tsarist officer and administrator General Grigorii Potemkin (1731–1791) for anticipating the modern sniper-scout. In his reforms of the Russian army that he introduced in the late eighteenth century, he encouraged the development of light, mobile units—Jäger regiments—and emphasized accurate shooting, the need to change fire positions, field craft, and tactical deception. Another significant Russian development, which has clear parallels with the raiding groups employed in the American War of Independence and the later American Civil War—the latter marking the incunabula of modern sniping and countersniping—was the use of Cossacks in a scouting role. These scouts, known as *plastuny*, were the eyes and ears of the regular Russian army, especially in the border regions, and were recruited from the Kuban and Black Sea Regiments. The name lives on in the Russian translation of the English "leopard crawl"—*po-plastunski*—to move like a *plastun*.

The first Soviet sniping school was set up in 1929 at Kuskovo, operating under the auspices of Obshchestvo sodeitsviia oborone i aviatsonno-khimicheskomu stroitel'stvu (OSOAVIAKHIM, The society for furthering the defense and aviation-chemical construction of the Soviet Union). By 1935, against the backdrop of a huge increase in competitive shooting, some 3,000 snipers had been trained for the Red Army. Progress continued, and in 1936 there were 11 sniping schools in the Soviet Union. By 1933 much of the expertise and requirements of sniping training had been put together in a Red Army manual, *Metodika strelkovoi podgotovki i kurs strel'b dlia podgotovki snaiperov* (The principles of rifle training and a course of marksmanship for the training of snipers). In forty-five-day courses, Soviet snipers were taught the importance of target selection, camouflage and concealment, and the impact of wind and distance on the fall of shot. Soviet snipers were trained to be able to engage targets with open sights up to a range of 1,000 meters and up to 1,500 meters with optical sights. Even for good rifle shots, armed with a reliable rifle and rounds with a high degree of ballistic consistency, this is outstanding marksmanship and was especially so in the 1930s. Soviet snipers were also expected to carry out reconnaissance missions, evaluate terrain and select future fire positions, and even engage low-flying enemy aircraft. The specifics of the Soviet sniper training program aside, the Soviet sniper, like his counterparts in other armies, developed the basic infantryman's skills of fieldcraft and marksmanship to such a high degree, that the trained sniper, to cite a British manual, "can be defined as a soldier, who is trained to locate an enemy, however well hidden, who can stalk or lie in wait for him unseen and who is, at the same time, an expert shot with the rifle. His object is to kill with one round."[6]

A serious consideration in sniping is the rifle to be used. In order to achieve greater accuracy and to avoid betraying the sniper's position by the ejection of an empty case (a feature of semiautomatic weapons), modern sniping rifles tend to be bolt operated. Considerations of accuracy led to semiautomatic rifles designed by Sergei Simonov, Vasilii Degtiarev, Colonel Nikolai Rukavishnikov, and Fedor Tokarev—some of the Soviet Union's most famous weapons designers—being rejected in favor of the Mosin 1891/1930, which in 1931 underwent further modifications such as an improved bore, reduced variations in dimension in production, a change in the shape of the stock, and the installation of an optical sight.[7] The original optical sight, the *pritsel teleskopicheskogo tipa* (PT), with x4 magnification, was soon replaced by the *vintovichnyi pritsel* (VP). In 1936 the VP was replaced by the *pritsel Emel'ianova* (PE) sight with x4.2 magnification. The final version was the PU with x3.5 magnification.[8] It was initially designed for the Tokarev semiautomatic rifle and by 1941 was fitted to the Mosin 1891/1930. Some idea of the growth in the importance of sniping doctrine in the Red Army can be seen in production quantities for the Mosin 1891/1930 rifle: 1932 (749 rifles), 1933 (1,347 rifles), 1934 (6,637 rifles), 1935 (12,742 rifles), 1936 (no data), 1937 (13,130 rifles), and 1938 (19,545 rifles).[9] Using specially selected ammunition, the Mosin 1891/1930 could achieve a 3-cm group at 100 meters, a 7.5-cm group at 200 meters, a 15.5-cm group at 300 meters, an 18-cm group at 400 meters, a 25-cm group at 500 meters, and a 35-cm group at 600 meters.[10]

In terms of training establishments, organization, rifles and optical equipment, and a coherent doctrine—*snaiperskoi terror* (sniper terror)—the Soviet Union was by far the best prepared of the combatants at the start of World War II. During the Spanish Civil War, shipments of the latest sniper rifles had been delivered to republican forces, and, along with other items of equipment and doctrine, their operational use had been thoroughly analyzed by the Soviet General Staff.[11] In fact, sniping had been an integral part of the concept of *malaia voina*—literally, "little war"—that had been developed in the 1920s by Soviet military thinkers such as M. V. Frunze, I. P. Uborevich, and A.I. Egorov. *Malaia voina* was a response to the need to find ways to counter the more technologically advanced Western states should they invade the Soviet Union. It envisaged small groups of men, acting on their own initiative, attacking the enemy, very much in the spirit of Potemkin's Jäger regiments. However, when the Red Army attacked Finland in 1939, the concept was reversed. The Red Army was cast in the role of the powerful invader, and the small Finnish army employed small groups of soldiers who, showing great initiative, plenty of patriotic fervour, and élan, provided a brilliant demonstration of *malaia voina*. Snipers played a major role in paralyzing and disrupting Soviet movement, and a number of memoirs refer to what Red Army soldiers called *kukushki* (cuckoos). A Finnish sniper would lie in a white sheet suspended in a tree, permit a Soviet patrol to pass, and then kill selected targets—officers, machine gunners, and signalers—from the rear. The tactic caused panic and disruption and greatly retarded the speed of the Soviet advance. In his preliminary report to Stalin on Red Army performance, Nikolai Voronov (army commander of the 2nd rank and head of Soviet artillery) acknowledged the impact of Finnish snipers on operations. He pointed out that "the snipers are exceptionally well trained, and they combine their fire well with handheld automatic weapons and machine guns."[12] In an earlier report prepared for the Soviet leadership it was noted that "losses are mainly inflicted by snipers, who are well camouflaged and frequently located in trees; by small groups of enemy moving around the flanks and attacking from the rear; [and] by mines, which the enemy lays in the night on the routes used by the infantry and transport."[13] The Winter War demonstrated the efficacy of sniper terror and at the same time highlighted the failure of the rigid ideological control of military decision-making that was to cost the Red Army dearly eighteen months later.

Before the war, sniper training had been dispersed among formations and units; it was now centralized under the control of *shkoly otlichnykh strelkov snaiperskoi podgotovki* (schools of outstanding marksmen in sniper training) in the military districts. Some idea of the training and administrative effort devoted to sniper training can be seen from the fact that from 1941 to 1944 some 428,335 snipers were trained and deployed.[14] In the life-and-death struggle the Red Army had no hesitation about training women for this role, and a total of 1,885 woman snipers passed through the schools. About 180 lost their lives.[15] Their tallies of killed Germans are impressively high, in keeping with those of the men. For example, according to one source, a single company of woman snipers that was part of 3rd Shock Army killed a total of 3,012 German soldiers.[16] Vasil' Bykov, a former *frontovik* and, arguably, the outstanding writer on the war theme in Soviet-Russian literature, offers a slightly different view of Soviet women at war from that which features in many Soviet accounts:

> Those who got to the regiments and battalions were not really taken seriously. Among the mass of men, in this purely male business that war is, they immediately discovered their complete uselessness, even the women in categories such as snipers who in the lull in fighting would move into no-man's-land in immediate proximity to the enemy. It is received wisdom that every sniper's shot meant a dead German. In reality, however, everything was completely different. Lying under the very nose of the enemy and opening fire was possible only for a matter of minutes. And a shot from one of these women's rifles did not always hit a target. But when active military operations were not being conducted at the front, sniper activity was the sole indicator that something was being done, and the commanders did not stint on the numbers in their reports.[17]

Soviet snipers are an important part of the battle of Stalingrad, not just because the urban environment, especially after the German aerial bombardment, was ideally suited to sniping but also because the highly personalized nature of this form of killing, amplified in a relentless flood of newspaper articles and other forms of propaganda, fed and nurtured the need to feel that the Germans were paying a heavy price for violating Mother Russia. The high point of Soviet activity, as disseminated then and now, remains the duel that according to many accounts took place between Major Konings and Vasilii Zaitsev, probably the best-known Soviet sniper of the Great Fatherland War.[18]

The Konings-Zaitsev Duel

The Konings-Zaitsev duel features in a large number of Western and Soviet histories and accounts of the Stalingrad battle. In fact, the story of the duel has been repeated and recycled so many times that challenging the accuracy of these accounts, let alone their veracity, is something of an uphill struggle. The background to the duel, endlessly propagated, resides in the apparent ease with which Soviet snipers were outmaneuvering any attempts by German 6th Army to counter the Soviet sniper threat; as a consequence, the German command at Stalingrad is said to have requested expert assistance. Major Konings, the head of the German Army's sniper school, was sent to eliminate Zaitsev.

This view is prominent in serious studies by Western and Soviet historians, for example, Alan Clark's *Barbarossa: The Russian-German Conflict 1941–1945* (1965); Vasilii Chuikov's memoirs, *Nachalo puti* (*The Beginning of the Road*, 1962); the various editions of A. M. Samsonov's *Stalingradskaia bitva* (*The Stalingrad Battle*); and other official histories. Especially important is Zaitsev's own biography, *Za Volgoi zemli dlia nas ne bylo: Zapiski snaipera* (*Beyond the Volga There Was No Land for Us: Notes of a Sniper*, 1971), which, in addition to providing a detailed account of his duel with Konings and other German snipers, is a rich source of insight into the fighting at Stalingrad in general and sniping in particular. Serious history and memoirs have set the tone for popular histories and film, which have continued to propagate the Soviet view of the duel and its outcome. In this regard, one can note, among others, William Craig's *Enemy at the Gates: The Battle for Stalingrad* (1973); Sergei Alekseev's *Gvardeiskii razgovor, rasskazy iz istorii Velikoi Otechestvennoi Voiny* (*Speaking with Soldiers: Stories from the History of the Great Fatherland War*, 1979[19]); Albert Axell's *Russia's Heroes: 1941–45* (2001); Andy Dougan's *The Hunting of Man: A History of the Sniper* (2004); and the film *Enemy at the Gates* (2001), directed by Jean-Jacques Annaud.

The Zaitsev Memoir

Primarily concerned with his experiences as a sniper at Stalingrad, Zaitsev's memoir is nevertheless rich in observations and insights into the nature of war and the Stalingrad battle itself and for those reasons may be seen as an important contribution to the literature dealing with Stalingrad. The memoir has an introduction written by Marshal Vasilii Chuikov, the commander of 62nd Army, which faced the brunt of the German assault in the city, who plays up the importance of the duel between Zaitsev and Konings. Zaitsev's title has relevance for the Stalingrad battle that for most readers will not be immediately obvious. Chuikov provides some hint to its real meaning when he writes: "There was nowhere to retreat; there was no land for us beyond the Volga."[20] The slogan—"There was no land for us beyond the Volga"—which was widely used at party meetings and agitation sessions among the troops during the battle, was a veiled threat to be interpreted in the context of Order № 227 (28 July 1942). There was to be no retreat because any retreat, unless authorized—and Stalin had made it clear that there would be no such authorization—would be regarded as an act of desertion to be punished by a firing squad. The Red Army was to stand and fight where it stood.

Initially Zaitsev joined the navy, transferring in September 1942 to the Red Army, where he served in 2nd Battalion, Regiment 1047 of 284th Rifle Division. During the night of 21–22 September 1942 Zaitsev crosses the river to Stalingrad with his unit. In the first instance the unit is deployed in ruins close to the Long Gully (*ovrag Dolgii*). Almost immediately the division faces the Germans in close-quarters battle. These experiences in the rubble provide Zaitsev, at this stage fighting as an ordinary infantry soldier, with the basis of the observations that make this memoir worth reading, quite apart from its account of the duel with Konings:

> The artillery and mortars have fallen silent. We're attacking again. We're waging an unequal battle. Hand-to-hand fighting starts, brutal and short. This is where the training came in useful that we were taught before the crossing. Again, there's a breather. We glance at the factory ruins: piles of bricks and twisted metal beams. And suddenly, I see, there is a little girl: so small, thin, about twelve years old. Her delicate little legs are grazed and bloodied, her dark blue dress, obviously secondhand, is torn, her tiny red boots, also ripped and worn on bare feet. The little girl is walking ahead of some wounded soldiers, leading them somewhere. Until then we had seen many tracks and trails among the ruins in the direction they were heading. A shell explodes with a bang, and splinters and small fragments of brick fly out in a fan. Explosive bullets click here as well. But the little girl continues to walk as if she notices nothing. I get down behind the machine gun, press on the trigger, and return the enemy's fire. The memory of that little girl will stay with me forever.[21]

Zaitsev is clearly exercised by the question of courage; there are a number of places in his memoir where he reflects on its essence and what it means for the infantry soldier or for the specialized task of the sniper. In these many observations and in the many incidents that befall Zaitsev, Order № 227 is ever present, hanging over the battlefield. When Zaitsev writes about the moment they cross over the Volga to Stalingrad, there is no mention of Order № 227 or that the order was read before they were deployed. However, this is the moment when the order or something similar would have been read to the troops. Later Zaitsev is buried with corpses and manages to extricate himself from the mass grave. When he makes it back to his unit, there is no suggestion that he has deserted or done anything wrong. The difficult problem of desertion is avoided because the battalion commander admits that they believed Zaitsev to be dead and buried him. Implied is the question of what happens to a soldier who is knocked unconscious in an explosion—surely a very common occurrence—and then turns up. In yet another incident, Zaitsev admits to having a panic attack, running off, and then recovering his composure. He relates an especially compromising incident that befalls another famous Stalingrad sniper, Viktor Medvedev, who is seized by Germans and dragged away but is successfully rescued by his comrades. In the climate engendered by Order № 227, these sorts of incidents are too readily construed as cowardice or desertion, and, indeed, on returning to their lines they learn that one of the officers has put it about that some of the snipers, among them Zaitsev as well as Medvedev, were under suspicion of having shirked their duty, a serious accusation. Zaitsev has to explain his absence. Later, Zaitsev notes that in their position they were almost surrounded and cut off; that for two days they were encircled. Is this another oblique way of attacking the presumption that soldiers who have been encircled are guilty of some crime?

Zaitsev tries to identify the nature of cowardice: "As a rule, those with a cowardly nature perish from a psychological point of view before their physical death because they don't think about how to kill the enemy but seek safety from him, and they perish. And how can it be any different? If you haven't killed the enemy, he'll kill you."[22] These discussions and digressions on the nature of fear and cowardice are an indirect yet effective way of dealing with Order № 227. Yet, for all the arbitrary nature of such orders, Zaitsev is well aware that cowards will let you down: "He who wants to survive in battle must first of all, without losing sight of fear, crush the coward in himself as a poisonous snake that can kill you ahead of time."[23]

On 21 October 1942, having demonstrated his marksmanship by killing two Germans with the standard-issue Soviet rifle at a range well beyond the skills of most infantrymen, Zaitsev is designated a divisional sniper. Whatever the Soviet propagandist's view of the various duels that took place between individual Soviet and German snipers, many tales of which were uncritically disseminated and often amplified in Western wartime reporting, Zaitsev evinces a healthy respect for the abilities of German snipers and their tactical abilities. That he can detach himself from the propaganda of Soviet military success and compel himself to concentrate on the German enemy as he finds him is further evidence of Zaitsev's mental strength and powers of concentration. In fact, he is very nearly killed by a German sniper when a bullet hits his helmet and shatters. Later one of Zaitsev's comrades, Sasha Griazev, also a trained sniper, is killed by a single shot. On the fieldcraft of German snipers, Zaitsev instructs us: "German snipers, as a rule, set up their firing positions in the depth of defense, whereas we move out to the very edge of the forward defense. They have many dummy firing positions. How does one determine the dummy ones from the ones in use? My limited experience hints at the answer: one needs good powers of observation and endurance."[24]

Like their Soviet counterparts, German snipers make every effort to kill Soviet commanders and artillery observers, thus reducing the effectiveness of Soviet battery fire. The effect of German snipers on the Soviet positions is clearly revealed in what a Red Army soldier tells Zaitsev: "'German snipers have pinned us down. You can't use the altillery periscope; they don't allow you to stick your head out. We've no idea where they are shooting from. Help us, Vasia.'"[25]

Zaitsev covers the duel with Konings in chapter 18 of his memoir ("The Duel"). News that the German high command in Berlin has sent the head of the Berlin sniper school to Stalingrad is gleaned from a German prisoner, and Zaitsev is placed on full alert by his divisional commander, Colonel Nikolai Batiuk. In what makes Zaitsev's memoir a classic among similar accounts of sniping and scouting, the author ponders over the problem of trying to track down and kill Konings before the German manages to locate and kill him. In Zaitsev's words:

> I divide the process of discovering the target in the enemy camp into two stages. The first begins with a study of the enemy's defense. Then I find out where, when, and in what circumstances our soldiers were wounded. In this instance I get a great deal of help from the medics. They tell me where the wounded soldier was picked up. I go there and seek out any eyewitnesses, and from them I get all the details concerning how the soldier was wounded. On the basis of this I can work out the enemy's fire plan. All this belongs to the first phase of determining where one must seek out the target. I call the second phase searching for the target. So as not to be picked up by the enemy sniper, I observe the territory with the help of the periscope or artillery tube. For this sort of work the telescopic sights on the rifle or binoculars are unsuitable. Experience indicates that there, where the enemy was active but where one can observe no movement at all, means that that is where the deadly predator is located. That is why I always tell my sniper friends that if I have not studied the situation or if I haven't talked with people, I make no move. As a sniper one needs to adhere to the principle expressed in the proverb: "Measure seven times, cut once." And in actual fact there is a lot of work required for a single shot. You have to acquire and study the enemy's character, study

> his strength, and probe for his weak spots, and only after that can you resolve the matter with a single shot.[26]

The first clear indication that Konings has arrived and deployed comes when two of Zaitsev's comrades, both experienced snipers, come off worst in an encounter with a German sniper: one has his optical sight destroyed; the other is wounded. Zaitsev is convinced that these are the hallmarks of his enemy. Now begins a four-day war of nerves. On the third day, Danilov, a *politruk* (political leader or instructor), insists on accompanying Zaitsev and his partner, Nikolai Kulikov. Despite, one assumes, some warnings from Zaitsev that Danilov must do exactly as he is told, Danilov believes that he has seen the German sniper and, momentarily breaking cover to indicate the German's position, is wounded. Zaitsev regards this as further evidence that they are indeed up against the German supersniper: "Of course, only an experienced sniper could shoot in such a way. I examined the enemy lines for a long time, but I could not find the ambush position. Over many days I had already studied the forward edge of the enemy's lines so that I immediately noted any new crater, any new parapet that appeared. Now I could see nothing new or suspicious at all."[27]

Zaitsev continues his observations of no-man's-land:

> Between the tank and the pillbox, on flat ground, just before the line of the German defense, there is a sheet of iron with a small pile of bricks. It has been there for ages; it's a familiar sight. I put myself in the position of the enemy: Where's the best place for a sniper position? Why not dig out a slit trench under that sheet of metal? During the night prepare a hidden route to it? Yes, in all probability, he's there, under the metal sheet, in no-man's-land. I decided to test this. I place a mitten on a plank and raise it. The German takes the bait! Excellent! I carefully lower the board into the trench, into the same position from which I raised it. I examine the hole. There's no angle on this; it's a direct hit, which means that the German is under the sheet, precisely.[28]

The duel is resolved in the afternoon of the fourth day. To quote Zaitsev:

> During the night we equipped the post. We stayed there until first light. The Germans maintained sporadic fire. Enemy mortars fired on the Volga crossing. Rockets soared into the sky. Later our artillery returned fire, and

> the German mortars fell silent. German bombers appeared. The sun rose. Kulikov fired off a blind shot. We had to arouse the sniper's interest. We decided to sit out the first half of the day; light reflecting from our scopes could give us away. In the afternoon our rifles were in the shade, while the direct light of the sun fell upon the German's position. Something sparkled by the edge of the sheet. Was this a piece of glass that just happened to be there, or was it the telescopic sight of a sniper's rifle? Very carefully, as only the most experienced sniper would do, Kulikov started to raise a helmet. The German fired. Kulikov raised himself for a brief moment, shouted loudly, and fell.
>
> The German probably thought that at last the Soviet sniper, the chief "hare" for whom he had been hunting the last four days, had been killed and stuck half of his head out from under the sheet. I fired. The German's head sank and the optical sight of his rifle sparkled in the sunlight.[29]

As soon as darkness fell, writes Zaitsev, Kulikov and he dragged the body of the dead German major out from under the iron sheet. The German's documents were removed and handed over to the divisional commander.

An Assessment of the Konings-Zaitsev Duel

Despite Zaitsev's detailed account of the duel and the hallmark of veracity given by the authority of a Soviet marshal, there are inconsistencies and lacunae in the historical record that unfortunately do raise questions about whether the duel ever took place. I say "unfortunately" because as a young soldier I was fascinated by the duel and took it for granted that these two evenly matched antagonists had stalked one another in the ruins of Stalingrad. That the sorts of duels described by Zaitsev, other Soviet snipers, and German snipers did take place on the Eastern front in World War II is not in doubt.

An obvious starting point is Zaitsev's memoir itself. Zaitsev goes out of his way to date various key moments in his military career: for example, he crosses the Volga on the night of 21–22 September 1942; he is formally accepted as a sniper on 21 October 1942; he and other members of his sniper group are deployed to the slopes east of Mamaev kurgan on 24 October 1942; on 10 February 1943 he is in hospital; and a day later, on 11 February 1943, he is promoted to junior lieutenant. Yet nowhere in his memoir does he provide precise dates for the four-day period of the duel with Konings. Given that Zaitsev can be bothered to cite the date when he crossed the Volga into the besieged city, his reticence concerning the dates for the duel with Konings, or at the very least the date on which he killed Konings and finally emerged victorious, is notable—even suspicious—by its absence. Not even the month in which this duel took place is indicated. It is not even clear whether the duel occurred in 1942 or 1943. Again, in view of the vast amount of interest in this duel then and long after the war, it is striking that no Soviet account provides the precise date on which Konings succumbed.

Recall the final day of the duel. Zaitsev says that Kulikov and he sat out the first half of the day so as to avoid betraying their position by sunlight reflecting on the telescopes of their rifles. In the afternoon the position of the sun was such that it now would betray Konings. Now, the sun rises in the east and sets in the west. If, therefore, the rising sun and sunlight in the morning posed a danger to Zaitsev, his ambush position must have been facing east; in other words, the fatal shot would have been fired *from* the west in an easterly direction. Likewise, if by the afternoon the position of the sun was now dangerously disadvantageous to Konings because it was in the west, then Konings would have been located in a firing position that faced west, not east. This configuration of Zaitsev's and Konings's relative positions is a complete reversal of the disposition of Soviet and German lines: the Germans were attacking from the west to the east; the Red Army, with its rear to the east, faced west in the direction of the attacking Germans. This should mean that for Konings the morning would have been the period of greatest risk of having his position betrayed by reflected sunlight, whereas the afternoon would have been the period of greatest risk for Zaitsev and Kulikov. It must be borne in mind that though the Germans faced east and the Soviet lines faced west, individual soldiers—typically scouts (*razvedchiki*) and snipers—could, because they fought highly individual battles, easily find themselves engaging the enemy from the direction of the main enemy lines, and vice versa. As far as one can tell, however, that particular configuration can be discounted for the Zaitsev-Konings duel because Zaitsev makes it clear in his memoir that Konings's firing position is in front of the main German forward edge of the battlefield, in no-man's-land. The other consideration regarding the dangers posed by sunlight is whether Konings or any other experienced sniper would have made such a cardinal error. Zaitsev shows himself to be aware of the hazard of sunlight. Are we to believe that his formidable opponent was not, and that he made this elementary and fatal error? Moreover, given Konings's demonstrated cunning, a piece of glass or optics sited in such a way as intentionally to reflect light would be an excellent way of attracting the attention of an enemy sniper in the hope that he would betray his position either by movement or a shot.

A final consideration concerns the body and documents of Konings. If Zaitsev had indeed managed to kill the top German sniper and had managed to recover the body and documents, the opening for Soviet wartime propaganda would have been enormous and irresistible. Photographs of the vanquished German's body, rifle, and personal documents would have been in every Soviet paper and would almost certainly have been reproduced by the British and American press. Yet we find nothing. Furthermore, if these documents were handed over to Colonel Batiuk, as claimed by Zaitsev, they would have been preserved not just as part of the divisional archive but as important historical documents in their own right, artifacts of the Stalingrad legend. I have yet to come across a single Soviet or post-Soviet source that provides any details of these documents or that even acknowledges their existence, apart from Zaitsev's account. Recent collections of declassified Russian documents make no reference to the duel at all. For example, one of the best collections is *Stalingradskaia epopeia: Materialy NKVD SSSR i voennoi tsenzury iz Tsentral'nogo arkhiva FSB RF (The Stalingrad Epic: Documentary Material of the NKVD of the USSR and Military Censorship from the Central Archive of the FSB of the Russian Federation*, 2000). This collection provides a mass of declassified Soviet material on, among other things, blocking detachments, executions, and desertion. This is precisely the sort of collection in which one would expect to find facsimiles of Konings's documents and Soviet directives and memoranda specifying the propaganda line to be adopted. Yet there is nothing.[30]

We might also consider the military records of Zaitsev and Konings. Zaitsev provides plenty of detail in his memoir that can be checked, among other resources, in the records of 284th Rifle Division, commanded by Colonel Batiuk, in which he served. Regarding Major Konings, there are serious grounds to doubt whether he existed. So far no trace has been found of any Major Konings in surviving Wehrmacht records.[31] Nor was there any German Army sniper school in Berlin or its environs at the moment when Konings was, according to the history of the duel, sent to Stalingrad.

When we compare the account of the duel given by Zaitsev with subsequent accounts, Soviet and Western, some glaring contradictions can be noted. For example, in *Barbarossa: The Russian-German Conflict 1941–1945*, Alan Clark cites a long extract dealing with the duel taken from the English translation of Vasilii Chuikov's memoirs, *The Beginning of the Road* (1963). Chuikov makes it clear that the German sniper was Major Konings,[32] whereas Clark states that the German sniper was Standartenführer SS Heinz Thorvald, the head of the snipers' school at Zossen.[33] Clark makes no mention of Konings. No SS units served at Stalingrad, but it is not inconceivable that an individual SS sniper might have been assigned this task. That such a deployment is not ruled out and is plausibly implied can be seen in the interrogation of Helmuth Ludwig, serving in 376th Infantry Division, who was captured on 5 December 1942. During his interrogation Ludwig mentioned that he had seen SS and SA troops in the Kessel:

> I must add, as I heard from the company commander, that a certain amount of soldiers from the SS and SA, apparently with the aim of strengthening and "raising the spirit" of the encircled units, are being brought in by these transport planes.
>
> I personally saw SS and SA soldiers, approximately 4–5 per company, in the units of 3rd [Infantry FE] Motorized Division that were at Novoalekseevka.[34]

Axell's account is marred by a distinct willingness to accept uncritically Soviet accounts of their snipers on the Eastern front in general and of Zaitsev's role in particular. A thoroughly misleading view, based on ignorance, of what is required for sniping is provided by Axell's remarks that accompany a photograph of Mila Pavlichenko, a female sniper. The photograph shows Pavlichenko's white face and hands without any camouflage cream or blackening and a rifle that that has also been untreated and thus will reflect light and betray the sniper's position. The sniper herself is wearing the standard soft hat worn in barracks. According to the caption, the sniper "lies in ambush." The claim is obviously preposterous: any sniper, German or Russian, who so flagrantly neglected the basic requirements of personal camouflage and concealment would soon be dead. Nor were snipers accompanied by photographers during operations. The photograph had clearly been stage-managed for propagandistic purposes. The misleading nature of Soviet photographs and the need to be on one's guard can be appreciated by comparing photographs used by Antony Beevor in *Stalingrad* and by Professor Samsonov in *Stalingradskaia bitva*, which throughout the Soviet period was regarded in the Soviet Union as the definitive study of the battle. Both Samsonov and Beevor use almost identical pictures of General Konstantin Rokossovskii. In the photograph used by Beevor, in the bottom right-hand corner are two men, one of whom is holding a camera and shown taking a picture of Rokossovskii.[35] In the photograph in Samsonov's book, the same two men have been erased.[36] Once alerted to this erasure, one can detect two hazy outlines created by the censor's editing. Whether the photographer was deleted from the photograph because he drew attention to the too obviously stage-managed nature of the photograph or whether he fell afoul of the NKVD and had to be retrospectively erased is anyone's guess.

Axell concedes in an endnote that there are doubts about whether Konings existed but offers no good reasons for why there are doubts.[37] There are also a number of basic errors in his account. He cites Zaitsev's full name as Vasilii *Alexandrovich* Zaitsev,[38] whereas Zaitsev's patronymic is given in his memoir as *Grigor'evich*.[39] Moreover, Axell claims that at the time of the duel Zaitsev was a "senior captain,"[40] whereas in fact, as Zaitsev himself makes clear in his memoir, he was promoted to the rank of junior lieutenant—*mladshii leitenant*—on Chuikov's order on 11 February 1943 after the German collapse.[41] Axell refers to the moment in the duel when Danilov the *politruk* was wounded, stating that "the bullet only grazed his scalp."[42] Zaitsev merely tells us that Danilov was wounded.[43] Axell also claims that Zaitsev and Kulikov retrieved the German sniper's rifle and kept it as a souvenir but handed over the German's documents to the divisional commander.[44] In his account (see above) Zaitsev says nothing about what became of the German's rifle, only that Konings's documents were passed on to the divisional commander.

In *The Hunting of Man: A History of the Sniper* Dougan provides a general account of attempts to kill accurately, starting with slings and arrows and moving up to the modern era of military and police sniping and countersniping. Although somewhat skeptical of the Zaitsev-Konings duel, some of his observations need to be treated with caution. For example, Dougan recounts a duel with a German sniper from which Mila Pavlichenko emerged victorious. According to Dougan's account, she recovered the German sniper's log book containing his record of kills. To quote Dougan: "This German had been active since Dunkirk and had killed more than 400 British and French soldiers before Mila Pavlichenko added him to her total in the Crimea."[45] The Soviet claim, based on what was in a German logbook, which, as far as one can tell, has never been made available, that a German sniper had managed to kill 400 British and French soldiers since Dunkirk needs to be treated with extreme caution. The German campaign against the British Expeditionary Force (BEF) and the French Army in the summer of 1940 was a brilliant demonstration of combined-arms warfare, the Blitzkrieg, pioneered by the Wehrmacht. France was conquered in an exceptionally short campaign of no more than six weeks, and the BEF by a miracle managed to evacuate the bulk of its troops from Dunkirk. Given the nature of the German campaign—fast-moving, armored columns, motorized infantry, and the air arm being used in support—the conditions for the static warfare required for snipers would not have existed, and certainly not for the prolonged period necessary to achieve anything like 400 kills. Again, the German campaigns in Greece, Crete, and North Africa followed the same pattern as the campaign in France in the summer of 1940: highly mobile with static defenses being bypassed. The French took no part in these campaigns. The inflation of the number of British and French soldiers killed by this unknown German sniper is intended to serve the purposes of Soviet propaganda. It is meant to imply that the British and French were soft targets: only the Red Army had the skill and courage to defeat the German sniper threat. Another problem with the claim that this German sniper had been active since Dunkirk concerns the provision of training and equipment of snipers in the Wehrmacht. There were indeed institutional wisdom, memories, and knowledge, but training and equipment were largely nonexistent.

Dougan's account of Zaitsev's career is flawed not just by a gross historical error—Dougan writes that the head of the Red Army's political department was receiving daily reports of the fighting in Stalingrad in 1941[46]—but by a glaring discrepancy between Zaitsev's memoir and some of the sources (unspecified) that Dougan uses in his book. Dougan notes that the Soviet propaganda machine had declared that in order to mark the anniversary of the October Revolution, Zaitsev would bring his score of German soldiers killed to 150. At the end of October, writes Dougan, Zaitsev had managed to kill 149 German soldiers.[47] Given that Zaitsev was only appointed a divisional sniper on 21 October 1942, it seems somewhat farfetched to believe that he achieved such a tally in ten days. An almost identical account is given by Antony Beevor in *Stalingrad*. Neither Beevor nor Dougan provides any source for this implausible story.[48]

The Konings-Zaitsev Duel in Soviet-Russian War Literature

Of the five best-known novels dedicated to the battle of Stalingrad in Soviet-Russian literature, only Grossman's shows any interest in the Zaitsev-Konings duel. There is nothing in Konstantin Simonov's *Dni i nochi* (*Days and Nights*, 1944), Viktor Nekrasov's *Vokopakh Stalingrada* (*In the Trenches of Stalingrad*, 1946),[49] or IUrii Bondarev's *Goriachii sneg* (*Hot Snow*, 1969). By contrast, Grossman's *Stalingradskie ocherki* (*The Stalingrad Sketches*), a collection of the author's articles written for the Red Army newspaper *Krasnaia zvezda* and published in 1943; *Za pravoe delo* (*For a Just Cause*, 1952); and *Zhizn' i sud'ba* (*Life and Fate*, 1988) show that Grossman was fully aware of snipers.

One of Grossman's best-known articles, *Glazami Chekhova* (*Through Chekhov's Eyes*, 1942), is based on time spent with Anatolii Chekhov, another famous Stalingrad sniper. Grossman's article is, in parts, technically convincing. He shows a complete grasp of the essential tasks of the sniper: to see without being seen and to kill without being killed. A comparison of the detailed notes made by Grossman in his wartime diary, based on time spent with Chekhov, with the actual article published in *Krasnaia zvezda* gives some idea of what worried the military censors.

Grossman's published article presents a softer image of Chekhov than that which emerges from the diary notes. Chekhov's home life suggested that he was one of the millions of social casualties caused by the huge changes inflicted on Soviet society before the war—even, in fact, that he may have harbored some grudge against Soviet power. The war offered him a new purpose and meaning. Well aware that the Germans were exploiting such grievances at Stalingrad and elsewhere, Grossman stressed the need for unity. According to Grossman, Chekhov understood this as well: "But on that night he understood for the first time in all its depth the terrible force of evil that had been brought to our country by the Germans. He grasped that the minor troubles and woes were nothing in comparison with the great national catastrophe."[50]

Grossman stresses that as a boy Chekhov had never even used a catapult and that he was reluctant to kill any living thing—the message was driven home by Grossman on a number of occasions—whereas in his diary Grossman merely notes that Chekhov had not used a catapult. The point here is to emphasize that Chekhov had been turned into a reluctant killer, a people's avenger, by the German invaders. In the article Grossman stresses Chekhov's love of books, yet in the diary entry he writes that Chekhov told the war correspondent: "My favorite books? In actual fact I read very little."[51] Nor does Grossman record that Chekhov spent many hours mastering the physics of light and optics. This is the sort of detail that owes more to Grossman's scientific background. In his article, Grossman stresses that initially the killing did not come easily to Chekhov, whereas in his diary Grossman records Chekhov telling him that he killed nine men on the first day.

Any qualms Chekhov had about killing German soldiers going for water must have disappeared very quickly since he was soon killing women as well, without any compunction. Chekhov told Grossman that the Germans sent out women and that he had killed two out of five.[52] These women were almost certainly Russian civilians either press-ganged into working for the Germans or collaborators. Chekhov had no way of knowing. He killed them anyway. Grossman records that "women live on Mamaev kurgan; they keep fires going and cook. Officers visit the girls."[53] In Grossman's article there is no reference to Chekhov's killing women. Presumably, the fact that Soviet soldiers were killing women was deemed not to help the Soviet propaganda effort at home and abroad since it might invite comparisons with the German invaders. It would also raise very awkward questions about why there was any collaboration at all.

One of Chekhov's victims may have been a Russian *Hiwi*. His dying words, in Russian, were: "Thank you, Stalingrad, that a Russian sniper killed me."[54] If Chekhov was close enough to hear one of his victims' last words in Russian, then he may well have been close enough to identify the women he killed as collaborators. Grossman records an encounter that Chekhov had with a German sniper. Observing the German lines, Chekhov noted that a small embrasure had appeared in a wall: "Chekhov realized that this meant a German sniper. 'Just look,' he whispered to the sergeant who had come to see him at work, and he squeezed the trigger. There was a shout and the clatter of boots as the German submachine gunners dragged away the body of the sniper who had not succeeded in firing a single round."[55] Chekhov had no way of knowing whether the German was a sniper, but the claim that he had killed an enemy sniper was presumably added for the benefit of the reader at home and abroad. A potential downside to Grossman's article in *Krasnaia zvezda* was that the Germans seemed—uncharacteristically—to take so long to realize what was happening, and their responses seemed woefully inadequate.

In *Stalingradskoe voisko* (*The Stalingrad Army*, 1943), Grossman relates a visit to a battalion located on the slopes of Mamaev kurgan. In places the distance separating the German lines from the Soviet lines is as little as 25 meters. Every movement takes place under the watchful eyes of snipers:

> Here everything is registered, each stone is a firing reference point. There are a lot of snipers here. . . . The tension of death and war reigns here, day and night. The Germans fully understand the importance of this sector in their defensive system. Here, so as to avoid the crack of a German sniper's bullet, you must not show yourself over the top of the edge of the trench. Here the Germans do not conserve their ammunition.[56]

Grossman identifies German snipers as being active and efficient in *For a Just Cause*: "During the night snipers and small groups of Germans armed with automatic weapons infiltrate into the inner city, picking their way through the ruins and bringing down heavy artillery fire on our positions and artillery headquarters."[57] The fact that German snipers targeted Soviet commanders in the same way that Zaitsev and his fellow snipers sought out German commanders and junior leaders is obvious in the following passage. A Soviet officer is just about to inspect the battalion's positions: "Having dispatched Shvedkov to regimental headquarters, he threw his overcoat over the top of his map case and artillery board so that a German sniper didn't pick him up straightaway."[58] German artillery forward observation officers were prime targets for Soviet snipers since killing them greatly reduced the effectiveness of artillery fire. Grossman's description of a German observer shows that he fully understands the vital role for both sides played by these observers. Attention to personal camouflage and concealment was every bit as important for observers as it was for snipers: "An NCO artillery observer wearing loose-fitting camouflaged overalls mottled with yellow, brown, and green oval shapes with a face veil covered in frayed strips of rag stood on the balcony of a four-story building facing the Volga."[59]

Grossman offers two accounts of Zaitsev's duel with an experienced German sniper, yet provides no name for the German. He merely notes "Zaitsev's lone battle with a major German sniper."[60] In his sixth notebook (Stalingrad 1942), he records the conclusion of the duel: "'He killed three of our men. He waited fifteen minutes. Our gully was empty, and he started to stand up. I can see that his rifle is on the ground. I stand right up. He sees me and understands. I fire.'"[61] In *Life and Fate* Grossman describes the denouement as follows:

> Zaitsev began to recount his duel with the German sniper at the foot of Mamaev kurgan, which had lasted several days. The German knew that Zaitsev was stalking him as he was stalking Zaitsev. Both seemed a match for the other, and neither of them could outwit the other.
>
> "On that day he killed three of our lads. I am sitting in a gully, and I do not fire off a single shot. Then he shoots for the last time, without missing. The soldier falls; he's on his side, his arm folded back. From their side a soldier comes with some papers. I'm sitting there, watching. And he, I know this, understands that if a sniper were waiting there he would kill the one with the papers, but the soldier passes. I realize that he cannot see the soldier he has killed and that he wants to take a look. It's quiet. A second German comes running past with a bucket. The gully

remains silent. About another sixteen minutes pass. He starts to stand up. Now he's standing. I stand fully up."

Once again reliving what had happened, Zaitsev stood up from behind the table. That particular expression of strength that flashed on his face now became its sole, its main, expression. This was no longer some good-natured, broad-shouldered lad. There was something powerful, leonine, malevolent in those flared nostrils, in the broad forehead, in eyes that were full of terrible, triumphant inspiration.

"He understood; he recognized me. And I fired."[62]

Both versions given by Grossman have little in common with the resolution given by Zaitsev in his memoir. Once again we have conflicting accounts and no obvious way of deciding which are accurate. Grossman's notebooks throw yet another wrench in the works since he records that the other snipers refer to Zaitsev as Vasilii *Ivanovich*, a third variation on the patronymic.[63] Another twist emerges in an extract from Grossman's diaries that was not published in the 1989 collection. Grossman refers to two soldiers who were sentenced to be shot but who had their sentences rescinded: one was a soldier with the name of Zaitsev; the other was named Murashev. The striking thing about this entry is that, according to Grossman, the same men went on to become the two best snipers in Stalingrad.[64] There is certainly nothing in Zaitsev's memoir about his having been sentenced to death. In the light of Grossman's diary entry, however, Zaitsev's noting that he is suspected of shirking his duty may well be a hint at something serious. Another tantalizing aspect to this story is that the extant archives of 10th Rifle Division NKVD also contain a reference to a Vasilii Ivanovich Zaitsev, who, according to a report dated 29 August 1942, had been absent from his unit for seven days.[65] When this particular Zaitsev turned up, he was without his rifle. The date of the report, however, rules out the possibility that this was Zaitsev the sniper.

The Wehrmacht Rediscovers the Art of Sniping

The massive use of Soviet snipers against the Wehrmacht in Russia after 22 June 1941 compelled the German army to rediscover the art of sniping in which it had once been a pioneer. To quote Peter Senich: "Without question, the effect of Soviet sharp shooting was the predominant influence determining the direction of the overall German sniping program from late 1941 until the end of the war in 1945."[66] It is not clear that any centralized German sniping school was ever established, so sniper instruction would have been of a largely improvised and ad hoc nature and carried on within German units, though toward the end of the war there is evidence of a more centralized approach (as discussed later in this chapter). In a brief article published in *Der Freiwillige*, Bernhard Jocher provides some details of early sniper training in the Wehrmacht. For example, he notes that snipers began their training with small-caliber weapons and then moved on to the heavier K-98. He points out that the semiautomatic rifle, the Gewehr 1943, was also adapted for sniping and fitted with a telescopic sight (x4 magnification).[67]

As the scale of the Soviet sniper threat emerged, the German Army made efforts to establish and to disseminate best practices in order to counter the threat and to improve as quickly as possible the training and operational effectiveness of German snipers. The Finnish Army, having inflicted mass casualties and massive disruption on the Red Army in the Winter War with its own snipers, and perhaps sensible of the fact that Soviet snipers were dangerous opponents, paid close attention to the methods and tactical ruses of their enemy. In May 1943 the Finnish Army summarized its experiences in sniper training and the current nature of the Soviet sniper threat in a document that the German Army had translated into German. The document, "*Finnische Erfahrungen bei der Scharfschützenausbildung*" (Finnish experiences in sniper training) sets out the basic approach for sniper training, the individual qualities required, methods of sniper deployment in defense and attack, observations on Soviet snipers, deception methods, and ways to counter the threat. Some of the methods used by Soviet snipers to cause soldiers to betray their position are noted:

> In order to accustom our men to carelessness, a position on our line has been maintained for eight days. The sniper's assistant has for some considerable period shoveled snow and afterward raised a helmet over the trench, or the sniper himself has placed a helmet in the trench of an open position in order to open fire from a different position. Once after an enemy sniper had crawled behind a stone, a dummy in full equipment was led back and forth. In places by means of heavy fire the enemy has tried to unsettle our men and get them to give away their positions. With this in mind he has also shot off unusually long bursts of machine-gun fire. The sniper has first zeroed his rifle at a certain distance, and only after *a few days* has he carried out very accurate application fire at the actual target.[68] [Emphasis in the original.]

The authors pay tribute to the marksmanship of Soviet snipers and cite numerous examples of accuracy:

> Determined by the width of the intermediate ground, the shooting ranges vary from 100 to 900 meters, but at times enemy snipers have even attempted shots at a range of 1,400 meters. The usual and most effective range is from 200 meters to 400 meters, but even at ranges from 600 meters to 700 meters the accuracy has been quite good.
>
> The readiness to engage moving targets and the rate of fire have also been good, which can be ascribed to the good training of the snipers and above all to the use of a rifle fitted with a telescopic sight. The rate of fire and the accuracy suggest that snipers who are located in houses are making use of special rests. Concerning the accuracy, the following examples may be cited: at ranges from 200 meters to 400 meters several periscopes and stereoscopes have been shot out; a sniper let off three rounds one after another at a stone about 10 cm x 10 cm that had been placed in the observation slit; on one occasion, as one of our machine-gun team commanders raised his hand over the snow wall in order to readjust an alarm wire, a sniper shot him in the hand at a range of 100 meters; in an observation slit that had been bored with a stick a sniper had several hits; various objects that our sentries had raised above the trenches as a test were as a rule hit; it has also happened that our observer watching through a periscope behind the snow wall has been shot at.[69]

Of relevance for the Zaitsev-Konings duel are the authors' observations concerning the exploitation of Soviet snipers in propaganda and the tally of claimed kills: "Decorations and rewards are issued for a definite number of 'kills.' Mind you, this propaganda is very optimistic in its evaluation of the performances and successes of snipers, who in all truth and in no way have achieved the results claimed."[70]

The document concludes with a series of recommendations intended to reduce the effectiveness of enemy snipers:

> Most of the losses that are caused by enemy snipers can be attributed to *carelessness*, insufficient exploitation of the terrain by our troops, or the circumstance that our men either wear only dirty snow camouflage jackets and hats or no snow camouflage clothing at all in exposed terrain. Losses due to our own carelessness can be avoided, and therefore every soldier

> must be *compelled* to exploit all possible means in order to make the task of enemy snipers as difficult as possible.
>
> The following countermeasures, among others, can be noted: cautious movement and painstaking exploitation of terrain in dangerous areas; the best possible camouflage; sufficiently deep fire and communications trenches; *warning signs* in trenches; poles across fire and communications trenches that make it necessary to bend the upper body when moving; *the use of helmets*; the use of clean and full snow camouflage suits in the front line; very careful selection as well as thorough digging in (with steel plates, sandbags, and so on) and camouflage of the fire positions; avoiding unnecessary shooting in observation posts; various, tested deception methods; intensification of our own sniper activity, for example, by means of the temporary deployment of snipers from the reserves; freeing our snipers from all other duties and their continual further training, especially where it concerns accuracy of fire; [and] the planned operation of other arms of service against enemy snipers when they cannot be destroyed by our own snipers.[71]

A later German assessment, issued under the auspices of the German high command in January 1944, shows that the Red Army used its snipers in conjunction with other arms. The assessment reports this development in a summary of a Soviet attack against units of German Army Group South:

> Shortly before first light and without any major preparatory artillery bombardment, the Russians attacked with mass armored forces. On the evening before, the enemy, making skillful use of terrain, had brought much larger infantry forces, interspersed with numerous snipers, right up to our forward edge of the battle area (about 80–100 meters). While at the start of the attack the bulk of the enemy tanks opened fire on the identified positions of the combat group at a range of about 200–400 meters, the first wave of tanks rolled over the position. At the same time enemy snipers prevented any move out of cover so that returning fire on the assaulting tanks with close-quarters weapons was made impossible. After the enemy tanks had succeeded in reaching the rear of our position, they turned against them. By means of hand grenades thrown from opened tank hatches and by rifle fire from snipers the gun crews on the position came under fire from the front and rear. Using this method the enemy managed to break up part of the forward edge of the battle area. At

that stage his tank and infantry reserves that had been held back attacked through the broken line farther into the depth of the defense.[72]

The author of the document made a number of recommendations, one of which was that "much greater significance is to be given to sniper operations. Snipers are to be trained to kill the commanders in enemy attacks."[73]

A major development for sniping in both the Wehrmacht and the SS came with an order issued by Hitler in August 1944 for the creation of a sniper badge: "The Führer has introduced a sniper badge for the Army and the SS. Herewith is the high level of achievement of the marksman armed with a rifle and his success in firing single shots acknowledged and serves at the same time as an incentive for the raising the performance hitherto achieved."[74]

The sniper's badge was allocated in three grades according to the number of kills. The basic badge depicted an eagle's head resting on two oak leaves. The sniper badge class 3 was awarded for a minimum of 20 confirmed kills, the sniper badge class 2 (edged in silver) for a minimum of 40 confirmed kills, and the sniper badge class 1 (edged in gold) for a minimum of 60 confirmed kills. A Wehrmacht document dated 27 August 1944 provides details of a typical sniper course that was to run for one month (18 September–21 October 1944) on the Munster troop training area.[75] Unfortunately, there are no details about the precise nature of the instruction. It seems likely that the accelerated emphasis on sniper training and deployment at this late stage in the war was linked to Hitler's determination to fight to the end and to use snipers to inflict as many casualties on the invading enemy as possible.

Soviet Snipers in German 6th Army Records

Extant records from German 6th Army headquarters and the various divisions, such as operational situation reports (*Tagesmeldungen*, *Lagemeldungen*, and *Zwischenmeldungen*), *Erlebnisberichte*, miscellaneous reports and orders (*Berichte* and *Befehle*), and formal intelligence assessments (*Feindnachrichtenblätter*), reveal that the commanders and soldiers of German 6th Army were fully aware of the threat posed by Soviet snipers and were doing everything within the limits of existing resources and the vagaries caused by extended lines of communication to deal with it.

The intelligence section at German 6th Army was responsible for preparing assessments of enemy units and developments. Three of these assessment documents, individually known as a *Feindnachrichtenblatt*, which cover the three critical months of September, October, and November, are in the German 6th Army records. The main theme is the obvious Soviet determination to fight on and the increasing harshness of the attrition battles in the city. In September's appreciation of the enemy it is noted that "the appearance of new troop formations in the enemy bridgeheads at Stalingrad, which have only been deployed in the last few days from the east bank of the Volga, and the ongoing addition of more reserves for the regiments that have already been fighting for some time on the west bank bear unambiguous witness to the will to commit to further determined resistance."[76]

Information derived from prisoners or deserters is summarized with a recommended course of action. Thus, the *Feindnachrichtenblatt* for September reports that Soviet prisoners have provided information concerning a 76-mm antitank gun with a muzzle velocity of 900 meters per second. The authors of the report request that any information about this gun along with any photographs be passed on to German 6th Army headquarters.[77] The significance of this observation lies in the fact that German 6th Army was monitoring very closely, as one would expect, any developments in Red Army infantry tactics and weaponry that might confer some advantage on its Soviet enemy. Consistent with this approach, the authors request more information about enemy reserve units, training schools, and establishments and areas. If Soviet snipers had been causing problems beyond the norm—snipers are after all an occupational hazard for infantrymen—one would expect to encounter some references to the problem.

Additional information concerning the situation facing German units in the city that is provided in September's *Feindnachrichtenblatt*, can be found in a report dated 25 September 1942, which was written by Major Menzel, a staff officer at German 6th Army headquarters.[78] Menzel was dispatched to the city by the chief of staff at German 6th Army headquarters with orders to visit 295th Infantry Division, 71st Infantry Division, 194th Infantry Regiment, an amalgamation of its 1st and 2nd Battalions, and the forward companies. The trip took place on 23 September 1942. Menzel notes the extreme proximity of the enemy and his alertness, yet there are no specific references to Soviet snipers.

October's *Feindnachrichtenblatt* (7 October 1942) notes that enemy resistance has stiffened. Once again there is detailed attention to any new tactical methods being employed by the Red Army. The following is noted:

> There is a slow, hardly noticeable moving right up to our own positions and the construction of tunnels right up to the barbed-wire obstacles,

> followed by a surprise detonation of the tunnel and the wire obstacle by means of elongated charges on a wide front. This is followed by the exploitation of the psychological effect in order to penetrate the position. The penetration will be carried out by day, mainly without any preparatory fire, and only with limited use of heavy infantry weapons. The Russians then proceed to barricade themselves in with sandbags that they have brought with them in the newly secured trenches. They then bring up heavy weapons.[79]

By closing the gap between the German and Soviet lines, the Soviet infantry make the task of providing close air support for the German ground forces by the Luftwaffe far more difficult since the margin of error is reduced and the chances of hitting their own troops a real risk. This move also has a profound psychological effect on the Germans since it reinforces the intention to close with and to destroy them. The reduced distances provide enormous opportunities for *razvedchiki* and snatch teams on both sides, quite apart from the snipers.

The November *Feindnachrichtenblatt* (dated 6 November 1942) notes the unremitting zeal of the Russians: "In spite of heavy losses, enemy resistance in Stalingrad shows no reduction in tenacity."[80] The three *Feindnachrichtenblätter* for September, October, and November cover the peak period of Soviet sniper activity. Yet there is nothing about the rise of Zaitsev or any other Soviet snipers to prominence. Given the casualties for which, according to Soviet sources, Zaitsev and his colleagues were responsible, the lack of references, if only to pour scorn on the number of Germans killed, is noteworthy.

The German Army made considerable efforts to record and to analyze its own combat performance with the aim of disseminating best practices throughout the army. Thus, a German 6th Army memorandum dated 5 November 1942 and signed by 6th Army's chief of staff, Generalleutnant Arthur Schmidt, notifies recipients that a dedicated staff officer will be dispatched to 6th Army and its divisions with the aim of bringing together the various lessons and experiences of the 1942 summer campaign.[81] Among the areas of combat that are to be reviewed and studied are the peculiarities of fighting in Fortress Stalingrad and in the inner city area, tactical combat experiences, and any other experiences.

A *Tagesmeldung* for 4 October 1942 from German 6th Army to VIII Army Corps provides some of the first references, albeit indirect ones, to Soviet snipers. Among the details for the return of captured enemy equipment one can note that eighteen Soviet sniper rifles (*Fernrohrgewehre*) have been seized, which will have been a welcome addition to the sniper and countersniping capabilities of the German units concerned.[82] Toward the end of October 1942 we encounter the clearest indication that German 6th Army is advocating measures that can reasonably be construed as countermeasures against the threat or increased threat of Soviet snipers. The *Tätigkeitsbericht*—a progress report—which was compiled by the command and training section at German 6th Army headquarters is a response to an *Erfahrungsbericht* of the 9th Machine Gun Battalion and was sent to Army Group B. The first paragraph of this brief response is significant:

> It has been proven that equipping individual soldiers with rifles fitted with telescopic sights *trains* their overall combat skills in observing the enemy, the recognition of targets, and their marksmanship (competitiveness). This is all the more important since mastery of this training area has almost been completely lost.
>
> Providing the troops in permanent positions with trench mirrors is vital for the approaching battle, which resembles a major event in the World War. German 6th Army submits an application for every division to be supplied with about 200 trench mirrors. The production of these by the troops themselves—quite apart from their improvised nature and thus their limited application—is not possible in the army's unpopulated area.[83]

The use of the word "*Wettkampf*" (competition) in this context might not be insignificant, since it conveys an idea of a duel, a competition between opposing snipers, the masters of the rubble. It also suggests recognition of the effectiveness of the Soviet policy that encourages rivalry among snipers so as to maximize enemy kills and a conscious attempt on the part of the Germans to emulate this policy. Exploiting this competitive element as a means to deal with enemy snipers with rewards for confirmed successes was used in units of 376th Infantry Division. To quote Horst Zank:

> In the open terrain it is especially dangerous to go to the forward positions in daytime or even to leave the gullies behind the main forward line and to move about in the coverless high terrain. There one has virtually no cover from view and, in particular, no protection from the Russian snipers who wait in ambush. As a result, our soldiers who are deployed forward in the

> trenches and antitank dugouts are practically pinned to the ground for days on end. Nevertheless, they are always trying by means of new tricks to make out the positions of the enemy snipers so as to eliminate them. In dealing with these enemy snipers, such as with antitank or antiaircraft guns, kills, confirmed by observers, are registered. As a reward there are special allocations of cigarettes or chocolate we commanders have, which are no longer available as normal rations. When several operational successes of this type against enemy snipers are confirmed, the well-deserved award of the Iron Cross, earned under such conditions, is made.[84]

One particular document in the German archives, *Ausbildungsvorshcrift für die Gebirgstruppen* (Training instructions for mountain troops), shows that among certain units the recognition of the value of snipers had not been totally lost. Referring to the problems of warfare in mountains, the author notes: "The lone rifleman and especially the sniper armed with a rifle fitted with a telescopic sight are, far more so than is the case in flat terrain, of decisive significance in the attack and in defense. In many instances there are strict limits to the support that can be made available by heavy infantry weapons and by artillery."[85]

The author also recognizes the classic problems of sniping—judging distance and the impact of mountain terrain: "Distances in high mountain terrain when looking up, down, and to the side are harder to assess than in flat terrain. Looking up, the distance is easily underestimated; looking down, it is overestimated."[86]

At the end of October 1942, in a lengthy order, *Befehl für den Kampf im Winter 1942/43* (Order for the winter battle, 1942–43), that was circulated to 6th Army divisions, there is further recognition by German 6th Army headquarters that sniping and countersniping would figure prominently in the static conditions. In a section devoted to training we find the following: "There is to be much greater value placed on observation of the terrain and the enemy by the individual soldier. The allocation of snipers and encouraging the competitive instincts of all soldiers are tried-and-tested training aids for this. The use of improvised trench mirrors prevents losses."[87] These training orders suggest that poor observation has facilitated the work of Soviet snipers and that poor trench discipline—insufficient camouflage and careless and unnecessary exposure of soldiers—has resulted in avoidable losses from Soviet snipers. Once again the theme of *Wettkampf* (competition) is being emphasized.

As the paper trail of situation reports and other documents moves downward, away from German 6th Army headquarters toward the divisions, regiments, and smaller subunits of 6th Army, the reporting of Soviet and German sniper activity becomes more pronounced. We even encounter the names of individual soldiers who have been killed and wounded by Soviet snipers. The sense of detachment that is necessarily and unavoidably present in documents generated at German 6th Army headquarters is greatly reduced, the sense of urgency all the greater. The reports and observations generated by the divisions and units lower in the Wehrmacht hierarchy bring us much closer to the front line and its perils, among which Soviet snipers, for all their efficiency as rifle killers, were just one.

German mobility on the steppe counted for very little in the suburbs and inner city, especially after the damage inflicted by the Luftwaffe attacks. Rubble, damaged buildings, and blocked streets all favored the defenders, not the attackers. German units encountered Soviet snipers from very early on in the battle. On days when major movements of men and equipment did not take place, sporadic harassing fire from mortars, artillery, and snipers was the norm. In a report prepared by the intelligence section of Panzer-Grenadier Regiment 64, dated 28 August 1942, intelligence officers identify a pattern of behavior that continued throughout the battle: "From 0800 hours noticeable quiet ensues in front of the combat group's entire sector. The enemy confines himself for the rest of the day to sniper activity and minimal harassing fire."[88] In an entry dated 1 September 1942, which appears to have been written some time after 1 September, there has been an escalation in sniper activity: "In the ensuing days enemy snipers are very active; there is also harassing fire coming from well-camouflaged tanks, antitank guns, and mortars on the outskirts of Spartakovka."[89] Later reports compiled on the basis of reports from survivors highlight the threat of snipers. In an entry dated 8 December 1942: "The enemy takes his revenge with the increased deployment of snipers, who make our lives hell. For all that, the mood of the troops remains good."[90] In his own account, Gefreiter Josef Maessen recalls a narrow escape that took place on 4 January 1943: "An explosive bullet hit the left edge of my steel helmet and shattered."[91] Maessen was lucky to survive: he had almost certainly been targeted by a Soviet sniper.

Soviet sniper activity features in the documents of 305th Infantry Division. German soldiers were warned to ensure that they maintained good fire and concealment discipline: "The repeatedly encountered belief of the troops—they only make themselves visible to the enemy by reconnaissance and firing—is to be firmly resisted. The best way to keep troublesome snipers at bay is by the deployment of one's own good marksmen (rifles with telescopic sights!)."[92]

Deprived of mobility in the city, the soldiers of 24th Panzer Division increasingly functioned as infantrymen. The need for their own snipers was soon realized: "Snipers must be deployed in every unit who, located at crucial points, must be able to keep up-to-date with special tasks."[93] Being an armored unit, 24th Panzer Division was probably not a high priority for the allocation of German or captured Soviet sniper rifles. Whatever the reasons, the lack of rifles fitted with telescopic sights was acutely felt, as is quite clear from a report dealing with the provision of weapons: "The absence of these weapons in the division was obvious and detrimental in many operations. Well-sited and camouflaged marksmen armed with rifles fitted with telescopic sights could have taken out many a Bolshevik firing from ambush positions in houses and cellars and consequently saved our troops unnecessary losses."[94]

Sixteenth Panzer Division also suffered from the attentions of Soviet snipers. In a report dated 3 August 1943, a soldier of 2nd Battalion, Panzer Grenadier Regiment 64, recalls what befell Hauptmann Alfred Mues on 17 November 1942: "Toward 1100 hours Knight's Cross holder Hauptmann Mues received a severe head wound from a sniper's bullet. On 23 November 1942 he died at the division's main casualty clearing station."[95] Hauptmann Mues was not an isolated example. The same soldier notes: "In the position nobody can raise his head too high; otherwise he'll be finished off by a sniper."[96] And a day after Hauptmann Mues received his fatal wound: "Enemy pressure continues unabated throughout the day. Snipers and registered mortars prevent any movement toward the combat group in daytime."[97]

The dominance of Soviet snipers in this sector is confirmed by Obergefreiter Hufschmidt's account, compiled after he was wounded and evacuated from Stalingrad: "The Russians must have had snipers over there. As soon as anything sticks out over the edge of the trench—even if just for a few seconds—a deadly accurate shot follows."[98] Later Hufschmidt, now wounded, recalls how he made his way to the rear while being targeted by a Soviet sniper:

> A larger splinter tears away our tent, which we have pulled tightly over our shell scrape as protection from the snowstorm. Quickly I try while there is still a bit of light to repair the damage. To do this I have to reach out a bit from the shell scrape. A second later I feel a blow against my left hand,

and there then follows a stinging pain in my wrist. My first thought is that I have been wounded in my artery. Indeed, the blood shoots up high but in a constant stream from the wound. My comrade binds my left arm and puts on an emergency dressing. Now I have to wait until evening. The blood loss is considerable. Hopefully, there'll be no major attack. Things are okay. As the darkness sets in, I get myself ready to move off to the platoon commander's bunker. Outside it remains quite light. It is a clear, starlit night. I can't go; otherwise the enemy will surely see me. In any case, I crawl away. I've got about 300 meters to cover.

Moving slowly, often with pauses, I move on from hole to hole. Along the way I see some comrades with their faces down on the snow: they've been shot in the head.

All of a sudden there is rifle fire from the other side. I press myself down into the snow as tightly as I can. I wonder whether they have seen me. When it becomes quiet once again, I crawl on further. Now there is a small mound in front of me, rising by about only a meter over the surface of the snow. I briefly weigh the situation: Should I go over it slowly or do it in one leap? I think of the comrades with head shots who are lying behind me. Finally I go for the leap. I am not quite on the ground once again when the typical sharp crack of an infantry rifle sounds like a whip over the terrain. Slowly I crawl on. Suddenly, however, I note that my right leg hurts when I push myself along.

I feel my knee: my hand is full of blood. So I have been hit a second time. The bullet wound is just over the knee joint. Now it takes a massive effort to go on, just another 100 meters, then I've made it.[99]

The exceptionally detailed and lengthy accounts of the role played by their respective divisions in the fighting at Stalingrad left to us by former officers of 94th Infantry Division (Hauptmann Rudolf Krell) and 76th Infantry Division (Major Grohe) add technical and personal detail to the role of snipers at Stalingrad. Krell's memoir reveals that his unit was aware of snipers and appropriately equipped. He notes, for example, that Grenadier Regiment 267 included a Luftwaffe battalion consisting of three companies of air-landing troops and one company of paratroopers. This subunit was liberally armed with automatic weapons and had trained snipers. In a section in which he summarized the experiences and lessons Krell notes the vital role played by German snipers: "In the forward edge of the battle area, dug-in sniper positions with alternate positions (six rifles fitted with telescopic sights per rifle company) kept the enemy and his forward lines at a distance. When he attacked, the enemy's officers and junior leaders, when identified, could be eliminated."[100]

One indicator of enemy sniper activity recorded by Grohe is implied in the many situation reports that note the loss of a soldier on days when most of the front line is quiet apart from occasional harassing fire. These relatively quiet days are characterized by recurring and similar phrases such as "*keine besonderen Vorkomnisse*," "*keine nennenswerten Ereignisse*," and "*keine wesentlichen Kampfhandlungen*," which can be more or less summed up as saying that there is nothing significant to report. Yet even on these quiet days when there was no significant enemy action to report, lone soldiers were dying, killed by a stray shell or felled by a sniper's bullet. Grohe's entries have something in common with the ending of Remarque's famous novel, *Im Westen nichts Neues* (*All Quiet on the Western Front*, 1929): "He died in October 1918, on a day which on the entire front was so uneventful and quiet that the Army Report for the day was limited to one sentence: there was nothing to report on the western front."[101] Grohe first notes the enhanced sniper threat when elements of 76th Infantry Division occupy a position formerly occupied by the 44th Infantry Division. The entry in the war diary for 28 December 1942 notes: "The position was extremely unsatisfactory as it ran across a wide-open plain without any cover and was completely observed by the enemy. There was one heated dugout per squadron, and the bulk of the men were located in holes in the ground covered with groundsheets. Throughout daylight no man can show himself, since enemy snipers are alert. There are continual losses."[102]

Cited by Grohe in the division's war diary, Obergefreiter Petznick, 5th Battery, Artillery Regiment 176, highlights the impact of Soviet snipers: "On 18 January 1943 the combat group took up new positions in open terrain in the area of Gumrak (southwest). Here too the Russians attacked with ever stronger forces. Every day losses were incurred from enemy snipers."[103]

A telephone message sent by the intelligence section of Infantry Regiment 178, a unit of 76th Infantry Division, reports a development in Soviet small arms that would have serious implications for any measures used to counter Soviet snipers, especially in urban areas:

> Russian paratroopers numbering about 16 men, who were dropped in the region of Kalach, are attempting to break through to the Russian lines in small groups. Among them is a commissar who is armed with a rifle fitted with a silencer. According to the statements of two of the captured

> paratroopers, the rifle makes no noise when fired. By means of intensified guard and security duties (the use of patrols), especially at night, the paratroopers are to be prevented from reaching the Russian lines. It is important to acquire the rifle fitted with a silencer being carried by the commissar.[104]

German and Soviet Sniping in German Divisional Histories

Regimental and divisional histories compiled by the survivors of German 6th Army contain a number of detailed accounts of sniping on the Eastern front. It is clear from these accounts that Soviet snipers were causing problems for these Stalingrad divisions well before they reached and perished on the Volga and that Soviet snipers continued to be a threat for the divisions reformed after February 1943. However, it is also a story of adaptation, training, and equipment. Having learned the lessons of sniping on the Eastern front, or rather having rediscovered them, the Wehrmacht in the latter half of the war on the Eastern front was proving to be a formidable practitioner of the art of sniping. The following tales of encounters with Soviet snipers and general observations are taken from histories of 3rd Infantry Division (mot.), 44th Infantry Division, 76th Infantry Division, 79th Infantry Division, 100th Jäger Division, 305th Infantry Division, and 16th Panzer Division.

That Soviet snipers and their innovative tactical use were highly effective before the urban battles in Stalingrad can be appreciated from an action in which 16th Panzer Division took part on 9 July 1941. For example, Wolfgang Werthen notes that "in turnip and corn fields the Russians let the tanks pass through, and then sniper fire was directed at the infantry from camouflaged positions. There were many head shots, and losses were high."[105] This bears a strong resemblance to the tactical deployment of Finnish snipers in the Winter War: permitting the enemy to advance so that he can be attacked from the rear. Later, at Stalingrad, Soviet snipers also made great efforts to exploit terrain to get as close as possible to German lines. In some instances, they were as close as 20 meters. To quote Werthen again: "When the Russians were not mounting an attack, they would crawl forward under cover of tank fire and dig themselves in about 20 meters in front of the German positions. Their snipers fired at any movement. Nor was there any peace during the night. The men's nerves were stretched to breaking point."[106]

One feature of the Soviet use of snipers at Stalingrad and later in the war was to deploy snipers en masse so as to defeat German attacks. Werthen provides an example of how a German attack was broken up by concentrated Soviet sniper fire on 31 May 1944:

> In the middle of the sector the enemy had dug in several machine guns and snipers and defended so well that our own attack was pinned down. Only now did our own tanks move forward. However, just before the exit from Markovka they were stopped by a defensive line of antitank guns. An attempt to bring together all the heavy weapons of 1st Battalion, Infantry Regiment 64, and to break into the sniper position with a heavy assault group failed with heavy losses.[107]

In his history of 3rd Infantry Division (mot.), Gerhard Dieckhoff notes the disruptive effect of Soviet snipers on German movement. The occupation of Nara Fominsk is made especially dangerous by Soviet snipers: "The Russians have sited snipers on chimneys and other high points who make any movement by day impossible."[108] Dieckhoff also provides a stunning example of Red Army cunning and fieldcraft when attacking German positions. A German position is attacked at night, and the Russians are seen only when they are some 4 to 5 meters in front of the German trenches. In order to get as close as possible to the German positions without being seen, the Russians have dug a tunnel under the deep snow, emerging right in front of the German positions so as to provide no warning of an attack.[109]

Friedrich Hauck paints a grim picture of the strains endured by the soldiers of 305th Infantry Division: "Snipers, small-arms and artillery fire, dive bombers, rain, cold nights, filth, vermin, and a lack of sleep sap the strength. Death lurked everywhere in this depressing wasteland of destroyed factories."[110] Hauptmann Kempter, a battalion commander, notes that "snipers and mortars fired at every single man."[111]

There is a tendency to regard sniping as exclusively long-range killing, yet in the urban environment much of the shooting would have been at very close range, often less than 100 meters, and the emphasis would have been less on outstanding marksmanship than on superb camouflage and a cool head. At such short ranges, telescopic sights would not have been essential. After the Western Allies landed in Normandy, the Germans used the dense cover of the boscage to get very close to enemy positions and kill at short range. These stalkers among the undergrowth were known in German as *Heckenschützen*, literally "hedge shooters," and they severely disrupted Allied movement much in the way that the Finns interdicted the Red Army in the Winter War. Friedrich

Dettmer, an officer in 44th Infantry Division, records that Soviet snipers, exploiting terrain and the detritus of war, would often come very close to German positions before shooting:

> In addition to the losses caused by continual enemy mortar and harassing artillery fire—which unfortunately could not be dealt with—the percentage of losses caused by Russian snipers increased. Some enemy tanks in front of the forward edge of the defense that had gone over mines or had been rendered immobile always provided these snipers with a hiding place, even though our own antitank shells had literally filled these tanks full of holes. After they had fired a shot, the snipers would disappear into cover dug out underneath the tanks so as to reappear immediately afterward. Our own resources were insufficient to mount an assault operation with the aim of incorporating these tanks as sniper positions into our own defense system or of destroying them for good by means of engineer explosives.[112]

The use of knocked-out tanks as hiding places for Soviet snipers is also a problem on another position commanded by Dettmer: "In the middle of December I had to take over the former Nechansky sector (left wing of the regiment). This was the worst position I encountered in the whole campaign. Right in front of us, about 50 meters, were eight knocked-out T-34 tanks in, on, and under which were Russians. Despite exceptional care our men suffered head shot after head shot."[113]

In Stalingrad 100th Jäger Division's first task was to take and hold spot height 102 (Mamaev kurgan) and attack the Red October Metal Factory. In these operations the assault troops encountered snipers who, in Neidhardt's words, "hid in wait behind every possible piece of cover for advancing soldiers."[114] In fact, the newly appointed battalion commander of 2nd Battalion, 54th Regiment, while inspecting the battalion lines was hit by a sniper on the northern slope of Mamaev kurgan.

In the newly re-formed 100th Jäger Division the sniping lessons and experience of Stalingrad had been learned and implemented. Neidhardt notes that May 1943, when the division was in a defensive position on the Strypa, was the time of the sniper and that some five to six confirmed kills were recorded every day.[115]

In this defensive phase we find further evidence of the remarkable camouflage skills of the Russian snipers and infantry. In the sector of 1st Battalion, Infantry Regiment 54, there was about a 300-meter strip of no-man's-land between the German forward line and the Russian positions. The German sector was somewhat back from a river. One night a sentry of 3rd Company noted the red glow of a cigarette in the area before him. He duly reported what he had seen. The next day the area was subjected to observation using binoculars. Nothing out of the ordinary was observed. That night a reconnaissance patrol was sent to the riverbank. The patrol had barely covered 10 meters from its own trenches when it encountered antipersonnel mines. An engineer patrol that was sent out later in the night was shot up and showered with hand grenades. It had to withdraw. It was clear to the German side that the Russians had managed to dig in right in front of the German company, so well, in fact, that the Germans had not had the slightest idea that the Russians were there. To quote Neidhardt: "The Russians had camouflaged everything so superbly that in spite of the most intense observation from several positions one could not ascertain where this nest of Russians was."[116] A determined effort by the Germans to clear out this nest led to the death and capture of 50 Russians. The author notes: "It appeared wholly improbable what the Russians had achieved in the limited time available to them. The camouflage and the faultless construction of the firing points were superb work right under the noses of the German soldiers. In any case, this was a warning that the enemy should not be underestimated."[117]

In yet another demonstration of the Russian resourcefulness in camouflage, the following incident is noted by Neidhardt. During the night the noise of vehicles could be heard. In the morning the Germans discovered that the Russians had created a wall of trees, a wood, behind which the vehicles moved at night.[118]

One other lesson learned from the Russians, and possibly the Finns, is that successful snipers must be recognized in situation reports and, subject to their meeting kill quotas, honored. Thus, Neidhardt notes that in May 1943 a sniper in 3rd Battalion, Infantry Regiment 227, has achieved 50 confirmed kills.[119] Two highly successful snipers are mentioned by name. In a Russian attack Oberjäger Pein shot some 20 Russians, specifically commanders, and was later awarded the Knight's Cross of the Iron Cross for 200 confirmed kills.[120] On 20 April 1945 Oberjäger Preiss, in the same regiment as Pein, was also awarded the Knight's Cross of the Iron Cross for 200 confirmed kills. Preiss only learned of his award in 1979.[121]

Surprisingly, given the nature of 76th Infantry Division's deployment in Stalingrad, there are no substantial references to either Soviet or German sniping in Jochen Löser's *Bittere Pflicht*. However, during the first operations in which 76th Infantry Division takes part on 2 July 1941, 1st Battalion, Infantry Regiment 203, sustains very heavy losses when crossing cornfields. The battalion lost 31 killed, among them the battalion commander and his adjutant, and 69 wounded.[122] The pattern and manner of the losses is identical to those incurred by 16th Panzer Division when crossing the same type of terrain and suggests the Soviet deployment of snipers, or more likely *Heckenschützen*, at ranges of not more than and probably a lot less than 150 meters. Extracts from a letter contained in supplementary archive material confirm that snipers were the cause of the high losses. In the letter, dated 6 July 1941, Gefreiter, later Oberleutnant, Bert Mauß-Auth fills in the details: "When crossing the River Pruth our 1st Battalion suffered heavy losses, including the battalion commander and adjutant, and so on. Russian snipers are everywhere, and they only shot at people with rank. Now all our officers have removed their shoulder badges of rank."[123]

In the winter battles of 1941–1942 Soviet snipers also caused problems. In the account of the lengthy battle to expand the bridgehead over the river Bachmut, Löser notes that "the enemy has erected barricade after barricade. Behind them are well-camouflaged Soviet snipers. They react to any movement."[124]

The encounter with Soviet snipers as recorded by the men of 76th Infantry Division confirms the pattern of behavior first noted in the trenches during World War I: that new arrivals, especially those with preconceived ideas, are at the greatest risk because they underestimate the danger and ignore the hard-won experience of others. Oberleutnant Robert Fink cites an example of just such behavior. Fink warns a newly arrived platoon commander that he will be well advised to settle in first so that he knows the routine in the front line. Forty-five minutes later, having received and ignored this excellent advice, the new platoon commander is dead. According to Fink:

> The soldiers merely report that the new platoon commander, immediately on his arrival, went up to a sentry and removed the veil that had been placed over the mounted binoculars as camouflage that stood next to the machine gun. He then asked the soldier whether he was frightened to look through the binoculars. He would show him how it's done, he said. With that he placed himself directly behind the binoculars and the very next moment fell to the ground with a shot directly through the center of his forehead.[125]

Oberleutnant Robert Fink also reports on the nature of some of the deserters: "We have numerous deserters. They inform us that they are Siberian snipers and that they have just arrived."[126] This is an interesting observation because the obvious assumption is that Soviet snipers, like snipers in other armies, would be the type of soldier selected for discipline and commitment and thus would be least likely to desert. Fink does not report whether these deserters brought their sniper rifles with them.

Defense, with its routines of changing sentries, standing to, sending out wire parties and patrols, delivery of rations, dispatch of runners, observation posts, and the arrival of soldiers new to the front line, is ideally suited to the predatory behavior of the sniper. In the last days of the war the ability of Soviet snipers to exploit the routines of defense to inflict casualties is evident in the following series of incidents. Leutnant Heinz-Georg Borchers, an officer at the headquarters of 1st Battalion, Grenadier Regiment 203, reports that with the onset of first light, 9 soldiers in a forward company position have been killed in quick succession. All died from shots to the stomach. There is no doubt that the deaths were caused by snipers:

> Hauptmann Röthe sent me to 1st Company. There I ascertained that a sentry had been standing on two ammunition boxes stacked up on another in order to be able to observe better in the period of first light. He was shot and fell back into the trench. His belt was visible from the cover. In my time of duty I had not seen any such thing. It was almost as if the command had been given: "Prepare to die." The second sentry followed after the first one had been killed. What was completely inexplicable was that the company commander was there. Hauptmann Röthe wanted to have the company commander relieved of his post, but he managed to escape his superior's wrath by virtue of being wounded.[127]

The incidents cited by Fink and Borchers suggest that though chance is a major factor in the selection of a sniper's targets, it is not all down to chance. Even small countermeasures and a willingness to learn very quickly made the difference between death and survival. Those sniper-aware and sniper-alert German soldiers who survived and their Red Army counterparts—the ones who did not do stupid things and listened to the veterans—acquired an instinctive sense of the threat.

Conclusion

The attention paid to developments in the use of Soviet weapons—small arms, patrols, mortars, and even rifles fitted with silencers—once again strengthens the view that if German subunits (forward companies and battalions) had been losing too many men from Soviet snipers and if those losses had been due to one particular individual, some mention of this activity would have appeared in the reports, war diaries, and situation reports. All the signs are that German 6th Army did everything in its power to respond to requests from the divisions for assistance in solving problems. One example can be noted here. So bad were the problems caused by the nighttime activity of Soviet aircraft—apart from anything else, German troops could not get any rest—that German 6th Army requested that the Luftwaffe do more to attack the airfields during the day.[128] Now, I suggest that this is precisely the sort of request that one would have expected to be made if Soviet snipers, among them Zaitsev, had been causing exceptional losses.

Another obvious and so far overlooked feature of the German military bureaucracy consists in the fact that the process of deploying Konings or Thorvald against Zaitsev would have been initiated by the German units in whose sectors the Soviet snipers were most active. Serious problems would have been noted and commented on in reports to divisional headquarters. Initially the divisions would have tried to respond to the Soviet threat by relying on their own resources. When that proved unsuccessful, an approach to German 6th Army headquarters would have been made. German 6th Army in turn would have made a request to German Army headquarters in Berlin to dispatch the necessary expert. Clearly this exchange of messages, from the problem's first being noted to the requests and notification that the expert sniper was on his way, would have generated signal traffic, some indication of what was going on. Yet we find no footprint among the routine operational traffic.

Nor do existing German records, above all those held by the Bundesarchiv-Militärarchiv, confirm the existence of any sniper school in Berlin (Zossen) or elsewhere, or indeed the existence of its putative head, Major Konings. Some evidence may yet turn up, but so far none has been uncovered.

What Vasilii Grossman has to say, or rather what he does not mention in his diaries and in *Life and Fate*, may also be significant. Grossman was a war correspondent who covered the Stalingrad battle for *Krasnaia zvezda*. In that capacity he was at the very heart of the Soviet propaganda machine. He was therefore very well placed to know whether the existence of Konings was concocted for propaganda purposes. It is noteworthy that Grossman does not mention any expert German sniper by name; he confines himself to the observation that Zaitsev fought and won a duel with an expert German sniper and leaves it at that. Grossman's colleague Konstantin Simonov, another famous war correspondent and big name at *Krasnaia zvezda*, has nothing to say on the subject. Moreover, the huge amounts of declassified NKVD reports that are now available are completely silent on the matter. Inconsistencies in Zaitsev's own account also raise questions for which there are no clear answers: the position of the sun as described on the fourth and final day of the duel is not exactly convincing, and the documents that Zaitsev says he removed from Konings's body have never been made available.

The success of the Finnish sniper Simo Häyhä (1905–2002) during the Winter War—it is claimed he killed about 500 Soviet soldiers—and the way in which he achieved cult status as a symbol of Finnish resistance and independence may well have inspired the Red Army propaganda apparatus to promote Zaitsev and other Soviet snipers in much the same way during the Great Fatherland War. The cult status that grows up around successful snipers can be seen in later conflicts. The U.S. Marine Corps sniper Carlos Norman Hathcock became a nightmare for the North Vietnamese, and the enemy offered a bounty for his death. More recently, Iraqi insurgents discovered that American soldiers and marines provided plenty of targets for urban sniping. In fact, these sorts of attacks carried out by Iraqi insurgents at very short ranges have something in common with the Stalingrad battle and the German *Heckenschützen* operating in the Normandy boscage. Iraqi insurgents have also promoted individual snipers for propaganda purposes. The attacks of one such sniper, known as Juba, were filmed and posted on the Internet. In Afghanistan there are some signs that the Taliban has realized the importance of sniping—in many ways a perfect insurgent tactic—though it has been very slow to realize its potential, and the North Atlantic Treaty Organization (NATO) coalition has largely managed to play down any Taliban successes in this area by careful censorship.

Quite apart from whether the Zaitsev-Konings duel took place, there are no obvious ways of verifying the numbers of German soldiers killed by Soviet snipers. Regarding the tallies of Germans killed at Stalingrad, Riazanov, who does not dispute the accounts of the Zaitsev-Konings duel, cites the numbers of Germans killed by named snipers. In Table 5.1 I have collated the numbers cited by Riazanov. Since Riazanov also supplies tallies of Germans killed on other parts of the Eastern front, I have included those as well.

Summarizing the total number of Germans killed by Soviet snipers at

Table 5.1 *Sniper Kills at Stalingrad and the Eastern Front*

Sniper	Operational Area	Number of Kills
Ivan Sidorenko	Baltic front	500+
Nikolai Il'in	Stalingrad	494/496*
Mikhail Budenkov	Baltic front	437
Fedor Okhlopkov	Baltic front	429
Fedor D'iachenko	Leningrad front	425
Stepan Petrenko	Baltic front	422
Vasilii Golosov	Eastern front	422
Nikolai Galushkin	Eastern front	418
Afanasii Gordienko	Eastern front	417
Fedor Kharchenko	Volkhovskii front	387
Petr Goncharov	Voronezhskii front	380
Abukhazhi Idrisov	2nd Baltic front	349
Filipp Rubakho	Black Sea Fleet	346
Leonid Butkevich	North-Caucasus front	345
Ivan Larkin	Eastern front	345**
Ivan Markin	Eastern front	340
Viktor Medvedev	Stalingrad & Ukrainian fronts	331/342*
Il'ia Grigor'ev	2nd Belorussian front	328
Zhambyl Tulaev	North-West front	313
Liudmila Pavlichenko	North-Caucasus front	309
Ivan Gorelikov	Briansk front	305
Ivan Antonov	Baltic front	302
Gennadii Velichko	South-West front	300+
Vasilii Zaitsev	Stalingrad	225/242*/300
Zikan	Stalingrad	224
Nikolai Semenov	Eastern front	218
Noi Adamiia	Eastern front	ca. 200
IA. Vilkhelms	Eastern front	190 (Riazanov, p. 52)
Titov	Eastern front	49 (Riazanov, p. 48)
Anatolii Chekhov	Stalingrad	40 (*Gody voiny*, p. 387)
Iakov Laptev	Eastern front	34 (Riazanov, p. 38)
Evgenii Raskovalov	Eastern front	32 (Riazanov, p. 40)
Nikolai Korsakov	Eastern front	30 (Riazanov, p. 41)
V. V. Kamenskikh	Eastern front	23 (Riazanov, p.44)

Source: The bulk of the information concerning sniper kills is taken from Oleg Riazanov, Istoriia

(continued on next page)

snaiperskogo iskusstva (Moscow: Bratishka, 2004), pp. 58–59. Information about sniper kills taken from other parts of Riazanov's book is indicated by the relevant page numbers.

*Earlier Riazanov cites the totals for Zaitsev as 242, for Medvedev as 342, and for Il'in as 496 (p. 41). In the account of Zaitsev's duel with Konings given by Sergei Alekseev (*Gvardeiskii razgovor, rasskazy iz istorii Velikoi Otechestvennoi voiny* [Moscow: Voenizdat, 1979]), the total number of Germans killed by Zaitsev is given as "nearly 300" (p. 115). In *Gody voiny* Grossman records that Zaitsev killed 225. See the story "The Stalingrad Army" (p. 65) and the diary entry (p. 358).

**Olga Khinn, ed., *Sluzhit' Rossii* (Moscow: biblioteka Il'i Reznika, 2001), p. 178.

Stalingrad, Riazanov claims that the 98 snipers in 13th Guards Rifle Division were responsible for killing 3,879 enemy soldiers. The 70 snipers in 39th Guards Rifle Division killed 2,572 enemy soldiers. In 62nd and 64th Armies, which defended the city, each sniper killed an average of 25–30 enemy soldiers. Over the course of the battle Soviet snipers killed about 10,000 German soldiers.[129] Riazanov provides no sources for the number of Germans killed.

Dougan argues that the duel between Zaitsev and Konings "stands or falls on two issues."[130] He quite rightly points out that the existence of a German telescopic sight—allegedly belonging to Konings—in the Red Army Museum proves nothing. For such purposes any sight would do. In any case, Zaitsev makes no mention in his memoir that either Kulikov or he took the German sniper's rifle. The absence of any reference to the duel in Soviet situation reports and operational memoranda, especially to Alexander Shcherbakov, who was head of the Soviet Information Bureau and head of the Red Army's Political Directorate between 1942 and 1945, may indeed indicate that the duel did not take place—not merely because there was no Konings but also because all paperwork relating to the planned exploitation of Zaitsev's name and the fabrication of the Konings identity for propaganda purposes has either been destroyed or has still not been declassified. Soviet propaganda campaigns were thoroughly planned in advance, and it would be reasonable to expect to come across at least some evidence of planning and how best to exploit Zaitsev's name in official documents. On the other hand, given the way the story of the Zaitsev-Konings duel has become embedded in Soviet, post-Soviet, and Western accounts of the battle and has become part of Russia's stock of national pride, it may now be impossible or very difficult for any official or archivist to sanction the release of archival material (or to confirm that it does not exist) that would undermine or destroy the published essentials of the duel.

6 German Recruitment of Soviet National Minorities, Deserters, and Prisoners on the Eastern Front and in Stalingrad

For these vehicles a captured Red Army soldier who preferred to work with the company or battery as a Hiwi rather than march off to a prisoner-of-war camp could always be quickly found. All these Grigoriis, Alekseis, Ivans, or whatever they were called proved themselves in the future, apart from some minor exceptions, to be loyal, willing helpers with an incredible talent for improvisation, who went through thick and thin with their new unit.

—Hanns Neidhardt, *Mit Tanne und Eichenlaub: Kriegschronik der 100. Jäger-Division vormals 100. leichte Infanterie-Division*

Attitudes and policies toward Soviet prisoners throughout the Wehrmacht were not always consistent with Nazi race ideology. This discrepancy can be seen most obviously in the willingness on the part of more enlightened Wehrmacht officers to exploit resentment toward the Soviet regime—the Vlasov case being by far the best known—or to raise units made up of Soviet ethnic minorities to fight the Red Army. By early November 1942, for example, plans were at an advanced stage to attach a reinforced battalion comprising soldiers drawn from Turkic and Caucasian ethnic groups under German command to each infantry division in German 6th Army. As losses mounted from the attrition warfare inside the Kessel, German 6th Army used Soviet prisoners in combat-support roles so that German soldiers could be deployed to replenish losses in combat units. In this chapter, I examine German policy toward Soviet prisoners and Soviet national minorities and the role played by these Soviet soldiers in maintaining German combat efficiency at Stalingrad. I also consider the Soviet response to German recruitment of Soviet citizens.

Introduction

While it is a matter of historical record that the Wehrmacht exploited resentment toward the Soviet regime, sometimes very effectively, one of the more interesting unknowns of the war on the Eastern front is to what extent the outcome would have been different had the Nazis adopted an occupation policy that from the outset was both universally consistent and pragmatic toward the inhabitants of the occupied territories instead of pursuing a race war regardless of some of the obvious disadvantages. The question clearly has exercised historians before, but such was the seething resentment toward Stalin's regime in, for example, Ukraine before, during, and after the war, the scale of collaboration, and a major cause thereof—the memory of collectivization—that the question automatically asserts itself whenever desertion, that other primary index of military dissatisfaction with Stalin, is broached.

Wehrmacht Policy and Ethnic Recruitment

Our knowledge and understanding of German recruitment of Soviet national minorities and the raising of units based on Soviet ethnicity owe much to the early scholarship of Joachim Hoffmann. Writing during the period of the Cold War, Hoffmann was unable to access Soviet archival sources and relied heavily on the holdings of the German military archive in Freiburg-im-Breisgau. The volume of declassified documents now available supplements and confirms the general Hoffmann analysis. Interpreting the problem of collaboration was indeed one of the weak spots in the Soviet response to the German invasion throughout the Cold War, certainly at the time when Hoffmann was writing. Even if some Russian authors of novels and historical monographs have broken with what used to be ritual Soviet ideological denunciations of collaboration, seeking instead to grasp its causes, the theme still arouses strong emotions in Russia. The scale of the problem is itself of the greatest interest since it raised insuperable questions for Soviet historians. To quote Hoffmann: "One of the most remarkable manifestations in the history of the German-Soviet war is to be seen in the fact that on the German side countless numbers of Soviet citizens—according to some official figures close to a million—and including as well captured Red Army soldiers and deserters and also enlisted civilians took part in a struggle against the government of their own country."[1]

The genesis and course of German thinking on the raising of ethnic units on the Eastern front is set out in some detail by Hoffman in *Die Ostlegionen 1941–1943: Turkotataren, Kaukasier und Wolgafinnen im deutschen Heer* (1981). Certain German officers, Rittmeister d.R. Dr. Pfleiderer, for example, advocated the creation of ethnic units, especially those made up of Russians and Ukrainians. His aim was to encourage a civil war in the Soviet Union. Indeed, this was Stalin's great fear and explains the ferocious measures adopted by the NKVD to combat desertion and what was regarded as treason. Pfleiderer also recognized that a Russian civil war would cause propaganda problems for the Western powers in their war against Germany.[2]

The evolution of German attitudes to the training and deployment of nationalist formations on the Eastern front is a story of official suspicion and bureaucratic obstacles, much like that encountered by Colonel Archibald (always known as David) Stirling, founder of the British Special Air Service (SAS), when trying to persuade senior British commanders in the Middle East of the importance of raising units to strike behind the German lines. Middle-ranking officers who came up with new ideas were perceived to be subversive of established order and procedures. Major Andreas Mayer-Mader, who together with Oberleutnant d.R. Professor Dr. Dr. Oberländer played an important role in running these ethnic units, was himself regarded with some suspicion by the German military establishment because he tolerated habits among the units that were at odds with normal military custom. His unconventional approach led to his being dubbed the "the Chinese major" by his officers.[3] It seems to me that Mayer-Mader is an excellent example of an adviser "going native," a problem and a risk when officers, detached from their units, start to identify too closely with the ethnic units they are training.

Eventually the burden of training and assessing the legions was given to 162nd Infantry Division, which was designated as Aufstellungs und Ausbildungsstab für ausländische Freiwilligen-Verbände aus sowjetrussischen Kriegsgefangenen (Deployment and training headquarters for foreign volunteer formations from Soviet prisoners of war).[4] The division was supervised by a very able German officer and specialist, Generalmajor Professor Dr. Ritter von Niedermayer. Having gone on research expeditions to Persia and India and enjoying mastery of the relevant languages, he was well qualified for the task. In World War I he had conspired with the German legation secretary Werner Otto von Hentig to cause an uprising against the British in Afghanistan. In fact, Niedermayer was precisely the type of official—culturally aware, able to show initiative, and with command of the relevant languages—that had played such a vital role in running the more remote regions of the British Empire.

The main policy document for the recruitment, training, supervision, and use of Soviet prisoners and other categories of Soviet peoples in Wehrmacht units on the Eastern front was "Verfügung über landeseigene Hilfskräfte im Osten" (Order concerning indigenous auxiliary forces in the East), which was published by OKH in August 1942. Hoffmann quite rightly notes that this document "was an important milestone on the way to recognition and parity of treatment of the volunteer formations."[5]

Considerations determining this policy were economic and military. Local inhabitants were needed to exploit the region's natural and agricultural resources, and former prisoners and volunteers were required to take over guard duties from German regular troops, who could then be used to strengthen frontline units. The document posited six categories of persons who, in varying degrees, might be suitable for assisting German war and economic aims: (a) the Turkic peoples and Cossacks (enjoying the same status and privileges as Wehrmacht units in the fight against the Bolsheviks); (b) indigenous security formations (to be used as rear security forces and to be deployed against fragments of the Red Army, bandits, and Bolshevik troublemakers); (c) protection squads in the operational area (the main task being guard and security duties); (d) released prisoners of war and local volunteers who worked as permanent support services in German units; (e) local inhabitants (who were to be used on an ad hoc basis to work on road repairs, snow clearing, and building military installations); and (f) prisoners of war, who were to be used on the same work as the people in (e). Among the disaffected whom the Wehrmacht sought to use against the Red Army were Georgians, Chechens, Uzbeks, Armenians, and Volga Tartars. Crimean Tartars were not entirely trusted, as can be seen from the restrictions applying to their deployment: "Crimean Tartars can be used in the Crimean area in security units in order to combat partisans and also for coastal protection duties. The use of Crimean Tartars as combat troops at the front is not permitted."[6] (Though in this regard, see the NKVD assessment of German policy later in the chapter.)

"Verfügung über landeseigene Hilfskräfte im Osten" defines two important categories of personnel who were to be used by the Wehrmacht. The first category was *Legionär* (legionnaire), which was the official designation for Caucasian peoples who served in the Turkic battalions. The second category was *Hilfswillige* (auxiliary), which applied to those indigenous inhabitants who had volunteered for service and to those discharged prisoners of war who served as a permanent part of the auxiliary service in the German army.[7] *Hilfswillige* were required to wear white armbands showing the words "Im Dienst der Deutschen Wehrmacht" (In the service of the German Wehrmacht).[8]

By the beginning of October 1942 the number of prisoners and deserters taken by German 6th Army, as well as the pressing need to make up the combat losses in the infantry divisions, compelled General Paulus to give the formal go-ahead for the use of Soviet prisoners of war in a whole range of tasks. In an order dated 8 October 1942 in which he cited the authority of "Verfügung über landeseigene Hilfskräfte im Osten," Paulus stipulated that prisoners were to be used as drivers, animal handlers, and technical personnel (including work as armorers) and were also to be employed in building and supply battalions.[9] Sixth Army's commander stressed that all unit commanders must provide the same standards of rations and accommodations that they provided for their own men. As regards the implementation of this order in 76th Infantry Division, Hauptmann Löser recorded that "the *Hilfswillige* receive the same rations as German soldiers, though without the special supplements."[10] Units were given until 27 October 1942 to report back to 6th Army headquarters on (1) the number of *Hilfswillige* incorporated in each unit; (2) the number of any other *Hilfswillige* employed in the units; and (3) the number of prisoners who permanently worked in prisoner units for the Wehrmacht.

Paulus had earlier, in any case, made a persuasive argument for the deployment of *Hilfswillige* in his memorandum "Erhöhung der Kampfkraft" (Raising combat strength), dated 6 October 1942.[11] He pointed out that there was no realistic chance of any substantial reinforcements before early 1943 and that, as a consequence, 6th Army would have to do everything it could to increase its own combat strength. The army commander made the following recommendations: (1) that certain units and formations be disbanded, that certain supply chains be abolished, and that others be reduced in size; (2) that German soldiers be replaced by *Hilfswillige* in those positions that would not be concerned with fighting; and (3) that the German soldiers made available by this process be incorporated into the infantry and that other special combat units be formed. The second recommendation, however desirable, was not sustainable in the long term, as events were to show. Moreover, in making this recommendation Paulus made no distinction between a *Hilfswillige* and a prisoner of war (*Kriegsgefangene*), which despite the attempt to make such a distinction (as discussed later) reflects the fact that a certain number of *Hilfswillige* may not have been willing to help but had no choice. For example, Paulus noted that *Hilfswillige* were to be employed as ammunition carriers and telephone cable layers, the sort of tasks that attracted the attention of Soviet snipers.[12] Their being specifically deployed for these especially dangerous and onerous tasks is hardly consistent with the demand that they be treated the same as German soldiers.

Surviving 6th Army files contain a number of documents that pertain to the use of Soviet ethnic minorities. On 11 October 1942 6th Army headquarters issued a document setting out the Wehrmacht's position toward Kalmucks and Cossacks, two ethnic groups present in large numbers in 6th Army's rear areas. The main policy considerations were quite clear: "In the interests of achieving pacification of the territory, with the minimal use of manpower, and its economic exploitation, as well as securing the security of the rear areas, the creation of the most friendly relations possible with the Cossacks and the Kalmucks is of prime importance."[13] A symbolic gesture was the granting of the right to carry traditional sabers and daggers. However, this right applied only to Cossacks and Kalmucks and not to the many Russians who had settled in these regions. Provision was also to be made for Cossacks and Kalmucks to retain firearms after they had been vetted and approved by the local German commanders. Such measures were not merely concessions to the ancient warrior ethos of the Cossacks; they also served as confidence-building measures, the aim being the eventual use of Cossack detachments as internal security units in the army's rear, the bulk of which was occupied by Don Cossacks.

The policy document, intended for limited circulation, was accompanied by a leaflet for general circulation among the troops. The leaflet—"Merkblatt für das Verhalten gegenüber Kosaken" (General guidelines for behavior toward Cossacks)—offered a brief history of the Don Cossacks. One can note that the leaflet applied only to the Don Cossacks, whereas the covering memorandum specifically highlighted both groups. One might see this a hint that for all the talk of the Kalmucks' being allies of the Wehrmacht, they did not merit the same degree of trust as did the Cossacks. It suggests that some ethnic groups were, to borrow a phrase, more equal than others. The leaflet's author underlined the ancient traditions of the Cossacks, their religious customs, their sense of their own freedom, their hostility toward Jews. and their recent and bitter hatred of the Soviet system: "Freedom-loving and proud, they have bitterly defended their hundreds-of-years-old rights and property against the Bolsheviks and made the heaviest of bloody sacrifices."[14] Once again the consequences of collectivization were readily and easily exploited by Wehrmacht propagandists. Readers were reminded that Cossack religious customs were to be respected at all times, and, unless there were grounds for behaving otherwise, the Cossacks of the region were to receive preferential treatment relative to the non-Cossacks. The whole tone of the leaflet is sensitive to Cossack traditions and grievances. Even where the operational demands of war must take priority, the authors fully understand the need to explain and to justify Wehrmacht actions. To quote the leaflet's final paragraph: "Unavoidable compulsory measures that must be taken for the continuation of the struggle and that will be accompanied by widespread and severe consequences for the local inhabitants are to be explained to the population."[15] These are effective recommendations, which, had they been implemented more widely, might well have cost the Red Army dear.

The raising and training of Turkic battalions, as laid down in "Verfügung über landeseigene Hilfskräfte im Osten," had direct consequences for 6th Army. On 6 November 1942 German 6th Army headquarters issued a warning order concerning the arrival of the first units. The divisions were informed that training of these battalions was under way in the rear and that the battalions, which had been told off for 76th, 94th, and 113th Infantry Divisions, were due to arrive in Chir for onward deployment. The provisional date for their arrival was the period 10–18 November 1942. All remaining infantry divisions in 6th Army, the warning order noted, including 100th Jäger Division, would receive a Turkic battalion sometime after December 1942.[16] Responsibility for the training of these Turkic battalions lay with 162nd Infantry Division, and Generalmajor Schmidt's warning order came with a detailed analysis of the training and other considerations that had been put together by one of that division's staff officers.[17]

"Überblick über Zustand und Verwendungsmöglichkeiten der Turkbtle" (Overview concerning the situation and deployment possibilities of Turkic battalions) is an impressive analysis of the potential of these troops and is remarkably free of any racial arrogance. The author, a staff officer in 162nd Infantry Division, follows the general guidelines laid down in "Verfügung über landeseigene Hilfskräfte im Osten" but is well aware of the need to be sensitive to the various religious and cultural contexts if any degree of success is to be achieved. The author demonstrates an acute understanding of the strengths and weaknesses of these units and how they can best be deployed to serve German interests. One of the main problems is that great cultural and religious differences exist among the Caucasian peoples, nor are their attitudes toward Russia and the Soviet Union the same. Accordingly, argues the author, a practical and flexible approach is required. An approach that might be acceptable for Armenians and Georgians, he warns, cannot be assumed to be suitable for Chechen and Tartar units, religion here being critical. These are precisely the same problems that confronted imperial British administrators in the Middle East and India and that confronted the U.S.-led coalition in Iraq and, currently, NATO forces in Afghanistan.

The recommended approach to the use of these troops is pragmatic and even cautious. The officer argues that initially they should be used in light tasks such as conducting sweeps of the rear areas—broadly analogous to the *zagraditel'naia sluzhba* and other internal security duties carried out by NKVD units—and flank protection. The bulk of recruits to these battalions are, however, considered to be militantly anti-Soviet. Their prime function is to be used in the liberation of their countries from Bolshevik rule: "Under German protection the legionnaires are fighting against Bolshevism for the liberation and self-determination of their homeland. They have been promised political self-rule and the free development of their national, cultural, and economic forces. Related to this is the abolition of the collective farms, questions of religious freedom, and respect for their customs and traditions."[18] These troops are not, the author insists, to be regarded as foreign legionnaires or mercenaries but at all times to be treated as patriots who are fighting for their homeland, the central propagandistic theme in *Svoboda* (Freedom), the Russian-language paper printed for these units. In this struggle they are to enjoy the "same rights and duties as the German soldier."[19]

Aware of the obvious advantages of raising such units, the author cannot, however, avoid sounding a note of warning. He reminds his readers that these people are not always to be trusted. They are adept at tricking gullible Germans, and "unreliable and incorrigible elements are always to be found."[20] Whatever the shortcomings and advantages of such units, the significance of the numbers being recruited and trained is beyond doubt. The command-and-control structure of the battalion consisted of 37 German officers and men, whereas the component of Turkic soldiers was 926 men of all ranks.[21] Bear in mind that the intention is to attach a Turkic battalion to each infantry division in 6th Army, 14 divisions in all, which means the total numbers are substantial, nearly an extra 13,000 troops. The deployment of three battalions to begin with was almost certainly intended to be an experimental trial prior to the main deployment. The combat performance of these battalions would have been monitored very closely and thoroughly evaluated before proceeding with the final deployment, as indicated by the request for detailed progress reports (*Erfahrungsberichte*) to be sent to 162nd Infantry Division in the rear.[22] The other point that can be made is that the time frame for deployment was almost certainly thrown into disarray by the Soviet counteroffensive (19 November

1942). In fact, there are no further references to these battalions in 6th Army files, and one must assume that because of the Soviet counteroffensive, no deployments were made at all.

Soviet Deserters at Stalingrad

The intelligence officers of German 6th Army, no less than their counterparts in the NKVD's Special Sections, closely monitored the numbers of Soviet deserters, seeing them as an important index of Soviet combat morale and performance. In order more precisely to evaluate Soviet morale, German 6th Army specifically requested that units, when submitting returns for numbers of Soviet prisoners, were to differentiate between prisoners (*Gefangene*) and deserters (*Überläufer*). A prisoner of war and a deserter, in other words, were not the same thing, a distinction that the NKVD could barely bring itself to recognize.

Between 23 August and 23 September 1942 the Germans dropped 100 million leaflets over Soviet lines in an attempt to accelerate the rate of Soviet desertion. The numbers of Soviet deserters over the period 14–23 September 1942 are shown in Table 6.1.

The report's compiler notes that the real figure is likely to be much higher since these figures are based on individual deserters or those in small groups.

Table 6.1 *Red Army Desertion Rates, 14–23 September 1942*

September 1942	Number of Deserters
14 September	89
15 September	86
16 September	87
17 September	195
18 September	105
19 September	204
20 September	183
21 September	135
22 September	146
23 September	53
Total deserters	1,283
Daily average	128.3

Source: AOK 6. Ic/Iprop. 26 September, "Flugblattpropaganda in den Feind, " BA-MA, RH 20-6/214/74.

Where large groups of prisoners were taken, it is pointed out, it was not possible to differentiate between those captured and those who deserted. However, "it was established that all the prisoners, almost without exception, were in possession of leaflets with passes."[23] One can assume that possession of these passes—utterly damning evidence as far as the NKVD was concerned—was evidence of intention to desert. Whether these figures are typical of September or whether they represent the high point of Soviet desertions and the officer has decided to highlight them is not clear. Whatever the reasons, there is a huge discrepancy between the German and Soviet assessments of desertion rates for the month of September. A Soviet source, cited by Antony Beevor, gives a total of 446 for this period.[24] The German total cited above is nearly three times higher and covers only a ten-day period in September. In an assessment of the Soviet units facing German 6th Army that was compiled in September 1942 it was noted that 115th Motorized Brigade had "a huge tendency toward desertion," and a similar comment was made about 173rd Rifle Division. "Numerous deserters" also came from 343rd Rifle Division.[25]

Numbers of deserters continued to be high in October. Major Menzel, a liaison officer attached to 6th Army, in a report dated 4 October 1942, noted that there were "many deserters."[26] Two days later Menzel was again noting "numerous enemy deserters."[27] Based on German reports, the minimum number of Soviet deserters for October 1942 was 824, though the actual figure could be much higher. This trend continued into November, when "many deserters" were still being recorded.[28] Among the flood of Soviet deserters were almost certainly some Soviet spies. Sixth Army intelligence issued the following warning: "On a number of occasions deserters come across who turned out to be agents with tasks sent by the Soviet leadership. Deserters who are suspected of spying are to be taken to AOK 6-Ic/AO. Continual surveillance of these Hiwis is important!"[29]

German archives confirm the general picture found in NKVD reports that even after the start of the Soviet counteroffensive, and indeed well after it, Soviet soldiers were still deserting to the Germans. This is revealed more clearly in the individual divisional reports. A *Morgenmeldung* from 384th Division dated 29 December 1942 notes that the division picked up 3 deserters.[30] As the end for German 6th Army drew near, Soviet soldiers were, astonishingly, still deserting to the Germans. In the period between 1 and 20 January 1943, 2 officers and 2 soldiers deserted,[31] and in a report dated 2 February 1943(!), which covered operations for the period from 21 January to the end of the month, 6 Soviet deserters were recorded.[32] Even more remarkable were the assessments of what the local population allegedly thought about the Germans: "The population utters only good things about German soldiers. There exists an inclination to desert."[33]

German 6th Army reports confirm the bitterness felt by many Soviet soldiers toward Order № 227, which was also identified by the NKVD in their secret assessments.[34] In a staff officer report that charted the progress of German 6th Army from Kharkov to Stalingrad it was noted that, as a result of Order № 227, the Soviet defenders had to choose between "death in battle and death from their own commissar."[35] In an activity report from 384th Division dated 22 January 1943, the intelligence section, even at this late stage, could note that:

> As before, the soldier, with the exception of a few activists, attacks only when there is a gun at his back. Deserters feel tricked by Russian propaganda, which presented a German withdrawal right to the borders of the Reich without a fight, and so they desert. Every military setback creates panic. Poor provision of rations adds to the mistrust. In all circumstances officers and *politruks* energetically and ruthlessly try to maintain and increase the martial spirit through endless political instruction. The search for suspected deserters is extensive. They are shot immediately.[36]

This bleak view of Soviet morale at such a late stage must be balanced by the determination of some Soviet prisoners, reported to German officers by their agents, to take the first opportunity to escape. Attempts to get information failed because of the prisoners' "marked communist attitude" and the fact that many of them were members of the Komsomol.[37]

One of the best data sets concerning the number of prisoners and deserters taken by a 6th Army unit was that compiled by 79th Infantry Division. The records cover the period from 2 September 1942 to 5 January 1943, a substantial period, and so permit certain trends to be observed. Table 6.2 provides a breakdown of the total number of deserters and prisoners taken by 79th Infantry Division.

The intelligence section at 79th Infantry Division also went to great lengths to identify the ethnicity of the prisoners they were capturing, as can be seen in Table 6.3.

The striking thing about this categorization by ethnicity is the large range of ethnic groups represented (24). This racial and cultural diversity can only

Table 6.2 *Total Number of Deserters and Prisoners Taken by 79th Infantry Division, September 1942–January 1943*

Month/Year	Deserters and Prisoners	Prisoners	Deserters
September 1942	1,911	1,520	391
October* 1942	329	258	71
November 1942	173	119	54
December 1942	32	17	15
January 1943	30	30	No data
Total	2,475	1,944	531 (21.5 percent)

Source: BA-MA, RH 26-79/149/197-285, and BA-MA, RH 26-79/150/289-395.

*The incomplete numbers for October 1942 are possibly due to the fact that the division was involved in very heavy fighting and that there was no time for collecting data, or to the fact that no prisoners were being taken in the relentless battle of attrition. Two conclusions can be drawn. First, the figure for September, for one division, strongly suggests that the overall number of deserters taken by all units of 6th Army in that month was in excess of the 1,283 cited in Table 6.1, which was in any case just for a ten-day period. Second, of those who were initially classified as prisoners, a number almost certainly made the decision to make some kind of deal with their captors. Unless the numbers of Soviet deserters have somehow, and for no obvious reason, been grossly underestimated, there is no other way of explaining the large number of *Hilfswillige* on the rations strength of 6th Army.

have complicated the already dire problems of Soviet command and control. At a most basic level there was the problem of language. How many of these soldiers classed as Soviet minorities could understand Russian, and how many Russian Red Army junior leaders spoke some of these languages well enough to command and, just as importantly, to inspire their subordinates and maintain morale? Such cultural and linguistic diversity would also have massively complicated the requirements of Soviet propagandists, whereas it provided ample opportunities for their German counterparts to exploit real and justified grievances. It can be noted that of the total of 1,911 captured over this period by 79th Infantry Division 1,157 (61 percent) were not ethnic Russians.

As a quick victory eluded the 6th Army and the war of attrition started to reduce its combat efficiency, every attempt was made to exploit Soviet prisoners. Rations returns from German 6th Army files reveal the numbers of *Hilfswillige* attached to the divisions of 6th Army in October and November 1942 (see Table 6.4).

Table 6.3 *Totals and Categorization by Ethnicity of Deserters and Prisoners Taken by 79th Infantry Division, September 1942*

Russian (754)	Azerbaijani (26)	Carpathian (6)
Uzbek (301)	Tadzhik (23)	Circassian (6)
Ukrainian (285)	Turkmen (20)	Bachek* (5)
Kazakh (223)	Chuvash (16)	Cherkass (5)
Cossack (96)	Chirchik (12	Jew (4)
Tartar (33)	Kirgiz (10)	Pole (2)
Kalmuck (32)	Armenian (9)	Urtmut (2)
Belorussian (31)	Georgian (9)	Burak (1)
Total deserters and prisoners taken = 1,911		

Source: BA-MA, RH 26-79/149/197-242.

*The German original is "Batscheke," which suggests an English transliteration from the Russian "Bachek."

The two data sets for October and November 1942 are the most comprehensive available. The increase in *Hilfswillige* that some divisions record for November suggests that some divisions—44th Infantry Division, for example—are having their allocations of *Hilfswillige* reduced in order that divisions under stress can be reinforced. Some data are available after these dates. A ration return dated 6 December 1942 cites a figure of 275,000 men for 6th Army, which includes 11,000 Romanians and 20,300 *Hilfswillige*. The number of *Hilfswillige* is about a third lower than the number shown in the ration returns for October and November 1942. No explanation is given for this drop.[38] There are three likely reasons: killed in action; death by starvation, which was starting to hit the regular units of 6th Army at this time; and desertion back across the Soviet lines. The total rations strength of German 6th Army on 18 December 1942 amounted to 249,600 men, which included 13,000 Romanians, 19,300 *Hilfswillige*, and approximately 6,000 wounded.[39] As of 1 January 1943 there were 1,227 *Hilfswillige* on the rations strength of 24th Panzer Division.[40] For October and November 1942 the figures had been, respectively, 1,431 and 1,675.

Yet the numbers of *Hilfswillige* attached to 6th Army's divisions, cited in Table 6.4, are significantly lower than those cited by Antony Beevor in *Stalingrad*:

> Sixth Army had over 50,000 Russian auxiliaries attached to its front line divisions, representing over a quarter of their strength. The 71st and 76th

Table 6.4 *Number of Hilfswillige Attached to the Divisions of German 6th Army, 18 October 1942* and 13 November 1942***

AOK 6 Divisions	18 October 1942	13 November 1942
3rd Infantry Division (mot.)	1,041	782 (–259)
60th Infantry Division (mot.)	873	479 (–394)
44th Infantry Division	3,964	1,670 (–2,294)
71st Infantry Division	1,764	2,219 (+455)
76th Infantry Division	2,776	4,988 (+2,212)
79th Infantry Division	No data†	1,683 (± unknown)
94th Infantry Division	2,640	2,581 (–59)
100th Jäger Division	1,851	2,092 (+241)
113th Infantry Division	1,897	2,245 (+348)
295th Infantry Division	2,553	No data retain as above
305th Infantry Division	1,891	1,562 (–329)
376th Infantry Division	2,072	2,608 (+536)
384th Infantry Division	1,670	1,765 (+95)
389th Infantry Division	1,176	2,021 (+845)
14th Panzer Division	528	934 (+406)
16th Panzer Division	467	1,461 (+994)
24th Panzer Division	1,431	1,675 (+244)
Total	28,594	30,765 (+2,171)

*Source for 18 October 1942: BA-MA, RH 20-6/226/60–66.

**Source for 13 November 1942: BA-MA, RH 20-6/229a/17–34.

†In the report it is noted that 79th Infantry has been involved in heavy fighting, and there has not been time to gather the necessary data.

> Infantry Divisions had over 8,000 Hiwis each, roughly the same number of men, by mid-November, as their total German strength. (There is no figure for the number of Hiwis attached to the rest of the Sixth Army and other ancillary formations, which, according to some estimates, would bring the total to over 70,000).[41]

The obvious question is: Just how many *Hilfswillige* were attached to 6th Army's divisions? Beevor's source for the claim of over 50,000 *Hilfswillige* attached to 6th Army's divisions is based on a data table in Manfred Kehrig's *Stalingrad*.[42] Beevor has taken the number cited by Kehrig under the relevant column (*Hilfsw./Zuget.*) to be the total number of *Hilfswillige* attached to each division when, in fact, the figure cited represents the total of *Hilfswillige* and *Zugeteilte* (attached), not just the total number of *Hilfswillige*. Although he does not provide a breakdown of the total number of *Hilfswillige* or *Zugeteilte* attached to each division, Kehrig makes a clear distinction between the two categories. Fortunately, the two reports for October and November 1942 that were compiled by 6th Army do distinguish between *Hilfswillige* and *Zugeteilte* in terms of numbers.

In the November report (13 November 1942) the reporting format begins with the relevant division followed by three paragraphs: (a), (b), and (c). In paragraph (a) the total rations strength for 376th Infantry Division is cited as 8,187 (the same as in Kehrig's table). Immediately below two categories are cited: *Hilfswillige* and *Zugeteilte*. The number of *Hilfswillige* is given as 2,608 and the number of *Zugeteilte* as 1,497. The total is 4,105, which is the composite figure cited by Kehrig. With regard to the other divisions, the same pattern can be observed. For example, the November report lists the number of *Hilfswillige* attached to 76th Infantry Division as 4,988 and the number of *Zugeteilte* as 3,045. The total is 8,033, as cited in Kehrig's table. Interestingly, with regard to 94th Infantry Division, there is no mention of *Zugeteilte* under paragraph (a), just *Hilfswillige*, and the number given is 2,581—as in Kehrig's table—though this is a number for *Hilfswillige* alone. Concerning 295th Infantry Division, there is no reference to *Hilfswillige*, just *Zugeteilte*, and the number is given as 50, as cited in Kehrig's table. Again, the entry for 305th Infantry Division has no reference to *Zugeteilte*, only *Hilfswillige*. A figure of 1,562 is given, as in Kehrig's table.

The omissions and inclusions in the November report show that a clear distinction is being made between *Hilfswillige* and *Zugeteilte* in the 6th Army original documents. Unusually for German documents, there is no precise breakdown for the personnel of these attached units, so complete certainty regarding their composition is not possible. *Zugeteilte* could be attached to German units, including Luftwaffe, and might include military personnel from Romanian, Croatian, or Italian units or forcibly conscripted civilians. Some indication of the composition of the attached units and personnel is, however, provided in the three war diaries translated in Chapters 2, 3, and 4. In an entry for 10 October 1942, Major Grohe notes that Road-Construction Battalion 540 has been attached to 76th Infantry Division and later (24 October 1942) details of a rations return refer to troops attached to 76th Infantry Division from the general army (*Heer*) reserve. Grohe also makes a clear distinction between *Hilfswillige* and *Zugeteilte* (28 October 1942). In the same diary Hauptmann Löser states that each company had about 12–15 *Hilfswillige* attached to it (31 December 1942). Even allowing for a general reduction in the number of *Hilfswillige* attached to 76th Infantry Division since November 1942, this would mean an overall figure much lower than that claimed by Beevor. Again, in the 76th Infantry Division war diary, Obergefreiter Petznick refers to attached soldiers who are German, not Soviet (10 January 1943). Rudolf Krell confirms the presence of a Ukrainian construction battalion and other workers from the Organization Todt. He also records that Romanian soldiers were being brought in and deployed as construction units (9 December 1942). A similar profile can be noted in the 16th Panzer Division history. The author notes that a Cossack platoon was attached to 24th Panzer Division and that remnants of 1st Romanian Cavalry Division and 20th Romanian Infantry Division were fighting alongside the Germans (24 January 1943).

In a footnote to his table Kehrig speculates that the *Zugeteilte* are probably prisoners of war ("*wohl Kgf.*"). Were that the case, it would account for the lack of any further details. Kehrig's explanation is also broadly consistent with "Verfügung über landeseigene Hilfskräfte im Osten," which provides for units to be made up of prisoners of war who are expressly to be used for building work, snow clearing, and road repairs. With regard to the use of *Kriegsgefangene*, the following prescription can be noted, however: "The deployment of prisoners of war in prisoner-of-war units (building and supply battalions) or in general work can take place. *They remain prisoners of war and are fundamentally to be treated as such.*"[43] In other words, and critical to the deployment of both *Hilfswillige* and *Kriegsgefangene* by German units, they are quite distinct categories subject to different levels of supervision and trust on the part of the German army. That this is the case is strongly supported by the exceptionally detailed combat and ration strengths return provided by 24th Panzer Division (the full table appears in Appendix E). In these returns *Hiwis* and *Kriegsgefangene* are listed separately from one another. Though not referred to as such, the total number of Romanians (373) would fall into the category of *Zugeteilte*. The other significant point that can be derived from these data is that only 25 *Hiwis*—of a total of 1,227—were serving in combat units. The vast majority was serving in a support role. This would support the view, for the reasons given, that attached units did not comprise *Kriegsgefangene*. Note, too, that there are no *Kriegsgefangene* in any of 24th Panzer Division's units or parts of those units deployed in a combat role. Given the appalling conditions of Soviet prisoners of war, acquiring the formal status of a *Hilfswillige* was an attractive option. In order to become recognized as a *Hilfswillige* a Soviet prisoner of war had first to be discharged (*entlassen*) as a prisoner of war.

Table 6.5 *Number of Zugeteilte (Attached) Serving with the Divisions of German 6th Army, 18 October 1942* and 13 November 1942***

AOK 6 Divisions	18 October 1942	13 November 1942
3rd Infantry Division (mot.)	2,500	3,748
60th Infantry Division (mot.)	4,211†	1,592
44th Infantry Division	880	695
71st Infantry Division	5,941	5,915
76th Infantry Division	5,706	3,045
79th Infantry Division	No data‡	335
94th Infantry Division	126	0
100th Jäger Division	0	40
113th Infantry Division	2,635	3,319
295th Infantry Division	0	50
305th Infantry Division	988	0
376th Infantry Division	3,302	1,497
384th Infantry Division	420	39
389th Infantry Division	0	358
14th Panzer Division	0	0
16th Panzer Division	5,016	382
24th Panzer Division	1,079	0
Total	32,804	21,015 (–11,789)

*Source for 18 October 1942: BA-MA, RH 20-6/226/60-66.

**Source for 13 November 1942: BA-MA, RH 20-6/229a/17-34.

†The first number—most likely 4—is not clear on the copy.

‡In the report it is noted that 79th Infantry has been involved in heavy fighting and there has not been time to gather the necessary data.

Ration returns based on the situation (*Stand*) on 18 October 1942 confirm the distinction between *Zugeteilte* and *Hilfswillige* made in "Verfügung über landeseigene Hilfskräfte im Osten." In this rations return the *Hilfswillige* are referred to as "*Russen*" and the *Zugeteilte* as "*Zugeteilte Einheiten*" (attached units). One other consideration emerges. If these *Zugeteilte* were prisoners of war, their concentration in such large numbers, close to the front, would have posed problems for the host division. Consider that in October 1942 71st and 76th Infantry Divisions had, respectively, 5,941 and 5,706 men classified as *Zugeteilte* working for or in their divisions (see Table 6.5). Concentrations of nearly 6,000 prisoners of war would have posed a severe security threat, especially for a division in close contact with the enemy.[44] The host German divisions would then have had to allocate men to maintain the necessary surveillance and order. Soldiers allocated to such duties from the division would necessarily have reduced the number of men deployed in the front line, thus weakening the division's combat performance. Such a deployment would also be a clear breach of the terms of use specified in the Paulus memorandum dated 6 October 1942 ("Erhöhung der Kampfkraft"). The total number of *Zugeteilte* serving in 6th Army divisions for October and November 1942 is cited in Table 6.5.

Assuming that the composite figure cited by Kehrig all represent *Hilfswillige* would indeed give a total of more than 50,000 (51,780) *Hilfswillige* attached to 6th Army. Overall, however, the number attached to 6th Army is significantly lower than 50,000, and in the case of 71st and 76th Infantry Divisions the number of attached *Hilfswillige* is much lower than that cited by Beevor. The total number of *Hilfswillige* reported as being attached to 6th Army for 6 December 1942 (20,300) and 18 December 1942 (19,300), though lower than the attached numbers for October 1942 (28,594) and November 1942 (30,765), are plausibly consistent with the earlier numbers.

One final point on units attached to German 6th Army can be noted. As noted earlier, it is not clear, given the inevitable disruption caused by the Soviet counteroffensive, whether all, if any, of the designated Turkic battalions reached their German divisions inside the Kessel.

Soviet Responses to German Recruitment of Deserters and the Formation of Nationalist Units

Soviet fears about traitors and deserters were deep-rooted. Their origins stem in part from the period before 1917 when the party was targeted by the tsarist secret police and from the Civil War and its aftermath. Two orders from the 1920s issued by the Cheka give some idea of the Soviet obsession with traitors and deserters and the methods used for dealing with them. In one order it is proposed that a list be drawn up of all persons in the command and headquarters staff of the army. The next step is to record the domicile of all of those persons' close relatives so that, in the event of treachery on the part of a commander, his family members can be arrested. The first part of the order states: "The arrested family members and the close relatives of those persons who have gone across to the enemy or who have committed acts of a treasonous character must be kept in concentration camps or in workhouses until the end of the Civil War in Russia."[45] A second order issued against the rising fear of Western intervention—the order begins with the warning that "global capital is preparing to inflict a new blow on us"—underlines Cheka fears concerning traitors. All dubious members of the command staff are to be strictly held to account, and all manifestations of counterrevolutionary activity among the soldiers are to be nipped in the bud.[46]

In fact, in all conflicts, internal or external, the search for traitors and deserters was a high priority. Consider, for example, the Russo-Finnish conflict, which in its catalog of problems anticipated the much bigger stresses that lay ahead. In a secret report commissioned by OKH to summarize the performance of the Red Army against the Finns in the Winter War of 1939–1940, various critical failings were noted, many being the direct consequences of Stalin's purges of the military leadership: "Inadequate initiative [and] predictable and clumsy operational handling caused the Russians considerable reverses at the beginning of the war. Their striving to stay, as far as possible, on tracks and the lack of experience in moving and fighting in forested areas made it possible for the mobile Finns repeatedly and successfully to attack the rear communications of their enemy."[47]

Regarding the Soviet conduct of reconnaissance, it was noted that "only selected people were ordered to take part in reconnaissance patrols, absolutely *no* volunteers (deserters)."[48] There is evidence that Soviet horror propaganda was counterproductive: "As the Finns were depicted in a particularly gruesome manner in propaganda, the Russian soldier feared being taken prisoner. On the other hand, if he withdrew he could bank on being shot by his superiors."[49] These observations suggest that the mind-set that gave rise to the formal creation of blocking detachments and other disciplinary measures was well established before the promulgation of Orders № 270 (1941) and № 227 (1942).

The large-scale desertion of Red Army soldiers and the obvious signs of willingness to collaborate with the German invader on the part of many civilians provoked a mixture of fear, ruthlessness, and panic among the Soviet leadership. Far worse than desertion—on one level desertion is a basic refusal to fight and risk one's life—was the readiness of Soviet soldiers (prisoners) and civilians to serve in the military formations of the invader. From the range of declassified material now available, one sees that the NKVD was well informed about the measures being taken by the Germans to recruit and to train a variety of units and detachments and devised any number of countermeasures to deal with the threat. Unfortunately for the NKVD and the Soviet regime, these countermeasures could not counter or remove the fact that many Soviet citizens rejected the claims on their loyalty made by the Soviet state. Collaboration and desertion obviously occurred for narrowly selfish motives, but the underlying cause was much deeper: a thorough disaffection from the Soviet state and its pre-1941 policies, especially collectivization.

What was taking place in the German-occupied territories, especially in Ukraine, Crimea, and the Baltic States, and later in the Don and Caucasus, confirmed the Soviet regime's suspicions that the national minorities, some of them numerically very large minorities, could not be trusted; that harsh measures were justified; and even that before 1941 they had not been severe enough. Even worse for the party was the fact that desertion, collaboration, and participation in German units were not confined to Ukrainians, Belorussians, and Kazakhs. Russians were well represented among the ranks of the deserters and *Hiwis*.

Strident claims of Soviet multiethnic unity in the face of fascist—very rarely Nazi—aggression may have made good copy for those with access to Soviet papers living in Soviet-controlled areas but hid the bitter war between nationalists and those loyal to the Soviet state in the German-occupied territories. In a report prepared by the Crimean District Committee of the Communist Party and sent to the Central Headquarters of the Partisan Movement there is a detailed assessment of Tartar nationalists.[50] In the extract cited the report's author notes that in the villages of Koush, Stilia, Khorbik, Kuru-Uzen', and Eni-Sala, among others, in the southern coastal region, the inhabitants are hostile to the partisans and actively assist the German-Romanian occupation forces.[51] In the mountain regions the Germans have formed volunteer detachments to combat partisans. The men wear either German or Romanian uniforms and are equipped with the weapons left behind after the Red Army withdrawal. The settlement of Koush is the center of German recruitment, and its detachment numbers about 345 Tartar deserters and local inhabitants.[52] Khasanov Osman, a former member of the party, was now the German-appointed *starosta*[53] of the Koush settlement and, according to the report, was now "plundering that part of the population loyal to Soviet power."[54] An alarming development for the Soviet side is that in April 1942 some 15,000 Tartar volunteers completed military training under German supervision and are to be sent to the front.[55] This NKVD intelligence assessment is thus at odds with the prohibition stated in "Verfügung über landeseigene Hilfskräfte im Osten" that Crimean Tartars not be sent to the front (see earlier in this chapter).

Despite the injections of obligatory scorn for the fascist invaders and their demagoguery, the report cannot hide the fact that German appeals to nationalism, autonomy, and the slogan "Crimea for the Tartars" are working. Once again collectivization, as it would throughout so much of the German-occupied territories, has returned to haunt the Soviet regime. The report notes that kulaks and nationalist elements repressed by Soviet power are now being actively recruited by the Germans, and assets and other private property seized by the Soviet regime are being returned to those dispossessed as kulaks.[56] The one piece of encouraging news from a Soviet perspective is that Tartars living in the steppe region are so far showing a greater loyalty to the Soviet regime than Tartars from the mountain parts of the Crimea.

A follow-up report in August 1942, prepared by Major G. T. Karanadze of the NKVD, goes into much greater detail about life and collaboration in German-occupied Crimea.[57] Karanadze confirms the alarming news that 15,000 Tartars have been recruited by the Germans. Another grave development can also be noted. Four large punitive detachments (*karatel'nye otriady*) have been formed: the Bakhchiel'skii detachment (382 men), Shelenskii detachment (765 men), Uskutskii detachment (437 men), and Karabiiailinskii detachment (300 men).[58] The usual anti-Soviet suspects served in these detachments—dispossessed kulaks, those repressed by Soviet power, and Red Army deserters—but Major Karanadze did not evade the really alarming fact that large numbers of communists and Komsomol members served in both the volunteer and punitive detachments. He concluded that "volunteer and punitive detachments render the Germans invaluable assistance in the provision of garrison duty, freeing up troop formations, and helping in the struggle against Soviet power."[59]

Along with the policy of raising volunteer and punitive detachments, the German occupation forces conferred a range of privileges on the Tartar population in order to secure its loyalty. For example, all Tartars serving in the Red Army who were captured were released by the Germans and permitted to return home. Seeking to exploit religion against Soviet atheism, the Germans actively encouraged the opening of mosques in villages. Whereas the Germans seized foodstuffs from non-Tartars, strict orders were given that Tartars were to be left alone.[60] Known Tartar nationalist leaders, some of whom had taken part in the Uskutskii uprising in 1930, helped to strengthen and to legitimize Tartar opposition to Soviet rule. Representatives of the Crimean émigré party, Milifirka, ipso facto counterrevolutionary in Soviet eyes, arrived in Crimea and held a conference in Simferopol. The conferees pushed the themes of Tartar independence, the hostility of Jews and communists toward

Tartars, and German liberation from the Bolshevik and Jewish yoke.[61] The conference also elected a Crimean government. Major Karanadze freely acknowledges the failings of the NKVD to counter German policies in the Crimea. Yet he does not quite seem to grasp, or perhaps finds himself constrained from being too frank in his report, that the speed and ease with which the Germans have implemented their policies of exploiting nationalism and ethnic recruitment were ably assisted by pre-1941 Soviet policies.

German entry into the Caucasus opened up new opportunities for recruitment among national minorities in and out of the Red Army. In a report to Shcherbakov, head of the Main Political Directorate of the Red Army, brigade commissar Khalil Nadorshin revealed the harsh contrast, once again, between the propaganda of multiethnic solidarity and where the real loyalties of substantial numbers of national minorities lay.[62] Whether a consequence of their indifference or hostility toward the Soviet state or a variable independent of political/ideological considerations, Nadorshin also cataloged a series of operational shortcomings associated with the deployment of non-Russian units in the Red Army.

Among the military formations that comprised the Northern Group of the Transcaucasian front were seven national divisions: two Georgian, three Azerbaijani, and two Armenian. In the divisions a substantial part of the rank and file and the junior commanders was made up of non-Russian nationalities, especially those from the Caucasus and Central Asia. In several formations, notes Nadorshin, whole infantry battalions, artillery battalions, and squadrons comprise non-Russian nationals.[63] Effective command and control, let alone the Soviet obsession with political-educational work (propaganda), were severely complicated by the fact that the bulk of the rank and file and junior commanders did not speak Russian. A portion of them is illiterate. Nadorshin blames the commanders and political staff for this state of affairs. They have, he claims, "failed to take into account the national peculiarities of these soldiers, their customs, and the way they live, and, as a consequence, they have, therefore, frequently permitted formalism in their approach to them and when working with them, and at times callousness and a coarse demeanour."[64]

Even granting Nadorshin's criticism of the commanders and political staff—they are surely responsible for this lamentable state of affairs—this is a remarkable admission and one that highlights the differences between the German and Soviet approaches to the Soviet Union's national populations. Given the long history of Russian interaction, not all friendly by any means, with the nationalities of Georgia, the Caucasus, and Central Asia, Soviet commanders enjoyed a huge head start over their German counterparts in their understanding of these people. Russia has enormous ethnological expertise in, and cultural awareness of, the Caucasus. Typical of tsarist Russia's commitment to understand its neighbors to the south and east was the establishment of a faculty of oriental languages at Saint Petersburg University in 1854. Throughout the latter half of the nineteenth century, Britain and Russia competed with one another for influence and control in this part of the world, the so-called Great Game. An important figure in tsarist Russian studies of this part of the world and India, and an acknowledged expert, was General Andrei Snesarev, who survived into the Soviet era. In the Soviet period his academic reputation counted for very little. Arrested by the NKVD on a charge of being part of a monarchist conspiracy, he died in a labor camp in 1937. Furthermore, two of Russia's greatest writers, Mikhail Lermontov (1814–1841) and Lev Tolstoy (1828–1910), wrote about the Russian encounter with the Caucasus. Lermontov's poems, "Cherkesy" (The Circassians, 1828) and "Kavkazskii plennik" (Prisoner in the Caucasus, 1828) among others, and the prose work *Geroi nashego vremeni* (*Hero of Our Time*, 1839–1840), together with Tolstoy's multifaceted portrait of a Caucasian warrior, *Khadzhi-Murat* (1912), helped to embed the Caucasus deep in Russian culture.

The Soviet problem in dealing with the tribes of the region did not arise from a lack of knowledge: it was essentially ideological, a determination to view these nationalities through the prism of Marxist-Leninist multiculturalism rather than to be cognizant of the fact that Georgians, Armenians, and Azerbaijanis had their distinct languages; customs; and, of course, religions, a corpus of knowledge that was well understood by nineteenth-century Russian soldiers, diplomats, and explorers. The Germans certainly had their ideologues, but in the process of understanding the Soviet national minorities and recruiting them for the German cause, German officers such as Major Mayer-Mader, Oberleutnant d.R. Professor Dr. Dr. Oberländer, and Generalmajor Professor Dr. Ritter von Niedermayer demonstrated a level of cultural sensitivity that was clearly absent among comparable Soviet commanders. Unlike their Soviet counterparts, who were hampered by the Soviet state's official and aggressive atheism, German officers and trainers were able to exploit the religious convictions of their trainees and win their confidence.

In battle, the performance of these national divisions was exceptionally weak. To quote Nadorshin: "In the units of these divisions there were mass episodes of desertion, self-harming, and betrayal of the Motherland."[65] So bad were two of the national divisions, 89th Armenian Division and 223rd Azerbaijani Division, that they had to be withdrawn. Regarding 223rd Azerbaijani Division, Nadorshin writes that 168 soldiers deserted along with their weapons and ammunition while on a march. Eighty-ninth Armenian Division showed itself to be unsteady at the slightest contact with the enemy. This was especially worrying because the division had spent ten months training.[66] Nadorshin allocates responsibility for this to the regimental commander, Lieutenant Colonel Andronik Sarkisian, and his deputies, who "instead of making severe demands of their subordinates cultivated an ethos of mutual responsibility and then started to smooth over and to hide the shortcomings in the scandalous state of affairs that was unfolding."[67] In the first encounter with the enemy, commanders lost control of their men, and "more than 400 deserted to the enemy."[68] In another unit, over an eight-day period from 5 to 13 October 1942, 160 soldiers deserted or tried to desert to the enemy.[69] The German approach was clearly working.

Not only was the German approach working but the scale and effort being devoted to volunteer and nationalist formations was, toward the end of 1942, being stepped up. On 15 November 1942 at 1115 hours a radio station in the German-occupied territories broadcast the following statement: "The national formations have already demonstrated their martial spirit in action. Formation of these units is continuing at ever-increasing volume. In their ranks, fighting against Bolshevism, are Ukrainians, Russians, Cossacks, and Caucasians."[70] Despite a halfhearted attempt to dismiss the claims as boasting, Senior Major Nikolai Selivanovskii nevertheless conceded in his subsequent report on the broadcast that all the intelligence data reaching him from a variety of sources indeed pointed to "the considerable scale of work being carried out in the formation of 'volunteer' detachments under German leadership."[71] Selivanovskii reported on German progress with regard to three nationalist formations: Cossack, Turkestan, and Ukrainian.

To facilitate the creation of Cossack units, the Germans enjoyed the services of a very able ally: the Cossack general Petr Krasnov. Krasnov immigrated to Germany in 1919, from where he continued his anti-Soviet activity. He was an obvious leader for the Cossack units envisaged by the German leadership. Krasnov, Selivanovskii notes, had visited the Don region, appealing to the Don and Kuban Cossacks, his "brother Cossacks," to join his detachments. A key element in Krasnov's recruitment drive was a pledge to abolish the collective farms after the war. The second formation noted by Selivanovskii was the Turkestan-Mohammedan Battalion (Turkestansko-magometanskii batal'on), which consisted of about 830 men recruited from prisoners of war. Lower- and middle-level command posts were occupied by Caucasians; senior command posts were filled by German officers. The detailed knowledge of the command structure, weapons, and names of commanders of a second battalion suggests that Soviet intelligence had a source in the unit itself. Selivanovskii challenges the view that these soldiers are in fact volunteers: "In actual fact the so-called volunteers joined the battalion out of fear of being executed and to save themselves from starving to death in prisoner-of-war camps. As a consequence, the mood among the overwhelming majority of the soldiers is anti-German."[72] These motivations make sense, but, as Selivanovskii would have known only too well, they would have earned no sympathy on the Soviet side and would not have prevented these volunteers from being regarded with profound suspicion on coming back under Soviet control, especially by their NKVD/SMERSH interrogators, who operated on the principle that all returners, *okruzhentsy*, legionnaires, and former prisoners were presumptively guilty. Concerning the formation of Ukrainian units, Selivanovskii is not so well informed. He is able to report, however, that the Germans are recruiting Ukrainian males between the ages of sixteen and forty-eight. The families of volunteers are given an extraordinary grant of 500 roubles and about 82 kilos (181 pounds) of flour and are freed from the obligation to provide the established tax of crops in kind. They also receive an allocation of the best land. Despite these material incentives, Selivanovskii notes that in the Kobylok settlement, in the Kursk district, with a population of 5,000, only 5 volunteers, all, in Selivanovskii's words, "inveterate hooligans," could be found.[73]

The NKVD made every effort to disrupt and undermine these German-recruited units. A plan drawn up by Senior Lieutenant Mikhail Ivanov (NKVD Directorate of the Krasnodar *raion*, or administrative region) envisaged sending an operational NKVD group to the Tula *raion*, where two Cossack squadrons were being trained.[74] The intention was to subvert the squadrons and draw them into the location of Red Army units. Infiltration by agents pretending to be deserters from the Red Army was one approach that was considered. A clear priority for the operational group was to ascertain from what part of the Kuban the Cossacks came and where their families lived. Having located the Cossack families, NKVD agent networks were instructed to find ways of luring some of them to the Black Sea region "so that familial ties could be exploited in order to undermine and to withdraw the squadrons."[75] There should be no doubt about what is meant by the intention to exploit familial ties. Threats and blackmail would be applied to the families if they failed to cooperate. The Cossacks themselves would be expected to desert to the Red Army to prevent these sanctions. They would then be interrogated, subjected to filtration, and almost certainly punished. Whatever the outcome, any families identified would be regarded as outcasts.

The expansion and potential threat of these nationalist movements were real enough. In 1941–1942 there were a total of nine national committees: Georgian, Armenian, Azerbaijani, Turkestan, North Caucasus, Volga Tartar, Kalmyk, Karachaev, and Russian, Estonian, Latvian, and Lithuanian national committees were formed in December 1942.[76] The FSB archival team points out that the national committees created formations that comprised "traitors of the Motherland [*Rodina*], deserters, and prisoners of war."[77] Now, the use of "Motherland" goes to the heart of the problem: Whose Motherland has been betrayed, Soviet or, say, Estonian? Estonian nationalists by their participation in a nationalist movement reject any notion of allegiance to the *Soviet* Motherland; their loyalty is to the *Estonian* Motherland. They regard themselves not as traitors but as defenders of their homelands from Soviet aggression. Soviet worries about these nationalist formations have two main causes. First, they make a real contribution to policing the rear areas, thus freeing Germans for the fight against the Red Army (as noted by Major Karanadze). Second, they serve as the ideological, practical (arms and experience), even spiritual base for movements of national liberation that did not disappear after the Red Army reoccupied their lands.

By December 1942 there are indications of a more centrally directed and coordinated attempt from Moscow to combat the German-trained nationalist formations and their controlling committees. This move by Moscow to tighten its grip perhaps reflects a growing sense that these formations could not lightly be dismissed and that information flows had hitherto been too disjointed, insufficiently detailed, and too slow in arriving. In a directive Abakumov set out the way forward. He realized that all efforts to neutralize or to destroy the nationalist formations had to be intelligence driven: "With the aim of combatting the measures taken by the Germans in this area, and with the aim of correctly implementing our own countermeasures, it is essential to possess the maximum amount of detailed information about all the so-called nationalist formations being created by the Germans which are operating or are situated opposite our sector of the front."[78]

To this end he required that all available information about the Russian National Army (Russkaia Natsional'naia Armiia), Ukrainian battalions, Cossack units, and all legions and detachments made up of the various nationalities be sent to the Directorate of Special Sections no later than 10 January 1943. A measure of the urgency now required is evident in Abakumov's stipulations that the appearance of any new nationalist formation on the front sector and the fact of the arrest of any person(s) belonging to these nationalist formations be reported by telegraph. Abakumov also stipulated a list of careful questions that should be put to any arrestees so as to harvest as much information as possible about the nationalist formations, for example, the names of the organizers, the route taken to the front, the maximum detailed personal information about the representatives of German intelligence, the state of morale, and details of any specific operations against partisans or the Red Army in which the arrestee's national formation took part.[79]

Despite the attention paid to the nationalist formations by the NKVD and its networks, it is the creation of the various Russian nationalist movements associated with the name of General Andrei Vlasov that prompts the deepest sense of unease among the Soviet leadership. Non-Russian nationalist movements were a serious threat, but if a Russian nationalist movement could gain recruits and momentum, the consequences for the survival of the Soviet Union could be catastrophic. The news, even after the Kursk battle, that General Vlasov as head of the Russian National Committee had concluded an agreement with the German government must have been alarming for the Soviet leadership.[80] Huge efforts were devoted to countering the appeal of the Russian Liberation Movement, infiltrating its ranks, discrediting its leadership cadre, and getting the recruits to desert.

There were also detailed and determined plans to kill General Vlasov. In July 1943 the Central Headquarters of the Partisan Movement issued orders that included, among other things, the requirement to "destroy Vlasov in the event that he should turn up in the subunit's area."[81] In August 1943 an assassination plan was drawn up by People's Commissar and Minister of State Security Vsevolod Merkulov, in which he set out a plan to kill Vlasov (referred to as Voron [Raven] in the document) should he visit various cities—among them Pskov, Smolensk, Minsk, and Vitebsk—in his capacity as head of the Russian National Committee.[82] Stalin, Laventii Beria, and Viacheslav Molotov were the sole recipients of the written proposal. Some idea of the scale and allocation of resources to this undertaking can be seen in the fact that Merkulov's plan involved 17 operational groups numbering more than 2,600 personnel. The FSB archivists point out that others not listed in the plan were also involved.[83] General Vlasov was not assassinated but fell into the hands of

SMERSH in 1945. He was executed by hanging in 1947. The threat posed to the Soviet state by the Russian National Committee and the Russian Liberation Army was military and political. The mere existence of a non-Soviet organization comprising Russians and dedicated to the liberation of Russia from Soviet power was a deadly threat. It is the idea of "liberation" that is so dangerous since it clearly identifies Soviet power, correctly, with tyranny and oppression. Only this fear can explain the extraordinary efforts to discredit Vlasov and his army so long after 1945.

Conclusion

Soviet accusations that *Hiwis*, members of the national committees, nationalist formations, those serving in antipartisan detachments, and Vlasov and his men were traitors might well fit a conventional narrative involving a conflict between two nontotalitarian states, but they are woefully inadequate when applied to what occurred on the Eastern front. My reading of Georgii Vladimov's *General i ego armiia* (*The General and His Army*, 1994) leaves me in no doubt about this.[84] In this regard, I fully concur with Joachim Hoffmann's interpretation of this overall phenomenon:

> Furthermore, the military cooperation of Soviet citizens—not merely those who belonged to national minorities but also Russians, Ukrainians, and Belorussians—with German troops assumed dimensions against which reproaches of treachery simply pale into insignificance. When during a great patriotic defensive war 700,000, indeed, according to the analysis of such a competent expert as the general with responsibility for volunteer formations at army headquarters, General of Cavalry Köstring, even a million or more of one's own soldiers actively rendered the alien intruders military duties, then it is a question of some elemental historic-political event that is least likely to be grasped by legal criteria or by expressions of moral outrage.[85]

Soviet expressions of outrage are also wholly inconsistent with the formation by the NKVD of organizations made up of captured German officers such as the Bund Deutscher Offiziere (The alliance of German officers) and Nationalkomitee Freies Deutschland (The national committee of free Germany) and the 1st Romanian Infantry Volunteer Division (Pervaia rumynskaia pekhotnaia dobrovol'cheskaia diviziia) formed of prisoners by the Red Army. The inspiration for these Soviet moves hardly needs explaining.

The training, supervision, and general deployment of *Hilfswillige* at Stalingrad involved a significant allocation of military resources. Nor was the use of *Hilfswillige* a risk-free option for German 6th Army. The apparent ease with which Soviet soldiers could desert to the Germans also made it possible for the NKVD to infiltrate its own agents in the other direction. Soviet deserters and prisoners, as German records show, did consider the option of getting back to their own lines. Just how much of a contribution did *Hilfswillige* make to the German defense effort once the ring was closed? The answer comes in two parts. The first involves an assessment of the practical gains; the second must consider the psychological and ideological effects on the Red Army.

As noted in "Verfügung über landeseigene Hilfskräfte im Osten," the Wehrmacht's general experience with *Hilfswillige* was good. Throughout German documents and divisional histories written after the war one can find miscellaneous comments on the use and effectiveness of *Hilfswillige* in various roles inside the Kessel. Such observations as these, though anecdotal, fragmentary, and incomplete, have the great advantage of having been made by officers with direct experience of working with *Hilfswillige* at the sharp end. There is also evidence that some kind of informal arrangement regarding the use of *Hilfswillige* existed before the publication of "Verfügung über landeseigene Hilfskräfte im Osten." Thus, in an incident that took place in August 1941, Hanns Neidhardt, the historian of 100th Jäger Division, comments on the behavior of *Hiwis*: "The ammunition issue point fortunately remained undetected. Russian *Hiwis* deployed as horse drivers proved themselves over and over again. They helped to recover wounded, dragged ammunition, and never thought to join their own countrymen."[86]

Neidhardt's remarks are supported by Jochen Löser, who argues that *Hiwis* made a substantial contribution to the combat-effectiveness of 76th Infantry Division. He notes, for example, that "many Russian soldiers voluntarily filled the gaps in our division and joined with us in the fight. In Stalingrad that was about 30 percent of the combat strength."[87] Later he observes that *Hiwis* formed the backbone of the supply chain.[88] From the point of view of military, national, and ideological allegiance, the ease with which former Soviet soldiers could change sides is troubling. To quote Löser: "Their attitude was incomprehensible: they fought just as well on the side of German soldiers as they had earlier fought in their Russian formations."[89] Löser cites a telling example of this phenomenon. Having eventually taken out a Soviet antitank-gun position that was causing a lot of problems, Löser and his men take two of the crew prisoner:

> At that time we already had few soldiers in our group, 4 or 5 at the most. We were desperately in need of ammunition carriers and machine gunners. We divided up both of these brave antitank gunners, and after about half an hour they were incorporated into this combat company and became part of the further attack on the height. The second gunner of one of the machine guns, the German soldier, was killed, and the Russian took his place as the second gunner on the machine gun and fired at his former comrades. We frequently had such experiences with these prisoners called *Hiwis*.[90]

Such behavior on the part of Red Army soldiers suggests either complete ignorance and confusion about the nature of the war aims or perhaps a willingness to do whatever is necessary in order to survive.

Major Grohe, another officer serving in 76th Infantry Division, notes that each company had some twelve to fifteen *Hilfswillige* attached to it. "Only a handful of them," points out Grohe, "desert so as to mix in with the civilian population in the ruins of Stalingrad."[91] In a report dated 31 October 1942 an officer from 24th Panzer Division comments on the measures to enhance the division's combat strength and the role of *Hilfswillige*: "The division tries to raise its combat strength by all kinds of improvised measures. Numerous *Hilfswillige* are deployed as skilled manual labor, drivers, cooks, and ammunition carriers. One or two have proven themselves as machine gunners; even whole fire teams have been made up of Russians."[92] From the same division we find further very positive appraisals of *Hilfswillige* in combat tasks: "The use of *Hilfswillige* as ammunition carriers, riflemen, and machine gunners, even as whole groups, has proved itself. They are good and hard fighters and good machine gunners and in house fighting are able to persuade those Russians still holding out in strongpoints to surrender."[93] The scale of the contribution made by *Hiwis* to sustaining the operational effectiveness of 6th Army's divisions is clear from a monthly prisoner-of-war report dated 7 October 1942, prepared by Ib (quartermaster) of 79th Infantry Division. As of 1 October 1942 it is recorded that a total of 1,289 prisoners are deployed for work, which included 555 prisoners on resupply duties, 169 building positions and accommodations, and 574 on miscellaneous work details.[94] Other work duties included the construction and maintenance of roads and bridges. Any manifestation of insubordination on the part of *Hiwis* resulted in harsh treatment. In a night march undertaken by 3rd Battalion, Grenadier Regiment 203, in order to break contact with the enemy, Russian *Hiwis* were reluctant to follow orders, not wanting to be separated from the German units to which they had been originally allocated. The German author notes: "The Russians, however, wanted to go with their companies and could only be prevented from doing this, in part, by beating them. There was no malice on our part here, but they believed that they had to go to where they had been."[95] Commenting on a photograph in his history of 16th Panzer Division, Günter Schmitz writes: "In the background there comes 'Ivan,' one of the many Russian *Hilfswillige*. In the course of the battles there were almost as many *Hiwis* in the division's ranks as Germans, proof of the fact that they were treated properly, at any rate among the troops on the front line."[96]

Gronow makes much the same point as Schmitz but underlines the fact that *Hilfswillige* did more than just drive vehicles or lay signal line: "The number of Russian *Hilfswillige* employed in 16th Panzer Division who in many a critical situation took up arms against the Bolsheviks was considerable. Later, outside Russia, they have also proved themselves."[97] If this was the common experience of 6th Army's divisions, then one must conclude that the effort and risks of using *Hilfswillige* were justified and that in both support and combat roles they made a substantial contribution to prolonging 6th Army's resistance to the Red Army. Indeed, the willingness of 6th Army to use *Hilfswillige* is another example of the general flexibility and adaptability that were found in the Wehrmacht.

NKVD and Red Army units were well aware that some of their erstwhile comrades in arms were fighting for the Germans. Not only did this prompt ever harsher disciplinary measures, with a diminishing return, but it can only have exerted a distorting effect on military performance. Demonstrations of loyalty became a necessary part of the tactical calculus. The scale of desertion in the early part of the battle (August–September 1942) suggests that a combination of German blandishments (leaflets and passes of safe conduct) and the threat of harsh penalties from their own side worked to the German advantage, and even after the Soviet counteroffensive Red Army soldiers were willing to desert. An entry in the war diary of 24th Panzer Division for 7 December 1942 suggests a plausible explanation: "A deserter who was picked up in the operational area of subgroup Beidel stated, among other things, that they have been told by the commissars that the Germans in the Stalingrad area have been encircled. The bulk of Russian soldiers do not believe these statements."[98] Soviet soldiers, in other words, did not trust their own side to tell them the truth.

Desertion was, of course, not the sole prerogative of Red Army soldiers, yet its scale in the Red Army made it a military problem with serious consequences. In a number of German records and memoirs there are references to Soviet attempts to get German soldiers to desert that had some success. As far as I am aware, no figures for the number of German deserters at Stalingrad have ever been published, before or after 1991. Sixth Army casualty returns list killed, wounded, and missing, but there are no specific references to German deserters (*Fahnenflüchtige*). The absence of any published data from the Russian side may well be intended to avoid embarrassing comparisons.

First and foremost, desertion on a large scale weakens whole sectors of the forward line, which requires that a sector either be abandoned or be reinforced from reserves. Bolshevik agitators and other subversive elements incited desertion from the tsarist army in World War I, behavior that undoubtedly assisted the German army. In mobile warfare the sudden defection of substantial forces will open gaps in the front and flanks that can be exploited and may prove catastrophic. Second, desertion on any scale attacks the morale of those who remain: it compels them to question their loyalties and priorities. Again, the Russian experience of World War I shows what can happen. Third, it does not follow that all deserters, as many Soviet and post-Soviet observers would have us believe, were simply opportunists or cowards. Many, especially Ukrainians, had bitter memories of collectivization. Others never accepted the legitimacy of the Soviet state, as in the case of the annexed Baltic States. Fourth, deserters, whether they be opportunists or those harboring justified grievances, can provide a ready source of manpower for the enemy. In this sense they are no different from captured enemy weapons and other war matériel, as the Germans demonstrated inside the Kessel. Fifth, the measures taken to deal with large-scale desertion, a far more ruthless disciplinary regime, as reflected in some of Stalin's wartime orders, run the risk of causing the very thing they are intended to stop. Where discipline is harsh and arbitrary, it destroys morale and stifles the exercise of command. Sixth, harsh measures quickly become known to the enemy, who will seek to exploit them, primarily, as is quite clear from the Eastern front, as a means of encouraging more deserters but also as part of his general propaganda campaign. Seventh, collaboration and desertion are themes that will continue to haunt a nation long after the guns have fallen silent.

The aftermath of 1945 in both France and the Soviet Union, and even now in the Russian Federation, bears witness to this prolonged expression of bitterness. If a number of recent Russian publications are in any way indicative of a general mood, then for a great many Russians, despite what appear to be mitigating circumstances, the word "*Hilfswillige*," more frequently used in its abbreviated form, "*Hiwis*," inspires contempt and loathing. It is not difficult to understand why. However, if Stalingrad eventually became one of the high points of Soviet arms, an iconic victory over Nazi Germany, it also revealed—desertion being but one symptom—a syllabus of structural weaknesses.

7 Behind the German and Soviet Lines: Espionage and Counterespionage at Stalingrad

Our counterintelligence measures must proceed from the assumption that as regards external appearance, a German agent will be indistinguishable from any serviceman of the Red Army. In this it is necessary to direct all attention to the most thorough verification of the documents and checking of the owner.

—Colonel Vladimir Egnarov, head of Intelligence Section, Main Directorate of NKVD troops for Security of the Rear, 31 July 1943

Stalingrad was far more than a battle between the divisions of German 6th Army and those of the Red Army. It was also a ferocious war of espionage and counterespionage waged at different levels—local, battalion, army, and front—in which the intelligence agencies of both sides tried to secure as much information as possible about their respective enemies and at the same time to disrupt the enemy's attempts to acquire valuable operational information and data. The ongoing program of publishing declassified reports being undertaken by the Federal'naia Sluzhba Bezopasnosti (FSB) of the Russian Federation, and others, means that a very detailed picture of this unseen war, hitherto obscured, now emerges in unprecedented detail. In this chapter, I examine German recruitment of Red Army prisoners for espionage, NKVD filtration and interrogation, internal security at Stalingrad, and sabotage and other types of missions organized by both sides.

Introduction

On 25 March 1942 a German plane, a Junkers 88, was shot down over the small village of Liapichevo in the area of Stalingrad while carrying out a reconnaissance flight. Captured and interrogated, the crew of four revealed that they were part of 2nd Intelligence Detachment of OKW; further, that since December 1941, 2nd Intelligence Detachment had been conducting reconnaissance of the deep Soviet rear areas of the Black Sea coast to Batumi, including

Stalingrad, Rostov, Saratov, Kamensk, and Piatigorsk. The crew also revealed that the specific task of this mission was to reconnoiter the Black Sea coast in order to identify the movements of military and trade shipping, their tonnage, the state of ports, and their defenses. Over the Stalingrad region the main tasks were to identify the rail and road routes used for the transport of troops and ammunition, the supply routes for Stalingrad's military industry, the delivery of arms to the front, and the presence of aerodromes on the approaches toward Stalingrad.[1] German reconnaissance flights deep over Soviet territory were almost certainly part of the intelligence-gathering process initiated by the German planners in preparation for the Wehrmacht's forthcoming summer campaign (Plan Blau). These flights marked the beginning of a long series of intelligence activities on the part of the Germans that began with the aerial reconnaissance of Stalingrad and its environs and ended with the officers of the Abwehr recruiting Soviet citizens, prisoners of war, civilians, and even children to spy on the Red Army.

NKVD Planning and Preparation for Espionage and Sabotage in Stalingrad

With or without the confirmation provided by the downed German air crew that Stalingrad ran the risk of being a target of the Wehrmacht's summer 1942 campaign, the NKVD, as early as October 1941, perceived a threat to the Stalingrad district. With the Soviet counteroffensive at Moscow stalled and the Germans showing signs of recovery, that threat was once again being taken seriously. In a report delivered on 11 February 1942 to the Stalingrad party committee, Major Alexander Voronin, head of the NKVD Directorate for the Stalingrad district, recommended that the time had come to seek permission from the State Committee for Defense to raise the security regime status of Stalingrad from category 2 (in place since 10 September 1940) to category 1. Since the start of the war, Voronin noted, Stalingrad had undergone numerous changes: it was now a major part of the Soviet defense industry, and with the evacuation of defense industries from the west its importance had grown; also, it was a major production site for artillery, tanks, mortars, artillery prime movers, and tank engines. The metallurgical factory, Red October, later in the year to be the site of ferocious fighting, produced the jet-rocket launchers, the BM-13, known more widely as the Katiusha. Stalingrad's population had also massively increased due to displaced persons, evacuations, and the greater concentrations of troops, which, as far as the city's defense committee was concerned, raised the internal security risks from "criminal and other suspicious elements."[2] To ease the security problem, Voronin and the city's defense committee argued:

> Bearing in mind that in the surrounding areas (*raiony*), the villages of Krasnai Sloboda, and Gorodishche, which are linked to the city by local transport and suburban communications, there are a considerable number of convicted persons and other criminal elements who are denied residence permits in the city of Stalingrad, we request that the State Committee for Defense, together with the introduction of security regime status of the first category, shall establish a 25-kilometer [15.5-mile] exclusion zone around the city.[3]

In his capacity as head of the Directorate of the NKVD for the Stalingrad district, Major Voronin was intimately involved in the detailed planning and preparations for the conduct of intelligence and sabotage operations in the German rear. He had earlier set out his preliminary recommendations in a memorandum dated 29 January 1942. To begin with, he envisaged the formation of partisan detachments. Seventy-eight partisan detachments were formed in the fifty-four regions of the district. Two detachments were formed in those regions where conditions for the conduct of partisan warfare were more suitable.[4] In order, one assumes, to ensure greater ideological loyalty and because of a need for secrecy, the bulk of the recruits were party members. Out of a total number of 2,466 partisans, 1,985 (80.5 percent) were members of the party, 109 (4.4 percent) were members of the Komsomol, and the remaining 309 (15 percent) were non–party members.[5] Major Voronin expressed some concern that non–party members amounted to only 15 percent of the detachments: "Partisans without party membership amount to 15 percent of the contingent, which without a doubt is insufficient. Bearing in mind that in the conditions of the Stalingrad district concealment in places will principally be the reliable connections in the populated areas, the proportion of non–party members in the detachments would be up to about 30 to 40 percent."[6] The low percentage of non–party members hints at something that by this stage in the war had already revealed itself with alarming and brutal clarity for the regime: the willingness of citizens from all strata of Soviet society, civilian and military, not only to withdraw active support for the Soviet regime but also to defect to the enemy when the opportunity arose and actively to work for his war aims against Soviet power. The low representation of partisans without party membership, which might reflect either apathy or hostility toward the party, would,

Table 7.1 *Civilian Posts Held by Nominated Heads of Partisan Detachments in Stalingrad District, January 1942*

Civilian Posts of Nominated Partisan Detachment Commanders	Number
Party secretaries of regional party committees	11
Chairmen of area councils	12
Chiefs of area sections, NKVD	6
Chairmen of collective farms	6
Directors of machine tractor stations	4
Directors of Soviet collective farms	3
Heads of militia sections	3
Managers of area land sections	3
Chairmen of village councils	4
Authorized heads of the Council of Soviet Commissars	1
Factory directors	3
Miscellaneous	22
Total	78

Source: OGB/1942/1/№ 792, p. 77.

as Voronin surmised, weaken support for the partisans under conditions of German occupation. On the other hand, and on the assumption that party members would not be so easily suborned, a high concentration of non–party members would make it easier for the Germans to recruit spies and others to serve their purposes. Another factor that weakened the effectiveness of these detachments was the fact that large numbers were being conscripted for service in the Red Army and thus disrupting training and planning. As one would expect, the command-political structure ("command-political" reflecting the ideological union of military and political in the Red Army and paramilitary structures) was dominated by party members, most of whom, when not directly employed by the party, held important positions in the regional and district infrastructure. I have collated the data for the civilian posts held by nominated partisan detachment commanders in Table 7.1.

Of the 78 detachment commissar posts, 55 are filled by party secretaries of regional party committees. This represents massive party dominance and reflects the importance placed by the party on the sound ideological line to be taken and the need to submit all decisions to the current party line in all matters. Of the remaining 23 posts, 5 were held by the chairmen of area councils,

2 by the directors of machine tractor stations, 2 by area prosecutors, and 11 by persons holding miscellaneous posts.[7]

Among the partisans, a total of 1,770 persons had served in the Red Army, 90 belonged to the red partisans during the Civil War, and 543 had no military training at all.[8] Training of partisans relied on the core program adopted for the so-called destroyer battalions (*istrebitel'nye batal'ony*). This included training in the use of explosives, the tactics of street fighting, reconnaissance, and the use of bayonets and sidearms. The basis of all instruction was to inculcate training and cohesion to the point that the groups could carry out operations in the enemy's rear. Supplies of rations for two to three months were allocated and were typically held in trading organizations and collective farms.

In addition to the partisan detachments being formed in the Stalingrad district, Voronin also provided details on the formation of sabotage groups; intelligence residencies, and the organization of clandestine communications in the enemy rear. Thus, in the 26 *raiony* of the Stalingrad district and in Stalingrad itself, a total of a 125 sabotage groups had been formed. Voronin set out the locations and tasks of these groups: "The groups have been organized in populated areas, located along railway lines and leveled roads, on water crossing points, in industrial enterprises, in electric power stations, in communications infrastructure, in entertainment venues, in the major population centers, and in other strategically important locations where it will be possible to inflict the most damaging blows on enemy personnel and equipment."[9]

The organization of these sabotage groups was to be carried out in accordance with the planning done by the Stalingrad Directorate of the NKVD. The main emphasis would be on the makeup of the groups, their tactical operation, and their clandestine operation in the conditions of the enemy rear. The training program provided for instruction in the use of explosives (the use of incendiary devices) and weapons (pistols and hand grenades).[10]

In the cities of Stalingrad, Astrakhan', and Kamyshin and other major population centers, thirteen intelligence residences were being created. Their aims were to penetrate, by means of spying, the command-and-control apparatus of the enemy, his intelligence agencies, and his military and industrial installations.[11] Voronin noted that in Stalingrad the intelligence residencies were to be created from the following operational sections: the counterintelligence section, secret-political section, and economic section of the Directorate of the NKVD.[12] Each residency would be equipped with a radio. In addition to the intelligence residencies, sabotage-terrorist residencies were also being created in the areas and cities of the district. One hundred seventy-eight residencies of this type had been created in 46 areas of the district with a total of 697 persons.[13] In the event that these groups lost contact with the agencies of the NKVD, they were to carry out independent sabotage attacks. Two further groups with specific tasks were also being considered. The first was a network of agents for spying on enemy lines of communications, which would be based in Stalingrad and Astrakhan'. As of late January 1942 suitably qualified candidates were under consideration. The second group concerned people who would be in a position to provide the partisans with assistance, specifically: information about the enemy, shelter, aid for ill and wounded partisans, and transport.[14]

Planning for effective clandestine communications in the enemy rear was based on a variety of methods so that some form of communication was still possible between the operatives behind their lines and their controllers in the event of enemy disruption. The system envisaged couriers and runners, people who could be used as mail drops, people in secret apartments, and others who could provide cover for illegal radios and signalers.[15] In his conclusion Voronin summarized the work in progress: (1) a thorough check was being conducted of the personnel in the partisan detachments, (2) the contacts of partisans who would be able to serve as cover in the enemy rear were being checked, (3) instructions for partisan detachment commanders concerning methods and tactics were being worked out, (4) places for possible operations under winter and spring conditions (areas with natural cover) were being studied, (5) destroyer groups were being formed, (6) selection of suitable candidates to serve as illegals behind the enemy lines was under way, and (7) selection of potential apartments for illegal radios and also candidates for radio operators was under way.[16]

The proposals submitted by Major Voronin met with general approval, though Ivan Serov, deputy people's commissar of the NKVD, who replied, made a number of observations on Voronin's earlier report. First, Serov argued that each detachment must have a chief of staff whose most important function would be operational planning. Second, he questioned the wisdom, under the conditions of German occupation, of allowing the relatives and other close ties of Soviet partisans to serve as cover for any length of time. Their dwellings would be vulnerable to raids and searches. Serov warned against allowing partisans to be dispersed alone, to use his words, "outside the detachment and the commander's field of vision."[17] Serov's objections were sound enough. In the conditions of partisan warfare, collaboration and treachery are ever-present risks. Partisans operating unsupervised for long periods might well be suborned and recruited by the Germans. Possibly for the same reason, Serov advised that when terrain conditions provided no cover, as for example on the steppe, partisans should be deployed across the lines for specific tasks and only for a few days. Third, partisans would be expected to conduct political agitation and to explain their actions among the local population. Killing traitors and henchmen of the occupation forces would also be one of their tasks. Fourth, Serov made a number of tactical suggestions concerning the conduct of operations. Two rendezvous points must be designated: one where partisans must assemble after a successful mission and another after a failed mission. Fifth, partisans must be taught to move on skis and how to operate ambushes. Sixth, he criticized the view that partisan detachments should have any links with the intelligence residencies. He argued, correctly, that such a connection could compromise the security of the residencies. All intelligence data and information necessary for a partisan operation must be secured by the partisans themselves. Seventh, Voronin's plans for runners and couriers envisaged using members of the local population living legally in enemy-occupied territory. The central flaw, as Serov pointed out, was that even relatively brief spells of absence would arouse suspicion. This risk mandated the use of illegal couriers and runners living underground who could be supplied with identity documents provided by the occupation forces. Eighth, Serov confirmed the need to execute traitors if they could not be brought back across the front line under escort.[18]

Notwithstanding Serov's objection to the use of lone agents operating independently, Voronin reconsidered this type of agent deployment later in the year (October 1942). In a general guidance document prepared for his subordinate agencies, Voronin noted that "practical intelligence work in the rear of the enemy has shown the enormous effectiveness of the work of lone agents, deployed across the front and entrusted with missions of short duration, and, additionally, the great value of intelligence data being secured by the female agent network, whose movement throughout occupied territory is caused fewer problems by the enemy."[19] Voronin recommended that lone agents be recruited and deployed for long-term work and that the percentage of female agents be not less than 50 to 60 percent of the agent networks.

Activation of Networks in the Stalingrad District

Voronin's detailed report on the preparations being made for partisan warfare, sabotage, and the setting up of intelligence residencies in the Stalingrad district and Serov's response reveal just how alarmed the Soviet authorities were at the possibility that Stalingrad and the district would become a target for German military operations. Red Army recruitment and the exigencies of war would seem to have reduced the number of partisan detachments and other formations available for deployment. Voronin envisaged 78 detachments consisting of a total of 2,466 partisans. By the beginning of the Stalingrad battle the numbers deployed were lower. Thirty-four partisan detachments and 19 underground groups had been formed in the Stalingrad district, with a total of 879 personnel.[20] As far as the occupied *raiony* of the Stalingrad district were concerned, the formations deployed were as follows:

> In the occupied *raiony* of the Stalingrad district the struggle was conducted by 8 partisan detachments (122 soldiers) and 9 underground groups (72 persons). In order to carry out underground work 40 communists had been left. Two hundred seventy-three Stalingrad communists and members of the Komsomol carried out intelligence and sabotage in the enemy rear under the control of the headquarters of the partisan movement attached to the Military Council of the Stalingrad Front.[21]

On 15 August 1942, eight days before the advanced columns of 16th Panzer Division reached the northern suburbs of Stalingrad, Voronin, now promoted to senior major, initiated preparations for the deployment of the intelligence residencies. Communications were to be established with the groups that had already been left behind the German lines. In order to get a current picture of German activities, interrogations of persons who had emerged from encirclement, escapees from the German-occupied territories, and any prisoners were to be conducted. Voronin and the NKVD sought specific details concerning the German rear areas: (1) the numbers and locations of German units; (2) the nature of the control regime established by the Germans and any published instructions; (3) the system of propaganda; (4) economic measures taken by the occupation forces; (5) details concerning the agencies of control and any anti-Soviet formations being created by the Germans; (6) the names of any traitors working for the enemy; (7) specific details and facts of brutality, violence, and plundering being carried out by the occupation forces; (8) the attitude of the population toward the occupation forces; (9) the identification of easily negotiable sectors on the front and routes providing access into the rear areas of the enemy; and (10) the political attitudes and morale among enemy troops.[22] This intelligence format more or less remained standard throughout the battle.

Analogous Intelligence and Sabotage Networks in Ukraine

Voronin provided no breakdown of the composition of these intelligence residencies. However, a detailed operational plan of work for intelligence agencies and sabotage groups designated for deployment in Ukraine and drawn up by an NKVD officer of the 4th Directorate, Major Nikolai Reshetov, gives some idea. The bulk of the residential agencies (*rezidentury*) consisted of three to five agents, one of whom was a trained radio operator. The total number of groups to be deployed was 15, with a total number of 59 agents. Teams were to be inserted in Kiev, Zhitomir, Stalino, Dnepropetrovsk, Kishenev, Odessa, Poltava, and other cities and towns. I have collated the data and present them in Table 7.2.

Groups designed specifically for sabotage missions tended to be slightly bigger, consisting of four to six agents. Reshetov noted that a total of eight such groups were deployed with a total of forty-one agents. I present full details in Table 7.3.

Table 7.2 *NKVD Intelligence Residencies for Deployment in Ukraine, August 1942*

Residency Code Name	Operational Area	Number in Group	Equipped with Radio
Boguntsy	Kiev	5	Yes
Mstiteli	Zhitomir	4	Yes
Maiskogo	Stalino	4	Yes
Pobediteli	Dnepropetrovsk	3	Yes
Druz'ia	Sumy	3	Yes
Chernomortsy	Nikolaev	4	Yes
Bessarabtsy	Kishinev	4	Yes
Kotovtsy	Kotovsk	4	Yes
Dnestrovtsy	Tiraspol'	5	Yes
Kirillova	Kamenets-Podol'skii	4	Yes
Patrioty	Odessa	3	Not indicated
Okhotniki	Kiev	4	Not indicated
Poltavtsy	Poltava	4	Yes
Slobozhan	Khar'kov	4	Yes
Vasil'eva	Kirovgrad	4	Yes

Source: OGB/1942/2/№ 1052, p. 141.

Table 7.3 NKVD *Sabotage Networks for Deployment in Ukraine, August 1942*

Code Name	Operational Area	Number in Group	Equipped with Radio
Donskie	Millerovo-Debal'tsevo-Voroshilovgrad	5	Yes
IUzhane	Poltava	5	Yes
Luch	Sumy	6	Yes
Mstiteli	Dnepropetrovsk	5	Yes
Lugantsy	Voroshilovgrad	4	Yes
Lesnye	Kiev	4	Yes
Shakhtery	Voroshilovgrad	6	Yes
Severnye	Khar'kov	6	Yes

Source: OGB/1942/2/№ 1052, p. 142.

Party Problems and Shortcomings Revealed

A resolution of the Stalingrad district Communist Party dated 19 August 1942 shows that a great deal of the advance planning, as envisaged by Voronin earlier in the year, had been implemented. For example, partisan groups were already operating in the *raiony* of Kalach-on-Don (west of Stalingrad), Tormosin (south of Kalach-on-Don), and Kotel'nikovo (southwest of Stalingrad) and carrying out the tasks required by the Red Army.[23] However, in the *raiony* of Verkhne-Kurmoiarskii, Chernyshkovskii (west of Stalingrad), and Perelazovskii (northwest of Stalingrad), effective organization of detachments had lapsed, and no supplies of rations and ammunitions had been laid down. Furthermore, the resolution was critical of the educational and instructional work being carried out. Members of the party and candidate members who had earlier volunteered for the detachments were now "under various pretexts . . . refusing to cross the front and operate behind enemy lines."[24] Worse still, "the *raion* party committees are not making such cowards and chatterboxes liable under the requirements of party responsibility and are not taking the necessary measures with regard to these people, as provided for by the order of the People's Commissar for Defense, Comrade Stalin, № 227."[25]

Various party officials in Perelazovskii, Kotel'nikovo, and Verkhne-Kurmoiarskii had, in the words of the resolution, "displayed personal cowardice and allowed the disintegration of the partisan detachments."[26] One obvious reason why the infrastructure of the partisan detachments had failed to work in these areas was because the party members responsible for organization and leadership had been evacuated to the east as the Germans advanced (or had left of their own volition). In fact, this was more or less admitted in the resolution when the second paragraph demanded that the area party committees "assemble all communists evacuated from the *raoiny*, create partisan detachments, and after a three- to five-day course of instruction send them behind the enemy lines to carry out their tasks."[27] It seems that the main purpose was not so much to achieve anything militarily worthwhile as to punish party officials deemed to have lost their nerve. They are, in the words of Stalin's Order № 227, being given a chance to expiate their sin against the Motherland. This is quite explicit in the case of Comrade Maksimov, the party secretary of the Verkhne-Kurmoiarskii *raion* committee who had been found guilty of allowing the disintegration of the partisan detachment for which he was responsible. The resolution recommended that Comrade Maksimov be advised of the verdict and that "the offer be put to him to assemble and instruct the detachment within five days, deploy it across the lines into the enemy rear, and conduct sabotage."[28]

Comrade Maksimov was being offered a lifeline—not much of one under the circumstances—but better than nothing. For Comrade Vitskov, there appeared to be no hope of escaping the firing squad. The wording of paragraph 10 of the resolution had all the hallmarks of a death sentence with no chance of appeal or reprieve:

> For failing to carry out the decisions of the District Committee of the All-Union Communist Party (b) of 28 July of this year on the formation of a partisan detachment, for allowing the disintegration of the detachment, and for displaying cowardice, the party's bureau resolves to remove the secretary of the Perelazovskii Area Committee of the All-Union Communist Party (b) Comrade Vitskov from the post of First Secretary of the Area Committee and to expel him from the ranks of the All-Union Communist Party (b). We request that the Central Committee of the All-Union Communist Party (b) confirm this decision.[29]

Much of this resolution seems to have been written with Stalin's Order № 227 in mind. The various expulsions were intended to demonstrate that the party committee of the Stalingrad District was acting with all due severity against cowards and shirkers. Even where there were useful suggestions, such as calling on Voronin to organize two-day seminars, the measures were too late.

Under German Occupation: A Preliminary Assessment

One of Senior Major Voronin's most important documents was concerned with the situation in the German rear in Stalingrad and the surrounding area. The report, dated 16 October 1942, was compiled for the commander of the Don Front, General Lieutenant Rokossovskii, and owed much to the work of the partisan detachments, intelligence residencies, and lone agents who had managed to infiltrate across the German lines.[30] Voronin's report contained a total of eight sections, each of which dealt with a specific aspect of the German occupation regime: data concerning enemy troops, the local agencies of control and the regime in the occupied territory, political measures in the occupied territory, the situation of the population in the occupied territory, brutality and violence inflicted on old men and women, fascist (very rarely referred to as Nazi) henchmen—traitors to the Motherland, fascist propaganda and the exploitation of religious prejudice, and Soviet patriots.

Voronin's sources and agents had clearly made considerable efforts to identify various levels of German headquarters in and outside Stalingrad. Key indicators were small, lightly armored vehicles; concentrations of German officers; and visible displays of communication networks. It is interesting to note that the various buildings now identified as serving as German headquarters—for example, a school on Nizhegorodskaia Street, a military school on Kholzunov Street, a clinic for railway workers on Kommunisticheskaia Street, or a maternity ward in the area of the Red October factory—were prefixed with the adjective *byvshii* (former). Although it is accurate to say that those buildings were not being used for their primary Soviet purposes, the use of *byvshii* implies that any Soviet connection had been eradicated, if only temporarily, and not just by the fact that the buildings were physically occupied by Germans. The use of *byvshii* seems to reflect a deeper sense of loss, of pain and anger that these buildings were occupied by the Germans. In addition to noting the location of long-range artillery batteries and antiaircraft guns, it was reported that "a large concentration of German troops is not noticeable in the central regions of the city. Small groups of submachine gunners, machine gunners, and mortar crews are mainly located in these areas."[31] Larger concentrations of German troops in groups of up to 300 men had been identified in Nevskaia, Medveditskaia, and Chernomorskaia Streets. The picture that emerges is that the very end of the German forward line was manned by small groups of German soldiers heavily armed with automatic weapons and able to dominate key pieces of ground. The larger concentrations of troops to their rear functioned as an immediate reserve to deal with, and clear out, any penetration of the German lines by Soviet assault groups. This was a valuable tactical insight for Soviet commanders planning attacks.

Underlining the willingness of Soviet prisoners to collaborate with their captors was the finding that the Germans were running short courses of instruction in the use of signal pistols. The aim was to send these signalers across the line so that targets could be marked for German mortars and artillery. The report noted that these courses were taking place in a small, wooded gully west of spot height 102 (Mamaev kurgan). One of the Soviet soldiers, a Russian with the surname Semenov from 38th Motor Rifle Brigade, had been identified as an instructor.[32]

Critical information for the potential to interdict the flow of German reinforcements and lines of communications were the details of German transport by rail and road. Voronin reported that "there is a constant flow of military train columns with troops and ammunition along the rail route from Sal'sk to the station at Kotel'nikovo. The movement of individual, minor train convoys gets to the station at Zhutovo (about 100–120 kilometers [62 to 75 miles] to the southwest of Stalingrad). Beyond that point the railway line is not used in the direction of Stalingrad."[33] From Kotel'nikovo men and ammunition were moved along a leveled dirt road. Over the period of 5–6 October a considerable concentration of enemy vehicles and infantry was observed in the gullies of this region.[34] Kotel'nikovo was identified as the main disembarkation point for men and equipment to Stalingrad.

Voronin provided a lot of detail about the dispositions and equipment of Romanian units. He observed, perhaps tellingly, that not all Romanian soldiers were equipped with boots; some were wearing light shoes.[35] Voronin's sources also indicated that the true scale of German and Romanian losses was being hidden:

> Graves are being dug not too deeply but in such a way that up to about six to ten bodies can be taken, and moreover, regardless of the fact that there are ten bodies, only one cross with the name of one soldier is inserted. This is being done apparently with the aim of hiding the actual losses in manpower. Every grave has a number, which is on the rear of the cross. When burials take place, a clerk working in the hospital comes to the grave and notes its number and the names of the buried soldiers in a special, secret book.[36]

Voronin's account of enemy dispositions and activity contained one observation that can be considered significant in the light of the Soviet counteroffensive of 19 November 1942. Soviet agents reported that the Germans were investing a huge amount of effort in building winter quarters (Red Army prisoners were being deployed to work on these bunkers in large numbers). The creation of what the Germans called Festung Stalingrad (Fortress Stalingrad) suggested that German 6th Army was still focused on taking the city—eventually—but that the German leaders realized they might have to sit out the winter before resuming their assault. This focus on the city would seem to be based on a disregard of the growing risk to German 6th Army's vulnerable flanks. For the Soviet planners now putting the finishing touches to Operation Uranus, this must have been a welcome indicator.

The nature of the occupational regime established by the Germans in Stalingrad and in the many villages and settlements in a large zone reaching back to the Don (to the west) and to the north and south was of major interest for the Special Sections of the NKVD. Voronin and his colleagues would want to know the locations of German counterespionage units, the level and nature of German confiscations, the severity of German measures for punishing violators of the occupational regime, and the ease with which it was possible for potential agents to move about. Also, as always, they showed an obsessive interest in traitors and those deemed to be collaborators.

The general German approach was to maintain a presence in various villages headed by a *starosta* and some five to seven members, all of whom were Russians. They were expected to maintain order and to report any signs of partisan activity. According to Voronin, "Those selected to be *starostas* and members of the police are recruited by the Germans from among traitors of the Motherland and from those former [*byvshii* (!)] Red Army soldiers who handed themselves over to the Germans. Such is the *starosta* of the settlement of Orekhovskii, Aleksandr Dolgov; senior policeman Aleksandr Klimov, the *starosta* of the Selivanovskii settlement; Ivan Sukhorukov, the *starosta* of the Maiorovskii settlement; Petr Denisov; and others."[37] *Starostas* were marked men. They were regarded as legitimate targets for assassination by Soviet agents and partisans.

Movement of local inhabitants was permitted from 0500 to 2000 hours in the region of their zone of occupation, but movement between one populated zone and another was not permitted without a pass issued by the local commandant's office. This required the recommendation of the *starosta*. Reasons for movement had to be stipulated, and movement was permitted only in daylight hours. Voronin noted that in the Kalmytskii Autonomous Republic, a large part of which was occupied by the Germans, bands of indigenous peoples were armed by the Germans and carrying out a policing role. They detained any suspicious persons and handed them over to the Germans. To quote Voronin: "These bands not infrequently exchange fire with the scouts of the Red Army."[38] Encouragingly, from Voronin's point of view, he reported that a young Russian woman simply referred to as "L" was able to move about the Stalingrad region without being subjected to rigorous security checks.[39]

Large numbers of civilians; displaced persons; refugees; and often, in Soviet jargon, "criminal elements" posed a massive security problem. One of the most important counterespionage measures that could be undertaken either by an occupier or by the internal security forces was the mass evacuation of civilians from a war zone. The Germans issued a steady stream of public notices warning the local population to abandon the city and to make for Kalach (most likely Kalach-on-Don) and Gumrak. They made it clear that bread would not be issued and that all available accommodations would be used by German troops. Civilians were ordered to abandon the city center by 7 October 1942. Those who ignored the order were liable to be shot. As the Germans were attempting to take the city in August 1942, the Stalingrad party's municipal committee adopted equally ruthless measures. A state of siege was declared, effective beginning at 2400 hours on 25 August 1942. Colonel Saraev, the head of the garrison and commander of 10th Rifle Division NKVD, was ordered to draw up a statute for maintaining order. The party municipal committee also intended that those seeking to exploit the chaos for plunder should receive swift and ruthless justice: "Persons engaged in looting and robbery are to be summarily shot at the scene of the crime. Those deliberately violating order and security in the city are to be handed over to a court of a military tribunal. The military prosecutor and the military tribunal are to consider all the evidence on violators of the established order in a period of siege within 24 hours."[40]

According to Voronin, all citizens forced to evacuate the city had to do so barefoot and hungry because "the Germans seized all foodstuffs, clothing, footwear, and bedding."[41] In the city civilians were forced to use their reserves of flour to bake bread for the Germans, and all warm clothing was taken. Voronin also recorded instances of plundering by non-Germans. Thus: "On 29–30 September [1942] a punitive detachment consisting of about thirty men, made up of Ukrainians or Poles in German uniform, burst into the area of Voroshilovskii *raion*. This detachment engaged in looting. The raiders turned all the inhabitants' pits and cellars upside down and took away literally everything hidden that they found. Whole vehicle loads of goods and foodstuffs were carted off."[42] This raid, and it was probably not an isolated example, could not have happened without the knowledge and approval of the Germans. Such raids were intended to terrorize the civilian population into submission and to encourage them to leave certain areas. Moreover, the fact that these raids were carried out by Ukrainians, Soviet citizens, and not Germans would have been intended to have a demoralizing effect on those remaining loyal to the Soviet state. In some cases it would induce a sense of hopelessness, passive disaffection, and apathy, or even defection to the enemy. It also made it possible for the Germans to deny responsibility at a later date, should it prove expedient, by claiming that these Ukrainians were renegades acting without German knowledge or approval.

Dispossession and forced evacuation were not the sole punishments inflicted on Soviet citizens in the German-occupied zones. Able-bodied civilians along with Red Army prisoners were made to work on military-related infrastructure: road repairs, defensive positions, and trenches. Voronin noted that the Germans conducted raids with the aim of rounding up able-bodied civilians to be used on these projects. The details of German behavior toward Soviet civilians in Stalingrad and in the small towns and settlements throughout the Stalingrad district are an important and largely unknown part of the Stalingrad story that has not received the attention it merits. Forced evacuations, conscription as labor, seizure of foodstuffs and clothing, and arbitrary and harsh disciplinary measures imposed by the Germans and their Soviet auxiliaries amount to a catalog of misery and hardship on a scale beyond that endured by the German-occupied nations of Western Europe. Food became a weapon of war, a means to manipulate and control. To quote Voronin:

> Throughout the region of Kletskaia, as indeed throughout other regions, the entire population was removed without the slightest reserves of foodstuffs and warm clothing, as a consequence of which there is starvation. Cases of gum and mouth diseases have been noted owing to a shortage of salt. Even the sparse food is prepared without salt. German soldiers, even if they do not employ direct violence against women, exploit the harsh conditions facing Russian women, and for salt they buy them for

> the night. The source bears witness to the fact that a woman in the settlement of Logovskii, Mariia Kalmykova, gave herself to a German for the night in return for a jug of salt.[43]

Voronin's concession that German soldiers did not rape Russian women was of course in complete contrast to Soviet wartime propaganda. However, in other parts of his report he cited examples of the rape of Russian women by Germans and Italians. Shortage of salt would appear to have been a minor problem. So bad were the shortages of food that "civilians, so as not to starve to death, creep out at night and head out to fields some several kilometers away and collect ears of wheat."[44] Even worse, "in every settlement the Germans have appointed a collective farm overseer who under the direct surveillance of the Germans employs the collective farm workers to harvest the grain. All the barns with grain, the stacks of grain, and hay in the fields are guarded by German sentries to prevent theft by Russians."[45] Voronin's accounts of the starving civilian population in the German rear and the harsh measures taken by the Germans to requisition as much grain as possible for immediate use bear an obvious resemblance to the Soviet forced collectivization of the early 1930s, with its far harsher seizures and quotas. In the huge area of the Stalingrad district, the predominantly steppe terrain offered little natural cover in the harsh winters and no refuge for partisans or persecuted civilians. Seizure of foodstuffs and clothing and evacuation from homes was a death sentence.[46] In February 1943, after the surrender, German soldiers would experience much the same treatment at the hands of the Red Army and starving and avaricious civilians.

Voronin's sources have been able to ascertain the names of a number of the German-appointed *starostas* and members of the auxiliary police. Fedor Andreevich Moldovanov, who worked as a tractor driver on a collective farm, was appointed *starosta* of the Khlebnyi settlement. Soviet justice did catch up with Moldovanov. On 30 June 1943 he was sentenced to ten years in a corrective labor camp by a military tribunal of the NKVD. He was rehabilitated on 25 September 1965.[47] Other appointees of the Germans were noted, such as Ivan Gostin (*starosta* of the Repin settlement), Georgii Dement'ev (former collective farm chairman and *starosta*), and Fedor Gorin (a *starosta*, arrested and sentenced to ten years, who died in captivity in 1943). One Russian, appointed as the senior police officer in the settlement of Orekhovo, told Voronin's source that he had given an oath of allegiance to Hitler and that "he considered himself to be a citizen of the German republic."[48] However, Voronin was also able to cite examples of Soviet patriotism and resistance to the Germans. The problem for him and his colleagues was trying to ascertain the level of treachery and support for Soviet power and whether the critical threshold had been reached beyond which countermeasures were superfluous since the occupied areas had been lost not just physically but also psychologically and ideologically.

Disrupting German Networks

Infiltration of the Abwehr and its agencies was a very high priority for the officers of the NKVD Special Sections. To this end agents were carefully selected and provided with convincing cover stories before being sent across the lines. Some individual case studies reveal a great deal about NKVD training methods, aims, and tradecraft. Consider, for example, the agent referred to as Taprakov.[49] On the night of 10 November 1942 Taprakov, accompanied by another agent whose name is given as Kuznetsov, is to cross the front.

In a briefing document that is personally addressed to Taprakov by his NKVD handler and that Taprakov signs, the agent is given specific tasks and instructions. Taprakov's primary mission is to infiltrate the German intelligence network. The agent is instructed to ascertain the names and posts of all the German officers involved in German intelligence and any servants involved in cooking and cleaning, especially those from the local population. The agent's primary task is stated as follows: "The main thing is that you are required to know all the agent network of the German intelligence organ in which you yourself will work, by surname, first names, and patronymic, and to report back to us in good time about any agent insertions into the rear of the Red Army and deep rear of the Soviet Union so that these agents can be liquidated."[50] Taprakov is also instructed by his Soviet handler that should he and others be inserted by parachute into Kazakh territory, he is to undermine the group and get it to hand itself over to the NKVD. Taprakov's cover story is that he is a Kazakh, the son of a peasant dispossessed by the NKVD, and that he has deserted the Red Army because of his anti-Soviet convictions.[51] This is an effective ploy because the bitterness over collectivization is a major factor in causing Red Army soldiers to desert to the Germans, especially those from parts of the Soviet Union where the death toll has been high (Ukraine and Kazakhstan, for example). It is also perhaps a cynical admission on the part of the very organs that played a role in forcing through Stalin's agricultural policies that the policies were disastrous. Taprakov's cover story is convincing and consistent with what German recruiters will already have observed and will expect to hear, and thus is likely to be believed.

Amid the worsening military situation and chaos, the Special Section of the NKVD on the Stalingrad front was nevertheless able to report some success in its efforts to disrupt German agent penetration. In a report dated 10 September 1942, the deputy head of the Special Section (Stalingrad front), Major Vladimir Kazakevich, summarized the results for the month of August 1942. Kazakevich notes, for example, that over the reported period a total of 110 German spies had been arrested: 97 were arrested on the front line, 3 were arrested in the rear of front and at transit assembly points, and 10 were uncovered as a result of the agent network.[52] A pointer for the success of NKVD blocking and filtration operations is the fact that the vast majority of these German agents (88 percent) were captured in the process of crossing the front line. Of 101 captured agents, 12 were from the command-and-leadership stratum, 76 were from the junior ranks, and 13 were identified as women. The civilian or military status of the remaining 10 agents was not given. According to Kazakevich, the main task of the German intelligence agencies was to undermine the ranks of the Red Army by encouraging soldiers to desert to the Germans and to collect information in the frontline zone.[53] Encouraging Red Army soldiers to desert was a highly effective way of undermining the Soviet defenses. Once desertion reached a certain level for a unit, it weakened the unit's effectiveness. The main danger for the Soviet command was that mass desertion would leave gaps in hastily improvised defenses, thus making it easier for the Germans to seize the city before major defense lines could be consolidated.

Kazakevich also reports a major counterintelligence success. On 9 August 1942 a German agent, equipped with a radio, surrendered to the Special Section of the Stalingrad front. The agent, whose surname is given as Shkarupin, was a former navigator in 200th Aviation Regiment of 40th Aviation Division. On the night of 22 July 1942 Shkarupin had been dropped by parachute behind the lines in the region of Stalingrad "with an intelligence-related task."[54] Shkarupin's capture attracted the attention of Abakumov (then a deputy people's commissar of the NKVD and eventually head of SMERSH in 1943). Realizing the significance of what had happened, Abakumov circulated a directive to other NKVD Special Sections. In his report, Abakumov provides no details of Shkarupin's activities over the eighteen-day period before he surrendered. Given Shkarupin's air force background, one can speculate that his task was to observe and, via radio, to report back on Soviet aircraft types and numbers in the Stalingrad region. The real bonus for Soviet counterintelligence were the many details of his recruitment and subsequent training provided by

Shkarupin because such information would enable the NKVD to build up a detailed picture of the modus operandi of the Abwehr: its training and intelligence objectives. Shkarupin told his Soviet interrogators that he had been in a prisoner-of-war camp in the region of Stuttgart and that, because he had been trained in the use of radio, he had been transferred to a concentration camp in Oranienburg. There, he had been drawn into an organization, the Combat Union of Russian Nationalists. Shkarupin had then been sent to a sabotage-intelligence training school in IAblon'.[55] Especially valuable for Soviet counterintelligence was the fact that Shkarupin was able to provide a detailed list of names of other agents with whom he had trained and who were being prepared for insertion behind the Soviet lines. Shkarupin's fate is not recorded. The firing squad was a distinct possibility, or he may have been used in a radio game in order to mislead his erstwhile masters.

Alongside efforts to interdict German agents, Kazakevich and his colleagues were aggressively pursuing other counterintelligence measures. Agents were being sent across the lines with the aim of penetrating the intelligence agencies of the enemy, and others were being deployed as stay-behind parties in the event of Red Army withdrawals.[56] Thus, in August 30 agents were sent into the enemy rear, 22 with counterintelligence assignments and 8 "with other tasks."[57] Kazakevich noted that 27 of these agents were newly recruited and 3 had been recruited from those returned from behind enemy lines. Kazakevich provides no indication whether these 3 agents had initially been recruited by the Germans and, having been turned, were being sent back across the lines. A total of 46 agents, signalers, and *rezidenty* had been sent across as part of the stay-behind groups.[58] In his report Kazakevich referred to what he called 'numerical information for the month of July and August 1942."[59] The precise nature of this information is not clear because the attached document mentioned by Kazakevich in his report has not been published. Speculation is not without risk, but I venture that the numerical data may well refer to the number of Red Army soldiers executed on the Stalingrad front in accordance with the provisions of Order № 227. If that is the case—and I underline that this is *speculation* on my part, not fact—the execution data cited in *Stalingradskaia epopeia*, often based on reports compiled by Kazakevich, could well understate the scale of executions on the Stalingrad and Don fronts.[60]

The scale and threat posed by German agents in and around Stalingrad mandated regular briefings for the Soviet General Staff and Main Political Directorate. In one such briefing, dated 24 September 1942, Abakumov reported on the heightened German threat at the moment of greatest danger for Stalingrad. At the time of his writing, German agents were seeking information about defensive positions, installations, communications, and the locations of tanks. Information about newly arrived Red Army units in the sectors of Ilovlinskaia-Kachalinskaia-Kotluban' and the right bank of the Volga north of Stalingrad was also being sought. Abakumov noted that between 23 and 26 August 1942 the Special Section of the Stalingrad front arrested a whole batch of German agents, Soviet prisoners recruited by the Germans. The intelligence tasks of these agents—the location and state of bridges, roads, and defensive installations and the location of major troop concentrations—were all consistent with large-scale offensive planning. Other German teams were tasked with attacking troop trains in the Volga basin area and disrupting links across the Volga. From a Soviet perspective, the scale of German intelligence activity must have seemed alarming and fully justified the harshest measures to disrupt it.[61]

German Intelligence Agencies of Interest to the NKVD

The steady stream of German agents being interdicted by the Special Sections in 1942 and later enabled the NKVD to identify some of the key German personnel involved in the recruitment and training of agents. In a widely disseminated report (7 October 1942), Abakumov revealed that a German officer by the name of Bruno Schultz operating within Abwehr Group 105 was largely responsible for agent training and recruitment. Under interrogation—and one can assume that NKVD interrogators did not permit themselves to be constrained or in any way hampered by irritating notions of human rights and individual dignity—captured agents provided names of other agents undergoing training, names of recruiters, and locations of safe houses and rendezvous points.[62] A list of the uncovered agent networks prepared by Schultz was attached to this report but has not been published by the FSB.

Abwehr Group 103 was another high-priority German intelligence target identified by Abakumov. The group was based in Elista (Kalmyk Autonomous SSR), and the main thrust of its intelligence activities were the Stalingrad, North Caucasian, and 4th Ukrainian fronts. Agents were primarily recruited from among Soviet prisoners and local civilians.[63] Abakumov's directive reveals a great deal of information about this group, including unit commanders, training, tasks, methods of infiltration, and even passwords to be used on exfiltration, which was almost certainly obtained from captured agents.

The NKVD also paid close attention to new ruses adopted by the Abwehr.

For example, the use of large groups masquerading as Red Army units and operating in the rear of the Red Army had been identified as a new and dangerous intelligence threat in the winter of 1942. In a directive circulated to the heads of all NKVD Special Sections, Abakumov reported that a group of twenty-two former Red Army soldiers captured by the Germans and recruited as agents had been detained on 7 March 1942 in the operational zone of 61st Army of the Western front. For nearly a whole month this group had moved about quite freely in the immediate rear and had been able to send back reports to its controllers. Abakumov quite rightly highlighted this as a serious counterintelligence failure:

> The fact that for a whole month close to the front a group of German agents with false documents and a radio station was able to turn up in various areas with impunity bears witness to the fact that the agent-informer network for exposing spies in the immediate rear of the front has still not been properly mobilized by the agencies of the Special Sections; that barrier-filtration work has been poor and that a thorough check of documents had not been organized; and that sufficiently decisive measures for the detention and filtration of suspicious persons are not being taken.

Abakumov also noted that the use of large groups was a new approach on the part of the Germans, one intended to create the impression that the unit was a legitimate Red Army subunit and thus to allay suspicions.[64]

An alarming development from the point of view of the NKVD, and further evidence of the flexibility and resourcefulness of German Abwehr recruiters, was the discovery of a special German school in which Soviet adolescents were being trained as saboteurs and spies. A circular of the NKVD Directorate of Special Sections reported the capture of thirteen-year-old N. I. Kuz'michev, who had managed to get into a reserve rifle regiment.[65] The trend of using adolescents had been isolated earlier in the year. In a report dated 20 February 1942, the NKVD noted: "Recently, immediately behind their lines, German intelligence has also organized a chain of intelligence schools for which are gathered children and adolescents in the age range from eight to fourteen years. These adolescents are mainly from families of parents who have been repressed by Soviet power, from criminal-hooligan elements, and homeless children."[66] In his report prepared for the Soviet leadership on NKVD activity in the liberated areas, dated 18 March 1943, Merkulov also noted the use of adolescents as agents: "A group of adolescents has been detained in the Kantemirovskii *raion* [Voronezh *oblast'*]—Filippovich, P. I. (born 1931); Filippovich, V.I. (born 1928); and Shevchenko, N. M. (born 1930)—which was deployed by the Germans across the front with the mission of blowing up the ammunition dumps left behind by the Germans and collecting intelligence data about the units of the Red Army."[67]

In addition to networks made up of Soviet prisoners and other defectors and even children, the Abwehr also deployed the exceptionally well-trained squads and units of the Brandenburg Division zbV. 800. The Brandenburg special forces were deployed at the start of Barbarossa, having established their effectiveness and efficiency against the Western Allies in the summer of 1940. The idea for this division came from an officer on Admiral Wilhelm Canaris's staff, Hauptmann Dr. Theodor von Hippel. He proposed that before the start of major operations a small unit be deployed behind the enemy lines with the aim of seizing objectives—especially bridges, passes, tunnels, route foci, and viaducts—before the enemy could destroy them so as to permit the unimpeded movement of German armored vehicles and other mechanized forces. The units would use all kinds of tricks and ruses to get close to the objective, overwhelm the defenders, deactivate the charges, and then hold the objective until the arrival of the main forces. In order to hide the real nature of these units, von Hippel proposed the name of *Baulehrkompanien* (Building/construction training companies).[68]

There is no evidence that the Brandenburg units were deployed in Stalingrad itself, but they were deployed with great success in the Caucasus, where they were used to seize mountain passes. They also made a significant contribution to the German advance in the Great Don Bend area and thus to the final advance to Stalingrad. The mere suspected presence of these units seemed to induce something approaching panic among the Soviet high command (a valuable contribution in its own right). In a directive issued by the commander of the Transcaucasian front, General Ivan Tiulenev, dated 22 August 1942, Red Army units guarding passes were warned of the danger posed by the Brandenburg units. Moreover, Tiulenev ordered that "all passes and routes be closed, and that no person be permitted to pass through. In every instance of the approach of our retreating groups and units, I am to be contacted for a decision once the passes have been closed."[69]

The Brandenburg zbV. 800 units soon discovered that long reconnaissance operations on foot in the steppe and Great Don Bend were ineffective because of the shortage of water, the lack of radio range, and the exhausting physical demands of such terrain. Using methods identical to those pioneered by the British SAS and Long Range Desert Group (LRDG) in North Africa, the organizers of the Brandenburg units realized that small mobile groups, often in captured American trucks supplied to the Red Army under Lend-Lease, were the best way to get results in the vast expanses of waterless steppe. Helmuth Spaeter provides an excellent example of how these units operated and how, in Red Army uniforms, they managed to bluff and trick their way through Soviet checkpoints to achieve their missions:

> The long-range reconnaissance patrol commanded by Hauptmann John in the Great Don Bend, which was still not occupied by German troops, got involved in a long interrogation by a Russian commissar in a village about 80 kilometers [50 miles] behind the enemy lines that was full of Russian troops. . . . After about three-quarters of an hour, this duel with psychological weapons between the commissar and the German interpreter had still not been decided when the interpreter took a final gamble and said: "If you do not believe me, contact Army HQ (the Russians)!" To which the commissar replied: "If I had a long-range radio link to there, I would have already done so!"
>
> With this, the decision went in favor of the German troops. As they left the village with some directions from the Russian lieutenant concerning the state and occupation of the next village that they would pass, the Germans acquired the best reconnaissance results possible. After leaving the village the troops, simulating a breakdown and waiting for the onset of darkness, headed west into the steppe and shortly before dawn reached their own lines. Approaching their own lines was always especially dangerous because of the risk of being fired on by one's own side. The use of American vehicles in this operation almost led to disaster. In 1942 these vehicles were not widely known throughout the Red Army since at that time the American deliveries had only just started. The appearance of such vehicles frequently led to inquisitive questions from Russian sentries. The vehicle drivers had consequently to speak the best possible Russian.[70]

Return of the NKVD to Liberated Territories

Soon after the Soviet counteroffensive, Operation Uranus, was launched, parts of the Stalingrad district were liberated from German occupation. This marked the beginning of a new phase in NKVD operations. In an order dated 28 November 1942, Voronin set out the immediate postoccupation tasks for the NKVD.[71] A high priority was to ascertain the full scale of collaboration with the Germans and the names of collaborators and to glean as much first-hand information as possible about the German occupation regime. Civilians were to be interrogated, and details of German economic exploitation, crimes, and brutality were to be recorded. Enemy prisoners were to be interrogated with a view to ascertaining political attitudes and morale, conditions in Germany, and the nature of propaganda. A high priority for both intelligence and counterpropaganda purposes and future penetration of German networks was the collection of copies of all blank German documents, public orders, and appeals to the local population as well as the diaries, letters, and photographs of enemy soldiers. Just how desperate and ruthless the NKVD could be regarding the issue of agent recruitment is revealed in Voronin's final paragraph. He stated:

> Members of the local population who remained in place during the enemy occupation are to be recruited for deployment behind the enemy lines. Recruitment for this category of agent network is permitted from among those accomplices of the enemy on the basis of their being exposed and subject to the condition that their families are evacuated to the deep rear and also that the person recruited shall be warned that in the event that he fails to carry out his obligatory tasks all members of his family are liable to repression.[72]

The decision to recruit civilians, accomplices of the German occupation forces or not, as agents to infiltrate the German lines seems to have been motivated, at least in part, by the determination to punish civilians for the mere fact of having lived in German-occupied territories. The threat to punish relatives bears the vindictive stamp of Order № 270.

Meanwhile, inside those areas of the Kessel still under German control, living conditions for both German soldiers and Soviet civilians was steadily deteriorating. In a document prepared by Voronin for distribution in early January 1943, the NKVD officer reported on the struggle to survive.[73] Voronin's sources provided plenty of detail on the state of German food and ammunition. For example, German prisoners reported that the scale of ammunition issue had fallen from 100 rounds of rifle ammunition and 4 grenades per day at the start of the encirclement (19 November 1942) to 30 rounds and 1 grenade. So bad was the situation that Soviet agents had reported that they had seen German soldiers collecting small-arms ammunition scattered about the streets and in dugouts. The lack of food was now critical. Agent Alekseev reported that German soldiers received about 100 grams (3.5 ounces) of bread per day; the Romanians did not even get that. The main source of food was now horse meat and carrion. Voronin noted: "On Zelenaia Street, in the presence of one of our agents, the Germans shot an exhausted horse and amid a fight dismembered it and dragged the pieces away to their dugouts. Local inhabitants say that the Germans have started to eat cats and dogs."[74]

Voronin's agents identified very weak morale among the Romanian and Croatian contingents. One Croatian seized by a Russian patrol stated that "the Croatian soldiers situated on the forward edge of the battle area do not want to fight and adopt a very negligent attitude toward their duties and do not surrender because the Germans shoot those trying to surrender from the rear."[75] German behavior exactly mirrored that of the NKVD *zagriaditel'nye otriady*, one of whose tasks was to open fire on Soviet units carrying out unauthorized withdrawals. Morale among Croatian and Romanian units was undoubtedly poor, yet at even at this stage, despite highlighting individual examples, German morale was still remarkably high given the physical and psychological conditions inside the Kessel. Voronin grudgingly conceded this when he reported that "despite the severe situation in which the surrounded Germans in Stalingrad find themselves, the command of the encircled formation is taking all measures in order to strengthen the defense line occupied by the Germans at the time in question and to build new fortifications."[76]

If German soldiers were suffering from acute shortages of rations and in some instances dying of hunger, starvation also stared Russian civilians in the face. Agent Pavlo reported on the dreadful plight of Demidova and her three children, who lived in a tractor factory and were at the extreme of exhaustion. In response to a question put to a woman about how she managed to survive, Agent Alekseev received the following answer: "'We live very badly here with the Germans. The Germans give us no food at all. We eat carrion, which for us as well as the Germans is in short supply. We've not seen bread for more than a month.'"[77] According to Agents Malinovskaia and Olia,[78] on 23 December 1942 the Germans carried out a reregistration of the civilian population. The purpose of this reregistration was to select civilians for work on defensive installations. These sorts of filtering and selection measures bear a strong resemblance to those implemented by the NKVD during the Terror Famine and during the mass deportations from Poland, the Baltic States, Ukraine, Belorussia, Kazakhstan, the Caucasus, and the lower Volga.

Voronin also reported details of repression and extreme violence carried out in the occupied area, though it is not clear whether these war crimes were committed by the regular German divisions of German 6th Army or by *Einsatzgruppen*. Having occupied the Voroshilovskii and Verkhne-Kurmorskii *raiony*, the Germans immediately embarked upon "the mass shooting of Jews."[79] In Liapichevo the Germans executed five children who had climbed into a German vehicle. Voronin also reported that in addition to the mass shootings of civilians and prisoners of war, "the occupiers raped women in front of their husbands and mothers and in the presence of their children."[80]

In a later memorandum, prepared after the German surrender and sent direct to NKVD boss Lavrentii Beria, Voronin provided additional information about life under German occupation and the ongoing nature of Soviet intelligence work. From the outset, the Germans made every effort to cajole and to force the civilian population to leave the city, the preferred destinations being Kalach (it is not clear whether this was Kalach or Kalach-on-Don) and Chir. Those who remained were subjected to periodic registrations and the issuance of residence documents in order to facilitate the exposure of Soviet agents. The Abwehr and other German agencies obviously reckoned with the possibility that some passes would eventually fall into Soviet hands and be copied. Periodic changes were therefore necessary in order to thwart NKVD plans.

Voronin, relying on the interrogation of the captured interpreter who worked for the German commandant's office, cited numerous examples of German pillaging. If the interpreter was to be believed, there was clear evidence of systematic and personal plunder by German individual soldiers and the German army: "On the admission of Lieutenant Auturgoph, the captured military interpreter attached to the commandant's office, the scale of plundering carried out by the Germans in Stalingrad exceeded everything that had occurred in the other populated zones and cities occupied by them in the Soviet Union."[81]

The German general designated to be the commandant of the city after its capture, Generalmajor Lenning, according to Voronin, had stolen a whole range of items—carpets, porcelain, silverware—that he took back to Khar'kov.[82] Voronin also noted that much of this pillage took place "with the active cooperation of German-appointed henchmen-*starostas*, *polizai*, and accomplices drawn from socially alien and criminal elements."[83]

The *Ukrainskie dobrovol'cheskie politseiskie otriady* (Ukrainian volunteer police detachments) were German-sponsored units whose members would have been a prime target for interrogation and filtration after the German surrender. Other Ukrainian units played a major role in the hunting down and killing of Jews:

> From the very first days of the occupation the Germans set about the extermination of those persons of Jewish nationality who had remained in the city and carried out harsh measures against communists, members of the Komsomol, and those suspected of engaging in partisan activity. For the most part the task of uncovering the Jews was done by German military police and the "Ukrainian Auxiliary Police." *No small role was played here by traitors from among the local residents. With the aim of searching out and destroying Jews, all apartments, cellars, trenches, and dugouts were checked.* For the most part the search for communists and members of the Komsomol was conducted by the Secret Field Police with the active participation and assistance of traitors to the Motherland in the service of the Germans.[84]

Various German reprisals against those suspected of being partisans or hostile to the Germans were also cited by Voronin. He noted that after the Germans were defeated dozens of the brutally mutilated corpses of Red Army personnel were found in the cellars of the main office of Factory № 221. Among them was "the body of a girl who had had her eyes gouged out and her right breast cut off by these monsters."[85] In the same area, in the presence of children, two female evacuees from Voroshilovgrad were raped and then shot.[86] Voronin cited many other examples of arbitrary violence and rape. Whether those responsible for these acts of violence were acting on their own initiative or whether the appearance of randomness was intended to hide an organized campaign of violence designed to terrorize the civilian population into submission is not obvious. Previous patterns of German occupation in cities in the West would suggest a combination of both random and organized violence, especially with the participation of the *Einsatzgruppen*, *Sicherheitsdienst*, and auxiliary police and antipartisan units made up of Soviet nationalities. Major Hans Speidel, who assumed control of the commandant's office after the departure of Generalmajor Lenning, underlined the arbitrary nature of violence: "All persons suspected of taking part in anti-German operations or being sympathetic toward Soviet power were shot on the spot."[87] However ruthless, this is not the same as rape or torture.

Not only did the Germans deport able-bodied men and women to Germany and parts of the Soviet Union as labor, they also removed agricultural and industrial resources from Stalingrad. Responsibility for the recording and con-

Table 7.4 *Category of Arrests in Stalingrad after the German Occupation, 20 March 1943*

Category of Arrestee	Number
Agents of German intelligence	46
Suspected of espionage	45
Polizai workers	68
Administrative personnel	28
Miscellaneous personnel	10
Volunteers in the German Army	172
Traitors	52
Deserters	19
Miscellaneous anti-Soviet elements	62
Total	502

Source: IA. F. Pogonii, i dr., *Stalingradskaia epopeia: Materialy NKVD SSSR i voennoi tsenzury iz Tsentral'nogo arkhiva FSB RF* (Moscow: Zvonnitsa-MG, 2000), p. 434.

fiscation of Soviet material lay with a special team, Wirtschaftserfassungskommando № 6. Attached to this group were a large number of informers, *litsa doveriia (Vertrauensleute)*, who were able to provide information about the location of industrial resources and property.[88] Nonferrous metals, some ferrous metals, lubricants, leather, and chemicals were all transported to the German rear and to Germany. Voronin estimated that some 12,000 to 20,000 metric tons (13,228 to 22,046 tons) of grain were removed from the main Stalingrad elevator.[89]

In his report to Beria, Voronin provided a detailed breakdown of those arrested in various categories of crime ranging from being a German agent to being an anti-Soviet element. I have collated the categories and numbers of arrests in Table 7.4.

The interesting thing here—and elsewhere—is the total absence of any reference to *Hiwis*. Given that at least 30,000 of them were known to have worked for the Germans, one must ask why there was no reference to *Hiwis* in this and in similar reports. "Volunteers in the German Army" could easily be a euphemism for "*Hiwis*." It is as if the use of the word "*Hiwi*" had been banned from Soviet documents so as not to draw attention to them. Was this intended to hide something sinister? Among the 502 arrested, Voronin noted that 17 were members and candidate members of the party and 46 were members of the Komsomol. Voronin then presented a breakdown of those arrested by social category. I present those data in Table 7.5. Note the very high percentage (70)

Table 7.5 *Social Category of Soviet Citizens Arrested by the NKVD in Stalingrad after the German Defeat*

Social Category	Number
Kulaks (*kulaki*)	3 (0.58 percent)
Traders (*torgovtsy*)	2 (0.40 percent)
Repressed by Soviet power (*repressirovannye*)	16 (3.19 percent)
Collective farm workers (*kolkhozniki*)	129 (25.7 percent)
Workers (*rabochie*)	186 (37.05 percent)
Office workers (*sluzhashchie*)	166 (33.06 percent)
Total	502

Source: IA. F. Pogonii, i dr., *Stalingradskaia epopeia: Materialy NKVD SSSR i voennoi tsenzury iz Tsentral'nogo arkhiva FSB RF* (Moscow: Zvonnitsa-MG, 2000), p. 434.

of arrests drawn from groups such as workers and office workers, who in many ways could be seen as the main beneficiaries of Soviet power and so more likely to remain loyal.

Immediately after the German surrender every effort was made to identify members of German intelligence and related personnel for purposes of interrogation. Voronin provided categories of those being investigated. I have collated those data in Table 7.6. Voronin points out that the posts of these officers have been revealed by the 'operational filtration of German Army volunteers and the personnel from the companies of the Ukrainian Auxiliary Police'.[90]

Reports prepared at the highest levels of the NKVD, especially because they were based on sources unavailable to junior NKVD officers, add enormously to our understanding of NKVD operations to uncover German agents, saboteurs, and accomplices of the Germans in Stalingrad and the surrounding district. One such assessment was prepared by Vsevolod Merkulov, a senior NKVD officer, on Stalin's orders and circulated to a small section of the Soviet leadership.[91] The value of Merkulov's report lies in the fact that he provided arrest and operational data not just for Stalingrad and its district (*oblast'*) but also for all other districts and autonomous republics liberated from the German occupation in early 1943. What emerges therefore is a detailed overview of collaboration and German agent penetration throughout the Soviet Union.

Merkulov noted that up to and including 10 March 1943, 30,750 people of various categories had been arrested by the NKVD and its operational groups. The data provided cover the Stalingrad, Voronezh, Rostov, Stavropol, Krasno-

Table 7.6 *Categories and Numbers of German Intelligence Personnel under Investigation*

Category of German Intelligence	Number
Abwehr	5
Members of Ic	23
Secret Field Police	8
Military police	4
Romanian intelligence	6
Military commandant personnel	4
Signals intelligence	4
Propaganda company personnel	3
Military courts	5
Miscellaneous personnel and interpreters	29
Total	91

Source: IA. F. Pogonii, i dr., *Stalingradskaia epopeia: Materialy NKVD SSSR i voennoi tsenzury iz Tsentral'nogo arkhiva FSB RF* (Moscow: Zvonnitsa-MG, 2000), pp. 434–435.

dar, Leningrad, Kalinin, and Orlov districts; Ukraine; and the Kalmyk, Kabardinian-Balkarian, and North-Ossetian Autonomous Soviet-Socialist Republics. I have collated all the data from Merkulov's report and present them in Table 7.7.

With regard to Stalingrad and the Stalingrad district, Merkulov reported that immediately after the German collapse at Stalingrad the NKVD and Red Army subunits conducted a sweep of cellars and ruined buildings and combed the main gullies and ravines in the city. The results were remarkable and highlight a little-known facet of the battle. To quote Merkulov: "In the course of these operations more than 5,000 German soldiers and officers were uncovered and detained. In a number of cases, they offered armed resistance when being detained."[92] Merkulov noted that a major role in collaborating with the German occupation forces was played by "former White Guards and the relatives of those persons who were repressed and dispossessed in the past."[93] Thus, according to Merkulov, I. V. Sergeev, the son of a White Guard who had been executed in 1937 on a charge of counterrevolutionary activity, "took an active part in all the measures of the occupation forces to uncover and to give away partisans [and] party and Soviet activists (he has been arrested)."[94]

The striking thing about these data is the huge number of those arrested on suspicion of having been accomplices (*posobniki*) of the German occupation forces, a total of 60.3 percent of all arrests. Even assuming that a portion

Table 7.7 *Categories of Arrests of Soviet Citizens by the NKVD in Liberated Territories*

Region of USSR	German Accomplices	German Agents	Bandits and Deserters	Miscellaneous Anti-Soviet Elements	Total
Stalingrad	1,423	479	78	470	2,450
Voronezh	2,861	218	319 deserters	528	3,926
Rostov	1,807	221	121	665	2,804
Stavropol	4,652	312	252	0	5,216
Krasnodar	3,011	309	1,480	1,200	6,000
Leningrad	60	19	0	30	109
Kalinin	122	30	0	24	176
Orlov	1,449	227	2,037 deserters	1,131	4,844
Ukraine SSR	1,591	94	21 deserters	62	1,768
Kalmyk ASSR	243	28	16	25	312*
Kab-Bal ASSR	538	160	524	507	1,729
North-Ossetian ASSR	506	100	298 deserters	38	942
Totals	18,263 (60.3 percent)	2,197 (7.25 percent)	5,146 (17 percent)	4,680 (15.45 percent)	30,286**

Source: OGB/1943/1/№ 1360, pp. 295–307.

Note: The data for Stalingrad to Orlov refer to the administrative districts as a whole and not exclusively to the city from which the district (*oblast'*) is named.

*The total for the Kalmyk Autonomous Soviet Socialist Republic is based on the categories cited in the source: 312, not 303.

**The total number of arrests based on all regions amounts to 30,286, not 30,750, as cited by Merkulov.

of those deemed to have abetted the German occupation did so out of conviction, others would have been forced to work for the Germans in their various trade capacities (builders, millers, cooks, and bricklayers). Others would have worked for the Germans in order to survive. Regardless of the precise motives, this figure suggests a high level of political disaffection from the Soviet state, ranging from outright hatred and participation in armed resistance to passive resistance and apathy.

An NKVD Assessment of Its Agent Networks

In a report dated 9 April 1943, some two months after the German collapse, Captain Boris Pol', the head of 4th Section of the NKVD Directorate for the Stalingrad district, provided an assessment of Soviet espionage and counterespionage carried out during the German occupation.[95] Pol' covered network deployment in the city, the agent networks in the rural *raiony* of the district, the work of the agent network sent into the enemy rear, failures and repression of networks by the enemy, cooperation with other NKVD directorates, intelligence work via prisoners of war, activity in the zones immediately to the rear of the front, and drew some fundamental conclusions.

Pol' and his colleagues prepared 51 agents to remain behind the German-occupied part of Stalingrad. They were deployed in the form of 9 intelligence residencies, a total of 43 agents and 8 lone agents. In view of the amount of work invested in the creation of these agent networks, the results were not that impressive. Twenty-seven agents remained in occupied territory "from whom over the entire period of military operations no material at all was received, and not one of the individual agents crossed the front line."[96] Pol' also noted that no sooner had the enemy entered regions of the city allocated to the Druzhnye and Volzhane networks than all radio contact was lost: "Attempts to reestablish contact with the intelligence networks by sending liaison agents across the front line achieved little in the way of positive results. The liaison agents did not discover the residencies in their former domiciles."[97] Worse still, from the NKVD's point of view, once the battle was over, none of the agents sent across the line could be found, and the buildings where they had been last known to have stayed had been destroyed. When the building that had housed the Druzhnye network was searched, no traces of any radio equipment or batteries could be found. The loss of contact with the networks could easily have been explained as a consequence of the fact that the agents had been killed in the aerial and artillery bombardments to which the city had been subjected by both sides. However, Pol' and his masters would have considered the possibility that the agent networks had been disrupted by the Germans and even that the agents had been captured and worked for the Germans. One factor that clearly played a role in effectively disrupting Soviet agent networks was the mass evacuation of the overwhelming majority of the civilian population from Stalingrad at the beginning of October 1942, a measure that, as Pol' reported, "included our entire agent network."[98]

In the rural parts of the district 145 agents were prepared and left behind the German lines, organized in 31 residencies with an additional 15 agents deployed as lone agents for a total of 160 agents. After the German surrender, 108 were found. Of the remaining 52, the Germans evacuated 48 into the deep rear, and 4 died.[99] Again, the results of these networks are far from impressive. To quote Pol':

> The residences left behind the enemy lines did not carry out any organized and systematic intelligence work. This can be explained basically by the lack of experience of the *rezidenty* selected in the majority of the *raiony* in conditions of the approaching war. At the same time, 6 of the 31 *rezidenty* were evacuated by the Germans to the deep rear, 4 *rezidenty* evaded the discharge of their duties, and 7 *rezidenty* displayed cowardice and did not lead their networks.[100]

Despite these poor results, Pol' nevertheless maintained that "the intelligence network carried out significant work in uncovering traitors and the accomplices of the occupiers and exposing the German agent network."[101] There is an obvious question to be addressed here: What should have been the priorities for NKVD networks behind the enemy lines? Dealing with traitors—killing the German-appointed *starostas* and others—undoubtedly satisfied a deep psychological need to eliminate traitors. It also acted as deterrence because those minded to work for the Germans had to reckon with the fact that the long arm of Soviet justice would catch up with them, and it signaled the presence of Soviet power in the occupied territories. However, killing traitors is no substitute for hard intelligence data and information and may even be something of a distraction because it creates the impression that valuable intelligence-rclated work is being carried out and masks the failure to acquire the real thing: information about the enemy and his intentions. The limited successes achieved by the agent networks in the rural areas could not hide another problem, and one acknowledged by Pol': "The fundamental conclusion to be derived from the experience of intelligence networks left behind in the rural regions is as follows: it is necessary to select higher-quality *rezidenty* because the success of the agent network depends to an enormous degree on their activity."[102]

Turning his attention to the work of the agent network in the enemy rear, Pol' recorded that up to 1 February 1943, 147 agents had been recruited and sent across the enemy lines. Of those agents, 12 were killed trying to cross the lines, 46 failed to return, and 7 returned wounded. Fourteen agents among the 46 nonreturners were located after the liberation of the occupied territory.[103] Overall, Pol' listed five categories of achievements:

1. Timely receipt of information concerning the political, economic, and administrative measures of the enemy
2. The exposure of 362 persons deemed to be traitors, active enemy accomplices, and other anti-Soviet elements
3. The receipt of valuable military intelligence data, which were passed on to the Red Army
4. The formation of a partisan detachment consisting of Red Army prisoners, a total of 30 men, with the participation of agents Olia and Malinovskaia
5. The distribution of 13,400 anti-German leaflets and the bringing across of 45 civilians, 32 Red Army prisoners, and 6 Romanian and 2 German soldiers "whose interrogation yielded valuable information in the realm of military-political intelligence."[104]

Once again, the value of female agents in operating behind the lines was stressed. According to Pol', "Their primary advantage consists in the fact that they can move about more freely in occupied territory and in the relative ease of providing them with a cover story (of the 46 nonreturning agents a mere 11 were women)."[105] A remarkable admission made by Pol' in his report was that "cases of our agent network being uncovered by German counterintelligence have not been ascertained."[106] This suggests that the NKVD networks were unable to penetrate the German counterintelligence apparatus and thus to monitor the success or failure of the Germans. Successful efforts on the part of German counterintelligence to uncover Soviet agents are clearly implied in the fact that Soviet agents were killed trying to infiltrate across the German lines, failed to return, or were wounded. Pol' noted that some of those originally listed as nonreturners were recovered after the liberation of occupied territory. One wonders just how many of these listed as nonreturners, eventually accounted for or otherwise, provided information to the Germans. This was a real possibility and one that did not appear to be taken seriously by Pol' in his assessment.

Many of the basic conclusions summarized by Pol' do, however, identify flaws and areas of agent work that required improvement. To this end, Pol' made seven recommendations:

(1) Every effort must be made to insert agents into the enemy's control structure. Getting agents into such positions also has another advantage for the NKVD: "The participation of an agent in the control agencies provides sufficient guarantee that the agent will not be evacuated into the depth of occupied territory and so creates the conditions for the implementation of our tasks."[107]
(2) In addition to purely intelligence-gathering tasks, the networks must engage in "active subversive activity aimed at the enemy."[108]
(3) The use of runners and couriers must be retained in the residencies, but communication centers independent of the residencies need to be created.
(4) Liaison couriers are to be sent across the line to the residencies so as to update them and where necessary to send intelligence material across the line of the front with couriers.
(5) *Rezident* heads are to recruit couriers to take material across the line of the front.
(6) As regards recruitment, persons with a command of German, members of the rural intelligentsia and collective farm administration, and those with civilian trades are the most suitable (millers and cobblers).
(7) Reserve *rezidenty* are to be left with the aim of conducting the independent recruitment of agents behind the enemy lines.

The first recommendation could be construed as an acknowledgment that the NKVD had earlier failed to get any agents inserted in such positions and thus explain why, as I suggested earlier, Pol' was unable to provide precise information on the number of Soviet agents uncovered by German counterintelligence. The third recommendation suggested that when one network was compromised, it led to others being compromised. Independent communication networks were a way of reducing the risk. The sixth recommendation clearly recognized that persons, for example, who spoke German were likely to be used as interpreters and thus to gain access to information. The downside was that German-speaking Russians were likely to be regarded with some degree of suspicion. Again, millers and cobblers were likely to be employed by the Germans in support of their logistical effort. One other weak link that Pol' did not consider was that possibly too much was expected from the networks, which led to their being compromised. Thus, agents who were primarily engaged in observation and the collection of data should generally have taken no part in sabotage or distributing leaflets. This operational principle was clearly recognized in the plan of work drawn up by Major Reshetov for purely intelligence agencies and sabotage groups to be deployed in Ukraine (see earlier in this chapter).

The Interrogation of the Chief of Staff of 305th Infantry Division, German 6th Army

German officers among the large contingent of German prisoners captured in February 1943 who were directly involved in espionage and counterespionage were of the greatest interest to the NKVD. They could provide a detailed account of the German organizational structure; information about operations in which they had been involved; names and details of Soviet citizens working for the relevant German agencies; and, critically, just how successful they had been and the degree to which NKVD operations had also been successful. Despite various lacunae, the interrogation record of Oberstleutnant i.G. Rudolf K. Paltzo, the chief of staff of 305th Infantry Division, is a good example of the information sought by the NKVD and of how valuable such interrogations were. Even where much of the information provided by prisoners was already known to the NKVD, the fact that its accuracy or veracity was corroborated by other sources was itself valuable.[109]

The record of Paltzo's interrogation reveals that he provided a great amount of detail about the Geheime Feldpolizei; the Sicherheitsdienst; the departments of the Abwehr and their various functions; and the Ic (staff designation for the tasks listed) section at divisional headquarters that dealt with reconnaissance, espionage, and sabotage prevention. He noted that Abwehr 2 controlled and deployed the German special forces unit Brandenburg zbV. 800, which had caused considerable disruption behind the Soviet lines and enjoyed a high success rate in its operations. Among the functions of the Sonderkommandos of the Sicherheitsdienst was "the implementation of punitive measures against Jews."[110] Paltzo confirmed not just that Jews had been singled out for repressive measures but that he, as an army officer, had known about it. This has much wider implications for the complicity of the German Army in National Socialist war crimes.

One of Paltzo's revelations concerning the *modus operandi* of Abwehr 2 would have been especially valuable for Soviet counter-intelligence. To quote Paltzo:

> I want to add that the deployment of an agent network, as a rule, occurs on the very same sectors of the front in each army. This is done because on that sector of the front where a network has once been deployed, the commander of the respective company and the head of the divisional Ic section know how to carry out this deployment and consequently a subsequent deployment from this side of the front cannot present any difficulties.[111]

This was valuable information for the NKVD because it meant that Soviet counterintelligence units could be concentrated to achieve maximum disruption of German agent deployment. It is, of course, possible that the NKVD had already observed a consistent pattern of deployment from the same sector. However, confirmation from the enemy was useful and, quite apart from anything else, reinforced the sense of institutional and professional pride among NKVD officers.

The German View of NKVD Operations: A Synopsis

Recruiting civilians and Red Army prisoners for spying and sabotage, promoting nationalist sympathies, and creating nationalist formations, German intelligence and counterintelligence agencies were well aware that a massive effort was being made by the NKVD to penetrate the German lines across the entire front. In one of its intelligence reports for October 1942 German 6th Army circulated details concerning the establishment of special units. The information had been passed on from Army Group Center. According to a prisoner, the Soviet 19th Rifle Division had four groups consisting of 10 to 20 each, 30 percent of whom were communists. They received special training and typically consisted of the following personnel: 1 officer, 3 NCOs, 1 mine specialist, 1 radio operator, 1 telephonist, 2 demolition specialists, and 1 interpreter. They wore German uniforms and typically penetrated up to 15 kilometers (9.3 miles) behind the German lines. By day they hid in woods. During the night they destroyed bridges, attacked convoys, and conducted reconnaissance. The report noted that these units were set up by officers of the NKVD's Special Section.[112]

Acting on information received from 6th Army headquarters, the intelligence officer of 79th Infantry Division circulated a warning about the threat posed by NKVD squads throughout the division and details of their activities in the divisional and neighboring sectors:

> During the night of 21 November two men are supposed to have been sent out through the position on the southwest corner of the metal factory next to the four small houses and to have returned on 23 November. Their primary task was to conduct a reconnaissance of observation posts and artillery positions.
>
> It has been established in a neighboring corps on the northern front that the Russians sent out similar agents in large numbers for several days through our own lines. They were deployed in groups of three and had the task of reconnoitering positions and camps. Generally speaking, specific points on the front are selected for the infiltration of these squads. These agents frequently make themselves out to be deserters. Later, after they have carried out their reconnaissance tasks, they are to escape and return back across the front line.[113]

In keeping with the experiences of his NKVD counterparts, the German intelligence officer realized that controlling the movements of the civilian population was one of the most effective ways to prevent agent penetration. He ordered that "as a matter of routine, any person, including civilians, in a combat zone is to be arrested" and that placards with the following warnings be posted in prominent locations: "Access to Stalingrad is strictly forbidden. Any person encountered will be shot dead without warning" and "Any civilian movement outside the villages is strictly forbidden. Any person encountered will be shot dead without warning."[114] Moreover, as a measure to undermine the false passes used by the NKVD, 79th Infantry Division's intelligence officer ordered that all passes issued to civilians either for entering Stalingrad or for movement between villages were to be regarded as invalid.

In an early-morning summary dated 27 December 1942, German 6th Army headquarters reported that on the western side of the front there had been heavy activity carried out by "fighting patrols in German uniforms with German-speaking soldiers."[115]

German 6th Army received additional information about NKVD sabotage squads from Army Group Hollidt, dated 30 December 1942. According to the report, special reconnaissance companies had been set up whose sole task was to gather information on Axis forces. For the observation missions, small groups were formed that might penetrate 40 to 60 kilometers (25 to 37 miles) behind the Axis lines. The specific reconnaissance tasks were determined by the division sending out the group. The report's author noted: "The 302nd Division from the Stalingrad sector on the order of a Colonel Ekimoiuk [the name is not clear in the German original] has formed several special groups from men of the reconnaissance companies. In some groups there are women. These operations are conducted by lone individuals or small groups in civilian clothing issued with light automatic weapons."[116] Units bigger than company size were also being deployed. For example, 503rd Infantry Regiment of 91st Infantry Division had the task of carrying out special tasks behind the lines up to a depth of 50 to 60 kilometers (31 to 37 miles). The report's author noted: "These tasks are carried out in order to seize prisoners, to destroy command posts and camps, and to attack lone supply and ammunition vehicles."[117]

In assessing the scale of German penetration of the Soviet line, Soviet intelligence officers frequently bemoaned the carelessness and negligence of Red Army units, which made the tasks of the German agent networks all the easier. German counterintelligence officers faced a similar problem of carelessness among their own soldiers. In a directive issued by the intelligence section of 79th Infantry Division on 2 January 1943, specifically dealing with counterespionage and sabotage measures, the intelligence officer highlighted numerous failings on the part of German soldiers:

> The many cases of espionage that have been uncovered in recent days make it absolutely clear that the enemy's intelligence service is especially active in the present situation. The activity of enemy spies is not only herewith made all the easier by insufficient control of the civilian population but is also demonstrably assisted by the credulity of German soldiers. Enemy agents have been able to move about undetected, elicit answers to their questions, and be transported in Wehrmacht vehicles. From this it can be assumed with certainty that the enemy, as a consequence of the repeatedly confirmed carelessness of our own troops, acquires from day to day a clear picture of the positions, accommodations, headquarters, supply points, state of the units, and more besides.[118]

The intelligence officer cited various examples of carelessness: Russian prisoners had been sent to Stalingrad to collect wood and been left unsupervised for six days; Germans wearing Russian informs and heading out on a reconnaissance patrol had been able "to move about in Stalingrad completely unhindered, to enter a headquarters and a gun position, and to conduct conversations with prisoners engaged in building work";[119] and weak security had enabled Russian prisoners to kill their guards and escape.

Sabotage and reconnaissance tasks were the standard work of both Abwehr and NKVD special operations. However, German intelligence reports also identified activity that as far as one can tell was peculiar to the NKVD. An intelligence report of Gruppe Pfeiffer drew attention to the deployment of NKVD female agents provided with poison:

> According to the latest information some Russian female agents are equipped with poison in powdered form. On completion of other tasks, they are to try to get employment in the kitchens of German troops. They are then supposed to poison food meant for soldiers. They have been instructed to flee immediately, before the outcome of the poisoning. Concerning the type of poison and its effects, nothing is known.
>
> The greatest care and constant surveillance is required when employing the local female workers.[120]

Army Group Hollidt reported that Russian intelligence agencies were using carrier pigeons. The final section of the report concluded: "Local inhabitants are to be informed that violations of this order will be mercilessly punished with the death penalty."[121] One final point is that news of NKVD retribution eventually reached the Germans. In an intelligence report of 384th Infantry Division it was noted: "In the territory formerly occupied by us, the NKVD is carrying out executions. Those we employed as *starostas* and *polizai* were shot; others were deported. Able-bodied men are being inducted into the Red Army. The female part of the population that is fit for work is being dispatched to labor projects."[122]

Conclusion

The scale of the threat posed by German agent networks in the period leading up to 22 June 1941 was all too clear to the NKVD. In an intelligence assessment made before the outbreak of hostilities by the 3rd Directorate of the NKO SSSR, it was noted that the Germans were successfully recruiting agents "from Ukrainian nationalists, Polish prisoners of war (officers and soldiers), Russian White Guards and emigrants, citizens of the Baltics, and even Jews.

Up to 10 percent of the agent network, as noted in the briefing documents, consisted of attractive young women. The average age of all agents did not exceed thirty years."[123] The age range must have been especially worrying for the NKVD because these were people who had been born and brought up in the Soviet state, yet were prepared to work for its destruction. The question bypassed is why. Nationalism, which had not been destroyed but driven underground, was one reason, and related to it was the lack of any sense of allegiance to the Soviet state. Another cause was the genocidal implementation of collectivization in the early 1930s. By the end of June 1941 German recruitment of agents among Soviet prisoners was also causing alarm and prompted a number of directives and orders issued specifically to deal with the threat posed by Soviet deserters and traitors. Order № 270 was just one such order.

By the summer of 1942, and certainly by the time German 6th Army was investing Stalingrad, the NKVD had built up a good idea of the German modus operandi. Notwithstanding the scale of the German espionage and agent threat, the FSB compilers of SMERSH criticized the German habit of using large numbers of poor-quality agents. They noted: "German intelligence aces reckoned that if only one out of ten successfully recruited agents carried out the task, there would be a successful outcome."[124] In Soviet counterintelligence jargon, this was known as *nastroika mashiny na krupnyi pomol*, which roughly translates as "running/tuning the machine on flour," or as we might say in English, "You cannot make a silk purse out of a sow's ear."[125] They noted, for example, that up to 8 August 1942, 11,765 enemy agents had been arrested.[126]

Even if large numbers of poorly trained agents did not achieve the immediate goals—and that outcome cannot be confirmed with any degree of certainty—flooding the Soviet rear with poorly trained agents possessed three clear advantages. First, it fanned the fears and paranoia of the NKVD that the Red Army was riddled with spies and deserters and that soldiers escaping from German captivity or returning from encirclement could not be trusted. Second, by exploiting the vast reservoir of captured Red Army manpower at their disposal, the Germans were able to overwhelm the Special Sections of the NKVD. Sweeps, arrests, interrogation, and filtration were time-consuming and labor-intensive operations. Regardless of the fact that a large percentage of hastily recruited Red Army soldiers handed themselves in to the NKVD, German intelligence officers knew that any such soldier would be the subject of profound suspicion. Clearly they would have preferred some hard intelligence data, but undermining trust and sowing suspicion were still a useful return on the investment. Moreover, the vast pool of poorly trained agents recruited and dispatched behind the Soviet lines provided excellent cover for the really well-trained and committed German agents who were undoubtedly also being sent. The huge scale of Soviet filtration and interrogation confirms the perceived German threat. Third, Abwehr recruiters were surely aware that a percentage of their new recruits were potentially unreliable and would surrender to the Soviet authorities at the first opportunity.[127] This provided an opportunity to mislead and to deceive the NKVD about German intentions.

Some idea of the basic but nevertheless potentially valuable tasks given to Red Army prisoners recruited by the Abwehr and given just minimal training is revealed in a report drafted by Abwehr Troop 304, a copy of which was sent to German 6th Army headquarters. Three agents crossed the line on the night of 8–9 December 1942 and were able to blend in with various Red Army stragglers and other units and thus to move about relatively freely. Of obvious value to the Abwehr was the knowledge that the headquarters of the Soviet 333rd Infantry Division was located in Sviridovskii and that an even bigger prize, the headquarters of 5th Army, was rumored to be in Shirkov. There was also evidence of Soviet retribution: the German-appointed *starosta* in Ostrovo had been shot. The agents were able to move about the Kalach area and the all-important bridge and to identify the traffic moving across. Already, in mid-December, vehicles and pedestrians were crossing the frozen Don. Another valuable discovery was that a new airfield was under construction at the Victory-of-October *sovkhoz*. Soviet morale also appeared to be good, according to the report; note though the caveat: "The rations of the Red Army soldiers were, for the greater part, derived from captured German supplies. Morale among the units that had still to be deployed can be characterized as good. There is much talk in general that great victories are to be expected."[128] These short-stay missions could provide valuable tactical information, though the intelligence value tended to be short-lived. An experienced intelligence officer could tease out a great deal of material. Moreover, if the resources were available to act on the information gained, real damage could be done. Divisional and army headquarters, noted in the report, were prime targets, and even if an air attack did not achieve total destruction, disruption of command and control even for brief spells could have serious consequences for the conduct of the battle. Even allowing for the vigilance of NKVD blocking detachments and other security patrols, the size of the operational area and the general comings and goings at the front and immediately behind it provided plenty of cover for the agents of both sides to exploit. A Red Army soldier recruited by the Abwehr who was then captured and revealed under interrogation by the NKVD that his task was to identify the location of major formation headquarters merely confirmed that he was engaged in one of the basic tasks of all intelligence agencies. The mass deployment of poorly trained agents was worth the effort and the risks.

The high quality of some German agents was, in any case, not in doubt. This was revealed in a detailed internal NKVD assessment of its own counterespionage work for the first half of 1943. Over this period (January–June 1943) NKVD units responsible for the security of the rear areas managed to arrest and to uncover 264 enemy agents. Forty-seven of those arrested had undergone special training in German intelligence schools.[129] Of the total agents apprehended by the NKVD, 37 were women, and 33 were youths.[130] The German training regimen was recognized as thorough and comprehensive and included, among other things, small-arms training, navigation and infiltration skills, and the knowledge necessary to identify major units and interunit boundaries. The training would typically last from one to six months. Saboteurs and signalers, in the case of the latter requiring the mastery of Morse code and encryption, underwent the longest training. Some of the tasks given to German agents could have had far-reaching consequences had they been successful. With an obvious assassination mission under consideration, one German agent was given the task of identifying the location of Marshal Georgii Zhukov.[131] In a plan similar to that which German counterintelligence believed was being plotted against them by female NKVD agents, German female agents planned to poison wounded soldiers and workers.[132]

The familiar pattern of German agent movement behind the Soviet lines can also be observed. To cite Colonel Vladimir Egnarov, the report's author: "The most qualified enemy agents, who operated in the uniforms of the command personnel of the Red Army, carried out their tasks under the guise of persons carrying out official duties, whereas those dressed in the uniform of Red Army soldiers and NCOs operated under the pretence of having escaped encirclement, lagged behind, or seeking out their units."[133]

No matter how well trained, the German agents avoiding detection often depended on the quality of the false documentation with which they were provided. If this documentation failed to withstand initial scrutiny at an NKVD or Red Army checkpoint, further checks would be made, and the agents ran the risk of being exposed. To quote Colonel Egnarov: "All these documents were identified as false without any difficulty when carefully examined. In many instances it was precisely this that facilitated the exposure of enemy agent networks."[134] In his final list of recommendations Colonel Egnarov stressed thorough verification of the documents and bearers as the single most effective measure for exposing German agents.[135] German-trained agents were valuable assets, so one had to ask whether it sometimes suited German controllers to sacrifice agents with the intention of misleading the NKVD and for other purposes. Poor documentation would more or less guarantee their detention and arrest. Colonel Egnarov recorded, for example, that during interrogation many German agents deliberately provided confusing statements, which they would repeatedly change.[136]

Despite the vast number of declassified documents that deal with Stalingrad, there are two obvious lacunae in our knowledge that pertain to the role of the NKVD. Of immediate relevance and interest is the fate of the Red Army soldiers—the *Hiwis*—who worked for the Germans inside the pocket. German 6th Army rations returns for November 1942 show that about 30,000 *Hiwis* were attached to the divisions of the 6th Army. Yet among the declassified reports published by the FSB we find nothing about what befell these Red Army prisoners after the German surrender in February 1943. One reason the NKVD and Red Army detachments conducted sweeps and searches of the ruins of Stalingrad and its gullies after the German surrender was to gather up Germans and *Hiwis* who had gone to ground. These searches must have been very thorough because the NKVD had a very good idea of the number of civilians in Stalingrad after the German surrender. See, for example, Table 7.8, based on NKVD documents for numbers and locations.

Precise figures for the number of civilians remaining in the parts occupied by the Germans raise the obvious question of why there are no corresponding figures for *Hiwis*. Bear in mind the assiduity with which the NKVD identified civilian collaborators and their category by class after territories were liberated. Yet we find nothing about *Hiwis*. What happened to these men after the German surrender? One cannot rule out the possibility of a large-scale, Katyn-style massacre somewhere in the steppe outside Stalingrad. In his memoir of 3rd Infantry Division (mot.), Gerhard Dieckhoff writes that after the division surrendered, *Hiwis* were killed on the spot ("*an Ort und Stelle umgelegt*").[137] The other possibility is that those captured and uncovered would have been subjected to a lengthy process of filtration and interrogation and would then have endured a range of penalties, including labor camp, dispatch to a penal battalion, or execution. This is speculation, but the fact is that the precise fate of these men remains unknown.

Table 7.8 *Numbers of Civilians Accounted for in Areas of Stalingrad after Liberation*

Area of Stalingrad	Number
Tractor factory	112
Barricade	123
Red October	128
Ermanskii	72
Dzerzhinskii	3,090
Voroshilov	4,120
Total	7,645*

Source: IA. F. Pogonii, i dr., *Stalingradskaia epopeia: Materialy NKVD SSSR i voennoi tsenzury iz Tsentral'nogo arkhiva FSB RF* (Moscow: Zvonnitsa-MG, 2000), p. 431.

*Voronin gives a total of 7,655.

In a Russian study published in 2008 there is some discussion of the fate of *Hiwis*—or some of them. The author notes that from the middle of December 1942 to 8 January 1943 more than 20,000 "former military personnel of the Red Army" who had been in German captivity were detained. He continues:

> On the basis of decisions made by the military councils of the fronts [Southwest, Don, and Stalingrad fronts], of the general number detained 8,867 were left for work in the rear areas; 7,786 were arrested by the Special Sections of the NKVD; and 8,950 persons were located at the armies' transit assembly points. The Special Sections of the NKVD carried out a thorough filtration of all former Soviet prisoners of war, uncovering the enemy agents among them while at the same time using them in the production camps of the Moscow-area coal fields.[138]

This is valuable clarification, yet it reveals nothing about what happened to those *Hiwis* captured after the German collapse in February 1943—though if the same procedures were adopted for those captured in February 1943, this would preclude a large-scale massacre.

Documents in both the Zolotarev and Zagorul'ko collections refer to the liberation of Red Army soldiers from German captivity and the way they were treated. In the documents, in keeping with standard Soviet jargon, these soldiers are typically referred to as *byvshii* (former) Red Army soldiers, or in large numbers and in special camps they are designated as a *spetskontingent* (special contingent). Even the slightest suspicion that these soldiers had collaborated

Table 7.9 *Initial Filtration Results in Camp № 123, Uriupinsk Stalingrad District, 25 March 1943*

Filtration	Number
Sent to RVK*	34
Arrested	15
Hospitalized	10
Died	1
Escaped	1
Total	61

Source: M. M. Zagorul'ko, ed., *Voennoplennye v Stalingrade 1943–1954: Dokumenty i Materialy*, tom 2: *Voennoplennye v SSSR, 1939–1956*, gosudarstvennoe uchrezhdenie (Volgograd: Izdatel', 2003), p. 99.

*RVK is the Raoinnyi voennyi komissariat, which dealt with recruitment and distribution of troops to units.

with the Germans—and the fact of capture alone was often enough to arouse suspicion—meant transfer to an NKVD filtration camp. In a directive of the Don Front Military Council to other subordinate military councils dated 29 January 1943, a formal reprimand was issued concerning the cavalier and lax attitude toward prisoner security. Point 5 of this directive sets out the tone and the measures to be adopted with regard to "former" Red Army soldiers: "Former Red Army personnel liberated from captivity are to be escorted to the assembly points under strict guard. Immediate measures are to be taken to clear out the rear areas of this category of persons, among whom there will be a great deal of mercenary scum and traitors."[139]

Given the numbers involved, camp capacity became a major problem. A directive from Deputy NKVD Commissar S. N. Kruglov in Moscow, dated 23 March 1943, ordered that Camp № 108 be made ready to accommodate 10,000 former Red Army soldiers who had been liberated from German captivity so as to facilitate their rapid filtration. Some *spetskontingent* prisoners were accommodated in Camp № 123 in Uriupinsk. In a report, the camp commandant, Major N. P. Batenkov, noted that 1,354 prisoners had been accepted into the camp since it had been set up. At the time of his writing the camp held 1,293 prisoners, of whom 466 had been subjected to filtration. Some results of the filtration process are cited in Table 7.9.

Table 7.9 shows that 34 members of the *spetskontingent* had been sent to the Raoinnyi voennyi komissariat (RVK), which implies that they had been found innocent of any wrongdoing and were being returned to a military unit. On the other hand, it might also imply that there were grounds for doubting their

Table 7.10 *Category of Arrests Carried out by Special Sections between 22 June and 1 December 1941*

Category of Arrestee	Number
Banditry and looting	4,214
Cowards and panicmongers	3,325
Deserters	13,887
Disseminators of false rumors	4,295
Saboteurs	669
Those with self-inflicted wounds	2,358
Spies	2,343
Traitors	4,647
Total arrested	35,738
Total executed of those arrested	14,473 (40.5 percent)

Source: G. Bezverkhnii, ed., *SMERSH: Istoricheskie ocherki i arkhivnye dokumenty* (Moscow: Izdatel'stvo Glavarkhiva Moskvy, 2003), p. 28.

loyalty and that some of these soldiers were to be sent to a penal unit. By the end of 1942, a total of 172,081 former Red Army soldiers passed through the filtration process in special camps. Of this number 150,512 (88 percent) were sent to the relevant regional recruitment commissariats for allocation to Red Army units.[140]

Some idea of the overall number of Red Army soldiers falling into the *spetskontingent* category is provided in a document dated 7 April 1943. The document deals with the allocation of prisoners of war and special-category detainees to various labor projects run by the NKVD. In the document it was noted that up to 1 April 1943 there were 47,696 persons in the *spetskontingent* category in the NKVD camps. The document provides details of the various industrial branches in which prisoners of war are working but conspicuously withholds any information concerning the industries to which the *spetskontingent* has been allocated.[141] The same withholding of any information concerning the *spetskontingent* and work allocation, medical attrition rates, and mortality can be noted in two other documents dated 17 August 1943[142] and January 1944.[143] There are two possible explanations for the absence of any data. The *spetskontingent* may have been working in especially dangerous branches of industry, and the mortality rates from such work combined with illness and exhaustion may have been especially high, as would have been the case, for example, in uranium and lead mining and deep coal mining.

Table 7.11 *Executions for the Period 22 June–10 October 1941**

Total Detained	Sent to Front	Total Arrested	Executed before Unit	Executed Other Than before Unit	Total Executions
657,364	632,486	25,878	3,321	6,880	10,201

Source: V. S. Khristoforov, *Stalingrad: Organy NKVD nakanune i v dni srazheniia* (Moscow: Moskovskie uchebniki, 2008), p. 85.

*Bear in mind that this period was before the harsher provisions of Order № 227 were enacted. If this rate of execution had been the norm on the Stalingrad and Don fronts from 1 August 1942–1 January 1943, it would imply a total of about 14,570 executions (taking the 3.5-month period from 22 June to 10 October 1941: 10,201 ÷ 3.5 = 2,914; 2,914 × 5 = 14,570).

The other lacuna in the history of Stalingrad is the absence of a fully collated list of the number of Red Army soldiers executed under the provisions of Order № 227. The data provided in *Stalingradskaia epopeia* are not exhaustive and may well understate the executions. By way of comparison, between 22 June and 1 December 1941 a total of 35,738 persons were arrested, of whom 14,473 were executed (40.5 percent). I have collated some of the available data in Table 7.10.

Khristoforov notes that over the period from 22 June to 10 October 1941 a total of 657,364 service personnel were detained by the NKVD and its Special Sections. Of those detained, 25,878 were arrested and the rest, 632,486, were allocated to units and sent to the front. Based on these figures, the total number of those arrested and those allocated to units would be 658,364. Of the 25,878 arrested, 10,201—3,321 of them in front of their units—were executed by shooting. I have compiled these data in Table 7.11.

In summing up this chapter, I might argue that the greatest intelligence failure on either side at Stalingrad was a German failure, and one that had nothing to do with the NKVD and its agent networks, which were too obsessed with exposing traitors and waging vendettas. German army assumptions that the Red Army had no further reserves led to a situation in which the obvious signs of a Soviet build-up on 6th Army's flanks were ignored or not taken seriously. This is the permanent problem with intelligence gathering and assessment. If commanders and their political masters have preconceptions about what the enemy will do, intelligence data that raise awkward questions will not be allowed to get in the way.

8 The Aftermath of Defeat: German Prisoners of War in the Soviet Camps

Now, there is nothing truer than the observation that all evil and painful experiences are expunged from the memory far more quickly than anything pleasant. I myself have essentially held this view. But here I must once again return to something unpleasant because in its awfulness it must remain unforgotten, and that is the terrible experience of hunger as a prisoner of war of the Russians. No powers of the imagination are sufficient to convey any idea with words how totally, and to the exclusion of everything else, each person who was affected in this situation was gripped with his whole being physically and psychologically by this hunger psychosis such that one, with the increasing duration of this mass phenomenon, was barely able to think straight.

—Rudolf Marks, 76th Infantry Division

The fact that the Wehrmacht and the other armed formations of National Socialist Germany, including the Waffen SS, entered the Soviet Union as invaders and conquerors should not be allowed to hide or to gloss over the high mortality rates endured by German prisoners of war in the Soviet camps, in prison hospitals, and as laborers in heavy industry. The precise figure of German dead in Soviet captivity is disputed, but it could be in the region of 1 million, about one-third of all those captured. The striking aspect to the story about German prisoners of war is that the last batch of prisoners, the bulk of whom were nonamnestied, only returned home—to a divided nation—as late as January 1956. Soviet documents reveal that German prisoners of war were forced to work in Soviet heavy industry, including defense-related industries. In addition, in order to supplement the labor of prisoners of war in the Soviet Union, able-bodied Germans, men and women, were deported from occupation zones under Soviet control to work as slave labor. Although the Soviet Union had not signed the Convention Relative to the Treatment of Prisoners of War (Geneva, 27 July 1929), which stipulated that prisoners of war must be repatriated as soon as possible after the cessation of hostilities, declassified

Soviet documents reveal that pressure from the International Red Cross Committee did help to accelerate the repatriation of some prisoners of war, especially in 1948. In this chapter, I begin with a general discussion of the theme of German prisoners of war before returning to the fate of German 6th Army prisoners of war.

Introduction

Today, looking back at World War II, I suspect that there is not much sympathy for German and other Axis soldiers captured by the Red Army and for what they endured in Soviet captivity. The privations and years of hardship would seem to be justified retribution—even too little—for the Holocaust, the German regime in the occupied territories, and a near total disregard for the welfare of Soviet prisoners taken by the Wehrmacht in the huge encirclement operations of 1941 and 1942. In Germany, the Soviet Union, and now Russia, the arguments about the way Red Army and German prisoners of war were treated by their respective captors continue to exercise German and Russian historians. Justified national grievances aside, they are right to be concerned because this is a part of World War II and its aftermath that remains largely unknown to English-speaking audiences. The mass of declassified Soviet documents now available adds enormously to our knowledge of what happened behind the Iron Curtain in the years after 1945. That so much about this theme has not been known before now is partly due to the fact that scholars, Russian and Western, have until very recently been denied access to Soviet documents.

Condemnations of capitalist exploitation of the workers were routine in Soviet propaganda. The Soviet state pledged to end the exploitation of man by man and banish the profit motive because once capitalism had been supplanted by an economic system based on the common ownership of the means of production, an era of peace and prosperity would ensue for all. This theory may have suited Western Marxists, yet among the many striking revelations that emerge from collections of Soviet documents is the entrepreneurial zeal with which the Soviet camp administrations sought to exploit the huge labor pool, civilian and military, at their disposal. Documented in this mass of material are detailed profit-and-loss accounts, requests for civilians to be deported to work as slave labor in the Soviet Union, and precise numbers of prisoners employed in the many branches of Soviet industry. Since the end of World War II we have tended to see the German camp system as the epitome of ruthless exploitation of prisoners; yet these Soviet documents reveal that organized slave labor—and it was highly organized—was not confined to National Socialist Germany. The Soviet Union proved itself to be equally adept in the matter of exploiting slave labor. The fate of German and other Axis prisoners in Soviet captivity is therefore not just another phase of World War II: it is a major theme within the ideological confrontation of the Cold War.

Mortality and the Question of Numbers

From the moment when selected German prisoners of war were repatriated—many of them because they had been deemed unfit for heavy physical work by the Soviet camp administration—accusations of harsh and arbitrary treatment in Soviet captivity started to accumulate. It was claimed that German prisoners were dying in large numbers; that they were being exploited as slave labor in violation of the legal instruments governing the treatment of prisoners of war; and that German soldiers, innocent of any wrongdoing, and on the flimsiest of evidence, were being charged and prosecuted as war criminals. Many of the survivors also provide great detail about the massive indoctrination and reeducation programs instigated by the NKVD, often with the use of turned prisoners, senior officers among them, and German communists who had fled Germany in the 1930s. These programs, ostensibly carried out as a way of promoting a spirit of antifascism among prisoners, were also designed to destroy any solidarity among them and thus to weaken resistance.[1] Antifascist programs were also essential in preparing the way for the cases being prepared against German prisoners under investigation as war criminals. Subverted prisoners were exploited as witnesses and suitably rewarded. Under the circumstances that obtained in the Soviet camps, food or an assurance of early repatriation were just two of the levers available to the NKVD to compel men to bear false witness against their fellows.

As a blanket term to apply to all captured Axis combatants, the term "prisoner of war" is somewhat misleading. Erwin Peter has attempted to refine the use of the term when applied to Germans and Austrians captured by the Red Army. In a first category he includes those German soldiers who were captured during the war while taking part in operations. These he regards as prisoners of war proper. In a second category he places German soldiers who ended up in Soviet captivity after the unconditional-surrender document was signed on 8 May 1945. These he calls *Kapitulationsgefangene* (capitulation prisoners). In Peter's third group we find huge numbers of German civilians—men, women, and children—who were deported and forcibly recruited as slave labor.[2] Theirs was a dreadful fate and a story that has not been fully told.

Declassified Soviet documents, for all the detail of numbers exploited, provide very little information about the scale of human misery.

The number of German and Soviet soldiers who ended up as prisoners of war between 22 June 1941 and 8 May 1945—and, in the case of Germans, after 8 May 1945—runs into millions. The number of Red Army soldiers captured by the Wehrmacht is in the region of 5.7 million, of whom 3.3 million died in captivity in Germany.[3] Concerning the total number of German soldiers who died in Soviet captivity, German and Soviet/Russian historians have not yet reached complete agreement. In one of the first major studies devoted to German prisoners of war published in the Russian Federation, Russian historian Major General Zolotarev tried to clarify this matter by citing a document drawn up in 1956 in which, according to him, "[is] given the total figures of all prisoners of war of European armies that passed through Soviet captivity and who were captured by Soviet troops over the entire period of the Great Fatherland War."[4] To quote Zolotarev:

> The statistics for prisoners of war of German nationality in this document turn out to be as follows. 2,388,443 prisoners of war, including 376 generals, 69,472 officers, and 2,318,595 NCOs and other ranks were captured, transferred to the camps of the Main Directorate for the Affairs of Prisoners of War and Internees of the Ministry of Internal Affairs, and accounted for individually. 2,031,743 persons were released and repatriated. Included in that figure were 277 generals, 65,063 officers, and 1,966,403 NCOs and other ranks. 356,687 Germans, among them 99 generals, 4,406 officers, and 352,182 NCOs and other ranks, died in captivity.[5]

Allowing for a slight discrepancy in the figure of those who died in captivity—Zolotarev cites a figure of 356,687, whereas the difference between the total captured (2,388,443) and those repatriated (2,031,743) is 356,700, which leaves 13 unaccounted for—these data should settle the argument. However, the major discrepancy occurs between the total in the 1956 document and an earlier acknowledgment by Zolotarev that "it is known that by the end of the war there were more than 3 million German soldiers, officers, and generals alone in Soviet captivity."[6] Returning to this figure of more than 3 million Germans in Soviet captivity, Zolotarev, citing a German source, notes the Germans claim that "by the end of the war 'more than three million German soldiers were already in Soviet captivity or had only just started their long and difficult path to Soviet camps. There, about a million of them died.'"[7] The mortality figures for Germans in Soviet captivity do indeed give a mortality rate of 14.9 percent, based on a total number of 2,388,443 and a total death toll of 356,687 (or 356,700). However, in view of the fact that both Zolotarev and German historians accept the figure of more than 3 million German soldiers in Soviet captivity at the end of the war, this leaves a minimum, assuming a total of 3 million German prisoners in all, of 611,557 German prisoners of war unaccounted for. Depending on how much higher than 3 million the figure of "more than 3 million" is, the total number unaccounted for could be in the region of 700,000. Based on the figure of 3 million, the death rate in captivity would then be 968,257 (32.27 percent), which more or less tallies with the German claim that one in three German prisoners died in Soviet captivity. Using data gathered by the German Red Cross, Erwin Peter gives the range of German prisoners taken by the Soviet Union as between 3.2 and 3.5 million, of whom 1.2 million, including 156,000 Austrians, died.[8]

Publicly and in declassified documents, Soviet agencies are highly sensitive to accusations or suggestions that German prisoners died of starvation in captivity. This may be due to the institutional memory of the Ukrainian genocide (the Holodomor) and the millions of victims who were deliberately starved to death in the 1930s, and thus accusations of parallels, or it may reflect the Soviet attempt to counter negative reports in the West and what it perceived to be Western Cold War propaganda. Zolotarev rejects claims made at an exhibition in Germany in 1995 that German prisoners were so hungry that they resorted to cannibalism. He ripostes: "For scientific proof of the facts of cannibalism exclusively documentary, convincing, and irrefutable confirmation is required."[9] The suggestion that cannibalism occurred is by no means farfetched. There were documented cases during the siege of Leningrad, and Soviet prosecutors considering the case against the German officers in charge of Dulag-205, the transit camp for Soviet prisoners of war in 6th Army's rear, heard evidence that cannibalism was widespread among desperate Red Army prisoners. It seems quite reasonable to assume that German soldiers in the same circumstances would also resort to cannibalism. Zolotarev's demand for hard documentary evidence can also be satisfied. Erwin Peter and his coauthor, the Russian historian Alexander Epifanow, reproduce a copy of a Soviet report dated 22 February 1943 and drafted by General Major Krivenko, the head of the NKVD's Escort Troops, to General Lieutenant Apollonov, another senior NKVD officer, in which Krivenko noted that lack of food for prisoners of war has led to an increase in cannibalism and that even the guard personnel have been attacked.[10] Three observations can be made here. First, Krivenko's reference to incidents affecting escort and guard troops is significant because hunger, starvation, and thus desperation among German prisoners were most acute after surrender, when no rations were made available for German prisoners on long, exhausting marches to staging posts (railheads) and camps. Second, Krivenko is drawing attention to an *increase* in cannibalism, not just some isolated instance recorded for the first time. Third, given the structure and the manner of passing information in Soviet bureaucracies—there is a marked tendency not to pass on anything negative—the fact that cannibalism is even mentioned in the report drawn up by a very senior NKVD officer suggests that the decision to write a report in which cannibalism is highlighted was prompted by rumors that it was taking place and that it was widespread.

The Legal and Administrative Approach of the Soviet Union to Axis Prisoners of War

The primary Soviet document setting out the treatment of prisoners of war is the *Spetsial'noe polozhenie o voennoplennykh* (Special Statute Concerning Prisoners of War), dated 1 July 1941. Certain provisions in the statute seem to owe something to the Convention Relative to the Treatment of Prisoners of War (Geneva, 27 July 1929), which the Soviet Union did not sign; thus, the statute represents a sanitized version of the earlier document. According to the statute, three categories of persons are to be recognized as prisoners of war: persons who are part of the armed forces of states in a condition of war with the Soviet Union (including citizens of those states interned on the territory of the Soviet Union); "persons comprising the personnel of armed detachments that do not belong to the armed forces of the enemy if they bear arms openly";[11] and civilians accompanying the armed forces of an enemy, such as war correspondents, suppliers, "and other persons captured during the course of military operations."[12] The first category is clear enough. Thereafter, difficulties arise. In view of the fact that the second category says nothing about Soviet citizens, it would seem to include German-raised antipartisan units recruited from Soviet civilians. Engaged in antipartisan operation in the German-occupied territories, these ad hoc units would have no need to conceal the fact that they were armed and so would fall within the definition of a prisoner of war. Moreover, this definition seems to proscribe any punitive measures against members of nationalist formations, especially non-Russians. The third category is also conveniently wide, to the point that any civilian taken prisoner could be construed as a prisoner of war. I suggest that "other persons" is specifically aimed at Soviet civilians working for the German armed forces. However, if they are to be regarded as prisoners of war, they cannot also be regarded as traitors (*predateli*).

The statute also stipulates that prisoners of war are not to be subjected to harsh treatment, that threats of violence and other forms of compulsion are not to be employed in order to secure information, and that items of clothing are not be removed from prisoners of war. According to the statute, valuable possessions and money may be removed from prisoners of war provided that an official receipt is issued by an authorized person.[13] Whatever the provisions of the statute regarding the proper treatment of Axis prisoners of war, the vast body of testimony provided by prisoners of war is full of accounts of arbitrary violence and theft of valuables (watches), footwear, and especially winter clothing. Violations of the statute seem to have been the norm, not the exception. In view of what prisoners captured at Stalingrad have to say about the availability of medical services, food, and adequate shelter, the specific provisions of the statute that deal with these matters bear no resemblance to what happened. Again, based on survivors' testimony, the provisions of the statute concerning access to regular mail and goods from abroad—it states that prisoners are permitted to receive various goods from their homeland or from neutral countries—seem almost fantastic.

Section IV of the statute, which deals with the arrangements governing the use of prisoners of war as labor (*Trudovoe ustroistvo voennoplennykh*), is clearly relevant for the mass deployment of German prisoners of war in Soviet industry. In this regard, note paragraph 20: "Prisoners of war from the rank and file and NCOs can be enlisted for work both in the camp and outside the camp in industry and in agriculture of the USSR on the basis of special rules devised by the Directorate of the NKVD USSR for the Affairs of Prisoners of War and Internees. Officers and prisoners of equal status can be enlisted for work with their agreement."[14] Again, as with the level of material provision for the welfare of prisoners, there is little evidence that the requirements of this paragraph were heeded.

The provisions of the Special Statute Concerning Prisoners of War do not seem to have struck a chord with certain members of the Red Army's Political Directorate. In a memorandum submitted to Deputy People's Commissar of Defense and Army Commissar of the 1st rank Lev Mekhlis on 15 August 1941, D. Manuil'skii reported that German officers and NCOs were subverting the discipline in the camp (south of Riazan') and inspiring resistance. In order to correct what he saw as an unacceptable state of affairs, Manuil'skii recommended that the hard core of Nazi officers, NCOs, and others be placed "in the same situation in which antifascists find themselves in the concentration camps in Germany" and that all forms of "superfluous humanity" be dispensed with. He also recommended that "any attempt to wage hostile agitation against the USSR be stopped with the harsh measures of wartime, in accordance with Soviet laws."[15]

As the war progressed, the measures taken against certain prisoners undoubtedly became much harsher. In September 1944, with a much larger prison population, special camps with a hard routine for prisoners of war were set up. These camps, so-called *rezhimnye lageria*, were primarily intended for three types of prisoners: those who were suspected of having committed atrocities; members of enemy intelligence, counterintelligence, and punitive agencies; and those who had made escape attempts.[16] Prisoners in *rezhimnye lageria* were made to work on tasks allocated by the directorate of the NKVD responsible for prisoners of war and internees. The working day lasted twelve hours, and work on projects related to the war effort was not expressly proscribed.[17] This point is important because prisoners, whether in a *rezhimnye lager'* or one of the standard prisoner-of-war camps, were made to work on war-related projects, a clear violation of international law.[18]

A document prepared by an engineer colonel serving in the NKVD in March 1944 (no specific date is cited) provides a detailed breakdown of the number of prisoners of war employed in various branches of Soviet industry.[19] Many of these industrial enterprises were directly related to the Soviet war effort. For example, a total of 3,600 prisoners of war were working in ammunition factories in Stalino and Aleksina. Another 4,152 were employed in the production of tanks, and 2,794 prisoners of war were working on port construction. Four hundred fourteen prisoners were working on the production of plywood for the aircraft industry. Forestry and wood processing accounted for 5,633 prisoners of war in various camps. Probably the most dangerous work for prisoners was the extraction of asbestos from open-cast pits in Sverdlovsk. A total of 3,104 were employed. Work in such conditions, and on the extraction of such a dangerous substance, was tantamount to a death sentence for prisoners, guards, and camp staff.

The insatiable demand for labor meant that all able-bodied Germans, civilian or military, within the reach of Soviet enforcement agencies were vulnerable and liable to labor conscription. In a memorandum dated 17 May 1946,

Sergei Kruglov, the Soviet minister for internal affairs, reported to Stalin that consideration was being given to the repatriation of 20,000 civilians to Germany because they were deemed unfit for work. These 20,000 German civilians were part of much larger contingent that, in accordance with two wartime resolutions of the State Defense Committee (16 December 1944 and 3 February 1945) had been rounded up in Romania, Yugoslavia, Bulgaria, Czechoslovakia, and Upper Silesia and forcibly deported to work as slave labor in Soviet industry. The total deported was 189,472, among whom there were 51,138 women.[20] The recommendation to Stalin that these 20,000 Germans be returned home was purely practical. They were unable to work, and the Soviet Union did not want to incur the costs or problems associated with holding on to them, and especially associated with large numbers dying. The fate of those German civilians who remained was not recorded. Likewise, the early repatriation of prisoners of war unfit for work was purely practical because the Soviet Union did not want the burden of having to look after them. At the time, of course, this looked like a humanitarian gesture when it was nothing of the kind. Zolotarev's brutal admission makes this unequivocally clear: "The repatriation of prisoners of war to their homeland at this stage was first and foremost dictated by the striving of MVD agencies to be rid of those persons incapable of working and such ballast as invalids and severely ill German soldiers."[21] These NKVD calculations are evident in a postwar order that stipulated that 27,500 Germans unfit for work be returned to Germany and that an equal number of physically healthy Germans be removed from the camps and prisons of the Ministerstvo vnutrennikh del (Ministry of Internal Affairs, or MVD) in Germany and be dispatched to the Soviet Union as replacements for work in coal mines in the eastern regions and on fuel construction projects.[22]

After 1945 prisoners of war fell into two categories: those deemed suitable for repatriation and those retained for labor (and other reasons). In a memorandum prepared in January 1949 Kruglov summarized the repatriation process so far. In 1948, for example, 647,295 prisoners of war were repatriated. This included 337,694 Germans, 173,606 Japanese, 98,956 Hungarians, 81,761 Romanians, 2,166 Koreans, 1,018 Austrians, 236 Czechoslovaks, 149 Poles, and a miscellaneous group of 1,709.[23] As of 1 January 1949 there were a total of 544,047 prisoners of war still being held in MVD camps and other institutions. Of this total, 421,221 were citizens of Germany. The report noted that the overwhelming majority of prisoners of war had been mobilized to work in the heavy industries. The allocation is given in Table 8.1.

Table 8.1 *Allocation of Prisoners of War to Soviet Industry, 1 January 1949*

Branch of Industry	Allocation
Coal mining	120,367
Road and rail construction	91,651
Heavy industry and military projects	90,224
Machine tools and aviation	25,425
Metal and chemicals	14,687
Total	342,354

Source: "Doklad MVD SSSR o kolichestvennom sostave voennoplennykh i ikh trudovomu ispol'zovanii po sostoianiiu na 1 ianvaria 1949 g," in Major General V. A. Zolotarev, ed., *Russkii Arkhiv: Velikaia Otechestvennaia*, vol. 13, no. 2, *Nemetskie voennoplennye v SSSR* 1941–1955 *gg.*, Sbornik dokumentov, Kniga pervaia (Moscow: TERRA, 1999), pp. 248–249.

Kruglov's January 1949 memorandum also reveals the degree to which the Soviet camp administration exploited the intellectual and technical expertise of German prisoners. Kruglov listed a whole series of research and development outcomes, many of which are clearly of major significance for the Soviet armed forces. For example, prisoners developed equipment that measured the rate of acceleration of torpedoes. This equipment was highly rated by the Ministry of Ship Construction. Methods for combating fighter aircraft by bombers were also highly regarded by the Soviet Air Ministry. Other developments were a new device for calculating vehicle suspension springs, meteorological research, enhanced coal-processing methods, a draft for a semiautomatic tube-rolling mill, a device for converting electric energy into rays or beams, spectrographic research in bauxite, a project for a printing press and casting equipment for duralumin, and a project for a bucket (dredge) for light metals.[24] The full memorandum has not been published, so the likelihood that German prisoners were working on really sensitive research, such as rockets, radar, and nuclear weapons cannot be excluded. The scale of this intellectual exploitation is remarkable and parallels much of what Alexander Solzhenitsyn described in his novel *V kruge pervom* (*First Circle*, 1968).

Antifascist Propaganda and Ideological Indoctrination among Prisoners of War

Among declassified Soviet material relating to prisoners of war are many documents that refer specifically to the ideological processing of prisoners of war. In a detailed summary of this work prepared by Lieutenant Colonel

Grishchuk in February 1951, which examines the antifascist program over the period 1942–1950, the author stresses its importance: "From the very beginning of its existence, political work among prisoners of war in the camp was conducted intermittently but with each passing year it assumed an ever wider scope and was valued by the camp's command and political apparatus as the most important work and having significance for the state."[25] One document, "Tipovaia programma frontovykh antifashistskikh shkol" (A typical program of a front antifascist schools), a course of antifascist propaganda drawn up in 1943, gives some idea of the specific ideological processing to which German prisoners of war were subjected: Section 1, "Lessons of the Two Years of War of Hitler's Germany with the Soviet Union"; Section 2, "Exposing the Theory and Practice of German Fascism"; Section 3, "The Soviet Union—the Land of Socialism"; Section 4, "The Tasks of German Antifascists in the Struggle for a Free and Independent Germany"; and Section 5, "The Tasks of Antifascist Activists in the Matter of the Reeducation of German Prisoners of War."[26]

The antifascist program was divided into two stages. The first stage covered the war and was concerned primarily with making a contribution to the war effort. This involved subverting German morale, civilian and military; encouraging desertion; propaganda aimed at provoking insurrection and opposition to the NS regime in Germany; and raising military units under Soviet control to take part in operations. Huge efforts were made to subvert German generals, especially those captured at Stalingrad in 1943. Overall, Soviet activity in this area is a carbon copy of what the Abwehr itself was doing on the Eastern front. In the statute regulating these operations (dated 1944) provision was also made for sending German prisoners of war back across the lines with the aim of undermining Wehrmacht morale.[27] Interestingly, however, the deployment of any officials of the FDK or the BDO across the lines in pursuit of such activities was forbidden, reflecting either the fact that they were not fully trusted or the fear that were they to fall into the hands of German counterespionage agencies, they would cooperate and be exploited for propaganda purposes. However, permission was granted for recently captured German prisoners of war, those, in the words of the statute, "not possessing any information about our troops and the conditions under which prisoners of war are being held in the camps," to be sent across the lines for purposes of undermining German morale.[28] This was a sound policy and one the Abwehr adopted from the moment it acquired large numbers of Soviet prisoners. The aim was to burden and mislead the Soviet counterintelligence agencies by sending large numbers of hastily recruited prisoner of war and agents across the Soviet lines. Now, with a large pool of prisoners, the NKVD and SMERSH were also playing the same game. For both sides, the use of a scattershot approach held the chance that some agent might deliver something useful.

In the second, post-1945 stage, the full weight of ideological processing could be brought to bear on prisoners prior to their eventual repatriation. The aims were (1) to expose the true aims of Germany in the war; (2) to expose German propaganda lies about the Soviet Union; (3) to explain the responsibility that Germany bore for what had happened in the war; and (4) to explain the basis of the Soviet socialist structure and on this basis to increase the number of prisoners of war who were favorably disposed toward the Soviet Union. Post-1945 the focus is on promoting the Soviet Union as the sole guarantor of peace and prosperity. Two key elements in post-1945 Soviet propaganda can be noted. The prisoners were to be inculcated with an understanding "of the necessity of the unity of the working class and its role as the grave digger of capitalism" and with a spirit of "hatred of nationalism [and] of anti-Soviet lies and a readiness to stand on the side of the progressive forces of their country, fighting for national and state independence."[29] We have here a marvelous example of Orwellian doublethink, or just plain hypocrisy. At a time when German prisoners of war were being bullied and harassed about the dangers of nationalism, Stalin and Commissar for Culture Andrei Zhdanov had launched a campaign to eradicate Western influences, scientific and cultural, from Soviet society and at the same time were promoting their particular view of Russian nationalism in a spirit of rabid xenophobia. Much of this campaign, the Zhdanovshchina, derived from the name of its principal author, was also markedly anti-Semitic and led to the murders of prominent Jewish artists.

Soviet propaganda among prisoners of war also exploited the exchange of letters between prisoners and home. To quote Grishchuk: "After the war these letters were used for disclosing the truth about Soviet captivity and the realities of Soviet life."[30] At the risk of sounding cynical, I take this to mean that selected German prisoners of war were encouraged to write well of their time in Soviet captivity and that NKVD officers in the respective occupation zones would ensure that the contents of the letter would be used to counter accusations of poor treatment in captivity. Promises of early repatriation and extra food would have been powerful incentives to cooperate.

Whether prisoners joined the block of antifascists out of conviction or opportunism, they were obliged to surrender all intellectual and moral autonomy. "Rekomendatsii dlia raboty antifashistskogo aktiva Krasnogorskogo lageria № 27" (Recommendations for the work of the antifascist activist group of Krasnogorsk Camp № 27), dated 23 October 1944, reveals the psychological state of mind of the German collaborators. It gives some idea of the brainwashing to which Oberst Boje (see chapter 9) and others would have been subjected. Above all, it documents the gruesome process of self-denial and self-debasement to which the antifascist activist must submit in order to be accepted. In this regard, note the second point: "Activists are responsible bearers of the political struggle, which they jointly conduct with all those bound to the Free Germany movement, and must make efforts to ensure that all members of the camp group implement a correct political line [*pravil'naia politicheskaia liniia*]."[31] And point 4: "Every activist is obliged and must always be able to function politically correctly [*politicheski pravil'no*] within the group of party activists and with complete responsibility for his actions."[32]

Those selected for antifascist training were intensively processed, undergoing a five-month course. The aim of the course was to produce a competent propagandist and agitator well versed in the fundamentals of Marxism-Leninism. The teaching plan for one such course is shown in Table 8.2. The course was based on an eight-hour day of instruction and ran from 1 December 1945 to 30 April 1946. In an attachment to the course program, the head of the school, Lieutenant Colonel Parfenov, noted that each course member had to allocate an additional two hours every evening (Sundays not included) to independent work, a total of 240 hours. Antifascists stridently denouncing the alleged revanchism of the Federal German Republic on their return home might well have served the overt propaganda aims of the Soviet Union, but other considerations came into play as well. NKVD officers carefully watched and assessed attendees with a view to recruitment as Soviet agents on returning home. This was the long-term threat posed to the Federal Republic of Germany (FDR) and the West by these post-1945 courses.

That NKVD recruiters were thinking along these lines is evident in a directive dated 18 August 1945. The directive's subject was the procedure for the repatriation of prisoners of war who had been used as camp agents and informers. The overwhelming priority was that the files of any agents liable for repatriation and "presenting an operational interest with a view to their possible use under cover" be sent to the Operational Directorate of the Main Directorate for the Affairs of Prisoners of War and Internees.[33] Regarding this category of prisoners, additional measures were specified: "Until further notice this category of agents is not to be given advance notice of the forthcom-

Table 8.2 *Teaching Plan of the Anti-Fascist Political School Attached to NKVD Special Installation № 40, Krasnogorsk, November 1945*

Subject	Lecture Hours	Group Discussion Hours	Work Class Hours	Total Hours
1. Dialectical and historical materialism	76	20	26	122
2. Basis of political economy				
(a) Capitalist system	32	—	20	52
(b) Soviet economics	28	14	—	42
3. Short course of history of USSR	92	24	30	146
4. Soviet structure	20	6	—	26
5. Short course of history of native land	54	10	26	90
6. The most important questions of current affairs	—	60	—	60
7. Political map of the world	24	—	—	24
8. Exams	—	—	28	28
Total hours for each part	326	134	130	590
9. Independent work	—	—	322	322
Total	326	134	452	912

Source: "Uchebnyi plan antifashistskoi politshkoly pri spetsob"ekte NKVD № 40 dlia 8 kursa [*sic*], noiabr' 1945 g," in Major General V. A. Zolotarev, ed., *Russkii Arkhiv: Velikaia Otechestvennaia*, vol. 13, no. 2, *Nemetskie voennoplennye v SSSR 1941–1955 gg.*, Sbornik dokumentov, Kniga pervaia (Moscow: TERRA, 1999), p. 342.

ing return home, and no arrangements concerning undercover work are to be made. They are not to be included among those subject to liberation, and the normal work with them in the camps is to continue."[34] Agents deemed to be of little value were to be repatriated in the normal way "without securing any obligations from them at departure in the form of a signature concerning illegal work with them."[35] Regarding a third category, it was noted: "In response to a statement from individual agents concerning a desire to continue working with us undercover, it shall be made clear to them that this request will be considered."[36]

Stalingrad: Captivity and Forced Labor

The precise number of Axis prisoners who fell into Soviet hands at Stalingrad is, even now, after all this time, still not agreed upon, even among Russian historians with more or less unfettered access to the necessary files and other archival material. One assessment is that up to 15 February 1943 there were about 138,000. However, it is noted that some of those captured had already been deported and that others had died en route to reception points. Thus, Zagorul'ko takes the view that "*up to the present time, the number of enemy soldiers and officers captured in the Stalingrad region has not been precisely calculated.*"[37] Alexander Epifanow provides a rough guide of 239,775 for the entire course of the battle, though Zagorul'ko, in responding to this figure, insists that "further research in NKVD USSR material and among the documents of army formations is necessary since this figure requires further checking."[38] A preliminary assessment of the total number of prisoners of war held in NKVD camps behind the front line (dated 4 February 1943 and submitted to Stalin) cited a total of 212,836 prisoners. But this was a figure for the total number of prisoners of war held over the course of the war up to 3 February 1943. Some of these prisoners would have been taken at Stalingrad and the surrounding area well before the final German surrender, but given the chaos in the immediate aftermath of the Axis collapse, it is unlikely that this figure reflects the full number taken at Stalingrad. One part of this assessment revealed the astonishing range of nationalities that had so far been taken prisoner. Among them were Frenchmen, Spaniards, Greeks, Estonians, Belgians, Dutch, Norwegians, and Swedes. There were also ninety-four Jews and three Americans listed as prisoners of war.[39]

The most obvious point that emerges from these documents, and one that confirms the testimony of German veterans, is the total chaos after the German collapse and the general lack of preparedness for coping with a huge influx of Axis prisoners. In a postwar survey of work by the directorate responsible for prisoners of war, there is ample confirmation of the chaos and appalling conditions that confronted Axis prisoners:

> The work of the reception points and frontline camps over this period took place in exceptionally difficult conditions. The situation was made worse by the fact that the agencies at the front, located in devastated territory that had only just been cleared of the enemy, were compelled to hold and provide for prisoners in the complete absence of any suitable accommodations, lack of, sometimes a complete lack of, any fuel, rations, clothing, transport, and other supplies. . . . Things were made even worse

> in connection with the fact that a contingent of the prisoners of war emerging from encirclement was utterly exhausted and weak, completely infected with lice, and wearing rags. Among them were many who were ill and suffering from frostbite, since the battle had taken place, as is known, in the harsh winter of 1942–1943.[40]

The effects of chaos and sheer overload were made worse by hatred of the Germans and indifference to their fate. In the words of the head of Reception Camp № 48 (Voronezh front) in a report to the MVD USSR in March 1943:

> The situation with food is exceptionally serious. For thirteen days we have had no bread or dry rations. The rations supply section of 38th Army provides no rations, in part because of the remoteness of the ration dumps but mainly because there is no wish to feed prisoners of war. . . . On 26 February 1943 two three-ton vehicles arrived with groats. One vehicle was unloaded for the Russian unit, but the representative of the supply section refused to unload the other. "I," he said, "have no wish to feed the Fritzes with groats; let them die." And the vehicle drove away.[41]

Such chaos and the lack of basic provision of shelter and food dramatically increased the chances that prisoners would die very soon after capture, and in the long term, once they had reached a proper camp. However, blame for German deaths after capture cannot be attributed solely to poor Soviet administration. Well before the final collapse German soldiers inside the Kessel had been surviving on reduced rations, and the majority were in a severely weakened state at the moment of capture. They were victims of Hitler's determination that German 6th Army resist to the last. Regardless of any sound military reasons for denying Paulus the chance to accept Soviet offers for a German surrender, the decision, nevertheless, condemned very large numbers of Axis soldiers and then prisoners of war to a cruel and miserable death. Some idea of the mortality rate can be been seen in the fact that of the 56,146 prisoners of war captured before the final collapse, from December 1942 up to February 1943, 595 died soon after arrival in the camps. En route to camps, 5,014 died, and 3,574 were handed over to evacuation hospitals.[42] A constant in all the misery and suffering endured by prisoners of war is the high death rate when in transit to camps. Exactly the same pattern can be observed in the administration of the Nazi camps.

The high point for prisoner mortality was March 1943, when 18,723 prisoners of war died of various causes, though the main cause was cited as dystrophy.[43] From 21 March to 1 April 1943 the mortality rate amounted to 41.2 percent; from 1 April to 10 April 1943 it was 33.6 percent. Over the period 10 April to 10 June 1943 the rate was 31 percent.[44] It can also be noted that over the period from February to November 1943, 31,194 prisoners of war died in prison hospitals.[45] At the end of the war prisoners were still dying, and where they were not dying, the rates of medical attrition remained high. Note, for example, the state of a convoy consisting of 763 German prisoners of war sent to Stalingrad in April 1945: "17 died en route, and another 11 in a very bad condition were immediately hospitalized. . . . Of the 667 prisoners given a medical examination, only 92 were found to be fit for heavy work and 115 for light work; a further 164 were found to be temporarily unsuitable for work."[46]

In Soviet documents there are not only acknowledgments of the scale of the administrative problem facing the Soviet authorities and their failure to cope with it but frank and shocking admissions concerning the way German prisoners of war were being treated by their captors. For example, in the memorandum to Stalin of 4 February 1943 there is confirmation that prisoners of war were not fed on the long marches to staging posts and that prisoners of war were the victims of arbitrary executions:

> It must be pointed out that while prisoners of war are under escort a number of arbitrary acts on the part of the guards have been permitted. So, for example, with the successful offensives of units of the Red Army on the Stalingrad, Voronezh, and Don fronts the front line changes on a daily basis and prisoners of war are escorted on foot for distances up to 150–200 kilometers [93–124 miles] to a reception point, and without being fed. Moreover, before they were captured, the prisoners state that they had received no food for four to seven days. As a result of the extreme exhaustion, prisoners of war would collapse along the way, and then the escorts, as a rule, would shoot them.[47]

The examples of arbitrary behavior cited in the report to Stalin were by no means isolated. The savagery and sadistic treatment to which German prisoners of war were subjected was so bad that even the head of reception point № 48 (Voronezh front) felt compelled to highlight it:

> Recently the prisoners of war have become very weak. They have to cover stages over 200 kilometers [124 miles], and along the way they are not fed

> for six to seven days. They get to the reception point: they collapse and die. Evacuation of prisoners of war from the front line is carried out in such a disgusting manner that even the escort guards are not provided with rations. They have nothing to eat for three days, and when they arrive at the reception point, they ask for something to eat, anything. . . . Along the way the prisoners of war are stripped of all clothing by anyone who can be bothered. Along the way they meet some command personnel [*komsostav*]. They ask the escort for two or three Germans. The guard hands them over, and they execute them on the spot. In the Directorate of 38th Army's rear at Iastrebovka, 32 prisoners of war were executed. . . . The escort of German prisoners of war has been entrusted to former military service personnel who are going together with the prisoners to a transit point for filtration. One part of the escorts had been with the Germans. Others were in the camps and suffered a great deal under the Germans and are now getting their own back. Another part is traitors and marauders. They treat the prisoners of war even worse: they rob them, strip them of their clothing, and kill them. Recently, as a general rule, the prisoners of war are 75 percent barefoot and 20 to 25 percent stripped of clothing. A dreadful situation is created. The prisoners of war arrive: there are no rations and no accommodations.[48]

That this report is not reproduced in toto suggests that some parts are even more shocking and deeply embarrassing for the Red Army. A particularly disturbing aspect to this account is that Soviet command personnel ask the escort guards for German prisoners and then kill them. This appalling incident, demonstrably a war crime, strikes me as an example of what can only be described as trophy or pleasure killing. There is no obvious reason why exhausted German prisoners should be removed from the column way behind the lines, where they posed no danger, and killed—effectively murdered—other than to satisfy the desires of men who had not experienced the dangers of frontline service but who nevertheless wanted to take life. I suspect that the killers were rear-echelon Soviet troops who wanted the thrill and pleasure of killing Germans with absolutely no risk to themselves. One can imagine these Soviet executioners posing with the corpses and being photographed. It is the revenge of the weak and humiliated, the desire, among others, to propitiate the sense of earlier failure and shame engendered by retreat and defeat. Grossman portrays a similar incident in *Life and Fate* after the German defeat at Stalingrad. A German prisoner is being beaten and kicked by a Soviet colonel, and another Soviet officer intercedes to stop the beating. His driver approves of the beating, telling his superior that he could shoot any one of them, which invites the reply: "'All right, all right. You should have shot them in 1941 when you were running from them without a glance backward, just as I did.'"[49]

The sustained lack of proper food before the surrender and the chaos and confusion that obtained after 3 February 1943 as thousands of Axis prisoners of war marched into captivity do provide some mitigating circumstances for the Soviet authorities and the problems they faced. Thereafter, the burden of responsibility falls on the Soviet camp administration. The critical factors determining whether a prisoner survived were his physical condition at the time of capture, the provision of adequate food in the camps, the availability of medical care, and the type of forced labor he was made to do.

Inspection reports of hospitals intended for prisoners of war in the Stalingrad district give some idea of the state of prisoner-of-war health in June 1943. In that month, although the inspections took place in the second half of May, six hospitals were inspected: special hospitals № 4939 (Beketovka), № 3249 (Rudnia), № 4950/6 (Stalingrad), № 4952 (Frolovo), № 4937 (Kapustin Iar), and № 283 (Dubovka). Medical services in the Beketovka hospital were provided largely by prisoner-of-war doctors. On the day of the inspection there were 2,358 patients. The physical state of the hospital was considered poor, and the ward designated for prisoners suffering from stomach and intestinal illnesses was overrun with flies. The report noted that the ill were washed infrequently, especially the severely ill. On the credit side, the kitchen area was clean, and hot food was prepared three times a day. The mortality rate was an average of 15 per day. The Rudnia hospital had 1,089 patients and scored well on all indices. Its average mortality rate in May was 7–10 patients a day, down from 40–50 a day in April. The Stalingrad hospital had 796 patients on the inspection day. The inspectors noted that there were difficulties caused by the fact that the head of the hospital was a Georgian, and because German was the language used by the German doctors, he was unable to maintain proper control. The inspectors noted that the German doctors inflated the numbers suffering from dystrophy to acquire an increase in rations. The patient mortality rate was an average of 7 per day. The Frolovo hospital accommodated 365 patients and met with the approval of the inspectors. Food was issued three times a day, and the mortality rate was 3–4 patients per day. In order to ensure that patients did not suffer from vitamin deficiencies, sorrel and nettles were included in the diet. In other hospitals infusions of pine were the norm. The Kapustin Iar hospital accommodated 160 prisoners. Medical provision was judged to be unsatisfactory. Among the failings were no furniture, a lack of surgical instruments, and a general lack of kitchen utensils. Lack of vehicle transport was critical. The hospital had to rely on nine horses, and given its remoteness from supply centers, there were frequent interruptions in the resupply of rations and the quality. The Dubovka hospital accommodated 631 patients and 312 convalescents. It attracted the most damning assessment: "The area of the hospital is filthy. Lice infestation was discovered in all the wards. The wards were dirty. There were huge volumes of flies. The toilet and cesspits were in an antihygienic state. The cooks slept in the kitchen accommodation."[50] The inspector was highly critical of the chief doctor, who had failed to take the necessary measures to put the hospital in order.

In other hospitals lack of proper heating in the winter was identified as a major problem. For example, in a report on special hospital № 5771 in the Stalingrad district it was noted that in some wards temperatures had fallen to 10–12°C (50–54°F), and in some it was down to freezing. During a period of severe frosts the temperature in wards ranged from 10°C to 3–4°C (50°F to 37–39°F), a huge burden for weak and ill prisoners.[51]

Mortality rates continued to be high throughout the war and beyond. An exceptionally detailed report on the state of hygiene and the provision of medical services in the four main NKVD prisoner-of-war camps in the Stalingrad district provided precise figures for deaths. The mortality rate in the four camps for the first five months of 1945 is shown in Table 8.3.

The mortality rate was acknowledged to be high. Various reasons were cited. First, there was a general shortage of suitably qualified medical personnel. Second, a large number of prisoners of war from outside the district and suffering from extreme exhaustion had arrived at the end of 1944, which had led to an unusually high death rate. The question is, why were prisoners of war in such acutely poor physical condition moved from one camp to another? The answer may well have had something to do with the arcane workings of Soviet bureaucracy: one camp administration realized that weak and dying prisoners of war were a liability and therefore sought to offload them in any way possible. Third, it was admitted that there was a mismatch between the quantity of available hospital beds and the number of patients, which, in the words of the report's authors, "created exceptionally great overcrowding in the distribution of sick prisoners of war in the living accommodations without the appropriate hospital conditions."[52] A fourth factor was interruptions to the supply of rations such that a proper dietary regimen could not be maintained. The same sporadic supply chain also led to an insufficient supply of medicines.

Table 8.3 *Mortality Rate of Prisoners of War in Four NKVD Camps (Stalingrad District), January–May 1945*

Month	Deaths
January	1,467
February	556
March	597
April	405
May	162
Total	3,187

Source: "Doklad UNKVD po Stalingradskoi oblasti v 4-i otdel GUPVI NKVD SSSR o sanitarnom sostoianii i meditsinskom obsluzhivanie lagerey dlia voennoplennykh," 2 iiunia 1945 g., № 83, in M. M. Zagorul'ko, ed., *Voennoplennye v Stalingrade 1943–1954*, p. 274.

Conditions for prisoners of war deemed to be fit for heavy labor also betray the same symptoms of official indifference and general neglect. In a report dated 24 April 1946 the authors point out that prisoners of war slept on the floor and that any bedding was filthy and unwashed.[53] In this particular camp the prisoners had to march 5 kilometers (3.1 miles) to the work site, setting off just after 0700 hours, which took about 1.5 hours because they had been given an inadequate breakfast. They then returned at 1700 hours. Throughout this working period, often in harsh winter conditions, they received no hot food at all. A rudimentary dinner was served on their return, and so the cycle began again. The report's author noted that there was ample opportunity for theft of food and the issue of short measure.

As in other parts of the Soviet economy, deported slave labor was used in the reconstruction of Stalingrad. On 26 April 1945 a convoy train bringing 763 German civilians, referred to as "mobilized Germans," arrived in Stalingrad for work in the oil industry.[54] In this context, "mobilized" should be take to mean that German civilians had been rounded up in the Soviet occupation zone and forcibly deported. More than half of those deported were older than 40, and 17 had died en route. A medical commission ascertained that only 92 of the arrivals were fit for heavy physical labor.[55] Thereafter, things got worse for these Germans. No thought had been given to beds and proper hospital accommodations, and despite an inspection carried out by an official of the Soviet Commissariat for Health in which all kinds of shortcomings were identified, nothing was done, and infection rates and mortality sharply increased

Table 8.4 *Age Range and Mortality Rates of German Civilians Deported to Stalingrad, 26 April–1 August 1945*

Age Range	Deaths
17–20	7
20–25	12
25–30	7
30–35	15
35–40	10
40–45	39
>45	152
Total	242

Source: "Dokladnaia zapiska UNKVD po Stalingradskoi oblasti v GUPVI NKVD SSSR o sostoianii rabochego batal'ona mobilizovannykh nemtsev № 2021 pri SMU № 1 Neftemashstroia," 14 avgusta 1945 g., № 88, in M. M. Zagorul'ko, ed., *Voennoplennye v Stalingrade 1943–1954*, p. 294.

among the Germans. From 26 April to 1 August 1945, 242 German civilians died of tuberculosis, dystrophy, heart-related illnesses, and other causes. The age range and mortality rates among them are provided in Table 8.4.

As the table shows, of the total of 763 German civilians deported from Germany, 17 died en route, and another 242 died after arrival, an overall mortality rate equal to 34 percent. The fact that the age range above 45 was not specified suggests to me that the Soviet administration had something to hide. It may well be that some of the deportees were much older than 45 and that it was felt this should not become too widely known, even internally. The death toll among these German civilians puts the fate of German prisoners of war into some kind of comparative context. If 34 percent of these deportees died en route to and in what amounted to incarceration in Stalingrad, it is not implausible to posit that German soldiers enduring much harsher conditions before and during captivity could have perished at comparable rates. Even after the death of so many German civilians, substantial improvements in food (quality and quantity) did not take place. It was acknowledged that the food was "insufficient to maintain the normal physical condition of the contingent."[56] The lack of proper medical provision, sufficient food, and accommodations were failings that could be directly attributed to the NKVD and the camp administration. This report is dated 14 August 1945, and one wonders just how many more deported German civilians died with the onset of autumn and winter, and indeed how many of them ever returned home. Survival rates are not mentioned.

Prisoners of war at Stalingrad, which would have included those captured in February 1943 and others transported from other parts of the Soviet Union and beyond, were exploited in virtually every industrial enterprise in the Stalingrad district. The scale of exploitation is remarkable, as can be seen in Tables 8.5 and 8.6, which show the branch of industry in which prisoners of war were deployed and the numbers.

Escape Attempts

As noted in chapter 1, some German soldiers tried to escape from the Kessel immediately before the end, though none of these escape attempts is known to have succeeded. Escape attempts continued in captivity. In fact, they are a recurring theme in documentation pertaining to Soviet prisoner-of-war camps. In a report dated 27 April 1943 various escape attempts carried out by prisoners of war in the Stalingrad district, some involving the murder of Soviet civilians, were listed. For example, on 10 February 1943 a woman, her son, and her daughter were killed (with the use of axes) in Kapustin Iar. Mother and daughter had also been raped. The investigators concluded that the murderers were three escaped German prisoners of war because when apprehended they had items of clothing on them taken from the victims.[57] During a move under escort, all three prisoners escaped. On 23 February 1943, again in Kapustin Iar, the bodies of a mother and son were found. Items of German origin close to the bodies implied German perpetrators. During the night of 4 March 1943, in the Pologoe Zaimishche settlement 2 kilometers (1.2 miles) from Prisoner of War Camp № 98, a family was robbed and beaten. The perpetrators were shot dead resisting arrest. On 28 February 1943 two prisoners escaped from their guards, murdered a *kolkhoz* worker, and severely injured his wife and son. Both escapees were shot while resisting arrest.

Escapes from camps in the Stalingrad district continued through the rest of the war and after May 1945. In a report covering the period January–October 1944 various escape attempts were recorded to have taken place from Camp № 123. Over this period 11 prisoners escaped in groups or individually. Of the 11 escapees, 9 were recaptured, typically after having been on the run for two to four days. The report provided details of the measures taken once an escape attempt was known to have occurred. Search groups were deployed to the most likely routes, water crossing points, and stations. Simultaneously, the relevant security agencies—NKVD, police, and railway police—were noti-

Table 8.5 *The Use of Prisoners of War in MVD Camp № 3621* (Stalingrad District) as of 10 October 1946*

Name of Agency	Ministry	Number of POWs
1-i Spetsstroitrest	Heavy industry	1,831
53-i Trest	Armaments USSR	1,988
25-i Trest	Heavy industry	798
Zavod № 221	Armaments USSR	194
OSMCh-STS	Heavy industry	1,170
Stalingrad Traktornyi zavod	Agricultural machinery	1,400
STZ № 1	Agricultural machinery	306
Kamyshinskii steklotarnyi zavod	Food industry	284
Sovkhoz «Buerachnyi»	Livestock rearing	166
Sovkhoz «Privolzhskii»	Farming	100
Total		8,237

Source: "Spravka OPVI UMVD Stalingradskoi oblasti o trudovomu ispol'zovanii voennoplennykh lagerey № 362 i 108 po sostoianiiu na 5 oktiabria 1946 g," № 153, in M. M. Zagorul'ko, ed., *Voennoplennye v Stalingrade 1943–1954*, p. 487.

*In the text of the document the camp number is cited as 3621, not 362, as in the document heading.

fied. In the first phase search groups extended their range to about 50 to 60 kilometers (31 to 37 miles). After that, searches were carried out at longer distances, 120 to 250 kilometers (75 to 155 miles).[58] Another report noted that in the third quarter of 1945, 16 prisoners escaped from camps in the Stalingrad district: 2 from Camp № 362, 9 from Camp № 163, 2 from Camp № 123, 2 from Camp № 50, and 1 from Camp № 36. Fifteen of the 16 were recaptured.[59] An important role in the apprehension of escaped prisoners of war was played by the *brigady sodeistviia* (assistance brigades). These were made up of members of the local population with an intimate knowledge of the surrounding area and the ability to identify strangers. An assessment of the assistance brigades, whose number increased toward the end of the war and afterward, acknowledged their role but admitted that their help was not always effective, though one member, Tinguta Kumeiko, in charge of a railway station, was awarded 150 roubles and thanked for his part in apprehending an escaped prisoner of war.[60] One factor favoring escape attempts was, according to a report dated January 1947, the general negligence of the MVD escort troops. From 10 August to 22 December 1946, 22 prisoners of war escaped from

Table 8.6 *The Use of Prisoners of War in MVD Camp № 108 (Stalingrad District) as of 10 October 1946*

Name of Agency	Ministry	Number of POWs
Zavod № 264	Transport construction	830
OSMU № 6	Heavy industry	531
Sel'elektro	Farming	26
Zavod № 91	Chemical industry	482
Stalgres	Electricity	562
Gushosdor	MVD SSR	310
Zavod im. Ermana	Forestry	489
Lesozavod	Communications	162
Lesobaza	Forestry	250
Vtorchermet	Ferrous metals	217
Krasnoarmeiskaia pristan'	River transport	273
Krasnoarmeiskii sudoremzavod	River transport	225
SVU-6 USVR st. Kotel'nikovo	Communications	348
Machtozavod	Electricity	251
SO KhOZO UMVD	Internal affairs	709
VSY № 2	Internal affairs	44
Rechstroi	River transport	603
Sudoremzavod	River transport	250
Zavod im. Kuibysheva	Forestry	356
Zavod gidroliznyi	Food preparation	137
Miasokombinat	Food industry	32
OSMCh-3	Building materials	491
UVSR-307	Military installations and naval bases	565
UMGB	MGB SSSR	283
UVSR-311	Military installations and naval bases	856
Stalingradskii kul'stroi	Council of Ministers RSFSR	460
USVR zh.d.	Communications	1,282
Oblupolkomzag	Procurements SSSR	45
SVU USVR st. Archeda	Communications	493
Detskaia zheleznaia doroga	Communications	79
Total		9,328

Source: "Spravka OPVI UMVD Stalingradskoi oblasti o trudovomu ispol'zovanii voennoplennykh lagerey № 362 i 108 po sostoianiiu na 5 oktiabria 1946 g," № 153, in M. M. Zagorul'ko, ed., *Voennoplennye v Stalingrade 1943–1954*, pp. 487–488.

Table 8.7 *Escapes from Camp № 108 for the Period 1944–1949*

Year	Escaped	Captured	On the Run
1944	10	10	0
1945	6	6	0
1946	37	35	2
1947	37	29	8
1948	10	7	3
1949	2	1	1
Total	102	88	14

Source: M. M. Zagorul'ko, ed., *Voennoplennye v Stalingrade 1943–1954*, p. 731.

Camp № 108. Only 4 were recaptured. Most of the escapes took place during work assignments outside the camp.[61] Despite the lax surveillance and, one assumes, measures taken to remedy this state of affairs, escapes from Camp № 108 continued after 1946. A report dated 21–22 February 1950 listed escapes for the period 1944–1949, as shown in Table 8.7. In one of the early escape attempts mentioned in this 1950 report, prisoners of war armed themselves with German weapons they found on the battlefield. Two were killed in an exchange of fire; a third was detained.[62]

Escapes, successful or otherwise, were the clearest rejection of the attempts by turned Germans and the Soviet camp administration to impose the Soviet worldview on prisoners through antifascist indoctrination. In a record of an antifascist meeting, one German activist stated that every normal prisoner of war knew that escape attempts were pointless. The Soviet chairman insisted on a resolution condemning such escapes as anti-Soviet: "Escapes can be carried out only by enemies of the Soviet Union who during the period of the Great Fatherland War took up arms and turned against the Soviet people and at the present time, finding themselves in captivity, are trying by any means possible to harm and to take revenge on the USSR."[63]

Repatriation of German Prisoners of War

Denied after the war, the reasons for the delayed repatriation of German prisoners of war are now acknowledged. First, German labor was required to restore the Soviet Union's infrastructure. Second, immediate repatriation of all prisoners of war would have denied the NKVD the chance to uncover war criminals, or what was understood in Soviet law to be war criminals, among prisoners. Third, the prolonged spell in captivity provided the chance to impose Soviet ideology on prisoners (and to pursue the agenda of talent spotting and agent recruitment). Another initial justification was that after the arrest of Hitler's successors, essentially Admiral Karl Doenitz and his colleagues, there was no effective government with which to conclude peace.[64]

The International Red Cross Committee interceded on behalf of prisoners of war. Its executive, Max Guber, wrote to Molotov, the Soviet foreign secretary. In his letter, dated 26 June 1946, Guber drew Molotov's attention to the fact that the International Red Cross Committee had earlier sent a memorandum to those states holding prisoners of war that had ratified the Convention Relative to the Treatment of Prisoners of War (27 July 1929). In his covering letter Guber pointed out, with an obvious and loud hint, that although the Soviet Union had *not* ratified the Convention Relative to the Treatment of Prisoners of War, the Soviet authorities might, nevertheless, find the contents of the memorandum addressed to those powers that had signed the convention to be of interest. The key element in the Guber memorandum was the reference to two articles pertaining to the repatriation of prisoners of war after the cessation of hostilities, specifically Articles 72 and 75. Article 72 provides for the repatriation of prisoners "who have been in captivity for a long time."[65] By the end of the 1940s this provision was assuming greater importance for the large numbers of German prisoners of war still being held in the Soviet Union. Concerning the obligations of belligerents, the fundamental principle of Article 75 is quite clear: "In any case, the repatriation of prisoners shall be effected as soon as possible after the conclusion of peace."[66] The Guber memorandum was ignored. However, the fact that the Soviet Union, alone among the victorious powers, had not ratified the Convention Relative to the Treatment of Prisoners of War was something of a diplomatic embarrassment, strengthening the view that the Soviet Union was behaving in an arbitrary manner and flouting the established norms of international law.

Anticipating that the Soviet delegation would be asked about the number of German prisoners of war still being held in the Soviet Union at a forthcoming meeting at the level of ministers of foreign affairs, Molotov, in a letter to Stalin dated 12 March 1947, stated that the total number of German prisoners of war currently held in the Soviet Union of all ranks was 988,500. Up to then 965,974 had already been repatriated. Molotov expressed the view that the Soviet Union should agree to publicize the number of German prisoners of war in the Soviet Union provided that the Western Allies agreed to do the same. Molotov concluded: "It is expedient to do this because the reactionary press

Table 8.8 *German Prisoners of War Held by the Western Allies and the Soviet Union According to a TASS Communiqué Published 13 March 1947*

State	POWs Held
USSR	890,532
France	631,483
UK	435,295
USA	30,976
Total	1,988,286

Source: "Soobshchenie TASS o chislennosti germanskikh voennoplennykh," in Major General V. A. Zolotarev, ed., *Russkii Arkhiv: Velikaia Otechestvennaia*, vol. 13, no. 2, *Nemetskie voennoplennye v SSSR 1941–1955 gg.*, Sbornik dokumentov, Kniga pervaia (Moscow: TERRA, 1999), p. 392.

and the German press under the control of the Allies is blowing this question out of all proportion, citing a figure of 5 million German prisoners of war in the Soviet Union."[67] On 13 March 1947 a TASS communiqué on the number of German prisoners of war held by the Western Allies and the Soviet Union was published in *Pravda*. The numbers are given in Table 8.8.

The TASS communiqué noted that 1,003,974 German prisoners of war had been returned since the German capitulation in 1945. This means that a total of 1,894,506 were held in all. In his letter to Stalin, Molotov stated that there were 988,500 German prisoners of war in the Soviet Union, whereas the TASS communiqué cited a figure of 890,532. That meant 97,968 prisoners of war remained unaccounted for. Another discrepancy can be noted in the numbers claimed to have been repatriated. In his letter, Molotov claimed that 965,974 prisoners of war had been "liberated from captivity at the present time."[68] The repatriations cited by TASS were 1,003,974, which left 38,000 prisoners of war unaccounted for.

The Soviet Union envisaged further repatriations in 1948. In a memorandum to Molotov, dated 10 July 1948, Kruglov, deputy chairman of the Council of Ministers of the USSR, cited the numbers of prisoners of war envisaged for repatriation in 1948. The numbers are provided in Table 8.9.

The cited total is 660,759, a shortfall of 6,000 prisoners of war based on the figures in Kruglov's memorandum to Molotov. After the 1948 repatriations were carried out on 1 January 1949 there would still be a total of 534,804 prisoners of war in the Soviet Union. The numbers and nationality are provided in Table 8.10. Therefore, the total number of prisoners of war held by the Soviet Union in 1948 before the repatriation would have been 660,759

Table 8.9 *Planned Repatriations of Prisoners of War from the Soviet Union for 1948*

Nationality	Number
German	343,961
Japanese	175,000
Hungarian	93,802
Romanian	40,946
Austrian	1,050
Total	660,759 (654,759)

Source: "Dokladnaia zapiska ministra vnutrennikh del SSSR S. Kruglova zamestiteliu predsedatelia soveta ministrov SSSR V. M. Molotovu o chislennosti voennoplennykh," 10 iiulia 1948 g., in Major General V. A. Zolotarev, ed., *Russkii Arkhiv: Velikaia Otechestvennaia*, vol. 13, no. 2, *Nemetskie voennoplennye v SSSR 1941–1955 gg.*, Sbornik dokumentov, Kniga pervaia (Moscow: TERRA, 1999), p. 421.

(654,759) + 534,804 = 1,195,563 (1,189,563). The total number of German prisoners of war = 765,182.

One way in which the Soviet Union sought to bypass the provisions of Article 75 of the Convention Relative to the Treatment of Prisoners of War and the pressures to conform with its former Western Allies, and thus retain prisoners of war for long as possible, was to delay the signing of any formal cessation of hostilities with Germany. Implicitly, the Soviet position was that there

Table 8.10 *Total Number of Prisoners of War in the Soviet Union as of 1 January 1949*

Nationality	Number
German	421,221
Japanese	91,563
Hungarian	7,478
Austrian	7,191
Miscellaneous	3,782
Romanian	3,569
Total	534,804

Source: "Dokladnaia zapiska ministra vnutrennikh del SSSR S. Kruglova zamestiteliu predsedatelia soveta ministrov SSSR V. M. Molotovu o chislennosti voennoplennykh," 10 iiulia 1948 g., in Major General V. A. Zolotarev, ed., *Russkii Arkhiv: Velikaia Otechestvennaia*, vol. 13, no. 2, *Nemetskie voennoplennye v SSSR 1941–1955 gg.*, Sbornik dokumentov, Kniga pervaia (Moscow: TERRA, 1999), p. 421.

were outstanding questions that had to be resolved and until such time as they had been resolved, no peace treaty with German could be concluded, and thus the final repatriation of German prisoners of war could not be completed. One unintended, or possibly intended, consequence of the failure to conclude a peace treaty was heightened tension between the Western Allies and the Soviet Union. The Soviet attempt to blockade Berlin was one example, the war in Korea another. In fact, the formal declaration ending the state of war between both German states and the Soviet Union was issued on 25 January 1955.[69] Promulgation of this decree paved the way for the final repatriation of all remaining German prisoners of war, including those condemned as war criminals.

Conclusion

Whether the final number of German prisoners of war who perished in Soviet captivity amounts to 1 million, about one-third of the total number of prisoners, or is more accurately represented by the lower figure of 356,687, the overall German experience of Soviet captivity is another dreadful chapter in the suffering of World War II. In the case of German 6th Army soldiers captured in the depths of winter, captivity meant exhausting marches to remote staging posts, no food en route, and harsh and sometimes sadistic treatment from guards and civilians. Spring and summer brought some relief, but the ravages of disease, exhaustion, and lack of food continued to cull survivors. Physical and medical burdens were exacerbated by forced labor and the relentless pressure to join one of the NKVD-front organizations for German prisoners of war and so-called antifascist propaganda. After May 1945 "*Heimat*" was a word that meant a far-off place to which one day some might return. A good many never saw it again, and among those who did, some had to wait thirteen years.

One can easily dismiss any concerns about the fate of German and other Axis prisoners of war in the Soviet Union by pointing out that the Wehrmacht invaded the Soviet Union and showed scant regard for the millions of Soviet prisoners it captured. Where evidence of war crimes could be gathered and was robust, it is right and proper that war criminals be punished, but no nation's soldiers, whether rank and file or senior commanders, can be the subject of punitive measures merely because they wore the uniform of a totalitarian regime. It seems to me that Zolotarev is quite wrong to hold every German soldier guilty because they took part in the war against the Soviet Union.[70] Is every member of the Red Army responsible for the invasion of

Poland, Katyn, and the mass rape of German women after the fall of Berlin in 1945?[71] And what about the fate of German civilians deported from their homes to a wretched existence as slave labor in Soviet industry? Are their relatives the sole ones to mourn their treatment? Hitler's reasons for attacking the Soviet Union cannot just be dismissed as the ravings of a madman: war is a fact of life in the existence of states. How an aggressor treats prisoners and civilians, a matter that since the end of the eighteenth century has led to the emergence of a corpus of legal instruments designed to ameliorate the prisoner of war's lot that even nonsignatories cannot entirely ignore, is another matter.

9 Return from the House of the Dead: The Arrest, Interrogation, and Repatriation of Oberst Boje (44th Infantry Division)

Head on the pillow, stuffed with shavings of wood: feet in jacket sleeve; coat on top of blanket and Glory be to Thee, O Lord. Another day over. Thank you I'm not spending tonight in the cells. Here it's still bearable.

—Alexander Solzhenitsyn, *One Day in the Life of Ivan Denisovich* (1962)

Oberst (Colonel) Arthur Boje was the commander of 134th Grenadier Regiment, part of 44th Infantry Division, commanded by Generalleutnant Deboi. At the end of January 1943 the remains of Boje's regiment surrendered to the Red Army, and Boje and his men became prisoners of war. After thirteen years as a prisoner Boje was one of the small group of German survivors that returned to Germany. One of the central themes of Boje's account of his time in Soviet captivity, *Stalins deutsche Agenten: Ein Kriegsgefangener berichtet* (*Stalin's German Agents: A German Prisoner of War Reports*), is the willingness, out of expediency or newfound conviction, of German soldiers, including many high-ranking officers, actively to collaborate with their Soviet captors in order to undermine the German war effort. Yet Boje's memoir goes way beyond the mere documentation of German collaboration. With the author's many insights on the nature of the Soviet system and the way people behaved in captivity, *Stalin's German Agents* is an underrated contribution to the genre of camp literature. In fact, Boje's memoir is, in my opinion, on a par with Alexander Solzhenitsyn's *Odin Den' v zhizni Ivana Denisovicha* (*One Day in the Life of Ivan Denisovich*, 1962) and *Gulag Archipelago* (1973, 1975, 1978) and Varlam Shalamov's *Kolymskie rasskazy* (*Kolyma Tales*, 1978).

Brief Biography of Oberst Arthur Boje (1895–1981)

Arthur Boje was born in Berlin on 3 August 1895. With the outbreak of war in August 1914 he joined the German Army, part, in fact, of that huge wave of volunteers that included Ernst Jünger, and was soon in action. Wounded early on, he was transferred to a reserve battalion of his regiment after his convalescence. On 2 August 1918 Boje was badly wounded and captured by the British during the heavy fighting at Dury. He was transferred to a British military hospital in Fulham and also spent some time in Redmires in Yorkshire. In all he spent some thirteen months in Britain. In his memoir, written after his return in 1956 from Soviet captivity, Boje writes of his learning about the total German collapse in May 1945 and how it brought back the moment of despair and grief he had earlier experienced when, in a hospital bed in London, he had learned of the German surrender in 1918:

> I had cause to think about 11 November 1918, on that day of the cease-fire in World War I, which I experienced as a wounded prisoner of war of the English in Fulham Military Hospital. At that time we could hear and see the carnival-like, effusive state of mind of the Londoners who, sporting colored paper hats and cardboard trumpets and with much racket celebrated the victory of the Entente on the plain streets of the British capital. Our station doctor, an older civilian, offered his hand to each one of us and said: "Can we shake hands on it?" To be sure, he meant it all in good faith. The station sister, an older professional nurse from Ireland, offered her opinion: "Oh, he is really a gentleman!" But we had no view about whether he was a gentleman or not. We lay wounded in our beds, and we felt more abandoned than before, when the war still continued. The senior sister, this sweet Irish woman, who had really cared for us and who made no secret of her liking for us Germans, shed tears of compassion.[1]

Boje was released from British captivity on 27 October 1919. On returning to Germany he held a number of teaching and operational posts in the police. By the mid-1930s Boje was back in the army. Toward the end of 1938 he was appointed commander of 3rd Battalion, Infantry Regiment 92. On 10 November 1938 Boje assumed command of 3rd Battalion, Infantry Regiment 76, and took part with this unit in the Polish campaign of 1939. He was then transferred to 3rd Battalion, Infantry Regiment 503, serving with this unit in the campaign against the British and French in the summer of 1940.

By now Boje was showing the kind of operational acumen and leadership qualities that were eventually to win him the Knight's Cross. On the Russian front, during the winter of 1941–1942, Boje personally led the remnants of his regiment in counterattacks. He was awarded the Knight's Cross (Ritterkreuz des Eisernen Kreuzes) on 5 February 1942, which added to an already impressive tally of military decorations going back to World War I: Iron Crosses in both world wars, the Infantry Assault Badge in Silver (Infanterie-Sturmabzeichen in Silber, awarded in 1940), and the German Cross in Gold (Deutsches Kreuz in Gold, awarded in 1941).

As commander of 134th Regiment, part of 44th Infantry Division, Boje fought in Stalingrad. In common with other divisions of 6th Army, 44th Infantry Division's support and logistics units were outside the Kessel after the Soviet attack on 19 November 1942, as a consequence of which 44th Infantry Division's mobility was severely restricted. The remnants of Boje's regiment surrendered on 29 January 1943. On 17 May 1947 Boje was arrested by the Military Tribunal of the Ministry of Internal Affairs of the Tartar ASSR. On 29 December 1947, on the basis of Part I of the Decree of the Presidium of the Supreme Soviet of the USSR, dated 19 April 1943, Boje was sentenced to twenty-five years for war crimes, specifically "for inflicting jointly with his subordinates a series of atrocities and crimes on the peaceful Soviet population."[2] Had the death penalty not been rescinded at that time in the Soviet Union, Boje would almost certainly have been executed instead of receiving a long prison sentence. Boje did not serve the full sentence and returned home to Germany on 14 January 1956 as part of a contingent of 450. However, as far as the Soviet authorities were concerned, Boje remained guilty of the crimes for which he had been sentenced in 1947. This is also the view in the Russian Federation, and Boje is unlikely ever to be rehabilitated. Oberst Arthur Boje died on 18 April 1981 in Hamburg.

Prisoner: Interrogation and Tribunal

Boje covers his arrest and the case against him in some detail in *Stalin's German Agents*. The Boje case is also extensively covered in SMERSH, the FSB's sixtieth-anniversary monograph published in 2003. Boje's memoir and SMERSH are the two main sources for the story of his arrest and trial. To begin with, Boje's account of his surrender differs dramatically from the account given in SMERSH. Boje notes that he and the other survivors of his regiment left their position and that they laid down their weapons. At this moment Generalleutnant Edler von Daniels (commander of 376th Infantry Division) was addressing some of his own men. Boje describes the moment thus:

> It was a sad procession that now set off along the street under the railway bridge in the direction of the Tsaritsyn gully. At this time, on both sides, Red Army soldiers stood armed with machine pistols. After we had covered a few hundred meters we had to stop, and from several sides cameramen approached us and took snapshots and filmed us.[3]

At this juncture, Boje writes, the officers and other ranks are split up. Boje lists the items in his rucksack: a second uniform; some shirts and collars, handkerchiefs; a packet of chocolate, and some cigarettes. There is no mention of any diary.[4] Now, consider the circumstances of Boje's capture given in SMERSH:

> Early on the frosty morning of 29 January 1943 in the ruins of a school on the outskirts of Stalingrad a reconnaissance patrol stumbled across something resembling a human being. It scrambled out of a crater with some difficulty. Its legs, wrapped in a child's blanket, slipped along the frozen remains of brick and concrete. The bottoms of a long, secondhand sheepskin coat caught on the twisted metal fittings. Through the holes of a dirty woman's shawl gray, watery eyes with a look of fear stared out at the soldiers. Only by the tabs of the torn and faded uniform could they guess that a German colonel was standing in front of them. Without any fuss he and the French leather suitcase that was found with him in the cellar were sent to the rear, to the Special Section.[5]

Apart from the date and the fact of capture, the two accounts are completely different. Boje's own account reflects a certain dignity of the moment: his men and he are defeated; they have lost the battle, but they surrender as soldiers. In the FSB account Boje is bereft of any dignity or soldierly honor. In clothing that we are to assume has been stolen from Soviet citizens, and even worse from women, Boje is shown as a half-frozen, filthy tramp.

According to the FSB account, Boje was being interrogated by a Special Section captain within a matter of hours. From Boje's point of view, the interrogation seems to be going well. Then a diary and photographs are laid on the table, and Boje's composure fails him. It is significant that Boje, who lists what he takes with him into captivity, makes no mention of a diary, or indeed of any photographs. In fact, given that he is marching into Soviet captivity, it would hardly have been a wise move to carry any kind of incriminating documents. The obvious solution would have been to destroy them. On the other hand, one cannot rule out the possibility that Boje omits the fact that he retained a diary, thereby implying that any future Soviet reference to a diary is unreliable evidence.

In his memoir Boje offers an explanation for the diary in question. En route to Moscow he meets a Soviet general who tells him that he, the general, has read his memoirs. Boje informs the general that he has not written his memoirs. The general counters that a book written by Boje was found among the belongings of a dead officer in Boje's regiment. Boje then explains that at the end of 1941 he compiled a commemorative book dealing with the regiment's campaign in Russia. The book contained brief summaries of various actions and photos taken by members of the regiment. The book was published by the Oldenburger Staatsverlag. Boje's claim is that this was the book that had fallen into Soviet hands. Moreover, the book dealing with the 1941 campaign in Russia was a follow-up volume to that dealing with the regiment's campaign in France, which also marked the regiment's 245th anniversary. Of this incident, Boje records in his memoir: "At that time I had no idea what a fateful role this book was about to have for me."[6]

Titled *The History of the 134th Infantry Regiment, or the Struggle of the Deutschmeister against the Soviets*, the diary laid before Boje was allegedly a history of the regiment before and after the invasion of Russia. I say "allegedly" because publication of extracts of the diary has been under the exclusive control of the FSB. I submitted a request to the FSB for access to Boje's diary, interrogation records, and other paperwork, but permission was denied. Since the diary is crucial to the case against Boje I have translated those extracts that were published in Russian in SMERSH. It would of course have been better to have had access to the German original, but the Russian translations from the German are all that are currently available. So they must suffice.

The first extract is dated 15 March 1941:

> When on 15 March 1941 in France, standing on the parade of the famous Deutschmeister Regiment during the unforgettable commemoration of its 245th anniversary, I gave an oath that the regiment would without doubt prove itself in the battles with the enemy, I at that time could not believe in what circumstances my hopes would be met.[7]

The second extract is dated 25 March 1941:

Loading begins on 25 March. The final good-bye, and the train slowly sets off. There's a continuous road through France. There is fertile soil and uninhabited spaces. The train soon enters the borders of Alsace. What order and cleanliness there is here! Germany! Everywhere we see work and people's joyful faces. What a difference! This is the apogee! The blows of a new era's pulse can be heard. . . . We head through the old German border. We are in Poland. Everywhere we see Jews. It has long been high time that that this country passed into the orderly hands of the Imperium.[8]

The third extract is dated 22 June 1941:

[On] 22 June the regiment occupies strongpoints; still one night to go, and then will begin the unprecedented struggle of order against disorder, of culture against the absence of culture, of good against bad. We are so grateful to the Führer that he noted the danger in time and the he will strike unexpectedly. Just one more night! The enemy is on the other side of the Bug. The watch hands move slowly. The sky starts to lighten. It is 0315 hours. Our artillery opens fire. Fire pours forth from hundreds of barrels. The forward groups leap into the boats and cross the Bug. The battle has started! The unexpected blow succeeds. The other riverbank is ours. Shots are heard. Here a house is on fire, there a haystack. Initial resistance is broken. Now onward, forward![9]

The fourth extract is undated but is stated to be a month later, July 1941:

All of us are surprised by how Russia looks. Many have lost all hope of a bread paradise in the Ukraine. We are indignant that we have seen "Soviets" in this paradise. There is a complete lack of roads; small clay houses covered with straw and small windows. Apart from a half-ruined peasant house, a pair of chickens, and a pig, the peasant has nothing. And this is called the Soviet paradise![10]

The fifth extract is dated November 1941:

The enemy is reinforcing. Movement becomes ever more difficult. We are bogged down in mud up to our knees. Vehicles and carts are hopelessly stuck or roll off to the side of the road. Day and night you hear shouts and cursing.[11]

The sixth extract is undated:

The Soviet paradise. What do we see in the Soviet paradise? The people have no religion or soul. The churches are destroyed or serve as barns. There is no trace of culture. Every one of us has one feeling—that is happiness that the Führer decided radically to change this depraved system. Victory. Keep our Führer safe![12]

The seventh extract is undated, but the reference to Kiev suggests August 1941:

Days off. There are not many days off in the war against the Soviets. But after the heated battles near Iurovka and Pochtovaia and on the southwestern edge of Kiev we regard these days off as the best days. How quickly, when joking, are these fierce battles forgotten. The warm August sun shines in the sky. Everyone is in shorts. The soldiers are engaged in their favorite pastime: taking care of their stomachs. It is amazing just what a soldier's stomach can digest. Ducks, chickens, geese: nothing can hide. They are hunted, chased after, and shot.[13]

The eighth abstract is not dated:

The attack on Dubno. . . . The heat of the sun is unbearable. There is a golden harvest in the fields. How wonderful is this wheat field. In endless ranks the gray columns move across the sands of the Volyn'. Like flour, the sand gets in your boots and makes every step unbearable. Sweat runs down your face and body in floods. It's dry in your mouth. Some water! Some water! But nothing can stop us! Neither heat nor sand, neither dust nor sweat. Farther and farther, we keep heading eastward.[14]

The ninth extract is not dated:

The main highway to the north. Communism in all the years of its existence has done nothing apart from the destruction of Europe, and Germany above all. Everywhere we see massive structures, barracks and

> barracks. We are met by long columns of prisoners of war. The Asiatic faces look at us. History has lost its mind! These hordes will conquer us?![15]

None of these extracts provides any evidence of war crimes or atrocities. In fact, Boje's assessment of the way communism has behaved—the destruction of churches and the low material standard of living—are not matters of dispute. One wonders whether some of Boje's diary entries had anything to say about the ravages of the Holodomor in Ukraine and are for that reason not cited. Boje's response to the photographs was to claim that they were the work of an officer from the propaganda department of 44th Infantry Division.[16] A turning point in Boje's interrogation and processing, at least as far as the NKVD and SMERSH were concerned, was the knowledge that Boje had commanded an SS battalion in between 1936 and 1938. Far more important for the NKVD's purposes was that the investigators were able to identify two soldiers—Major Pohl, the commander of 1st Battalion, 134th Infantry Regiment, and Unteroffizier Paul Suchitsch of 2nd Artillery Battalion—who could provide statements purporting to support accusations of atrocities carried out on Boje's orders.

With the insertion of Suchitsch and Pohl in the interrogation process, extracts from Boje's diary are now followed by extracts from interrogation statements made by Suchitsch and Pohl. So immediately after the sixth extract from Boje's diary Suchitsch states the following:

> Some 15–20 kilometers [9 to 12 miles] from the town of Dergachi, in an populated area the name of which I cannot remember, the whole population on the orders of Oberst Boje was herded into the synagogue. The synagogue was mined and blown up along with all the people inside. . . . On 13 July in the populated area of Nesolon', 30 kilometers [19 miles] to the east of Novgorod-Volynskii, Oberst Boje ordered that the church be blown up. . . . In approximately the first half of the month of August 1941, along the Krupoli–Berezan' road, about 10 kilometres [6 miles] from the Berezan' station, a *sovkhoz* was set alight and more than 300 prisoners of the Red Army war were shot, among whom the majority were women. Oberst Boje kept shouting: "What does an armed woman mean? That's our enemy."[17]

Immediately after Boje's seventh extract Suchitsch states the following:

> In the first half of August near the city of Kiev Oberst Boje traveled around

the field in his vehicle and shot prisoners of war with his rifle; that is, he hunted them. He killed ten of them. I saw this myself.[18]

Immediately after Boje's eighth extract Major Pohl states:

In the city of Dubno 134th Regiment captured many Russian tanks and four tank crews. On the orders of Oberst Boje, they were shot. In the town the soldiers plundered the civilian population. On his orders all the monuments, statues, and busts of Soviet leaders were destroyed by the men.[19]

Immediately after Boje's ninth extract Suchitsch makes the following statement:

Near the village of Krupoli, next to a lake with reeds, 5 commissars were shot on the orders of Oberst Boje. I witnessed this myself since I was with a sergeant from our company on a round-up in the reeds. There—I can't remember the name of the populated area—Oberst Boje shot dead an officer who had hidden in a haystack. In order to make a point, the corpse lay unburied. Among the soldiers there were rumors that the corpse was that of an official in the GPU [Gosurdastvennoe politicheskoe upravlenie, or State Political Directorate]. Earlier in the reinforced position of IAnov, on the other side of the river Bug, behind some concrete reinforcements, a group of Red Army soldiers and commanders was formed up, about 20 men. Oberst Boje ordered that they be shot.[20]

As far as the Soviet counterintelligence officers, Captain Savel'ev and Lieutenant Colonel Puzyrev, were concerned, the diary, the photographs, and the testimonies of Pohl and Suchitsch, as well as that of a Hauptmann Krause and a Leutnant Grostman (though nothing is cited from the latter two's testimony), constituted prima facie evidence of Boje's responsibility for war crimes. Before considering Boje's account of his interrogation, one obvious error in the FSB material needs to be pointed out. On a first mention, Paul Suchitsch's rank is given as Unteroffizier, an NCO rank. Thereafter, he is referred to as an Oberleutnant (first lieutenant). This rank inconsistency may well be an innocent error, or it may stem from the belief of those making the case against Boje that the testimony of his fellow officers would carry more weight than that of a cook NCO. Boje gives Suchitsch's rank as Unteroffizier, a cook in Artillery Regiment 96.[21] If Boje is correct, then Suchitsch's testimony starts to look vulnerable because Suchitsch claims that he personally saw Boje kill Soviet soldiers on at least two occasions. If Suchitsch was a cook in an artillery battalion, it is highly unlikely that he would have seen some of the things he claims to have seen—not absolutely impossible, just unlikely—because as a cook he would have been in the rear echelons of 134th Regiment, not with its frontline formations, essentially the infantry. An artillery unit would tend to be some way back from the front.

Boje has some forewarning that a case may be made against him because he is transferred to the Lubianka for interrogation, sharing a cell with Generalmajor Schmidt, who is also accused of having committed war crimes. The subjects of Boje's first interrogation are the war crimes that he and his regiment are supposed to have carried out in the summer campaign of 1941. Boje rejects any such accusation, maintaining that the provisions of the various international agreements—the Hague and Geneva Conventions—were observed. As far as the interrogator is concerned, the commemorative 1941 booklet is telling evidence of war crimes. Boje suspects that accusations of crimes are part of a psychological process to make him more cooperative and indeed to secure from him as much information as possible about other prisoners. The main psychological blow aimed at Boje is the news from his interrogator that General von Seydlitz–Kurzbach has called on captured German officers to join the BDO and fight Hitler. Boje's refusal to sign the declaration results in his being brought face-to-face with General Mel'nikov, one of the NKVD's senior officers. Mel'nikov resumed the line that Boje's commemorative book was evidence of atrocities and propaganda. When Boje continues to adhere to his earlier and future explanations of the book's purposes, Mel'nikov reacts with violence. In Boje's words, Mel'nikov "came around the table and struck me several times in the face with his fist."[22] As Boje readily admits, others have endured much worse. The aim of this limited, controlled, targeted violence is to inflict psychological pressure on the victim, to inflict a sense of helplessness that is likely to be especially acute when inflicted on those accustomed to taking control and making decisions. Similar measures were applied in the Krasnogorsk camp. For example, administrative posts and other positions with greater access to privileges were held by German communists and prisoners, some of whom were German deserters. Boje concluded that it was part of the punishment, a psychological conditioning, to place rank-and-file deserters in charge of German officers so as to "destroy the dignity of the person by all means."[23]

The case against Boje is finally initiated in Camp № 7125:

> A Soviet senior lieutenant, hitherto unknown to me, had me informed through an interpreter that I was under suspicion of numerous war crimes and that I was henceforth a prisoner under investigation and that I had to answer the questions put to me. As I could expect, my commemorative booklet with its accounts and photos, already mentioned numerous times, would form the basis of the accusations of war crimes.[24]

Boje's interrogation lasts several weeks. Various witnesses who had served in 44th Infantry Division are summoned. Some of these witnesses are not referred to in the FSB account. Thus, Boje recalls the testimony of the assistant medical officer, Suchanek, who served in 132nd Infantry Regiment. According to Suchanek, his regiment arrived in a settlement that had been taken in battle by Boje's regiment, where they found many destroyed houses and corpses. Boje dismisses this as an example of appalling naïveté. Destroyed houses and corpses are the consequences of war. He then attempts to undermine Suchanek's credibility as a witness. He says that Suchanek claimed that he, Boje, had ordered a Soviet battery and commander that had been captured by Boje's regiment to turn his guns around and open fire on his men. Suchanek is asked by Boje to explain how he could have known about this since he was not there. Suchanek replies that he heard about it.[25] Boje explains, he writes, that the sole truth in this account was that one of his infantry companies, led by Oberleutnant Klaus Vormann, had captured a Soviet artillery battery during the battle in the Surovikino position, for which Vormann was awarded the Knight's Cross.[26] Suchanek goes on to claim that Boje gave the order to plunder the town of Zwiahel in the summer of 1941. Boje says that there was nothing to loot and that the seizure of foodstuffs could not be construed as looting, as meant by Suchanek.[27] Suchanek then maintains that during the massive encirclement battle for Kiev, Boje let commissars and several hundred Red Army prisoners be shot.[28] When asked how he knows, Suchanek merely replies that there was talk of this having happened.

According to Boje, he is also denounced by two junior officers: Leutnant Eberhard and Leutnant Mylo von Schweinichen. Eberhard claims that Boje incited opposition to the Soviet authorities, specifically that he sought to organize a hunger strike against Soviet war-crimes proceedings; Von Schweinichen accuses Boje of having spread fascist propaganda.[29] Boje also refers to two written statements made by witnesses that are read to him: one from a Russian woman and the other from Paul Suchitsch. The Russian woman, a widow, claims that Boje shot her husband in July 1941. In a statement to the Soviet commission investigating German war crimes, she, whose surname is given as Mikhailovskaia, makes the following claim: "In July 1941, the regiment commander Boje shot my husband for having links with the partisans. Moreover, the dwellings of many inhabitants were burned down on his orders."[30] An unnamed witness of the village in which this is supposed to have occurred states: "In July 1941, on the orders of Oberst Boje, a church and twelve dwellings were burned down. The villagers ran away to the forest, pursued by the Germans."[31] The aspect to these testimonies that strikes one as suspect is that both witnesses are able to name Boje. There is a suspicion that the SMERSH investigators provided the names so as to enhance the veracity of the witness statements. Assuming that Boje ordered these measures and that he shot this woman's husband, it would not have been in his interests to let his name be known.

If Boje is to be believed, Suchitsch has been placed in charge of the work company in one of the camps, an important position in the prisoner hierarchy and one that would provide all kinds of special privileges. On this basis, Suchitsch's statements may be regarded as somehow tainted. A former police officer, and thus a person experienced in the ways and wiles of interrogators, Boje identifies the main approach used in Suchitsch's testimony: "His statements always rested in some way on actual occurrences, but always presented in a way that incriminated me."[32] For example, on 22 June 1941 the engineer platoon of Boje's regiment was deployed to capture a strong Russian bunker. However, it took several days to achieve the goal and capture prisoners. According to Suchitsch, Boje then ordered that these prisoners be shot. Boje accepts the Suchitsch version with the exception of the shooting order: "The engineer platoon was able only after several days to report back to the regiment, which meanwhile was engaged in a battle some miles east of the river Bug, by which time the prisoners had long been handed over to a prisoner-of-war collection point."[33] Suchitsch also claims, like Suchanek, that Boje gave the order that commissars and prisoners of war be shot at Kiev. Boje later learns that Suchitsch cannot be brought before him because he has been struck by lightning while sheltering from a storm. Boje admits that he derives a certain satisfaction from this, seeing it as an act of divine judgment. In his own account of his interrogation, Boje makes no mention of any testimony from Major Eberhard Pohl, which may indicate that he is not aware that Pohl has made statements against him or that he has chosen to withhold the information. One cannot rule out the possibility that Pohl and Boje were brought together in a face-to-face confrontation (*ochnaia stavka*). Given that Major Pohl was also a holder of the Knight's Cross (awarded on 17 December 1942), the NKVD and SMERSH interrogators would have regarded him as a powerful and credible witness in their battle of wills with Boje, one intended to break Boje's will to resist.

Despite what the NKVD and SMERSH by now regarded as overwhelming evidence against Boje, he still refused to acknowledge any guilt. In the FSB account Boje is now accused of trying to save himself by providing information on senior officers from German 6th Army. According to the FSB account, Boje denounced Paulus:

> I became acquainted with Generalfeldmarschall Paulus before the war, on exercises. Then he was a general and chief of staff of a tank corps. Here in the camp he is respected and honored by everyone. He will not discuss political themes in general since he considers that he is being monitored. The Generalfeldmarschall will never undertake anything against Germany and its government. He will never be drawn into the BDO. He views this as treachery.[34]

Boje goes on to make similar comments about Generalleutnant Strecker. Of his divisional commander, Generalmajor Deboi, Boje reports:

> Generalmajor Deboi is a convinced national socialist and enemy of the BDO. But he does not believe in Germany's military victory, and it could be possible to get him to cooperate.[35]

Boje's observations about Paulus, Strecker, and Deboi hardly constitute treachery. In view of what Boje writes of his own attitude toward the BND, he may well be trying to deter the NKVD and SMERSH from any attempt to recruit Paulus and others for the purposes of Soviet propaganda.

As further evidence of Boje's willingness to cooperate with SMERSH, the FSB account includes a report, referred to as a *donos*, by Boje on General Deboi. The report is dated 23 October 1943, and the source, Boje, is referred to by the code name "Zapadnik":

> Generalmajor Deboi belongs to a category of officers that relates most positively to the existing German government. In his capacity as a soldier

and a commander, he enjoys great authority among his subordinates, and his commanders have much regard for his opinions. All those who have had contact with him characterize him as a firm, independent officer dedicated to his duty, a man with a particularly clear mode of thinking. His political views are completely national socialist, and he is one of those officers who is most devoted to national socialism. I consider him to be a person who at the present time would be unable to change his views, and if he decides to do anything, then he does it wholeheartedly. This view of him was formed at the time when he commanded our division. In the personal sphere he is exceptionally reserved and does not become closely involved with any people connected with him in his duties. His relations with those in his immediate entourage have a dry, formal character.

At the moment when Hitler came to power he had the rank of major and was only promoted to the rank of general in the spring of 1942. That is, his military career has achieved its development especially recently. He has recently been the commander of 44th [Infantry] Division.[36]

This is hardly character assassination from Boje. It is a highly favorable assessment of Deboi, and one that might well persuade an NKVD officer in search of recruits for the BND to go elsewhere.

If the FSB account of Boje's interrogation is to be believed, Boje agreed to cooperate with Soviet counterintelligence. A not-very-legible copy of what purports to be Boje's handwritten and signed, though undated, agreement to work for the Soviet authorities is also presented as evidence. In the interests of accuracy I cite my transcription of the German followed by my English translation:

Hierdurch verpflichte ich mich, alle bisherigen und zukünftigen Gespräche und alle Verhandlungen mit Dienststellen der russischen Behörden streng geheim zu halten. Besonders sollen alle Fragen der Zusammenarbeit mit der Sowjet-Regierung jeder Art hierunter fallen. Es ist mir bekannt, daß eine Nichteinhaltung dieser Verpflichtung eine strenge Ahndung erfährt. Boje.[37]

Herewith I undertake to maintain strict secrecy about all previous and all future discussions and all negotiations with the official agencies of the Russian authorities. In particular this shall include all questions of cooperation of any kind with the Soviet government. I know that a failure on my part to honor this obligation shall lead to a severe punishment. Boje.

Assuming that I have accurately transcribed and translated the handwritten German, it is by no means clear that the document signed by Boje does indeed constitute an agreement to cooperate with Soviet counterintelligence. In terms of the general wording, the document does not commit Boje to cooperate with Soviet counterintelligence because there is no explicit reference to any Soviet counterintelligence agency. The agreement, such as it is, merely stipulates that Boje is to remain silent about his past and future discussions with "the official agencies of the Russian authorities." Interestingly, and tellingly, the fact that the NKVD and SMERSH interrogators conflate "the official agencies of the Russian authorities" with Soviet counterintelligence reveals a great deal about the Soviet state and where executive power resides. The real significance of this document for SMERSH is that Boje has *signed* a piece of paper. In other words, he has crossed a psychological threshold, which, as far as SMERSH is concerned, makes Boje *their man*. I suspect that Boje, the former police officer, not exactly a neophyte in these forms of psychological tactics, grasped the dangers but deemed them necessary.

Boje does not deny that he signed an agreement with the Soviet authorities. In his memoir he refers to an incident that occurred while he was in a special camp in Krasnogorsk. This was Camp № 2, the so-called Antifa Schule (Antifascist school). He is brought before the camp commandant, Colonel Voronov, and reprimanded for his failure to cooperate with the agencies of the Soviet Union despite the fact that he earlier gave a written undertaking to do so. At this stage Boje is accused of conducting a conspiracy against the Soviet Union and threatened with the death penalty. This threat would almost certainly have been made under the provisions of Article 58 of the 1926 RSFSR Criminal Code. Boje's view is that the main aim of this pressure, at this stage, is to force him to work as an informer.[38]

Boje is finally sentenced as a war criminal on 29 December 1947 in a tribunal that took place in the Joschkar-Ola Camp. The administrative mechanism before which Boje was brought was the troika, the same Soviet institution that had already sentenced hundreds of thousands of victims, Soviet and non-Soviet, guilty and innocent, to death and to hellish and long terms of imprisonment. The rough and brutal nature of this Soviet procedure and its ugly cynicism are apparent when Boje tries to challenge the accusation that he shot dead a woman's husband. He is merely dismissed with the assertion that "one doesn't lie in the Soviet Union,"[39] which closely resembles another cynical claim often heard during the Soviet period: that "innocent people are not imprisoned in the Soviet Union." The tribunal concludes with four questions being put to Boje:

1. Did you shoot the husband of the woman [unnamed but given as Mikhailovskaia above] in Nesolon?
2. Did you permit libraries in Rovno to be plundered?
3. Did you allow Russian prisoners of war to be shot in the Kiev encirclement battle?
4. Did you force a Russian battery commander to redeploy his guns and open fire on his own people?[40]

Boje recalls the verdict thus:

I was taken into a side room. After a few minutes I was taken into the hall again. The members of the court came in, and the senior lieutenant read out the judgment, prepared typewritten text. The interpreter translated and placed the document in front of me for me to sign. Therewith I was convicted of the war-crimes charges and sentenced to twenty-five years in a corrective-labor camp. I had the right of appeal against this sentence to a higher authority, for which I applied in accordance with the procedure. Then I was dismissed.[41]

Capture Shock, Bund Deutscher Offiziere, and Nationalkomitee Freies Deutschland

Capture shock and subsequent captivity can cause a soldier of any rank to reassess his relationship with his superiors, his fellow soldiers, and his country. This is one reason why the Germans were able to recruit disaffected Red Army prisoners to serve in the Vlasov units and to be trained as German spies. The NKVD clearly had similar plans, and much of Boje's memoir deals with the various pressures exerted by the NKVD to recruit senior German officers to serve in the BDO.

In the first instance, capture shock expresses itself in the loss of a will to live. Soldiers who proved to be brave and resourceful in combat, who endured hunger and cold, now seem to abandon the struggle to survive. Running parallel with this psychological collapse, new forces are starting to shape behavior. The sense of collective responsibility, one of 6th Army's great strengths, is starting to fail: "When people are forced to do without warmth, food, care, and love, then the barriers put in place by education and custom, by practice and example, fall away. Then man stands naked in all his need before dreadful realities that he would never have dared to imagine."[42] In these circumstances the captors possess all the aces. Active, not merely passive, collaboration is inevitable. Boje repeatedly returns to the question of how German soldiers could be turned so easily against their own side in so short a period of time. The Soviet authorities themselves are surprised: "At the front these soldiers had withstood all the stresses, but now some kind of mass collapse in their basic convictions had occurred that stunned even the Soviet commissars and made them suspicious. For them, it was scarcely conceivable that German officers, partly also without the application of any pressure, had succumbed to their rat-catching methods."[43]

Soldiers take orders from their officers and commanders. As prisoners, they now take orders from their captors. Capture creates an authority vacuum that has to be filled. The captors have replaced their own commanders, and the habits of obedience can be exploited. This further suggests to me that those soldiers who have shown a willingness to challenge their own side—that is, they have preserved some sense of their individual identity and moral autonomy—are better able to resist the approaches and pressures of their captors. Later in the same camp, when the son of Wilhelm Pieck, the German communist, appears in the uniform of an NKVD captain, Boje records that he is deeply shocked to see and hear German soldiers, who only a few months ago were fighting at the front, stand up and give this man a rapturous welcome and sing communist songs. The role of the German communist émigrés is critical here because they help to allay any sense of guilt that the German officer is betraying Germany. They help to undermine prisoner solidarity and impose the captors' narrative on the prisoners. Romanian and Italian communists were used in much the same way against Romanian and Italian prisoners.[44] In the early 1970s, Jane Fonda's willingness to be exploited by the North Vietnamese authorities for propaganda purposes and to undermine the morale of American prisoners would amount to the same ploy. In all these cases, Cicero's apocryphal warning about the dangers of the traitor within the gate come to mind.

Some examples of German prisoners' collaboration with their Soviet captors are indeed remarkable for the apparent total transformation in the men's actions and subsequent behavior. In the Krasnogorsk camp Boje encounters an SS prisoner, a Leutnant Schauer, who, according to Major Hahn, the highly decorated pilot, made it clear that if Schauer encountered his own father, also serving at the front, he would kill him.[45] In the Antifa camp Boje encounters large numbers of German soldiers who have gone over to the Soviet side. Boje overhears a conversation: certain German soldiers, dressed in Russian uniforms, were taken by their Soviet masters to the German center front, which was in the midst of severe withdrawal battles. Now in German uniforms, they crossed the German lines with instructions to lead retreating German units in the wrong direction and thus to cause them to fall into Soviet hands. This happened on many occasions. They had also plundered the bodies of their fellow Germans. Boje recalls his disgust:

> It was unnerving to have to listen to all this. However, what for a German soldier represented the height of unimaginable behavior was the fact that this group of traitors had also applied to be awarded Russian military decorations.[46]

On the theme of collaboration, Boje's ire is directed at the way senior German officers behave in Soviet captivity. The number of German generals and other senior officers who did throw in their lot with the Soviet intelligence and propaganda agencies is indeed striking. Boje records some of the defections from the ranks of 6th Army: General von Seydlitz-Kurzbach (LI Corps commander), Generalmajor Martin Lattman (14th Panzer Division), Generalleutnant Edler von Daniels (376th Infantry Division), Generalleutnant Carl Rodenburg (76th Infantry Division), Generalleutnant Arno von Lenski (24th Panzer Division), and Oberst Albrecht Czimatis (305th Infantry Division). Boje first learns of General von Seydlitz-Kurzbach's defection in the Lubianka. The news is undoubtedly intended to weaken his resistance to the idea of collaboration. Nevertheless, the news must come as a great shock because everything in his biography—a name associated with the best of the Prussian military tradition, a highly successful and decorated commander—speaks of loyalty to Hitler and the Nazi state.

Boje is present when Generalleutnant Rodenburg gives a long speech in which he seeks to explain his decision to join the BDO. His main argument rests on the need to end the war as soon as possible and prevent further loss of life. As Boje rejoins in his memoir, Rodenburg seems oblivious to the fact that the main purpose of bringing about a German collapse is not only to end the war but also to further the postwar geopolitical and ideological ambitions of the Soviet Union. To quote Boje: "That this markedly dashing, youthfully slim general with all the airs and graces of a Prussian officer and the masterfully worn monocle had deserted to the Russians and was now trying to get us to do the same thing was incomprehensible."[47]

Jochen Löser, the main author of *Bittere Pflicht*, offers a completely different view of Generalleutnant Rodenburg's conduct in Soviet captivity. Löser praises his former divisional commander, writing that Rodenburg had to endure much in Soviet captivity "because of his upright convictions."[48] Rodenburg himself states that he opposed attempts to get him to join the BDO and that "I myself was arrested on a charge of plotting against the BDO."[49] This seems to weaken the case against Rodenburg, though none of his statements amounts to an emphatic denial that he ever joined the BDO. He also reports that, as happened to Boje, he was condemned to death, a sentence that, since the death penalty had then been abolished in the Soviet Union, was, dare one say it, commuted to twenty-five years of forced labor.[50]

Either Löser, who was not captured at Stalingrad, allowed himself to be used by Rodenburg or Boje's accusation of collaboration is an unjustified slur. In the absence of complete access to Rodenburg's interrogation and other records kept by the NKVD and the Soviet camp administration, which are held in the Russian State Military Archive, there is no effective way to determine which of the two assessment's—Löser's or Boje's—is the truth or even close to the truth. If Rodenburg delivered the address that Boje says he did, Rodenburg has a case to answer, or at the very least some explaining to do. On the other hand, Rodenburg may have taken the view that such were the agonies endured by 6th Army inside the Kessel that he was released from any loyalty owed to the NS state. Unfortunately, silence on this matter or any dissembling would suggest that for all the calls of *gebieterische Pflicht* that von Seydlitz-Kurzbach sought to impose on Paulus at the critical hour and that, if Boje is to believed, Rodenburg sought to impose on fellow officers in captivity, there is some residual sense of guilt and even shame for having got too close to the NKVD creation, the BDO, and for having become, if only fleetingly, its tool in an equally sordid cause.

Oberst Czimatis, according to Boje, collaborates with the Soviet authorities in order to get back to Germany as soon as possible. Worse is to come for Boje and other loyal German officers. In December 1944, fifty generals and Paulus sign a leaflet—"Anruf an Volk und Wehrmacht"—calling on German commanders to put an end to the Hitler dictatorship. Millions of these leaflets are dropped over the German lines. Boje's personal response to this is predictable, though he clearly ignores the case of Vlasov and the willingness of *Hilfswillige* to assist 6th Army:

> There is no precedent in man's entire history where soldiers in captivity acted against their own Fatherland as well as their own comrades and countrymen with whom they had bravely fought against the enemy before

they were captured. Such behavior for German soldiers would have been inconceivable before the war.[51]

Some German officers who had initially resisted signing later capitulated and signed. General Graf von Hülsen, an officer from a family with a proud name, even went so far as to address the German people over the radio, urging them to turn their weapons against Hitler.[52]

Behind the scenes von Seydlitz–Kurzbach was planning to go much further in his attempts to ingratiate himself with his new masters than Boje could have imagined. In February 1944, Seydlitz drafted a long memorandum, addressed to General Mel'nikov, on how to strengthen the role of the BDO and the NFD. The substance and tone of the von Seydlitz–Kurzbach memorandum reveal the extent of the total volte-face undergone by its author. Whatever the nature of the Nazi state, one that von Seydlitz-Kurzbach was willing to serve—and did serve until his capture—von Seydlitz–Kurzbach shows himself ready to ignore the totalitarian nature of the Soviet state and its own murderous policies (Holodomor, the Great Terror, Katyn). In his memorandum, von Seydlitz–Kurzbach claims that the Soviet Union has no intention of imposing communist ideas by violence on the German people—a view, he says, that is fully shared by German communists: "German communists have also declared that they do not intend to impose an unacceptable policy on the German people with the assistance of Soviet arms."[53] Some of the von Seydlitz–Kurzbach proposals for postwar Germany simply sidestep the nature of German war crimes, first and most obviously the Holocaust, and the fact that Germany will have to answer for them. For example, von Seydlitz–Kurzbach seriously contemplates the possibility that Germany could be liberated by an armed formation of the National Committee and that such a formation would render the various occupation regimes of the Allies with their demarcation lines and zones of influence unnecessary.[54] Von Seydlitz–Kurzbach, in trying to avert the occupation of Germany, shares something in common with the anti-Hitler conspiracy in Germany itself. Both parties seemed to believe that Germany could escape the consequences of occupation, whereas it was the policy of the Allies that Germany, unlike in 1918, be occupied and held to account. It is possible that von Seydlitz–Kurzbach knew and understood full well what lay in store for Germany—occupation, division, and retribution—and that those parts of his memorandum in which he talks of partnership and cooperation and even that German fears of Bolshevism are unjustified were an attempt to head off the worst. This view of von Seydlitz–Kurzbach's behavior in captivity would place him and some of his fellow officers among the patriots, those who have Germany's interests at heart. Boje and many others who have remained true to their soldierly duty under the pressure of Soviet captivity naturally find such an interpretation grotesque. They remain rightly perplexed and outraged by how von Seydlitz–Kurzbach, an officer who had clearly benefited from the NS state, could suddenly transfer his loyalties to the enemy. Moreover, the way the Red Army behaved as it entered Prussia and in the aftermath of the fall of Berlin, the mass deportation of Germans from Poland and Czechoslovakia, and the forcible imposition of communist regimes on states after the Nazi occupation can only have confirmed the Boje view that von Seydlitz–Kurzbach and other senior officers were thoroughly dishonorable opportunists who knew what was coming and wanted to secure the best possible position for themselves in postwar Germany.

Stalins deutsche Agenten as a Contribution to Camp Literature

The primary value of Boje's memoir inheres in the author's account of his capture at Stalingrad, the attempts by the NKVD to attract senior officers to the BND, and Boje's interrogation and subsequent sentencing as a war criminal. Regardless, *Stalins deutsche Agenten* deserves to be seen as a major contribution to the genre of camp literature, whether the camp was a Nazi concentration camp or a Soviet forced-labor camp. Boje, the former police officer (and possibly for that reason), shows himself to be an astute observer of the way men and women behave under stress. One of the striking changes noted by Boje as men transit from being part of an army, a cohesive hierarchical body, to captivity is the psychological dislocation caused by capture, what can be called capture shock. In Solzhenitsyn's work this is the moment of arrest, the nighttime removal by the NKVD. For some German soldiers there remains the option of suicide rather than enduring Soviet captivity. Boje writes that he admires the standpoint of those who opt for suicide and that he rejects any criticism of their action based on religious or other grounds. For himself and the others who reject this catastrophic solution, he gives the reasons:

> In our weak bodies some faint hope glimmered that there would still some other way out, to escape with our lives even in captivity.[55]

Religion appears as an important theme in this book: the celebration of Christmas in the Kessel, the role of bread, and the longing for meaning in the aftermath of defeat. One asks: How are these German soldiers, like Boje, to reconcile religious faith with the ambitions of the Nazis and the Vernichtungskrieg?

Transiting through the various camps, Boje presents a gallery of individuals, including many non-Russians who have been caught up in the Soviet penal system. The Italians, German allies, form a tightly knit group held together by their faith and the remarkable ministrations of Father Brevi, a Jesuit priest. Boje notes the same group cohesion among Japanese prisoners. He praises their demeanor and self-discipline. From his own observations and those of others, Boje concludes that the Japanese represent their nation in a way that is superior to the prisoners of all other nationalities in Soviet captivity. In one of the camp hospitals he encounters a German woman, a Volksdeutsche, who married a Russian. Before the war she was repatriated to Pommern. When the Red Army occupied the area she was deported to the Soviet Union, and her children were taken away from her. In the arrival of one group of young girls and their teachers from a Lyceum class in Reval, we see evidence of the post-1945 Sovietization policies of territories reoccupied by the Red Army:

> They were attractive fair-haired girls, well dressed and certainly from a higher social stratum, who had been shipped here because of their alleged political machinations by the "liberators" of the Baltic States.[56]

Boje is right to fear the worst for these girls in the appalling circumstances of the Soviet camps, where they would be vulnerable to all kinds of sexual predators.

Many of Boje's observations and experiences in the camps confirm those that appear in the works of famous Russian writers, especially as they concern orphaned children and professional criminal elements. For example, Boje is struck by the fact that the criminals love to hear stories, the theme of one of Shalamov's sketches in *Kolyma Tales*. The favorite story is *Le Comte de Monte-Cristo* (*The Count of Monte Cristo*, 1844) by Alexandre Dumas.[57] Boje explains their reaction in terms that could easily be construed as culture shock. To quote Boje:

> The effect, especially on the young criminals, was stunning. I had the impression that for these uneducated people it was not merely a question of the sensation alone. I think they were driven by a need for knowledge,

> like primitive peoples who for the first time have come into contact with a higher culture and sophisticated civilization.[58]

Yet, this need for stories, for the fantastic and unbelievable, is by no means confined to the uneducated criminal stratum of Russia. In his time in Vorkuta, Boje encounters a Dr. Beck, who, according to his own account, was a lawyer in Berlin and who for various unspecified reasons was arrested by the Soviet occupation authorities in Berlin, ending up in Vorkuta. As it turns out, Beck is a fantasist but an astonishing storyteller who entrances his listeners with his adventures and accounts of far-flung places. Even well-educated listeners with highly developed critical faculties succumb to Beck's stories. Beck's success as a storyteller is based on the circumstances of captivity. People want to be distracted from their present; they want to suspend disbelief. In a sense they collude with the storyteller. The other aspect to Beck's success relates to the circumstances of information deprivation that obtain in the camps. In such circumstances the fantasist has an advantage, which might also explain why rumors are so readily believed when they are taken as the sole source of news from outside. Thus, rumors circulate that the American fleet has entered the Black Sea and bombarded the coast; that a plane seen circling overhead is an American reconnaissance plane. To quote Boje:

> One simply cannot imagine the sorts of confusing thoughts that spin around in the heads of people thousands of kilometers away from their homelands, with practically no thought of the desperately desired return home and leading a prisoner's existence. These are thoughts the same as hallucinations similar to the fata morgana in the wastelands. I myself have succumbed to imaginings so crazy that I would be too embarrassed to write them down.[59]

The Soviet authorities who control the flow of news and information circulating in the camps are also storytellers. Their story is not one of fantastic adventures but an ideological narrative—a just and noble struggle of the Soviet people against the evil invaders—that they seek to impose on the prisoners so that they can be co-opted to serve Soviet interests. The Beck phenomenon confirms the longevity of the powerful and basic drive to tell stories and to listen to them and, depressingly, the fact that large numbers of human beings, apparently regardless of educational level, can, in certain circumstances, be persuaded to accept just about any ideological or political narrative, even more so when the narrative is directly or indirectly supported by some authority source. Soviet success, albeit the methods were far harsher, in attracting German officers to work for the BDO and NFD anticipates the results of the famous experiment conducted by Stanley Milgram and the less well-known one carried out by Solomon Asch on opinion forming and social pressure.

The Milgram experiment is well known, and its conduct and conclusions require no comment. In the Asch experiment nine men were shown a straight line marked on a card. They were then shown a second card marked with three lines of varying lengths. They were asked to identify which of the three lines was the same length as the single line on the first card. The experiment is repeated until one of the volunteers finds himself disagreeing with all the other volunteers. What he does not know is that his selection of the line is correct but that the other volunteers have been briefed to give the wrong answer. The aim of the experiment is to see how the lone individual who has chosen the correct line will respond to group pressure to conform. To conform, he must give the incorrect answer. The individual, as Asch notes, now finds himself caught between two opposing forces: "the evidence of his senses and the unanimous opinion of a group of his peers. Also, he must declare his judgements in public, before a majority which has also stated its position publicly."[60] Asch repeated this experiment at three higher-education institutions. The data are remarkable. When individuals were not under pressure, errors in comparison occurred less than 1 percent of the time. Under group pressure, the rate of errors leaped to 36.8 percent. Even those individuals who suspected that the others who went along with the pressure to give incorrect answers were sheep, they themselves still went along with the scam rather than rebel. Asch made other findings. He noted that some individuals saw their difference from others as a shortcoming and one that must be hidden. Moreover, it was found that those individuals, perhaps something of a misnomer, who did conform underestimated the rate at which they conformed. "That we have found," Asch concluded, "the tendency to conformity in our society so strong that reasonably intelligent and well-meaning young people are willing to call white black is a matter of concern."[61] If such levels of conformity could be achieved in the Asch experiment in the pleasant and benign circumstances of an American university in the 1950s, the pressures on German prisoners in NKVD-controlled camps would have been immeasurably greater, especially with subjects already habituated to years of military discipline and operating in a hierarchical organization.

Some part of the reaction to isolation from the outside world and brainwashing can be seen in the greater awareness of the natural world. The narrative of nature asserts itself in descriptions of the passage of seasons and the beauties of the wilderness. Boje's memoir contains many references to natural phenomena: the cold, clear night sky; the northern lights; a thunderstorm and a fire in the steppe; and the vastness of Russian forests. The prisoner who can perceive these treasures among the trials of the camp can be strengthened and inured to his plight. Quite apart, however, from its beauty, the natural world has another advantage. For the prisoner subjected to ideological and propagandistic processing, the natural world provides confirmation of objective standards and eternal truths, a refuge from the bombardment of lies.

Conclusion

The Soviet case against Oberst Boje is not a compelling one. From the moment of his capture the NKVD and later the SMERSH investigators worked on a presumption of guilt, along the lines of "the guilty man will receive a fair trial—well, a trial at any rate." The diary extracts cited by the FSB provide no evidence of war crimes. Certainly they are evidence of martial jubilation, *Siegesrausch*, as the Wehrmacht rolled up the Red Army and captured large numbers of Soviet prisoners in the summer of 1941. It is a reasonable assumption that if there were really incriminating evidence in the diary and photos—evidence that could directly and unequivocally be attributed to Oberst Boje—the FSB would have cited it in order to remove any doubts and to silence potential objectors. The corpses of Red Army soldiers and shelled buildings are not per se evidence of war crimes; they could be merely the evidence of war in all its horrors. Nor do the witness statements of Boje's fellow Germans inspire confidence in their veracity or accuracy. It is highly unlikely that Unteroffizier Paul Suchitsch, a cook NCO, would have been in a position to have seen the deeds he claims to have to seen. His rank is also a matter of dispute. Boje refers to him as an NCO. On a first mention the FSB account gives his rank as an *Unteroffizier* (corporal); he is later referred to as an *Oberleutnant* (first lieutenant). Major Pohl's testimony may or may not be true, and no details of any attempt by Boje to challenge Pohl are given. As for Dr. Suchanek, his testimony relies on hearsay and rumor and is hardly credible. The problem with all the witnesses is the degree to which they were subjected to coercion and pressure by the NKVD and SMERSH case officers, themselves under pressure to get results. In the harsh conditions of captivity, food is the lever that can make most men do things they would not normally do.[62] Add to this the ideological and propagandistic assault to which the prisoners were subjected, and their testimony starts to look very unreliable. The final hearing—the troika—is a mechanistic procedure dating back to the early days of the Soviet Union and used throughout Stalin's Great Terror. It is explicitly designed to expedite the speedy condemnation and punishment of prisoners in the cause of revolutionary and party justice. The revolutionary troika is not concerned with the forensic analysis of detail and statements with the view to getting the truth, as must be quite clear from the procedure used against Boje. Recall the cynical response to Boje's wish to have the evidence of the widow challenged in the hearing: "One doesn't lie in the Soviet Union."

Boje was repatriated to Germany in January 1956 as a nonamnestied war criminal with a request from the Soviet authorities that he be questioned with regard to the accusations against him and that the relevant files be considered by a competent court in his permanent domicile. Boje and all other returning prisoners were questioned by representatives of the Foreign Ministry. In an interim memorandum dated 24 January 1956 it was noted that "an initial, to be sure somewhat superficial examination of the cases that was initiated after the arrival of the nonamnestied prisoners in Friedland or in Hannoversch-Münden has revealed that by far the biggest part of these nonamnestied prisoners have committed no crimes or misdemeanors in the context of German laws."[63] All the nonamnestied prisoners were interviewed by the legal office of the German Red Cross concerning their sentences, and a report was submitted to the Foreign Ministry. As far as one can tell, no action was taken against Boje because the initial assessment of the Foreign Ministry report was upheld.

Oberst Arthur Boje enjoyed a remarkable military career. In two world wars he proved himself to be an outstanding soldier. His military record and decorations speak for themselves. His military career is also a complete military career in ways that the careers of most professional soldiers cannot be. Boje knew the bitter taste of defeat and the humiliation of captivity, and what as far as I can see are unjust accusations that he was a war criminal—and, of course, he also knew the heady days of German Army glory in World War II. Unless and until the FSB places all the material it holds in the public domain, the full truth of the Boje case may never be known. In the absence of full and complete disclosure, there are clearly problems in assessing the strength of the case against Boje. So the task is to filter what evidence is available and to try to arrive at some conclusion. The notes and the photos that, according to the Soviet version, were found on Boje at the time of his capture were a gift to his captors. Even if, as I have argued, the material placed in the public domain by the FSB provides no evidence of war crimes carried out on the orders of Boje or by Boje himself, the material made it much easier for the NKVD and SMERSH to make a case. I say "make a case" quite deliberately. By the time of Boje's capture in January 1943 the Soviet security agencies were experts in the process of fabricating cases against those deemed to be enemies of the regime. That is not to say that there were not war criminals who deserved to punished but that the Soviet legal and security system in the Lenin and Stalin years operated on the principle of "*les rubiat—shchepki letiat*" (literally, "cut down trees and chips fly," or, as we would say in English, "you can't make an omelet without breaking an egg").[64] Operationally, and catastrophically for many millions, this meant that guilt was determined by notions of class war rather than by any objective standards. For Boje and other German prisoners suspected of war crimes in the circumstances of the Great Fatherland War, this also meant that any presumption of innocence until proven guilty, a policy never much respected in Soviet jurisprudence in any case, was jettisoned in favor of likely to be guilty and almost certainly not innocent.

10 Reconciliation

I never heard anything again from any of my comrades in the Kessel. Were they killed in battle; did they freeze, starve, or perish in captivity? The same things could have happened to me. The tragedy of Stalingrad and the uncertain fate of my comrades have been a psychological burden all my life. Fate decreed that I survived. Otherwise, today, my name would be inscribed on a block of granite at Rossoschka: Johannes Petzold, year of birth 1918.

—Johannes Petzold, *Namen für Rossoschka—Schicksale aus Stalingrad*

In these concluding remarks I examine the work of the German War Graves Commission in formally identifying and burying the remains of German soldiers posted as killed and missing at Stalingrad. I then turn to the themes of good and evil, which two former enemies explore in a drawing and an essay, respectively: the famous *Stalingrad-Madonna* (1942) by Kurt Reuber and *Sikstinskaia Madonna* (*The Sistine Madonna*, 1989) by Vasilii Grossman.

Stalingrad, especially the uncertainty concerning the fate of loved ones, continued to blight the lives of the relatives of German soldiers long after the end of World War II. Wives, children, mothers, fathers, brothers, and sisters, desperate for news—any news—tried with varying degrees of success to ascertain the fate of soldiers posted as killed or missing. The role played by the Deutsches Rotes Kreuz (German Red Cross, DRK) and Die Deutsche Dienststelle für die Benachrichtigung der nächsten Angehörigen von Gefallenen der ehemaligen deutschen Wehrmacht (the official german agency for the notification of the next of kin of those killed in the former German armed forces) was exemplary. Among these searches, played out against the background of the Cold War, and frequently subjected to its priorities, there are some success stories, but for the most part it is a story, or many stories, of fruitless searches and waiting in vain. Some idea of what this meant is reflected in the title of Arno Surminski's book *Vaterland ohne Väter* (*Fatherland without Fathers*, 2004).

A remarkable and moving development in these individual quests for news has been the patient diplomacy and unceasing efforts of the Volksbund Deutsche Kriegsgräberfürsorge, the German War Graves Commission, not only to find, to exhume, and to rebury the remains of German soldiers killed in the battle but also to reconcile the two former enemies. The commission's real opportunity came in 1991 with the collapse of the Soviet Union. Negotiations, not always easy by any means, were conducted with the authorities in both Volgograd and Moscow. Some Russians did not want work to begin until after the fiftieth anniversary of the end of the Great Fatherland War in 1995, and other Russians expressed anger that a special site was to be created for German war dead but nothing for Russian war dead. The German War Graves Commission therefore proposed to create a Russian cemetery adjacent to the German one.

The eventual location selected for the new cemetery-memorial site was the former Wehrmacht burial ground close to the village of Rossoschka, 30 kilometers (19 miles) and slightly northwest of Volgograd. The German memorial site is a series of granite blocks, 140 in all, on which are inscribed the names of all German soldiers killed or missing or who died in captivity. The formal inauguration of the cemetery took place on 15 May 1999. The German War Graves Commission also had a memorial erected to the villagers of the two villages, Malaia and Bol'shaia Rossoschka, who were listed as killed and missing. Tracking down the names of soldiers was severely hampered by the fact that many of the identity tags had been stolen and sold as black-market souvenirs (apparently there is a thriving market for them). By February 1999, however, the names of some 150,000 German soldiers listed as killed and wounded had been recorded in a memorial collection, *Gesamtnamenbuch Wolgograd-Rossoschka* (Complete Book of Names Volgograd-Rossoschka). On 9 September 2006 there was an opening ceremony to mark the laying of the first 107 blocks. This official opening of the first phase of the Rossoschka cemetery-memorial site attracted some 400 visitors, the bulk of whom were relatives of the killed and missing.

The reactions of surviving relatives and veterans to the Rossoschka site underline just how deeply the experiences of Stalingrad, directly and indirectly, have marked post-1945 Germany, probably more than any other defeat suffered by the Wehrmacht in World War II. Indeed, the full impact is clearly and very movingly revealed in an outstanding collection of reminiscences, personal experiences, and family letters to and from the Kessel published by the German War Graves Commission under the heading *Namen für Rossoschka—Schicksale aus Stalingrad* (Names for Rossoschka—fates from Stalingrad, 2008).

Namen für Rossoschka rescues German soldiers from ideological oblivion. German soldiers who were killed or listed as missing at Stalingrad emerge not as the Nazi automata of Allied propaganda but as men with wives and children. One reason why the experiences of soldiers and families recorded in *Namen für Rossoschka* are so compelling is because the collection deals with the almost unbearable disruption inflicted on German families, as on all families caught up in a global war. In reading *Namen für Rossoschka* we, the former enemies of Germany in World War II, recognize our own losses and the suffering shared in common, whatever the righteousness of the cause. An extract from *Namen für Rossoschka* illustrates the point. Karin Bohl recollects her father's last leave and his day of departure for Stalingrad. He was reported missing in December 1942.

> The closer the day of departure, the more unsettled and sadder my father became. Then the day of departure arrived. I was going to the kindergarten and my brother to school. We went into our yard and looked up at the open window in which my father was standing. He was crying. I could see a tear fall from above onto the roof above the house door. I never saw my father again. He remained in Stalingrad. But I've never forgotten that last tear.[1]

In conditions of total war, during a life-and-death struggle, it seems scarcely relevant whether enemy civilians suffer the loss of loved ones, whether their sons or fathers live or die. After the war it matters very much because grief softens and renders the human heart open to guilt, to the acknowledgment of complicity and responsibility and the possibility of moral redemption and reconciliation. A former enemy who is denied the chance publicly to grieve because he is always taunted with reminders that he was the aggressor or because of the application of misguided notions of collective guilt is cruelly denied the chance to regain his full humanity. Moreover, the process of internal reconciliation, as important in the healing process as it is between nations, cannot run its course if one group—in Germany, for example—dictates that there is something improper or ideologically dubious in acknowledging that Germans were also victims of the NS regime and of the war in general and its aftermath, and that their fellow Germans must remain in something like a permanent state of shame. This tendency is revealed in an interview with Guido Knopp, the series narrator and a historian in his own right, attached to Sebastian Dehnhardt's generally excellent *Stalingrad* trilogy.

In the course of this interview Knopp goes so far as to assert that Stalingrad was a war crime ("*ein Kriegsverbrechen per se*" [a war crime in itself]), in effect turning all soldiers of 6th Army into potential war criminals. War crimes were committed by members of 6th Army at Stalingrad and also by the Red Army, but the German investment of Stalingrad was not a war crime (*Kriegsverbrechen*) per se but an operation of war (*Kriegsunternehmen*). This is a critical distinction. Both NS-Germany and the Lenin-Stalin state were odious, totalitarian regimes. But even odious, totalitarian regimes have the right, in common with all states, to wage war. *Jus ad bellum* is not exlusively the legal instrument of liberal democracies.

As a former soldier, I admire military prowess and professionalism. The manner in which German 6th Army fought and perished—the German words *Untergang* or *Überbewältigung* strike me as a more precise characterization than the English "defeat"—inspires admiration. If Winston Churchill, during some of the darkest days of early 1942, could pay tribute in the House of Commons to the outstanding generalship of Generalfeldmarschall Erwin Rommel, then seventy years after the German collapse at Stalingrad, recognition of the soldierly virtues of German 6th Army is perfectly in order. Indeed, such recognition is demanded by historical objectivity and fully consistent with it.[2]

Military historians should perhaps confine their judgments to matters temporal, to the raw material of history—facts, data, numbers, divisions, units, operations, tactics, and critical thresholds—and leave ruminations spiritual and theological to theologians. That said, the human experience of Stalingrad—German, Soviet, Russian, Italian, Romanian, Croatian, civilian, and soldier—cannot grasp the nature of what occurred without recourse to what one might call incorporeal factors. The problem is further complicated by the fact that the boundaries between good and evil or right and wrong are blurred and overlap. German 6th Army was the aggressor: it was the army of a regime whose purposes were conquest, extermination, and exploitation. The military successes of formations such as 6th Army created huge rear areas of occupation in which, away from prying eyes, Hitler's extermination squads perfected and carried out their plans of murder and genocide. German 6th Army was an accessory to these campaigns, an indirect instrument of terror. Yet the Soviet Union also perpetrated genocide: the Holodomor in the early 1930s. It invaded Finland, and under the provisions of the Soviet-German Non-Aggression Pact it forcibly annexed the Baltic States of Lithuania, Estonia, and Latvia. On 17 September 1939 the Red Army invaded Poland. Six months later, beginning in March 1940, at Katyn and other sites, the NKVD systematically murdered 21,857 Poles deemed to be incorrigible class enemies. During the war the NKVD, acting on Stalin's orders, deported from their homelands very large numbers of Soviet minorities deemed to be potential enemies. In fact, one of the first in a series of major war time deportations struck the Stalingrad district in 1941 when 7,170 families comprising 26,245 people were deported.[3] Over the period of 3–20 September 1941, a staggering total of 376,717 people were deported from the Volga region.[4] These NKVD prophylactic security deportations clearly anticipate the identical measures carried out by the German occupation forces in Stalingrad. After Berlin fell the Red Army engaged in an orgy of mass rape, using it as a weapon to terrorize the civilian population and to degrade German women. Are all former members of the NKVD, SMERSH, and the Red Army deemed to be guilty of these crimes? Or is the notion of collective guilt to be applied only to the vanquished?

On the questions of good and evil and human behavior in war and what one might call the ineffable zone, by which I mean the zone of human behavior that cannot easily be apprehended by rational means, two Stalingrad veterans, one German, the other a Soviet writer, sought to make some sense of the experiences of war, and Stalingrad in particular, by recourse to the madonna and child. The first interpretation is represented in Kurt Reuber's famous *Stalingrad-Madonna*, which Reuber, a medical officer in 16th Panzer Division, sketched for his fellow soldiers during Christmas 1942 inside the Kessel. Since 1983 the drawing has been housed in the Kaiser Wilhelm Memorial Church in Berlin. The second interpretation is derived from Grossman's short essay *Sikstinskaia Madonna* (*The Sistine Madonna*, 1989), which the author wrote in 1955 after he had visited an exhibition of Raphael's paintings in the Pushkin Museum.

Reuber's madonna and child drawing (charcoal on paper) is a mixture of light and darkness. The faces of the child and mother are bathed in light, yet dark areas are ubiquitous. The mother's unusually large right hand rests behind the child's head. The overall effect of this drawing evokes a womb, a place of refuge and safety. Are we to see the Kessel, or parts of it, as a safe haven? The drawing with its caption of "Light, Life, and Love," a reference to the Gospel of Saint John, is a bittersweet reminder for German soldiers of what they are missing, the longing for home and hearth. The sketch captures the terrible vulnerability of the mother and child, and of the German soldiers inside the Kessel. It is an appeal for God's protection. In word and image, light seems to dominate: light to grasp the meaning of their predicament; light as the basis of life and love. The emphasis on light at this time of year—

the winter solstice has just occurred—hints at some ritual long predating Christianity. The passing of the shortest day of the year heralds the beginning of the end of darkness, the return to light, life, and love, to rebirth. It is therefore a restatement of an eternal cycle, and within that the binary oppositions that characterize and drive human action: light and darkness, life and death, love and hate, good and evil, and war and peace. Without darkness, there is no light; death cannot exist without life, nor love without hate, and what is war without peace? Theoretically these distinctions are conveniently precise and to that extent misleading. They are convenient shorthand. Reuber, the theologian, apprehends that in the middle of life there is death; that love and hate are not so easily separated; that in light there is shadow; that even in the darkest night, light finds a refuge. The mother's visage is not directed at the onlooker; her eyes appear closed, as if she reflects on the fate that awaits her Son. Yet we feel her gaze and the terrible anxiety she feels for the child. "Why hast thou come here?"—she asks the German soldiers—"Why hast thou laid waste the Russian lands with fire and sword?"

I suggest that the full significance of Reuber's *Stalingrad-Madonna* can be grasped only in conjunction with his other sketches made on the Eastern front, especially those of children. His sketches of Russian adults confront us—by "us" I mean Westerners—with something that is at once incomprehensible yet at the same time overwhelmingly familiar. Reuber's Russian portraits are insights into a type of human suffering that Westerners have no means to measure or to judge. It is not just the misery and suffering of the war; it is the war that the Soviet regime has waged against its own people. In a letter to Friedrich Heiler, his theology teacher, dated 31 August 1941, Reuber pulls no punches about what has befallen the Soviet people under communism:

> Everything that one would never dare to believe is surpassed in the naked shattering facts. . . . These day-to-day experiences are so depressing that one is often driven to the abyss of nothing. What a flood of blood and tears of terror of the soul and body have passed over these lands. There is hardly a house where the monster has not celebrated his orgies. Where is the person to be found? This is a people without any human dignity.[5]

Contemplating Reuber's portraits of little boys and girls is almost unbearable. These children have seen and experienced things that no little boy or girl should ever have to see or to experience. We see it in their young, wise eyes:

little Nina, Klava, Shura, and Alexandra, and above all in the all-knowing gaze of little Natasha. Contemplating Reuber's portraits, we can at least grasp the truly demented and satanic creeds according to which these people were regarded as less than human or, during the Holodomor, as class enemies to be exterminated. Nor are the Soviet and Nazi regimes the sole purveyors of misery. Reading Reuber's account of how he protected and consoled a terrified little Nina during a bombardment, I, *waschechter* Englishman, was forced to remember that little German boys and girls, also innocent of any wrongdoing, were similarly terrified and killed when German cities, Hamburg and Dresden among them, were incinerated and subjected to the full force of total war. I am well aware of the rational military justification for these raids, but nevertheless I cannot shake off a sense of shame or remove a splinter of guilt.

Reuber's Madonna is an expression of reconciliation. The drawing talks to former foes and friends, acknowledging the suffering shared by all in war. In my opinion, however, the reconciliation theme extends beyond mastering the pain of war. Reuber's madonna and his letters home accept that in this world wars come and go; that innocents, frequently children, will suffer. For example, in a letter to his wife that he wrote while in Soviet captivity (25 December 1943), Reuber dwells on the words of Franz Marc, who was killed in World War I. Marc wrote that "every one of us has a great longing for peace. But what do the majority conceive in conditions of peace? They pursue conditions once again inimical to peace!"[6]

Vasilii Grossman, the great chronicler of Stalingrad and Soviet totalitarianism, readily concedes that the word "immortal" is overused in relation to many works of art but admits that he can find no other single word that can encapsulate Raphael's *Madonna*. The power of the painting, Grossman argues, inheres in its impact on all people and the longevity of this impact. That so many people of all classes and groups have viewed this painting and that they can react to it suggests a common humanity that transcends individual wickedness. (I wonder whether Grossman ever considered that this notion of common humanity might equally apply to Stalin, Eichmann, and the Katyn murderers.) Grossman also stresses the huge changes that have taken place since the painting was created: the rise and fall of European empires; the publication of Newton's *Principia*, Galileo's *Discorsi*, and Einstein's "On the Electrodynamics of Moving Bodies." Yet the painting speaks to all new generations. Grossman identifies what he sees as the secret of the painting and its power:

> In his *Madonna* Raphael has revealed the secret of maternal beauty. But this is not the source of the inexhaustible life of Raphael's painting. It consists in the fact that the body and face of the young woman are her soul because the madonna is so beautiful. In this visual representation of the maternal soul there is something that cannot be apprehended by human consciousness.[7]

Every age that views Raphael's *Madonna* sees its own age and its own suffering: the madonna weeps as her child is starved to death in the Holodomor; as children are separated from their mothers in the Great Terror, are orphaned in war, and perish in the ghettos and gas chambers of the Holocaust. Yet the painting builds bridges to times past and times to come. To quote Grossman: "Man recognizes himself, his cross, and suddenly understands the extraordinary connection of the ages, the link with what lives today, with everything that was and that has expired and with everything that will be."[8] Reuber's *Stalingrad-Madonna* and Raphael's *Madonna* return us to the past and point to the future. Both works seem to be inside and outside time, and timelessness and eternity mesmerize mortal human beings. Westerners can ponder the work of Reuber and Raphael and reflect on the nature of time and suffering. Russians can ponder something incomparably greater than these two works of art. Surrounded by steppe, the great Volga is not just the symbolism and substance of time. Forever flowing, she remains the omniscient witness, washing away the sins of the invader and soothing the hurts of Mother Russia.

APPENDIX A: FINNISH EXPERIENCE IN THE TRAINING OF SNIPERS

The original document was written in Finnish and then translated into German for circulation among German units on the Eastern front. It is a detailed analysis of the methods used by Soviet snipers. My translation into English is based on the German translation. The archive reference is BA-MA, RH 68/1. All emphasis is in the original.

Ref: Sniper Training 8 May 1943

I. Training and Deployment of Enemy Snipers

On the basis of statements made by deserters and from captured enemy manuals, the following general points about the enemy sniper, and from our point of view about defensive measures, can be made.

Individual Qualities of the Sniper

Regarding his psychological qualities as well as his physical performance, the sniper must be a first-class soldier. Only a steadfast individual, and one who is utterly determined, suits the role of a sniper.

In the *assault* the sniper's place is some 10–15 meters behind the fire control position, his mission to lie in wait for enemy officers as well as for the gunners of light and standard machine guns.

In the defense his place is either on the ground or in a tree, better still on the boundary lines of the front sector, respectively, on the open flanks, and his mission is to destroy enemy leaders and soldiers entrusted with special tasks who are momentarily visible.

As part of patrols, the sniper's place is in the middle of the patrol, and his mission consists in supporting the security units. In any battle he withdraws a bit to the rear in order better to be able to select his targets.

Snipers always operate *in pairs*. One of the snipers is responsible for observation with a telescope and estimating distances; the other shoots. They remain in visual and hand-signal contact with one another and are supported by ordinary riflemen. Their alternative positions, of which there are *many*, are about 20 meters removed from the actual fire positions. The center point in these positions is determined by the field of fire and the opportunities for camouflage. Regarding fire nests in trees, the enemy seeks out thick, bushy ones that offer cover from view.

In order to be able to determine the nature of the situation and to acquire enemy targets by isolated, often insignificant signs, the sniper must possess a highly developed gift for observation and be highly alert. According to one account, a sniper was able to discover his enemy in winter by signs of his breathing behind a stone or bush, and another specifically, because the latter had dropped crumbs that birds picked up under the tree.

The sniper, particularly in the defense, must evince patience and tenacity. Since the enemy conducts himself in an especially cautious manner, he must often lie in wait for hours on end in the hope that an enemy observer will give himself away in the observation slit of a fire position or in the trench by a careless movement. The battle with the enemy is a battle of endurance where the decisive factor is who makes the first careless movement or who fires too soon.

The necessary skill in the exploitation of terrain and independent, exceptionally rapid behavior adapted to changing conditions presuppose a thorough tactical training among snipers. In all situations he must be able to decide for himself which enemy targets are to be dealt with first. He must often rely exclusively on himself and must fight without any direct link with his command post.

Snipers require special training in the art of concealment. A well-developed training in the use of shooting tables and in the use of improved methods of calculating and sketching is especially necessary for the sniper.

Finally, the value of a willing dedication to his work with all its laws [?] and exertions is particularly highlighted, for which propaganda in the papers on and behind the front line will be made. Decorations and rewards are issued for a definite number of "kills." Mind you, this propaganda is very optimistic in its evaluation of the performances and successes of snipers, who in all truth and in no way have achieved the results claimed.

Situation and Replacement of Snipers

Taking into account that the protracted battle, often in severe conditions, requires a high level of psychological and physical performance, the clothing, rations, and time for the sniper to recuperate must be especially generous.

The training of new snipers should be entrusted to experienced snipers and, indeed, on days when the latter are free of any operational duties.

Snipers and Reconnaissance

On reconnaissance, snipers are merely to be deployed on their own task. It is by far the most expedient to allocate them to large reconnaissance patrols and, to be sure, in pairs.

When the reconnaissance patrol withdraws, both the snipers follow the main group and lie in wait for remote targets. At times it has proved itself expedient to deploy the snipers as an intermediate patrol in the same direction from which one expects the enemy to appear. In this way they can support the activities of the head of the patrol, clearing the way ahead for them.

In battle, the snipers take up positions from which they can cover the development of the battle by the main group. The one sniper destroys individual enemy targets; the other silences enemy machine-gun nests.

After preliminary assessment of the terrain, snipers change their positions one after another, thus deceiving the enemy.

When breaking contact with the enemy, both snipers as well as other soldiers, armed with automatic weapons, can be deployed to provide cover. However, it must be noted that the use of automatic weapons will draw enemy fire on the snipers, and for that reason automatic weapons are to be set some way to the side.

Snipers in the Attack

In our own attacks snipers are primarily to be deployed for the destruction of those enemy targets that provide the biggest obstruction to our advance. This can be best accomplished when the snipers operate *on the flank*.

Snipers are to be briefed not only with their own deployment in the battle formation and its tasks in the advance and the assault but also with the overall mission of the formation.

In the assault the snipers are, primarily, to take out officers, fire controllers, and machine-gun and antitank-gun teams. Should it not be possible to silence the target, the snipers are to indicate the targets to machine-gun, mortar, and antitank crews by means of tracer and immediately change their position.

In an enemy counterattack, the division of work between the snipers is as follows: one destroys weapons, the other the enemy's manpower, primarily officers, automatic-weapon crews, and snipers. The activity of one's own assault troops should be supported by snipers. Accurate rifle fire in enemy embrasures makes it possible for the assault troops to break into the fire positions of the enemy.

Snipers in the Defensive Battle

The sniper's fire positions vary according to the situation and range. In a long-range battle, snipers are located on the switch lines; indeed, if necessary, they push farther forward. In a battle at shorter distances, they can also be located behind the forward line in the event that there is dominant ground.

II. Own Observations on Enemy Snipers

Concerning the activity of enemy snipers as well as the intensification of our own corresponding countermeasures, the following experiences have been noted.

Organization of Enemy Sniper Activity

Among the main factors for the effectiveness of enemy sniper activity is primarily the good weapon (rifle with telescopic sight) and secondarily the concentrated use of snipers, combined with the generous use of the same. Indeed, according to statements from prisoners, there exist sniper groups of a sniper company simply consisting of 3–5 (earlier 2 men), but it turns out that the rear formations place their snipers at the disposal of the frontline troops. Reserve units have also deployed their forces with the aim of destroying enemy targets in order thereby to win fame for their units. In such a way the enemy has put together fantastic achievements for its snipers, which, among other things, have been reflected in frontline newspapers.

As far as the massive deployment and the positions of snipers are concerned, then enemy sniper activity is not bound by any hard-and-fast rules. Most recently, snipers have been appearing in small groups (4 men), but each sniper has nevertheless his own position, which he abandons at a specific time, in order to move to another.

Snipers' Shooting Locations

The preconditions for sniping vary, naturally, according to the front sectors, but generally speaking one can say that the enemy adapts himself with exceptional skill to local conditions and always bears in mind that keeping his fire positions concealed is of the greatest importance in not attracting attention. Regarding the fire positions of enemy snipers, the following observations have been made.

The sniper normally waits in a well-camouflaged dugout or a covered position that is in contact with the trenches. Both open positions and dugouts are provided with one or several tiny shooting gaps. The sniper's face cannot be seen, and when he discharges a shot, only the slightest puff of snow can be seen in front of the shooting slit. The sniper does not fire directly out of the dugout but to the side of the actual line of fire in order to deceive the enemy or to provide himself with cover.

In one instance the snipers appeared to have been located in the rear of the dugout or of a covered fire position so that shooting occurred through the front part of the same. This assumption is confirmed by the fact that the sound of the discharge has not been detected.

If the sniper is set up in a trench, then he lies in wait through a tiny shooting slit in the embrasure, which is exceptionally difficult to find.

At times snipers lie in wait forward of the positions or behind the trenches, even, indeed, on the roofs of dugouts, in which case the gain of a superior field of fire in low-lying terrain has been of prime importance.

On moonlit nights, snipers in one direction in intervening ground have been discovered. Flares, to illuminate the area immediately to the front, have then been put up from our positions.

Ruined buildings offer snipers good fire positions, and the shooting occurs through the gaps in the roof and cellar. By removing a number of bricks in the walls, fire and observation slits have often been created.

Snipers have also hidden themselves in stacks of beams and piles of wood.

During last summer, several enemy snipers were shot down from trees, but in winter they have avoided tree positions.

The enemy's snipers appear to carry out their mission with exceptional patience and tenacity and have superb equipment at their disposal. This can be concluded from the fact that they have been able to spot the slightest movement at long distances and also that they confine themselves to carefully selected, certain, and visible targets. *Generally speaking, they seem to bother only with targets they are likely to hit.* Likewise, the coordination as well as the allocation of tasks among several snipers appears to be good. At times two snipers have lain in wait for the same target since it has happened that two men walking alongside one another have been hit. On one occasion our sniper had just taken aim at his opponent when another enemy sniper shattered his rifle. The sniper's accomplice not only busies himself with observation but also with deceiving the enemy. He uses every possible means to entice observers and sentries. Examples of this are cited below in the section titled "Deception."

Enemy snipers have used dumdum rounds. These make it more difficult to ascertain the firing point but make it easier for the enemy to identify the point of impact.

Period of Activity

Enemy sniper activity has been at its most active on sunny, clear days and in winter after snow has drifted, when fire and communication trenches are snowed up or have just been cleared. Likewise, the enemy's snipers have proved to be very active during light snowfall and at last light, and indeed, as our men demonstrate a lack of caution when moving about, the rifle fitted with a telescopic sight loses nothing in accuracy. They have also tried to exploit the careless movement of our men at mealtimes.

During daylight hours, the snipers have preferred morning and midday.

Shooting Distances and Performances

Determined by the width of the intermediate ground, the shooting ranges vary from 100 to 900 meters, but at times enemy snipers have even attempted shots at a range of 1,400 meters. The usual and most effective range is from 200 to 400 meters, but even at ranges from 600 to 700 meters, the accuracy has been quite good.

The readiness to engage moving targets and the rate of fire have also been good, which can be ascribed to the good training of the snipers and above all to the use of a rifle fitted with a telescopic sight. The rate of fire and the accuracy suggest that snipers who are located in houses are making use of special rests. Concerning the accuracy, the following examples may be cited:

At ranges from 200 to 400 meters, several periscopes and stereoscopes have been shot out.

A sniper let off three rounds one after another at a stone about 10 x 10 cm [4 x 4 inches), which had been placed in the observation slit.

On one occasion, as one of our machine-gun team commanders raised his hand over the snow wall in order to readjust an alarm wire, a sniper shot him in the hand at a range of 100 meters.

In an observation slit that had been bored with a stick, a sniper had several hits.

Various objects that our sentries raised above the trenches as a test were, as a rule, hit.

It has also happened that our observer watching through a periscope behind the snow wall has been shot at.

Deception

Enemy snipers have made use of, among others, the following methods of deception:

In order to accustom our men to carelessness, a position on our line has been maintained for 8 days.

The sniper's assistant has for some considerable period shoveled snow and afterward raised a helmet over the trench, or the sniper himself has placed a helmet in the trench of an open position in order to open fire from a different position.

Once, after an enemy sniper had crawled behind a stone, a dummy in full equipment was led back and forth.

In places, by means of heavy fire, the enemy has tried to unsettle our men and get them to give away their positions. With this in mind he has also shot off unusually long bursts of machine-gun fire.

The sniper has first zeroed his rifle at a certain distance, and only after *a few days* has he carried out very accurate application fire at the actual target.

Our Countermeasures

Most of the losses that are caused by enemy snipers can be attributed to *carelessness*, insufficient exploitation of the terrain by our troops, or the circumstance that our men either wear only dirty snow camouflage jackets and hats or no snow camouflage clothing at all in exposed terrain. Losses due to our own carelessness can be avoided, and therefore every soldier must be *compelled* to exploit all possible means in order to make the task of enemy snipers as difficult as possible.

The following countermeasures, among others, can be noted:

- Cautious movement and painstaking exploitation of terrain in dangerous areas
- The best possible camouflage
- Sufficiently deep fire and communications trenches
- *Warning signs* in trenches
- Poles across fire and communications trenches that make it necessary to bend the upper body when moving
- *The use of helmets*
- The use of clean and full snow camouflage suits in the front line
- Very careful selection as well as thorough digging in (with steel plates, sandbags, and so on) and camouflage of the fire positions
- Avoid unnecessary shooting in observation posts, various, tested deception methods
- Intensification of our own sniper activity, for example, by means of the temporary deployment of snipers from the reserves
- Freeing our snipers from all other duties and their continual further training, especially where it concerns accuracy of fire
- The planned operation of other arms of service against enemy snipers when they cannot be destroyed by our own snipers

APPENDIX B: TRANSLATION OF CHAPTER 18 ("THE DUEL") OF VASILII ZAITSEV'S MEMOIR

During the night our scouts dragged in a German prisoner in a sack. When interrogated, he let it be known that the German command had been seriously alarmed by the operations of our snipers. The head of the German sniper school, Major Konings, had flown in from Berlin and had been set the task of killing above all, in the words of the prisoner, the number-one Soviet sniper.

The divisional commander, Colonel Batiuk, was in a good mood.

"For our lads, this major will be easy"—he joked—"The Führer ought to have flown in himself. It would be a bit more interesting to hunt after that one. Is that right, Zaitsev?"

"Right enough, Comrade Colonel," I say. And I thought to myself that this is easy to say, but he is the head of the school, so it seems; a deadly enemy.

"Whatever, this supersniper must be destroyed"—the divisional commander said, now in a severe tone of voice—"But just make sure that you operate carefully. Use your brains."

Already, I had learned quickly how to figure out the signature of German snipers. From the way they fired and their camouflage I was able without much difficulty to distinguish the more experienced marksmen from the beginners, the cowards from the persistent and the resolute. However, the character of the head of the sniper school remained a mystery for me for a long time. Our day-to-day observations came up with nothing specific. It was difficult to say in which sector he was. In all probability, he changed his position frequently and was carefully seeking me out, as I was him.

Without calling off the search for the Berlin supersniper, I tried to analyze my best experience and the experience of my comrades so as to come up with a solid solution. Experience dictated that without the assistance of the lads in the trenches—the riflemen, machine gunners, engineers, and signalers—one could not count on success.

Frequently, after a German sniper had been discovered and his location had been determined, I would summon, let's say, a machine gunner and give him a telescope, and I myself would pick up the trench periscope. I would indicate the most visible object and start to direct the machine gunner's gaze according to various reference points. And at that moment when the machine gunner sees the German sniper and is convinced just how cunningly he is camouflaged, that machine gunner becomes your able assistant.

Source: Vasilii Zaitsev, *Za Volgoi zemli dlia nas ne bylo: Zapiski snaipera* (Moscow: DOSAAF, 1971), pp. 199–212.

An hour or two hours are spent on such a demonstration. A number of snipers reproached me: "Soldiers don't need this demonstration. If you need an assistant, the company commander will just issue the order, and any soldier will come to you as he is told." All that's true, but I am appealing to the soldier's heart, to his awareness, his conscience. And when we understand one another well enough, you derive a psychological reward and success.

Apart from that, when we are preparing dummy positions, setting up models, his use of camouflage gives me the chance to study each soldier, to find out who is capable of what. Another soldier, one sees, shows initiative, is bold, but is not suitable as an assistant. You cannot rely on such a soldier in a long struggle. After the first dangerous encounter he'll find a reason to leave you under the pretext of a more important matter. In essence, his reserves of courage are exhausted. One quite often comes across such characters among our novice snipers as well.

It is far more difficult to unravel the characters of the enemy snipers. One thing is clear to me: all of them are unyielding. I have found my way of dealing with them. You prepare a good puppet, locate it where it is not immediately visible, and begin to move it about. The puppet, like a man, must change its poses. Alongside the puppet is your well-camouflaged position. The enemy sniper fires a round at the puppet, but it remains "alive." And now we see the really determined character revealed. He fires a second shot and then gets ready to fire a third, but before the third shot he becomes the target.

Experienced enemy snipers occupy their positions under cover of fire and accompanied by two to three assistants. Confronted with such a "wolf," I pretend to be a novice, more accurately a simple soldier, and in such a way I undermine his vigilance, or I play jokes on him. So after a shot I show him the results of his shooting with the standard signs, as is done on the range during training. The German sniper quickly gets used to this target and ceases taking any notice of it. And as soon as his attention is distracted by other objects, I instantly occupy the place of the target. Several seconds are required for this. Throwing the target to one side, I catch the enemy sniper in the telescopic sight of my rifle.

I divide the process of discovering the target in the enemy camp into two stages. The first begins with a study of the enemy's defense. Then I find out where, when, and in what circumstances our soldiers were wounded. In this instance I get a great deal of help from the medics. They tell me where the wounded soldier was picked up. I go there and seek out any eyewitnesses, and from them I get all the details concerning how the soldier was wounded. On this basis, I can work out the enemy's fire plan. All this belongs to the first phase of determining where one must seek out the target. I call the second phase searching for the target. So as not to be picked up by the enemy sniper, I observe the territory with the help of the periscope or artillery telescope. For this sort of work the telescopic sights on the rifle or binoculars are unsuitable. Experience indicates that where the enemy was active but where one can observe no movement at all means that that is where the deadly predator is located. That is why I always tell my sniper friends that if you've not studied the situation or not talked with people: don't make a move. As a sniper, one needs to adhere to the principle expressed in the proverb: measure seven times, cut once. And in actual fact there is a lot of work required for a single shot. You have to acquire and study the enemy's character, study his strength, probe for his weak spots; only after that can you settle the matter with a single shot.

Success in observation can be achieved only by practical work on the ground. In a combat situation, these skills are not easily acquired. Every move onto the position must be secured by strict camouflage. A sniper who cannot observe from a camouflaged position is no longer a sniper, just a live target for the enemy.

You move out onto the forward edge of the battle area, camouflage yourself, lie like a stone. Observe, study the terrain, and draw a sketch indicating special objects on it. If during the process of observation you reveal yourself by some careless movement of your head and give yourself away to the enemy and don't manage to hide in time, remember, you have made a blunder. For your error you'll get a bullet in the head, yours alone. Such is a sniper's life.

This is why in the training of snipers I lay the main emphasis on remaining undetected and camouflage.

Every sniper has own tactics, methods; his own tricks and inventiveness. But all snipers, be they novices or experienced ones, must always remember that to your front there is a tactically mature, dynamic, resourceful, and extremely good rifle shot. He must be outthought, dragged into a complicated struggle, and so tied to the selected position. How is this to be achieved? Think up false moves, distract his attention, muddle your tracks, irritate him by deliberate movements, and tire out his powers of visual concentration. Even in a long-term system of defense I am against setting up a permanent sniper post. The sniper is a nomad; he appears suddenly where the enemy does not expect him. One must fight for the initiative in battle. Tricks alone will not give you the enemy if you lack the confidence to pay for these cunning twists by accurate and determined fire.

On one occasion in the area of the refrigeration plant in the location of the 6th Company's defense, the snipers Nikolai Kulikov and Galifan Abzalov did not notice any signs of life in the course of a whole day. They were sitting in a trench under a railway line. And it was only on the second day that they fixed some tinned food to a piece of rope and placed them in no-man's-land before daybreak. One end of the rope remained in the trench. The sun rose, and the tins started banging right under the noses of the Germans. They started to look out. First one head appeared, then a second. The snipers fired at each one. An hour later the whole process repeated itself. In such a way Kulikov and Abzalov had by evening knocked out a whole enemy section.

One time in a relatively quiet period, I met two snipers, Afinogenov and Shcherbina, among the ruins of the forward edge of the battlefield. They came toward me sluggishly. We greeted one another, left the track to one side, sat on a stone, and had a smoke.

"Where are you heading?"—I asked.

"To the company lines. The Germans are hiding, not showing anything; perhaps they are resting"—replied Shcherbina.

"There's no point in leaving"—I said—"this is a good time to register fire."

The lads agreed, and we set off to the area of the rifle ranges. Along the way it came to light that both of them had not once registered fire on possible targets. They did not see any point. They would simply head out among the ruins along the whole forward edge of the battle area and, having noted an enemy, would open fire. This frequently resulted in misses. It could not be anything different. You cannot determine the distance to the target at once, no available range data were prepared in advance, and the target appears for only a few seconds: hence the misses. You have to prepare several posts in advance, study well the terrain ahead, note the various orienting features, and determine the distance to them. Then in the quiet periods you'll have success as well.

We got to the factory settlement and went into a ruined building. My reserve position was here. I indicated to my comrades where the enemy strongpoints, machine-gun positions, heavy weapons set for firing over open sights, observation posts, and battle outposts were located and said—"As you can see, a sniper does not need to know that much about the enemy's defense. I come to the position, locate the necessary page in my notebook, make the necessary corrections in the fire plan, and wait for a suitable moment. For a well-trained sniper, it is sufficient that the target appears for a short while. In that time you have to line up, take aim, and fire off a shot without missing."

It was four o'clock in the afternoon.

"This is when the Germans have their dinner"—I said, turning to my comrades—"they're always on time."

And I pulled a piece of plywood from out of the trench wall. A fire plan was written on it. Over time several of the figures had faded. I got a piece of pencil and rewrote the numbers; then I set the necessary range, got ready for a shot, and waited. My comrades observed the enemy positions through the trench periscopes. We sat in silence, carefully following the enemy's movements. An hour passed. The passion and enthusiasm of my comrades started to weaken. They were bored by the monotony and wanted to move to another position to talk to the soldiers.

"Wait!"—I silenced them—"No talking in an ambush."

My friends were silent. Several minutes passed after that. A head appeared in the German trench. I fired at once. A German helmet landed on the parapet. From the trench, where the head had appeared, a digging tool started banging about. The second, surviving German was making his trench deeper.

On one occasion, I did not have the option of killing Germans of my choice. There would be times when I would see my old acquaintances through my optical sight. Observing the enemy's behavior was a passion of mine. So you'll see some puffed-up German officer, strutting about and trying to look important, who chases the soldiers about all over the place with imperious gestures. They carry out his will, wishes, and caprices to the letter. But he doesn't know that he has only seconds to live. I see his fine lips; even teeth; wide, heavy chin; and fleshy nose. At times I have the feeling that I have seized a snake by the head; that it wriggles, but my hand squeezes: and a shot rings out.

Among the snipers in our division, a rule has been established. We meet up in one of the bunkers and sum up the day's work, mull over our ideas, and report back any new changes in the enemy's tactics.

We made some calculations. In order to let off an aimed shot, a sniper requires ten seconds at most. So in a minute a sniper can fire off five rounds. To reload the rifle takes about twenty, thirty seconds. One can appreciate that over the period of a minute, ten snipers can kill fifty enemy soldiers. Among us snipers, Sasha Kolen'tev is considered to be the highest level of specialist. We respect him. We know that he has completed the course at the Moscow sniper school and knows the rules for using a sniper rifle with a telescopic sight inside out. And on one occasion he opened his gas-mask bag and emptied out ammunition, a grenade, a dirty piece of rag—known as a towel—then he took out a small package bound in leather, opened it up, and started to read out words to us, which I wrote down in my notebook: "The road to an accurate shot is a small path along the edge of a steep bank of a bottomless chasm. Setting out on a duel, every sniper is aware of tension, as if he stands on the edge of a stone on one leg alone. So as to hold out on the edge of the chasm on the sharp stone, one needs, it goes without saying, courage, training, calm, and cold-bloodedness. Such a feeling possessed me. The man who emerges as the victor of the duel is the one who first of all conquers himself."

So, weighing up and thinking about our experience, my comrades and I sought a way of bringing about a decisive duel with the supersniper from Berlin who so far had skilfully and cleverly outplayed us.

And on one of those days it happened that the German sniper smashed the optical sight of Morozov, a friend of mine from the Urals, and wounded Shaikin. Morozov and Shaikin were experienced snipers. They had emerged victorious in the most protracted and difficult situations. Now there could be no doubts: they had stumbled across the German supersniper, the one I was looking for.

At first light I set off with Nikolai Kulikov to the same positions where our comrades had been the day before. The familiar forward edge of the enemy's line, studied for days on end, lay in front of me; nothing new. The day was coming to a close. Suddenly a helmet unexpectedly appeared from a German trench and slowly moved along the line of the trench. Should I fire? No; this was a ruse. The helmet rocked about unnaturally. It almost certainly was being carried by the sniper's assistant, while the sniper himself waited in the hope that I would give myself away with a shot.

We sat in silence until darkness.

"Where can this damned sniper be camouflaged?"—asked Kulikov, as we under cover of darkness, left the ambush.

"That's the whole point"—I said.

"And what if he's not here? Perhaps he went ages ago?"—Kulikov expressed his doubts.

But by the patience shown by our enemy, who throughout the whole day had remained undetected, I somehow guessed that the Berlin sniper was here. Exceptional vigilance was required.

A second day passed. Whose nerves would prove to be the stronger? Who would outwit whom?

Nikolai Kulikov, my loyal frontline friend, was also enthusiastic about this duel. He no longer doubted that the enemy was in front of us and firmly believed in our success.

In the evening a letter from Vladivostok was waiting for me in the dugout. Comrades had written—"We've heard of your heroic exploits on the banks of the Volga. We're proud of you—our pupil."

I felt ill at ease. I felt like breaking the frontline custom and reading the letter alone. Our comrades write about "heroic deeds," and here this day you're hunting for one German without any real plan. ... But Kulikov and Medvedev butted in—"A letter from the Pacific Ocean, read it out!"

I had to read it.

It seemed that it was not the letter, but a wave from the Pacific Ocean washed into the bunker, arousing many dear memories. Then Viktor Medvedev said—"We have to write straight back. Write to them, Vasia, from all of us. Tell them that we won't shame our naval honor."

On the third day, Danilov, the *politruk*, accompanied us to the ambush.

The morning begins as usual. The nighttime gloom is dispersed, and with every minute the enemy's positions become more distinct.

Next to us a battle rages, shells whistle through the air, but using our optical equipment we keep a firm eye on what is happening to our front.

"There he is. I'll point with a finger!" exclaims the *politruk* suddenly. He barely, literally for a second, raises himself above the parapet, but that is enough. Fortunately, the bullet only wounds the *politruk*.

Of course, only an experienced sniper can shoot in such a way. I examine the enemy lines for a long time, but I cannot find the ambush position. Over many days I had already studied the forward edge of the enemy's lines so that I immediately noted any new crater, any new parapet that appeared. Now I can see nothing new or suspicious at all.

But given how quickly the shot was fired, I conclude that the sniper is somewhere in front of us.

I continue my observations. To the left is a knocked-out tank, to the right a pillbox. Is the German in the tank? No; an experienced sniper would not occupy that. In the pillbox? Again, no: the firing slit is closed.

Between the tank and the pillbox, on flat ground, just before the line of the German defense, is a sheet of iron with a small pile of bricks. It has been there for ages; it's a familiar sight. I put myself in the position of the enemy: Where's the best place for a sniper position? Why not dig out a slit trench under that sheet of metal? During the night prepare a hidden route to it?

Yes, in all probability, he's there, under the metal sheet, in no-man's-land.

I decide to test this. I place a mitten on a plank and raise it. The German takes the bait! Excellent! I carefully lower the board into the trench, into the same position from which I raised it. I examine the hole. There's no angle on this; it's a direct hit, which means that the German is under the sheet, precisely.

"The viper's there"—alongside me, Nikolai Kulikov's quiet voice carries from the ambush.

Now we have to entice him out, just the slightest edge of a head. There's no point in trying that now. He's hardly going to move out of that excellent position now. His character is now well known.

During the night we equip the post. We stay there until first light. The Germans maintain sporadic fire. Enemy mortars fire on the Volga crossing. Rockets soar into the sky. Later our artillery returns fire, and the German mortars fall silent. German bombers appear. The sun rises. Kulikov fires off a blind shot. We have to arouse the sniper's interest. We decide to sit out the first half of the day; light reflecting from our scopes could give us away. In the afternoon our rifles are in the shade while the direct light of the sun falls upon the German's position. Something sparkles by the edge of the sheet. Is this a piece of glass that just happens to be there, or is it the telescopic sight of a sniper's rifle?

Very carefully, as only the most experienced sniper would do, Kulikov starts to raise a helmet. The German fires. Kulikov raises himself for a brief moment, shouts loudly, and falls.

The German probably thinks that at last the Soviet sniper, the chief "hare" [in Russian Zaitsev's name suggests hare] for whom he had been hunting the last four days, has been killed and sticks half of his head out from under the sheet. I fire. The German's head sinks, and the optical sight of his rifle sparkles in the sunlight.

Kulikov lies on the bottom of the trench and bursts out laughing.

"Let's go"—I shout at him.

Nikolai gets a grip and crawls after me toward the reserve position, and the Germans pour down artillery fire onto our ambush position.

As soon as it got dark, our lads on this sector attacked the Germans. At the height of the battle Kulikov and I dragged the body of the dead German major out from under the iron sheet. We removed his documents and handed them over to the divisional commander.

"I was certain that you would bring this German bird down"—said Colonel Batiuk—"but there's another task for you, Zaitsev. Tomorrow a German offensive is expected on one sector. Chuikov has ordered that a group of the best snipers be put together and be used to disrupt the attack. How many lads have you got ready?"

"Thirteen men."

The divisional commander thought for a bit and then said—"So that means thirteen against hundreds. Can you cope?"

"We'll try"—I answered.

APPENDIX C

Memorandum of the Deputy of the People's Commissar of Internal Affairs of the USSR General Lieutenant A. N. Apollonov to the People's Commissar of Internal Affairs of the USSR, L. P. Beria, Concerning the Impossibility of Allocating Snipers from NKVD Personnel for Bringing Up to Strength the Sniper Subunits, Units, and Formations of the Red Army

[No earlier than 30 June 1943]

For the period up to 30 June of this year, NKVD troops have a total of 25, 410 snipers on their strength with a holding of 18,421 sniper rifles. In the units, 27,604 snipers have been trained with this number of sniper rifles. Of those trained, 19,932 have seen active operational deployment in the units of the Red Army.

During their operational service, 216,640 enemy officers and soldiers have been killed by NKVD snipers. Our own losses amount to 1,158, of whom 375 have been killed, 770 wounded, and 13 reported as missing.

In the draft resolution concerning the development of sniping in the Red Army, which has been proposed by Comrade Shchadenko, it is envisaged that 15,000 snipers from the NKVD be assigned to the sniper subunits being formed in the units and formations of the Red Army in order to bring them up to strength.

I consider it to be impossible to allocate 15,000 snipers from NKVD units in order to bring Red Army units up to strength. Our snipers carry out the duties of guarding state borders, protecting railway infrastructure and industrial enterprises, discharging convoy duty, and participating in operations carried out by the troops. Our snipers do this on an equal footing with all other soldiers. As a consequence any such allocation would weaken the operational readiness of the snipers to a considerable degree.

Moreover, this will reduce the general level of personnel among the troops, which as of 30 June of this year stands at 106,000 soldiers.

I consider it expedient to formalize the practice that has been established among NKVD units of sending snipers to the front for operational service, having required the NKVD of the USSR to maintain a permanent presence at the front of no less than 100 snipers and replacing them every 15–20 days.

Such a measure will considerably facilitate the destruction of enemy soldiers and officers at the front and will strengthen the units of the NKVD.

Deputy People's Commissar of Internal Affairs, USSR

General Lieutenant A. N. Apollonov

Source: *Organy gosudarstvennoi bezopasnosti SSSR v Velikoi Otechestvennoi Voine: Sbornik dokumentov*, Tom chetvertyi, kniga 1, *Sekrety Operatsii "Tsitadel'" 1 ianvaria–30 iiunia 1943 goda*, izdatel'stvo "Rus'", Moscow, 2008, pp.646-647.

APPENDIX D: VASILII GROSSMAN, *GLAZAMI CHEKHOVA* (*THROUGH CHEKHOV'S EYES*), 16 NOVEMBER 1942, STALINGRAD FRONT

For many days and for many nights these all-seeing eyes had been looking down onto the city from the fifth floor of the ruined apartment block. These eyes observed the street, the square, and the dozens of blocks, with their collapsed floors and ceilings, the empty, dead doorways, full of deceptive silence. These brown, round, almost yellow, greenish eyes—one cannot make out whether they are light or dark—observe the distant hills pitted with German dugouts; they consider the smoke from fires and kitchens, the vehicles and horse-drawn carts approaching the city from the west. Sometimes it is very quiet, and then you can hear in the building opposite, where the Germans are, small pieces of plaster falling down. Sometimes you can hear German conversation and the scraping of German boots. But sometimes the bombing and the shooting are so powerful that you have to bend your ear toward a comrade and shout at the top of your voice, and the comrade spreads his hands as if to say, "I can't hear."

Anatolii Chekhov is in his twentieth year. He has not had much of a happy life. The son of worker in a chemical factory, this young man with a precise mind, a kind heart, and exceptional abilities, who enjoyed books, something of an expert in and lover of geography, someone who dreamed of journeys, liked by his comrades and neighbors, who had won the affections of the aloof, older workers by his readiness to help the unfortunate, had since the age of ten come to know the dark side of life. His father was a drunk who treated his wife, son, and daughters harshly and unfairly. A couple of years before the war, Anatolii Chekhov left school, where he had excelled in all subjects, and went to work in a factory in Kazan. He quickly and easily mastered a whole range of specialties, becoming an electrician, a gas welder, and an accumulator technician, an irreplaceable worker respected by everyone.

On 29 March 1942 he was summoned to the military administrator's office, and he requested a posting to the sniper school. "Generally speaking, when I was a boy I never used a catapult or anything. I could never bring myself to fire at anything living," he said. "Well, even though I passed everything with top marks in the sniper school, I made a right mess the first time on the range. Out of a possible 50 points, I got 9. The lieutenant said to me, "Excellent in everything apart from bad in the shooting. Nothing will become of you."

But Chekhov was not about to weaken. In addition to the daytime course hours, he

---

Source: Vasilii Grossman, *Gody voiny* (Moscow: Izdatel'stvo Pravda, 1989), pp. 40–48.

put in extra hours at night. For hours on end he studied theory and studied his rifle. He had a great respect for theory and believed in the power of books. He thoroughly studied the principles of optics and, just like a real physicist, could talk about the laws of refraction of light, sketch the complex path of a ray of light through the nine lenses of the optical sight. He understood the internal theoretical principles of all devices: both the turns on the range wheel and the links with the sight bar, which was raised when aiming, with the horizontal threads. Moreover, Chekhov perceived the large, wide, fourfold magnified image from the standpoint not only of a marksman but also of a physicist.

The lieutenant was mistaken. When shooting with his rifle at moving targets, Chekhov hit the head of the small, quick-moving figure with all three allocated rounds. He finished the sniper school with top marks, at the top of the course. He immediately volunteered for a frontline unit, though he remained as an instructor to teach students conventional and sniping marksmanship, the use of submachine guns, and various types of grenades. As was his custom, whether at school, in a factory, or in the military art, he easily and completely mastered the understanding of various subjects.

This young man, liked by everyone for his decency and devotion to his mother and sisters, who as a boy had never used a catapult because, in his own words, "I could never bring myself to fire at anything living," desperately wanted to go to the front.

"I merely wanted to become that sort of person who himself killed the enemy," Chekhov told me.

On the march he trained himself to judge distances without the use of an optical sight. Anatolii would guess, "How many metres to that tree?" and would check it out by walking the number of steps. To begin with, it was a complete disaster, but gradually he learned to determine large distances with the naked eye to within two or three meters. And this simple skill helped him in war no less than the knowledge of complicated optics and the laws governing the movement of a ray of light through a combination of nine double convex and concave lenses. He learned to see the most idyllic landscape as a combination of range markers. For him, birch trees, rosebushes, or windmills became positions from which an enemy could appear and helped him quickly and precisely to adjust the range wheel.

During his first days in Stalingrad, Chekhov commanded an infantry section and then a mortar platoon. Chekhov would set himself tasks and would solve them himself with precision and intelligence. In these decisions he would bring not only his strong, young hands and legs, his clear and focused eyes to bear but also his mind. He thought intensely, quickly, with difficulty, as was perhaps not the case when he solved the most complicated tasks in physics and algebra that a teacher could roll out in order to terrify schoolchildren.

From the very first battles he ceased to see the battle as the chaos of fire and noise and learned to guess what it was that the enemy was trying to achieve.

"Was it terrible in those first days? No, I had the sort of feeling that I was teaching the soldiers how to camouflage things, to shoot, to advance, almost as if it was not war."

Conversations at the front frequently turned to the question of courage. Often this sort of conversation would become a heated argument. Some would say that courage is oblivion that comes in battle. Others candidly stated that when carrying out brave acts, they experienced very little fear; they got a grip on themselves and forced themselves by the strength of will to carry out their duty, and having raised their heads, they moved forward to meet death. A third would say, "I am brave because I have assured myself that I'll never be killed."

Capitan Kozlov, a very brave man who on many occasions had led his motor-rifle battalion in the heaviest attacks, told me that he, on the contrary, was brave from the fact that he was convinced of his own death and that it was all the same to him whether death called today or tomorrow. Many took the view that the source of bravery was getting used to danger, an indifference to danger that came from being under fire the whole time. For a majority, the underlying source of bravery and contempt for death was to be found in the sense of duty, hatred for the enemy, a desire to avenge the terrible sufferings that had been brought by the occupiers of our country. Young people say that they would carry out heroic deeds from a desire for glory. To some it seems that in battle they are being watched by friends, loved ones, and sweethearts. One elderly divisional commander, a man of great courage, in response to the request of his adjutant that he move away from the zone under fire, said with a laugh, "I love my two children so strongly that nothing can kill me."

I think there is nothing to argue about with the men at the front about the nature of courage. Every brave man is brave in his own way. Great and wide is the mighty tree of courage, its thousands of branches, interwoven with one another, rising high to the heavens the glory of our army, of our great people.

Yet if each person is brave in his own way, the self-regarding coward is always reduced to the same thing: a slavish submission to the instinct of preserving his stomach. The man who runs away from the battlefield today will tomorrow run out of a burning building, having abandoned his old mother, wife, and small children to the flames.

Concerning Chekhov, I noted still one other feature of courage, the most simple, it seems, the most complete, the most robust: he was innately, from his very nature, completely alien to any sense of the fear of death, much in the same way that the fear of heights is alien to an eagle.

He received his sniper rifle just before evening. He thought long and hard about what positions he should take up: whether to go in the cellar, whether to set up on the first floor, or whether to take cover in the pile of bricks that had been blown out of the wall of a high-rise building by a high-explosive shell. Slowly and curiously, he inspected the buildings of the forward edge of our defense: the windows with burned strips of curtain, the fittings dangling down in twisted iron; the sagging beams of the intermediate ceilings; fragments of trelliswork and the nickel frames of the spouses' double beds blackened by flames. His curious and perfect eye caught and fixed the minor details. He noted the bicycles hanging on the walls over the chasm of five crumbled stories; he noted the blackened splinters of the greenish crystal wineglasses, the pieces of mirror, and the reddish and scorched ends of the palm date trees on the windowsills; the buckled pieces of tin plate, dispersed by the hot air of the fire as if they were light sheets of paper; the exposed black cables sticking out from under the ground; the thick water pipes: the muscles and bones of the city. Chekhov made his choice: he went through the main doors of a large block and climbed up the still remaining staircase. In places the steps were shattered; on the small squares of the stairways in the rectangular, burned-out doors, empty doorways were visible; the stories could be identified only by the different paint on the walls. A flat on the second floor was painted pink; on the third floor it was dark blue, and on the fourth floor it was pistachio green with brown paneling. Chekhov climbed up to the area of the fifth floor. This was what he had been looking for. The caved-in wall opened up a wide panorama. Directly to the front and slightly to the side stood the blocks of houses occupied by the Germans; to the left ran a straight, wide road; about 700 meters farther on was the start of a square. This was all German. Chekhov set himself up on a stairway square next to the sharp end of a protruding piece of wall, in such a way that the shadow of the end fell on him and he became completely invisible in the shadow, whereas everything around him was illuminated by sunlight. He laid his rifle on the decorated cast-iron rails. He looked below. As a rule he would select orientation points, but there were very few. Two German soldiers came walking along the deserted street. They stopped about 100 meters from Chekhov's position. For four minutes the young man looked at the Germans. He hesitated. This was that strange sense of indecision known to practically all snipers before that first shot. Chekhov had been told about this by the famous Pchelintsev, who had come to the sniper school and recalled his first shot as a sniper, as a hunter, at a German soldier.

Night set in quickly. The light blue sky became dark blue. The high, burned-out buildings stood there like gray, silent corpses. The moon rose. It was at its zenith: large and clear; like a tank man's wide, steel mirror, indifferently reflecting the cruel image of the battle. The moon was a honey-yellow color, full, and its light, like dry white wax separated from the honey, seemed to lack substance, without taste, smell, or warmth. This fine film of waxy white light lay on the dead city, on the hundreds of windowless buildings, on the asphalted streets and squares, which sparkled like ice. Chekhov recalled those books about the ruins of ancient cities, and a terrible, bitter pain squeezed his young heart. To him it seemed that he was struggling for breath, so poignant, so agonizing was the desire to see this city free; to see it once more come to life, full of noise and joy; to bring all those thousands of girls back from the cold steppe who, wrapped up in their fur coats, waited for passing vehicles on the highway; to bring back those boys and girls, with their sense of mature seriousness watching the troops heading toward Stalingrad; to bring back those old men wrapped up in old women's clothing; to bring back the city's old women wearing their sons' greatcoats over their unfastened cardigans.

A shadow flashed across the ledge. A large Siberian cat with its tail up walked noiselessly past. It glanced at Chekhov, its eye sparkling like electric blue fire. Somewhere at the end of the street a dog started barking, then a second and a third. Then the angry voice of a German could be heard; then a pistol shot, the despairing yelp of a dog, and again the bad-tempered, uneasy, and determined barking. Loyal to the places they lived in, these dogs prevented the Germans from groping about the apartments during the night. Chekhov got up and took a look: quick, dark figures flicked through the shadow of the street. The Germans were carrying bags and cushions. There was no way of taking a shot. The light from the shot would immediately give away the sniper's position. "What are our lot looking at?" Chekhov thought with longing, and no sooner had he thought this than somewhere to the side a Soviet machine gun opened up a heavy weight of fire with a vengeance. Chekhov stood up and cautiously, trying not to break any of the glass splinters that glinted in the moonlight, went downstairs. An infantry section was accommodated in the building's cellar. The sergeant was sleeping on a metal bed frame; the soldiers lay on half-scorched fragments of plush and silk blankets. Chekhov poured some tea into a tin mug. The pot had only just boiled, and the edge of the mug burned his mouth. Chekhov did not feel like eating and turned down the porridge. He sat on some bricks, noticing the ashtray with the inscription: "Wife, do not upset your husband" and listened in the dark corner to the Red Army soldier from Stalingrad talking about life before the war: about the cinemas and what they showed, about the waterworks, about the beach, about the theater, about the elephant from the zoo that had perished in the bombing, about the dance halls, and about those gorgeous girls. And listening to all this, Chekhov once again saw in front of him a picture of the dead Stalingrad, illuminated by a full moon. Early on, from his childhood years, he had known the harshness of life. "My father would often shout—and it was difficult for me to read and learn my lessons. I had no private space at all," he told me sadly. But on that night he understood for the first time in all its depth the terrible force of evil that had been brought to our country by the Germans. He grasped that the minor troubles and woes were nothing in comparison with the great national catastrophe. And his young and decent heart was on fire: it burned him.

The sergeant woke up. The bedsprings started to squeak, and he asked, "Well, Chekhov, have you killed many Germans on your first day?"

Chekhov sat thinking, then suddenly said to the soldiers who had just returned from sentry duty and who had put on a record, "Lads, I request that you don't play any records today."

In the morning he was up before first light. He drank or ate nothing. He merely poured some water into a bottle, put some dry rations in his pocket, and went up to his post. He lay on the cold stones of the hall stairway and waited. It became light. Everything was bathed in light, and so great was the life force of the young morning sun that even the unfortunate city, so it seemed, smiled quietly and in sadness. Only under the protruding wall where Chekov lay was there cold, gray shadow. A German came out from the corner of a building with an enamel bucket. Somewhat later Chekhov realized that at this time the soldiers would always come and go with buckets, fetching water for the officers to wash. Chekhov adjusted the range screw, brought up the crossed threads and brought the sight to four centimeters [1.6 inches] in front of the soldier's nose, and fired. Something dark flashed out from underneath the cap, the head snapped back, the bucket fell from his hands, and the soldier fell to the ground. Chekov was shaken. A minute later another German soldier came out from the corner with binoculars in his hands. Chekhov squeezed the trigger. Then a third German appeared. He wanted to get to the German on the floor with the bucket, but he did not make it. "Three," said Chekhov, and became calm. On that day Chekhov's eyes saw a great deal. He identified the road used by the Germans to get to the headquarters located in the housing block, which stood to one side of where the soldiers would always run with some white paper in their hands, some report. He identified the road used by the Germans to bring ammunition to the housing block opposite where the submachine gunners and medium machine gunners were. He identified the road used by the Germans to bring food, and water for washing and drinking. For lunch, the Germans ate cold food. Chekhov knew what they ate, morning and day: bread and tinned food. At dinnertime the Germans would open up with heavy mortar fire and would keep it going for about thirty to forty minutes and afterward would shout in unison: "Rus, time for lunch!" This invitation to acknowledge some kind of truce enraged Chekhov. It struck him, as a happy lad with a sense of humor, as repulsive that the Germans were trying to play games with him in this tragically destroyed, unhappy, and dead city. This offended the purity of his soul, and during the dinner hour he was especially merciless. He quickly learned to distinguish between the officers and the men. The officers had forage caps; they wore no waist belts and wore ankle-high boots. He could immediately make out the soldiers by their boots, belts, and soft caps. He wanted to make sure that the Germans were not able to walk about the city without bending and crouching, so that they could not drink fresh water, so that they had to go without breakfast and dinner. He ground his teeth from a desire to force them to the ground. Chekhov, this young lad who loved books and geography, who dreamed of journeys to far-off places, this tender son and brother who had never used a catapult as a boy because "he could never bring myself to fire at anything living," became something terrible: the destroyer of the occupiers. Is this not where the iron, holy logic of the Great Fatherland War is?

Toward the end of the first day, Chekhov caught sight of an officer. The officer moved confidently. Soldiers armed with submachine guns came running out of the buildings and stood to attention in front of him. And once again Chekhov adjusted the range drum, raised the crossed threads. The officer's head snapped back, and he fell on his side with his boots toward Chekhov.

Chekhov noted that he found it easier to shoot at a running man than at one standing: the bullet hit the target on the head. He made one small discovery that helped to render him invisible to the enemy. A sniper was most frequently discovered by the flash of the shot when firing, but Chekhov always fired against a white background and made sure that the barrel of the rifle was about fourteen to twenty centimeters [six to eight inches] back from the edge of the wall. Against the white background, the flash of the shot was not visible.

Now he only wanted one thing: to make sure that the Germans could not walk about Stalingrad without bending and crouching. He wanted to bend them to the ground, to push them into the very earth. And he achieved his goal. Toward the end of the first day, the Germans were not walking but running, and by the end of the second day they had started to crawl. No soldier went for water for the officer in the morning. The small road along which the Germans used to go for drinking water became deserted. They had to go without fresh water and use foul water from the boilers. On the evening of the second day, while squeezing the trigger, Chekhov said, "Seventeen."

That evening the German submachine gunners got no supper. Chekhov went downstairs. The lads put on a record, ate some porridge, and listened to a record—"The Tiny, Dark Blue Shawl." Then they all sang "The Sea Stretched out before Us." The Germans opened up with furious fire, firing away with mortars, guns, and mounted machine guns. The hungry submachine gunners fired away with a real stubborn vengeance. They had given up shouting, "Rus, time for dinner!"

The blows of picks and shovels could be heard all night long. The Germans were digging communications trenches in the frozen ground. On the third morning Chekhov noted many changes. The Germans had brought two trenches right up to the asphalt strip of the road. They were going without water, but they wanted to bring up ammunition in these trenches. "Well, I have forced you to the ground," thought Chekhov. In the wall of the building opposite, he immediately caught sight of a small embrasure. Yesterday it had not been there. Chekhov realized that this meant a German sniper. "Just look," he whispered to the sergeant, who had come to see him at work, and squeezed the trigger. There was a shout and the clatter of boots as the German submachine gunners dragged away the body of the sniper, who had not succeeded in firing a single round. Chekhov occupied a trench. The Germans crawled to the asphalt, ran across the road, and jumped into the second trench. Chekhov started to fire at the moment when they emerged on the asphalt. The first German crawled back into the trench.

"Well, I have forced you into the ground," said Chekhov.

On the eighth day Chekhov had all the roads leading to the German buildings under his control. Now it was time to change his position. The Germans had stopped moving about and shooting. He lay on the square, and his young eyes took in Stalingrad destroyed by the Germans. The young lad who could not bring himself to fire at "anything living" from a catapult had become, in accordance with the iron and holy logic of the Fatherland War, a terrible person, an avenger.

APPENDIX E: COMBAT AND RATION STRENGTHS OF 24TH PANZER DIVISION, 1 JANUARY 1943

Truppenteil/ Troop Formation	Gefechtsstärken/Combat Strengths							Verpflegungsstärken/Ration Strengths							
	Offz.	Beamte	Uffz.	Mannsch.	Rumänen	**Hlfsw.**	Summe	Offz.	Beamte	Uffz.	Mannsch.	Rumänen	**Hlfsw.**	**Kgf.**	Summe
Stb. 24 P. D.	0	0	0	0	0	**0**	0	18	7	33	114	2	**7**	**0**	181
Pz. Rgt. 24	20	0	137	247	0	**0**	404	26	5	275	535	24	**24**	**0**	889
Pz. Gr. Rgt. 21	11	1	70	294	46	**6**	428	11	1	74	295	46	**3**	**11**	441
Pz. Gr. Rgt. 26	5	0	41	174	94	**16**	330	7	0	55	256	94	**22**	**0**	434
Kradsc/Abt 4	10	0	124	509	37	**0**	680	11	2	142	541	42	**57**	**0**	795
Pz. AR. 89	24	0	89	429	0	**3**	545	24	3	113	517	0	**19**	**0**	676
IV. AR. 89	10	0	28	168	0	**0**	206	10	2	44	195	2	**5**	**0**	258
Pz. Pi. Btl. 40	3	2	11	73	33	**0**	122	3	2	20	130	33	**16**	**0**	204
Pz. Jg. Abt. 40	6	1	37	242	0	**0**	286	7	3	58	303	0	**7**	**20**	398
Pz. N. A. 86	3	0	24	124	0	**0**	151	5	2	31	133	0	**12**	**0**	183
Div. Sup. Tr. 40	0	0	0	0	0	**0**	0	18	7	82	440	16	**79**	**0**	642
San. Kp. 1/40	0	0	0	0	0	**0**	0	8	2	23	165	13	**2**	**0**	213
Div. V. A. 40	0	0	0	0	0	**0**	0	0	4	7	34	0	**16**	**0**	61
Bäck. Kp. 40	0	0	0	0	0	**0**	0	1	0	17	102	0	**7**	**16**	143
Schl. Kp. 40	0	0	0	0	0	**0**	0	1	1	5	38	0	**2**	**8**	55
Feldpost 40	0	0	0	0	0	**0**	0	0	14	0	5	0	**0**	**0**	19
Feldg. Tr. 40	0	0	0	0	0	**0**	0	3	0	21	8	0	**1**	**0**	33
St. 94. I. D.*	0	0	0	0	0	**0**	0	17	33	121	513	0	**132**	**0**	816

Gr. Rgt. 267	17	0	116	587	30	**0**	750	26	3	264	1,029	30	**442**	**20**	1,814
Gr. Rgt. 274	14	0	61	375	0	**0**	450	20	3	153	609	50	**246**	**71**	1,152
Art. Rgt. 194	11	0	116	294	0	**0**	421	11	1	141	375	0	**128**	**0**	656
Pi. Batl. 194	2	0	4	27	21	**0**	54	8	1	36	426	21	**0**	**194**	686
Insgesamt	136	4	858	3,543	261	**25**	**4,827**	235	96	1,715	6,763	373	**1,227**	**340**	**10,749**

Source: Gefechts—und Verpflegungsstärken der 24. Panzer-Division am 1. Januar 1943, BA-MA, RH 27-24/6.

Note: The total ration strength of 24th Panzer Division and all incorporated units on 1 January 1943 was 10,749. The total combat strength was 4,827, leaving a total noncombatant strength of 5,922. Inside the Kessel the distinction between combatant and noncombatant would have been somewhat academic, especially toward the end as units and various formations were being disbanded and amalgamated in order to supplement frontline losses. Formations of 94th Infantry Division, for example, have been incorporated into 24th Panzer Division.

*Part of the document before St. (Stab/HQ) has been erased.

Key to personnel headings:

Offz. = Officers
Beamte = Civilian officials
Uffz. = NCOs
Mannsch. = Soldiers
Rumänen = Romanians
Hlfsw. = *Hilfswillige*
Kgf. = *Kriegsgefangene*
Summe = Subtotal
Insgesamt = Complete Totals

Key to German troop formation abbreviations:

Stb. 24 P. D. = HQ 24th Panzer Division
Pz. Gr. Rgt. 24 = Panzer Regiment 24
Pz. Gr. Rgt. 21 = Panzer Grenadier Regiment 21
Pz. Gr. Rgt. 26 = Panzer Grenadier Regiment 26
Krads./Abt. 4 = Rifle Motorcycle Section 4
Pz. A. R. 89 = Panzer Artillery Regiment 89
IV.A. R. 89 = 4th Battalion Artillery Regiment 89
Pz. Pi. Btl. 40 = Panzer Engineer Battalion 40
Pz. Jg. Abt. 40 = Tank Destroyer Battalion 40
Pz. N. A. 86 = Panzer Signal Section 86
Div. Sup. Tr. 40 = Command Section Divisional Supply Troop 40
San. Kp. 1/40 = Medical Company 1/40
Div. V. A. 40 = Divisional Advance Guard
Bäck. Kp. 40 = Bakery Company 40
Schl. Kp. 40 = Butcher Company 40
Feldpost 40 = Field Post Office 40
Feldg. Tr. 40 = Military Police Troop 40
St. 94. I. D. = Elements of 94th Infantry Division HQ
Gr. Rgt. 267 = Grenadier Regiment 267
Gr. Rgt. 274 = Grenadier Regiment 274
Art. Rgt. 194 = Artillery Regiment 194
Pi. Batl. 194 = Engineer Battalion 194

APPENDIX F
GLOSSARY OF GERMAN RANKS

Generalfeldmarschall (Field Marshal)
Generaloberst (Colonel General)
General (General)
Generalleutnant (Lieutenant General)
Generalmajor (Major General)
Oberst (Colonel)
Oberstleutnant (Lieutenant Colonel)
Major (Major)
Oberstabsveterinär (Senior Veterinary Officer, Major)
Hauptmann (Captain)
Rittmeister (Captain Cavalry)
Stabszahlmeister (Paymaster, civilian with the rank of captain)
Oberleutnant (First Lieuteant)
Leutnant (Lieutenant)
Stabsfeldwebel (Warrant Officer)
Hauptwachtmeister (Warrant Officer in regimental police)
Oberfeldwebel (Staff Sergeant)
Wachtmeister (Staff Sergeant)
Feldwebel (Senior Sergeant)
Unteroffizier (Noncommissioned Officer, approximately Sergeant)
Obergefreiter/Oberjäger (Corporal)
Gefreiter (Lance Corporal)
Soldat/Jäger/Grenadier (Private Soldier)

NOTES

Chapter 1. The Battle of Stalingrad in Post–Cold War Perspective

1. Günter Schmitz, *Die 16. Panzer-Division 1938–1945: Bewaffnung, Einsätze, Männer*, (Friedberg: Podzun-Pallas-Verlag, ca. 1976), p. 105.

2. Vasilii Grossman, *Za pravoe delo* (Moscow: Sovetskii pisatel', 1989), p. 356.

3. Bericht über eine Fahrt nach Stalingrad, 25 September 1942, Bundesarchiv-Militärarchiv, Freiburg-im-Breisgau, RH 20-6/213/172. Hereinafter future references to this archive will be given as BA-MA followed by the document's archival signature.

4. Hanns Neidhardt, *Mit Tanne und Eichenlaub: Kriegschronik der 100. Jäger-Division vormals 100. leichte Infanterie-Division* (Graz-Stuttgart: Leopold Stocker Verlag, 1981), p. 180.

5. Paul Carell, *Stalingrad: Sieg und Untergang der 6. Armee*, Sonderausgabe (München: F. A. Herbig, 2003). p. 147.

6. David M. Glantz with Jonathan M. House, *The Stalingrad Trilogy*, vol. 1: *To the Gates of Stalingrad: Soviet-German Combat Operations April–August 1942* (Lawrence: University Press of Kansas, 2009), p. 219.

7. Neidhardt, *Mit Tanne und Eichenlaub*, p. 201.

8. On the severity of the weather endured at Stalingrad, Sänger states that "from 19 November 1942 until 1 February 1943 the Russian winter brought temperatures of between –30 and –40 degrees every day." Hans Sänger, *zusammengestellt von Die 79. Infanterie Division* (Friedberg: Podzun-Pallas-Verlag, n.d.), p. 132. This is a much colder and more prolonged spell of cold weather than that noted by Grohe. Weather observations given by Neidhardt are more consistent with those given by Grohe. In Neidhardt's words, "The first snow fell on the 16th [November]. It had already been cold for some time, with nighttime temperatures often below freezing. Now 'General Winter' attacked properly for the first time. And further to the rear, in the small gullies, away from the streets, many a trudging runner caught sight of moving gray shadows: the first wolves! There was still no howling from them in the night, and they dared not get to close to the accommodations. But how much longer would this last?" Neidhardt, *Mit Tanne und Eichenlaub*, p. 218. The issue of roads and tracks being rendered unusable by snow and ice was taken very seriously by 6th Army. On 10 October 1942 6 Army headquarters issued three detailed formats for reporting winter road conditions. This first format consisted of an 11-point scale to indicate the depth of snow and any icing on roads. On this scale x indicated nothing to report, 4 indicated snow under 15 centimeters (6 inches), 5 indicated a snow depth greater than 15 cm, and 6 indicated deep snowdrifts. The second scale was a 7-point scale for road mainte-

nance, and a third 10-point scale was used to report the suitability of roads for light and heavy vehicles, tracked vehicles, and horses. See Schlüssel für Straßenzustandsmeldungen, 10 October 1942, BA-MA, RH 20-6/224/187.

9. Horst Zank (376th Infantry Division) challenges the widely accepted view that German soldiers were issued inadequate winter clothing. In his memoir he writes that the issue of winter clothing (1942–1943) was more than adequate (p. 24), and later, in a letter home (10 November 1942), he extols its high quality: "Unpleasant about the weather is this always cold wind that blows across the open steppe. But this year our winter equipment is fantastic." See Horst Zank, *Stalingrad: Kessel und Gefangenschaft*, dritte Auflage (Hamburg, Berlin, Bonn: Verlag E. S. Mittler & Sohn, 2001), p. 77.

10. Major Menzel, BA-MA, RH 20-6/213/174.

11. Ibid.

12. Jochen Löser, *Bittere Pflicht: Kampf und Untergang der 76. Berlin-Brandenburgischen Infanterie Division* (Osnabrück: Biblio Verlag, 1986), p. 212.

13. Friedrich Wilhelm Hauck, *Eine Deutsche Division in Russland und Italien: 305. Infanteriedivision* 1941–1945 (Dorheim: Podzun-Verlag, 1975), pp. 70–71.

14. Neidhardt, *Mit Tanne und Eichenlaub*, p. 214.

15. Gerhard Dieckhoff, *3. Infanterie-Division, 3. Infanterie-Division (mot.), 3. Panzergrenadier-Division* (Göttingen: Erich Börries Verlag, 1960), p. 220.

16. Ibid.

17. Nachträge zu *Bittere Pflicht*, BA-MA, Band 1, O11b, 76a-1, p. 35.

18. Löser, *Bittere Pflicht*, pp. 174 and 182.

19. Antony Beevor, *Stalingrad* (London: Penguin, 1999), p. xiv.

20. Ibid., p. 364.

21. Ibid., p. 26.

22. "Doklad nachal'nika artillerii Krasnoi Armii narodnomu komissaru oborony ob itogakh i ispol'zovanii boevogo opyta sovetsko-finliandskoi voiny," 1 April 1940 g., in N. L. Volkovskii, ed., *Tainy i uroki zimnei voiny, 1939–1940, Po dokumentam rasskrechennykh arkhivov* (Sankt-Peterburg: Poligon, 2000), p. 396.

23. "Prikazanie shtaba 9-i armii komandiram soedinenii ob organizatsii razvedki, nochnykh deistvii i boia v lesy," № 030/op, 21 December 1939 g., in Volkovskii, ed., *Tainy i uroki zimnei voiny, 1939–1940*, p. 207.

24. Catherine Andreyev, *Vlasov and the Russian Liberation Movement: Soviet Reality and Émigré Theories* (London: Cambridge University Press, 1987), p. 26.

25. Beevor, *Stalingrad*, p. 222.

26. At the start of the battle Paulus held the rank of General der Panzertruppen. On 30 November 1942 he was promoted to Generaloberst and on 31 January 1943 he was promoted to Generalfeldmarschall.

27. Beevor, *Stalingrad*, p. 228 .

28. Manfred Kehrig, *Stalingrad: Analyse und Dokumentation einer Schlacht*, Beiträge zur Militär-Kriegsgeschichte, Band 15, Herausgegeben vom Militärgeschichtlichen Forschungsamt (Stuttgart: Deutsche Verlags-Anstalt, 1974), p. 565. The full text of the *Denkschrift* is cited as an appendix, pp. 564–567.

29. Ibid., p. 566.

30. Ibid., p. 567 (emphasis in the original).

31. Ibid., p. 246.

32. Glantz, *The Stalingrad Trilogy*, vol. 1, p. 319.

33. Ibid., p. 3.

34. Ibid., p. 212.

35. Ibid.

36. Ibid., p. 345.

37. Ibid., p. 389.

38. Vasilii Grossman, *Zhizn' i sud'ba* (Moscow: Sovetskii pisatel', 1990), p. 289.

39. David M. Glantz with Jonathan M. House, *The Stalingrad Trilogy*, vol. 2: *Armageddon in Stalingrad, September–November 1942* (Lawrence: University Press of Kansas, 2009), p. 168.

40. During the Cold War the battle was also the subject of a number of films: *Stalingradskaia bitva* (The Stalingrad battle, 1949), directed by Vladimir Petrov; *Soldaty* (Soldiers, 1956), based on Viktor Nekrasov's story "In the Trenches of Stalingrad" and directed by Aleksandr Ivanov; *Hunde, wollt ihr ewig leben?* (Dogs, do you want to live forever?, 1959), based on the novel by Fritz Wöss and directed by Frank Wisbar; *Velikaia bitva na Volge* (The great battle on the Volga, 1962), directed by Mariia Slavinskaia (shown in the DDR as *Die grosse Schlacht an der Wolga*, 1963); and *Stalingrad* (1990), directed by Iurii Ozerov. The first post-Soviet Russian film about the battle will be *Stalingrad*, directed by Fedor Bondarchuk. The film is due for release in October 2013.

41. David R. Stone, review of *Enemy at the Gates*, http://www.h-net.org/reviews/showrev.php?id=15019, June 2002.

42. Helena Wanin, letter to Heinz Werner Hübner, Direktor WDR, Betreff.: Die Fernsehserie, *Der unvergessene Krieg*, 7 October 1981, BA-MA, Nachträge zu *Bittere Pflicht*, Band 6, O11b, 76a-6, pp. 2–7.

43. "Iz prikaza narkoma oborony SSSR № 0391 o faktax podmeny vospitatel'noi raboty v Krasnoi Armii repressiiami, 4 oktiabria 1941 g.," *Organy gosudarstvennoi bezopasnosti SSSR v Velikoi Otechestvennoi voine*, tom vtoroi, kniga 2, № 592, 1 September–31 December 1941 g., izdatel'stvo "Rus'" (Moscow, 2000), p. 164. On a first citation of a report from this series, the full title will be given. Thereafter an abbreviated citation format will be used to refer to material from these volumes: title (OGB) followed by year, 1 or 2 to indicate the first or second half of the year, the report number as cited in the original volume, and volume page numbers. Minus the full title, the above citation in abbreviated format would be OGB/1941/2/№ 592, p. 164.

44. General M. Gareev, "Pod vidom poiska istoricheskoi pravdy," *Voenno-istoricheskii zhurnal* 12 (2005): 9–15.

45. Evgenii Viktorovich Kovyrshin, "K voprosu o zagraditel'nykh otriadakh v Krasnoi Armii." This article was downloaded from the web site of the Ministry of Defense of the Russian Federation, http://mil.ru, 27 April 2010.

46. "Prikaz narodnogo komissara oborony Soiuza SSR № 227 o priniatii mer po ukrepleniiu poriadka i povysheniiu distsipliny v voiskakh," 28 iiulia 1942 g., OGB/1942/2/№ 1027, p. 79. The full text of Order № 227, with a slightly abbreviated title, was first published in 1988. See I. Stalin, "Prikaz Narodnogo komissara oborony Soiuza SSR, № 227, 28 iiulia 1942 g.," *Voenno-istoricheskii zhurnal* 8 (1988): 73–75.

47. Kovyrshin, "K voprosu o zagraditel'nykh otriadakh v Krasnoi Armii," p. 1.

48. Ibid., p. 5.

49. "Soobshchenie OO NKVD STF v UOO NKVD SSSR o khode realizatsii prikaza № 227 i reagirovanii na nego lichnogo sostava 4-i tankovoi armii, 14 avgusta 1942 g." See IA. F. Pogonii, i dr., *Stalingradskaia epopeia: Materialy NKVD*

SSSR i voennoi tsenzury iz Tsentral'nogo arkhiva FSB RF (Moscow: Zvonnitsa-MG, 2000), pp. 180–182.

50. "Spravka OO NKVD STF v UOO NKVD SSSR o deiatel'nosti zagraditel'nykh otriadov Stalingradskogo i Donskogo frontov [ne ranee 15 oktiabria 1942 g.]," *Stalingradskaia epopeia*, p. 230.

51. "Postanovlenie Gosudarstvennogo Komiteta Oborony № 187ss o preobrazovanii organov Tret'ego upravleniia NKO SSSR v osobye otdely NKVD SSSR, 17 iiulia 1941 g.," *OGB/1941/2/№* 411, p. 338.

52. "Direktiva Upravleniia osobykh otdelov NKVD SSSR № 39212 ob usilenii raboty zagraditel'nykh otriadov po vyiavleniiu i razoblacheniiu cherez liniiu fronta, 28 iiulia 1941 g.," *OGB/1941/2/№* 452, p. 412.

53. "Direktiva Stavki VGK № 001919 komanduiushchim voiskami frontov, armiiami, komandiram divizii, glavnokomanduiushchemu voiskami IUgo-Zapadnogo napravlenii o sozdanii zagraditel'nykh otriadov v strel'kovykh diviziiakh, 12 sentiabria 1941 g., *OGB/1941/2/№* 550, p. 86.

54. "Spravka 4-go otdela UNKVD po Kalininskoi oblasti ob organizatsii i deiatel'nosti istrebitel'nykh batal'onov na territorii oblasti, 10 dekabria 1941 g.," *OGB/1941/2/№* 726, p. 396. Khristoforov provides some support for this view, confirming that the NKVD was in charge of the blocking detachments. Moreover, he notes that these formations on the Stalingrad and Southeastern fronts were made up of reliable Red Army soldiers and commanders and that "officers of the Special Sections of the NKVD SSSR who had been tried and tested in battle were appointed as commanders of these blocking detachments." V. S. Khristoforov, *Stalingrad: Organy NKVD nakanune i v dni srazhenii* (Moscow: Moskovskie uchebniki, 2008), p. 88.

55. "Iz zhurnala boevykh deistvii 272-go strelkovogo polka 10-i strelkovoi divizii vnutrennikh voisk NKVD za period s 23 avgusta po 26 sentiabria 1942 g.," *OGB/1942/2/№* 1120, p. 290.

56. Ibid., pp. 294–295.

57. "Predstavlenie Voennogo soveta Stalingradskogo fronta № 0820 v GKO SSSR o nagrazhdenii 10-i strelkovoi vnutrennikh voisk NKVD ordenom Lenina za otvagu i geroizm, proiavlennye ee lichnym sostavom v boiakh za g. Stalingrad, 12 noiabria 1942 g," *OGB/1942/2№* 1197, p. 458.

58. Ibid.

59. "Soobshchenie NKVD SSSR № 1611/B v GKO i General'nyi shtab Krasnoi Armii ob obstanovke v g. Stalingrade, 22 sentiabria 1942 g.," *OGB/1942/2/№* 1113, p. 269.

60. *Merkblatt für den Ortskampf*, BA-MA, RH 26-305/14/50–51.

61. Ibid., p. 50.

62. Ibid.

63. Ibid.

64. Ibid., p. 51.

65. Glantz, *The Stalingrad Trilogy*, vol. 2, pp. 166–167.

66. David R. Stone, "Stalingrad and the Evolution of Soviet Urban Warfare," abstract, *Journal of Slavic Military Studies* 22 (2009): 195.

67. See Order № 307, "Prikaz ob ustanovlenii polnogo edinonachaliia i uprazdnenii instituta voennykh komissarov v Krasnoi Armii, 9 oktiabria 1942 g.," *Stalingradskaia epopeia*, p. 451.

68. "OKH/GenStdH/Abt FrHOst (I) vom 29.8.1942, betr. Gedanken zur Weiterentwicklung der Feindlage im Herbst und Winter," cited in Kehrig, *Stalingrad*, pp. 550–551.

69. Stone, 'Stalingrad and the Evolution of Soviet Urban Warfare," p. 197.

70. Iurii Rybalkin, *Operatsiia «X» Sovetskaia voennaia pomoshch' respublikanskoi Ispanii, 1936–1939* (Moscow: AIRO-XX, 2000), p. 107.

71. Ibid., p. 116.

72. Ibid., pp. 52–53.

73. Carell, *Stalingrad: Sieg und Untergang der 6. Armee*, pp. 73–74.

74. Der Kampf um Höhe 61, 6, BA-MA, RH 26-76/41/5.

75. Ibid., p. 9.

76. Ibid.

77. Ibid., p. 10.

78. Ibid., p. 7.

79. Abwehrkampf des III/203 unter Führung von Herrn Hauptm. Gerstenberg in der Zeit von 15.10-26.11.1942, BA-MA, RH 26-76/41.

80. Ibid.

81. Volksbund Deutsche Kriegsgräberfürsorge e.V., Kassel, hrsg., *Namen für Rossoschka: Schicksale aus Stalingrad*, 2nd. ed. (Pößneck: GGP Media GmbH, 2008), pp. 172–173.

82. Löser, *Bittere Pflicht*, p. 211.

83. Ibid., p. 244.

84. Ibid.

85. See Zank, *Stalingrad: Kessel und Gefangenschaft*, p. 44.

86. Neues russisches Kampfverfahren für Stosstrupps, 6.11.1942, BA-MA, RH 26-76/41.

87. Viktor Nekrasov, *Stalingrad* (Frankfurt/Main: Possev-Verlag, 1981), p. 181.

88. See "Dokladnaia zapiska V. Abakumova A. Vyshinskomu o zverskom otnoshenii nemetskikh voennosluzhashchikh k sovetskim voennoplennym, 2 sentiabria 1943 g.," *Stalingradskaia epopeia*, pp. 356–363.

89. *Federalnyi Arkhiv, Federalnaia Sluzhba Bezopasnosti Rossiiskoi Federatsii, Ugolovnoe Delo Po Obvineniiu Kerperta i dr.* Arkhiv № K-99468, delo 159, list 182. For a detailed analysis of the interrogations of the German officers, see Frank Ellis, "Dulag-205: The German Army's Death Camp for Soviet Prisoners at Stalingrad," *Journal of Slavic Military Studies* 19, no. 1 (March 2006): 123–148.

90. *Federalnyi Arkhiv, Federalnaia Sluzhba Bezopasnosti Rossiiskoi Federatsii, Ugolovnoe Delo Po Obvineniiu Kerperta i dr.* Arkhiv № K-99468, delo 159, listy 217–219.

91. "Ukaz Prezidiuma Verkhovnogo Soveta SSSR o merakh nakazaniia dlia nemetsko-fashistskikh zlodeev, vinovnykh v ubiistvakh i istaizaniiakh sovetskogo grazhdanskogo naseleniia i plennykh krasnoarmeitsev, dlia sphionov, izmennikov Rodine iz chisla sovetskikh grazhdan i dlia ikh posobnikov, 19 aprelia 1943 g.," *Organy gosudarstvennoi bezopasnosti SSSR v Velikoi Otechestvennoi voine*, tom chetvertyi, kniga 1, № 1398, 1 ianvaria–30 iiunia 1943 goda, izdatel'stvo "Rus'" (Moscow, 2008), pp. 401–402. This decree was promulgated under the provisions of Stalin's Order № 0283, which is document № 1398.

92. OGB/1943/1/p. 403.

93. Eric Lomax, *The Railway Man* (London: Vintage, 1996), p. 74.

94. In 2006 I completed a brief trip on board HMS *Gloucester*, one of the Royal Navy's type 42 destroyers and the latest ship to carry the Gloucester name. The ship's padre informed me that when the ship reached Crete he would conduct a special memorial service for Kenneth Macdonald, one of a small group of sailors who survived the sinking of HMS *Gloucester* on 22 May 1941 during the Bat-

tle of Crete. Just before sailing the padre had received the urn with Kenneth Macdonald's ashes—he died in 2006—and the culmination of the service would be the commitment of the urn to the deep over the spot where HMS *Gloucester* had gone down. Along with the urn the padre had also been given Kenneth Macdonald's memoir, *A Bandsman and Barbed Wire: Experiences and Recollections May 1941–May 1945*. As soon as I read this memoir, I realized that it was an important historical document. Many of Macdonald's experiences immediately after and during capture and upon release are consistent with those of prisoners of war of other combatant nations.

95. Vasilii Grossman, *Gody voiny*, izdatel'stvo (Moscow: Pravda, 1989), p. 281. This entry is taken from the second of Grossman's wartime diaries (September 1941, the Briansk front). All his diaries covering the war were published in this volume.

96. Friedrich Dettmer, *Stalingrad: Ein Rückblick nach 60 Jahren* (Nürnberg: Buchdienst Südtirol, 2003), p. 169.

97. Ibid., p. 170.

98. Khristoforov, *Stalingrad*, p. 108.

99. Zank, *Stalingrad: Kessel und Gefangenschaft*, p. 91.

100. Ibid., p. 132.

101. Ibid., p. 138.

102. On the snow-covered steppe, the recovery of ration bombs and other airdropped supplies was made much more difficult by the fact that parachutes were white.

103. Dieckhoff, *3. Infanterie-Division*, p. 238.

104. Neidhardt, *Mit Tanne und Eichenlaub*, p. 229.

105. Carell, *Stalingrad: Sieg und Untergang der 6. Armee*, p. 211.

106. Aussage des Fw. Michael Horvath, Feldgend. Trupp 100, BA-MA, RH 26/76/41.

107. Arthur Boje, *Stalins deutsche Agenten. Ein Kriegsgefangener berichtet* (Verlag, Graz-Stuttgart: Leopold Stocker, 2002), p. 82.

108. Freifrau Mady von Schilling, "Betreuung der Stalingradkämpfer—Abwicklungsstab Stalingrad," BA-MA, Nachträge zu *Bittere Pflicht*, Band 6, O11b, 76a-6, p. 15.

109. Ibid., p. 16.

110. Boje, *Stalins deutsche Agenten*, p. 88.

Chapter 2. 16th Panzer Division inside Fortress Stalingrad, 19 November 1942–2 February 1943

1. This document is based on various personal accounts and other sources and was compiled and written by Leutnant von Gronow, the assistant adjutant of Panzer Engineer Battalion 16, 16th Panzer Division. He is also referred to in Wolfgang Werthen, *Geschichte der 16.Panzer-Division* (Bad Nauheim: Podzun-Verlag, 1958), p. 280.

2. In the left margin of this account is a handwritten entry that indicates that it was 1st platoon, 1st Company, 16th Panzer Engineer Battalion. This incident is referred to in detail by both Glantz and Beevor. Glantz notes that the Soviet gun crews, consisting of barely trained and hastily mobilized civilian women, had no chance against the professionals of 16th Panzer Division and were brutally dispatched and achieved nothing for their sacrifice (see David M. Glantz with Jonathan M. House, *The Stalingrad Trilogy*, vol. 1: *To the Gates of Stalingrad: Soviet-German Combat Operations April–August 1942* [Lawrence: University Press of Kansas, 2009, p. 336]). Beevor, for reasons that

are not clear, draws a parallel between these Russian civilians and the apocryphal, ancient races of warrior women mentioned by Herodotus (see Antony Beevor, *Stalingrad* [London: Penguin, 1999], p. 108). The relevant point is that however willing these women were to make their contribution to the defense of Stalingrad, Komsomol-style enthusiasm was no substitute for professionalism.

3. This failed Soviet attack over the period 31 October–3 November 1942 is referred to in detail in a 6th Army report. The Germans took some 521 prisoners and destroyed a total of 14 boats (of various sizes). They seized 4 antitank guns, 10 mortars, 38 machine guns, and 450 handheld firearms. The report noted that other boats were damaged, but the onset of darkness made a precise count impossible. See AOK. 6. Ia. 3 November 1942, BA-MA, RH 20-6/227/180. Given that Operation Uranus is only 16 days away, can this failed Soviet landing be seen as a diversionary attack intended to focus 6th Army's attention on the city rather than on its threatened flanks?

4. Note that Major Grohe reports snow on 19 October 1942 (see chapter 4).

5. The equanimity with which the author accepts that encirclement is an occupational hazard in a war of mobility is in striking contrast to the paranoia and suspicion with which Soviet troops were treated by the NKVD if they were encircled and managed to escape.

6. I take this to be the ratio of officers to NCOs to soldiers.

7. "Long" refers to the long-barreled gun on this type of tank.

8. This speculative and deeply personal response to the physical and psychological pressures of war in the Kessel demonstrates a striking similarity with some of the passages to be found in the writing of the German World War I veteran Ernst Jünger, such as those, for example, in Jünger's long essay *Der Kampf als inneres Erlebnis* (Combat as an inner experience, 1922).

9. Note that the original states 300th Infantry Division. I take that to be an error.

10. The hedgehog was a tactical response to massed Soviet attacks used to ensure all-around defense. In open steppe terrain, machine guns would be deployed at the cardinal compass points, and heavy weapons where available would be deployed to cover tank approaches.

Chapter 3. "And There Are No Pages That Tell of These Heroic Deeds": 94th Infantry Division

1. The preface was probably written about 1968–1969. The author's identity is not given.

2. Throughout this document there are references to attachments (*Anlagen*), which were not included with the original document.

3. That this unit was armed with assault rifles (*Sturmgewehre*) in late 1942 is historically interesting because production of these weapons, and then fairly limited, did not start until later 1943–1944. Assuming Krell is not mistaken, these weapons could have been early prototypes.

4. These guns were likely to have been the 88-mm, which turned out to be the most effective antitank gun in World War II.

5. Commanded by Leutnant Urban, hence the reference.

6. The Todt Organization, named after Dr. Fritz Todt (1891–1942), was responsible for large-scale building

projects all over the Third Reich and in the German-occupied territories.

7. Krell's assessment of Soviet assault tactics—unimaginative, repetitious, predictable, costly in lives, and often for no obvious gain—matches Jochen Löser's.

8. These two paragraphs sum up as well as anything the remarkable qualities of the German infantry, the professionalism of its junior leaders, and the acknowledgment by the German higher command that it could not, nor should it, attempt to micromanage the defensive battle. These differences underline critical and decisive differences in German and Soviet attitudes toward training and command and were prominent throughout the war.

9. Generalmajor Martin Lattman was the commander of 14th Panzer Division, not the commander of 389th Infantry Division, as stated here by Krell. However, on 19 January 1943, Lattmann assumed temporary command of 389th Infantry Division, replacing Generalmajor Erich Magnus who nevertheless still retained the title of divisional commander.

Chapter 4. Eternal Glory: The End of 76th Berlin-Brandenburg Infantry Division

1. In the original documents the data are not presented in tables. For purposes of clarity and ease of reading, I have presented them in tabular format.

2. Such was the success of the Blitzkrieg—a highly mechanized form of warfare—that one can easily lose sight of the degree to which German 6th Army and other formations relied on horses. As these horses succumbed to cold and starvation and eventually were eaten, the infantry units were unable to move heavy weapons, ammunition, and wounded.

3. Throughout this document there are references to attachments (*Anlagen*) that were not included with the war diary. Some of these attachments refer to divisional documents, others to those emanating from 6th Army Headquarters.

4. The 100th Division referred to here is 100th Jäger Division.

5. Note that this is just the beginning of October, before the onset of winter proper, and with another four months to go.

6. In the original, "*westl.*" has been crossed out, and what appears to be "*ostwärts*" has been written in over the word.

7. The order referred to is most likely to be "Erhöhung der Kampfkraft," 6 October 1942, BA-MA, RH 20-6/224/9-15.

8. Here and elsewhere in this document the distinction between prisoners of war (*Kriegsgefangene*) and *Hilfswillige* (auxiliaries) is not always properly made. The distinction is discussed in chapter 6.

9. "Verhalten gegenüber Kosaken und Kalmücken," 11 October 1942, BA-MA, RH 20-6/225/36. Referred to in chapter 6.

10. The aim of these quick-reaction units was as follows: "The task of the emergency units/quick-reaction units is the inculcation of an aggressive spirit in all those formations that are not immediately involved in combat and the strengthening of the bonds between combat troops and those assisting the combat troops, the temporary relief at the front of deployed units, and the additional deployment in critical periods." See OKH Org. Abt., 08.10.1942, Grundlegender Befehl Nr.1 (Hebung der Gefechtsstärke), BA-MA, RH 20-6/220/65. In all, a total of 100 *Alarmeinheiten* were formed in 6th Army, with a combined total of 11,131 officers and men.

11. This paragraph refers to a German

6th Army circular and attachment dated 22 October 1942. In the circular it is noted that pictures of undamaged German tanks, self-propelled guns, and artillery pieces falling into enemy hands are being published in foreign newspapers. There are obvious concerns about the propaganda damage being done to the Wehrmacht: "Towns or other larger places in which significant supplies of ammunition, rations, and other special supplies are stored must be fought for to the utmost. It is a crime—be they destroyed or otherwise—to abandon them to the enemy." See BA-MA, RH 20-6/226/20–22.

12. Combat strength (4,809) + attached units (5,706) + Russian *Hilfswillige* (2,776) = 13,291. I assume that the difference between 13,291 and 12,125, a total of 1,166 men, is accounted for by the troops from the general reserve.

13. Typically, corduroy tracks are made up of logs laid across muddy and wet terrain, especially during Russia's mud season (*rasputitsa*), which can then be crossed by wheeled vehicles. These were common in western Russia, where wood was plentiful, but in the steppe region the shortage of timber would have made their construction very difficult. Moreover, the requirement to use wood for tracks would have faced a rival claim for fuel for winter dugouts.

14. Heightened enemy surveillance of German radio traffic is consistent with future operational planning (an offensive); thus, German measures to reduce radio traffic, and so deny the enemy useful information, are consistent with the fact that some intelligence officers in 6th Army suspect that a large-scale offensive may be likely.

15. This refers to "Befehl für den Kampf im Winter 1942/43," 29th October 1942, BA-MA, RH 20-6/220/6–24. This is a detailed report that deals with tasks, operations of the formations, and combat in winter positions. Paulus clearly fails to take into account the state of the troops and their exhaustion.

16. An order issued and signed by Paulus ("Betr.: Kampfführung im Winter," 30 October 1942) passed on Hitler's thoughts to 6th Army. The opening remarks leave no doubt at all that Hitler and his senior commanders had failed to identify any threat of a major Soviet counteroffensive in the weeks ahead: "At the present time the Russians are hardly in the position to initiate a major offensive with wide-ranging operational objectives" (BA-MA, RH 20-6/227/63). Despite the apparent conviction that the Red Army has exhausted its offensive potential, Paulus stresses the need for determined defense and refers to the "*heilige Aufgabe*" (holy mission) to repulse all enemy attacks. Mediating Hitler's views on Russian potential in this order to 6th Army, Paulus nevertheless betrays a hunch that something is in the offing.

17. The order originated from 6th Army's chief of staff (see BA-MA, RH 20-6/228/32).

18. Löser's report provides clear evidence that a large-scale operation is being planned by the enemy, at least on the sector of 76th Infantry Division.

19. This attachment refers to the detailed report issued by 6th Army Headquarters, 6th November 1942, "Überblick über Zustand und Verwendungsmöglichkeiten der Turkbtle," BA-MA, RH 20-6/228/69–87, which is analyzed in chapter 6.

20. This attachment refers to Führerbefehl No. 2, 6 November 1942.

Hitler warns the men of 6th Army to expect an attack on the following day to mark the Bolshevik Revolution. The order is to be read out to all officers and men on 6 November 1942 (see BA-MA, RH 20-6/228/48).

21. Dinafü is a military abbreviation for *Divisionnachschubsführung* (divisional supply headquarters).

22. The significant point here is that there is no suggestion that the soldiers of another division who have been separated from their units in the course of the battle are in any way guilty or under suspicion of attempting to desert. This is in striking contrast to the way these soldiers would have been treated had they been in the Red Army.

23. The light field howitzer 16 entered service with the German army in 1916.

24. This reference to "foreign security troops" is likely a comment on Germany's Romanian allies.

25. The battle for height 61.6 was discussed in chapter 1.

26. Parts of this remarkable engagement were discussed in chapter 1.

27. "*Ratschbumm*" is German army onomatopoeic slang for the Soviet antitank gun.

28. Soviet mines were made of wood with an explosive filling. In *Bittere Pflicht* Löser notes that since in the open steppe there was no firewood, German soldiers, having removed the detonator, would use the mine's wooden case and explosive filling as fuel. Jochen Löser, *Bittere Pflicht: Kampf und Untergang der 76. Berlin-Brandenburgischen Infanterie Division* (Osnabrück: Biblio Verlag, 1986), p. 227.

29. "Sewing machine" was one of the nicknames given to small, light Soviet aircraft that would fly over German positions at night, dropping bombs and leaflets. The nickname referred to the droning engine noise.

30. Father, later Monsignor, Josef Kayser features prominently in the history of 76th Infantry Division, both before and after Stalingrad, providing comfort to the sick and wounded. One of the more remarkable incidents recalled by Father Kayser concerns his first encounter with the Red Army at the moment of surrender. To quote him: "I did not walk away but approached the Russians and suddenly stood face to face with 5 young men. Behind them stood another soldier with a different type of headwear, indicating a higher rank, a lieutenant. The 5 young men raised their weapons. I made a sign of a large cross and shouted at them in Russian: 'I am a priest: Christ is also arisen in war!' Then they threw their machine pistols away. To be honest, I thought to myself, 'If only you had a machine pistol now! With one burst you would be able to finish them off.' But at the sign of my cross they had thrown their weapons down! But I still expected a shot. Then they put their arms round my neck and kissed me on the right cheek, on the left cheek, and on the mouth and said: 'In truth, he is once again arisen!'" Quoted in Löser, *Bittere Pflicht*, p. 234.

31. Once again we can note the crucial difference in the way the two armies treated their troops who had been encircled and managed to fight their way back to their own lines.

32. This term is used in the original document. "*Hilfswirtschaft*," translated as economic aid or assistance, probably refers to a part of the German supply chain.

Chapter 5. K-98 vs. Mosin M 1891/1930: German and Soviet Snipers at Stalingrad and on the Eastern Front

1. Major H. Hesketh-Prichard, *Sniping in France: With Notes on the Scientific Training of Scouts, Observers and Snipers*, with a foreword by General Lord Horne of Stirkoke (London: Hutchinson & Co, 1920), pp. 28 and 31.

2. Ibid., p. 2.

3. Ibid.

4. Ibid. (emphasis in the original).

5. Translated as *Snaiping vo Frantsii: sluzhba sverkhmetkikh strelkov v mirovuiu voinu na Zapadno-evropeiskom fronte* (Moscow: Gosvoenizdat, 1924).

6. *Infantry Training*, vol. 1: Infantry Platoon Weapons Pamphlet № 10, "Sniping," 1951, p. 3.

7. In his excellent account of German snipers, Peter Senich refers to the Soviet sniper rifle as the Mosin-Nagant M91/30, whereas Russian sources refer to the rifle as the Mosin M91/30. See Peter R. Senich, *The German Sniper 1914–1945* (Boulder, CO: Paladin Press, and London and Melbourne: Arms and Armour Press, 1982). Nagant (*Nagan* in Russian) was the Belgian arms manufacturer that designed the revolver used in the Soviet Union. The Mosin rifle was designed by Sergei Ivanovich Mosin and entered service with the tsarist army in 1891.

8. Among the sources consulted I could find no explanation of PU. I suggest it could be something such as *pritsel ustanovlennyi* (mounted sight).

9. Oleg Riazanov, *Istoriia snaiperskogo iskusstva* (Moscow: Bratishka, 2004), p. 25. According to Senich, 53,195 sniper rifles were produced in 1942 alone. See *The German Sniper 1914–1945*, p. 407.

10. Riazanov, *Istoriia snaiperskogo iskusstva*, p. 28. For those who may not be familiar with what is meant by "grouping" in marksmanship, the following explanation will be in order. Good grouping is the ability of the marksman to achieve the smallest possible spread of shots on a target. So if a marksman fires five shots at a target from a distance of 100 meters, and all five shots fall within a circle with a maximum diameter of, say, 2 inches, that would be regarded as a good group because the shots are consistently hitting the same part of the target. (Modern rifles firing high-quality ammunition will achieve even smaller groups.) Another marksman who, using ammunition from the same batch and shooting at the same range, achieved a 10-inch group would be regarded as being an inferior rifle shot. The primary reason for poor grouping can normally be attributed to poor holding. Zeroing is the process whereby the marksman ensures that at a set range, conveniently and normally 100 meters, his shots will hit the part of the target selected. Throughout zeroing and grouping the marksman always takes the same point of aim. Typically on the range this will be a small, highly visible point on the center of the target. At this stage in the process it is not essential that all the shots hit the center of the target. What is critical is that all the shots fired land on the same part of the target and are as tightly bunched together as possible (a good group). The smaller and tighter the groups achieved, the better because any corrections made to the lateral and vertical screws on either the iron/open or telescopic sights will ensure a greater degree of accuracy. So the marksman fires five shots at the target at

a range of 100 meters. He aims for the center of the white circle on the center of the target. He notes that all five shots have tightly clustered in a 2-inch group. Taking the center of the five shots fired as the basis for corrections (the mean point of impact), he notes that the center of his group is 5 inches high and 5 inches to the left. In order to ensure that his MPI is consistent and statistically as accurate as possible, he will fire four or five groups of five rounds per group. He then takes the mean of all the MPIs and uses these data as the basis for making any changes. That done, the marksman can now adjust the elevation and lateral screws on the rifle's telescopic sight and fire a confirmation group of five shots. Theoretically, he should now achieve the same group, all tightly clustered in and around the center of the target. Grouping will be influenced by the rifle; the ballistic consistency and features of the ammunition; the skill of the marksman (the sequence of firing the shot); and, at longer ranges, by light, wind, and other meteorological factors. As the range increases, the group size will also increase. With fewer working and moving parts than a semiautomatic rifle—factors that influence grouping—the bolt-operated rifle is the best option for a sniper rifle. Moreover, spent rifle cases, ejected when firing a semiautomatic rifle, can, in certain circumstances, betray the sniper's position to an observer or enemy sniper.

11. Iurii Rybalkin, *Operatsiia «X» Sovetskaia voennaia pomoshch' respublikanskoi Ispanii, 1936–1939* (Moscow: AIRO-XX, 2000), p. 107, p. 116.

12. N. L. Volkovskii, ed., *Tainy i uroki zimnei voiny, 1939–1940, Po dokumentam rasskrechennykh arkhivov* (Sankt-Peterburg: Poligon, 2000), p. 397.

13. "Doklad upolnomochennogo narodnogo komissariata oborony narodnomu komissaru oborony o rezul'tatakh proverki v chastiakh 8-i armii," 10 January 1940 g., in Volkovskii, ed., *Tainy i uroki zimnei voiny, 1939–1940*, p. 265.

14. Riazanov, *Istoriia snaiperskogo iskusstva*, p. 36.

15. Ibid.

16. Ibid.

17. Vasil' Bykov, "'Za rodinu! Za Stalina': Tsena proshedshikh boev," *Rodina* 5 (1995): p. 33.

18. Sniper training was also taken very seriously in NKVD units. In the first half of 1942 Colonel Saraev, the commander of 10th Rifle Division NKVD, ordered that "before 30 May 1942 snipers are to be assembled, having trained one sniper for each section" (see "Prikazy 10 Strelkovoi Div. Vnutr. Voisk NKVD-SSSR Po lichnomu sostavu. Nachato 01.01.1942 g. Okoncheno 01. 06.1942 g.," Rossiiskii Gosudarstvennyi Voennyi Arkhiv [Russian state military archive] fond 38759, opis' 1, delo 1, list 180). Saraev also confirmed the importance of using snipers against enemy aircraft (see ibid., list 167). The scale of sniper training and deployment in NKVD units can be appreciated from a report sent to Beria in June 1943 by General Lieutenant A. N. Apollonov, a senior NKVD officer. In his report Apollonov states that as of the end of June 1943 the NKVD has a total of 25,410 snipers and a total of 18,421 sniper rifles. The following successes and losses are claimed: "During the tour of duty 216,640 enemy soldiers and officers have been killed by NKVD snipers. Our own losses amounted to 1,158, of whom 375 were killed, 770 wounded, and 13 reported as missing." № 1489, "Dokladnaia zapiska zamestitelia narod-

nogo komissara vnutrennikh del SSSR general-leitenanta A. N. Apollonova narodnomu komissaru vnutrennikh del SSSR L.P.Berii o nevozmozhnosti vydeleniia snaiperov iz sostava voisk NKVD na ukomplektovanie snaiperskikh podrazdelenii chastei i soedinenii Krasnoi Armii' ne panee 30 iiunia 1943 g.," *Organy gosudarstvennoi bezopasnosti SSSR v Velikoi Otechestvennoi Voine: Sbornik dokumentov*, tom chetvertyi, kniga 1, *Sekrety Operatsii "Tsitadel,"* 1 January–30 June 1943 g., izdatel'stvo "Rus'" (Moscow, 2008), p. 646.

19. The story that deals with the duel is "Berlinskaia znamenitost'" (The Berlin celebrity), Sergei Alekseev, *Gvardeiskii razgovor, rasskazy iz istorii Velikoi Otechestvennoi Voiny* (Speaking with soldiers: Stories from the history of the Great Fatherland War) (Moscow: Voenizdat, 1979), pp. 115–117.

20. Vasilii Zaitsev, *Zapiski snaipera: za Volgoi zemli dlia nas ne bylo* (Moscow: DOSAAF, 1971), p. 5.

21. Ibid., p. 44.

22. Ibid., p. 93.

23. Ibid., p. 96.

24. Ibid., p. 127.

25. Ibid., p. 165.

26. Ibid., p. 202.

27. Ibid., pp. 209–210.

28. Ibid., p. 210.

29. Ibid., pp. 210–211.

30. Nor does the second book in the third volume of a collection of declassified NKVD documents include anything about the duel or its outcome. See *Organy gosudarstvennoi besopasnosti SSSR v Velikoi Otechestvennoi Voine: Sbornik dokumentov*, tom 3, kniga 2, *Ot oborony k nastupleniiu 1 iiulia–31 dekabria 1942 goda*, izdatel'stvo "Rus'" (Moscow, 2003). This collection does, however, contain a directive from the NKVD directorate that underlines the exceptional importance attached to securing all captured enemy documents, such as internal passports and other forms of identification, and then passing them on to higher NKVD formations, precisely what has not happened in the case of the dead German sniper. See № 1149, "Ukazanie UNKVD po Stalingradskoi oblasti № 85107 Astrakhanskomu OKPO i PO NKVD o napravlenii v adres Upravleniia trofeinykh i dobytykh u protivnika dokumentov i otlichitel'nykh znakov," 9 October 1942 g., pp. 350–351.

31. On one of my visits to the Bundesarchiv-Militärarchiv in Freiburg-im-Breisgau I discussed the question of whether Major Konings existed and the availability of any extant records pertaining to his German Army career with Dr. Manfred Kehrig, then the head of the archive, and one of the archivists.

32. See Vasilii Chuikov, *The Beginning of the Road*, trans. Harold Silver (London: Macgibbon & Kee, 1963), p. 142.

33. Alan Clark, *Barbarossa: The Russian-German Conflict 1941–1945* (Middlesex: Penguin, 1966), p. 278. In a second edition of *Barbarossa* (1985), Clark still cites Thorvald as the sniper (p. 243).

34. "Donesenie OO NKVD DF v UOO NKVD SSSR s protokolom doprosa voennoplennogo G. Liudviga, 9 dekabria 1942 g.," *Stalingradskaia epopeia: Materialy NKVD SSSR i voennoi tsenzury iz Tsentral'nogo arkhiva FSB RF* (Moscow: Zvonnitsa-MG, 2000), p. 299.

35. Antony Beevor, *Stalingrad* (London: Penguin, 1999). The photograph used by Beevor is between pages 334 and 335.

36. A. M. Samsonov, *Stalingradskaia bitva*, 4th ed. (Moscow: Nauka, 1989), p. 349.

37. Albert Axell, *Russia's Heroes: 1941–45* (London: Constable & Robinson, 2002), p. 254.

38. Ibid., p. 101.

39. Zaitsev, *Zapiski snaipera*, p. 6.

40. Axell, *Russia's Heroes*, p. 102.

41. Zaitsev, *Zapiski snaipera*, p. 216.

42. Axell, *Russia's Heroes*, p. 105.

43. Zaitsev, *Zapiski snaipera*, p. 209.

44. Axell, *Russia's Heroes*, p. 107.

45. Andy Dougan, *The Hunting of Man: A History of the Sniper* (London: Fourth Estate, 2004), p. 234.

46. Ibid., p. 236.

47. Ibid.

48. Beevor, *Stalingrad*. For Beevor's discussion of the role of Soviet snipers and the Zaitsev-Konings duel, see pp. 203–205. Surprisingly, given the theme, there is no reference in *Stalingrad* to Zaitsev's memoir, and the work is not listed in the sources. This omission is remedied in Antony Beevor and Luba Vinogradova, *A Writer at War: Vasily Grossman with the Red Army 1941–1945* (London: The Harvill Press, 2005), which is Vinogradova's translation of Grossman's diaries and notebooks with a commentary by Beevor.

49. Nekrasov points out that after Chuikov had been given a private showing of the film version of the novel, generals from the political department complained about the absence of any reference to Zaitsev. See Viktor Nekrasov, *Stalingrad* (Frankfurt-am-Main: Possev-Verlag, 1981), p. 454.

50. Vasilii Grossman, *Gody voiny*, izdatel'stvo (Moscow: Pravda, 1989), p.45.

51. Ibid., p. 385.

52. Ibid., p. 386.

53. Ibid., p. 387.

54. Ibid.

55. Ibid., p. 48.

56. Ibid., pp. 63–64.

57. Vasilii Grossman, *Za pravoe delo* (Moscow: Sovetskii pisatel', 1989), p. 561.

58. Ibid., p. 592.

59. Ibid., p. 599.

60. Grossman, *Gody voiny*, p. 359.

61. Ibid.

62. Vasilii Grossman, *Zhizn' i sud'ba* (Moscow: Sovetskii pisatel', 1990), pp. 174–175.

63. Grossman, *Gody voiny*, p. 358. It can also be noted that in *A Writer at War*, Beevor and Vinogradova also cite Zaitsev's patronymic with the initial "I" (p. 353).

64. Beevor and Vinogradova, *A Writer at War*, p. 159.

65. "O narushenii prikaza Tov. Stalina № 227 ot 28 iiulia 1942 g. Kr-tsem Zaitsevym Vasilem Ivanovichem," 29 August 1942, *Rossiiskii Gosudarstvennyi Voennyi Arkhiv*, fond 38759, Opis' 2, delo 2, list 171.

66. Senich, *The German Sniper 1914–1945*, p. ix. That the Wehrmacht (and the Luftwaffe) has reapplied itself to relearn the art of sniping is evident from two high-quality German World War II sniper training films, both of which can be seen on the Internet. See Das Oberkommando der Luftwaffe, Filmgruppe des Gen. d. Fl. Ausb. Film No. 668, *Scharfschütze im Einsatz—die unsichtbare Waffe* (The sniper on operations—the invisible weapon), Frühjahr 1944, and *Scharfschütze in der Geländeausbildung—Meister der Tarnung und Täuschung* (The sniper on fieldcraft training—masters of camouflage and deception).

67. Berhard Jocher, "Die Scharfschützen der Deutschen Wehrmacht," *Freiwillige* 9 (2000): 15–16.

68. Finnische Erfahrungen bei der

Scharfschützenausbildung, 8 May 1943, BA-MA, RH 68/1. A full English translation of this document is included in this book as Appendix A.

69. Ibid.

70. Ibid.

71. Ibid. (emphasis in the original).

72. Oberkommando des Heeres, Ausbildingshinweis Nr. 15, Zusammenarbeit russischer Scharfschützen mit Panzern im Angriff und Erfahrungen bei der Abwehr russischen Großangriffe, 18 January 1944, BA-MA, RH 2/2816/1.

73. Ibid., RH 2/2816/4.

74. "Befehl des Führers über die Einführung eines Scharfschützenabzeichens, 20th August 1944," *Freiwillige* 12 (2000): 12.

75. "Stellv. Generalkommando X.A.K. (Wehrkreiskommando X), Abteilung Ia/Ausb., Scharfschützenausbildung," Hamburg, 27 August 1944. I would like to thank Herr Bühm, an archivist at the Bundesarchiv-Militärarchiv, for providing me with a copy of this document.

76. Feindnachrichtenblatt "Stalingrad Nr. 9," 23 September 1942, BA-MA, RH 20-6/213/80.

77. Ibid., RH 20-6/213/81.

78. Bericht über eine Fahrt, 25 September 1942, BA-MA, RH 20-6/213/172–176.

79. Feindnachrichtenblatt "Stalingrad Nr. 10," 7 October 1942, BA-MA, RH 20-6/224/65. Vasilii Grossman provides an account of this behavior on the slopes of Mamaev kurgan as the Red Army moves closer to the German lines: "And the Germans sense that the time is close when neither a sniper nor a machine gunner will be of any use. And they are terrified by the thud of the spades. They want that sound to cease, even if only for a little while, even a minute." *Gody voiny*, p. 64.

80. Feindnachrichtenblatt "Stalingrad Nr. 12," 6 November 1942, BA-MA, RH 20-6/228/118. There is a reference to a second *Feindnachrichtenblatt* for October, Nr. 11, dated 23 October 1942, which is, as far as this author can tell, no longer available.

81. Sixth Army memorandum, 5 November 1942, BA-MA, RH 20-6/228/32.

82. Tagesmeldung, 4 October 1942, BA-MA, RH 20-6/215/24.

83. Tätigkeitsbericht, 25 October 1942, BA-MA, RH 20-6/226/128 (emphasis in the original).

84. Horst Zank, *Stalingrad: Kessel und Gefangenschaft*, 3. Auflage (Hamburg, Berlin, Bonn: Verlag E. S. Mittler & Sohn, 2001), p. 47.

85. Ausbildungsvorshcrift für die Gebirgstruppen (A.V.G), Heft III, Vorläufiger Entwurf, [no date], BA-MA, RHD 4/374/3, paragraph 368, p. 159.

86. Ibid.

87. Befehl für den Kampf im Winter 1942/43, 29 October 1942, BA-MA/RH 20-6/220/21.

88. Gefechtsbericht der Kampfgruppe Krumpen über den Kampf um Stalingrad, Panzer-Grenadier-Regiment 64 Abt.Ic, 28 August 1942, BA-MA, RH 27-16/43, p. 8. We find a similar report referring to enemy sniper activity dated 30 August 1942, p. 9.

89. Ibid., p. 10.

90. II PZ. Gren.Regt.64 Abt. Ic Betr: Gefechtsberichte "Stalingrad" O.U., 5 August 1943, BA-MA, RH 27-16/43, p. 5.

91. Gefreiter Josef Maessen, 14 April 1943, BA-MA, RH 27-16/43.

92. "Merkblatt für die Verteidigung," Ia, 305th Infantry Division, 5 September 1942, BA-MA, RH 26-305/14/33.

93. 24th Panzer Division, Betr: Besonders zu beachtende Führungs—und Aus-

bildungshinweise, 31 October 1942, BA-MA, RH 27-24/3, p. 4. The need to deploy snipers was also made quite clear in Erfahrungen in Kampf um Stalingrad, Anlage zu 24.Pz.-Div. Ia Nr 365/42 geh. v. 11.10.1942 (dated 11 October but should be 11 November 1942). See BA-MA, RH 27-24/3, p. 1. In the same document we also find the following appreciation of trench mirrors: "The Russian trench mirror has proved itself as a tool for observing the presence of enemy snipers" (p. 1). The report notes that the enemy's two most dangerous weapons are his antitank rifles and his snipers (p. 5).

94. Anlage zu 24. Pz.-Div. Abt. Ia Nr.377/42/geh. v. 15.11.1942, Erfahrungen im Kampf um Stalingrad c.a. Waffentechnische Erfahrungen I.) Zielfernrohrgewehre, BA-MA, RH 27-24/3/p. 13. The demand for good-quality optical instruments among the divisions of German 6th Army either to replace damaged and destroyed equipment or to add to the inventory must have been considerable. Some idea of the demand can be seen from a list of equipment requirements for just one division, 79th Infantry Division, dated 7 October 1942. Among the resupply requests are listed various optical instruments—range finders, optical sights for machine guns, telescopic sights and mounts—a total of 160 miscellaneous items. See Anlage zur Beurteilung der Versorgungslage. Bedarf an Waffen und Grossgerät, BA-MA, RH 26-79/149.

95. BA-MA, RH 27-16/12.

96. Ibid., RH27-16/39/13.

97. Ibid.

98. Ibid., 46, p. 5.

99. Ibid., pp. 6–7.

100. Rudolf Krell, Verteidigung im Nordriegel des Kessels Stalingrad, BA-MA, RH 26-94/113, p. 24.

101. Erich Maria Remarque, *Im Westen nichts Neues* (Köln: Kiepenheuer & Witsch, 1984), p. 263.

102. Major Grohe, Kriegstagebuch der 76 I.D.vom 01.10.42-23.01.43, BA-MA, RH 26-76/40, p. 56.

103. Ibid., p. 72.

104. I.R. 178 Ic. Fernspruch E., 13 October 1942, BA-MA, RH 26-76/41. Riazanov notes that NKVD snipers were equipped with a silencer known as a *Bramit*. See *Istoriia snaiperskogo iskusstva*, p. 48. These snipers would have belonged to units such as *otdel'naia motostrelkovaia brigada osobogo naznacheniia* [OMSBON, Independent motor-rifle brigade of special designation]). One of their main tasks was to conduct sabotage in the enemy rear. The commissar with the silencer may well have been part of such a unit.

105. Wolfgang Werthen, *Geschichte der 16. Panzer-Division*, hrsg vom Kameradschaftsbund 16. Panzer und Infanterie-Division Kameradenhilfswerk e.V. (Bad Nauheim: Podzun-Verlag, 1958), p. 50.

106. Ibid., p. 111.

107. Ibid., p. 215.

108. Gerhard Dieckhoff, *3. Infanterie-Division, 3. Infanterie-Division (mot.), 3. Panzergrenadier-Division* (Göttingen: Erich Börries Verlag, 1960), p. 139.

109. Ibid., p. 165.

110. Friedrich Wilhelm Hauck, *Eine Deutsche Division in Russland und Italien: 305. Infanteriedivision 1941–1945* (Dorheim: Podzun-Verlag, 1975), p. 74.

111. Ibid., p. 75.

112. Friedrich Dettmer, *Stalingrad: Ein Rückblick nach 60 Jahren* (Nürnberg: Buchdienst Südtirol, 2003), pp. 30–31.

113. Ibid., p. 67.

114. Hanns Neidhardt, *Mit Tanne und*

Eichenlaub: Kriegschronik der 100. Jäger-Division vormals 100. leichte Infanterie-Division (Graz-Stuttgart: Leopold Stocker Verlag, 1981), p. 211.

115. Ibid., p. 318.

116. Ibid., p. 319.

117. Ibid.

118. Ibid., p. 321.

119. Ibid., p. 322.

120. Ibid., p. 390.

121. Ibid., p. 395.

122. Jochen Löser, *Bittere Pflicht: Kampf und Untergang der 76. Berlin-Brandenburgischen Infanterie Division* (Osnabrück: Biblio Verlag, 1986), p. 79.

123. BA-MA, Nachträge zu *Bittere Pflicht*, Band 4, O11b, 76a-4, no page number.

124. Ibid., p. 8.

125. Ibid., p. 200.

126. Ibid., p. 199.

127. Ibid., para. 4, Erlebnisbericht.

128. In the report it is noted that "the troops cannot get any rest." See German 6th Army, Ia, 15 October 1942, BA-MA, RH 20-6/225/49.

129. Riazanov, *Istoriia snaiperskogo iskusstva*, p. 45.

130. Dougan, *The Hunting of Man*, p. 238.

Chapter 6. German Recruitment of Soviet National Minorities, Deserters, and Prisoners on the Eastern Front and in Stalingrad

1. Joachim Hoffmann, *Die Ostlegionen 1941–1943: Turkotataren, Kaukasier und Wolgafinnen im deutschen Heer*, 2nd ed. (Freiburg: Verlag Rombach, 1981), p. 11.

2. Ibid., p. 23.

3. Ibid., p. 28.

4. Ibid., pp. 61–62.

5. Ibid., p. 54.

6. "Verfügung über landeseigene Hilfskräfte im Osten," Oberkommando des Heeres, GenStdH/Org. Abt (II) Nr. 8000/42 geh. August 1942. Rotes Heft. BA-MA, RHD 7/8a-2/5.

7. Ibid., 2/6.

8. Ibid., 2/30.

9. "Einsatz von Kriegsgefangenen bei der Truppe," 8 October 1942, BA-MA, RH 20-6/224/185.

10. Major Grohe, Kriegstagebuch der 76 I.D.vom 01.10.42-23.01.43, BA-MA RH 26-76/40/9.

11. "Erhöhung der Kampfkraft," 6 October 1942, BA-MA, RH 20-6/224/9–15.

12. Ibid., p. 12. Things moved quickly. On 10 October 1942 Generalleutnant Schmidt, 6th Army's chief of staff, informed Army Group B of preliminary measures on the use of Russian *Hilfswillige* in divisional artillery. "Erhöhung der Kampfkraft," 10 October 1942, BA-MA, RH, 20-6/224/141.

13. "Verhalten gegenüber Kosaken und Kalmücken," 11 October 1942, BA-MA, RH 20-6/225/36.

14. "Merkblatt für das Verhalten gegenüber Kosaken," BA-MA, RH 20-6/225/37.

15. Ibid.

16. AOK 6. Ia Nr.4425/42 g.Kdos, 6 November 1942, BA-MA, RH 20-6/228/68.

17. "Überblick über Zustand und Verwendungsmöglichkeiten der Turkbtle," BA-MA, RH 20-6/228/69–87.

18. Ibid., p. 70.

19. Ibid.

20. Ibid., p. 71. There is an explicit warning of such dangers in "Verfügung über Landeseigene Hilfskräfte im Osten": "The good experiences, which, for the greater part, the troops have had with *Hilfswillige* must not in any way lead to reckless trust and a neglect of the need to

be vigilant in defensive measures. The troops must constantly bear in mind that in difficult situations and when experiencing local setbacks, unreliable elements among the *Hilfswillige* in the army can inflict serious damage, and that the enemy will routinely attempt to insert agents in this manner. The deployment of female *Hilfswillige* is forbidden. Those *Hilfswillige* who go absent are to be dealt with as deserters" (p. 7). The potential dangers posed by the use of *Hilfswillige* are evident in an order issued by 79th Infantry Division: "The discharge of Hilfswillige is forbidden. If Hilfswillige are deemed to be superfluous, then they are to report to the Intelligence Section at Divisional Headquarters. Russian prisoners of war who move about in the main combat zone and are not employed as *Hilfswillige* among the units are to be shot dead on sight [*sind sofort zu erschießen*]," 79th Infantry Division, I/c 2/43 secret, Divisional Headquarters, 2 January 1943, Hans Sänger, *Die 79. Infanterie Division* (Friedberg: Podzun-Pallas-Verlag, n.d.), pp. 124–127.

21. "Überblick über Zustand und Verwendungsmöglichkeiten der Turkbtle," p. 76.

22. Ibid., p. 73.

23. AOK 6. Ic/Iprop. 26 September 1942, Flugblattpropaganda in den Feind, BA-MA, RH 20-6/214/74.

24. Antony Beevor, *Stalingrad* (London, Penguin, 1999), p. 171. Beevor quite rightly notes that "Dobronin's [NKVD officer] acknowledgement of the statistical difficulties should certainly be remembered when looking at the total of 446 desertions during September" (p. 171).

25. Anlage 3 zum Feindnachrichtenblatt "Stalingrad Nr. 9," Gliederung und Kampfwert der Feindverbände vor 6. Armee. Stand 23 September 1942, BA-MA, RH 20-6/213/84–87.

26. AOK 6. to OKH Op. Abt. Report from Major Menzel, 4 October 1942, BA-MA, RH 20-6/215/33.

27. AOK 6. to OKW./Op. Abt. 6 October 1942, BA-MA, RH 20-6/224/20.

28. AOK 6. Ic. 6 November 1942. Feindnachrichtenblatt "Stalingrad Nr. 12," BA-MA, RH 20-6/228/118.

29. Ibid., p. 119

30. 384 Infantry Division, Morgenmeldung, 29 December 1942, BA-MA, RH 26/384/32/71.

31. 384 Infantry Division, Tätigkeitsbericht Nr. 2 der Abtlg. Ic, 1 January 1943, 21 January 1943, 22 January 1943, BA-MA, RH 26/384/33.

32. Ibid., Nr. 3 (21–31 January 1943), 2 February 1943, p. 33.

33. Ibid., p. 33, s.3.

34. See, among others, "Soobshchenie OO NKVD STF v UOO NKVD SSSR 'O khode realizatsii prikaza № 227 i reagirovanii na nego lichnogo sostava 4-oi tankovoi armii' 14 avgusta 1942 g.," *Stalingradskaia epopeia*, pp. 180–182.

35. AOK 6 HQ, *Von Charkow bis Stalingrad*, BA-MA, RH 20-6/216/72 .

36. Tätigkeitsbericht, 22nd January 1943, BA-MA, RH 26/384/33.

37. 384 Division, *V. Mann–Einsätze*, 13 December 1942, BA-MA, RH 26/384/32/16.

38. Verpflegungsstärken A. O.K. 6 im Kessel, 6 December 1942, BA-MA RH 20-6/239/226.

39. Manfred Kehrig, *Stalingrad: Analyse und Dokumentation einer Schlacht*, Beiträge zur Militär-Kriegsgeschichte, Band 15, Herausgegeben vom Militärgeschichtlichen Forschungsamt (Stuttgart: Deutsche Verlags-Anstalt, 1974), p. 604.

40. Gefechts- und Verpflegungsstärken der 24. Panzer Division am 1. 1943, BA-MA RH 27-24/6.

41. Beevor, *Stalingrad*, p. 184.

42. Kehrig, "Personal- und Materialstärkeangaben der 6. Armee Stand Mitte November 1942," *Stalingrad*, pp. 662–663.

43. Verfügung über landeseigene Hilfskräfte im Osten, BA-MA, RHD 7/8a-2/pp. 5–6 (emphasis added).

44. This is an ancient problem. At Agincourt in 1415, the English king, Henry V, was confronted with a similar security threat to the immediate rear of his army. Fearing that large numbers of French prisoners were about to rearm themselves and attack the English, Henry V ordered that the French prisoners be put to death.

45. "Prikaz VChK (bez nomera), 'O zalozhnikakh iz semei voennosluzhashchikh, sovershivshikh izmenu rodine,'" № 50 [1920], in A. N. IAkovlev *et al.*, eds., *Lubianka: organy VChk-OGPU-NKVD-NKGB-MGB-KGB 1917–1991 spravochnik*, in the series "Demokratiia," *Rossiia. XX VEK, Dokumenty* (Moscow: Mezhdunarodnyi fond, 2003), pp. 375–376.

46. "Prikaz VChk № 261, 'O rabote organov VChK v Krasnoi Armii, 21 avgusta 1921 g.,'" № 62, in ibid., pp. 389–390.

47. Oberkommando des Heeres (OKH), *Erfahrungen aus dem finnisch-russischen Kriege*, 2 October 1940, BA-MA, RH 20-6/475/11. The fact that volunteering to be part of a reconnaissance patrol would invite suspicions of attempting to desert speaks for itself.

48. Ibid., p. 12 (emphasis in the original). In the period leading up to the sixtieth anniversary of the Great Patriotic War, the Russian State Military Archive held a small exhibition dedicated to the Soviet-Finnish Winter War of 1939–1940. Desertion was a major theme in the exhibits. On one leaflet was a picture of a Red Army soldier with his rifle slung upside down on his back with the bayonet pointing toward the ground and his hands up. Underneath the photo the caption says: "Throw down your rifle/Comrade Red Army men—save your life!/Surrender to the Finns. In Finland we live very well/Surrender; then this pointless war will be over." In an exceptionally detailed and comprehensive study of the collaboration of Soviet citizens in Wehrmacht units, the author reveals that during the Russo-Finnish war the Finns attempted, with some success, to recruit Soviet deserters to fight against the Red Army. See S. I. Drobiazko, *Pod znamemani vraga: Antisovetskie formirovaniia v sostave germanskikh vooruzhennykh sil, 1941–1945 gg.* (Moscow: Eksmo, 2005). One of the architects of this plan was B. Bazhanov, who fled the Soviet Union in 1928. He subsequently met Marshal Mannerheim, who gave permission for an attempt to raise a unit made up of Soviet deserters. Bazhanov discusses this venture in his book *Vospominaniia byvshego sekretaria Stalina* (Moscow: SOFINTA, 1990).

49. OKH, *Erfahrungen aus dem finnisch-russischen Kriege*, 2 October 1940, BA-MA, RH 20-6/475/12.

50. № 1002, "Iz doklada Krymskogo obkoma partii v TsK VKP (b) i Tsentral'nyi shtab partizanskogo dvizheniia o bor'be krymskikh partizan v tylu u nemtsev i predatel'skoi roli tatarskikh natsionalistov, 7 iiulia 1942 g.," *Organy gosudarstvennoi bezopasnosti SSSR v Velikoi Otechestvennoi voine*, tom tretii, Kniga 2, 1 iiulia–31 dekabria 1942 goda, izdatel'stvo

"Rus'" (Moscow, 2003), pp. 19–21.

51. Ibid., p.20.

52. Ibid.

53. In the German-occupied territories, *starostas* were individuals appointed by the Germans to pass on German orders; to act as intermediaries between the local population and the German occupation forces; and to inform the Germans about, for example, partisan activity in the region. They were regarded as traitors and were often killed by partisans.

54. Ibid.

55. Ibid.

56. Ibid., p. 21.

57. "Iz dokladnoi zapiski NKVD Krymskoi ASSR v NKVD SSSR o politiko-moral'nom sostoianii naseleniia Kryma [avgust 1942 g.]," OGB/1942/2/№ 1075, pp. 192–202.

58. Ibid., pp. 193–194.

59. Ibid., p. 194.

60. Ibid.

61. Ibid., p. 195.

62. "Donesenie nachal'nika otdela Severnoi gruppy voisk Zakavkazkogo fronta brigadnogo komissara Kh. S. Nadorshina nachal'niku Glavnogo politicheskogo upravleniia Krasnoi Armii A. S. Shcherbakovu o sostoianii natsional'nykh divizii v sostave Severnoi gruppy voisk Zakavkazkogo fronta, 18 oktiabria 1942 g.," OGB/1942/2/№ 1166, pp. 399–402.

63. Ibid., p. 399.

64. Ibid.

65. Ibid., p. 400.

66. Ibid.

67. Ibid., pp. 400–401.

68. Ibid., p. 401.

69. Ibid., p. 402.

70. "Soobshchenie nachal'nika OO NKVD Stalingradskogo fronta № 3228/S nachal'niku UNKVD po Stalingradskoi oblasti o sozdanii nemtsami «dobrovol'cheskikh» formirovanii na vremenno okkupirovannoi territorii SSSR, 18 noiabria 1942 g.," OGB/1942/2/№ 1202, p. 468.

71. Ibid.

72. Ibid., p. 472.

73. Ibid., p. 473.

74. "Plan meropriiatii 4-go otdela UNKVD po Krasnodarskomu kraiu po razlozheniiu i vyvodu v raspolozhenie chastei Krasnoi Armii dvukh kazach'ikh eskadronov, sformirovannykh nemtsami, 28 noiabria 1942 g.," OGB/1942/2/№ 1213, pp. 490–492.

75. Ibid., p. 491.

76. The Japanese intelligence services were also busy recruiting special service detachments made up of the nationalities living in the border regions of the north. Natural hunters and with an intimate knowledge of the terrain, these tribal recruits were ideally suited to a wide range of intelligence-related tasks. See "Direktiva NKVD SSSR № 52/4610 o merakh po preduprezhdeniiu i presecheniiu podryvnoi deiatel'nosti «otriadov osobogo naznacheniia», sozdannykh iaponskoi razvedkoi iz predstavitelei narodnostei Severa, prozhivaiushchikh v prigranichnykh s SSSR raionakh, 16 aprelia 1942 g.," OGB/1942/1/№ 893, pp. 358–361.

77. "Direktiva NKVD SSSR № 558 o poryadke predstavleniia materialov i informatsii o deiatel'nosti sozdannykh nemtsami «natsional'nykh formirovanii», 11 dekabria 1942 g.," OGB/1942/2/№ 1231, p. 527.

78. Ibid., p. 525.

79. Ibid., p. 526.

80. "Spetssoobshchenie Chetvertogo upravleniia NKGB SSSR narodnomu komissaru gosudarstvennoi bezopasnosti

SSSR V. N. Merkulovu o dogovore mezhdu pravitel'strvom Germanii i tak nazyvaemym Russkim natsional'nym komitetom, 11 avgusta 1943 g.," OGB/1942/2/№ 1556, pp. 222–223.

81. "Iz ukazaniia nachal'nika TsShPD № 1941 o neobkhodimosti razlozheniia formirovanii ROA i likvidatsii izmennika Rodiny A. A. Vlasova, 9 iiulia 1943 g.," OGB/1943/2/№ 1505, p. 77.

82. "Dokladnaia zapiska NKGB SSSR № 1767/M v GKO SSSR s predlozheniem o likvidatsii izmennika Rodiny A.A. Vlasova, 27 avgusta 1943 g.," OGB/1943/2/№ 1583, pp. 288–293.

83. Ibid., p. 293.

84. For an analysis of the Vlasov/loyalty theme in Vladimov's novel, see Frank Ellis, *The Damned and the Dead: The Eastern Front through the Eyes of Soviet and Russian Novelists* (Lawrence: University Press of Kansas, 2011), pp. 232–254.

85. Hoffmann, *Die Ostlegionen* 1941–1943, pp. 78–79. There is a remarkable encounter between units of 76th Infantry Division and Soviet civilians described in Jochen Löser's *Bittere Pflicht*. All attempts to speak Russian to these villagers come to nothing until German soldiers hear some of the villagers speaking German with a Swabian accent. It turns out these villagers are the direct descendants of Germans brought to Russia by Catherine the Great. The locals inform the Germans that all the men have been taken away and that German-speaking parachutists—almost certainly NKVD provocateurs—sought their help. They beg the divisional Catholic priest, Josef Kayser, to stay and be their priest. See Löser, *Bittere Pflicht: Kampf und Untergang der 76. Berlin-Brandenburgischen Infanterie Division* (Osnabrück: Biblio Verlag, 1986), pp. 105–107.

86. Hanns Neidhardt, *Mit Tanne und Eichenlaub: Kriegschronik der 100. Jäger-Division vormals 100. leichte Infanterie-Division* (Graz-Stuttgart: Leopold Stocker Verlag, 1981), p. 73. Well before 100th Jäger Division was committed to the battle in the city, a shortage of manpower was a problem. *Hiwis* were now essential: "The regiments were merged, and one tried with all kinds of improvisation to maintain somewhat the combat strength. The supply chains were combed, and Ukrainian and Russian *Hiwis* were used as drivers in greater numbers" (Neidhardt, p. 201).

87. Löser, *Bittere Pflicht*, p. xiii.

88. Ibid., pp. 181–182.

89. Ibid.

90. Ibid., p. 206.

91. BA-MA, RH 26-76/40/58.

92. BA-MA, RH 27-24/3/23.

93. Ibid., p. 19.

94. Kriegsgefangenen-Monatsmeldung, 79 Infanterie-Division, 7 October 1942, BA-MA, RH 26-79/149. In this report, which was sent to XI Army Corps, a clear distinction is made between a prisoner of war (*Kriegsgefangener*) and a deserter (*Überläufer*). In the report, there are references to Dulags (transit camps), among them, Dulag-205. Confirming the security risk posed by prisoners of war the report's author states that: "All prisoners of war are guarded by the troops".

95. "Der Kampf um Höhe 61,6," BA-MA, RH 26-76/41/6.

96. Günter Schmitz, *Die 16. Panzer-Division 1938–1945: Bewaffnung, Einsätze, Männer* (Friedberg: Podzun-Pallas-Verlag, ca. 1976), p. 110.

97. "Der Kampf der 16. Panzer-Division in der Festung Stalingrad in der Zeit vom 19. November 1942 bis 2. Februar 1943," BA-MA, RH 27-16/52 /37.

98. BA-MA, RH 27-24/5/166.

Chapter 7. Behind the German and Soviet Lines: Espionage and Counterespionage at Stalingrad

1. "Soobshchenie NKVD SSSR № 548/B v GKO i General'nyi shtab Krasnoi Armii o pokazaniiakh chlenov ekipazha sbitogo pod g. Stalingradom nemetskogo razvedyvatel'nogo samoleta," 31 marta 1942 g., *Organy gosudarstvennoi bezopasnosti SSSR v Velikoi Otechestvennoi voine*, tom tretii, Kniga 1, № 872, 1 ianvaria–30 iiunia 1942 goda, izdatel'stvo "Rus'" (Moscow, 2003), pp. 307–308.

2. "Iz protokola № 210 zasedaniia Stalingradskogo gorodskogo komiteta oborony o neobkhodimosti otneseniia g. Stalingrada k rezhimnoi mestnosti pervoi kategorii," 11 fevralia 1942 g., OGB/1942/1/№ 802, p. 113.

3. Ibid.

4. "Dokladnaia zapiska UNKVD po Stalingradskoi oblasti № 85013 nachal'niku 2-go otdela NKVD SSSR ob organizatsiia razvedyvatel'noi i diversionnoi raboty v tylu protivnika," 29 ianvaria 1942 g., OGB/1942/1/№ 792, p. 76.

5. Ibid.

6. Ibid., p. 77.

7. Ibid.

8. Ibid.

9. Ibid., p. 78.

10. Ibid.

11. Ibid., p. 79.

12. Ibid.

13. Ibid.

14. Ibid.

15. Ibid.

16. Ibid., p. 80.

17. "Ukazanie zamestitelia narodnogo komissara vnutrennikh del SSSR № 55/64 nachal'niku UNKVD Stalingradskoi oblasti ob organizatsii partizanskikh formirovaniia, diversionno-razvedyvatel'noi seti i agenturnoi sviazi v tylu protivnika," 7 fevralia 1942 g., OGB/1942/1/№ 798, p. 95.

18. Ibid., pp. 95–96.

19. "Orientirovka UNKVD po Stalingradskoi oblasti № 85120 v podchinennye organy ob organizatsii raboty agentov-odinochek, perebrasyvaemykh cherez liniiu fronta s kratkosrochnymi zadaniiami," oktiabr' 1942, OGB/1942/2/№ 1177, p. 425.

20. OGB/1942/1/№ 798, p. 95.

21. Ibid., p. 95.

22. "Ukazanie UNKVD po Stalingradskoi oblasti № 85046 nachal'nikam operativnykh grupp UNKVD pri osobykh otdelakh armii Stalingradskogo fronta ob izmeneniakh v rabote operativnykh grupp," 15 avgusta 1942 g., OGB/1942/2/№ 1053, p. 144.

23. "Iz postanovleniia biuro Stalingradskogo obkoma VKP (b) o khode komplektovaniia partizanskikh otriadov i razvertyvaniia ikh boevoi deiatel'nosti v tylu nemetsko-fashistskikh okkupantov," 19 avgusta 1942 g., OGB/1942/2/№ 1055, p. 148.

24. Ibid.

25. Ibid., p. 149.

26. Ibid.

27. Ibid.

28. Ibid., p. 150.

29. Ibid.

30. "Razvedyvatel'naia svodka UNKVD Stalingradskoi oblasti № 10 (85111) kommanduiushchemu Donskim frontom general-leitenantu K.K. Rokossovskomu o polozhenii v tylu protivnika po sostoianiiu na," 15 oktiabria 1942 g., 16 oktiabria 1942, OGB/1942/2/№ 1163, pp. 380–392.

31. Ibid., p. 381.

32. Ibid.

33. Ibid.
34. Ibid.
35. Ibid., p. 382.
36. Ibid., p. 383.
37. Ibid., p. 385.
38. Ibid.
39. Ibid.
40. "Iz protokola zasedaniia Stalingradskogo gorodskogo komiteta oborony," 25 avgusta 1942, OGB/1942/2/№ 1063, pp. 166–167.
41. OGB/1942/2/№ 1163, p. 386.
42. Ibid.
43. Ibid., pp. 387–388.
44. Ibid., p. 388.
45. Ibid.
46. Some idea of the appalling fate and conditions that struck the civilian population is also revealed in the history of the German 100th Jäger Division: "Along the streets one constantly saw the corpses of men, women, and children, struck dead by shell fire and dead from exhaustion and hunger. How these poor souls that had made it to the rear managed to make ends meet remained unresolved. They had practically nothing to eat, and they were certainly unable to take large amounts of provisions with them on their flight from the city, and even then this small amount was taken from them. For all that, this was a minor tragedy occurring on the periphery of the great catastrophe itself." Hanns Neidhardt, *Mit Tanne und Eichenlaub: Kriegschronik der 100. Jäger-Division vormals 100. leichte Infanterie-Division* (Graz-Stuttgart: Leopold Stocker Verlag, 1981), p. 218.
47. OGB/1942/2/№ 1163, p. 389.
48. Ibid., p. 390.
49. "Zadanie razvedyvatel'nogo otdeleniia Upravleniia voisk NKVD po okhrane tyla Donskogo fronta zafrontovomu agentu «Taprakovu», perebrasyvaemomu v tyl protivnika," 9 noiabria 1942 g., OGB/1942/2/№ 1186, p. 439.
50. Ibid., p. 440.
51. "Legenda zafrontovomu agentu «Taprakovu», napravliamemomu s zadaniem v tyl protivnika," 9 noiabria 1942 g., OGB/1942/2/№ 1187, p. 441.
52. "Soobshchenie OO NKVD Stalingradskogo fronta v NKVD SSSR ob itogakh raboty za," avgust 1942 g., OGB/1942/2/№ 1187, p. 227.
53. OGB/1942/2/№ 1089, p. 228.
54. "Direktiva NKVD SSSR № 359 o priniatii mer po rozysku i arestu agentov nemetskoi razvedki, obuchavshikhsia v razvedyvatel'no-diversionnoi shkole v m. IAblon' Liublinskogo voevodstva (Pol'sha)," 27 avgusta 1942 g., OGB/1942/2/№ 1066, p. 172.
55. Ibid.
56. OGB/1942/2/№ 1089, p. 228.
57. Ibid.
58. Ibid.
59. Ibid.
60. See, for example, "Spravka OO NKVD STF v UOO NKVD SSSR o deiatel'nosti zagraditel'nykh otriadov Stalingradskogo i Donskogo frontov [ne panee 15 oktiabria]," 1942 g., and "Dokladnaia zapiska OO NKVD DF v UOO NKVD SSSR o rabote osoborganov po bor'be s trusami i panikerami v chastiakh Donskogo fronta za period s 1 oktiabria 1942 goda po 1 ianvaria 1943 goda," 17 fevralia 1943 g., in IA. F. Pogonii, i dr., *Stalingradskaia epopeia: Materialy NKVD SSSR i voennoi tsenzury iz Tsentral'nogo arkhiva FSB RF* (Moscow: Zvonnitsa-MG, 2000)*Stalingradskaia epopeia*, pp. 230–232 and 403–410.
61. "Soobshchenie Upravleniia osobykh otdelov NKVD SSSR № 16/45367 v

General'nyi shtab i Glavnoe politicheskoe upravlenie Krasnoi Armii ob aktivizatsii razvedyvatel'no-diversionnoi deiatel'nosti protivnika na uchastkakh Stalingradskogo fronta," 24 sentiabria 1942 g., OGB/1942/2/№ 1118, pp. 285–287.

62. "Direktiva NKVD SSSR № 431 o merakh po rozysku i arestu agentury germanskoi voennoi razvedki, podgotovlennoi abvergruppoi 105," 7 oktiabria 1942 g., OGB/1942/2/№ 1143, p. 343.

63. "Direktiva NKVD SSSR № 544 o merakh pozysku i arestu agentov abvergruppy 103," 3 dekabria 1942, OGB/1942/2/№ 1219, p. 503.

64. "Direktiva NKVD SSSR № 108 ob usilenii tshchatel'noi proverki vyzyvaiushchikh podozrenie grupp voennosluzhashchikh dlia vyiavleniia nemetskoi agentury, napravliaemoi v prifrontovuiu polosu pod vidom podrazdelenii Krasnoi Armii," 13 marta 1942 g. , OGB/1942/1/№ 848, pp. 256–257.

65. "Orientirovka Upravleniia osobykh otdelov NKVD SSSR № 16/22128 o deistvuiushchei v g. Mtsenske nemetskoi razvedyvatel'noi shkole, gotoviashchei podrostkov dlia sovershеniia shpionskikh i diversionnykh aktsii v chastiakh Krasnoi Armii," 5 iiunia 1942 g., OGB/1942/1/№ 970, p. 527.

66. "Ukazanie NKVD SSSR № 66 ob usilenii operativno-chekistskoi raboty po vyiavlenii agentury razvedyvatel'nykh organov voiuiushchikh s SSSR stran," 20 fevralia 1942, OGB/1942/1/№ 812, p. 142.

67. "Zapiska NKVD SSSR v GKO o vyiavlenii i likvidatsii sphionov, diversantov, nemetskikh posobnikov i band v gorodakh i raionakh, osvobozhdennykh Krasnoi Armiei ot voisk protivnika," 18 marta 1943 g., OGB/1943/1/№ 1360, p. 297.

68. Helmuth Spaeter, *Die Brandenburger: eine deutsche Kommandotruppe zbV 800*, 2. teilw.überarbeitete Auflage mit Personen—und Sachregister (München: Verlagsagentur Walther Angerer, 1982).

69. "Direktiva komanduiushchego voiskami Zakavkaskogo fronta komanduiushchim armiiami fronta o protivodeistvii spetsial'nym gruppam protivnika i ustanovlenii rezhimnykh mer v raoinakh pervalov Glavnogo Kavkazskogo khrebta," 22 avgusta 1942 g., OGB/1942/2/№ 1059, p. 160.

70. Spaeter, *Die Brandenburger*, pp. 180–181.

71. "Ukazanie UNKVD po Stalingradskoi oblasti № 85155 nachal'nikam raiotdelenii NKVD oblasti o provedenii agenturno-operativnykh meropriiatii v osvobozhdennykh ot okkupatsi naselennykh punktakh," 28 noiabria 1942 g., OGB/1942/2/№ 1211, p. 486.

72. Ibid., p. 487.

73. "Iz svodki UNKVD Stalingradskoi oblasti № 16 o polozhenii v tylu protivnika," [ne panee 5 ianvaria 1943 g.,] OGB/1943/1/№ 1261, p. 40.

74. Ibid.

75. Ibid., p. 41.

76. Ibid., p. 42.

77. Ibid.

78. Agents Malinovskaia and Olia successfully infiltrated a group of collaborators working for the Germans in Stalingrad and the Stalingrad district, mainly *starostas* and members of the auxiliary police. The agents managed to secure full details of the collaborators' identities, and nine persons were arrested. See "Iz spravki 4-go otdela UNKVD Stalingradskoi oblasti o rabote otdela za fevral' 1943 g.," 19 marta 1943 g., OGB/1943/1/№ 1362, p. 313.

79. OGB/1943/1/№ 1261, p. 44.

80. Ibid.

81. "Iz dokladnoi zapiski UNKVD SSSR SO v NKVD SSSR «o polozhenii v g. Stalingrade v period ego chastichnoi okkupatsii i posle izgnaniia okkupantov»," 1 aprelia 1943 g., *Stalingradskaia epopeia*, p. 419.

82. Ibid., p. 420. I can find no trace of any German *Generalmajor* with the name Lenning among the senior officers at Stalingrad. One possibility is that the Russian transliteration is a corruption of the name Lenski and is therefore a reference to Generalmajor Arno von Lenski, the commander of 24th Panzer Division.

83. Ibid.

84. Ibid. (emphasis added), p. 421.

85. Ibid., pp. 422–423.

86. Ibid., p. 423.

87. Ibid., p. 425.

88. Ibid., p. 428.

89. Ibid., pp. 427–428.

90. Ibid., p. 434.

91. "Zapiska NKVD SSSR v GKO o vyiavlenii i likvidatsii sphionov, diversantov, nemetskikh posobnikov i band v gorodakh i raionakh, osvobozhdennykh Krasnoi Armiei ot voisk protivnika," 18 marta 1943 g., *OGB/1943/1/№* 1360, pp. 295–307. An earlier NKVD report (not before 23 February 1943) provided details of battles between NKVD detachments and groups of German soldiers holding out in ruins in Stalingrad after 3 February 1943. There were clashes in the region of the Barrikady factory, the Red October marketplace, and the Red October factory. See "Iz istoricheskogo formuliara 21-i strelkovoi brigady voisk NKVD ob operativno-sluzhebnoi deiatel'nosti po okhrane tyla Donskogo fronta i v g. Stalingrade v period za dekabr' 1942 g.–fevral' 1943 g.," *OGB/1943/1/№* 1324, p. 205.

92. *OGB/1943/1/№* 1360, p. 296.

93. Ibid.

94. Ibid., p. 296.

95. "Iz spravki 4-go otdela UNKVD po Stalingradskoi oblasti ob operativno-chekistskoi rabote na vremenno okkupirovannoi protivnikom territorii," 9 aprelia 1943 g., *OGB/1943/1/№* 1384, pp. 366–371.

96. Ibid., p. 366.

97. Ibid., p. 367.

98. Ibid.

99. Ibid.

100. Ibid.

101. Ibid.

102. Ibid., p. 368.

103. Ibid.

104. Ibid.

105. Ibid., p. 369.

106. Ibid.

107. Ibid., p. 370.

108. Ibid.

109. "Iz protokola doprosa byvshego nachal'nika shtaba 305-i pekhotnoi divizii podpolkovnika R. Tal'ttso o strukture abvera, sluzhby bezopasnosti i SD, tainoi Polevoi politsii (GFP) i metodakh ikh razvedyvatel'noi i kontrrazvedyvatel'noi deiatel'nosti," 10 aprelia 1943 g., *OGB/1943/1/№* 1386, pp. 373–380. The Russian transliterated surname cited here is almost certainly a transcription error. In *Stalingrad*, for example, Manfred Kehrig refers to an Oberstleutnant i. G. Paltzo (pp. 94, 97, 103, and 112). Furthermore, on various Internet sites the operations officer (Ia) of 305th Infantry Division is named as Oberstleutnant i. G. Rudolf Karl Paltzo. See, for example, http://www.stalingrad.net/german-hq/division-Ia/operations_officers.htm (accessed 28 November 2012).

110. Ibid., p. 376.

111. Ibid., p. 378.

112. Feindnachrichtenblatt "Stalingrad Nr. 10," 7 October 1942, BA-MA, RH 20-6/224/64.

113. "79th Infantry Division, Ic 513/42 secret, 26 November 1942," Hans Sänger, *Die 79. Infanterie Division* (Friedberg: Podzun-Pallas-Verlag, n.d.), pp. 97–98.

114. Ibid.

115. AOK 6: "Funkspruch an Herresgruppe Don," 27 December 1942, BA-MA, RH 20-6/240/179.

116. Betr.: "Sowjetrussische Einheiten mit besonderen Aufgaben," 30 December 1942, BA-MA, RH 20-6/235/164.

117. Ibid.

118. "79th Infantry Division, Ic 2/43, secret, Protection from Espionage and Sabotage, 2 January 1943," Sänger, *Die 79. Infanterie Division*, pp. 124–127.

119. Ibid.

120. "Führungsordnungen Nr. 1," Gruppe Pfeiffer Ia, 5 January 1943, BA-MA, RH-20-6/235/163.

121. Betr.: "Brieftaubenverkehr," 11 January 1943, BA-MA, RH 20-6/235/211.

122. "Tätigkeitsbericht der Abt. Ic für die Zeit vom 10.12.42.–31.12.1942," 18.01.1943, BA-MA, RH 26-384/32/3–4.

123. G. Bezverkhnii, ed., SMERSH: *Istoricheskie ocherki i arkhivnye dokumenty* (Moscow: Izdatel'stvo Glavarkhiva Moskvy, 2003), p. 18.

124. Ibid., p. 31.

125. Ibid.

126. Ibid.

127. If Red Army soldiers who had been recruited by German intelligence believed that surrendering themselves to the Soviet authorities on crossing the lines would earn any goodwill, they were probably deluding themselves. For example, on 25 February 1942 a group of ten Red Army soldiers recruited by the Abwehr for attacks on railway lines handed themselves in. On 20 July 1942, after enduring all the rigors of NKVD interrogation, each of the ten men was sentenced to ten years in a labor camp with five years' loss of rights by a military tribunal of the Western front. See "Spetssoobshchenie Osobogo otdela NKVD 61-i armii Zapadnogo fronta № 775 v Osobyi otdel fronta o iavke s povinnoi diversionnoi gruppy, sformirovannoi nemtsami iz sostava byvshikh voennosluzhashchikh sovetskikh voisk," [ne panee 25 fevralia 1942 g.,] *OGB/1942/1/№* 817, pp. 157–161.

128. "V.-Mann-Einsätze," 13 December 1942, BA-MA, RH 26-384/32/16.

129. "Iz obzora razvedyvatel'nogo otdela Glavnogo upravleniia voisk NKVD po okhrane tyla Deistvuiushchei Krasnoi Armii o rezul'tatakh bor'by s vrazheskoi agentury za pervoe polugodie 1943 g.," *OGB/1943/2/№* 1535, p. 161.

130. Ibid.

131. Ibid., p. 165.

132. Ibid.

133. Ibid., p. 163.

134. Ibid., p. 163.

135. Ibid., p. 166.

136. Ibid., p. 163.

137. Gerhard Dieckhoff, *3. Infanterie-Division, 3. Infanterie-Division (mot.), 3. Panzergrenadier-Division* (Göttingen: Erich Börries Verlag, 1960), p. 241.

138. V. S. Khristoforov, *Stalingrad: Organy NKVD nakanune i v dni srazhenii* (Moscow: Moskovskie uchebniki, 2008), p. 127.

139. "Direktiva Voennogo soveta Donskogo fronta voennym sovetam armii o narusheniiakh v obrashchenii s voennoplennymi i spetskontingentom i merakh po ikh ustraneniiu," 29 ianvaria 1943 g., in M.M. Zagorul'ko, ed., *Voennoplennye v Stalingrade 1943–1954: Doku-*

menty i Materialy, tom 2, *Voennoplennye v SSSR, 1939–1956*, gosudarstvennoe uchrezhdenie Izdatel', № 3 (Volgograd, 2003), p. 62.

140. Ibid., p. 878.

141. "Spravka o vydeleniia voennoplennykh i spetskontingentov, soderzhashchikhsia v lageriakh NKVD, dlia trudispol'zovaniia narkomatami na," 1 aprelia 1943 g, in Major General V. A. Zolotarev, ed., *Russkii Arkhiv: Velikaia Otechestvennaia*, vol. 13, no. 2, *Nemetskie voennoplennye v SSSR 1941–1955 gg.*, Sbornik dokumentov, Kniga pervaia, TERRA, № 7 (Moscow, 1999), p. 173.

142. "Ob''iasnitel'naia zapiska k svedeniiam po trudoispol'zovaniiu voennoplennykh za iiun 1943 goda," № 19, in ibid., p. 193.

143. "Ob''iasnitel'naia zapiska k svodnym svedeniiam po trudovomu ispol'zovaniiu voennoplennykh i spetskontingenta na dekabr' 1943 g.," in ibid., p. 200.

Chapter 8. The Aftermath of Defeat: German Prisoners of War in the Soviet Camps

1. For example, one Soviet camp official proposed that Romanian and Hungarian prisoners of war should be housed in better accommodations than German prisoners of war and should receive better clothing and food than Germans. He also recommended that hot food be issued to Romanian and Hungarian prisoners of war ahead of Germans. See "Rasporiazhenie rukovodstva lageria № 163 nachal'nikam lagernykh otdelenii ob uluchshenii uslovii razmeshcheniia, snabzheniia i bytovogo obsluzhivaniia voennoplennykh vengrov i rumyn, 22 maia 1946 g.," № 135, in M. M. Zagorul'ko, ed., *Voennoplennye v Stalingrade 1943–1954: Dokumenty i Materialy*, tom 2: *Voennoplennye v SSSR, 1939–1956*, gosudarstvennoe uchrezhdenie Izdatel' (Volgograd, 2003), p. 429.

2. Erwin Peter and Alexander E. Epifanow, *Stalins Kriegsgefangene: Ihr Schicksal in Erinnerungen und nach russischen Archiven*, 2nd ed. (Graz-Stuttgart: Leopold Stocker Verlag, 1998), p. 11.

3. Major General V. A. Zolotarev, ed., *Russkii Arkhiv: Velikaia Otechestvennaia*, vol. 13, no. 2, *Nemetskie voennoplennye v SSSR 1941–1955 gg.*, Sbornik dokumentov, Kniga pervaia (Moscow: TERRA, 1999), p. 15.

4. Ibid., p. 9.

5. Ibid.

6. Ibid., p. 7.

7. Ibid., p. 9.

8. Peter and Epifanow, *Stalins Kriegsgefangene*, p. 14.

9. Zolotarev, *Nemetskie voennoplennye v SSSR 1941–1955 gg.*, p. 9.

10. Peter, *Stalins Kriegsgefangene*, p. 18.

11. "Spetsial'noe polozhenie o voennoplennykh', 1 iiulia 1941 g.," *Organy gosudarstvennoi bezopasnosti SSSR v Velikoi Otechestvennoi voine*, tom vtoroi, Kniga 1, № 347, 22 iiunia–31 avgusta 1941 goda, izdatel'stvo "Rus'" (Moscow, 2000), p. 141.

12. Ibid.

13. Ibid., p. 142.

14. Ibid., p. 144.

15. "Dokladnaia zapiska sotrudnika politicheskogo upravleniia D. Z. Manuil'skogo zamestiteliu narodnogo komissara oborony L. Z. Mekhlisu o rezhime v lageriakh dlia nemetskikh voennoplennykh i ikh politicheskikh nastroeniiakh, 15 avgusta 1941," in V. A. Zolotarev et al., eds., *Russkii Arkhiv: Velikaia Otechestvennaia. Nemetskie voennoplennye v SSSR: Dokumenty i materialy.*

1941–1955 *gg*. T 24 (13-2) (Moscow: TERRA, 1999), p. 72.

16. "Polozhenie o rezhimnykh lageriakh NKVD dlia voennoplennykh," in ibid., p. 88.

17. Ibid., p. 90.

18. In his introductory essay Zagorul'ko acknowledges that prisoners of war were used in the production of military goods: "At factory № 264, as well as being engaged on restoration and repair work, 45 percent of all the shells shipped out by the factory and 80 percent of all of the hulls of self-propelled guns were processed by prisoners of war for the nine months of 1944. In such a way, in violation of international law, prisoners of war were used in military production." See "Zhizn' i rabota voennoplennykh v Stalingrade," in Zagorul'ko, ed., *Voennoplennye v Stalingrade* 1943–1954, pp. 18–19.

19. "Spravka o chislennosti voennoplennykh, zaniatykh na rabotakh v otdel'nykh otrasliakh promyshlennosti po sostoianiiu na 1 marta 1944, mart 1944 g.," in Zolotarev et al., eds., *Nemetskie voennoplennye v SSSR* 1941–1955 *gg*., p. 201.

20. "Dokladnaia zapiska ministra vnutrennikh del o repatriatsii netrudosposobnykh internirovannykh i mobilizovannykh nemtsev v Germaniiu, 17 maia 1946 g.," in ibid., p. 244.

21. Ibid., p. 359.

22. "Prikaz ministra vnutrennikh del soiuza SSR № 001196 o zavoze iz germanii 27,500 nemtsev, soderzhashchikhsia v tiur'makh i spetslageriakh MVD, i vyvoze v Germaniiu takogo zhe kolichestva bol'nykh i netrudosposobnykh voennoplennykh i internirovannykh nemetskoi natsional'nost', 26 dekabriia 1946 g.," in ibid., p. 385.

23. "Doklad MVD SSSR o kolichestvennom sostave voennoplennykh i ikh trudovomu ispol'zovanii po sostoianiiu na 1 ianvaria 1949 g," in ibid., p. 248.

24. Ibid., p. 249.

25. "Doklad zamestitlia nachal'nika upravleniia lageria podpolkovnika Grishchuka o deiatel'nosti operativno-peresyl'nogo lageria № 27 MVD SSSR za period 1942–1950 gg.," in ibid., p. 343.

26. "Tipovaia programma frontovykh antifashistskikh shkol', 1943 g," in ibid., pp. 308–309.

27. "Polozhenie ob ispol'zovanii na frontakh upolnomochennykh natsional'nogo komiteta «Svobodnaia Germaniia» (voennoplennykh) i chlenov «Soiuza nemetskikh ofitserov» dlia razlozheniia voisk protivnika, 1944 g.," in ibid., pp. 329–332.

28. Ibid., p. 330.

29. Ibid., p. 350.

30. Ibid., p. 351.

31. "Rekomendatsii dlia raboty antifashistskogo aktiva Krasnogorskogo lageria № 27, 23 oktiabria 1944 g," in ibid., p. 323.

32. Ibid., pp. 323–324.

33. "Direktiva narodnogo komissara vnutrennikh del soiuza SSR № 138 narodnym komissaram vnutrennikh del soiuznykh i avtonomnykh respublik, nachal'nikam UNKVD kraev i oblastei o poriadke repatriatsii voennoplennykh, ispol'zovavshikhsia v kachestve lagernykh agentov i osvedomitelei, 18 avgusta 1945 g.," in ibid., p. 368.

34. Ibid.

35. Ibid.

36. Ibid.

37. Zagorul'ko, ed., *Voennoplennye v Stalingrade* 1943–1954, p. 9 (emphasis in the original).

38. Ibid.

39. "Dokladnaia zapiska rukovodstva NKVD SSSR predsedateliu Gosudarstvennogo Komiteta Oborony I. V. Stalinu o chislennosti voennoplennykh, nakhodiashchikhsia v statsionarnykh lageriakh i priemnykh punktakh NKVD v prifrontovoi polose, 4 fevralia 1943 g.," № 6, in ibid., p. 65.

40. "Iz obzora GUPVI MVD SSSR o rabote ego frontovykh organov za 1942–1943 gg.," in ibid., p. 74.

41. Ibid., pp. 75-76.

42. Ibid., p. 8.

43. Ibid., p. 10.

44. Ibid.

45. Ibid.

46. Ibid., p. 13.

47. Ibid., p. 66. In a later report (26 February 1943) on the state of Camp № 98, the poor physical condition of the prisoners of war was attributed to the long marches, typically 150 to 200 kilometers (93 to 124 miles). It was noted, however, that there were instances of prisoners of war having to march 500 kilometers (311 miles) to camps and staging posts and, as in the case of the shorter marches, without being fed for two to five days. See "Doklad upravleniia lageria dlia voennoplennykh № 98 nachal'niku UPVI NKVD SSSR general-maioru I. A. Petrovu o sanitarnom-bytovom sostoianii lageria i rabote ego lechebno-sanitarnykh uchrezhdenie za period s 29 dekabria 1942 g. do 26 fevralia 1943 g," № 19, in ibid., p. 89.

48. Ibid., p. 76.

49. Vasilii Grossman, *Zhizn' i sud'ba* (Moscow: Sovetskii pisatel', 1990), p. 537.

50. "Dokladnaia zapiska nachal'nika UNKVD po Stalingradskoi oblasti polkovnika gosbezopasnosti V. S. Proshina v NKVD SSSR o sostoianii spetsgospitalei dlia voennoplennykh, pasnolozhennykh na territorii oblasti, 3 iiunia 1943 g.," № 32, in Zagorul'ko, ed., *Voennoplennye v Stalingrade 1943–1954*, p. 113.

51. "Donesenie rukovodstva spetsgospitalia № 5771 v UNKVD po Stalingradskoi oblasti o provedennoi rabote i sostoianii gospitalia, ne panee, 1 marta 1945 g.," № 80, in ibid., p. 259.

52. Ibid., p. 274.

53. "Raport nachal'nika 7-go lagernogo otdeleniia lageria № 108 kapitana Murynkina nachal'niku lageria A. A. Fedrovu o rezul'tatakh obsledovaniia bytovykh usloviia i mesta raboty voennoplennykh, otkomandirovannykh na drovozagotovki v KhOZO UMVD po Stalingradskoi oblasti, 24 aprelia 1946 g," № 130, in ibid., p. 423.

54. "Dokladnaia zapiska UNKVD po Stalingradskoi oblasti v GUPVI NKVD SSSR o sostoianii rabochego batal'ona mobilizovannykh nemtsev № 2021 pri SMU № 1 Neftemashstroia, 14 avgusta 1945 g.," № 88, in ibid., p. 294.

55. Ibid.

56. Ibid., p. 295.

57. "Donesenie nachal'nika Upravleniia lagerei voennoplennykh na territorii Stalingradskoi oblasti podpolkovnika gosbezopasnosti N.N.Smirnova v UPVI NKVD SSSR o faktakh grabezha i ubiistva sovetskikh grazhdan voennoplennymi, bezhavshimi iz lagerey, 27 aprelia 1943 g.," № 29, in ibid., p. 105.

58. "Otchetnyi doklad upravleniia lageria № 123 v UPVI NKVD SSSR o deiatel'nosti za period s ianvaria po oktiabr' 1944 g., 6 noiabria 1944 g.," № 75, in ibid., p. 231.

59. "Dokladnaia zapiska OPVI UNKVD Stalingradskoi oblasti nachal'niku Upravleniia o prodelannoi rabote za III

kvartal 1945 g.," 9 noiabria 1945 g., № 95, in ibid., p. 321.

60. "Doklad UMVD po Stalingradskoi oblasti v GUPVI MVD SSSR o rabote lageria № 108 za period s 1943 g. po 1 ianvaria 1950 g," № 234, in ibid., p. 732.

61. "Doklad upravleniia lageria № 108 o sostoianii okhrany i rezhima voennoplennykh za II polugodie 1946 g., ne ranee 1 ianvaria 1947 g.," № 163, in ibid., pp. 514–515.

62. Ibid., p. 732.

63. "Protokol obshchego sobraniia antifashistov 2-go lagernogo otdeleniia lageria № 362, 16 iiulia 1947 g.," № 173, in ibid., p. 550.

64. Zolotarev et al., eds., *Nemetskie voennoplennye v SSSR 1941–1955 gg.*, p. 358.

65. "Convention Relative to the Treatment of Prisoners of War, with Annex," Signed at Geneva. July 27, 1929, League of Nations, *Treaty Series*, vol. 118, no. 2734, pp. 343–409.

66. Ibid., p. 387.

67. "Pis'mo V. M. Molotova I. V. Stalinu s informatsiei o kolichestve nemetskikh voennoplennykh, 12 marta 1947 g," in Zolotarev et al., eds., *Nemetskie voennoplennye v SSSR 1941–1955 gg.*, p. 391.

68. Ibid., p. 392.

69. "Ukaz presidiuma verkhovnogo soveta SSSR o prekrashchenii sostoianii voiny mezhdu Sovetskim soiuzom i Germaniei, 25 ianvaria 1955 g.," in ibid., pp. 469–470.

70. Ibid., p. 9.

71. On 20 April 1945, less than three weeks before the final German collapse, Stalin issued a directive in which he demanded that Soviet troops change their attitude toward Germans, civilian and military. It is highly unlikely that this directive could ever have brought about an immediate change in attitudes on the part of the Red Army toward Germans. The hatred, the anger, and the desire for revenge, inflamed by German atrocities and reinforced by Soviet propaganda, became all the stronger the closer the end came. One manifestation of this revenge, denied by the Soviet authorities and their Russian Federation successors, was the mass rape of German women in Berlin. Stalin's directive at such a late stage in the war is a typical example of his duplicity and mendacity in his management of the Soviet bureaucracy. In any case, the large-scale and illegal deportation of German civilians after the war to the Soviet Union for use as, effectively, slave labor in Soviet industry is hardly consistent with Stalin's call for "a more humane attitude toward Germans." See "Direktiva Stavki verkhovnogo glavnokomandovaniia RKKA № 11072 ob izmenenii otnosheniia voisk Krasnoi Armii k nemetskim voennoplennym i grazhdanskomu nasleniiu, 20 aprelia 1945 g.," in ibid., p. 62. In the Zolotarev collection, immediately below the text of this directive is a reference to the Soviet magazine *Novoe vremia* 15 (1944): 15. Whether this is intended to indicate that Stalin's directive was first issued and placed in the public domain in 1944, not April 1945, is not clear.

Chapter 9. Return from the House of the Dead: The Arrest, Interrogation, and Repatriation of Oberst Boje (44th Infantry Division)

1. Arthur Boje, *Stalins deutsche Agenten. Ein Kriegsgefangener berichtet* (Graz-Stuttgart: Leopold Stocker Verlag, 2002), p. 107.

2. Correspondence received from the FSB in connection with an application to consult Boje's interrogation record.

3. Boje, *Stalins deutsche Agenten*, p. 16.

4. Ibid., p. 17.

5. G. Bezverkhnii, ed., SMERSH: *Istoricheskie ocherki i arkhivnye dokumenty* (Moscow: Izdatel'stvo Glavarkhiva Moskvy, 2003), pp. 222–223.

6. Boje, *Stalins deutsche Agenten*, p. 32.

7. Bezverkhnii, ed., SMERSH, p. 223.

8. Ibid., pp. 223–224.

9. Ibid., p. 224.

10. Ibid.

11. Ibid.

12. Ibid.

13. Ibid., p. 225

14. Ibid.

15. Ibid.

16. Ibid., p. 224

17. Ibid.

18. Ibid., p. 225

19. Ibid.

20. Ibid., pp. 225–226.

21. Boje, *Stalins deutsche Agenten*, p. 127.

22. Ibid., p. 67.

23. Ibid., p. 34.

24. Ibid., p. 126.

25. Ibid.

26. Ibid.

27. Ibid., p. 127.

28. Ibid.

29. Ibid.

30. Bezverkhnii, ed., SMERSH, p. 227.

31. Ibid.

32. Boje, *Stalins deutsche Agenten*, p. 128.

33. Ibid.

34. Bezverkhnii, ed., SMERSH, p. 226. The 6th Army commander's suspicion that he was being monitored was entirely correct. Over the period from 31 January to 4 February 1943, Paulus, along with his chief of staff, Generalleutnant Arthur Schmidt, and his adjutant, Oberst Wilhelm Adam, were incarcerated in temporary accommodations immediately after they were captured. Over this period, Senior Lieutenant Tarabrin, a German interpreter attached to the Special Section of the Don front, was given the task of monitoring the exchanges between Paulus and his staff. See "Dnevnik-otchet operupolnomochennogo KRO OO NKVD Donskogo fronta starshego leitenanta gosbezopasnosti E. A. Tarabrina o nakhozhdenii i obshchenii s generalami nemetskoi armii, kotorye byli vziaty v plen voiskami 64-i armii v g. Stalingrade," *Organy gosudarstvennoi bezopasnosti SSSR v Velikoi Otechestvennoi voine*, tom chetvertyi, Kniga 1, № 1299, 1 ianvaria–30 iiunia 1943 goda, izdatel'stvo "Rus'" (Moscow, 2008), pp. 135–144.

35. Bezverkhnii, ed., SMERSH, p. 226.

36. Ibid.

37. Ibid.

38. Boje, *Stalins deutsche Agenten*, p. 92.

39. Ibid., p. 135.

40. Ibid.

41. Ibid., p. 136.

42. Ibid., p. 23.

43. Ibid., p. 94.

44. In Eugenio Corti's epic, *The Red Horse*, Italian prisoners captured on the Eastern front are subjected to the same ideological processing by Italian communists. During his interrogation by an Italian communist, Michele Tintori reflects on the nature of communism and fascism: "*He must have left Italy he despised fascism, great. But once in Russia, after finding out that communism is incomparably worse—if only because it's endlessly more bloody than the clownishness of fascism—instead of getting out, which would have made sense, look at him, he's preferred to lower himself to being the*

inquisitor of his countrymen for the Communists." Eugenio Corti, *The Red Horse* (*Il Cavallo rosso*, 1983) (San Francisco: Ignatius Press, 2002), p. 447 (emphasis in original).

45. Boje, *Stalins deutsche Agenten*, p. 71.

46. Ibid., p. 93.

47. Ibid., pp. 82–83.

48. Jochen Löser, *Bittere Pflicht: Kampf und Untergang der 76. Berlin-Brandenburgischen Infanterie Division* (Osnabrück: Biblio Verlag, 1986), p. 237.

49. Ibid., p. 454.

50. Ibid., p. 455.

51. Boje, *Stalins deutsche Agenten*, p. 105.

52. Ibid., p. 106.

53. "Soprovoditel'naia zapiska Val'tera fon Zaidlitsa k memorandumu ob ispravlenii i usilenii raboty natsional'nogo komiteta «Svobodnaia Germaniia» i «Soiuza nemetskikh ofitserov», 26 fevralia 1944 g.," in Major General V. A. Zolotarev, ed., *Russkii Arkhiv: Velikaia Otechestvennaia*, vol. 13, no. 2, *Nemetskie voennoplennye v SSSR 1941–1955 gg.*, Sbornik dokumentov, Kniga pervaia, TERRA, № 18 (Moscow, 1999), pp. 173, 315.

54. Ibid., p. 318.

55. Boje, *Stalins deutsche Agenten*, p. 16.

56. Ibid., p. 170. Boje's observations about the presence of prisoners from the Baltic States in one of the camps are consistent with the mass deportation of people from those states that occurred toward the end of the 1940s. In May 1948, the Soviet occupation forces, in pursuit of a policy of removing so-called class enemies, deported some 49,331 Lithuanians. Another 31,917 were deported in March 1949. As part of the same operation, 42,149 were deported from Latvia and 20,173 were deported from Estonia. See Timothy Snyder, *Bloodlands: Europe between Hitler and Stalin* (London: The Bodley Head, 2010), p. 329.

57. The popularity of *The Count of Monte Cristo* is confirmed in Viktor Astaf'ev's war novel *Prokliaty i ubity* (*The Damned and the Dead*, 1992–1994), part 1, chapter 3. Astaf'ev describes Red Army recruits, housed in appalling accommodations and treated little better than labor-camp inmates, as being entranced by the story's combination of treachery, adventure, betrayal, and individual triumph. Given the themes and plot of the Dumas novel, it is easy to see why such a novel would appeal to those who feel oppressed. In her study of camp literature, Leona Toker also confirms the especial appeal of *The Count of Monte Cristo* for prisoners: it was almost as if the novel inspired escape attempts. See Leona Toker, *Return from the Archipelago: Narratives of Gulag Survivors* (Bloomington and Indianapolis: Indiana University Press, 2000), p. 86.

58. Boje, *Stalins deutsche Agenten*, pp. 141–142.

59. Ibid., p. 155.

60. Solomon E. Asch, "Opinions and Social Pressure," in Alexander Thomas, ed., *Papers on Socialization and Attitudes selected from* Scientific American (Reading, England: W.H. Freeman and Company, 1974), p. 30.

61. Ibid., p. 32.

62. Rudolf Marks was captured by the Red Army on 7 February 1945 near Küstrin. Earlier in the war he had served in 76th Infantry Division. He provides a detailed two-part essay of his time as a prisoner, much of which is consistent with what we find in Boje's book. Permanent, gnawing hunger is cited by Marks as the worst memory of his time as a prisoner of war and as such is clearly

open to being exploited by the NKVD. He is especially alert to what he regards as breaches of international legal instruments governing prisoners of war, of which all the victors of World War II were guilty in varying degrees. Marks is convinced that "among the Allies the opinion was very widespread that a collective punishment had been inflicted on the German people because of Hitler's crimes that would itself exclude the application of the Hague Conventions from being applied for the benefit of the Germans." He also points out that it was repeatedly emphasized that a nonapplication of the Hague Conventions represented a permissible reprisal in response to the many violations of international law by Germans during the war. He also vigorously contests the view that since the central German power apparatus had collapsed in 1945 the Allies were in some way liberated from applying the norms of international law to Germany. In 1949, the decisive year for many German prisoners in terms of charges and interrogations, Marks finds himself the victim of various charges, specifically that as a military judge he was responsible for condemning partisans to death. Even if, as in the case of Marks, these charges are eventually dropped, the aim of the NKVD is not to seek any punishment where there are prima facie grounds for bringing a case, with the application of due process, but perversely to punish an arrestee by due process, or for what passes as due process, by subjecting the arrestee to prolonged interrogation and isolation. This suggests a presumption of guilt, not of innocence until proven guilty. Rudolf Marks, "Als Zwangsarbeiter in russischer Kriegsgefangenschaft—Gedanken und Erinnerungen," 10 November 1982, Nachträge zu *Bittere Pflicht*, BA-MA, Band 6, O11b, 76a-6, Part I, pp. 1–13, and Part II, pp. 1–15.

63. Aufzeichnung from Legationsrat Hergt, Betr.: "Behandlung der von der Sowjetischen nichtamnestierten Gefangenen," Auswärtiges Amt/Politisches Archiv, B12, Band 1931, Aufzeichnung/204/514-01/76/520/56/24 Januar 1956.

64. This is conceded by the FSB. To quote from SMERSH: "Unfortunately in the activity of the agencies of state security of the USSR over the period from 1930–1950, the principle of *les rubiat—shchepki letiat* obtained, which not infrequently led to the conviction of innocent people" (Bezverkhnii, ed., SMERSH, p. 328). The time frame of 1930–1950 implies that this operational principle somehow started with the rise of Stalin, when in fact it was first established and applied by Lenin and Trotskii immediately after 1917.

Chapter 10. Reconciliation

1. Volksbund Deutsche Kriegsgräberfürsorge e.V., Kassel, hrsg., *Namen für Rossoschka—Schicksale aus Stalingrad*, GGP Media GmbH, 2 Auflage (Pößneck, 2008), p. 37.

2. Churchill paid tribute to Rommel at a time when everything was going very badly for Britain. To quote the prime minister: "I cannot tell what the position at the present moment is on the Western front in Cyrenaica. We have a very daring and skilful opponent against us, and, may I say across the havoc of war, a great general." Winston S. Churchill, *The Second World War*, vol. 4: *The Hinge of Fate* (London: Cassell & Co., 1951), p. 59.

3. № 559, "Dokladnaia zapiska Stal-

ingradskogo oblastnogo operativnogo shtaba NKVD SSSR ob itogakh operatsii po pereseleniiu nemtsev za predely oblasti', 15 sentiabria 1941 g.," *Organy gosudarstvennoi bezopasnosti SSSR v Velikoi Otechestvennoi voina*, tom vtoroi, Kniga 2, *Nachalo*, 1 sentiabria–31 dekabria 1941 goda, Izadatel'stvo Rus', Moscow, 2000, pp. 106–111.

4. "№ 507, "Ukaz Prezidiuma Verkhovnogo Soveta SSSR o pereselenii nemtsev, prozhivaiushchikh v raionakh Povolzh'ia', 28 avgusta 1941 g.," *Organy gosudarstvennoi bezopasnosti SSSR v Velikoi Otechestvennoi voina*, tom vtoroi, Kniga 1, *Nachalo*, 22 iiunia–31 avgusta 1941 goda, Izadatel'stvo Rus', Moscow, 2000, pp. 539–540, 541.

5. Martin Kruse, hrsg., *Die Stalingrad-Madonna: Das Werk Kurt Reubers als Dokument der Versöhnung*, 3. überarb. Auflage (Hannover: Lutherisches Verlagshaus, 1996), p. 72.

6. Ibid., p. 63.

7. Vasilii Grossman, "Sikstinskaia Madonna," *Neskol'ko pechal'nykh dnei* (Moscow: Sovremennik, 1989), p. 395.

8. Ibid., p. 397.

BIBLIOGRAPHY

1. Bundesarchiv-Militärarchiv, Freiburg-im-Breisgau

Divisional Diaries and Accounts of Battles

Abwehrkampf des III/203 unter Führung von Herrn Hauptm. Gerstenberg in der Zeit von 15.10–26.11.1942. BA-MA, RH 26-76/41.

Beiträge zur Geschichte der 94. Inf. Div. bei den Kämpfen um Stalingrad 1942–43. BA-MA, RH 26-94/113.

Der Kampf der 16. Panzer-Division in der Festung Stalingrad in der Zeit vom 19. November 1942 bis 2. Februar 1943. BA-MA, RH 27-16/52.

Der Kampf um Höhe 61, 6. BA-MA, RH 26-76/41/5.

Gefechtsbericht der Kampfgruppe Krumpen über den Kampf um Stalingrad, Panzer-Grenadier-Regiment 64 Abt.Ic, 28 August 1942. BA-MA, RH 27-16/43.

Kriegestagebuch der 76 I.D. vom 01.10.42–23.01.43. BA-MA, RH 26-76/40.

Nachträge zu *Bittere Pflicht: Kampf und Untergang der 76. Berlin-Brandenburgischen Infanterie-Division*. BA-MA, 6 Bände, O11b, 76a-1-6.

Intelligence Reports and Summaries

Abwehr-Trupp 304b/AOK 6, V.-Mann-Einsätze, 13 December 1942. BA-MA, RH 26-384/32/16.

AOK 6, Funkspruch an Heeresgruppe Don, 27 December 1942. BA-MA, RH 20-6/240/179.

AOK 6, Ic/Iprop, 26 September 1942, Flugblattpropaganda in den Feind. BA-MA, RH 20-6/214/74.

Brieftaubenverkehr, 11 January 1943. BA-MA, RH 20-6/235/211.

Feindnachrichtenblatt "Stalingrad Nr. 9," 23 September 1942. BA-MA, RH 20-6/213/80.

Feindnachrichtenblatt "Stalingrad Nr. 10," 7 October 1942. BA-MA, RH 20-6/224/65.

Feindnachrichtenblatt "Stalingrad Nr. 12," 6 November 1942. BA-MA, RH 20-6/228/118.

I.R. 178 Ic. Fernspruch E. 13 October 1942. BA-MA, RH 26-76/41.

Neues russisches Kampfverfahren für Stosstrupps, 6.11.1942. BA-MA, RH 26-76/41.

79 Infantry Division, Ib Div.Gef.St., 7.10.1942. Betr.: Kriegsgefangenen-Monatsmeldung. BA-MA, RH 26-79/149/pp. 197–242, 26–79/150/pp. 289–395.

Sowjetische Einheiten mit besonderen Aufgaben, 30 December 1942. BA-MA, RH 20-6/235/164.

384 Infantry Division, Abt.Ic, Tätigkeitsbericht der Abt. Ic für dir Zeit vom 10.12.42–31.12.42, 18 January 1943. BA-MA, RH 26-384/32/pp.3–4.

384 Infantry Division, Ic, Tätigkeitsbericht Nr. 3 (für die Zeit vom 21.–31.1.1943), 2 February 1943. BA-MA, RH 26/384/33/pp. 1–4.
384 Infantry Division, Morgenmeldung, 29 December 1942. BA-MA, RH 26/384/32/71.
384 Infantry Division, Tätigkeitsbericht, Nr. 2 der Abtlg. Ic, für die Zeit vom 1.1.43 bis 20.1.43, 22 January 1943. BA-MA, RH 26/384/33/pp. 1–3.

Miscellaneous

Aussage des Fw. Michael Horvath, Feldgend. Trupp 100. BA-MA, RH 26-76/41.
Bericht über eine Fahrt nach Stalingrad, 25 September 1942. BA-MA, RH 20-6/213/172.
Marks, Rudolf. "Als Zwangsarbeiter in russischer Kriegsgefangenschaft—Gedanken und Erinnerungen." 10 November 1982. Nachträge zu *Bittere Pflicht: Kampf und Untergang der 76. Berlin-Brandenburgischen Infanterie-Division.* BA-MA, Band 6, O11b, 76a-6, Part I, pp. 1–13, and Part II, pp. 1–15
Schlüssel für Straßenzustandsmeldungen, 10 October 1942. BA-MA, RH 20-6/224/187.
von Schilling, Freifrau Mady. "Betreuung der Stalingradkämpfer—Abwicklungsstab Stalingrad." Nachträge zu *Bittere Pflicht: Kampf und Untergang der 76. Berlin-Brandenburgischen Infanterie-Division.* BA-MA, Band 6, O11b, 76a-6, pp. 1–24.

Operational Assessments, Directives, and Guidelines

Anlage zu 24. Pz.-Div. Abt. Ia Nr. 377/42/geh. v. 15.11.1942, Erfahrungen im Kampf um Stalingrad c.a. Waffentechnische Erfahrungen I.) Zielfernrohrgewehre. BA-MA, RH 27-24/3.
Anlage zur Beurteilung der Versorgungslage. Bedarf an Waffen und Grossgerät. BA-MA, RH 26-79/149.
AOK 6. Ia Nr. 4425/42 g.Kdos. 6 November 1942. BA-MA, RH 20-6/228/68.
AOK 6. to OKW./Op. Abt. 6 October 1942. BA-MA, RH 20-6/224/20.
Befehl für den Kampf im Winter 1942/43, 29 October 1942. BA-MA, RH 20-6/220/21.
Einsatz von Kriegsgefangenen bei der Truppe, 8 October 1942. BA-MA, RH 20-6/224/185.
Erfahrungen aus dem finnisch-russischen Kriege, Oberkommando des Heeres (OKH), 2 October 1940. BA-MA, RH 20-6/475/11.
Erhöhung der Kampfkraft, 6 October 1942. BA-MA, RH 20-6/224/9–15.
Erhöhung der Kampfkraft, 10 October 1942. BA-MA, RH 20-6/224/141.
Führungsordnungen Nr. 1, Gruppe Pfeiffer Ia, 5 January 1943. BA-MA, RH 20-6/235/163.
Meldungen über Verpflegungs—und Gefechtsstärken der Divisionen, 24 October 1942. BA-MA, RH 20-6/226/60–68.
Merkblatt für das Verhalten gegenüber Kosaken. BA-MA, RH 20-6/225/37.
Merkblatt für den Ortskampf. BA-MA, RH 26-305/14/50–51.
Merkblatt für die Verteidigung, Ia, 305th Infantry Division, 5 September 1942. BA-MA, RH 26-305/14/33.
OKH Org. Abt., 08.10.1942, Grundlegender Befehl Nr. 1 (Hebung der Gefechtsstärke). BA-MA, RH 20-6/220/65.

Tagesmeldung, 4 October 1942. BA-MA RH 20-6/215/24.
24th Panzer Division, Betr: Besonders zu beachtende Führungs—und Ausbildungshinweise, 31 October 1942. BA-MA, RH 27-24/3.
Überblick über Zustand und Verwendungsmöglichkeiten der Turkbtle. BA-MA, RH 20-6/228/69–87.
Verfügung über Prikaz seigene Hilfskräfte im Osten. BA-MA, RHD 7/8a/2 (1942).
Verhalten gegenüber Kosaken und Kalmücken, 11 October 1942, BA-MA, RH 20-6/225/36.
Verpflegungs—und Gefechtsstärken, 13 November 1942. BA-MA, RH 20-6/229a/17–36.
V.O./OKH. Bei AOK.6, 4 October 1942. BA-MA, RH 20-6/215/33.

Sniping

Ausbildungsvorshcrift für die Gebirgstruppen (A.V.G), Heft III, Vorläufiger Entwurf, (undatiert). BA-MA, RHD 4/374/3.
Finnische Erfahrungen bei der Scharfschützenausbildung. 8 May 1943. BA-MA, RH 68/1.
Oberkommando des Heeres, Ausbildingshinweis Nr. 15, Zusammenarbeit russischer Scharfschützen mit Panzern im Angriff und Erfahrungen bei der Abwehr russischen Gro angriffe, 18 January 1944. BA-MA, RH 2/2816/1.

2. Federalnyi Arkhiv, Federalnaia Sluzhba Bezopasnosti Rossiiskoi Federatsii, Ugolovnoe Delo Po Obvineniiu Kerperta i dr. Arkhiv No. K-99468

O narushenii prikaza Tov. Stalina No. 227 ot 28 iiulia 1942 g. Kr-tsem Zaitsevym Vasilem Ivanovichem, 29.08.1942, Rossiiskii Gosudarstvennyi Voennyi Arkhiv, fond 38759, Opis' 2, delo 2, list 171.

3. Auswärtiges Amt

Aufzeichnung from Legationsrat Hergt, Betr.: "Behandlung der von der Sowjetischen nichtamnestierten Gefangenen," Januar 1956, Auswärtiges Amt/Politisches Archiv/B12/Band 1931/Aufzeichnung/204/514-01/76/520/56/24.

4. Published Sources

Alekseev, Sergei. *Gvardeiskii razgovor: Rasskazy iz istorii Velikoi Otechestvennoi voiny.* Moscow: Voenizdat, 1979.
Andreyev, Catherine. *Vlasov and the Russian Liberation Movement: Soviet Reality and Émigré Theories.* London: Cambridge University Press, 1987.
Asch, Solomon E. "Opinions and Social Pressure." In Alexander Thomas, ed., *Papers on Socialization and Attitudes selected from* Scientific American. Reading, England: W. H. Freeman and Company, 1974, pp. 29–33.
Axell, Albert. *Russia's Heroes: 1941–45.* London: Constable & Robinson, 2002.
Beevor, Antony. *Stalingrad.* London: Penguin, 1999.
Beevor, Antony, and Luba Vinogradova. *A Writer at War: Vasiliy Grossman with the Red Army 1941–1945.* London: The Harvill Press, 2005.

Boje, Arthur. *Stalins deutsche Agenten. Ein Kriegsgefangener berichtet*. Graz-Stuttgart: Leopold Stocker Verlag, 2002.

Carell, Paul. *Stalingrad: Sieg und Untergang der 6. Armee*, Sonderausgabe. München: F. A. Herbig, 2003.

Chuikov, Vasilii. *The Beginning of the Road*. Trans. Harold Silver. London: Macgibbon & Kee, 1963.

Churchill, Winston S. *The Second World War*, vol. 4: *The Hinge of Fate*. London: Cassell & Co., 1951.

Clark, Alan, *Barbarossa: The Russian-German Conflict 1941–1945*. Middlesex: Penguin, 1966.

Dettmer, Friedrich, Otto Jaus, and Helmut Tolkmitt. *Die 44. Infanterie-Division Reichs-Grenadier-Division Hoch- und Deutschmester 1938–1945*. Friedberg: Podzun-Pallas-Verlag, 1979.

———. *Stalingrad: Ein Rückblick nach 60 Jahren*. Nürnberg: Buchdienst Südtirol, 2003.

Dieckhoff, Gerhard. *3. Infanterie-Division, 3. Infanterie-Division (mot.), 3. Panzergrenadier-Division*. Göttingen: Erich Börries Verlag, 1960.

"Dokladnaia zapiska zamestitelia narodnogo komissara vnutrennikh del SSSR general-leitenanta A. N. Apollonova narodnomu komissaru vnutrennikh del SSSR L.P.Berii o nevozmozhnosti vydeleniia snaiperov iz sostava voisk NKVD na ukomplektovanie snaiperskikh podrazdelenii chastei i soedinenii Krasnoi Armii' ne panee 30 iiunia 1943 g." *Organy gosudarstvennoi bezopasnosti SSSR v Velikoi Otechestvennoi Voine: Sbornik dokumentov*, tom chetvertyi, kniga 1, *Sekrety Operatsii "Tsitadel'" 1 ianvaria–30 iiunia 1943 goda*, izdatel'stvo "Rus.'" Moscow, 2008, pp. 646–647.

Dougan, Andy. *The Hunting of Man: A History of the Sniper*. London: Fourth Estate, 2004.

Drobiazko, S.I. *Pod znamemani vraga: Antisovetskie formirovaniia v sostave germanskikh vooruzhennykh sil, 1941–1945 gg*. Moscow: Eksmo, 2005.

Glantz, David M., with Jonathan M. House. *The Stalingrad Trilogy*, vol. 1: *To the Gates of Stalingrad: Soviet-German Combat Operations April–August 1942*. Lawrence: University Press of Kansas, 2009.

———. *The Stalingrad Trilogy*, vol. 2: *Armageddon in Stalingrad, September–November 1942*. Lawrence: University Press of Kansas, 2009.

Grossman, Vasilii. *Za pravoe delo*. Moscow: Sovetskii pisatel', 1989.

———. *Zhizn' i sud'ba*. Moscow: Sovetskii pisatel', 1990.

———. *Gody voiny*. Moscow: izdatel'stvo Pravda, 1989.

Hauck, Friedrich Wilhelm. *Eine Deutsche Division in Russland und Italien: 305. Infanteriedivision 1941–1945*. Dorheim: Podzun-Verlag, 1975.

Hesketh-Prichard, Major H. *Sniping in France: With Notes on the Scientific Training of Scouts, Observers and Snipers*, with a foreword by General Lord Horne of Stirkoke. London: Hutchinson & Co, 1920.

Hilger, Andreas. *Deutsche Kriegsgefangene in der Sowjetunion, 1941–1956: Kriegsgefangenpolitik, Lageralltag und Erinnerung*, Schriften der Bibliothek für Zeitgeschichte—Neue Folge, Hrsg. von Gerhard Hirschfeld, Band 11. Klartext Verlag, Essen, 2000.

Hoffmann, Joachim. *Die Ostlegionen 1941–1943: Turkotataren, Kaukasier und Wolgafinnen im deutschen Heer*, 2., unveränderte Auflage. Freiburg: Verlag Rombach, 1981.

Infantry Training, vol. 1: Infantry Platoon Weapons Pamphlet No. 10, "Sniping," 1951.

Jocher, Bernhard. "Die Scharfschützen der Deutschen Wehrmacht." *Der Freiwillige* 9 (2000): 15–16.

Kehrig, Manfred. *Stalingrad: Analyse und Dokumentation einer Schlacht.* Beiträge zur Militär-Kriegsgeschichte, Band 15, Herausgegeben vom Militärgeschichtlichen Forschungsamt. Stuttgart: Deutsche Verlags-Anstalt, 1974.

Khristoforov, V. S. *Stalingrad: Organy NKVD nakanune i v dni srazheniia.* Moscow: Moskovskie uchebniki, 2008.

Kruse, Martin, hrsg. *Die Stalingrad-Madonna: Das Werk Kurt Reubers als Dokument der Versöhnung*, 3., überarb. Auflage. Hannover: Lutherisches Verlagshaus, 1996.

Löser, Jochen. *Bittere Pflicht: Kampf und Untergang der 76. Berlin-Branderburgischen Infanterie Division*, unter Mitarbeit der Chronisten Fritz Bente, Bert Mauß-Auth, Gerhard Gutmacher, und von Werner Brandt, Wilhelm Kauffeld, Reinhold Fellmer, Mady von Schilling, Johannes Schmoll, Ernst von Schroeder, Erich Tomaszewski sowie von Msgr. Josef Kayser, und Jochen Klepper unter der Schirmherrschaft von Carl Rodenburg, Kommandeur der 76. Infanterie-Division in Stalingrad, Kameradschaft 76. Inf. Div. e.V. Osnabrück: Biblio Verlag, 1986.

Macdonald, Kenneth R., R.M., *A Bandsman and Barbed Wire: Experiences and Recollections, May 1941–May 1945* (unpublished diary).

Maschke, Erich, hrsg. "Leiter der Wissenschaftlichen Kommission für deutsche Kriegsgefangenengeschichte," *Zur Geschichte der deutschen Kriegsgefangenen des Zweiten Weltkrieges*, Gert Robel, Band VIII, *Die deutschen Kriegsgefangenen in der Sowjetunion: Antifa.* München: Verlag Ernst und Werner Gieseking, Bielefeld, 1974.

Neidhardt, Hanns. *Mit Tanne und Eichenlaub: Kriegschronik der 100. Jäger-Division vormals 100. leichte Infanterie-Division.* Graz-Stuttgart: Leopold Stocker Verlag, 1981.

Nekrasov, Viktor. *Stalingrad.* Frankfurt/Main: Possev-Verlag, 1981.

Nölke, Hans. zusammengestellt—betextet—bearbeitet, *Die 71. Infanterie-Division im Zweiten Weltkrieg 1939–1945: Fotos, Karten und Texts von den Kämpfen einer niedersächsischen Infanterie-Division* "DIE GLÜCKHAFTE," als Manuskript gedruckt bei Druckhaus Pinkvoß. Hannover, 1984.

Organy gosudarstvennoi bezopasnosti SSSR v Velikoi Otechestvennoi Voine: Sbornik dokumentov, tom vtoroi, kniga 1, *Nachalo 22 iiunia–31 avgusta* 1941 *goda*, izdatel'stvo "Rus.'" Moscow, 2000.

Organy gosudarstvennoi bezopasnosti SSSR v Velikoi Otechestvennoi Voine: Sbornik dokumentov, tom vtoroi, kniga 2, *Nachalo 1 sentiabria–31 dekabria 1941 goda*, izdatel'stvo "Rus.'" Moscow, 2000.

Organy gosudarstvennoi bezopasnosti SSSR v Velikoi Otechestvennoi Voine: Sbornik dokumentov, tom tretii, kniga 1, *Krushenie "Blitzkriga" 1 ianvaria–30 iiunia 1942 goda*, izdatel'stvo "Rus.'" Moscow, 2003.

Organy gosudarstvennoi bezopasnosti SSSR v Velikoi Otechestvennoi Voine: Sbornik dokumentov, tom tretii, kniga 2, *Ot oborony k nastupleniiu 1 iiulia–31 dekabria 1942 goda*, izdatel'stvo "Rus.'" Moscow, 2003.

Organy gosudarstvennoi bezopasnosti SSSR v Velikoi Otechestvennoi Voine: Sbornik dokumentov, tom chetvertyi, kniga 1, *Sekrety Operatsii "Tsitadel'" 1 ianvaria–30 iiunia 1943 goda*, izdatel'stvo "Rus.'" Moscow, 2008.

Peter, Erwin, and Alexander E. Epifanow. *Stalins Kriegsgefangene: Ihr Schicksal in Erinnerungen und nach russischen Archiven*, 2. Auflage. Graz-Stuttgart: Leopold Stocker Verlag, 1998.

Pogonii, IA. F., i dr. *Stalingradskaia epopeia: Materialy NKVD SSSR i voennoi tsenzury iz Tsentral'nogo arkhiva FSB RF*. Moscow: Zvonnitsa-MG, 2000.

Remarque, Erich Maria. *Im Westen nichts Neues*. Köln: Kiepenheuer & Witsch, 1984.

Riazanov, Oleg. *Istoriia snaiperskogo iskusstva*. Moscow: Bratishka, 2004.

Rybalkin, Iurii. *Operatsiia «X» Sovetskaia voennaia pomoshch' respublikanskoi Ispanii, 1936–1939*. Moscow: AIRO-XX, 2000.

Samsonov, A. M. *Stalingradskaia bitva*, 4th ed. Moscow: Nauka, 1989.

Sänger, Hans. *Bildband 2 der 79. Infanterie-Division Tapfer und Treu 1939–1945*, herausgegeben im Einverständnis mit dem Traditionsverband der 79. Infanterie-Division e.V. Limburg/Lahn von Hans Sänger, C. A. Starke Verlag, Limburg an der Lahn, circa 1982.

Sänger, Hans, *zusammengestellt von Die 79. Infanterie Division*. Friedberg: Podzun-Pallas-Verlag, n.d.

Schmitz, Günter. *Die 16. Panzer-Division 1938–1945: Bewaffnung, Einsätze, Männer*. Friedberg: Podzun-Pallas-Verlag, ca. 1976.

Senich, Peter R. *The German Sniper 1914–1945*. Boulder, CO: Paladin Press and and London and Melbourne: Arms and Armour Press, 1982.

Snyder, Timothy. *Bloodlands: Europe between Hitler and Stalin*. London: The Bodley Head, 2010.

Spaeter, Helmuth. *Die Brandenburger: eine deutsche Kommandotruppe zbV 800*, 2. teilw.überarbeitete Auflage mit Personen—und Sachregister. München: Verlagsagentur Walther Angerer, 1982.

Volkovskii, N. L., ed. *Tainy i uroki zimnei voiny, 1939–1940, Po dokumentam rasskrechennykh arkhivov*. Sankt-Peterburg: Poligon, 2000.

Volksbund Deutsche Kriegsgräberfürsorge e.V., Kassel, hrsg. *Namen für Rossoschka: Schicksale aus Stalingrad*, 2 Auflage. Pößneck: GGP Media GmbH, 2008.

Werthen, Wolfgang. *Geschichte der 16. Panzer-Division*, hrsg vom Kameradschaftsbund 16. Panzer und Infanterie-Division Kameradenhilfswerk e.V. Bad Nauheim: Podzun-Verlag, 1958.

Zagorul'ko, M. M., ed. *Voennoplennye v Stalingrade 1943–1954: Dokumenty i Materialy*, tom 2: *Voennoplennye v SSSR, 1939–1956*, gosudarstvennoe uchrezhdenie. Volgograd: Izdatel', 2003.

Zank, Horst. *Stalingrad: Kessel und Gefangenschaft*, dritte Auflage. Hamburg, Berlin, Bonn: Verlag E.S. Mittler & Sohn, 2001.

Zolotarev, Major General V. A., ed. *Russkii Arkhiv: Velikaia Otechestvennaia*, vol. 13 (2): *Nemetskie voennoplennye v SSSR 1941–1955 gg.* Sbornik dokumentov, Kniga pervaia. Moscow: TERRA, 1999.

INDEX